P9-ARN-565

Business Plans Handbook

Business Plans Handbook

A COMPILATION OF ACTUAL BUSINESS PLANS DEVELOPED BY BUSINESSES THROUGHOUT NORTH AMERICA

VOLUME

10

Lynn Pearce,
Project Editor

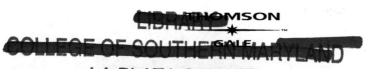

Detroit • New York • San Francisco • San Diego • New Haven, Conn. • Waterville, Maine • London • Munich

Business Plans Handbook, 10th Volume

Editorial
Lynn M. Pearce

Product Design
Mike Logusz

Composition and Electronic Capture
Keith Helmling

Typesetter
Shelly Andrews

For more information, contact
The Gale Group, Inc.
27500 Drake Rd.
Farmington Hills, MI 48331-3535
Or you can visit our Internet site at
http://www.gale.com

LIBRARY OF CONGRESS CATALOGING-IN-PUBLICATION DATA

ISBN 0-7876-6485-5
ISSN 1084-4473

Printed in the United States of America
10 9 8 7 6 5 4 3 2

Contents

Business Plans

Appendixes

Highlights

Business Plans Handbook, Volume 10 (BPH-10) is a collection of actual business plans compiled by entrepreneurs seeking funding for small businesses throughout North America. For those looking for examples of how to approach, structure, and compose their own business plans, *BPH-10* presents 20 sample plans, including plans for the following businesses:

- Automotive Repair Service
- Bioterrorism Prevention Organization
- Bistro and Wine Bar
- Coatings Inspection Company
- Event Photography Service
- Golf Grip Manufacturer
- Holistic Health Center
- Housing Rehabilitation Company
- Litigation Services Company
- Medical Equipment Producer
- Mural Company
- Structural Genomics Software Provider

FEATURES AND BENEFITS

BPH-10 offers many features not provided by other business planning references including:

- Twenty business plans, each of which represent an owner's successful attempt at clarifying (for themselves and others) the reasons that the business should exist or expand and why a lender should fund the enterprise.

- Two fictional plans that are used by business counselors at a prominent small business development organization as examples for their clients. (You will find these in the Business Plan Template Appendix.)

- An expanded directory section that includes: listings for venture capital and finance companies, which specialize in funding start-up and second-stage small business ventures, and a comprehensive listing of Service Corps of Retired Executives (SCORE) offices. In addition, the Appendix also contains updated listings of all Small Business Development Centers (SBDCs); associations of interest to entrepreneurs; Small Business Administration (SBA) Regional Offices; and consultants specializing in small business planning and advice. It is strongly advised that you consult supporting organizations while planning your business, as they can provide a wealth of useful information.

- A Small Business Term Glossary to help you decipher the sometimes confusing terminology used by lenders and others in the financial and small business communities.

- A cumulative index, outlining each plan profiled in the complete *Business Plans Handbook* series.

- A Business Plan Template which serves as a model to help you construct your own business plan. This generic outline lists all the essential elements of a complete business plan and their components, including the Summary, Business History and Industry Outlook, Market Examination, Competition, Marketing, Administration and Management, Financial Information, and other key sections. Use this guide as a starting point for compiling your plan.

- Extensive financial documentation required to solicit funding from small business lenders. *BPH-10* contains the most comprehensive financial data within the series to date. You will find examples of: Cash Flows, Balance Sheets, Income Projections, and other financial information included with the textual portions of the plan.

Introduction

Perhaps the most important aspect of business planning is simply *doing* it. More and more business owners are beginning to compile business plans even if they don't need a bank loan. Others discover the value of planning when they *must* provide a business plan for the bank. The sheer act of putting thoughts on paper seems to clarify priorities and provide focus. Sometimes business owners completely change strategies when compiling their plan, deciding on a different product mix or advertising scheme after finding that their assumptions were incorrect. This kind of healthy thinking and re-thinking via business planning is becoming the norm. The editors of *Business Plans Handbook, Volume 10 (BPH-10)* sincerely hope that this latest addition to the series is a helpful tool in the successful completion of your business plan, no matter what the reason for creating it.

This tenth volume, like each volume in the series, offers genuine business plans used by real people. *BPH-10* provides 20 business plans used by actual entrepreneurs to gain funding support for their new businesses. The business and personal names and addresses and general locations have been changed to protect the privacy of the plan authors.

NEW BUSINESS OPPORTUNITIES

As in other volumes in the series, *BPH-10* finds entrepreneurs engaged in a wide variety of creative endeavors. Examples include a proposal for a bioterrorism prevention organization; a holistic health and wellness center; and a housing rehabilitation company. In addition, several e-commerce based plans are provided, including an Internet and network security solution provider, an online customer service support company, and a company that offers routing and navigation software.

Comprehensive financial documentation has become increasingly important as today's entrepreneurs compete for the finite resources of business lenders. Our plans illustrate the financial data generally required of loan applicants, including Income Statements, Financial Projections, Cash Flows, and Balance Sheets.

ENHANCED APPENDIXES

In an effort to provide the most relevant and valuable information for our readers, we have updated the coverage of small business resources. For instance, you will find: a directory section, which includes listings of all of the Service Corps of Retired Executives (SCORE) offices; an informative glossary, which includes small business terms; and a cumulative index, outlining each plan profiled in the complete *Business Plans Handbook* series. In addition we have updated the list of Small Business Development Centers (SBDCs); Small Business Administration Regional Offices; venture capital and finance companies, which specialize in funding start-up and second-stage small business enterprises; associations of interest to entrepreneurs; and consultants, specializing in small business advice and planning. For your reference, we have also reprinted the business plan template, which provides a comprehensive overview of the essential components of a business plan and two fictional plans used by small business counselors.

SERIES INFORMATION

If you already have the first nine volumes of *BPH*, with this tenth volume, you will now have a collection of over 240 real business plans (not including the one updated plan in the second volume, whose original appeared in the first, or the two fictional plans in the Business Plan Template Appendix section of the second, third, fourth, fifth, sixth, and seventh volumes); contact information for hundreds of organizations and agencies offering business expertise; a helpful business plan template; a foreword providing advice and instruction to entrepreneurs on how to begin their research; more than 1,500 citations to valuable small business development material; and a comprehensive glossary of terms to help the business planner navigate the sometimes confusing language of entrepreneurship.

ACKNOWLEDGMENTS

The Editors wish to sincerely thank the many contributors to *BPH-10*, including:

- Alice Ahearn and Erin Pushman, Health-E-ssentials, LLC
- Lisa Bastian, Bastian Public Relations
- Dr. Daniel Burnett, Mr. Loy Hong Chia, Dr. Shane Mangrum, and George Ivanov, TheraNova
- Ken Carrasco, Ken Carrasco Consulting
- Collision Experts, Inc.
- Concord Business Development Inc., Vancouver, B.C.
- Eugene E. Doerr, III, Chief Executive Officer, REOD, LLC
- José J. Haresco, D. Rey Banatao, Sandra Waugh, and Sean Mooney, Quicksilver Genomics
- Steve R. Hartmann, Saint Louis University
- Sol D. Kanthack, brightroom, Inc.
- Jerome Katz, Cook School of Business, Saint Louis University
- Kristofer G. Knapstein, Sundern Development, LLC
- Karen and Ken Ko-Bas, Ko-Bas Painting
- Lyn Kondrako
- Sidney Oster, John Szypula, and Rominder Varma, SportsTek
- Jeff Russell, live e-care
- Ray Smalley, VenPlan Inc.
- Rick Solak
- Brian J. Sroub, AQUI Systems, Inc.
- Diane Tarshis, Burton Décor
- Linda Zolten Wood, Zolten Wood Design

The Editors would also like to express their gratitude to Shelly Andrews, Contributing Editor & Typesetter, for her talent, dedication, and hard work on behalf of this publication.

COMMENTS WELCOME

Your comments on *Business Plans Handbook* are appreciated. Please direct all correspondence, suggestions for future volumes of *BPH*, and other recommendations to the following:

Managing Editor, Business Product
Business Plans Handbook
The Gale Group
27500 Drake Rd.
Farmington Hills, MI 48331-3535

Phone: (248)699-4253
Fax: (248)699-8052
Toll-Free: 800-347-GALE
E-mail: BusinessProducts@gale.com

Automotive Repair Service

BUSINESS PLAN

COLLISION EXPERTS INC.

711 West Grand Boulevard
Detroit, Michigan 48202

Our mission is to act as an integral part of the business community in providing a valuable service to retail, business, and community clients. We intend to provide a level of professional autobody repair and refinishing to our clients that is unmatched in our marketplace. Our service integrity and customer satisfaction practices will result in an ongoing loyal client following across the business community markets we serve.

EXECUTIVE SUMMARY

Collision Experts Vision Statement

Collision Experts Incorporated has set forth to become a preferred provider of professional autobody repair in the Detroit marketplace. It is our belief that delivering a legacy of premium services will result in an ongoing profitable business enterprise in the highly commoditized automotive services market.

Our 30-year legacy of service to our customers demonstrates this philosophy for success.

Mission & Quality Management

Our mission is to act as an integral part of the business community in providing a valuable service to retail, business, and community clients. We intend to provide a level of professional autobody repair and refinishing to our clients that is unmatched in our marketplace. Our service integrity and customer satisfaction practices will result in an ongoing loyal client following across the business community markets we serve. Leveraging our business practices, personal management styles, and unique perspectives enable our business to succeed in this dynamic environment.

Business Summary

Collision Experts Incorporated (CEI) provides a comprehensive set of autobody repair and refinishing services. We provide a comprehensive set of services to benefit multiple clients and business community segments. The business community segments we serve vary widely and distinctly from segment to segment.

It is our view that the competitive pressures impacting our business and the uniqueness of our services creates positive competitive force. Our service delivery policies differ from the norm in that our primary competitors behave in an "industry standard" production model. Although our services are delivered in an industry-standard "insurance-work" business model, our services are delivered in a manner that dictate "doing it right the first time, to keep a customer coming back" as opposed to "hoping a customer is satisfied and accepts the basic level of quality required to get it out the door."

Each of our market segments we compete in have individual service and quality requirements from our set of services offered. The following business community segments are indicative of the communities we serve:

Business Community Segments

- Municipal vehicle fleets
- Retail consumers
- Corporate vehicle fleets
- Community churches and non-profit organization fleet vehicles
- Auction-house transactions
- Selective custom work

REVENUE MODEL

Our business is based on an hourly rate revenue model, based on industry norms, with a moderate degree of complexity. Complexities in our business model are primarily based on continuously changing corporate policy/rate modifications with partner-insurance companies.

Clients are charged based on estimated time and materials required to complete repair in a timely, professional manner to our exacting quality standards.

Market pricing for hourly rate and repair time-allowance standards are used in our pricing model. Industry standard pricing is set forth by industry organization publications and OEM aftermarket repair guidelines. All pricing is normalized to the Southeastern Michigan market-pricing norms and are based on time-studies performed by industry associations and acquired local competitive and labor knowledge. Organizations providing valuable information include Motors Manuals, ADP, and Mitchell Manuals.

CEI's major focus is in providing a high quality service to ensure repeat customers and to foster a relationship built on trust with each of our clients served.

Our revenue model can be characterized quite simply. Throughput, throughput, throughput. We must deliver multiple finished vehicles per day, 341 working days per year. We must continuously have 8-12 cars on our lot rotating through the production/repair process with additional vehicles in inventory reserve.

PRIMARY BUSINESS CHALLENGES

In this business plan we have chosen to focus on our primary business challenges. We are constantly faced with day-to-day events that cause distraction from our core efforts. The following challenges keep us up at night and drive our behavior on a day-to-day basis.

- Competitive Environment
- Commodity pricing
- Economic factors
- Insurance partner policies (downward pricing pressures)
- State, Municipal, and Federal regulatory environment
- Downward pressure on profit margins
- Cost containment
- Skilled employee/resources (acquiring and retaining reliable, competent employees)
- Industry currency (staying abreast of industry trends and taking proactive action)

PROMOTIONAL CONSIDERATIONS

Initially our brand advertising required localized regional promotions leveraging regional and mass-market type business communication vehicles. However, while a consistent client base developed and community presence was established, we were able to evolve into a highly targeted model for communicating our services and brand messages to our market and associated business community segments. This model for promotional and community communication strategies has resulted in a highly effective, low budget business process. We believe that the communication and follow-up through reliable demonstration of services and client satisfaction has enabled our continued, manageable growth without having to rely on internal and external resources to manage complex promotional strategies on an ongoing basis.

Our primary brand communications are delivered to our target business community and clients through a simple, time-tested method of touching the right consumer at the right moment. A blend of simple, effective messages are delivered through the following:

- Word-of-mouth
- At-location roadside signage
- Highly targeted community messaging (community and regional newspapers, etc.)
- Local church organization newsletters
- Targeted communications to municipal agencies and corporate fleet managers (letters and commendation examples)

BUSINESS INTERDEPENDENCIES

Our business relationships in this industry will make or break our enterprise on a long-term basis. We must have the ability to work, with integrity, in a coordinated manner with business partners that touch all aspects of our enterprise.

Business Partners

Our largest concern and single most interdependent business partner is the insurance agency community we provide services and contract with at the corporate and retail client level. Our clients demand the best and we provide it. We must have the ability to operate at many levels. To this end we participate in industry standard setting organization certification, industry action groups, and consumer advocate organizations to ensure adherence to industry standards and to exceed client expectations.

Many insurance agencies have preferred service providers' programs that we currently participate in and intend to participate in for the foreseeable duration of our business operations.

Some other companies and business partners that have significant influence and co-reliance on our operations and ultimately, our success, include automotive (OE and aftermarket) companies, towing services, regional and local utility service providers, and the automotive repair aftermarket supply chain.

Service Providers

We are only as good as our relationships with other service providers of associated services. On occasion we will not be able to provide custom or specialized services primarily due to specialized customer requirements. For example, a municipal police vehicle may need specialized computer installation our facility is not licensed to perform. This need requires us to rely on contract or labor services through an "outsourcing" agreement. At which point we would contract a provider to repair the damage and pass the costs and associated billing needs to client. We must maintain a trust-based relationship with these providers as we are only as good as the services they provide. The client only sees us and is dependent on us to get the whole job done. Clients are not interested in hearing a story on who's to blame if something is not "right."

Business Systems

- Automotive OEM
- Financial
- Insurance
- Regulatory and Safety

LOCATION & FACILITIES

CEI operates out of an existing automotive repair facility in Southeastern Michigan. Our location is based on a primary thoroughfare in a suburban Detroit area.

Our existing repair facilities and adjacent existing office is our primary occupancy and location for providing services, which is owned by the partners. Our operations have the ability to provide comprehensive service to our clients. Our facilities currently support the following primary client needs:

Extensive remove, replace, rebuild services, including:

- Exterior (structural cosmetic components)
- Interior (structural and cosmetic components)
- Vehicle structural repair (frame and subassembly)

Basic and custom painting and refinishing, including:

- Exterior prep and finish painting

Our facilities are able to support these needs and provide service through the leverage of onsite, state-of-the-art technologies featuring the following:

- High-tech paint facility (dust-free, electrostatic, high-temp curing technology)
- Frame repair equipment (full-service, automotive-grade, non-commercial vehicles)
- 10 professionally staffed, service repair bays
- State-of-the-art office technologies to support financial, repair, and regulatory complexities

CRITICAL SUCCESS FACTORS

Our business is a family business. Our ability to operate as a cohesive unit and manage personalities and financial integrity is tantamount to our success. However, external factors are the primary drivers and result in implications to enable or disable our success. The ongoing operations of our enterprise are reliant on the following five factors:

- Manage business continuity
- Continually expand customer base
- Retain best people
- Maintain stature in community
- Comply with and exceed reasonable regulatory and community expectations

COMMUNITY INVOLVEMENT

CEI is dedicated to providing high quality services to the retail consumer and business community. It is our intention and common practice to play an integral role in our business and business partner community, with our adjacent residential neighborhood community playing the most important role. Our physical location and business practices require us to take a multi-disciplinary view when considering our success as an enterprise. We must abide by and play a leadership role in addressing local neighborhood community standards for business behavior while taking consideration for business needs and compliance with state, local, and federal regulations for air, noise, water pollution, and recycling regulation. Our policies for exceeding requirements to clear regulatory hurdles to the satisfaction of our neighborhood and local governments has resulted in a win-win-win relationship.

Our policies for financial and resource support of local, school, religious, sporting, and academic activities allows us to provide an environment of mutual trust and reciprocity.

After all we live here, too.

FINANCIAL CONSIDERATIONS

Categorically, operating expenses fall into the following five categories:

Operational Expenditures

1. Administrative:
Legal Counsel
Promotional/marketing
Accounting
Interest and other items

2. Facilities:
Utilities (communications, electrical, gas, water, sewer)
Specialized Equipment (Shop-owned tools/equipment, paint, and frame repair equipment)
Specialized Recycling and Disposal Services

3. Human Resources:
Compensation (hourly pay, benefits, fringe benefits/bonus program)

4. Part and Non-Part Inventories:
Miscellaneous (general assembly parts, general non-part shop supplies)

5. Vehicle Expenditures:
Business-Owned Vehicle (business continuity required vehicles)

Bioterrorism Prevention Organization

BUSINESS PLAN

BIOTERRORISM & INFECTIONS PREVENTION ORGANIZATION

2307 Lincoln Avenue, Suite 14
Charlottesville, Virginia 22902

The BIPO is a private not-for-profit organization dedicated to the education and training of the public regarding the Bioterrorism prevention and response plans. The goal of the organization is to deter the use of biological agents by terrorists: Minimize the advantage of the potential effective use of any biological pathogen by terrorists through cultivating and enhancing our nation's public health infrastructure to ensure prompt identification of a threat and an appropriate response.

- EXECUTIVE SUMMARY
- PRESENT SITUATION
- PRODUCT STRATEGY
- MARKET ANALYSIS
- MARKETING PLAN
- SALES PROJECTIONS & PRICING STRATEGY
- ORGANIZATION OVERVIEW

BIOTERRORISM PREVENTION ORGANIZATION BUSINESS PLAN

EXECUTIVE SUMMARY

Mission

The BIPO's (Bioterrorism & Infections Prevention Organization) mission is "to provide public health and healthcare facilities with the tools needed for preparedness, response, recovery, and mitigation of intentional or naturally occurring outbreaks."

Organization Overview

The BIPO, a private not-for-profit organization dedicated to the education and training of public regarding the Bioterrorism prevention and response plans, has been preparing for Bioterrorism type infections long before the events of September 11, 2001. However, after the events of September 11, 2001, Bioterrorism awareness skyrocketed. It is for these reasons the Bioterrorism department decided to expand its operations.

The goal of the organization is to deter the use of biological agents by terrorists: Minimize the advantage of the potential effective use of any biological pathogen by terrorists through cultivating and enhancing our nation's public health infrastructure to ensure prompt identification of a threat and an appropriate response.

Business Objectives

The primary objective is to come up with a Marketing plan for a multimedia informational CD-ROM entitled, "Be Prepared for Bioterrorism." The marketing plan takes into consideration a multi-distribution channel approach, including e-commerce, along with partnering with other professional organizations in an attempt to get this information into the hands of as many public health professionals as possible.

Current Product

The current product is a narrative multimedia CD-ROM, which contains a Bioterrorism preparation kit, with a checklist for Bioterrorism "readiness." The toolkit is customized by state and includes important emergency phone numbers along with other information on what to do in the case of a terrorist attack or viral outbreak.

Advertising & Promotion

Advertising and promotion efforts will focus primarily on prospective customers over the Internet through various public health organizations such as the Professional Epidemiology Network, the National Disaster Medical Systems, the Infectious Disease Society of America, along with others. Promotions also will include ways to increase website traffic and will utilize mass mailings to target potential customers.

PRESENT SITUATION

Currently the University of Virginia Bioterrorism Center is looking for a Business Plan or E-Commerce solution for the University of Virginia School of Public Health that incorporates the delivery and sales of digital multimedia presentations that include information regarding Bioterrorism preparation and response plans relayed over the Internet. The plan discussed in this document concerns the first product of this effort the "Be Prepared for the Unexpected—CD-ROM," although a number of other products are planned.

Presently, the School of Public Health is working with the Professional Epidemiology Network (PEN). PEN is a nonprofit, international organization that worked with the School of Public Health in putting together an informational CD-ROM on Bioterrorism. It is being distributed as "Be Prepared for the Unexpected—CD-ROM." Currently, this CD-ROM is available from PEN for $8 (members) or $15 (non-members).

Vision

Our vision is to provide a comprehensive and coordinated training and preparedness program across the full continuum of public health activities in the United States to protect Americans from both the intentional use of biological agents and emerging infections.

Goals & Objectives

The objective of the plan will include documenting the necessary processes to distribute digital multimedia information through multiple distribution channels, including Amazon.com, a proposal to set up an "in-house" E-Commerce solution, along with other direct marketing and distribution channels.

The plan will include everything from the reproduction of the media, the presence on the Internet, to the plans for the distribution of product through various methods. Initial plans include what is necessary to distribute the media via Amazon.com, while researching other possible markets, and E-Commerce solutions.

PRODUCT STRATEGY

Overall the product strategy is to deliver digital documentation and multimedia presentations on a CD-ROM regarding Bioterrorism preparedness and reaction plans. The initial product focuses on targeting Public Health Professionals, Infection Control Professionals, Nurses, and Physicians. Response plans address Bioterrorism agents such as anthrax, smallpox, and plague.

In the future, specialized media also will be created for each agent which will include: history, signs, symptoms, diagnosis, isolation, treatment, prophylaxis, and vaccination.

Current Product Description

The current product is a multimedia CD-ROM that includes information and documents regarding Bioterrorism readiness and response plans. The product includes clinical fact sheets on anthrax, smallpox, botulism, and plague. It also has fact sheets from the Center of Disease Control and information from the Department of Defense. The CD-ROM also includes a Mass Casualty Disaster Plan Checklist.

PEN and the University of Virginia's School of Public Health estimate that over 80 percent of the population can view a CD-ROM from a computer. So in the event of an actual Bioterrorism attack, in which the Internet, Telephones, Libraries, or other means of gathering data may not be available, you would still have a CD-ROM from which the data could be printed as well. The initial product also includes some history and several photos of the various diseases themselves.

Maps are also included on the CD-ROM with customized templates for Bioterrorism readiness plans or "Templates for Healthcare Professionals." By clicking on a state, it will bring up a customized template for each state including important phone numbers such as the FBI and CDC emergency response offices.

Upcoming New Products

The highlighted product below is the first product in this effort and includes a collection of resources to assist a healthcare facility in Bioterrorism preparedness. The others listed are new products in the pipeline, some of them recently completed. The primary focus and strategy of the other products is to target other audiences with specific information pertaining to their area of expertise. Some of the CD-ROMs are specific to a particular disease and include: history, signs and symptoms, diagnosis, isolation, treatment, prophylaxis and vaccination. See the chart below for specific information.

Title	Audience	Content	Length	Estimated Date of Completion
Be Prepared for Bioterrorism	Infection Control Professionals	Collection of resources to assist a healthcare facility in bioterrorism preparedness.	N/A	Completed
Bioterrorism Agent Epidemiology: Anthrax Smallpox, and Plague	Nurses and Infections Control Professionals	Bioterrorism preparedness and the epidemiology of three of CDC's Category A agents: anthrax, smallpox, and plague.	1 hour	Completed
Epidemiology of Anthrax	Physicians and Nurse Practitioners	History, signs and symptoms, diagnosis, isolation, treatment, prophylaxis, and vaccination.	1 hour	4/15/05
Epidemiology of Smallpox	Physicians and Nurse Practitioners	History, signs and symptoms, diagnosis, isolation, treatment, prophylaxis and vaccination.	1 hour	Undetermined (Summer 2005)
Epidemiology of Botulism and Tularemia	Physicians and Nurse Practitioners	History, signs and symptoms, diagnosis, isolation, treatment, prophylaxis and vaccination.	1 hour	Undetermined (Fall 2005)
Epidemiology of Plague and Viral Hemorrhagic Fevers	Physicians and Nurse Practitioners	History, signs and symptoms, diagnosis, isolation, treatment, prophylaxis and vaccination.	1 hour	Undetermined (Spring 2006)
Public Health Preparedness	General Public	Description of the role of the public health in the community and in bioterrorism preparedness.	30 minutes	Completed
Bioterrorism Preparedness	Public Health Professionals	Bioterrorism threat analysis and history.	1 hour	Completed
Bioterrorism Reference Cards (Size: 4 x 6)	Healthcare and Public Health Professionals	Pocket-sized reference cards containing medical information including decontamination, isolation, treatment, prophylaxis, and vaccination recommendations. Nine two-sided 4 x 6 inch cards	N/A	In progress—estimated completion 5/15/2004

Research & Development

Obtain Copyrights—on the CD-ROMs that are exclusive property of the university, law already copyrights them. However, it is not a bad idea to obtain an official copyright to have one on file.

For the CD-ROMs that contain public data as well as that of the university, it may be possible to add value to the public information to the point a copyright can be obtained based on a "derivative work." That is if you "add value" to the product by perhaps adding an indexing system, or other way to retrieve the data through some sort of software or enhanced interface, the CD-ROM may be eligible to obtain an official copyright.

The current copyright filing fee is $30. See the United States Copyright Library of Congress at http://www.loc.gov/copyright/ for more information on copyrights.

Delivery Modes

DVDs—Although DVDs hold approximately six times more data, there are not nearly as many people using them yet. One of the main reasons for putting the data on a CD-ROM was that over 90 percent of those surveyed had access to CD-ROM drives. On future surveys a question about DVDs will be added.

Long term, DVDs are the way the market is going. Therefore, not until the School of Public Health has all of the initial CD-ROMs it is planning on creating completed, should it look at DVDs as a "value-added" product. It also will be necessary to add additional quality, as we will be charging a slightly higher price for the media to cover cost.

PDAs or Personal Digital Assistants—Also known as Palm Pilots (brand name). In future CD-ROMs the School of Public Health will look into adding a section of the CD-ROM that can be downloaded onto a PDA. Granted, not all individuals have PDA's, but in a time of disaster this might be the single best thing to which they do have access. PEN is currently in the process of performing a survey on PDAs.

Easy Access Web Links on the CD-ROMs—The Bioterrorism department needs to put easy access hyperlink buttons on the CD-ROMs that take individuals directly to the website. This will give the individual the opportunity to see what "new" or other products are being offered on the website, and will assist with keeping the website in front of the customer's eyes.

MARKET ANALYSIS

The market will vary with the actual data that resides on the individual CD-ROMs. For the purposes of this plan we are focusing on "Be Prepared for Bioterrorism." As the other products are completed, it will need to be decided which of the following markets the product fits in and which markets to target. There will always be some overlap.

We have identified three distinct markets from which to work. The goal should be to work from the primary market and then expand into the secondary and tertiary markets as the organization evolves.

General Market Definitions and Customer Profiles

Primary Market—This would include Infection Control Professionals, along with everyone directly involved in the Public Health Industry.

> *Infection Control Professionals*—There are currently approximately 6,400 hospitals in the United States. Each one is by law required to have an Infection Control Professional on staff. Some of the smaller hospitals may share the position, whereas some of the larger hospitals may have more than one. One average it is about one per hospital. Information provided by Jessica Blaine, Director of Marketing, PEN. This is PEN's primary customer base.

Public Health Professionals—There are approximately 3,000 Public Health offices in the United States. The Bioterrorism department has a list of these offices as many of them were involved in the initial technology survey sent out.

Secondary Market—This would include a subset of the entire Healthcare Industry. Since the Healthcare Industry is so broad, it would have to be segregated. It would include, but not be limited to, nurses, especially nurses within the Infection Control area. It would include first response Healthcare workers such as doctors and nurses that work in the emergency department. It would also include students of infection control. Many of these individuals are members of the organizations listed in the Marketing Plan, and for the sake of concentration should be pursued directly through those organizations.

Tertiary Market—Special CD-ROMs with information could be tailored toward Fire Fighters, Police Officers, and other public "first" responders.

For Fire Fighters, the IAFF (International Association of Fire Fighters) would be an excellent place to pursue (http://www.iaff.org/). The IAFF represents more than 240,000 professional fire fighters and emergency medical personnel in the United States and Canada.

For Police Officers the best resource would be NAPO, or National Association of Police Officers, http://www.napo.org/. The NAPO is now the strongest unified voice supporting law enforcement officers in the United States. NAPO represents more than 225,000 sworn law enforcement officers.

This market also would include the general public. The general public should be pursued through ads and distribution on major websites, and good placement in search engines.

Competition

The primary competition for this CD-ROM is the Center for Disease Control public domain data. However, this CD-ROM does add value and puts all of the data in one place so you do not have to sift through the information. Nor does the CDC offer information in video format. Another selling point for the CD-ROM is that the Internet and/or CDC may not be available in event of crises, whereas an individual or group of individuals would always have the CD-ROM readily available at or near their computer.

Risks

The "Be Prepared for Bioterrorism" CD-ROM is not copyrighted. If you copyright it, then people shouldn't copy it, except in accordance with applicable laws. A recommendation is to revise the CD-ROM and/or future CD-ROMs so that the information within can legally be copyrighted. This has been summarized previously in the Research and Development section.

Technology Access Survey Information

A survey by Philip J. Ferguson, Ph.D., and M.P.H. Associate Director of Science, was conducted to find out how many Physicians have access to Technology and the Internet, and how the Physicians prefer to train. The results indicated that 90 percent of the Healthcare workers surveyed had access to a CD-ROM drive either at work or at home.

The survey also indicated approximately 5 percent prefer training on a CD-ROM, and 51 percent preferred training on the Internet.

MARKETING PLAN

The marketing plan proposed a multi-channel distribution approach. This means that BIPO will sell its products through a variety of outlets or channels in order to most efficiently get its products before the key markets. This initially includes direct sales through PEN and other professional organizations, as well as the BIPO e-commerce website, and sales through distribution on major websites.

Direct Sales Marketing Information

The goal of the direct marketing plan is to partner with other organizations that are "already in the business." This will give the university direct contact with the primary, secondary, and tertiary markets, and those most apt to purchase these types of materials.

The following organizations need to be contacted directly to find out about possible partnerships, web links, newsletter, and conference information. Many of these organizations hold regular conferences and exhibits. Information needs to be gathered as to what is necessary to get CD-ROMs promoted, possible product demonstrations, or sample handouts.

Each of these organizations also has websites and it may be possible to add links from their website to the School of Public Health's Bioterrorism website.

Organization	Description	Market	Estimated Numbers
PEN—Professional Epidemiology Network	Primary customer base is Infection Control Professionals and those interested in the Infection Control field.	Primary	Approximately 14,000 members.
APHA—American Public Health Association http://www.apha.org/	An association of individuals and organizations working to improve the public's health and to achieve equity in health status for all.	Primary and Secondary	50,000 members from over 50 occupations of public health.
NDMS—National Disaster Medical System http://www.oep-ndms.dhhs.gov/index.html	The overall purpose of the NDMS is to establish a single, integrated national medical response capability for assisting state and local authorities in dealing with the medical and health effects of major disasters.	Primary, Secondary, and Tertiary	More than 7,000 physicians, nurses, paramedics, pharmacists, and other allied healthcare personnel serve as members of the NDMS disaster response teams.
IDSA—Infectious Disease Society of America http://www.idsociety.org/	IDSA's mission is to promote and recognize excellence in patient care, education, research, public health, and the prevention of infectious diseases.	Primary and Secondary	Annual Conference held in October. October 2001 Attendance approximately 3,300.
OPHS—Office of Public Health and Science, U.S. Department of Health and Human Services http://www.surgeongeneral.gov/ophs/	OPHS serves as the Senior Advisor on public health and science issues to the Secretary of Health and Human Services. This site has links to many public health office and organizations.	Primary, Secondary, and Tertiary	Many links and addresses to other Public Health Offices. Emergency Preparedness Offices, etc. Could be excellent resource for mass mailings.

NACCHO—National Association of County and City Health Officials http://www.naccho.org/	NACCHO provides education, information, research, and technical assistance to local health departments and facilitates partnerships among local, state, and federal agencies in order to promote and strengthen public health.	Primary, Secondary, and Tertiary	Serves all of the nearly 3,000 local health departments nationwide. Approximately 500 attend the annual conference.
MMRS—Metropolitan Medical Response System. http://www.mmrs.hhs.gov/	Managed by the Office of Emergency Preparedness (OEP). The primary focus is to develop or enhance existing emergency preparedness systems. The goal is to coordinate the efforts of local law enforcement, fire, HAZMAT, EMS, hospital, public health, and other personnel to improve response capabilities in the event of a terrorist attack. The number one goal is to integrate biological preparedness into the overall planning process.	Primary, Secondary, and Tertiary	Membership unknown, however, various events are held every month. Bioterrorism Preparedness is a primary focus.

Commerce Marketing Strategy

This strategy depends on getting the BIPO name to individuals who are surfing the Internet and interested in Bioterrorism. To give an indication of the current size of this audience, www.bioterrorism.uv.edu recorded 2,758 page views in the month of February. Of those, 2,081 were unique visitors and the average time spent looking was 2 minutes and 29 seconds (Information supplied by John Masterson, Webmaster, University of Virginia).

Since the majority of page referrals come from search engines, especially from the first few entries returned from a search engine, it is important to be one of the first sites returned. At this point BIPO is doing quite well.

See the results listed below when you search on the term "Bioterrorism" with the following search engines:

- Google.com—The Center for Disease Control comes up first and University of Virginia's website comes up as the 2nd link on the search list.
- Looksmart.com—University of Virginia comes up 1st
- Lycos.com—University of Virginia comes up 2nd
- Yahoo.com—University of Virginia comes up 4th
- Netscape.com—University of Virginia come 13th

There are several techniques the center could use to build on this strategy, like finding similar words to search on to generate hits. See the examples below.

- Biological Warfare—Searched Google, first 50 hits and none of them were from the University of Virginia.
- Anthrax—Searched Google, first 50 hits and none of them were from the University of Virginia.
- Small Pox—Searched Google, first 50 hits had a University of Virginia pdf file posted, however, there was not a link to the university's website.

The center also could partner with other organization websites with similar interests to set up links to the University of Virginia's website. Examples may include:

- Department of Defense
- Centers of Disease Control

- Other universities
- American Medical Association—This URL is an Index to Bioterrorism Resources and contains links to other Bioterrorism related sites. http://www.ama-assn.org/ama/pub/category/6671.html
- Office of Public Health and Science—http://www.surgeongeneral.gov/ophs/
- Office of Emergency Preparedness—http://ndms.dhhs.gov/

Consult with University of Virginia's webmaster John Masterson for guidance and tips for generating hits.

Amazon.com Marketing Information

Amazon.com's website also has been researched as a place to offer our products. See the Amazon information below. Amazon pays 45 percent of suggested retail. If the university sets the price at $15.00, the School of Public Health will net $6.75 per CD-ROM.

Requirements to get set up with Amazon:

- Set "suggested retail" price assuming the university will net 45% of that.
- Obtain ISBN number for CD-ROM.
- Join the Amazon.com "Advantage Plan."
- Customize the site with the information you want to present to the public.

Amazon.com Pros and Cons

Pros: It is free and there are no initial overhead costs other than the product.

- Little or no maintenance involved.
- No variable cost—exact cost/profit per CD-ROM is known up front.
- No third-party shipping hassles; Amazon handles it.

Cons: Little or no control over how many people see your advertisement.

- Amazon.com only pays 45% of sale price.
- You must deal on "their" terms.

Production & Delivery

Production

The School of Public Health's Bioterrorism department worked with PEN in putting together a master copy of the CD-ROM. From the master, multiple copies of the CD-ROM can be made.

See a summary of the pricing below for the various lot numbers. These numbers include CD-ROM replication, a jewel case with assembly and shrinkwrap, a 4-color one-sided jewel case insert, and a cardboard mailer. See Appendix E for a complete summary of pricing and options.

Lot	Price Each
500	$2.80
1,000	$1.90
2,000	$1.75
3,000	$1.67
5,000	$1.58
10,000	$1.45

Delivery

The method of sale will depend on the delivery method. For all deliveries that require individual CD-ROMs to be shipped, it is recommended that the Bioterrorism department use a sheltered workshop. Amy Ruler of the Bioterrorism department recommended GPM. See GPM's information below.

Organization Name:	GPM
Contact:	Fred Louver
Address:	6475 Washington Boulevard Columbia, MO 65203
Telphone Number:	(800) 455-9054
Pricing:	$.10 per Envelope
Includes:	Affixing Labels Postage Metering—Would Require Necessary Reimbursement Shipping

The Bioterrorism department would be responsible for supplying the labels, materials, and envelopes. This would mean the Bioterrorism department should build into their system a way to print labels for the orders taken on the BIPO website.

SALES PROJECTIONS & PRICING STRATEGY

See below the multi-tiered pricing strategy and sales projection strategy. The current pricing strategy is priced somewhat low, and revolves a lot around PEN's current pricing structure. It is designed to try and get a fair price for the CD-ROMs, while offering discounts and quantity pricing to individuals that belong to professional health organizations.

Pricing Strategy

This pricing strategy is based on attracting individuals that belong to various professional healthcare associations. Also included is "conference pricing," whereas it may be possible to get an organization to sponsor purchasing a few hundred of the CD-ROMs at an even larger discount. This would give the university an opportunity to get its name out there and generate more business for future products, especially if the CD-ROMs contained direct links back to the Bioterrorism website.

See below two other somewhat comparable products listed on Barnes and Noble and Amazon.

Amazon.com

21st Century Germs, Germ Warfare, Anthrax, and Bioterrorism: Fort Detrick Official Medical Management Handbook plus Complete Guide to Nuclear, Biological, and Chemical Terrorism (book and CD-ROM)

List Price: $39.95

Amazon Price: $39.95

Barnes and Noble

Germs: Biological Weapons and America's Secret War (CD-ROM)

Retail Price: $30.00

Barnes & Noble Price: $24.00

You Save: $6.00 (20%)

Readers' Advantage Price: $22.80

With the exception of the "conference pricing," the prices below are the same prices PEN is charging. However, as long as the products are not identical, it would be possible to have a higher "suggested retail." Since at this point the products are identical, it is recommended the university charge the same price as PEN.

Pricing Method	Price	Description
Suggested Retail/nonmembership Barnes & Noble and Amazon Pricing	$15.00	This is the price to be charged to all individuals who are not members of the following organizations. The Bioterrorism department will need to come up with the list of the organizations to which it wants to give the discount.
Membership Pricing	$8.00	Again, the Bioterrorism department will need to decide what organizations it wants to give discounts. It is recommended to give discounts to all organizations it is interested in partnering with.
Conference Pricing—When purchasing 500 CD-ROMs or more. This also takes into consideration when purchasing newly manufactured CD-ROMs, a lot of 500 is generally the lowest price break.	$6.00	This is designed to sell the CD-ROMs in bulk. This will allow the department to make a profit, along with the hope of gaining a customer that will purchase future products such as CME credits, etc., especially since the CD-ROM will contain links back to the university's Bioterrorism website.

Sales Projection Method

Given there is not any historical data to project sales, a theoretical method was applied to all groups in the multi-distribution channel. That is a hypothetical "group member"/reachable ratio or "web visits"/sales ratio was used. That was based on a theoretical number of individuals that might possibly be reached within a given organization.

For instance, organizations such as APHA that have 50,000 members, the individuals are very spread out, thus harder to reach all 50,000. Therefore it was assigned a lower member/reachable ratio. Markets that are dense were assigned higher percentages, as it is easier to hit the masses all at once (i.e., if you could show your product at a conference, it would "hit" a very high percentage of the people).

From here an arbitrary number of 3 percent was assigned across the board. This number could be high for some markets, but is probably low for most. The theory is that of all the qualified individuals that actually see the product, 3 percent of them would buy it. In some of the organizations membership was unknown, therefore a conservative arbitrary number was applied. Again, this is a very conservative approach and focuses on making back expenditures, however, retains the flexibility for higher sales.

Please note: These numbers are based on one product only, "Be Prepared for Bioterrorism." As the product line expands, so will the markets and therefore so will the sales. Consequently, it is imperative to target the markets based on the current product line.

See Appendix A for the actual numbers that were assigned.

Sales Projection Summary

The sales projection summary in Appendix A totaled 1,818. This is the number of this particular CD-ROM that is being used as a first-year baseline. Also, scenarios for various amounts of sales can be found in Appendix B.

For the purposes of this plan a baseline price of $10.00 per CD-ROM has been established. That is an average sale price of $10.00 that includes shipping and handling. The reason for the average is some of the CD-ROMs on the Bioterrorism website may be sold at $15.00, however, many will be sold at $8.00. While on Amazon.com the net sale price after Amazon's commissions will only be $6.75, and the conference price is $6.00.

**Again, the reason for the above prices is because this is the exact price PEN is charging for the exact same CD-ROM that in turn contains PEN references. If the Bioterrorism department modifies the CD-ROM, whereas it is a different CD-ROM, and can obtain a copyright, the department will have much more flexibility over the price and how the CD-ROM is sold.*

ORGANIZATION OVERVIEW

Location

University of Virginia, School of Public Health
Center for the Study of Bioterrorism and Emerging Infections
Charlottesville, VA 22902

Legal Business Description

University of Virginia, School of Public Health Center for the Study of Bioterrorism and Emerging Infections is a private not-for-profit organization dedicated to the education and training of the public regarding the Bioterrorism prevention and response plans.

Management Team

Edward Delgado
Business Plan Developer
E-mail: edelgado@comcast.net

Pat Clebe, RN, MSN, CIC
Infectious Disease Specialist
E-mail: pclebe@uv.edu

R. John Kletcha, Ph.D., M.P.H.
Director
E-mail: rjkletcha@uv.edu

Amy Ruler, B.S.B.A.
Web Development Specialist/Business Manager
E-mail: aruler@uv.edu

Jerry S. Rutgers, M.P.H.
Associate Director of Management and Training
E-mail: jrutgers@uv.edu

James White, B.A.
Multimedia Developer
E-mail: jwhite@uv.edu

Philip J. Ferguson, Ph.D., M.P.H.
Associate Director of Science
E-mail: pjferguson@uv.edu

Lakeisha Walker, B.A.
Research Assistant
E-mail: lwalker@uv.edu

Daniel B. Portnoy, Ph.D., C.I.H.
Associate Professor in Environmental and Occupational Health
E-mail: portnoy@uv.edu

Tayanna Brown
Secretary/Receptionist
E-mail: tbrown@uv.edu

Michael V. Jennings, M.D.
Infectious Disease Consultant

Roy Jorgenson, Financial Coordinator
rjorgenson@uv.edu

Strategic Alliances

PEN—Professional Epidemiology Network
1595 M Street, SW, Suite 400, Washington, D.C. 20005-4006, Telephone: 202-789-4590, Fax: 202-789-4599.

PEN Company Overview—PEN is a multi-disciplinary, voluntary, international organization. PEN promotes wellness and prevents illness and infection worldwide by advancing healthcare epidemiology through education, collaboration, research, practice, and credentialing. PEN also offers courses that count towards Continuing Education (CE) credits.

PEN is also in the business of marketing information regarding healthcare and infection control. PEN handed out approximately 2,000 of the "Be Prepared for Bioterrorism" CD-ROMs at their 2001 "Annual Educational Conference." At this conference there was actually a specified section on Bioterrorism. This year's conference will be held in June and will include many of the same people that attended last year's conference, however, it will not contain a section on Bioterrorism.

The Director of Marketing at PEN, Jessica Blaine, has agreed to share marketing numbers and information with University of Virginia as both organizations have a common interest in marketing Education.

Appendix A

Sales Projections from Sales Projection Summary. Results of Exact Sales Projection Method Used.

1st Year Sales Projections from Various Distribution Channels for "Be Prepared for Bioterrorism" CD-ROM only

Organization	Total Number of Members	Arbitrary Estimated Percentage to Actually Reach in Market	Number of Members Actually Reached Based on the Estimated %	Estimated Number of CD-ROM Sales Projected Based on Sales of 3% of the Market Reached
PEN—Approx. 3,000 members already have the CD-ROM from the conference, this number has been deducted from the "Actual Number to Reach."	14,000	75%	7,500	225
APHA—50,000 members from over 50 occupations of public health. Note: Not as much of a primary market as PEN.	50,000	20%	10,000	300

Appendix A

Continued...

Organization	Total Number of Members	Arbitrary Estimated Percentage to Actually Reach in Market	Number of Members Actually Reached Based on the Estimated %	Estimated Number of CD-ROM Sales Projected Based on Sales of 3% of the Market Reached
NDMS—7,000+ physicians, nurses, paramedics, pharmacists, and other allied healthcare personnel serve as members of the NDMS disaster response teams.	7,000	50%	3,500	105
IDSA—Annual Conference held in October. October 2001 attendance approx. 3,300.	3,300	100%	3,300	99
OPHS—Serves as the Senior Advisor on public health and science issues to the Secretary of Health and Human Services. This site has links to many public health office and organizations.	unknown	unknown	unknown	100
NACCHO—Serves all of the nearly 3,000 local health departments nationwide. Approximately 500 attend the annual conference.	3,000	100%	3,000	90
MMRS—Membership unknown, however, various events are held every month. Bioterrorism Preparedness is a primary focus.	unknown	unknown	unknown	100
BIPO—E-Commerce Marketing Strategy, based on web visits per month, total "visits" were multiplied by 12 to come up with an annual amount. Increased visits would mean increased sales.	24,972	100%	24,972	749
Amazon.com	unknown	unknown	unknown	50
			TOTAL	**1,818**

Appendix B

Break Even/Profit Point Based on 1st Year's Estimated Sales

Sales Breakeven Summary for Initial CD-ROM	
U-V's Estimated Average Gross Sale per CD-ROM	$8.00
Plus $2.00 Shipping and Handling	$2.00
Total Estimated Gross Sale per CD-ROM	**$10.00**
Less U-V's Estimated Cost per CD-ROM *(Based on 1,000 Lot Purchase = $1.90 per CD-ROM + 1.00 shipping and handling)*	$2.90
Initial Gross Profit per CD-ROM	**$7.10**
Less University Expenses	
Less 10% of Gross Profit per CD-ROM Goes to the School	$0.71
Less 12% Gross Profit per CD-ROM Goes to the University	$0.85
78% Goes to the School of Public Health = Gross Profit per CD-ROM	**$5.54**
Initial Start-up Cost	
Estimated CD-ROM Programming Cost	$6,400
Merchant's 1st Year Annual Start-up Cost	$1,662.40
Mass Mailing to 5,000 Addresses at .25 each	$1,250.00
Total Start-up Cost	**$9,312.40**
Number of CD-ROM Sales Necessary for the School of Public Health to Break Even	1,682
Initial Number of Estimated CD-ROMs to be Sold	1,818
Difference	+136
Net Profit	**$755.68**

Appendix C

Profit/Loss Scenarios Based on Number of CD-ROMs Sold

Profit/Loss vs. Sales		**500**	**1,000**	**2,000**	**3,000**	**5,000**
U-V's Estimated Average Gross Sales per CD-ROM	$8.00	$4,000	$8,000	$16,000	$24,000	$40,000
Plus $2.00 Shipping and Handling	$2.00	$1,000	$2,000	$4,000	$6,000	$10,000
Total Estimated Gross Sales per CD-ROM	$10.00	$5,000	$10,000	$20,000	$30,000	$50,000
Less U-V's Estimated Cost per CD-ROM Based on 1,000 Lot Purchase = $1.90 per CD-ROM + 1.00 shipping and handling	$2.90	$1,450	$2,900	$5,800	$8,700	$14,500
Initial Gross Profit per CD-ROM	$7.10	$3,550	$7,100	$14,200	$21,300	$35,500
Less University Expenses						
Less 10% Of Gross Profit per CD-ROM Goes to the School	$0.71	$355	$710	$1,420	$2,130	$3,550

Appendix C

Continued...

Profit/Loss vs. Sales		**500**	**1,000**	**2,000**	**3,000**	**5,000**
Less 12% Gross Profit per CD-ROM Goes to the University	$0.85	$426	$852	$1,704	$2,556	$4,260
78% Goes to the School of Public Health = Gross Profit per CD-ROM	$5.54	$2,769	$5,538	$11,076	$16,614	$27,690
Less Initial Start-up Cost						
Estimated CD-ROM Programming Cost		$6,400	$6,400	$6,400	$6,400	$6,400
Merchant's 1st Year Annual Start-up Cost		$1,662	$1,662	$1,662	$1,662	$1,662
Mass Mailing to 5,000 Addresses @ .25 Each		$1,250	$1,250	$1,250	$1,250	$1,250
Profit/Loss		**-$6,543**	**-$3,774**	**$1,764**	**$7,302**	**$18,378**

Appendix D

Verisign Merchant Account Start-up Cost and Cost per Transaction

Cost of Merchant Account using Verisign	**One-Time Initial Start-up Cost**	**Monthly Cost**	**Annual Cost**	**Additional Transaction Cost for more than 500 Transactions per Month**	**Total First-Year Annual Cost**
Payflow Link for lower volume selling, signup fee up to 500 transactions per month; includes credit card and electronic check processing	$179.00				$179.00
Annual cost to use Payflow Link program			$349.00		$349.00
Monthly charge		$19.95			$239.40
One-time cost to purchase 128 bit secure socket layer software	$895.00				$895.00
Total annual first-year cost based on less than 500 transactions per month					**$1,662.40**
Total first-year cost per month, total cost divided by 12 to establish monthly baseline based on less than 500 transactions per month					**$138.53**

Economies of Scale...		**Number of Transactions per Month**	**Cost per Transaction**
		100	$1.39
		200	$0.69
		300	$0.46
		400	$0.35
		500	$0.28
		600	$0.33
		700	$0.30
		800	$0.27
		900	$0.25
		1,000	$0.24
		1,500	$0.19
		2,000	$0.17
		3,000	$0.15
		4,000	$0.13
Optional toll free 24 x 7 support per month	**$495.00**	**5,000**	**$0.13**

Appendix E

CD-ROM Replication and Packaging Prices

CD-ROM Replication Pricing Approx. 10-Day Turn Around	Quantity	Price	Price Each
	500	$849	$1.70
	1,000	$899	$0.90
	2,000	$1,499	$0.75
	3,000	$1,999	$0.67
	5,000	$2,999	$0.60
	10,000	$4,499	$0.45

Price includes 3-color CD-ROM Label.

Packaging Options	Price Each
Jewelcase with assembly and shrinkwrap	$0.25
Tyvek Sleeve with window and flap	$0.20
Tyvek Sleeve without window and flap	$0.10
Plastic Sleeve	$0.12

	Tray Only	2-Panel	2-Panel	4-Panel
Jewelcase Insert Price List	**4-color on front, nothing on back**	**4-color on front, black on back**	**4-color on front, 4-color on back**	**4-color on front, black on back**
1,000+	0.50	0.80	1.00	0.95
500-999	0.60	0.90	1.25	1.10
300-499	0.70	1.10	1.40	1.25
100-299	0.80	1.20	1.50	1.40
50-99	1.25	1.75	2.05	1.95

Cardboard CD-ROM Mailers Price List	Blank	1-Color	2-Color	4-Color
1,000	0.25	2.70	2.82	3.83
5,000	0.23	0.66	0.70	0.92
10,000	0.21	0.42	0.44	0.55
25,000	0.20	0.27	0.32	0.33
50,000	0.19	0.21	0.21	0.24
100,000	0.18	0.19	0.19	0.19
Film		$95.00	$165.00	$375.00

For the purposes of this project, the highlighted prices and quantities were used. The reason for the Jewelcase insert is for a barcode and/or logo if required for an ISBN number. Therefore, see the cost per CD-ROM in lots of 1,000. It might be possible to find better and/or package pricing once the final configuration is known. **$1.90**

Appendix F

Technology Access Survey Information

The following survey was sent to three separate groups, physicians who belong to AMA, infection control practitioners who belong to PEN, and state and local health departments. A random sample was drawn to develop the mailing list for the physicians and the infection control practitioners. The survey sent to public health professions was not random, but sent to state health department epidemiologists, all local health departments, and the 120 cities that received government funded BT training prior to September 11, 2001. The department received approximately 1,000 surveys back from each of the groups. Information provided by Philip J. Ferguson, Ph.D., M.P.H., Associate Director of Science.

Physician Access to Technology at Work or Home

Technology Access	Work % (n)	Home % (n)	Either Location % (n)
Computer with CD-ROM	78.5 (884)	91.0 (1052)	91.4 (1089)
Computer with Internet	84.9 (968)	92.6 (1070)	95.1 (1133)

Preferred Method of Training by Physician Specialty for Bioterrorism Preparedness

	Family Practice % (n)	Emergency Medicine % (n)	Internal Medicine % (n)	Infectious Disease % (n)
Professional Meeting	26.8 (151)	22.7 (158)	24.1 (102)	27.1 (214)
Journal Article	14.4 (81)	11.7 (81)	13.2 (56)	15.8 (125)
Grand Rounds	6.21 (35)	4.60 (32)	14.4 (61)	12.4 (98)
Inservice	10.3 (58)	8.20 (57)	11.3 (48)	4.94 (39)
Internet	8.16 (46)	7.19 (50)	7.08 (30)	8.24 (65)
Video	6.56 (37)	10.8 (75)	8.25 (35)	7.10 (56)
CD-ROM	7.27 (41)	9.35 (65)	7.31 (31)	5.32 (42)
Table Top	6.21 (35)	9.35 (65)	2.83 (12)	7.35 (58)
Audio Recording	6.74 (38)	9.50 (66)	3.77 (16)	3.55 (28)
Case Presentation	4.79 (27)	5.04 (35)	5.42 (23)	4.69 (37)
Satellite teleconference	2.66 (15)	1.58 (11)	2.36 (10)	3.42 (27)

Table included participants who selected three or less preferred methods of educational delivery.

Preferred Method of Training for Bioterrorism Preparedness by Location for Infection Control Practitioners

	Rural % (n)	Urban % (n)	Suburban % (n)
Professional Meeting	61.1 (253)	57.0 (254)	62.0 (152)
Video	38.6 (160)	27.6 (123)	30.2 (74)
Satellite teleconference	32.4 (134)	26.5 (118)	29.4 (72)
Formal Class	17.4 (72)	25.3 (113)	26.1 (64)
Internet	25.6 (106)	19.5 (87)	22.0 (54)
Table Top	15.7 (65)	24.7 (110)	25.7 (63)
Journal Article	21.3 (88)	23.1 (103)	19.2 (47)
Case Presentation	17.9 (74)	21.7 (97)	20.0 (49)
Inservice	17.4 (72)	16.6 (74)	15.9 (39)
CD-ROM	17.4 (72)	13.0 (58)	11.8 (29)
Grand Rounds	3.4 (14)	8.1 (36)	6.5 (16)
Audio Recording	2.2 (9)	4.3 (19)	1.2 (3)

Table includes participants who selected three or less preferred methods for delivery of educational materials.

Preferred Method of Reference Material Provision for Bioterrorism Preparedness for Public Health

	State-PH % (n)	Local-PH % (n)	120City-PH % (n)	Total
Internet	59.2 (45)	51.4 (415)	51.1 (115)	51.8 (575)
Hotline/Helpline	21.1 (16)	56.6 (457)	36.0 (81)	50.0 (554)
Textbook	39.5 (30)	30.2 (244)	33.3 (75)	31.5 (349)
Pocket Card	14.5 (11)	15.6 (126)	22.2 (50)	16.9 (187)
FAX On Demand	6.6 (5)	13.2 (107)	8.9 (20)	11.9 (132)
CD-ROM	2.6 (2)	4.8 (39)	4.9 (11)	4.7 (52)
Journal Article	23.7 (18)	1.9 (15)	5.8 (13)	4.1 (46)
Electronic Organizer	5.3 (4)	1.5 (12)	5.8 (13)	2.6 (29)

Table included participants who selected three or less preferred methods of educational delivery.

Appendix G

Website Disaster Recovery Considerations

Disaster Recovery—A contingency plan for the Bioterrorism website needs to be looked at. After all, we are talking about disasters. Various "what if" scenarios need to be taken into account and The School of Public Health needs to decide what is mission critical and what still needs to function in a time of disaster. From there the school can decide the best option to pursue in the case of a disaster. Scenarios that should be taken into consideration are…

What if the website was hacked by a terrorist at the same time biological agents are released?

What if the data center or point where the server resides in Charlottesville is gone via a natural or intentional disaster?

What if Charlottesville, or the University of Virginia were gone? This also pertains to the CDC. Where would the public turn to for direction?

Although these are scenarios that may be unlikely, they need to be addressed, and at least the appropriate risk assigned to them. People thought the World Trade Center bombing was unlikely as well. If it were not for contingency plan regulations mandated by the SEC, many of those companies may have not been able to do business for weeks or months.

Possible options could include a second data center or server setup at another site out-of-state. This could reside at another U-V location. This server could be used to do load balancing, or just used as a fail-over server in case of emergency.

Many third-party companies offer facilities that you can go to with your backups and restore your setup in a disaster mode. These types of companies supply floor space, servers, and network connections out-of-state that can be accessed in case of a disaster.

Either way the university needs to decide how important this is, research the cost, and do a cost benefit analysis for the various options.

Appendix H

Summary of "To Do's" and Recommendations

1. Research the possibility of obtaining a copyright.
   This would require re-programming the CD-ROM and removing the PEN segments from the CD-ROM and replacing them with the Bioterrorism department's material.
2. Add "hot links" to the CD-ROMs that take the user back to the Bioterrorism website.
   This will help keep the website in front of the customer and allow them to view additional products.
3. Add a PDA downloadable section to the CD-ROMs.
   This will add value to the CD-ROMs and position the university in the future as PDAs become more popular.
4. Contact the organizations listed in Direct Sales and Marketing Information.

   Inquire about:

   - Getting hot links from their website to the University of Virginia's Bioterrorism website. It may be necessary to add a link from your website to theirs.
   - Get key individuals sample copies of the CD-ROMs and find out if their membership would be interested.
   - See if they will sponsor something in their newsletters.
   - Inquire about upcoming conferences and find out what is necessary to exhibit the product.
5. Work on getting more words recognized on search engines. See BIPO E-Commerce Marketing Strategy.
6. Obtain ISBN number.
7. Contact Barnes and Noble about marketing through their bookstores and website.
8. Add another CD-ROM to the product line tailored toward the "Tertiary" market, which includes Fire Fighters, Police Officers, and other public "1st" responders. See General Market Definitions and Customer Profiles.

9. Do an informational mass mailing to the 3,000 public health offices in the United States. Include information on the CD-ROM, website information, etc.

10. Once initial product line is complete, research implications of DVDs. This will add value, as more video time is available, however, fewer DVD players are in use.

Bistro and Wine Bar

BUSINESS PLAN

THE WINE BISTRO

3700 Johnston Boulevard
Springfield, Missouri 65804

Thanks to this plan, the restaurant owner received $35,000 in an operating loan and $30,000 in a term loan. The business is a bistro and wine bar offering customers first-rate food and wines along with a comfortable, elegant atmosphere in which to dine, meet friends, or have a drink after work.

BISTRO AND WINE BAR BUSINESS PLAN

EXECUTIVE SUMMARY

We are seeking $35,000 in an operating loan and $30,000 in a term loan. The owner will provide $15,000 in equity.

After almost 15 years in the restaurant business, Mr. Roberts is looking to open a conveniently located bistro and wine bar that will offer its lucky customers first-rate food and wines along with a comfortable yet elegant atmosphere in which to dine, meet friends, or have a drink after work.

Mr. Roberts has found an excellent spot strategically located in downtown Springfield. The restaurant will be within walking distance of two courthouses, several large office buildings, as well as many downtown businesses. Two up-scale hotels are located nearby: one with 198 rooms is located one half block away while the Best Western Hotel is only a block and a half away.

Mr. Roberts plans to take over a location that was previously a restaurant. The owner of the building will sell the equipment and furnishings at a discount. The previous business closed due to a change of priorities of the previous owner. The restaurant has been closed for three months.

The restaurant is projected to generate $100,000 in profits before taxes in the first year, after owner's draw.

THE BUSINESS

Mission Statement

Our goal at the Wine Bistro is to bring to the Springfield area a restaurant that will provide excellent food and wine at a reasonable price in a comfortable but refined atmosphere. In the summertime, patrons can dine outside in one of two patios—either the all non-smoking patio, or downwind in the cigar lounge.

Customers will find the bistro conveniently located in the center of the downtown area near two courthouses. It will be an excellent place for business people and lawyers located nearby to come for a delicious lunch and a good quality glass of wine. It will be an appropriate place to take clients: the perfect place for a lunch meeting.

Description

The Business at a Glance
Legal Name: The Wine Bistro
Type: Service
Product/Service: Restaurant and wine bar
Form: Corporation, not yet registered
Status: Start-up
Ownership: 100% by Mr. Roberts
Facility: 12,000 square feet on two floors plus patio in the summertime

The Products and Services

The Wine Bistro will offer clients high-end dining at a reasonable price. We will have 40 seats, plus two patios in the summertime with up to 50 more seats.

When customers enter the restaurant in the foyer, there will be a comfortable couch and coffee table where people can wait for a table or for their friends. Once inside the restaurant there is a bar with a large picture window and ten bar stools where patrons can also wait for a table or just have a drink after work. On the main level past the bar there is room for ten seats at three or four tables. Upstairs there is an "L" shaped dining area, with two sections. One section has five tables, while the other has four to five tables, for a total of 40 seats. The restaurant is broken up into smaller areas that allow the customer more intimate dining and chatting with friends.

Unique Selling Proposition

Our first priority is quality and presentation of the food. We will use the freshest local ingredients. For example, many of our cheeses will come from the local dairy, while we shop at the local Farmer's Market for fresh produce.

In the summer we will operate two patios. It will be the only place in Springfield with a non-smoking patio and also an outdoor cigar lounge.

Strategy

Our strategy will rely on the experience and proven track record of Mr. Roberts. We will take over a location where previously a restaurant was operated. Unlike the previous owner of the restaurant, we will bring to the venture experience, commitment, a sufficient amount of capital, and local goodwill.

The owner of the building bought the restaurant equipment and the fixtures from the previous tenant. We will be able to purchase these at a discount. The owner is interested in finding a new tenant for the location and has committed to waiving the first month's rent and will contribute to initial advertising.

Regulations

We will need a liquor license. There is already an existing license from the previous owners. We can use the old license for 90 days. We will be able to get our own license during this time. There will be no interruption in coverage.

THE MARKET

Market Overview

Though there are three other restaurants in Springfield that offer high-end dining, the Springfield area is large enough to comfortably support another restaurant offering high-quality food and service.

A key way we will reach our market is through our excellent location. There are two courthouses nearby; one is two blocks away while the other is three blocks away. Within walking distance is a regional building, the Centre (a large theatre), a new theatre soon to be opened called the Theatre, and a Mutual Life branch with about 100 employees. The Sheridan, a 198-room hotel, is only half a block away, while the Best Western Hotel is only one-and-a-half blocks away. There are many local shops nearby. The Farmer's Market is close by, and also a small mall and fitness center.

Key Market Trends

As the baby boom generation continues to age, and their children grow up, baby boomers have more free time and money to go out to dinner. Fast-food restaurants, the domain of young families, have fallen out of favor as many boomers now demand more nutritional, higher-quality food. Fine dining allows people to socialize and relax as they meet friends over excellent food and a fine glass of wine.

Competition

Our direct competitors consist of the following:

- The Salmon Bar serves nouveau cuisine with low prices but very small portions. They have only been open 8 months but people haven't been very receptive to it.
- LaCosta is part of a chain of restaurants. They have reasonable prices and serve

reasonable food. They have close to 200 seats in a Mediterranean-style dining room. They offer a fair wine list that is relatively expensive. The food is consistently middle-of-the-road while the service isn't very consistent.

- The Seafood Place is a well-known restaurant with a good reputation. It's been in business for 15 years. It's located right downtown. It offers good food at about the same price that we will have. They have a small wine list. They only have 60 seats.

Fine Dining in Springfield

Competitor	**Number of seats**
The Salmon Bar	100 seats
LaCosta	200 seats
The Seafood Place	60 seats
Total	**360 seats**

Competitive Analysis

The Wine Bistro will offer its clients consistently excellent food and service, along with an exceptional wine list. The staff will be knowledgeable about wines and be able to suggest the best wines to go with a particular meal. Unlike the Salmon Bar where servings are artistic but meager, we will offer our clients the aesthetics of food as well as high-quality taste and reasonable portioning.

LaCosta, which is part of a chain of restaurants, is less able to control the quality of food and service. As owner/operator, Mr. Roberts will be able to monitor all aspects of the restaurant and ensure high quality. Regulars of our establishment will get to know him and the staff and will enjoy a friendly atmosphere that may be missing from a chain restaurant.

The Seafood Place is an example of a successful Springfield restaurant. However, it can only offer 60 seats. We can benefit from the Seafood Place clients who may be looking for variety in their dining experience.

MARKET STRATEGY

Marketing Plan

The Wine Bistro will look to a particular segment of the community for customers. Perhaps our strongest advantage is our location in the business area of Springfield. We will build on the customers that Mr. Roberts has developed over many years in the business. For new customers our food and service will speak for itself; people will return based on the quality of experience of their first meal at the Wine Bistro.

We intend to become a recognized and active participant in the local community. Already, from working and living in the area, Mr. Roberts is well known in the community. The Wine Bistro will build on this and take an active part in promoting the well being of the area by hiring locally trained chefs, graduates from local colleges, and by buying locally. There is a strong sense of community in Springfield from which we can all benefit.

Market Positioning

Our position in the market will be entry-level fine dining. The atmosphere will be a casual yet refined atmosphere. People will feel comfortable coming for dinner but they will also feel that they are going somewhere special. Though there will be no dress code, no one will feel overdressed if they decide to dress for a special occasion.

Pricing Strategy

In the Springfield area we will lean towards a higher end price. Though we will be less expensive than LaCosta, we will be positioned in the mid to high-end range. However, customers will be able to taste the value in each dish we serve. We will use only premium ingredients. Food costs will be a third of the price of each plate.

Advertising and Promotion

We will have a grand opening party to promote the opening of the restaurant. We will do a direct mailing of 1,000 names, addresses, and e-mails that Mr. Roberts has collected from previous customers. We will also contact lawyers from offices located around the courthouses, as well as local businesses. We have allocated $1,500 for the Grand Opening Party and mailing. The Grand Opening will consist of an open house where people will be invited to visit the restaurant, meet Mr. Roberts, and the chef. During this event, hors d'oeuvres and wine and beer will be served.

The owner of the building has committed to doing some advertising for the Grand Opening as well.

Also, as an annual event we will be holding the Big Brothers Gala Event. This is a fundraiser for the organization with contributors paying $200 a plate. This gives us a chance to support an important organization, as well as giving the restaurant high exposure in the community. The dinner takes place in late February giving us a boost during the slow season.

Restaurant Loading Forecast
December 2001 Loading Forecast

	Mon	Tue	Wed	Thu	Fri	Sat	Monthly
% Loading							
Lunches	50%	50%	75%	50%	100%	25%	
Dinners	50%	50%	75%	75%	150%	150%	
Total Seats	**40**						
Number of Meals							
Lunches	20	20	30	20	40	10	602
Dinners	20	20	30	30	60	30	946
November 2001 Loading estimated at 40% of December							**40%**
Lunches							241
Dinners							376
January and February 2002 Loading estimated at 65% of December							**65%**
Lunches							391
Dinners							615
March 2002 Loading estimated at 80% of December							**80%**
Lunches							482
Dinners							757
April and May 2002 Loading estimated at 100% of December							**100%**
Lunches							602
Dinners							946
June, July, and August 2002 Loading estimated at 130% of December							**130%**
Lunches							783
Dinners							1,230
September, October, and November 2002 Loading estimated at 100% of December							**100%**
Lunches							602
Dinners							946

Risks

There are three basic reasons why a restaurant fails. They are:

- **Lack of management skills of the owner.** Many new restaurant owners don't have a good understanding of or experience in restaurant business. Mr. Roberts has worked almost 15 years in the industry and worked for a range of restaurant types from start-up restaurants to established restaurants. During the past three years he has been the General Manager of Rosa's Place Restaurant in Springfield.
- **The menu and atmosphere don't match.** We will match up-scale atmosphere with fine food and wine.
- **Under capitalization.** Many restaurant owners forget about the need for working capital. They overestimate how busy they will be and end up going out of business in the first six months.
- **Poor location.** We have a great location, especially for lunch. We feel confident that lunch will bring dinner. Many people will come for lunch because lunch is cheaper then decide to come back with their wife or husband for dinner.

Rewards and Opportunities

This represents an excellent opportunity to open a restaurant in a previously successful location with experienced and seasoned management.

OPERATIONS PLAN

Management

Mr. Roberts, Owner/Operator—Mr. Roberts has almost 15 years of experience in the restaurant business. Over the past three years he has been the manager of the award-winning restaurant Rosa's Place. From his many years of experience working in many different establishments he has gained a wealth of knowledge managing a successful restaurant.

Advisors

- Lawyer: Mr. Dave Smith, Springfield
- Accountant: GH Accounting Services, Springfield
- Bank: CitiBank, Springfield

Personnel Plan

The core staff is the manager and the chef. Other staff will be added based on actual customer requirements. The plan below is based on supporting the sales plan forecasted in the previous section.

				Headcount
Position	**Monthly Rate**	**Start**	**Oct-01**	**Nov-01**
Manager	2,200	-	-	1
Chef	2,200	-	-	1
Waiters	1,300	-	-	3
Part-time Cook	1,300	-	-	2
Part-time Dishwasher	800	-	-	1
Bartender	1,300	-	-	1
Total Staff		**0**	**0**	**9**

Location and Facilities

The Wine Bistro will be located at 3700 Johnston Boulevard as part of the Market Village, a six-unit complex. This location has 12,000 square feet plus another 12,000 square feet of patio in the summertime. It is an excellent location in the middle of downtown Springfield, close to two courthouses, many office buildings, and other local businesses, as well as two high-end hotels and the farmer's market.

Implementation Schedule

We hope to have the money in place by October 1 so we can open the restaurant by November 1. We will need one month to get things up and started. The owner of the building will waive the rent for the first month. We plan to have the Grand Opening during the second Sunday in November. We will be open for business during the previous week at a lower level. We can use this time to make sure everything is in working order.

November 1 is the latest we can open for this year and still benefit from the busy Christmas season. If there is a delay we will need to wait until next spring to avoid the slow winter season.

FINANCIAL PLAN

Investment Funds—Sources and Uses

Sources of Funds

Operating Line	10.00%	$35,000
Term Loan	8.00%	$30,000
Equity Investment		$15,000
Total Sources of Funds		**$80,000**

Uses of Funds	
Capital Equipment Purchases	$34,000
Deposits (Utilities, last month rent)	$4,500
Opening promotion and advertising	$3,000
Inventory—liquor and food	$7,000
Working Capital	$31,500
Total Uses of Funds	**$80,000**

Projected Balance Sheet

Period Ending	Opening Sep-2001	Year 1 Sep-2002	Year 2 Sep-2003	Year 3 Sep-2004
Assets				
Current Assets				
Cash	3,450	59,259	144,546	229,716
Accounts Receivable	-	-	-	-
Inventory	7,000	3,577	3,577	3,577
Other Short-Term Assets	4,550	4,550	4,550	4,550
Total Current Assets	**15,000**	**67,386**	**152,673**	**237,843**
Fixed Assets				
Plant and Equipment	-	34,000	34,000	34,000
Accumulated Depreciation	-	3,400	9,520	14,416
Total Plant and Equipment	**-**	**30,600**	**24,480**	**19,584**
Total Assets	**15,000**	**97,986**	**177,153**	**257,427**
Liabilities and Equity				
Current Liabilities	-	-	-	-
Short-Term Loans	-	-	-	-
Accounts Payable	-	-	-	-
Other Liabilities	-	-	-	-
Total Current Liabilities	**-**	**-**	**-**	**-**
Long-Term Liabilities				
Term Loan	-	24,500	18,500	12,500
Total Long-Term Liabilities	**-**	**24,500**	**18,500**	**12,500**
Total Liabilities	**-**	**24,500**	**18,500**	**12,500**
Owners' Equity				
Capital Input	15,000	15,000	15,000	15,000
Retained Earnings	-	58,486	143,653	229,927
Total Owners' Equity	**15,000**	**73,486**	**158,653**	**244,927**
Total Equity and Liabilities	**15,000**	**97,986**	**177,153**	**257,427**

Note: Short-term assets are deposits on utilities and last month's rent.

Project Income Statement

	Year 1	Year 2	Year 3
Period Ending	**Sep-2002**	**Sep-2003**	**Sep-2004**
Sales	478,548	552,120	552,120
Cost of Sales	161,208	185,992	185,992
Gross Margin	**317,339**	**366,128**	**366,128**
	66%	66%	66%
Operating Expense			
Salaries	14,300	156,000	156,000
Benefits and Employer Deductions	14,300	15,600	15,600
Rent	23,375	25,500	25,500
Common Expense	900	900	900
Taxes	6,600	6,600	6,600
Utilities	6,900	6,900	6,900
Repair and Maintenance Equipment	600	600	600
Phone	720	720	720
Office Supplies	360	360	360
Business Licenses	2,500	-	-
Liquor Licenses	800	-	-
Cleaners and Chemicals	1,550	600	600
Legal and Accounting Fees	2,200	1,200	1,200
Bank Fees	60	60	60
Advertising	2,500	1,200	1,200
Grand Opening	1,500	-	-
Credit Card Discounts	9,571	11,042	11,042
Total Operating Expenses	**217,436**	**227,282**	**227,282**
	45%	41%	41%
Operating Profit (PBIT)	**99,903**	**138,845**	**138,845**
	21%	25%	25%
Interest	3,847	1,700	1,220
Depreciation	3,400	6,120	4,896
Profit before Tax	**92,657**	**131,025**	**132,729**
Provision for Income Tax	34,170	45,859	46,455
Profit after Tax	**58,486**	**85,167**	**86,274**
	12%	15%	16%

Breakeven Analysis

Selling Price	$29.72	average per meal	*unit = meal*
Direct Costs	$10.01	average per meal	
Fixed Costs	$18,840	per month at beginning of second year	
Break Even Point	956	meals per month	
Normal Rate	1,548	meals per month at beginning of second year	

Meals per Month	$/month Fixed Cost	$/month Total Cost	$/month Revenue	$/month Profit
0	$18,840	18,840	-	(18,840)
478	$18,840	23,626	14,205	(9,420)
956	$18,840	28,411	28,411	-
1,434	$18,840	33,196	42,616	9,420
1,912	$18,840	37,982	56,822	18,840

Business Ratios

Profit Ratios	**Year 1**	**Year 2**	**Year 3**
Gross Margin	66.3%	66.3%	66.3%
Operating Profit Margin	20.9%	25.1%	25.1%
Net Profit After Tax Margin	12.2%	15.4%	15.6%
Return on Assets (After Tax)	59.7%	48.1%	33.5%
Return on Equity (After Tax)	79.6%	53.7%	35.2%
Activity Ratios			
Collection Days	-	-	-
Inventory Turnover	45	52	52
Debt Ratios			
Debt to Net Worth	0	0	0
Short-Term Liabilities to Liabilities	-	-	-
Liquidity Ratios			
Quick Ratio	67,386	152,673	237,843
Net Working Capital	26	82	114
Other Ratios			
Assets to Sales	0	0	1
Debt to Assets	0	0	-
Sales/Net Worth	7	3	2

Notes:

Current Ratio = Current Assets / Current Liabilities

Quick Ratio = (Cash + Receivables + Other Assets) / Current Liabilities

Net Working Capital = Current Assets - Current Liabilities

Interest Coverage = Operating Profit (PBIT) / Interest

The page left intentionally blank to accommodate tabular matter following.

Income Statement

	Start Month	Oct-01	Nov-01	Dec-01	Jan-02	Feb-02	Mar-02
		1	2	3	4	5	6
Sales							
Units							
Lunches		-	241	602	391	391	482
Dinners		-	378	946	615	615	757
Sales	**Unit Price**						
Lunches	$17.50	-	4,218	10,535	6,843	6,843	8,435
Dinners	$37.50	-	14,175	35,475	23,063	23,063	28,388
Total Sales ($)		**-**	**18,393**	**46,010**	**29,905**	**29,905**	**36,823**
Cost of Sales	**% of Sales**						
Lunches	36%	-	1,518	3,793	2,463	2,463	3,037
Dinners	36%	-	4,678	11,707	7,611	7,611	9,368
Total Cost of Sales		**-**	**6,196**	**15,499**	**10,074**	**10074**	**12,404**
Gross Margin		**-**	**12,196**	**30,511**	**19,831**	**24,418**	**30,511**
			66%	66%	66%	66%	66%

Apr-02	May-02	Jun-02	Jul-02	Aug-02	Sep-02
7	**8**	**9**	**10**	**11**	**12**
602	602	783	783	783	602
946	946	1,230	1,230	1,230	946
10,535	10,535	13,703	13,703	13,703	10,535
35,475	35,475	46,125	46,125	46,125	35,475
46,010	**46,010**	**59,828**	**59,828**	**59,828**	**46,010**
3,793	3,793	4,933	4,933	4,933	3,793
11,707	11,707	15,221	15,221	15,221	11,707
15,499	**15,499**	**20,154**	**20,154**	**20,154**	**15,499**
30,511	**39,673**	**39,673**	**39,673**	**39,673**	**30,511**
66%	66%	66%	66%	66%	66%

Operating Expense

	Oct-01	Nov-01	Dec-01	Jan-02	Feb-02	Mar-02
Salaries	-	13,000	13,000	13,000	13,000	13,000
Benefits and Employer Deductions	-	1,300	1,300	1,300	1,300	1,300
Rent	-	2,125	2,125	2,125	2,125	2,125
Common Expense	75	75	75	75	75	75
Taxes	550	550	550	550	550	550
Utilities	575	575	575	575	575	575
Repair and Maintenance Equipment	50	50	50	50	50	50
Phone	60	60	60	60	60	60
Office Supplies	30	30	30	30	30	30
Business Licenses	2,500	-	-	-	-	-
Liquor Licenses	800	-	-	-	-	-
Cleaners and Chemicals	1,000	-	-	-	-	-
Legal and Accounting Fees	1,000	-	-	-	-	-
Bank Fees	5	5	5	5	5	5
Advertising	-	1,500	100	100	100	100
Grand Opening	-	1,500	-	-	-	-
Credit Card Discounts	-	368	920	598	598	736
Total Operating Expenses	**-**	**6,645**	**21,188**	**18,840**	**18,518**	**18,656**
Operating Profit (PBIT)	**(6,645)**	**(8,991)**	**11,670**	**1,313**	**1,313**	**5,762**
		-49%	25%	4%	4%	16%
Interest	492	488	443	398	395	350
Depreciation	283	283	283	283	283	283
Profit before Tax	**(7,420)**	**(9,763)**	**10,944**	**631**	**635**	**5,128**
Provision for Income Tax	-	-	-	-	-	1,795
Profit after Tax	**(7,420)**	**(9,763)**	**10,944**	**631**	**635**	**3,333**
		-53%	24%	2%	2%	9%

Apr-02	May-02	Jun-02	Jul-02	Aug-02	Sep-02
13,000	13,000	13,000	13,000	13,000	13,000
1,300	1,300	1,300	1,300	1,300	1,300
2,125	2,125	2,125	2,125	2,125	2,125
75	75	75	75	75	75
550	550	550	550	550	550
575	575	575	575	575	575
50	50	50	50	50	50
60	60	60	60	60	60
30	30	30	30	30	30
-	-	-	-	-	1,200
-	-	-	-	-	-
-	-	-	-	-	-
-	-	-	-	-	-
5	5	5	5	5	5
100	100	100	100	100	100
-	-	-	-	-	-
920	920	1,197	1,197	1,197	920
18,840	**18,840**	**18,840**	**19,117**	**19,917**	**19,117**
11,670	**11,670**	**20,557**	**20,557**	**20,557**	**10,470**
25%	25%	34%	34%	34%	23%
305	260	215	170	167	163
283	283	283	283	283	283
11,082	**11,127**	**20,058**	**20,103**	**20,107**	**10,024**
3,879	3,894	7,020	7,036	7,037	3,508
7,203	**7,233**	**13,038**	**13,067**	**13,069**	**6,515**
16%	16%	22%	22%	22%	14%

Cash Flow

			Oct-01	Nov-01	Dec-01	Jan-02	Feb-02
Profit After Tax			**(7,420)**	**(9,763)**	**10,944**	**631**	**635**
Plus:							
Depreciation			283	283	283	283	283
Change in Accounts Payable			-	-	-	-	-
Inc (Dec) Other Liabilities			-	-	-	-	-
Operating Line (repayment)			35,000	-	(5,000)	(5,000)	-
Term Loan (repayment)			30,000	(500)	(500)	(500)	(500)
Equity Input		15,000					
Subtotal			**65,283**	**(217)**	**(5,217)**	**(5,217)**	**(217)**
Less:							
Change in Accounts Rec			-	-	-	-	-
Change in Inventory			-	(1,430)	(1,993)	(1,252)	-
Inc (Dec) in Other ST Assets			-	-	-	-	-
Capital Expenditures			34,000	-	-	-	-
Dividends			-	-	-	-	-
Subtotal			**34,000**	**(1,430)**	**(1,993)**	**(1,252)**	**-**
Net Cash Flow			**23,863**	**(8,550)**	**7,720**	**3,333**	**418**
Cash Balance		3,450	27,313	18,763	26,484	23,151	23,569
Mininum Cash Balance	$18,763						
Occurs in Month	Nov-01						

Mar-02	Apr-02	May-02
3,333	**7,203**	**7,233**
283	283	283
-	-	-
-	-	-
(5,000)	(5,000)	(5,000)
(500)	(500)	(500)
(5,217)	**(5,217)**	**(5,217)**
-	-	-
538	714	-
-	-	-
-	-	-
-	-	-
538	**714**	**-**
2,421	**1,273**	**2,016**
21,147	22,420	24,436

Coatings Inspection Company

BUSINESS PLAN

PROFESSIONAL COATINGS SERVICES, INC.

34000 Jackson Boulevard
Chicago, Illinois 60601

Professional Coatings Services (PCS) is in the business of doing third-party inspections for major coatings projects. These major coatings projects are on industrial units such as bridges, water towers, pipelines, etc. The benefit of having a third-party inspector on industrial coatings projects is that this person can make sure that the work is being performed properly and no shortcuts are being taken.

COATINGS INSPECTION COMPANY BUSINESS PLAN

EXECUTIVE SUMMARY

Professional Coatings Services (PCS) is in the business of doing third-party inspections for major coatings projects. These major coatings projects are on industrial units such as bridges, water towers, pipelines, etc. PCS inspectors will receive training from the National Association of Corrosion Engineers (NACE), which is widely recognized as being the best training program in the industry. The benefit of having a third-party inspector on industrial coatings projects is that this person can make sure that the work is being performed properly and no shortcuts are being taken. The coating application companies performing the work are on flat fee contracts, which create an incentive for these companies to cut corners to finish the job as quickly as possible. The sooner they finish the job, the bigger the profit they make.

PCS will be able to gain contracts immediately because PCS is a company created with the purpose of transferring the ownership of a family business from one generation to the next. The current family business in place is Sullivan, Inc., which was founded by Mark Sullivan, Sr., in 1988. The company currently employs Mark Sullivan, Sr., Mark Sullivan, Jr., and five other people as well as Mark Sullivan, III, during the summers.

Mark Sullivan, Sr., is seventy-years old and has done no estate planning for the business. Since the start-up costs are low for inspection services, one of the best options available to the family is to simply start another business (PCS) that would gradually take over the duties on the jobs of Sullivan, Inc. This strategy would allow for a smooth transition that does not result in a large amount of estate taxes for the next generation.

PCS will continue to be located in Chicago, Illinois, but can send inspectors to anywhere they may be needed in the U.S., and possibly globally. The firm has extensive experience in such areas as refinery and chemical plants, water treatment plants, storage tanks, pipelines, bridges, and overpasses.

PCS will build on the foundation of Sullivan, Inc., by developing inspectors that have the additional benefit of being able to identify and report to the customer potentially costly situations through their Occupational Safety and Health Administration (OSHA), Lead, and Hazardous Waste Operations and Emergency Response Standard (HAZWOPER) training. These inspectors are not the safety authority on these jobs because the coating contractors are the ones that must have a safety person to watch their operations. However, the legal system is set up in such a way that a worker getting hurt on the job can sue their employer as well as the place where the work is being performed. The PCS inspector, being someone that is in areas where few others will go, offers the customer an extra observer of working conditions. This way the company can be made aware of potentially bad situations and work to get them corrected before they become a catastrophe. PCS's distinctive competence is its higher level of professionalization stemming from its ability and willingness to train and develop its employees, as well as offer them financial security, thus turning them into the best trained and most professional inspectors available.

MISSION STATEMENT

Professional Coatings Services's mission is to become the premier coatings inspection firm in the industry by having the industry's most highly trained and professional workforce. The company's success will be built on the successes of its employees. Success will be obtained by providing employees with the best training available. We are selling the skills of individuals and thus want to have the best in the industry. Our people will be on the job site from the pre-job inspection to the final inspection using industry best practices to ensure that the coating system put in place achieves its optimal service life. Our employees also will be able to identify many safety or environmental issues that may come up on a coatings project. This added benefit will ensure that our customers are made aware of small issues that could become major issues in connection with their coatings project. Our customers can be assured when a Professional Coatings Services inspector is on the job that the job will run smoothly and correctly.

Services

Professional Coatings Services (PCS) will offer a complete package of services to assist a customer in the completion of a coatings project. PCS's employees will go through a number of different training and certification programs in order to be able to discuss with customers the wide array of issues that may come up in connection with a coatings project on their site. The services available will include:

1. **Coatings inspection:** This service ensures that the coatings procedures taking place are being completed according to specifications. Inspection takes place beginning with initial site assessment through to final inspection. PCS inspectors will ensure that the coatings contractor is in compliance with all specification requirements throughout the length of the coatings project. If an issue of nonconformance occurs, the PCS inspector would report the incidence to the customer. Customers will be matched with an inspector whose training level is necessary for the complexity of the job being performed.

2. **Failure analysis and Expert witness:** This service will be for customers that have a coatings failure that they want to have evaluated so as to determine the cause of the failure. Once the failure analysis is performed, the inspector can provide expert witness for the customer; however, expert witness is rarely used because the majority of cases are settled out of court. Only certified inspectors from the National Association of Corrosion Engineers (NACE) will be provided for such projects because if the matter goes all the way to court, having someone with NACE certification gives the best credentials for an opinion that will need to be upheld.

The main source of income for PCS will come from the coatings inspection service. Failure analysis and expert witness services have the highest margins but are sporadic and not something that can continuously sustain the company. PCS will be active in obtaining coatings inspection jobs and passive in pursuit of failure analysis jobs.

INDUSTRY & COMPETITION

The outlook for the coatings industry is good because rust will continue to occur. Eventually coatings will fail and have to be redone because coatings have a finite lifespan. The recent downturn in the economy has caused the government to cut back on its maintenance spending, particularly in transportation. However, PCS's main focus will not be in the government sector. Cutbacks in the private sector can be expected, but past experience has shown that the private sector suffers less impact than the government sector.

According to a study conducted by BM Technologies Incorporated and funded by the Federal Highway Administration, the corrosion control services industry is estimated to be a $1.2 billion industry. A search in the consultants directory of the *Journal for Protective Coatings and Linings* produced by the Steel Structures Painting Council reveals that there are 133 organizations offering coatings inspection services.

In the Midwest, there are few inspection firms. Sullivan, Inc. is the only firm located in Chicago. The closest competitor is Farmer & Associates. In the 17 years that Sullivan, Inc., has been in existence, the company has not competed against Farmer & Associates for a job. PCS's biggest possible threat of local competition will come from individuals that might decide to start up in the area due to low barriers of entry, such as no licensing requirements, low start-up costs, etc. Someone trying to start up in the area would have some difficulties because Sullivan, Inc., already holds many of the lucrative contracts. It would be more advantageous for someone to start up in another place where they would have no local competition.

Of all the firms offering coatings inspection, there is only one firm, Expert Corrosion Specialists, that is public. Expert Corrosion Specialists offers several different types of services such as coatings inspection, cathodic protection, and engineering services. Expert Corrosion Specialists, however, is not likely to be a player in the industry much longer due to their dire financial situation. The company reported in its last 10K filing dated September 30, 2003, that the company "may file, or may have no alternative but to file, bankruptcy or insolvency proceedings or pursue a sale or sales of assets to satisfy creditors."

Of the privately held companies, C-Pro Company is the largest. KTA is based out of Pittsburgh, Pennsylvania. They have been in business since 1949 and compete for jobs all over the U.S. Their services include coatings inspection, inspection instrument sales, lab testing, engineering services, and coating and environmental training. Discussions with former employees of KTA revealed that KTA does little to develop their employees. KTA has a common practice of hiring people out of local painters' union halls and putting them on coatings jobs as inspectors for KTA. These people have knowledge of how to apply the paint but typically have little to no knowledge of how to read a specification or work inspection instruments.

The most significant barrier to entry that PCS will face is name recognition. Firms such as C-Pro Company have been around long enough to have their name known in the industry. There will be a tendency on the part of the customer to want to go with the established name in the industry. However, some of the practices that KTA and others have pursued have begun to erode that name. KTA had an inspector get caught last summer taking a $5,000 bribe on a government job and is facing prison time. Expert Corrosion Specialists was caught with some accounting irregularities in the wake of Enron and thus are under constant scrutiny by the SEC. These events give PCS a window of opportunity to establish its name as the premier inspection company without the negatives attached.

PCS's competitive advantage will come from its commitment to its employees. PCS will develop a culture of continuous learning where hard work receives just rewards. PCS employees will know that they are a valuable part of the company and will have a vested interest in the success of the company. PCS's efforts in such things as training, insurance, scholarships, and bonus systems will work together to solidify PCS's commitment to its employees. Other companies will not be able to duplicate the genuine culture developed at PCS.

MARKETING STRATEGY

Promotion

PCS will immediately subcontract two jobs from Sullivan, Inc. The first job will be a chemical plant. Mark Sullivan, Jr., is currently working at this facility and has developed a strong relationship with the customer there. There are four years left on the 5-year contract signed with the chemical plant to take care of all their inspection needs.

The other job that will be subcontracted from Sullivan, Inc., is a refinery. This job provides nearly year-round fulltime employment of one inspector. At times this job will require two fulltime inspectors.

Each year PCS will add one new major contract. Possible contracts for the near future of PCS could be in the transportation and construction sectors. The important part is in making sure that PCS has qualified employees to put on the job. Jobs will not be taken if PCS cannot put a competent and well-trained inspector on the job.

Initially, promotion will be done by obtaining leads from coatings manufacturers, coatings contractors, and general contractors. Mark Sullivan, Jr., has solid contacts in each of the above sectors. Contacts that we currently have from the coating manufacturer's side are Barry Williams and Cynthia Smythe, who own the company YBK, Inc. Coatings manufacturers like to have third-party inspection to ensure that their coating is applied properly. Proper application results in a coating system that achieves its full service life. When a customer has a coating applied and that coating lasts its full service life without any problems, the customer is likely to do repeat business with the manufacturer of the coating as well as the inspection firm.

Within the coatings contractors we have contacts within many of the companies. Coatings contractors will give us leads when they know there will be third-party inspection required on a job and they want to try to get an inspection company on the job that will be fair. General contractors can actually become customers when they hire third-party inspection to protect their interests. Otherwise the general contractors can recommend good third-party inspection to their customers. This group is a newly developed market for us. Mark Sullivan, Jr., has made this contact with a general contractor and developed a good rapport with people there that he is trying to cultivate into a long-term contract with them.

Current promotion within Sullivan, Inc., is passive, and over the past month Mark Sullivan, Jr., has been called about three different jobs that led to work for the company. The next step for PCS will be to take an active approach in selling. One way of doing that will be to host seminars in the area and invite potential customers to these seminars. This way PCS can educate potential customers on the value of inspection and the benefits they can receive from it.

It will be important for PCS to hire on people as soon as possible to replace Mark Sullivan, Jr., on his inspection job because he will be much more valuable as a salesman. He will be able to go visit customers and follow up on leads. If he is able to sell to people in a passive role, he should be able to work great in an active role. Eventually, however, PCS will hire on a fulltime person to take on the selling and let Mark Sullivan, Jr., move into more of an overall business role in the company. The timing of this hire will be decided by Mark Sullivan, Jr., and Mark Sullivan, III, when they determine that the company has the manpower necessary to expand.

This person will have the sole responsibility of seeking out more work for PCS. This person will do such things as cold calling, on-site visits, and brochure mailings. This person will have to be trained in the same manner that an inspector would be so that this person can speak intelligently about what exactly it is that we provide to the customer. It also will be helpful for this person to be knowledgeable so that when they make on-site visits they can identify problem areas to show a customer right there. It is likely that this person will be someone that will be moved from an inspector within the company to the salesperson.

On most jobs, the PCS inspector will have to be a teacher of sorts. This is because most customers have no training or experience with coatings, nor do they have the time to learn anything about them. Working with coatings takes detailed knowledge of chemicals and reactions involved in the process. An inexperienced customer would have to take a lot of their valuable time to bring themselves up to speed before a coatings project takes place. PCS relieves the customer from having to take the time to learn the process, and avoid the headaches that can come from dealing with the entire process. Even the customers that have the knowledge and training of coatings can benefit from not having to take the time to watch every step of the coatings project. These experienced customers can focus on other, more important tasks that must be dealt with in their facility.

Another important aspect for PCS management and employees to work on is to write technical articles to be published in different trade magazines, such as *Materials Planning* and the *Journal of Protective Coatings and Linings*. Incentives will be put in place to encourage all those working at PCS to actively seek to have work published. This will enhance the prestige of the organization and the individual, making both more marketable.

Pricing

Currently there are no local competitors for PCS. The closest competitor is Farmer & Associates. For as long as Sullivan, Inc., has been operating in this area, the company has never bid on the same jobs as Farmer & Associates. This is important because the competitors that try to compete with PCS in this area must charge the customer a per diem and mileage. PCS will thus be able to demand a higher per hour price because it will still be cheaper for the customer to pay the extra per hour price rather than paying a lower per hour price and pay per diem and mileage. PCS will intentionally work on growth in the Midwest area to exploit this advantage. However, there inevitably will be contacts made in other parts of the country and even the world that will require PCS to charge a per diem and travel. The distinction is that these jobs will come from customers that are seeking us out and are thus willing to pay to have us come to them.

PCS delivers more service and protection to the customer than its competitors by putting the best trained and most professional inspectors on the job. PCS non-certified inspectors will cost $50 per hour on regular time and $60 per on overtime. This rate is around $5 per hour more than other firms. Customers will be paying a little more per hour for a PCS inspector, but the customer will be getting more peace of mind with a PCS inspector. Customers can be assured that they will be getting more for their money from a PCS inspector.

OPERATIONAL PLAN

PCS will begin operations out of Mark Sullivan, Jr.'s home in the Midwest. The company will be incorporated as an S Corporation. Most of the work of the business is done on the road, at the customer's location. Work performed at the office will be mostly administrative. The office will be open from 8:00A.M. to 5:00P.M. every day but Mark Sullivan, Jr., and Mark Sullivan, III, will be available by cell phone 24 hours a day.

The business will start with two officers and one employee. Two men will be out in the field working while another attends to the needs of the office and business in general. The one in the office will also be qualified to sit in on jobs if necessary. At the beginning of the calendar year 2004, the company will take on another inspector to accommodate another job.

All employees will be put on a salary to ensure that they have a steady source of income. Employees also will have health insurance available through the company. One of the key components of this company will be to have an environment of security and trust for the employees. The current job environment for a coatings inspector is uncertain because they are typically hired on a job to job basis. PCS wants its employees to be focused on their job and not worrying about from where their next job might come. PCS wants to shift the inspector's focus to ensuring the success of the business. This shift can take place by giving the inspector a salary and health insurance, which takes away the inspector's worries so that he/she can focus on the quality of their work for the company.

The payment policy of PCS will be to have customers pay every thirty days for services rendered. Some customers will inevitably pay late and it will be up to PCS management to ensure that bills are paid. Once customers become 60 days late on a payment, any PCS inspectors on that job will be immediately removed. If the debt makes it out to 90 days overdue, legal action may be considered to obtain the funds. It also will be the policy of PCS to discontinue any future business with customers that exceed the 90 days overdue threshold.

Training

All PCS employees will be at the Coating Inspection Technician level, which is successful completion of NACE CIP level one training, or higher. It is important for the employees to have at least a level one training because we want our customers to know that they are getting someone that knows how to inspect versus someone that used to paint but has no knowledge of inspection. PCS also will offer the added benefit of having inspectors trained in other areas so they can offer an extra set of trained eyes for the customer. This is important because typically the inspector is the only person going into the coatings project area besides the crew of the coatings application company. These additional benefits are:

1. **Occupational safety awareness:** Inspectors would be trained to identify and report safety hazards to the customer. Although the painting contractor is responsible for the safety of its employees, PCS's customers could be sued for allowing an unsafe working condition to exist on their property. Keeping the customer aware of any safety concerns and ways to correct them so that compliance is achieved will reduce the chances of an incident occurring that could be costly to our customer. All PCS employees will have completed the OSHA construction safety and health 30-hour course. This will ensure that the inspectors understand the major issues to look for on a construction site to keep everyone in compliance with OSHA regulations.

2. **Environmental issues awareness:** The most sought after service in this area is the understanding of lead removal laws since many projects will deal with the removal of former coating systems that are lead-based. PCS inspectors will have Lead Worker Training and HAZWOPER training in order to consult the customer on key issues of concern. These training programs will aid the inspector in being able to identify noncompliance in the field to report to the customer. Keeping the customer aware of any noncompliance can reduce the chances of costly lawsuits or possible government actions. PCS inspectors get lead and hazardous materials training offered at the state level by a third-party company. The company used would be Specialized Training Resources, Inc., which is the company currently used by Sullivan, Inc. Should any EPA training programs become available, PCS would seek EPA certification for its inspectors.

MANAGEMENT & ORGANIZATION

The three individuals that will be the first to work for PCS are Mark Sullivan, Jr., Mark Sullivan, III, and David Miller. Mark Sullivan, Jr., and David Miller are both NACE certified coatings inspectors. Mark Sullivan, III, has completed NACE level one training. Mark Sullivan, Jr., also has certifications for lead work and hazardous materials. David Miller is a former nuclear power plant inspector. Mark Sullivan, III, graduates with a Master of Business Administration degree in May 2004 and will then pursue a law degree.

Mark Sullivan, Jr., will be the senior inspector and president of the company. His duties will be to deal with questions and comments from the inspectors and clients. He also will handle all of the duties of obtaining new customers in the beginning. Mark Sullivan, III, will be the CEO of the company and deal with all the day-to-day administrative duties of the company. He also will have to handle customer phone calls and may need to sit in on jobs from time to time. Employee and customer problems or concerns can be addressed to Mark Sullivan, Jr., or Mark Sullivan, III.

Event Photography Service

BUSINESS PLAN

BRIGHTROOM, INC.

6400 Hollis Street, Suite 10
Emeryville, California 94608

brightroom doesn't take the pictures, but we work with those who do. By providing a digital infrastructure, brightroom increases photography revenue while reducing costs and eliminating time consuming, non-core business activities. brightroom enables the photographer to focus on the portion of the process where they add the most value and derive the most benefit—taking pictures.

- OVERVIEW
- MARKET OPPORTUNITY
- BRIGHTROOM'S SOLUTION
- ENTRY STRATEGY
- OTHER SEGMENTS
- SALES & MARKETING
- BETA TEST
- CUSTOMERS, ALLIANCES, & SUPPLIERS
- INDUSTRY OVERVIEW
- REVENUE MODEL
- FINANCIAL PROJECTIONS
- CURRENT STATUS & FUNDING REQUIREMENTS
- MANAGEMENT TEAM
- ADVISORY BOARD

EVENT PHOTOGRAPHY SERVICE BUSINESS PLAN

OVERVIEW

brightroom is the first fully scalable, online event photography solution.

brightroom's revolutionary process will enhance the experience, success, and personalization of any event. brightroom doesn't take the pictures, but we work with those who do. By providing a digital infrastructure, brightroom increases photography revenue while reducing costs and eliminating time consuming, non-core business activities. brightroom enables the photographer to focus on the portion of the process where they add the most value and derive the most benefit—taking pictures.

Additionally, brightroom will leverage its unique position in the photograph fulfillment process to engage in online and traditional marketing activities with the end consumer.

MARKET OPPORTUNITY

The event photography market is large: In the participatory sports event segment—brightroom's targeted entry point—there are in excess of 120 million registrations for an estimated 500,000 events annually. Industry sources report that nearly 80 percent of these participants have Internet access.

The ability to handle both film and digital formats at the outset will leave brightroom well positioned in the market with key established relationships as the market migrates to digital photography. Worldwide professional digital still photographic exposures are projected to grow from approximately 600 million in 1997 to over 3.8 billion in 2002. The professional worldwide photo image processing market is expected to grow from $10.8 billion in 1997 to approximately $14.9 billion in 2002.

Event photography is a profitable business: Based on proprietary market research, brightroom estimates gross margins can approach 50 percent in its target market from photo purchasing alone. As the medium converts to digital technologies, costs associated with development and processing will reduce significantly further enhancing margins. Ancillary revenue opportunities from direct and e-mail marketing also greatly enhance the revenue streams. It is estimated that over 40 percent of U.S. households have some sort of professional photograph taken each year. Consumers want to view and order their photos online: A recent study by Jupiter Research states that 73 percent of online consumers would like to be able view and share their photos with others online and via e-mail.

A digital solution is superior to existing methods: The current practice of sorting proof sheets and mailing thumbnails is inefficient, time consuming, and yields fewer orders. Not only are these proofs hard to evaluate for purchase, this model also restricts the audience: brightroom's solution allows for easier viewing as well as viral marketing of proofs, resulting in higher purchase rates.

Backend technology and business infrastructure are outside of the photographer's core competence: Photographers add value almost exclusively through the act of actually taking pictures. The remainder of the development process—processing negatives and printing photographs—is already outsourced to professional labs. The final pieces of the puzzle—mailing proofs, fulfilling orders, and handling payments—are similarly viewed as low value added by the photographer. The brightroom solution reduces costs and streamlines the process for professional photographers, allowing them to concentrate exclusively on the business of taking pictures.

Establishing and maintaining an e-commerce presence is still prohibitively expensive for small businesses: A recent study by the Gartner Group estimated that the average e-commerce site takes five months—and costs $1 million—to develop. In addition, there are ongoing, nontrivial costs to maintain the site and process orders. Not surprisingly, less than 5 percent of small businesses conduct sales online. By using brightroom's turnkey solution, event photographers will be able to achieve greater returns without significant up-front costs.

Order processing and fulfillment creates other significant revenue opportunities: Through the process of printing photographs, e-mailing users, driving traffic to websites where proofs are posted, and mailing prints, brightroom will capitalize off of its relationship with the end consumer. brightroom will leverage its knowledge of the end user and this relationship to realize significant revenue through online and traditional marketing activities.

BRIGHTROOM'S SOLUTION

Products and Services

brightroom offers a suite of commerce-enabling services for event photography including:

- Scanning and uploading of film photos or direct uploading of digital photos from any computer.
- Sorting and indexing of proofs.
- Online hosting at brightroom.com of photos in a digital format or remote hosting of photos on partner's website through brightroom's engineering architecture.
- E-mail notification to customers providing a unique hyperlink to view and order their prints online.
- Printing and mailing of "thumbnail" proof order forms.
- E-commerce and traditional offline order processing (phone, mail, fax).

brightroom will access, through outsource partnerships, such traditional services as:

- Development, printing and digitizing of roll film.
- Photo printing and shipping to fulfill customer orders.

Furthermore, brightroom's service offers numerous features targeted at event coordinators and their participants:

- An event homepage on brightroom where participants will come to search for and view their event photos. This page can contain links back to the event's homepage or other event promotions.
- brightroom can help the event coordinator manage their registrations and participant contact through its e-mails and mailings to customers.
- A unique, customized page for each participant containing personal elements such as race results and personal photos to view, share, and order.
- The ability to upload additional photographs and personalize photographs with captions.
- Album creation: as users participate in numerous events, their number of personalized pages increases.
- A "send to a friend" feature whereby participants can e-mail friends with their personal pages or digital postcards for additional viewing and ordering opportunities.

Benefits to the event coordinator

- Enabling participants to view, share, and order their personal event photos enhances event experience and satisfaction and leads to increased participation in future events.
- The brightroom solution makes event photography a profitable, more efficient and viable option where it was previously cost prohibitive through traditional methods.

- brightroom increases the event coordinators subsequent and ongoing contact with participants.

Benefits to the photographer

By relying on brightroom for all non-core business and fulfillment activities, professional photographers experience numerous advantages:

- Reduced proof and printing costs.
- Reduced time to consumer.
- Allows photographer to focus on their core business—taking photos.
- Increased purchase and re-order transactions and revenue through viral marketing of proofs—digital storage and circulation of photos allows a larger number of interested parties to view proofs and order prints (as opposed to the conventional system where a single set of proofs is mailed to an individual).
- Choice and flexibility in utilizing the brightroom suite of services.
- Detailed account, revenue, and campaign information to help them better manage their business through the brightroom solution.

Benefits to the end consumer

- Faster turnaround time.
- Consumers enjoy a more convenient way to share proofs and order prints. The brightroom solution is completely hassle free, including additional print ordering at any time in the future.
- Consumers can participate in specially targeted offers—a coupon on a pair of running shoes from an online sports retailer for anyone ordering a picture of a running race, for example.

Benefits to e-tailer/commerce partners

- brightroom enables commerce partners the ability to access a targeted demographic of potential customers via e-mail, direct mail, and co-branded advertisement campaigns. For example, by hosting the proofs from a marathon on a co-branded sporting goods site (as well as potentially including an incentive offer with each completed photograph order) the traffic generated by runners—as well as through viral activities—will be valuable to the retailer.

ENTRY STRATEGY

While brightroom's strategy benefits significantly from the widespread adoption of digital photography as a standard, its entry strategy encompasses existing film and photography technology. Through aggressive marketing and account acquisition, brightroom will be positioned as the dominant backend for the professional event photography industry. Attractive markets for brightroom include professional photography in the following areas: running road races and other competitive event photos such as biking and triathlons (at the finish, during the race), corporate events and trade shows, group skiing photos, wedding photos, graduations, and school portraits, as well as any other event photos. brightroom has targeted participatory athletic events (i.e. running, cycling, mountain biking, walking, swimming, triathlons) as a compelling entry point due to the size and structure of this market. With over 120 million registrations for an estimated 500,000 participatory events annually nationwide, this segment offers the ability to gain market share rapidly while proving the brightroom business model. The brightroom team's breadth of contacts makes the following geographic markets attractive primary candidates: Chicago, Dallas/Fort Worth, New York City, and San Francisco.

OTHER SEGMENTS

School Events and Graduation Photos

There were 12,436 portrait studio establishments in operation in 1994, according to the U.S. Census Bureau. These establishments employed roughly 75,000 people and earned nearly $3.2 billion in revenues. The industry includes portrait photographers, school photographers, home photographers, passport photographers, and video photographers. Specific portrait services include family portraits, wedding photos, passport photos, glamour photos, school photos, and team photos.

The professional portrait industry is segmented into two major categories and numerous subcategories of portraits. The first group is school portraits, which are further divided among kindergarten to grade 11 students, high school seniors, high school prom, and college. The second group, non-school, encompasses wedding, family, adult, daycare/nursery school, sports/team, children outside of school, glamour, class/family reunion, pet, hospital baby, church directory, and executive.

Conventions and Corporate Events

Conventions, trade shows, and corporate-sponsored events represent attractive segments for brightroom. Photo opportunities for these events range from fixed event contracts to corporate group photos. Three of the top convention markets in the U.S., Las Vegas, Chicago, and Atlanta, generated over 9.5 billion participants and nearly $10 billion in revenues in 1999 alone.

SALES & MARKETING

brightroom will market directly to event coordinators to secure long-term contracts. brightroom will then use local photographers as subcontractors to take pictures or will leverage these contracts with existing event photography firms in order to gain additional races and events with which these firms have established relationships. brightroom will partner opportunistically with existing event photographers.

Additionally, brightroom will advertise and market at trade shows and through trade organizations such as the Road Race Management Race Directors' Meeting and Trade Exhibition, Professional Photographers Association (ppa.com) and Photo Marketing Association International (pmai.org), through industry publications such as Professional Photographer, through direct contact with professional photographers, and by phone, mail, and e-mail.

BETA TEST: The Wacky Snacky 5K

On February 20, brightroom rolled out a beta test of its site and service with the Wacky Snacky, a 5k road race with approximately 1,300 runners in Chicago, in order to test site functionality and key aspects of the business model. Even with limited participant information—we didn't have access to registration or contact information and our promotion was limited to inclusion of a flyer in race packets—our site received over 1,500 unique visitors in the two weeks following the race as well as extremely positive feedback.

While the purpose of the trial was not to test our ecommerce functionality (the site allowed users to download pictures for free), brightroom actually received orders for over 40 photographs. By February 25, the company was officially post-revenue.

Additionally, based on the success of the Wacky Snacky trial, brightroom received a commitment from Chicago Special Events to utilize the brightroom solution for more than twenty participatory sporting events they produce annually.

CUSTOMERS, ALLIANCES, & SUPPLIERS

Customers

brightroom customers fall into three categories: 1) event coordinators and the businesses that produce events 2) photographers and photography businesses and 3) the end consumer.

brightroom has demonstrated the validity of its business model through the relationships it has formed through operations to date. Notably, based on the success of our pilot road race, brightroom has received commitments to photograph over 20 athletic events for Chicago Special Events Marketing with an excess of 150,000 participants. Also, EnviroSports has similarly committed to use the brightroom solution for the 30 marquee events that it produces throughout California and Washington including the Embarcadero 10k, the Alcatraz Triathalon, the Death Valley Marathon, and the Race Across California Enviro.

brightroom has also received a high degree of interest in partnerships from business development contacts at the Houston Marathon, the Chicago Race for the Cure (as well as the national organization—108 events total), the AIDS Ride (nine different events nationwide), and others.

Alliances

brightroom is in favorable discussions with online sporting goods companies such as fogdog.com and MVP.com. An arrangement with one such sports retailer could entail anything from a straight affiliate deal to direct or e-mail marketing to actual hosting of participant proofs on a co-branded sporting goods website.

Suppliers

For its development and fulfillment operations, brightroom has explored a variety of options for suppliers including Candid Color Systems, Kodak minilabs, and retail solutions.

Candid Color Systems, located in Oklahoma, is the largest U.S. digital minilab and currently provides event photography development and fulfillment for MarathonFoto as well as other, smaller operations. Candid provides an incrementally superior solution and service in terms of response time and product including captions. Additionally, Kodak's minilab in San Leandro, California, and other Internet-based retail operations (Seattle Filmworks, ofoto, etc.) provide viable alternatives which also offer competitive development costs.

By outsourcing a portion of fulfillment to a retail outlet affords brightroom the flexibility in its product offering: for example, brightroom could use one supplier to develop film, another one to print photos, and a third one for special orders such as printing photos on mousepads or T-shirts.

In short, there are a number of competitively priced options which will keep film development and print fulfillment costs well within acceptable parameters.

INDUSTRY OVERVIEW

There are an increasing number of venture-backed players such as Shutterfly.com (Jim Clark), Snapfish.com (CMGI), ofoto (Barksdale Group), Phototrust.com, Photoaccess.com, photoprint.com, PhotoPoint.com, ClubPhoto.com, ememories.com, PhotoLoft.com, and Zing.com (Kleiner Perkins), as well as established players such as Kodak and HP working to address the $14.2 billion consumer photo-processing market. These current models are similar in that they enable individual consumers to host and share their amateur photos on their respective sites. They are targeting the individual, nonprofessional consumer market.

Competition could come from the emergence of digital minilabs. Digital minilabs are forecasted to account for about 15 percent of the minilabs in the U.S. by 2002. Candid Color Systems in Oklahoma is an example of such a facility. Established in 1972, Candid is an example of a traditional minilab that is slowly making the transition from traditional photo processing methods to the digital format. However, as a photofinisher they derive their revenues primarily from the printing and finishing aspects—a highly competitive market.

Eprints.com is currently providing online hosting services for wedding photographers but has not capitalized on the potential industry aggregation and customer acquisition power of the brightroom model. Two brothers founded the company in June 1997. Based in Rhode Island, eprints.com does not appear to have significant financing or an aggressive growth strategy. Additionally, there are a few nascent players such as Primeshot (Arlington, Virginia), Photozone (Seattle), and Cyberpix (Dallas). While each of these competitors has a brochure-ware type web presence, none has appeared to achieve scale or traction in its business model. Furthermore, their strategies differ from brightroom's in key elements—entry segments are significantly unfocused and unproven, and dependence on either digital or film form. Both Photozone and Cyberpix offer services for a digital format exclusively at present—digital photography does not currently lend itself to the speed and scale of race photography. Primeshot is working to build a network of event photographers from the ground up—a slow and costly proposition.

REVENUE MODEL

brightroom's revenue will come from two primary sources: revenue from photography (i.e., sales of photos and pre-paid photography contracts) and revenue from registration and list management and advertising and direct-mail and e-mail activities.

In instances where brightroom owns the contract directly with the event, brightroom will either subcontract the photography or share a percentage of the revenue based on print ordering. In instances where the event photographer owns the contract, brightroom will partner to provide its backend infrastructure and receive a share of the revenue for its services.

Additionally, brightroom will generate a significant revenue stream by leveraging its relationship with, and deep knowledge of, the end consumer. During the proof viewing and print ordering process, brightroom will contact these users on a number of occasions through e-mail and traditional mail channels: importantly, each of these contacts is extremely likely to gain the undivided attention of the subject since it includes or concerns his or her personal picture.

For instance, through e-mailing users with a hyperlink to a site featuring proofs, brightroom can offer compelling, personalized offers as well as subsequently driving Internet traffic to a particular website to view the proofs. By contacting users through conventional mail initially with thumbnail proofs and subsequently with prints they have ordered, brightroom has the ability to present highly targeted promotions relating to the users' demographic information or relevant activities based on the content of the picture (e.g. specific promotions targeted at runners, skiers, newlyweds, etc.).

FINANCIAL PROJECTIONS

In forecasting revenues and expenses over a four-and-a-half-year period, brightroom anticipates significant initial expenditures related to building engineering infrastructure and product development and expenses associated with increased staffing to support brightroom's rapid growth.

Consolidated Projections of Operations

	2000*	2001	2002	2003	2004
Revenue	427,361	4,591,136	9,413,854	16,822,386	31,013,058
Cost of Sales	255,048	2,297,505	3,300,098	5,050,690	7,758,692
Gross Profit	**172,313**	**2,293,631**	**6,113,756**	**11,771,696**	**23,254,366**
Operating Expenses					
Sales and Marketing	30,365	103,317	115,498	184,498	323,573
Human Resources	597,500	2,832,500	3,957,500	4,316,185	4,587,500
Product Development	575,829	649,241	769,929	870,549	1,071,038
General and Administrative	117,342	193,342	193,954	193,342	193,342
Total Operating Expenses	1,321,036	3,778,400	5,036,881	5,564,574	6,175,453
Operating Income (Loss)	**-1,148,723**	**-1,484,769**	**1,076,875**	**6,207,122**	**17,078,913**

*May-Dec

CURRENT STATUS & FUNDING REQUIREMENTS

Since its founding in mid-January, brightroom has evolved quickly as a company while gaining a deep understanding of the event photography market. Among other important milestones, brightroom conducted a field trial of its business model with a beta website in early February which validated the business model. Furthermore, business development activities have continued in earnest, with commitments secured for over 50 events in California, Washington, Chicago, and Texas encompassing nearly 200,000 participants.

The company will be headquartered in Berkeley, California, brightroom is incorporated in the state of Delaware and has retained the firm of Weil, Gotshal & Manges LLP for legal services. brightroom has retained the legal services of Conley Rose & Tayon and is currently in the process of filing for patent protection for key elements of its core business.

brightroom has been funded entirely by the founding partners to date and is seeking $1-2 million in first round financing. This capital will be used for continued development and marketing expenses including costs associated with hardware and software, recruitment and salaries, operations, and sales-related activities.

MANAGEMENT TEAM

brightroom has assembled a founding team with diverse, complementary skills which will allow the company to craft and execute strategy successfully. In addition to a broad range of abilities and experiences, the individuals also present a history of collective accomplishment, having worked together on significant projects prior to brightroom.

Burch LaPrade, CEO
Burch is responsible for shaping the company through building a team and driving strategy including product development.

He brings significant experience at early stage Internet start-ups, having shaped and executed marketing and business development strategies at GetawayZone and flyswat during product development and initial launch. Additionally, while receiving his M.B.A. at the University of California at Berkeley, Burch completed numerous Internet marketing consulting projects as part of the Management of Technology certificate program.

Prior to graduate school, Burch was a police officer for the city of Berkeley. In addition to patrol, he worked in various special assignments during his five-year tenure, including Narcotics, the Special Response Team, and as a negotiator for the SWAT team. Burch received his undergraduate degree in Economics from Yale University.

Sol Kanthack, President

At brightroom, Sol is responsible for overall business model development, identifying and forging strategic alliances, and day-to-day operations including financing decisions. Sol has several years of sales, marketing, and financial experience with notable firms such as Merrill Lynch and J. P. Morgan. Most recently he worked as an integral part of the business development team at flyswat, a venture-backed start-up, and as a student associate evaluating business plans with Trident Capital, a well-established venture capital firm investing primarily in business-to-business e-commerce.

Sol will receive his M.B.A. from the University of Chicago Graduate School of Business in June. While at the GSB, Sol was chosen to participate in the very selective Kauffman Entrepreneurial Internship Program that sponsors students to work with start-up companies. He was also honored as the sole second-year student at the GSB to receive the ARAMARK/Joe Neubauer Scholarship for Entrepreneurship. Additionally, he has been very active as a Co-chair of the Entrepreneurship and Venture Capital Group, forging new inroads for the GSB's Entrepreneurial efforts. Sol received a B.B.A. in Finance from Texas Christian University.

Rich Snipes, CTO

Rich is responsible for technical architecture and development of the brightroom web presence. In addition, Rich is charged with building the brightroom engineering team and managing relationships with third-party technical support groups.

Rich's background includes significant design and development experience with both Internet and intranet-based solutions including database design and integration as well as front-end architecture and deployment. He has led development efforts in all phases, from design, through implementation, to testing.

Rich was awarded Dean's List and Gamma Kappa Alpha honors at the University of North Carolina where he received bachelor's degrees in Physics and Economics.

Molly Kanthack, Vice President of Sales/Marketing

Molly's background in sales and marketing at notable media, fashion, and sports organizations such as Walt Disney, Calvin Klein, and TYR Sport, Inc., will help drive brightroom's client acquisition and retention and strategic marketing efforts.

Molly was the co-founder of the Event Marketing department at a Walt Disney subsidiary. She organized and managed large trade shows and special events while obtaining corporate sponsorships and alliances. At Calvin Klein, Molly organized seminars and trade shows to further establish brand awareness with the consumer market and also worked on major media marketing campaigns with premier fashion publications. At TYR Sport, in the Sales and Marketing division, Molly was the sales manager of Illinois, increasing sales by 25 percent in the first quarter alone. Most recently, Molly was appointed by the Deputy Dean to manage one of the University of Chicago's fundraising programs by establishing and developing major corporate and alumni relations.

Molly was a scholarship athlete in Texas Christian University's world-class Division IA track and field program while completing her dual degree in Advertising/Public Relations and Psychology.

Chris Miller, Business Development
Chris has a background in law. Licensed as an attorney since 1997 in Texas, he has several years' experience in both litigation and transactional commercial practice. Most recently he worked with Weil, Gotshal & Manges, L.L.P. in Houston. Business development responsibilities with brightroom include identification and development of strategic partnerships and alliances.

Legal responsibilities with brightroom include drafting and review of miscellaneous contracts, service agreements, and related transactions. He is also responsible for basic corporate governance matters and human resources matters.

Chris received his undergraduate degree from Texas Christian University and his J.D. from the University of Houston Law Center.

ADVISORY BOARD

Jim Moliski, Co-Founder and Chief Operating Officer of Optomail
Jim is a pioneer in the business of e-mail permission marketing. He currently serves as COO of Optomail, a venture-backed permission marketing firm in Japan. Previously, as Employee #2 and Product Manager for MarketHome Inc., a U.S. firm in the same space, Jim spearheaded product and business development, resulting in a successful sale to that ClickAction (NASDAQ: CLAC) in July 1999. Previously, Jim worked at Mercer Management Consulting, where he participated in a variety of marketing cases for large U.S. and international companies. Jim received a B.S. from the University of Pennsylvania and an M.B.A. from the Haas School of Business, University of California - Berkeley.

Stephen S. Beitler, Managing Director Trident Capital
Mr. Beitler joined Trident Capital in 1998 as a Managing Director. From 1993 to 1998, Mr. Beitler was Assistant Corporate Controller at Sears, Roebuck & Co. From 1989 to 1994, Mr. Beitler was Corporate Director-Strategy and Development at Helene Curtis Industries, Inc., a subsidiary of Unilever. Earlier in his career, Mr. Beitler was an Intelligence Officer in the Green Berets, and served as the Assistant to the Under Secretary of Defense (Acquisition) and Intelligence Officer to the Secretary of Defense and the Chairman of the Joint Chiefs of Staff.

Mr. Beitler earned his B.A. from the School of International Service at the American University and his M.S.S.I. from the Defense Intelligence College. Mr. Beitler also completed graduate work at the University of Chicago.

Fertilizer & Commodity Chemicals Company

BUSINESS PLAN

AGRONIX ORGANICS, INC.

1666 West 75th Avenue, 2nd Floor
Vancouver, British Columbia V6P 6G2
Canada

Agronix Organics, Inc., plans on becoming a leading biotechnology firm, licensing technology for the conversion of common agricultural residue into environmentally friendly, bio-stabilized organic fertilizers and soil-enhancers, plus a host of related products. This plan, created by Concord Business Development, Inc., of Vancouver, raised $1.7 million for the company.

HIGHTLIGHTS

Industry and Sector: Biotechnology/Fertilizers, Commodity Chemicals

Mission Statement
Agronix Organics, Inc., will be a leading biotechnology firm, licensing technology for the conversion of common agricultural residue into environmentally friendly, bio-stabilized organic fertilizers and soil-enhancers, and a range of commodity chemicals produced on-demand, including ethanol for alternative fuel use. First to market with technology that offers significant advances over existing commercial methods and which uses only naturally occurring microbes during the enclosed channel bioconversion process, the company will work on a global, regional, national, and multinational basis in licensing the technology and in ongoing equity participation with licensees.

Singular Features
Fully bio-converted organic fertilizers and other products that meet or exceed criteria in current and proposed legislation; turnkey commercial-scale operations; rapid product turn-around time. Flexible, economically viable, on-demand production of chemicals to meet market requirements. Use of only naturally occurring (not genetically modified) microbes. Heavy metal contaminants changed from water-soluble to water-insoluble form.

Target Market
Technology transfer licensing program for qualified investors in North America and Europe, followed by Asia and South America.

Capital Requirements
Agronix Organics, Inc., is currently seeking US$5 million from both private and public sources to implement its global strategy.

Use of Proceeds
Research and development costs; formulation and calibration plant, product development, and general and administrative costs; marketing of the company's Technology Transfer Licensing program.

Management Projections
By the end of Year 1, the company expects revenues to be US$0.76 million; US$7.80 million by the end of Year 2; and US$34.12 million by the end of Year 3.

EXECUTIVE SUMMARY

Vision: Completing the Cycle

The problems associated with organic waste—such as animal manures, crop residues, and industrial waste—are not new. However, recent events, such as at Walkerton, Ontario, where seven people died from water contaminated by animal manure leachates, have raised many concerns about the approach Canada, the United States, and other industrial countries have chosen to deal with organic waste.

To make a significant contribution to resolving environmental pollution associated with organic waste, it is necessary to understand how Nature works. Any long-term viable solution has to be determined in accordance with how naturally produced matter is recycled through extremely small steps into essential compounds such as CO_2, H_2O, and minerals. For example, the production of plant constituents through photosynthesis is the result of several hundred minute steps, each requiring very small amounts of energy. Dead leaves on the ground are used in part by soil fauna to produce soil fauna biomass, and the least biodegradable materials are released for additional biological and chemical transformations by soil microorganisms, exoenzymes, and chemical reactions. Eventually, they are further decomposed by soil enzymes and soil microbes into more bio-resistant soil organic matter. At all of these steps, some components of the starting material are transformed into CO_2 and H_2O, but most are transformed into compounds that are more resistant to biodegradation.

It is also important to realize that the process takes time—simply adding raw agricultural residue to the soil makes it more depleted in organic matter than it was at the time the residue was incorporated. Any "artificial" process used to speed this up must increase the beneficial uses while retarding as much as possible the production of water-soluble materials or gases that contribute to air and water pollution. As well, until now, technology for the production of energy or chemicals from organic material has usually used anaerobic digestion to produce methane or fermentation to produce ethanol—and both processes have a negative impact on the environment by releasing carbon, nitrogen, and sulphur-based gases into the atmosphere and by significantly increasing the water solubility of residual organic and inorganic matter.

On the other hand, the company's technology for fully optimized bioconversion of organic residues into fully bio-stabilized organic matter follows Nature's path in producing a variety of components based on the chemical composition and biological and chemical reactivity of the source material. In this process, the amount of water-soluble organic and inorganic matter is reduced and the production of CO_2 and H_2O is limited.

Products and Services

The company's technology consists of two technical processes that can be operated independently or in conjunction with one another. Sources of material include agricultural residue, raw livestock manures, and other organic residues (olive sludge, brewers residue, etc.). Using these technologies and working with the company's strategic partners, Agronix Organics, Inc., will develop turnkey agricultural residue processing plants for licensing to investors with the option of equity investment.

Bio-Conversion Reactor (BCR) System
Ready for industry launch, this bioconversion process goes beyond what is possible with composting and produces fully sanitized and bio-stabilized organic matter suitable for use as value-added agricultural and gardening products, soil conditioners, growth substrates and enhanced, organically based fertilizers. During the process—which takes less than half the time as the closest comparative technology—no pollution or residue is produced and the end product is completely safe for the environment.

Bio-Chemical Integrated Recycling (BCIR) System
At the engineering stage (post laboratory), this environmentally friendly process has been proven to extract from bio-residue more than 65 chemical commodities suitable for sale to industry, including ethanol as a fuel additive or alternative. Other products include: polymers, surfactants, lubricants, alternative fuels, de-icers, adhesives, pharmaceuticals, and agro-chemical product ingredients.

Marketing Strategy

Agronix Organics, Inc., will deploy its BCR technology into the North American and European market first, closely followed by its BCIR technology (in the final phases of testing). Marketing will then continue into China, Southeast Asia, Australia, New Zealand, and South America. To take advantage of the multinational and multi-industry applications of the two technologies, the company is in the process of developing a three-part, highly flexible Technology Transfer and Licensing Structure that includes the following:

Technology Transfer Region Agreements

Based nationally or within economic communities (such as Western Europe), these agreements will take the form of either a License or Joint Venture between Agronix Organics, Inc., and one or more companies or government agencies. Any agreements would center on the ability of the candidate(s) to quickly establish the program within the region defined, taking into account the impact that cultural, regulatory, and language implications would have on the market entry process. Production and sales would be organized independently within each region. Agreements would include both processes, the Bio-Conversion Reactor (BCR) System and Bio-Chemical Integrated Recycling (BCIR) System.

Regions will be established based on strategic partnerships, organic residue availability, and the quality and efficiencies of processing the residues into value-added products for the specific region.

Sales and Distribution Territory Agreements

As the company's BCR and BCIR Systems generally serve different markets, they will have separate Sales and Distribution Territory licenses, although the same group may subscribe to both. For the BCR System, the Sales and Distribution Territory Agreements will follow natural boundaries (based on what crops are grown and the weather) rather than political ones, allowing Agronix Organics, Inc., and its regional Technology Transfer Licensee to tie into many existing marketing networks and channels of distribution. An example is the Pacific Northwest of North America. An estimated US$1 to US$2 million is required for a Sales and Distribution Territory; likely companies are established industry sector distributors or marketing organizations.

Production Area Licenses

Within each Sales and Distribution Territory there may be several Production Area License Plants with either or both BCR or BCIR operating licenses. Each license will be tied to a pre-established organic residue collection area that will supply the raw material required for that plant and the dedicated products it will produce.

An estimated US$7 million will be required for a Production Area License; likely investors will be large food processors and co-ventures by groups of livestock farmers. Government funding programs may be available for some ventures. Usually covered under a Technology Transfer Region Agreement, Production Area Licenses may precede such agreements.

BCR System

The company's initial per region target segments include licensing to companies producing end products for:

- Commercial farmers, including certified and non-certified organic farmers.
- Nurseries and greenhouses, including those serving the organic farming market.
- Lawn maintenance companies.
- Parks and municipalities.
- Golf courses.
- Lawn and garden retail suppliers and home gardeners.

Competition in these areas comes from other non-chemical fertilizers and soil-enhancers and chemical fertilizers. Depending on local and national regulations and the source material used, the end product may be able to be labeled as "organic," a positive factor for marketing to organic farmers and some home gardeners (both in direct purchases and as a selling factor in choosing gardening services).

BCIR System

As the company's BCIR System is an "on-demand" method of producing chemical commodities, chemicals to be produced can be matched closely to market demand. Due to anti-pollution legislation and alternative fuel source initiatives and tax breaks introduced by most developed countries, the company expects that ethanol will be a popular end product for companies licensing the BCIR System.

Industry Analysis

The ultimate success of Agronix Organics's technology and the commercial end products of that technology are subject to trends in several overlapping market categories:

- **Availability and uses for the agricultural wastes that provide the source raw material for the company's BCR and BCIR Systems.** A 1998 report estimates that Minnesota alone produces 13.6 million dry tons of agricultural waste annually, mostly corn stover. This type of production is due to the tendency towards fewer and larger, more specialized farms, which are unable to recycle their own waste. From the National Agricultural Statistics Service (United States): "There were over 2.17 million U.S. farms in 2000, down 0.9 percent from 1999. The average farm size increased to 434 acres. Farms with annual sales of over $100,000 accounted for 16.1 percent of all farms and for 56.1 percent of land in farms, averaging 1,516 acres."
- **Fertilizers and other soil enhancers for agricultural and home and garden use, including chemical-based and composted products.** In the United States, fertilizer purchases amount to about 6 percent of total farm production costs. In 1997, U.S. farmers spent $10.9 billion on chemical fertilizers, up 18 percent over 1994. The increase was due to increased fertilizer prices, increased planted acres, and increased application rates for corn over 1994. Chemical fertilizers are facing increasingly stringent government controls due to the pollution they can cause and that they don't restore the soil as organically based fertilizer can.
- **Global growth in organic farming as a market for BCR System products.** International Federation of Organic Agriculture Movements (IFOAM), the international umbrella organization of organic agriculture organizations, has around 750 member organizations and institutions in 104 countries...their February 2001 survey stated that about 15.8 million hectares are managed organically worldwide with the largest being in Australia at 7.6 million hectares. Consumer demand is increasing, making organic agriculture more viable. Total retail sales should have reached almost US$20 billion in 2000.
- **Commodity chemicals market in general (market for end product of the BCIR System), and specifically, agricultural crops grown to produce material previously supplied by the petrochemical industry.** A 1999 United States report sets the goal of at least 10 percent of basic chemical building blocks from plant-derived renewables instead of from fossil fuel sources by 2020 and 50 percent by 2050. Already ethanol production is the third largest use of U.S. corn, utilizing about 7 percent of the corn crop and adding $4.5 billion to U.S. farm income annually.

Organizational Development

Agronix Organics, Inc., is in the process of further developing its management base and adding key marketing staff, advisors, and associates, while bringing in specialists on a contract basis to handle aspects of the development process. At this time, the company depends on members of its Board of Directors for advice and occasional operational assistance and works in concert with both the scientific contingent guided by Dr. Daniel and the equipment/facility engineering team(s) managed by Mr. Carl Genesis.

Key Relationships

Agronix Organics has to date successfully negotiated several key strategic agreements:

1. Partnership agreement with BioMax Inc. of Quebec, Canada, in which BioMax has agreed to manufacture channel-composting systems on a worldwide basis, incorporating proprietary changes exclusive to Agronix Organics, Inc. Strategic partner Premier Tech will be responsible for building all of the heavy equipment for the operations; Elite Technologies Inc. will develop the process control and quality assurance software.

2. Agreement with DRD Consultants ("Dr. Daniel") of Ottawa, Canada, in which Agronix Organics, Inc., was able to acquire the proprietary technology developed by DRD Consultants for the treatment of organic residues.

3. Discussions between Agronix Organics, Inc., and Agriculture and Agri-Food Canada (AAFC) to complete the development of the formulations for the BCIR System. This preliminary Collaborative Research Agreement gives Agronix Organics, Inc., the exclusive world leadership position for this exciting technology.

4. Agreement with Carleton University for process engineering of the BCIR System (to build BCIR plants).

5. The Farm Credit Corporation ("FCC") of Canada has agreed in principle to provide 100 percent financing for the company's first commercial plant and all subsequent plants to be constructed in Canada, provided it falls within their mandate. This will be accomplished by a joint venture agreement where 50 percent will be owned by participating farmers and 50 percent by Agronix Organics, Inc.

Competition

Agronix Organics, Inc., will be first to market with technology that has significant advantages from a marketing and regulatory standpoint over existing processes for the production of organic fertilizers (and related products) and commodity chemicals from common agricultural residue. No pollution is caused by either process and there are no waste by-products; the microbes used in the company's BCR System are naturally occurring, not genetically modified; any heavy metals in the source material for the BCR System are changed from water-soluble form to water-insoluble; and last, the reagents used in the BCIR System are environmentally friendly.

Such is the growing demand for environmentally safe fertilizers and chemicals, the global marketplace will support many more companies than currently exist for both these technologies—being first to market means that Agronix Organics, Inc., will be able to establish optimal operations, both from a supply and market standpoint.

BCR System

For its BCR System, Agronix Organics, Inc., faces competition from established manufacturers of organically based fertilizers and soil enhancers and manufacturers of chemical fertilizers for agriculture and home and garden use. While chemical fertilizers have a large market share, their use is facing increasingly stringent controls; as well, organically derived fertilizers are more acceptable than chemical fertilizers to a growing segment of the population.

Examined in the competitive analysis are Vivendi Environnement (USFilter/IPS) and Bedminster AB, established companies with composting operations worldwide that primarily use municipal waste in their processes, and International Bio-Recovery Corp, a Canadian start-up company. Key differentiators for the company's BCR System is the production of a fully mature bio-stabilized product (doesn't require aging) in a very short time span without any pollution or waste created and which meets or exceeds current and proposed legislation. Unlike standard composting, with the company's BCR System, heavy metals are bound in a water-insoluble form, fully protecting the environment. In addition, the company is focusing on underutilized agricultural residue as the source material, not municipal waste.

BCIR System

For its BCIR System, the company faces competition from companies involved in the production of chemicals from crops and crop waste (such as corn stover), as well as those producing chemicals from fossil fuels and other sources. Looked at are Power Energy Fuels Inc., Archer Daniels Midland, and Arkenol Inc., all of which produce ethanol for use as a gasoline additive or replacement. Differentiators for the company's BCIR System: no pollution or waste material is produced during the process and the company's process is not only more flexible in the types of chemicals that are produced (able to change to meet market demands), but the process itself is less expensive.

Use of Proceeds

During Year 1, proceeds will be used for:

- Research and development costs, including final engineering of the BCIR System.
- Construction of a working formulation and calibration plant.
- Implementation of the company's strategic marketing plan.
- General and administrative costs.
- Office and communications costs.
- Building the Agronix Organics, Inc., website.

Exit Strategy

Agronix Organics, Inc., offers investors a strong exit strategy based on Technology Transfer Region sales in Europe, China, Southeast Asia, Australia, New Zealand, and South America. The company is in the process of applying for listing on the NASDAQ BB. After the first plant is built, the company will move up to NASDAQ Small Cap, and with additional plants, to Large Cap.

COMPANY OVERVIEW

History

RCA Trading Co. (RCA Trading) was incorporated under the laws of the state of Florida on May 6, 1996. It was formed as a "blind pool" or "blank check" company for the purpose of seeking to complete a merger or business acquisition transaction. As of the end of its fiscal year ending December 31, 2000, the company had entered into an Agreement for Share Exchange ("Exchange Agreement") dated October 16, 2000, with American Waste Recovery, Inc., (AWR) a private Nevada corporation. On June 11, 2001, RCA Trading changed its name to Agronix Organics, Inc.

Presently, Agronix Organics, Inc., is a development stage biotechnology firm licensing technology for the conversion of common agricultural residue into environmentally friendly, bio-stabilized organic fertilizers and soil-enhancers, and a range of commodity chemicals on-demand, including ethanol for alternative fuel use. The company will be involved in the setup and operation of these manufacturing plants on a global basis through ongoing equity participation with licensees.

Corporate Data

Date of Incorporation	January 2000
Name of Incorporation	Agronix Organics, Inc.
State of Incorporation	Florida
Statement of Purpose	Agronix Organics, Inc., is a biotechnology firm generating its income by regionally licensing its technology and by means of ongoing equity participation.
Principal Place of Business	1666 West 75th Avenue - 2nd Floor Vancouver, BC, Canada V6P 6G2 www.AgronixOrganicsinc.com
Telephone	(604) 714-1606
Fax	(604) 714-1605
E-mail	sales@AgronixOrganicsinc.com
Fiscal Year End	December 31
Board of Directors	Peter J. Bartlett—Chairman Brian Hofferman—President/Director Dr. Henri Daniel—Director Peter Desmond—Director
Corporate Attorney	McCarthy Trench (Vancouver, BC) Frascona, Joiner, Goodman and Greenstein P.C. (Boulder, CO)
Corporate Accountant	Grant Thornton International (Vancouver, BC) Sharp & Co. (Vancouver, BC)

Goals

Strategic Goals

Through hierarchal licensing agreements and equity investments, and supported by a global marketing force, Agronix Organics, Inc., will become a leading supplier of turnkey plants for the utilization of common agricultural residues and the production of organic fertilizer and soil enhancers as well as a range of commodity chemicals.

Year 1: Sales of at least one Technology Transfer Region agreement and the building of one BCR plant; processing revenues of US$235 per tonne; and general revenues of US$0.76 million and assets of US$8.6 million.

Year 2: Total of 2 Technology Transfer Region agreements, 3 BCR plants and 3 BCIR plants in operation; processing revenues of US$370 per tonne; and general revenues of US$7.8 million and assets of US$31.7 million.

Year 3: Total of 4 Technology Transfer Region agreements, 8 BCR plants and 7 BCIR plants in operation; processing revenues of US$416 per tonne; and general revenues of US$34 million and assets of US$69.8 million.

Agronix Organics, Inc., will achieve these goals through:

- Aggressive marketing of licenses for the turnkey operations.
- Being first to market with superior technology and maintaining that lead through continued research into bioconversion processes and provision for current licensees to benefit from any advances.
- Provision of standardized quality assurance programs as conditions of the license, including proprietary operational software, centralized testing, on- and offline technical and marketing support, and comprehensive training.
- Private label, branding, and co-branding initiatives.
- Participation in industry associations and programs.

- Active participation in government and multinational programs, including: sustainable agriculture, environmental reclamation, alternative energy, crop-based renewable resources, etc.
- Establishing close and productive relationships with strategic partners.

Short-Term Goals

The key tactics to achieve these goals over the next year are to:

- Establish a formulation and calibration plant in Canada for commercial testing of the BCR System, marketing, and training purposes, and the development of formal operational procedures and quality assurance programs.
- Complete the process engineering and operational procedures for the BCIR System technology and build a bench test plant.
- Build the company's website for marketing and technology support.
- Build an enthusiastic, achievement-oriented sales and marketing team with backgrounds in biology and experience and contacts within the agricultural industry, especially in the supply chain, for value-added products for the industry.
- Implement the company's strategic marketing plan within North America, including conducting market research to identify suitable locations for the company's plants based on supply of source materials, competition, and market demand for the bioconversion products.

Management Team

Agronix Organics has assembled a management team with impressive industry experience and contacts. In addition the company has assembled an advisory board, which consists of leading research scientists in the biotechnology industry.

Peter J. Bartlett, Chairman, Director

Peter Bartlett is the Chairman and a Director of the company. He is a co-founder of a number of restaurant companies, including Pizza Patio and Elephant and Castle. Mr. Bartlett is involved in a number of community and charitable services, for which he was honored by the Government of Canada which conferred upon him the 125th Centennial Medal of Honor for contributions to the development of Canadian society. He was recently appointed to the presidency of Variety Club International, a worldwide charity that supports children in need. Mr. Bartlett is a resident of Vancouver, B.C., Canada.

Brian Hofferman, President, CEO, Director

Brian Hofferman is the President, Chief Executive Officer, and a Director of the company. Mr. Hofferman is a founder of the company and has worked for the company since its inception. He has been an investor and developer for the past 20 years. Mr. Hofferman has a combined Economics and Commerce degree (Hons.) from Simon Fraser University and a law degree from the University of British Columbia. He is a resident of Vancouver, B.C. Canada.

Dr. Henri Daniel, Director

Dr. Henri Daniel is a director of the company. He has been a research scientist with the Research Branch of Agriculture and Agri-Food Canada since 1974 and since 1990 he has been leading a study on the impact of bio-solids on soil agro-ecological functions and the development of value-added products from residual and naturally occurring organic matters. Dr. Daniel obtained a B.Sc. in 1981 from the University of Ottawa in plant biology and biochemistry; a Masters in Science in 1985 from the University of Montreal in Palynology, Paleoecology, and Pedology; and a Ph.D. in 1989 from McGill University in Soil Sciences. He is a resident of Chelsea, Quebec.

Peter Desmond, Director
Mr. Desmond is a company Director. He has extensive international business management and marketing experience in the Waste and Sewage treatment industry. He is currently Chairman of Watercare Services, a billion dollar company, and is also Chairman of four other corporations, two of which are related to the waste industry. He holds directorships in five other corporations, including a billion dollar infrastructure company. He was previously the Chairman of one of New Zealand's first composting companies and is a New Zealand "Fellow" of the Institute of Directors. He is a resident of Auckland, New Zealand.

Ron Bain, Secretary/Treasurer
Ron Bain is a founder and the Secretary/Treasurer of the company. He studied Business, Economics and Marketing at Sheridan College in Ontario and has an extensive background as a business development manager and brand manager with major multinational companies. He is also President of Offshore Seafarm Systems Inc., an advanced technology development company which produces sea pen systems for the aquaculture industry. He is a resident of Vancouver, B.C., Canada.

Technical Advisory Board

Dr. Henri Daniel—*See Directors and Officers.*

Dr. Morris Schmidt
Dr. Schmidt obtained his B.Sc., M.Sc., and Ph.D. in Soil Chemistry from McGill University. At present he is the Emeritus Distinguished Research Scientist with Agriculture Canada. He is the co-author of the book *Humic Substances in the Environment* and the co-editor of the books *Soil Organic Matter* and *Interaction of Soil Minerals with Natural Organics and Microbes*. He has authored over 300 referred scientific papers and has received numerous awards and honors for his work in Soil Science. He is adjunct professor of Soil Science at the University of Guelph and has acted as an advisor to CIDA, Agriculture Canada, and the U.S. Department of Agriculture.

Dr. Theodore Paris
Dr. Paris is a research scientist with the Eastern Cereal and Oilseed Research Centre of Agriculture and Agri-Food Canada. He holds a M.Sc. in Agricultural Microbiology and a Ph.D. in Agronomy and Soil Fertility, both from Laval University. He is the author or co-author of 40 reports and studies on fertilizer effects and responses, plant productivity, composting, and soil management.

Carl Genesis
Mr. Genesis is the President of BioMax Inc., a company he created in 1987. He is a Professional Engineer, who received his B.Sc. in Mechanical Engineering from Laval University. Mr. Genesis has collaborated and initiated numerous composting projects in Quebec, and BioMax introduced the first in-vessel composting system in Quebec. He has been the Secretary-Treasurer of the Association Quebecoise des Industriels du Compostage (AQIC) as well as the Vice President of the Canadian Council of Canada (CCC-Quebec).

Philip Donaldson
Philip Donaldson is a chemical engineer and holds a P.Eng. along with a Bachelor of Arts. He has an extensive background in real estate development and investments through his company White Chapel Enterprises Ltd. He is a resident of Vancouver, B.C., Canada.

Business Advisory Board

Peter Desmond—*See Directors and Officers.*

Ron Bain—*See Directors and Officers.*

Ron Nelson
Ron Nelson is a graduate in Urban Land Economics from the University of British Columbia and is President of Ronald Nelson and Associates, a mortgage banker. Ron holds numerous designations relating to the mortgage and financing industry. He is experienced in producing financial models for plant expansion and international licensing.

SAGE (Strategic Advancement for Growth Enterprises, Inc.)
Principals Victor Long, Darcie Buzzer, and Tim Randall collectively have extensive experience in strategic resource development, pre- and post-production marketing, and e-marketing in the manufacturing and retail industries.

Strategic Alliances and Relationships

Agronix Organics, Inc., has developed key alliances with companies possessing the technological depth and industry experience necessary for rapid development of the company's agricultural residue processing plants:

BioMax Inc.
Based in Quebec, BioMax Inc. has developed a range of composting technology and services, and has recognized expertise in the development, construction, commercialization, and service of organic waste processing plants. Their most advanced system, RoboCompost III, was the starting point to which Agronix Organics, Inc., added proprietary improvements to develop the company's BCR System.

Agronix Organics, Inc., has acquired 20 percent (with the option of an additional 30 percent) of BioMax's third-generation RoboCompost technology and all improvements to that technology. BioMax will be responsible for process engineering and overseeing manufacturing of the turnkey bioconversion plants.

From a risk assessment by Agriculture and Agri-Food Canada (February 2001): "...BioMax's Technology is certainly the most advanced technology from an engineering perspective for the bio-conversion of organic residues. However, at this time the abiotic and biotic conditions required to fully optimize the bioconversion process is not met by the BioMax equipment. ... However, the equipment components of BioMax can easily be modified using [Agronix Organics, Inc.'s] proprietary technology without any fundamental changes. ... [and] will result in an increase of at least 20 percent in productivity for the first generation ... it could be increased by 50 to 60 percent in the second and third generation...will allow reduction of the bioconversion time from 21 days or more to 8 to 10 days...."

www.biomax.qc.ca

Premier Tech
Agronix Organics, Inc., and BioMax Inc. have contracted with Premier Tech for building all the heavy equipment required for the company's turnkey agricultural residue processing plants. Headquartered in Quebec, Premier Tech is a 75-year-old company with a multidisciplinary team of over 1,300 engineers, chemists, agronomists, technicians, plant workers, and sales and marketing specialists. With five business units, products and services include a full range of screening, sizing, and recycling equipment (through its business unit Erin Systems); development, manufacturing, and marketing of product handling, palletizing and packaging systems, custom design, and manufacture of mechanical equipment and systems; and a range of value-added agricultural/horticultural products. They sell to North American and European markets.

Premier Tech is "committed to supplying what their customers need through the ability of their business units to work as a team, delivering integrated product and services."

www.premiertech.com

Elite Technologies, Inc.
Elite Technologies is comprised of instrumentation and automation specialists, providing equipment and support software design, development, acquisition, installation, optimization, start-up, maintenance, and training services. For the company's turnkey plants, Agronix Organics, Inc., has contracted with Elite for development, installation, and optimization of the process monitoring and quality assurance software, as well as preparation of instrument data sheets and other quality assurance and training material.

Recent customers of Elite Technologies, Inc., include Merk Frost, AFG, Johnson & Johnson, JM Smucker, Noranda, Bombardier, and Grace Canada.

Organizational Development

Agronix Organics's organizational development needs will center on the ability to meet the company's financial requirements and market coverage objectives, particularly in the short term. Much of this strength is already accounted for within the founding group, but will be augmented as developing technology license relationships are solidified and specific knowledge of regional markets is required.

Personnel will be required for:

- Management and administrative functions.
- Communication and coordination functions.
- Process and product research and development.
- Operational safety and quality assurance.
- Marketing (staff and contractors).

Where top- and mid-level management and marketing capabilities are constrained by lack of direct geographic/political/industry sector experience, government implications, or language barrier limitations, the company will add the needed people though an aggressive recruitment plan. As well, the company's marketing plan, especially at the Technology Transfer Region Agreement level, is designed to allow rapid expansion into different geo-political areas.

Estimated Personnel Required

Personnel Type	Year 1	Year 2	Year 3
Research and Development	4	5	5
Sales and Marketing	7	8	11
General and Administrative	8	10	10

For maximum flexibility, Agronix Organics, Inc., will use contractors for market research and for market/industry development, forming teams within each targeted area (multilingual where required). These teams would coordinate with and report to the company's marketing staff. Duties would include analysis of regulatory issues, government policies, industry, market or field science orientation, market entry challenges, the distribution process unique to each area, and preparation of contingency plans.

Agronix Organics, Inc., recognizes that ultimately, the success of individual operations is key to the success of the organization as a whole. For each Technology Transfer Region, an acceptance criterion and interrelational template will be established and refined, helping to secure only highly qualified groups. Care will be taken that all objectives coincide, equally addressing the needs of the prospective Technology Transfer Region Licensees as well as those of the much smaller Production Area Licensees and Sales and Distribution Territory Licensees.

Organizational Chart

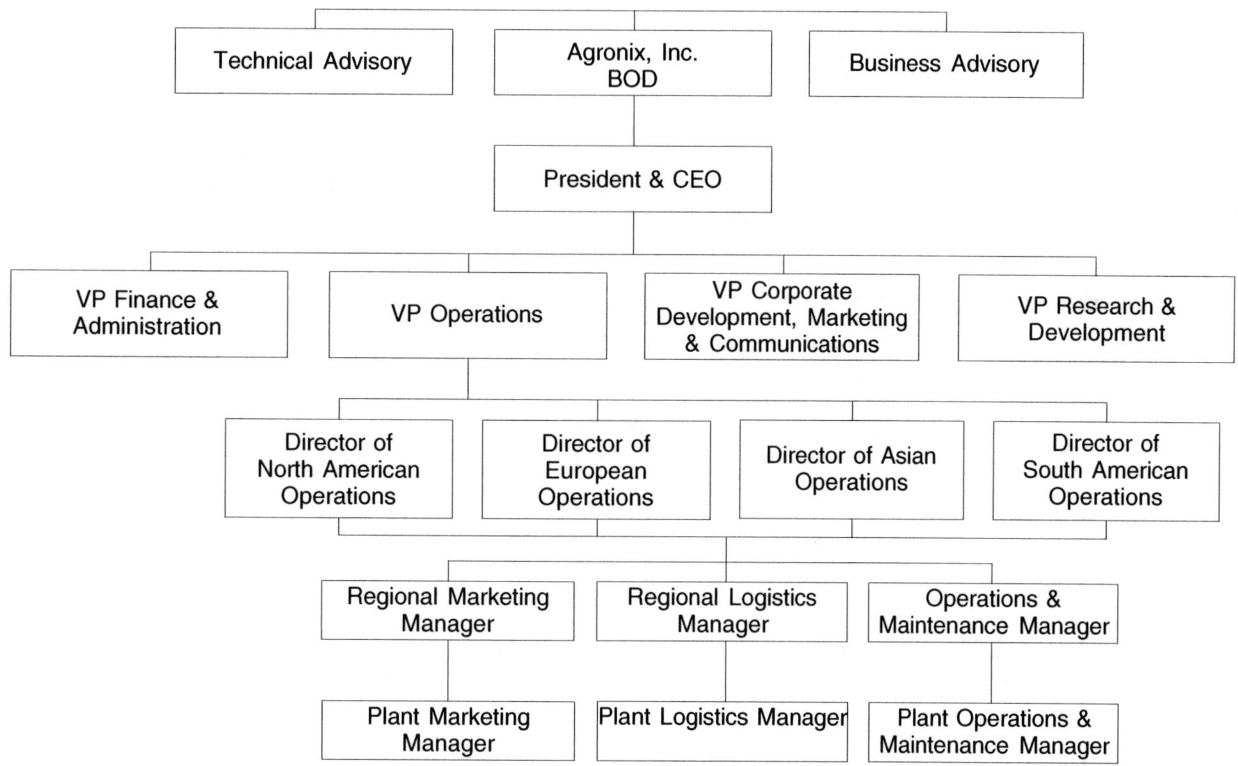

Food, Diet, & Nutrition Company

BUSINESS PLAN

THINK THIN WEIGHT LOSS CORPORATION

541 Howe Street, Third Floor
Vancouver, British Columbia V6C 2C2
Canada

Think Thin Weight Loss Corporation is a leading provider of products and programs in the diet and nutrition industry. This plan, created by Concord Business Development, Inc., of Vancouver, raised over $4 million for the company.

- FINANCIAL HIGHLIGHTS
- CORPORATE SUMMARY
- MANUFACTURING & DISTRIBUTION
- COMPANY OVERVIEW
- THINK THIN PRODUCTS/PROGRAM

FINANCIAL HIGHLIGHTS

Industry

Food, diet, and nutrition products.

Mission Statement

Think Thin Weight Loss Corporation is a leading provider of products and programs in the diet and nutrition industry. By offering a superior product line, employing innovative marketing techniques, and developing strategic partnerships with manufacturers and distributors, the company will maintain an uncompromising commitment to quality while ensuring a fair return to shareholders.

Strategic Partnership

Think Thin has entered into a strategic partnership with Garden State Nutritionals, one of the top five largest dietary and nutrition product producers, marketers, and distributors in the world. Think Thin is in negotiations with a number of profitable diet and nutrition-related companies to acquire further products that will add significant revenues to the parent corporation.

Target Market

The U.S. population concerned with health and weight issues.

Capital Requirements

Initial seed round of US$1 million; Phase 2 is US$3 million; Phase 3, which includes product launch, is US$5 million.

Use of Proceeds

Product Development and Sales and Marketing.

Management Projections

By the end of Year 1, the company expects revenues to be $32,976,673; by the end of Year 2, revenues are expected to be $55,280,112; and by the end of Year 3, $70,719,527.

Projected Revenues	**Year 1**	**Year 2**	**Year 3**
Net Income (loss)	$120,480	$4,156,067	$6,373,541
Sales Revenue	$32,976,673	$55,280,112	$70,719,527

CORPORATE SUMMARY

The Opportunity

Think Thin presents the investor with the opportunity to participate in the significant profits of the recession-proof diet and nutrition market. The diet and nutrition products industry is experiencing a powerful trend toward consolidation and financial growth.

Vision

The mandate of the Think Thin Weight Loss Corporation is to identify, develop, or acquire innovative products and programs in the diet and nutrition industry. Dr. Louie Scar, the co-creator of the best-selling diet of all time, the Atkins Diet, developed the initial concept for Think Thin. The business direction of the corporation has evolved from the concept of a single diet product to include a broad-based spectrum of products in the diet and nutrition industry that have solid profit potential. Think Thin Weight Loss Corporation is committed to providing safe, effective, and clinically proven health and weight loss products.

Strategic Partnership

Think Thin has successfully negotiated a key strategic partnership with Garden State Nutritionals, a division of Vitaquest International of New Jersey in which Garden State Nutritionals will supply valuable manufacturing, distribution, and marketing. Garden State is a world leader in private label and custom manufacturing of dietary supplement products. Garden State's 225,000 square foot manufacturing facility is able to produce up to 1.5 million bottles of finished packaged goods per week and will fulfill the expected demand for Think Thin's products.

Founded in 1977, Garden State and its affiliate divisions, Windmill Health Products and Celmark International Inc., serve hundreds of leading marketers and distributors in more than 35 countries worldwide, including Australia, Western Europe, Japan, and much of the Pacific Rim, with a distribution of 25,000 pharmacies, health food stores, supermarkets, mass merchants, electronic retailers, and an active mail-order database of two million. Producing more than 4,500 custom products, Garden State has helped pioneer many state-of-the-art technologies in dietary supplement formulations. These include its Betacoat™ and Cellugel™ micro coating systems, bi-layer tablet technology, and its new Phased Control™ time-release delivery system.

Products and Services

Americans spend $50 billion a year on weight loss and nutritional products that for the most part do not work. People are ready for products that will produce results that are healthy, convenient, satisfying, and fit well into today's busy lifestyle. Think Thin is currently in negotiations with a number of weight loss and nutritional product companies that fit this profile. The first of these targeted acquisitions is the Ultimate Lean Routine and Fat Fighter line of products from One World Networks Integrated Technologies Inc. These products were successfully launched in 2000 with revenues of over $8 million in the first year, and over $25 million in the second year. Revenues for the third and current year are projected to be over $40 million. The revenue from these products is predominantly derived from direct response marketing, which has established a base of over 463,000 customers in two years. Think Thin will expand the considerable success of the Ultimate Lean Routine and Fat Fighter line by introducing these products to the retail market, using the powerful distribution network of Garden State, its strategic partner.

Ultimate Lean Routine and Fat Fighter Products

Greg Isaacs, the inventor of "The Ultimate Lean Routine," is one of Hollywood's most recognized fitness and health gurus. Celebrities that he has trained include Russell Crowe, Melanie Griffith, and Pierce Brosnan. As a high profile fitness figure, Greg Isaacs garners numerous valuable press and promotional opportunities for the Ultimate Lean Routine brands. The Ultimate Lean Routine and Fat Fighter brands encompass close to twenty nutritional and dietary-related products including: energy bars, dietary bars, powder form weight loss shakes, powder form energy shakes, multi-vitamin/multi-mineral capsules.

The Think Thin Diet

The Think Thin Program is a meal replacement system of prepared drinks that goes beyond simply reducing calories: it reduces hunger and provides a satisfying sense of fullness. Building on 20 years of experience with the remarkable properties of the Mediterranean diet, the company's new weight loss program is fully developed and has been embraced by the medical community. The company's Think Thin canned or bottled meal replacement drinks will be available to the public through retail outlets, online sales, and in conjunction with medical and clinical programs. The cost of each beverage will be comparable to that of Slim-Fast products and other competitors.

The Think Thin Program has been reviewed by the dean of American Nutrition Professor Tony Vanderhelm, M.D., founder of the American Society for Clinical Nutrition, founding Director of the National Institutes of Health and Obesity Research Center, and Emeritus Medical Director of the Vanderhelm Clinic at St. Luke's-Roosevelt Hospital in New York City. Dr. Vanderhelm was also a consultant to the Surgeon General of the United States on human nutrition. Dr. Vanderhelm is on the company's Advisory Board.

MANUFACTURING & DISTRIBUTION

Garden State Nutritionals

As a leading producer of more than $1 billion in finished retail product per year, processing more than 5 billion doses annually and producing up to 1.5 million bottles of finished package goods per week, Garden State is uniquely qualified to provide support to Think Thin. Garden State's comprehensive suite of support services include product concept, formulation, laboratory services, package and label design, regulatory affairs, and merchandising services.

Garden State Nutritionals has an established distribution network of 25,000 retail chain accounts. These established client bases, well-developed distribution channels, and state-of-the-art technology infrastructure provide a valuable complement to Think Thin's sales efforts. Think Thin plans to leverage Garden State's distribution strength to accelerate its market penetration across all of its target markets.

Target Market

Think Thin is entering a recession-proof boom market. Currently, 15 percent to 35 percent of adults are on diets, and Americans spend $30 billion to $50 billion a year trying to lose weight. Since 1998 dietary supplement sales are estimated to be growing at a rate of 10-12 percent annually.

- 40 percent of women and 25 percent of men are seeking to lose weight.
- 30 percent each are actively seeking to maintain current weight.
- Most people have attempted to diet using more than one method; on average dieters try one method or another for about six months at the rate of more than one per year for two years.

Studies show that low-carb/high-protein diets such as the Think Thin Program are more popular with consumers—and the Think Thin Program has significant advantages over other such diets. Over half (54%) of popular low-carb/high-protein diet users say that their weight loss to date has either met their goal or exceeded their expectations, compared to only 22 percent of those on a low-fat diet plan.

Marketing Strategy

Think Thin will market its nationally advertised, medically validated line of diet products (the Think Thin Drink, Ultimate Lean Routine, and Fat Fighter) that combine the most popular form of weight loss diet in America today—low carbohydrate, high protein. The company's strategy is to build on the revenue and branding momentum created with the Ultimate Lean Routine and Fat Fighter product lines by taking them to the national retail markets using the distribution network of its strategic partner, Garden State.

For the rollout of the Think Thin products, the company will deploy marketing initiatives aimed at both the general public and the medical community. To ensure the development of a highly effective strategy, Think Thin has entered into an agreement with Greg Louis, the acknowledged marketing genius behind the branding of Tommy Hilfiger, USA Today, ESPN, MTV, and Lean Cuisine, among others. To further complement its marketing and distribution efforts, Think Thin will also be utilizing the well-established relationships Garden State has developed to effectively deliver the company's products to its target markets.

The company's marketing strategy will include high-impact advertising, long-term branding and community building, and expanding its expected solid base of medical support.

- Establish brand awareness
  —With the public
  —With the medical community
- Differentiate the company's products from the competition
  —Safe, appetite reducing, high compliance weight loss diet with an effective weight maintenance component
- Develop medical partnerships and support clinical research into weight loss using the company's products

Competition

Atkins Nutritionals

Atkins Nutritionals' low carbohydrate diet bears the closest comparison to the company's Think Thin Program and over the past two years the company has added a product line of drinks, bars, and supplements to what was originally just a diet book. Atkins' primary weakness is the high level of saturated fats that the diet allows and 30 years of criticism by the medical community for both the content of the diet and lack of research into its long-term effects. Atkins' strength is that the diet tends to work better than most and is generally well liked by its users (at least in comparison with other diets).

Slim-Fast Foods

The company's products offer a low-calorie meal replacement that generally follows accepted guidelines for nutrition, albeit with a too-low fat content if the product were the only food source. Their main weakness is that the diet doesn't work any better than any other low-calorie diet...which means that over the long term and for most people, it doesn't work at all AND is difficult to stay on for any length of time. Slim-Fast Foods sold in 2000 for $2.4 billion dollars (acquired by Unilever).

Think Thin Advantage

The strong product line, experienced marketing team, and celebrity and medical endorsements enjoyed by Think Thin will position the company as a leader in the diet and nutrition industry.

COMPANY OVERVIEW

Management Team

Think Thin has assembled a team of experienced medical, management, and marketing professionals with extensive knowledge and experience in public markets and the medical and weight loss field.

Chad H. Steinfeld, Chief Executive Officer and Director

Mr. Steinfeld was the Chairman and CEO of CCA Companies Incorporated and Chairman and CEO of Harwick Companies, Inc., which employed several thousand people worldwide. Chad Steinfeld has built, developed, or operated more than 50 restaurants including Tavern on the Green, which has rapidly evolved into the world's highest grossing restaurant, Maxwell's Plum, and many others. He has also developed health spas and theme parks in North America, Europe, and Asia, including Great Adventure in New Jersey, which is the world's largest independent theme park.

Chad Steinfeld has served as President and Chief Executive Officer of Kitchens of Sara Lee, the world's largest bakery. Mr. Steinfeld was also a Director, Member of the Executive Committee, and Vice President of Consolidated Foods, the parent company of Sara Lee that is ranked within the top 30 companies of the Fortune 500 companies in the United States of America.

Dr. Louie Scar, Chairman of the Board of Directors
The creator of the Think Thin Weight Loss System, Dr. Louie Scar, has researched diet products and appetite control through diet modification for over 30 years. Dr. Scar was the co-creator of the best selling diet of all time, the Atkins Diet.

Working with his associate, Dr. Dudley Whit, Chief Cardiologist at Harvard University, Dr. Scar achieved world recognition for the prominent role he played in the first-ever international telecommunication transmission of EKG, from Africa to the U.S., opening up a new era of medical communications and consultation.

Sally Lida, President, Director
Sally Lida holds a Cum Laude Baccalaureate Psychology degree from Stony Brook University. She worked for a number of years in research for the Psycho-Physiology Laboratory at Stony Brook, where she received awards for her independent research.

While an executive at DynaTech Nutritionals, she worked on the creation of a formula for the Ultra Herbal Power Slim weight loss product. At DynaTech, Ms. Lida set up an extensive multi-level marketing program, bringing on board a major celebrity endorser.

Greg Louis, Vice-Chairman, Marketing Director, and Director
The youngest inductee into the Art Directors Hall of Fame, Greg Louis is a communications guru—the acknowledged marketing genius behind the branding of Tommy Hilfiger, USA Today, ESPN, MTV, and Lean Cuisine.

Mr. Louis was the founder of Louis USA, a $425 million full-service agency with offices in New York, Chicago, Houston, and Los Angeles.

Kate Whitney, Secretary, Treasurer, and Director
Ms. Whitney brings considerable corporate administration experience in both private and public companies to the Think Thin team. Ms. Whitney has worked for the following firms: Pattinson & Brewer in England; Cowan, Lipson & Rumney in England; Tupper & Adams in Canada; Legal Freelance Centre in Canada; Ferguson Gifford in Canada; Jones McCloy Peterson in Canada; and Coglon Wizinsky Dadson & Co. in Canada.

Clark Peterson, Director
A graduate of the University of Miami School of Law, Mr. Peterson practiced law for nine years before co-founding Lums Inc., a restaurant chain that grew into 450 units. In 1969, Mr. Peterson purchased Caesars Palace, a 500-room hotel on the Las Vegas strip. Under his guidance, Caesars Palace in Las Vegas grew to 1750 rooms; he subsequently built Caesars Palace at Tahoe, Nevada, and Atlantic City. In 1990, Mr. Peterson became the Chairman and CEO of the MGM Grand Hotels in Las Vegas.

Clark Peterson has acquired and developed two honeymoon hotels in the Pennsylvania Poconos: Paradise Steam and Cove Haven. In 1984, he started Regent Airlines, a transcontinental luxury airline, which was sold in 1987 to Kirk Kerkorian, principal shareholder of the MGM Motion Picture Studio.

Donald Milne, Director
Mr. Milne is the current Chairman of the IndieProd company. Mr. Milne has been the producer of numerous box office hits such as "Air America," "Footloose," and "L.A. Story" to name but a few. Prior to forming IndieProd, Mr. Milne was Head of Production and President of Columbia Pictures. During his tenure at Columbia, Mr. Milne supervised such projects as "Midnight Express," "The China Syndrome," "Close Encounters of the Third Kind," and "Kramer vs. Kramer."

During Mr. Milne's career, he has garnered 84 Academy Award nominations, of which he received 26. Mr. Milne is a Founding Trustee and Board Member of the Sundance Film Institute in Sundance, Utah, and a Trustee and Board Member of the Museum of Contemporary Art in Los Angeles, California.

Advisory Board

Dr. Tony Vanderhelm, M.D.
Dr. Tony Vanderhelm is Professor Emeritus of Medicine at Columbia University's College of Physicians and Surgeons. Considered the dean of American nutrition, Professor Vanderhelm is the founder of the American Society for Clinical Nutrition, the founding director of the National Institute of Health and Obesity Research Center, and the Founding Medical Director of the Vanderhelm Clinic at St. Luke's-Roosevelt Hospital in New York City.

Professor Vanderhelm was also a consultant to the Surgeon General of the United States on human nutrition and served on the Food and Nutrition Board for the National Academy of Science. The author of over 200 papers in the field of weight and nutrition, Professor Vanderhelm is the recipient of the Distinguished Physician Award from the American College of Physicians.

Dr. James L. Gilford, M.D.
After completing his M.D. at George Washington University, Dr. Gilford enjoyed a long and illustrious career in the Public Service ranks. Early in his career, he headed the national Accident Prevention Program, leading the push for mandatory auto safety belts. After other high-ranking appointments, Dr. Gilford was tapped to become Surgeon General before being appointed Commissioner of the FDA.

Dr. Gilford received numerous honors for his career in public service, including honorary doctorates from the University of Michigan and Emory University, and the coveted Bronfman Prize of the American Public Health Association, the highest public health award in the U.S.

Robert H. Cotter, Ph.D., M.Sc.
Over the course of his impressive career, Mr. Cotter has held senior and consulting positions at leading laboratories responsible for the development and manufacturing processes of numerous pharmaceutical products. He is currently President of Cotter & Fay, Inc., specializing in pharmaceutical plant design, engineering, construction and start-up, and is the President/Principal of a technical consulting service to the chemical process industries, with an emphasis on pertinent regulatory agency requirements.

Maria A. Tolban, Ph.D., R.D.
Dr. Tolban is a registered dietitian and a member of the American Dietetic Association since 1980. She has worked as a clinical and research dietitian and taught graduate college courses in nutrition, counseling, and training. Much of her research as been focused on diets from other cultures and countries and their role in disease prevention and weight control, and she has concentrated her research on diets from the Mediterranean region. An associate of Dr. Scar, they have worked together on appetite control, weight reduction, and nutrition product development since 1985.

Strategic Partnership: Garden State Nutritionals

With the dietary and supplements market set to reach revenues in excess of $12 billion by the end of 2001, Garden State Nutritionals has remained at the forefront of bringing innovative products to meet market changes. For 30 years, this privately-owned corporation has strategically developed, manufactured, marketed, and distributed over 500 nutritional supplements. Garden State Nutritionals is a division of Vitaquest International Inc., one of the largest custom vitamin manufacturers in the USA, and Celmark International Inc., a marketing company that specializes in selling nutritional supplements through electronic media and direct response. Vitaquest manufactures over 4,500 custom products in the United States and in 35 countries.

Garden State is located in a modern, 225,000 square-foot building in West Caldwell, New Jersey. This state-of-the-art facility manufactures and packages a wide range of tablets, caplets, two-piece capsules, chewable wafers, effervescents, powdered formulations, liquids and topicals. A total commitment to quality and Good Manufacturing Practices (GMP) is evident by the fact that Garden State received an "A" rating by the National Nutritional Foods Association, the TGA-Certificate of Manufacturing from the Therapeutic Goods Association of Australia and the ACERIS-Quality Assurance Certificate from the Academy of Clinical Environmental Research and Information Services.

Garden State's dietary products are sold nationwide to over 25,000 retail chain accounts. As a marketing driven company, Garden State offers its customers cutting-edge products with value-added services. Such services include: technical advice, expertise from their scientific advisory board, promotions, national advertising and public relation campaigns via television, radio, and print. Garden State offers a full line of multi- and single vitamins and minerals, function-specific products, specialty products for weight loss, energy, herbal teas and supplements, sports nutrition, lotions and oils, and homeopathic products.

Garden State Nutritionals Management

Keith I. Frank, CEO
In his principal duties as CEO of Garden State, Mr. Frank is responsible for overseeing sales and marketing. In his role with Think Thin, Keith Frank is instrumental in identifying key acquisition targets that will considerably enhance the profitability of the company. Mr. Frank graduated from American University with a degree in Marketing Management.

Garden State Nutritionals Research and Development Team

Garden State's research and development team will collaborate with Think Thin to conduct clinical investigations of Think Thin's proposed products. Garden State has assembled a reputable and capable research and development team who are uniquely suited to qualify the products presented by Think Thin. The members of Garden State's research and development team include:

Jan Benedict, Vice President of Marketing and Sales
Mr. Benedict is responsible for formulating, developing, and marketing nutritional and botanical products for all segments of the nutritional market, including: multi-level marketing (MLM), direct sales, electronic media, health care professional, and Internet companies. Jan Benedict is a respected lecturer in North America, has a degree in Chemistry from the University of Notre Dame, and has completed graduate studies in business administration and marketing from the universities of Minnesota and Pennsylvania.

Rick Hendell, Senior Vice President
Prior to joining Garden State, Rick Hendell gained nearly 25 years of experience in all phases of the natural products industry, including product development, manufacturing, research, sales, and marketing. He is a multiple patent holder in enzyme delivery technologies. Mr. Hendell is a well regarded speaker for seminars and lectures worldwide. Rick majored in biology and chemistry at Fairleigh Dickinson University and William Patterson College.

Seymour "Sy" D. Lavelle, Senior Vice President of Scientific Affairs
Dr. Lavelle serves as Senior Vice President of Scientific Affairs and is responsible for Quality Control, Analytical Development, and Quality Assurance as well as Regulatory/ Information Services for Garden State. Previously employed with Squibb and Johnson & Johnson (Ortho Pharmaceutical Corporation and the R.W. Johnson Pharmaceutical Research Institute), Dr. Lavelle has authored or co-authored over 36 publications and over 80 U.S. patents. Dr. Lavelle has served as an adjunct Professor at the University of Kentucky, holds a Ph.D. in Pharmaceutical Chemistry from the University of Wisconsin, and a B.S. in Pharmacy from Brooklyn College of Pharmacy.

THINK THIN PRODUCTS/ PROGRAM

Nutritional Products

The company's program consists of dietary and nutritional products, including a revolutionary meal replacement formula that reduces appetite. The multiple products Think Thin Weight Loss Corporation initially proposes to acquire and develop in the retail market include:

Lean Routine™ Products

- Pure Energy plus Shake
- Fat Neutralizer
- Carb Blocker
- Weight Away
- Pure Nutrition
- Enerplex™ for Women
- Enerplex™ for Men
- Age Change™
- Mind Grow™
- Soy Bars™ Peanut Butter Crunch Bars
- Soy Bars™ Honey Nut Bars
- Lean Body Guide
- 20 Body Shaping Secrets Guide

Fat Fighter™Products

- Fat Fighter™
- Desire Fighter™
- Fat Fighter System Weight Away
- Fat Fighter System Fat Neutralizer
- Joy of Carbs Guide

The Think Thin meal replacement prepared drink consists of a precise balance between various constituents of foods, mainly carbohydrates, proteins, and fats. Developed by Dr. Louie Scar (the co-creator of the Atkins Diet), the formula for Think Thin is a major departure from competing products currently in the marketplace. In addition to supplying a full range of other nutrients, the products contain the highest level of "healthy" fat possible derived from olive oil. Based on the Harvard University Mediterranean Diet concept, 20 years of field experience, and supported by current mainstream dietary research, it has been concluded that the level and type of fat in the Think Thin product is not harmful. The meal replacement formula's combination of fatty acids and the ratio of various nutrients aid in appetite reduction in a safe and natural way. Because the Think Thin Drink contains only natural food constituents, it does not need to undergo a lengthy FDA approval process.

Differentiating Factors

The company's Think Thin Program can be clearly differentiated from the competition:

- Especially endorsed by leaders in the medical community (unlike the Atkins Diet, which has faced 30 years of criticism).
- Safe weight loss using a natural, monounsaturated fat source (the olive), (unlike the high saturated fats of the Atkins Diet plan).
- An all-in-one product for ease of use and conceptual simplicity (unlike the Atkins Diet line of products with separate vitamin supplements and other products).
- Appetite reduction—due to healthy fat content—so people follow the diet better and stay on it longer (unlike Slim-Fast's low-fat diet which has no appetite reduction).
- Key component of the product is all-natural olive oil, appealing to the growing number of consumers interested in, and even insisting on, natural ingredients and preferring "herbal" treatments.
- Effective, safe, high-compliance weight maintenance plan that follows the Harvard University Mediterranean diet pyramid. A high proportion of the weight stays off.
- It is something new: a new product without the stigma—and failures—associated in the public's mind with other diets.
- It is something old: the romance of the Mediterranean diet and a simpler, healthier way of life.

Components of the Think Thin Drink

- **Carbohydrates**—low carbohydrate (similar to the Atkins Diet), approximately 30 grams per day rather than the usual 150 grams.
- **Protein**—high levels of protein from skim milk or soy. Levels will be in accordance with what is currently considered safe by the medical profession.
- **Fat**—highest level of monounsaturated fats allowable; derived from olive oil.
- **Vitamins and minerals added**—three cans of the company's Think Thin drink (equivalent to total dietary replacement) will contain 100 percent of the RDA for vitamins and minerals.
- **Calorie content per can**—approximately 400 calories. Three cans of the company's Think Thin drink (equivalent to total dietary replacement) meet the National Institutes of Health recommendation for a low-calorie diet that promotes a safe rate of weight loss.
- **Think Thin breakfast** followed by normal lunch, dinner, and snacks. Total calorie reduction conforms to the lesser amount (500 kcal/day) recommended by the National Institutes of Health for the treatment of overweight by low-calorie diet. Weight loss will be approximately 1 to 2 lbs. per week depending on activity level and degree of overweight.
- **Think Thin breakfast and lunch** followed by normal dinner and snacks. Total calorie reduction conforms to the higher amount (1000 kcal/day) recommended by the National Institutes of Health for the treatment of overweight by low-calorie diet. Weight loss will be approximately 2 to 3 lbs. per week depending on activity level and degree of overweight.

Golf Grip Manufacturer

BUSINESS PLAN PROGRIP

P.O. Box 4567
Atlanta, Georgia 30314

ProGrip's mission is to develop and actively seek out innovative and advanced technologies that can be marketed and sold to the approximately $150 billion global wholesale sporting goods industry, to become a premier provider of quality and unique athletic products, and to establish a strong reputation for offering creative solutions to the needs of athletes and sports enthusiasts.

- EXECUTIVE SUMMARY
- COMPANY OVERVIEW
- MARKET OPPORTUNITY
- COMPETITIVE ANALYSIS
- PRODUCT & POSITIONING
- MARKETING STRATEGY
- MANUFACTURING & DISTRIBUTION
- MANAGEMENT
- THE OFFERING

EXECUTIVE SUMMARY

The Opportunity

ProGrip develops and actively seeks out innovative and advanced technologies that are marketed and sold to the $150 billion global wholesale sporting goods market. Its first line of products, the Impress golf grip line, provides an elegant design that solves the serious and unmet problems a golfer experiences when his or her club makes impact with the ball (or the ground). Specifically, the revolutionary design that ProGrip exclusively owns significantly reduces harmful shock and vibration for the user while preserving the "feel" of the club. For the approximately 27 million U.S. golfers, this results in greater comfort and swing control, a reduction in the risk of repetitive stress injuries, less fatigue, and more rounds of golf played for more years. As a community, golfers are extremely passionate about the sport and are very receptive to innovative technologies that promise to improve their performance or enjoyment of the game. The Impress grip provides a level performance that meets or exceeds that provided by other anti-vibration devices and, in addition, provides many other advantages, including customization, a greater degree of style selectivity and durability, and easy, noninvasive installation.

This is a unique and superior investment opportunity for the following reasons:

- **Large, Established, and Identifiable Market.** 26.7 million Americans currently play golf (66 million worldwide). Approximately 51 percent of U.S. players are "core" golfers, accounting for 88 percent of the 586 million rounds of golf played annually. Of this core segment, over 46 percent are "avid" golfers, defined as those who annually play at least 25 rounds. Although avid golfers comprise the smallest player segment (25%), they account for over 50 percent of all golf-related spending. ProGrip will initially be targeting this core golfer segment, with particular focus paid to avid golfers.

- **Expected Market Growth.** This market is expected to grow due to increasing interest from nontraditional golfers (i.e., juniors and women) and two population trends 1) the aging of Baby Boomers, and 2) the emergence of the Echo Boom generation (those born between 1977 and 1995).

- **Frequency of Golf Injuries.** 87 percent of golfers reporting golf-related injuries suffer from maladies of the hand, wrist, or elbow. Many of these injuries are caused by harmful shock and vibration and may be prevented with the appropriate equipment—such as the proper grip.

- **Proven Need for a Vibration Solution.** In a random sample of over 150 golfers, 73 percent of respondents claimed that shock and vibration reduced both their enjoyment and performance of the game. Of those golfers using anti-vibration devices, 75 percent to 98 percent feel that the devices are not effective. Only 7 percent of golfers claimed that their grips are effective at reducing shock and vibration.

- **Underserved Market.** The vast majority of research and development to date has focused only on the club head and the shaft. The third part of the club, the grip, has been virtually ignored and has undergone very little change or innovation.

- **Technology-Focused Consumers.** The rapid evolution of technology in the golf equipment industry accelerates the rate at which golfers purchase new clubs and other equipment, and it has also created a market that is very accepting of new technologies. 83 percent of respondents in our survey said they are interested in a new anti-vibration grip technology.

- **Proven Science Behind the Product.** The Impress grip design is a descendant of a hammer grip technology that decreases repetitive stress injuries and fatigue as well as increases productivity of its users. That technology is currently the basis for several premium hammers on the market that are generating over $30 million of annual sales. Dr. Dennis Williams, a plasma-physicist, the Chief Scientist for Atlanta-based SuperTech, Inc., and a minority shareholder of ProGrip, developed both the hammer and golf grip technologies.

- **Disruptive Technology.** In a survey conducted by the company, the Impress grip was rated up to 87 percent better than two competing grips in all observed categories. 96 percent rated it to be equal or superior in performance to the Comfort grip made by Baker/GolfLife, currently the market leader in golf grips.

- **Relationship with Golfworld International.** After trying a prototype of the Impress grip, Golfworld CEO John Danko provided ProGrip with valuable resources for its product and market research and pledged to publish a paper on the Impress grip design in *Golfworld Magazine*, the industry's largest technical journal with over 125,000 subscribers.

- **Initial Seed Funding Secured.** ProGrip has received a $100,000 funding commitment from the PGOT CORP® Ludington Fund, Ltd. Additionally, to date the shareholders of the company have personally invested over $15,000 towards the venture.

- **Mitigated Risks.** ProGrip has researched the market, operational, and product risks associated with the Impress grip and has taken many steps to mitigate them, including conducting extensive market and product surveys, building a strong Board of Advisors, and establishing important relationships with such firms as Freightways, Golfworld, Morgan Field & Rice, Advance Elastic Corporation, Jones & Puch, Calypso, and Dow Chemical. Each of these firms is a leader in its respective market. These steps, as well as others that will be implemented, will help to insure the long-term success of the company and an attractive financial return for ProGrip's shareholders.

Product and Benefits

The revolutionary new design of ProGrip's premium golf grips—the Impress grip line—has several unique advantages over other products currently on the market, including:

- **Effectiveness**—The Impress grip was rated 87 percent more effective than a standard grip at reducing shock and vibration while maintaining the balance and "feel" of the club and control of the swing.
- **Versatility**—The ability to create an anti-vibration grip with conventional manufacturing methods, using any commercially viable materials, and for any type of club (graphite or steel, wood or iron).
- **Convenience**—The grip is noninvasive to the club and it is installed like other slip-on grips.
- **Value**—While the Impress grip will be priced at a premium to most other golf grips, it offers consumers a less expensive alternative to other (non-grip) anti-vibration solutions. Consumer research shows that golfers are willing to pay a premium price for the benefits offered by the Impress grip.
- **Customization**—ProGrip introduces a new concept in grip design—Precise Shock Reduction (PSR). Golfers can now select a grip with the degree of anti-vibration quality that best suits their game, setting a new standard in customization that will precisely meet the needs of individual golfers.

The Market

ProGrip's primary market for the Impress golf grip is the approximately 35 million core golfers worldwide (13.7 million in the U.S.), who purchase grips through original equipment manufacturers (OEMs), distributors, mail-order houses, golf pro shops, and specialty golf retailers. In 2000, worldwide golf grip sales represented approximately $350 million. While the golf equipment market as a whole has contracted since 1997, the golf grip market has exhibited moderate growth due to golfers delaying new club purchases and instead purchasing grips in the aftermarket (the re-grip market) to replace older and worn grips on existing clubs.

In addition to the golf grip technology, ProGrip is in negotiations with Georgia State University to license a related grip technology developed by Dr. Williams that can be utilized for other sports instruments such as baseball bats and tennis racquets. These and other potential uses for the technology are expected to bring the total worldwide market for the Impress grip to over $500 million and represent approximately $43 million in sales for ProGrip by 2006. Beyond that, ProGrip will continue to acquire and develop innovative solutions for athletes and sports enthusiasts in the $150 billion global sports equipment market.

Competitive Strategy/Barriers to Entry

Due to the extremely competitive nature of the golf equipment market, ProGrip recognizes the vital need to create sustainable competitive advantages. This will be accomplished through the following:

- Securing intellectual property protection for the company's proprietary technology and trademarks.
- Outsourcing all phases of manufacturing, warehousing, and distribution to maintain flexibility in design and production, eliminate the need for extensive fixed assets, and leverage excess capacity.
- Bringing aggressive and innovative sales and marketing techniques to the mature and conservative golf grip market, thereby quickly establishing the ProGrip and Impress grip brands as well as building a sense of community among ProGrip's customers.
- Rapid rollout of new technology-based sports and leisure products into profitable markets.

Financial Summary and Offering

Set forth below is a summary of our projected financial information. The summary financial projections for the years ended December 31, 2002 through 2006 were derived from our financial projections.

	Projected Fiscal Year Ended December 31,				
	2002	**2003**	**2004**	**2005**	**2006**
	(in thousands, except total units sold)				
Net revenues	$185.50	$3,335.60	$10,371.10	$23,746.30	$42,578.20
Cost of revenues	110.7	2,050.90	6,802.30	16,113.90	29,569.80
Gross profit	74.8	1,284.70	3,568.70	7,632.50	13,008.40
Operating expenses					
Marketing and selling	390	840	1,346.70	3,562.00	5,904.10
General and administrative	49	650	1,050.00	1,750.00	2,750.00
Other	30.1	202.2	374.1	556.5	780.7
Operating income (loss)	-394.4	-407.6	797.9	1,764.00	3,573.60
Net Income (loss)	($372.30)	($412.10)	$755.00	$1,162.90	$2,362.80
Total units sold	**49,219**	**911,523**	**3,023,242**	**7,161,718**	**13,142,150**

As a result of ProGrip's unique technology and the attractiveness of the golf grip market, the company will reach positive cash flow in fiscal year 2004. ProGrip is seeking $750,000 in capital commitments to fund the company's initial launch. In return, the investor(s) will receive ownership of ProGrip in the form of preferred stock with a very attractive projected return on his or her original investment in five years. This return will be realized most likely from an acquisition of ProGrip by a large sports equipment company or through an IPO.

COMPANY OVERVIEW

Background

The revolutionary design for the Impress grip was developed by Dr. Dennis Williams, Ph.D., a plasma-physicist and the Chief Scientist for an Atlanta-based nanotechnology firm. While working on his doctorate, Dr. Williams became intrigued with the idea of developing a hammer that could actually hit harder. Based upon this research, he developed a radical new grip design that significantly reduces the shock and vibration felt in the hand, wrist, and elbow from impact with a target, thereby reducing fatigue and repetitive stress disorders. Simultaneously, the technology allows the hammer to provide greater momentum transfer. That is, it "hits harder" than before. By simultaneously decreasing the shock and vibration felt by the user and increasing the momentum transfer, the user experiences a significant increase in productivity and comfort. In addition, the grips can be incorporated into existing products with standard, commercially accepted materials, utilize conventional manufacturing methods, and look and feel like an ordinary hammer grip. This technology is owned by Georgia State University and is the basis for several premium hammers currently on the market that are generating over an estimated $30 million in annual revenues. Since a hammer is, in essence, simply an elongated impact instrument, Dr. Williams then sought similar uses for his radical new design.

The Company

ProGrip owns a derivative technology from the one developed by Dr. Williams for hammers that the company has applied to golf clubs. The company's first product, the Impress line of premium golf grips, has a revolutionary design that significantly reduces shock and vibration to the user while maintaining a level of performance that equals or exceeds that of existing products. The company will offer a variety of custom shock-absorbing models, all of which will feature several advantages over existing grips in the market. Our grips will initially be sold to distributors, as well as mail-order houses, golf pro shops, and specialty golf retailers that serve those golfers seeking to replace grips that have become worn and slick due to prolonged use. After gaining sufficient market acceptance, ProGrip grips will be sold to original equipment manufacturers (OEMs) for installation onto new clubs (woods, irons, and putters) and club sets.

ProGrip's mission is to develop and actively seek out innovative and advanced technologies that can be marketed and sold to the approximately $150 billion global wholesale sporting goods industry, to become a premier provider of quality and unique athletic products, and to establish a strong reputation for offering creative solutions to the needs of athletes and sports enthusiasts.

The company's short-term growth strategy is to:

- Initially focus primarily on the re-grip market for golf grips and on selected OEMs. While the re-grip market represents only about one-half of volume sales, it provides the greatest profit margins for manufacturers. Flynt Grips, a reputable brand, successfully used the strategy of focusing on this market for its launch in 1996. In addition, the largest OEMs such as Allegra will not use new suppliers until there is sufficient demand present in the marketplace. Therefore, ProGrip will focus initially on smaller OEMs such as Golf Authority and those focused on the women and junior markets, such as ProWomen Golf and Premier Golf.

- Rapidly build its share of the golf club grip market by leveraging its unique technology. The golf market is very accepting of new technologies and core golfers are especially eager for innovative products. In many cases a golf product's "mystique," such as the following among men for the Lady Precept MC golf ball, can lead to phenomenal success. In less than one year, the Lady Precept MC went from a cult product in Alabama to the #2 selling golf ball in the United States, with over a 6 percent share of the retail market. ProGrip will focus on the advanced design of its Impress grip and its unique benefits in all product marketing and initially build word-of-mouth through proven, as well as innovative, grass roots efforts.

- Introduce new golf grip designs and models that best meet the needs of golfers. ProGrip must quickly expand its golf product line to meet the needs of a very diverse customer base. Golf is a game that is played by both men and women and by a variety of age groups. In fact, women and juniors are golf's fastest growing segments. The flexibility of the Impress grip technology provides the company with a number of product design choices that can be marketed to specific golfer segments.

- Implement innovative marketing techniques to build consumer awareness and acceptance. Building demand is vital for getting initial orders from distributors and OEMs. The golf grip market is a mature one and historically very conservative. The company will utilize marketing techniques that will differentiate the company and the Impress grip from the competition.

- Expand its relationship with Golfworld International. Golfworld is based in Atlanta, Georgia and is the world's largest direct marketer and superstore retailer of golf equipment. The company founded the golf component industry in 1967 and since then has grown to become the leading retailer worldwide of all major brands of golf equipment. In addition, Golfworld mails over 13 million catalogues annually. Golfworld's CEO, Mr. John Danko, has tried the Impress grip and expressed his support for both the technology and the company.

ProGrip's long-term growth strategy is to:

- Build a strong brand in the sports market that represents quality, performance, and innovation. A strong reputation in the sports equipment industry will not only help the company seek out additional technologies, but also enter new sports segments.

- Strongly pursue the junior, women, and senior sports markets with products specific to them and their preferences. These markets have been the fastest growing segments since 1986. In addition, these market segments should derive the most benefit from an anti-vibration sports technology. Seniors suffer more from ailments such as arthritis that are compounded by harmful shock and vibration and women suffer greater incidences of elbow ailments than do male golfers.

- Develop new product designs based on our current technology that can be applied to other sports markets. The company will leverage its experience with golf grips to expand its Impress line of grips to other sports markets such as baseball and tennis. These products will be important additions to the company's product lines.

- Develop new solutions for athletes and sports enthusiasts. ProGrip will expand its portfolio of technologies and broaden its product mix within the broader sports equipment industry. Developing or acquiring new products will provide ProGrip with its long-term growth.

- Expand the company's sales internationally. Golf, baseball, and tennis are each sports with large numbers of enthusiasts overseas. Some of the largest markets for sports apart from the U.S., and that the company will target, include: Canada, France, Germany, Japan, and Mexico.

Current Status

First, ProGrip competed in the Atlanta PGOT CORP® Competition on December 6, 2001, and was voted First Runner-Up by a panel of distinguished venture capitalists and business leaders. Subsequently, the PGOT CORP® Ludington Fund, Ltd. announced its commitment to make a $100,000 investment in ProGrip, pending completion of the requisite documentation. The decision to make an investment in two competitors instead of just the first place team is unique for the PGOT CORP® Competition and was prompted by the Funds' confidence in ProGrip's business plan and management team.

Second, ProGrip has formalized its relationship with Dr. Williams, the inventor of the technology behind the Impress grip. In exchange for a 17.5 percent equity ownership in the company, a $7,500 note with a five-year term, and a seat on ProGrip's board of directors, Dr. Williams has agreed to sell all rights to the golf grip technology to ProGrip. In addition, Dr. Williams will provide his services to the company as needed to insure ProGrip's growth and ultimate success. These services include, but are not limited to, designing and creating an advanced prototype of the Impress grip, speaking with potential customers and investors, designing grips and equipment for other sports uses, and other advice and support as may be needed.

Third, ProGrip is in negotiations with Georgia State University to license a related hammer grip technology that Dr. Williams developed. This technology provides many of the same advantages as the Impress grip with the added benefit that it can provide greater momentum transfer; that is, the sports implement can actually hit harder. This technology has a patent filed in 1997 that is currently pending, although several of the major claims have been allowed as of February 2002, and covers the original hammer grip design as well as designs for similar grips that can be used on baseball bats and tennis racquets, as well as possibly other as yet undefined uses. This derivative technology will provide the company with valuable future products that will help ensure its long-term growth. The design for the golf grip is sufficiently different from the hammer design such that ownership did not fall to Georgia State University but to Dr. Williams directly, and now to ProGrip.

Fourth, ProGrip and Dr. Williams are working closely with Joseph Murphy, an engineer with SportsCreate LLC, on creating a number of revolutionary designs for the Impress grip. Several issues are being considered in choosing the most appropriate designs, including anti-vibration effectiveness, versatility, manufacturing practicality, cost, comfort, durability, and distinctiveness. Mr. Murphy is formerly the Director of Engineering and a 9-year veteran of Cutting Edge, an Atlanta-based professional design firm with such distinguished clients as Adidas, Boeing, Cingular, Dell, General Motors, Hewlett Packard, Shell, Sprint, and Sun. These designs will be used in creating advanced prototypes with which we can conduct additional product research and testing manufacturing methods.

Fifth, ProGrip secured its membership with the Golf Clubcraft Association and will join other organizations that will contribute to the company's success, including the Golf Merchandisers Association, the National Golf Foundation (NGF), and the United States Golf Association (USGA).

ProGrip has clearly identified an attractive opportunity with its innovative golf grip design. Accordingly, we are taking the necessary next steps to bring the company's product to market, including:

- Securing protection for our intellectual property.
- Conducting additional product and market research, including focus groups.
- Identifying and establishing relationships with potential customers.
- Creating marketing materials and campaigns.
- Securing additional financing.

MARKET OPPORTUNITY

Overview

In a market survey conducted by ProGrip, more than one-third of respondents claimed they had suffered a golf-related injury, and 87 percent of those suffered maladies of the hand, wrist, or elbow. Medial Epicondylitis ("Golfer's Elbow") and injuries to the hand and wrist are often associated with repetitive shock and vibration. In addition to contributing to injuries, the shock and vibration associated with striking the ball or ground can detract from a golfer's enjoyment of the game. In fact, 73 percent of respondents said that shock and vibration detracted from their enjoyment and performance of the game. Using appropriate equipment, such as an effective anti-vibration grip, can reduce the likelihood of injury, increase enjoyment of the game, and enhance a golfer's performance.

The rapid evolution of technology in the golf equipment industry accelerates the rate at which golfers purchase new clubs and other equipment, and it has also created a market that is very accepting of new technologies. Although there are three parts to every golf club (the head, the shaft, and the grip), the vast majority of research and development and innovation have focused on the head and the shaft. However, 94 percent of golfers surveyed stated that their grips play an important role in their enjoyment of the game. In terms of innovation that has occurred in the grip market, manufacturers have offered simple, materials-based products (such as the Flynt grip) instead of focusing on design solutions. Anti-shock products that do currently exist are frequently expensive, invasive to the club, add weight, or not particularly effective. In support of this, 87 percent of golfers surveyed indicated their interest in a new anti-shock grip design and only 7 percent claimed that their grips are effective at reducing shock and vibration. To address this underserved market, ProGrip's Impress grip contains an innovative, proprietary design that affordably solves the problem of harmful shock and vibration, that can improve sports health, that increases overall performance, and that enhances a golfer's enjoyment of the game.

Market Size and Segmentation

For true lovers of the game, golf is not simply a sport—it's an obsession. In the U.S., 26.7 million golfers—including more than one of every six adults—currently play golf. Approximately 51 percent are considered core golfers, and nearly half of this core segment are avid golfers, defined as those who annually play at least 25 rounds. In addition, there are an estimated 2.9 million golfers between the ages of 5-17, a segment that plays more rounds of golf (and will continue to play for years to come) than the average adult golfer.

Golf Participation in the U.S.

Due to the large size of the market and the wild popularity of the sport, golfers are a closely researched and clearly identifiable group. The following information illustrates some summary statistics regarding golf participation in the U.S. in 2000, as published by the National Golf Foundation.

U.S. Core and Junior Golfers on the Rise
(in thousands)

Golfer	1996	1997	1998	1999	2000	CAGR
Core (avids and moderates)	11,350	13,499	13,870	13,730	13,675	4.80%
Occasional	11,626	10,619	10,410	10,680	10,960	-1.50%
Junior (12-17)	1,761	2,356	2,147	2,036	2,065	4.10%
All Golfers	**24,737**	**26,474**	**26,427**	**26,446**	**26,700**	**1.70%**
Rounds Played	477,000	547,000	528,000	564,000	586,000	5.30%
Golf Facilities	14.3	14.6	14.9	15.2	15.5	1.90%
Golf Courses	15.7	16	16.4	16.7	17.1	2.20%

We are encouraged by the dramatic increase in the number of core golfers—that is, those golfers aged 18 and above who play eight or more rounds per year. The core golfer segment has shown tremendous growth over the last five years, increasing by over 20 percent, or at a compound annual rate of 4.8 percent. Of this core segment, over 46 percent are "avid" golfers, defined as those who annually play at least 25 rounds. Although avid golfers comprise the smallest player segment (25%), they account for over 50 percent of all golf-related spending.

We are also encouraged by the rapid growth in the number of total rounds played by golfers annually. The more rounds a golfer plays, the more rapidly his or her golf grip will suffer excessive wear and, ultimately, the more frequently he or she will have to re-grip.

With 87 percent of the core segment male, and with over two-thirds of the households earning $50,000 or more, core golfers represent an attractive, and demographically identifiable, primary target market. ProGrip will initially be targeting this core golfer segment, with particular focus paid to avid golfers. The segment is educated, committed to the game, and informed regarding trends in golf technology. However, despite the core golfers' financial wherewithal, many have recently been delaying the purchase of new golf clubs and other equipment, preferring instead to preserve their current set of clubs. Therefore, golfers have been re-gripping their clubs at a higher rate, leading to a 5 percent growth in grip sales despite a contraction in the overall golf equipment industry. Thus, the timing is ideal for an innovative and lower-priced anti-vibration solution such as the Impress grip.

Future growth in the industry will be fueled by two trends, 1) increasing interest from nontraditional golfers, and 2) shifting population trends. We point out the consistently high number of new players of golf each year. Attracting roughly 2.2 million new golfers annually, the sport has witnessed resurgence in popularity. Young, exciting, and successful personalities like Tiger Woods and Sergio Garcia, and international grudge matches like the Ryder Cup, have helped give rise to tremendous interest and participation in golf. According to the NGF, the total number of Junior golfers increased by over 4 percent per annum in the past five years. In addition, the successes of the Ladies Professional Golf Association (the "LPGA") Tour and such female golfers as Annika Sorenstam of Sweden have increased the appeal of the sport to women. These markets are expected to be particularly receptive to the comfort and athletic health benefits of ProGrip's Impress grip.

More than most other sports, golf stands to benefit from upcoming favorable demographic trends. In particular, over the next several years: 1) the aging of Baby Boomers (those born between 1946 and 1964) and 2) the emergence of the Echo Boom generation (those born between 1977 and 1995) will impact the sport of golf. As golfers age, they tend to play golf more often and spend more money on the sport, particularly in the over-50 age group. In addition, they become more health conscious and become more susceptible to such ailments as arthritis. Accordingly, because a majority of Baby Boomers are entering their 40s and 50s, the company expects interest in and spending on golf to increase along with a greater need for golf products that provide greater comfort in addition to performance enhancement. Further, because Echo Boomers are beginning to enter their 20s, the age most golfers begin to play the sport, the company believes they will further increase their participation in and spending on golf.

The Golf Grip Industry

Every time a golfer buys a new club, he or she buys a new golf grip installed on the club. In addition, golfers purchase replacement grips for their clubs as the original grips age or become worn from use. According to ProGrip's survey, golfers re-grip their clubs on average every six months to a year. Annually, golfers spend approximately $22 billion on equipment and fees in the U.S. Global golf grip sales are estimated to be $350 million, of which $140 million represents grip sales in the U.S. Roughly two-thirds of grip sales are to OEMs with the remainder being sold in the aftermarket for club re-grips. Golfers typically pay between $1.50 and $5.50 per club to re-grip them, exclusive of labor, and golfers carry on average 12 clubs in his or her bag.

Market Research

In addition to secondary research from a variety of sources, ProGrip conducted two primary research studies to ascertain golfers' needs and preferences, reactions to the Impress grip, and purchase intentions. The studies included a golf grip market survey involving 151 respondents and comparative consumer trials of 30 golfers.

Market Survey

ProGrip administered a market survey to 151 golfers. The survey was administered at two Golfworld stores in Atlanta, Georgia. The sample is considered representative of the core market segment for golf equipment and accessories. (See "Demographics" below.) Respondents were asked a series of 42 questions to determine demographics, skill level, golf-related injuries, equipment usage and satisfaction, preferred characteristics, and price sensitivity. The data was manually entered into a spreadsheet and analyzed with statistical software. Following is a summary of the analysis.

Demographics

89 percent of respondents were male, 11 percent were female. The median household income was between $60K and $80K, with 18 percent representing the less than $40K segment and roughly 17 percent representing the greater than $125K segment. Nearly 63 percent of respondents were between the ages of 30 and 60. 15.2 percent rated themselves beginners, 51 percent as intermediate, 32.5 percent as advanced, and 1.3 percent as professional. The demographics correspond to those of the target core golfer segment.

Golfers Who Re-grip

79.5 percent of respondents said they re-grip their clubs every two years or more frequently. 52.3 percent said they re-grip annually, and 14.6 percent said they re-grip their clubs every 6 months.

Effect of Shock and Role of Grips

73.3 percent of all respondents claimed that shock and vibration detracted from their enjoyment of the game. Additionally, 72.5 percent of all respondents claimed that shock and vibration reduced their performance. 94 percent of all respondents claimed that their golf grips played an important role in their enjoyment of the game, and 72 percent of those claimed the role was very important.

Anti-Vibration Equipment Effectiveness and Awareness

59 percent of respondents have tried gloves to reduce shock and vibration, but only 31

percent of those who have used gloves say they were effective at reducing shock and vibration. Of those who have used shaft inserts (33.8% of the sample), only one-third said they were effective in reducing shock. Nearly half of respondents have used graphite shafts, but only about half of those claimed they were effective at reducing shock and vibration. Oversized clubs were used by 41.1 percent of respondents, with about 44 percent of the users claiming effectiveness in shock reduction. Finally, of those who have tried grips currently on the market that claim to reduce vibration (22.5% of the sample), less than one-third of them said they were effective. Of those who were aware of anti-vibration grips currently on the market, less than half (47%) identified the Flynt grip as an anti-vibration grip, 11 percent identified Mercury, 5 percent identified GolfLife, and 5 percent identified Plex. (Figures do not add up to 100 because some respondents did not identify a specific brand of grip.)

Price Sensitivity and Purchase Intent

Currently, golfers in the target segment claimed to spend $6.22 per club, on average, to re-grip their clubs. The same segment claimed they were willing to pay, on average, $4.44 for a new anti-vibration grip. The difference between current spending and willingness to pay is due to 1) respondents' reluctance to admit a higher willingness to pay, and 2) to labor costs associated with re-gripping for those in the sample who do not re-grip their own clubs. Adjusting for labor costs and percentages of those who did not re-grip themselves, a new anti-shock grip priced at $4.79 would be priced attractively for the target segment.

Ranking of Golf Grip Attributes Used in Purchase Decision

The survey asked respondents to rate the importance of six attributes of golf grips: quality, price, material, appearance, technology, and brand. The results in the table below indicate the most significant discriminator is product quality. Product technology, however, was the second most significant attribute. Material, appearance, price, and brand were rated third through sixth, respectively. The results suggest flexibility in pricing and brand with respect to product quality and technology. (In other words, golfers would pay more for a high quality product that uses the latest technology and would readily switch brands.)

Golfers Ratings of Attributes Importance in Selecting a Golf Grip

	Grip Quality Rating	Grip Price Rating	Grip Material Rating	Grip Appearance Rating	Grip Technology Rating	Grip Brand Rating
Valid	151	151	151	151	151	151
Missing	0	0	0	0	0	0
Mean	3.87	2.94	3.51	3	3.68	2.64

Note: Ratings were on a scale of 1 (not important) to 4 (high importance).

Consumer Trials

ProGrip administered a controlled trial to 30 golfers at the driving range located at Golfworld's corporate headquarters in Atlanta, Georgia. The trial consisted of each golfer taking as many swings as he or she liked with each of three golf clubs. The clubs were identical with the exception of the grip. The grips included a standard Lee grip, a GolfLife Comfort grip (a comfort grip also identified as an "anti-shock" grip by market survey respondents), and the prototype Impress grip. Upon completion of the trial, each golfer was asked to complete a comparative survey of several observed attributes, and to add comments with respect to the ProGrip grip.

Descriptive Statistics

The Impress grip outperformed the standard grip (Lee) and the anti-vibration grip (GolfLife) decisively in all areas. In terms of comfort, the ProGrip grip scored an average 4.62 on a scale of 1 to 6. The score was 20 percent higher than the GolfLife anti-vibration grip and 58 percent higher than the Lee standard grip. The Impress grip scored 4.39 for control, 21 percent higher than GolfLife and 39 percent higher than Lee. A score of 4.66 on performance was 23 percent higher than GolfLife and 45 percent higher than Lee. In terms of preference, the Impress grip scored 4.61, which was 23 percent higher than GolfLife's score and 54 percent higher than Lee. Most telling was the rating for shock reduction: ProGrip's score of 4.93 was 31 percent higher than GolfLife and 87 percent higher than Lee.

COMPETITIVE ANALYSIS

Overview

The golf equipment industry is highly competitive. There are numerous companies competing in various segments of the golf equipment markets including those which manufacture and sell golf grips to OEMs as a component of new clubs, and alternatively to retailers. Retail grips are, in turn, sold to golfers who need to replace old or worn grips. Some of the company's competitors have greater brand name recognition, more extensive engineering, manufacturing and marketing capabilities, and greater financial, technological, and personnel resources than the company. ProGrip will be competing primarily on the basis of product quality, product specifications and design, on-time deliveries, customer relationships, price, and brand name recognition.

The golf industry is generally characterized by rapid and widespread imitation of popular technologies, designs, and product concepts. ProGrip may face competition from manufacturers introducing new or innovative products or successfully promoting golf grips that achieve market acceptance. Therefore, in order to compete effectively in the long-term, ProGrip must continue introducing innovative products and designs, differentiate itself in the marketplace, and create lasting competitive advantages.

Competition

ProGrip competes with a number of established golf grip manufacturers. The company's primary competitors include Baker/GolfLife and GolfMax, with estimated worldwide market shares of 56 percent and 20 percent, respectively, and who dominate the larger OEM firms such as Allegra and Made Well. In addition, there are at least a dozen smaller golf grip manufacturers that primarily sell into the re-grip market. Of these, ProGrip will be primarily competing against Van Grips and Flynt Grips, since each boasts products with anti-vibration qualities. Finally, ProGrip will be competing against other, non-grip, anti-vibration solutions currently on the market, including oversized club heads, graphite shafts, and Atlas's Ultra product. However, despite the fiercely competitive nature of the market, ProGrip is confident, based upon the success of Flynt Grips, that its Impress line of premium golf grips can gain significant market acceptance.

Established in 1977, Flynt Incorporated entered the sports equipment industry as a maker of tennis racquet strings. The company's technological advances in string filaments propelled Flynt to its position as one of the leading suppliers of quality tennis racquet strings in the world. In the 1980s, Flynt revolutionized the tennis grip market, replacing leather grips with a synthetic grip made from a proprietary polymer called Elastom ETM®, resulting in 20 U.S. and foreign patents.

In 1996, Flynt entered the golf industry with a line of golf grips made with Elastom ETM®. Initially, the company penetrated the golf industry as an aftermarket product for golf club re-gripping. As a result of the distinctive feel and slip-resistance of the grip, as well as its purported anti-vibration qualities, Flynt quickly made inroads with major golf club manufacturers and now serves as one of the preferred OEMs for golf grips. Flynt's success has also led to widespread imitation among the larger manufacturers. Flynt currently commands the highest premium price in the marketplace for its grips, with standard grip prices ranging from $2.95 to $5.50, with higher prices for putter grips.

The Impress grip, being a design innovation rather than merely a change to the materials of the grip, provides a number of advantages over any other grip currently in the market, and it has several compelling advantages over other anti-vibration solutions. In addition, ProGrip can utilize standard manufacturing methods in the production of its Impress grips. These advantages, combined with the innovative sales and marketing techniques that the company plans to utilize, will help insure ProGrip's success in the golf grip market.

PRODUCT & POSITIONING

Product Summary

ProGrip owns a revolutionary golf grip that significantly reduces the shock and vibration that results from striking the ball or the ground. The grip has been designed to dissipate the pattern of vibration specific to golf clubs before it reaches the hand, as opposed to dampening the vibration between the grip and the hand. The ultimate effect is a preservation of the "feel" of the club and the sense of control, while reducing injuries and stress that can result from profound continuous impacts. The sections below explain the various grips that will be offered and how they will be positioned in the market.

The Impress Grip

The physical principles and behavior of the Impress grip are identical to the anti-vibration grip developed for hammers by Dr. Williams, although the design takes on a different form. The Impress grip uses the physical structure and properties of the club shaft to absorb specific frequency vibrations within the grip itself, while still transferring other frequencies so that the "feel" of the club is not sacrificed. This design-based solution to shock and vibration provides a number of distinct advantages over other products, including:

- **A significant reduction of harmful shock and vibration felt by a golfer.** In the trial tests for the Impress grip, golfers found it reduced shock and vibration 87 percent more than standard grips.
- **The ability to create an anti-vibration grip with conventional manufacturing methods, using any commercially viable materials, and for any type of club (graphite or steel, wood or iron).** This will provide flexibility in manufacturing and help keep costs to a minimum. This benefit also expands our market beyond a single type of club—Ultra is only used with steel shafts.
- **The grip is nondestructive and noninvasive to the club, and it is installed like any other grip.** The Ultra product requires the use or purchase of steel shafts. Other solutions introduce additional devices onto the club.
- **A significant decrease in cost to the consumer from many other nongrip anti-vibration solutions.** The Ultra product costs over 3 times more than a premium golf grip. Oversized club heads are even more expensive.
- **An introduction of a completely new concept to the grip market, Precise Shock Reduction (PSR).** This refers to ProGrip's ability to manufacture grips that have anti-shock qualities of varying degrees, customizable to suit the particular grip characteristics desired by a diverse market.

These improvements strongly differentiate the Impress grip from its competition. The Impress grip simply makes golf more enjoyable for the average player. Since the Impress grip works on all clubs and is installed in a normal fashion, it may address both the OEM and re-grip markets.

The innovative design of the Impress grip allows the company to manufacture and offer the product with a wide range of materials without losing its anti-vibration qualities. Golfers prefer grips with a distinctive set of features, including: size, texture, comfort, materials, durability, and tackiness. ProGrip's grip technology is extremely versatile and will allow the company to offer products that best meet the specific needs of golfers.

The company intends to provide consumers with the concept of Precise Shock Reduction (PSR), an option that is available to golfers only with the ProGrip grip. With PSR, players will have the ability to choose a grip with the level of vibration absorption that best suits their needs, in the size and style of grip that they prefer. Specifically, for men and women, standard size grips will be initially available as well as a men's mid-size grip, with the golfer's choice of three levels of PSR. A total of 18 SKUs will be introduced initially, at an average retail price of $5.00. Eventually, men's jumbo and women's mid-size grips will be introduced, increasing the total number of SKU's to 30. By comparison, Flynt has 54 SKUs, of which 37 are non-putter grips, and GolfMax reports a total of 64 models.

Positioning

The Impress grip will be positioned as a premium product competing with standard and high-end grip products in the re-grip market, and later in the OEM market. ProGrip's various product offerings will be promoted as high performance grips based on a revolutionary design that significantly reduces shock and vibration, has a comfortable feel, mitigates the risks of sports-related injuries, and that can improve a player's performance and enjoyment of the game. ProGrip is currently in the process of developing unique looking designs for the Impress grip and also choosing the most appropriate materials with which to make the grip that will provide a unique feel and a high degree of durability. The company will always maintain itself as a provider of premium products that innovatively meets the needs of its customers.

MARKETING STRATEGY

Strategic Overview

Beyond product development, ProGrip creates value primarily through the marketing stage. (Manufacturing and distribution will be outsourced.) Building demand plays a central role to the acceptance of the Impress grip in the marketplace and the success of the company. Retailers and OEMs will not purchase component products without demonstrated demand from the market, and golfers will not be motivated to switch brands unless they are convinced of the benefits of a new product. Therefore, ProGrip will pursue grass roots, traditional, and innovative marketing and sales strategies to aggressively build acceptance of and demand for its premium line of Impress grips. Based on a careful review of other standard and premium grips and of other anti-vibration devices, ProGrip will price its Impress line at a premium. Market data indicate a high willingness to pay a premium for innovative products—particularly for grips, which are relatively low-priced compared to golf clubs and their other components.

Build Regional Demand

ProGrip will concentrate building demand in the top ten states in the country with the most number of golfers age twelve and higher. In descending order, those states are: California, New York, Pennsylvania, Michigan, Illinois, Ohio, Georgia, Florida, Wisconsin, and Minnesota.

The company will then expand its focus to include selected markets within other states and offer the Impress grip nationwide by late 2003. The company will eventually expand sales globally and intends to enter into joint venture agreements with foreign distributors and retailers of golf equipment, starting with Japan and the UK.

Channel Selection (Market/Distribution/ Retail)

Half of all golf grip sales are made through the re-grip market—to golfers who put new grips on existing clubs. The other half are sold to OEMs who install the grips as components of new clubs. ProGrip's strategy involves first penetrating the re-grip market and then gradually entering the OEM market. The sequential approach is favored for two reasons. First, the re-grip market offers higher margins. Second, the OEM market is a difficult market for new products to enter. Consumer demand created in the golf equipment components market (i.e., grips, heads, shafts) is what typically drives OEM club manufacturers to eventually offer new product components on their clubs. Additionally, Flynt (a relative newcomer to golf grips) used the sequential strategy to introduce its line of golf grips in 1996 and has since established itself as a reputable brand. Allegra, a major golf OEM, now installs Flynt grips on some of its clubs.

Initial channels include those distributors and retailers who cater to the re-grip market. ProGrip will pursue relations with over 400 retailers and distributors of golf equipment nationwide, concentrating on those doing business in the ten key states that have the most golfers. The intent is to develop strong relationships similar to the one ProGrip currently has and continues to build with Golfworld. Winning the support of retailers' sales forces and teaching pros who influence consumer decisions will be vital, and that support will come through their understanding of the benefits of the Impress grip. To accomplish this, ProGrip will teach distributors and retailers, their sales forces, and teaching pros the benefits of the Impress grip through a training video, product demonstrations, and sales representatives. (The video and product demos will also be used for promotion to consumers.) Finally, ProGrip will keep our retail and distribution partners informed of our marketing campaigns and promotions to ensure they are familiar with the demand levels we generate.

Private Label

ProGrip will explore opportunities to enter into private label agreements with major retailers in the U.S. such as Golfworld and Winners. Golfworld has already expressed interest in such a venture.

Promotion

In the golf equipment industry in general and the re-grip market in particular, it is extremely important to build product demand at a grass roots level in order to gain user acceptance. This is because golfers' purchase decisions are heavily influenced by the advice of friends, pro shop sales agents, and local teaching professionals, as well as through the emulation of golf professionals who succeed while using particular products. To build a "buzz" around the Impress grip, ProGrip has developed and will implement grass roots and viral marketing tactics concentrated in the ten key golf states. Such tactics include traditional approaches like buying print and broadcast ads, publishing articles on the Impress technology in influential journals, developing relations with local pros and teaching them about our product, distributing our training video, direct mailing, conducting product demonstrations at prominent and well-visited driving ranges, golf courses, and country clubs, and finally seeking pro usage on prominent tours. ProGrip will also employ innovative approaches to promote understanding of importance of re-gripping one's clubs and to build customer loyalty to the Impress grip. Two such approaches are "Re-Grip Day" and the "ProGrip Community." After initial market penetration, the company will pursue top-tier pro endorsement, broadcast sponsorship, and additional co-branding opportunities.

Print Promotions

The company will pursue editorial coverage and advertisements in golf and trade publications as well as general consumer magazines and newspapers worldwide. These include *Golf Digest, Golf Magazine, Sports Illustrated,* the *Wall Street Journal,* and *USA Today*. The cost of a full-page advertisement in *Golf Digest* and *Golf Week* are $60,000 and $17,500 respectively. Additionally, the company will use other media to convey the benefits of the technology to key industry influencers. For example, Golfworld CEO John Danko offered to publish an article on the Impress technology in Golfworld's Clubcraft magazine, the largest technical journal in the trade with a nationwide subscriber base of 125,000. Readership includes respected and influential equipment specialists and sales representatives.

Broadcast Promotions

The company intends to utilize 30 and 60-second direct television commercials on national stations such as ESPN and the Golf Channel as well as radio advertising, once the brand gains a foothold with core golfers. Advertising will include a series of innovative commercials to run during major golf tournaments and other golf-related programs.

Use of Impress by Professionals

The company will win support from local teaching professionals who are key opinion leaders in their respective golfing communities through leveraging existing relationships between ProGrip and several key industry contacts. ProGrip industry contacts include manufacturers and distributors (e.g., GolfSmith, Golf Authority, and Head), golf courses (Myrtle Beach, Cedar Grove in Atlanta, and the Atlanta Country Club), and acquaintances of PGA members such as Ben Crenshaw and Tom Kite. ProGrip will seek wide-ranging use of the Impress grip from many second-tier pro golfers. The company also considers the Buy.com Tour (formerly the Nike Tour) and the PGA Senior Tour as the two best opportunities for Impress grip trial by top-tier pros. Pro usage of a golf product (second tier and top tier) can spur extremely effective word-of-mouth marketing in the golf equipment industry.

Re-Grip Day

ProGrip will host "Re-Grip Day" at major corporate campuses and office complexes. Golfers will be encouraged to bring in their clubs to have them re-gripped by ProGrip representatives at our portable workshops. A short video loop will provide useful information, and representatives will help golfers select the right grips for their clubs. Golfers can learn how to perform the relatively easy task of re-gripping their own clubs, or they can simply drop off their clubs and return later to pick them up with the new Impress grips installed.

The ProGrip Community

Golfers who express interest in or purchase one of the company's products will receive informational newsletters on golf issues related to technology, performance, and health, and they will receive ProGrip promotional offers. This will be part of ProGrip's campaign aimed at building and maintaining a community following. The company has already developed a database of hundreds of potential customers, which continues to grow. The information was collected from market research and includes contact information as well as demographic and behavioral data.

Sponsorship

Sponsorship of selected golf tournaments and the Golf Channel's weekly instructional program, "Living Room Lessons" as well as other golf-related events with wide exposure would serve to build continued brand recognition among the golf community.

Co-Branding Opportunities

ProGrip has already initiated discussions with Walt Disney Corporation for the licensed use of certain of its copyrighted characters on its grips marketed for junior golfers. In addition, the company will seek to license characters from the Cartoon Channel and Nickelodeon, two media brands popular among young people.

PGA Golfer Endorsement

Formal endorsements from top-tier golf professionals are an important strategy for golf products to gain acceptance from amateur golfers, although the expense necessitates demonstrated acceptance on at least a regional level. The company will eventually seek endorsement from a top-25 ranked professional golfer on the PGA Tour to promote its product lines and build brand strength.

Additional Promotional Activities

The company will engage in a variety of additional promotional activities to sell and market its products. Such activities include 1) consumer sweepstakes; 2) promotional giveaways with certain purchases, including items such as instructional videos and audiotapes; and 3) promotional campaigns. Working with Golfworld, the company has already conducted the first such promotion—a drawing for a $100 Golfworld gift certificate for participants of one of our market research surveys.

Pricing

Primary consumer research has shown that golfers will pay a premium for technology-based products that reduce shock and vibration and promise to improve their game. The research specifically indicates that the average Impress grip could be priced attractively at $5.00, comparable to the pricing of other premium grips, which range from (roughly) $4.50-$5.50 per grip.

MANUFACTURING & DISTRIBUTION

Industry and Channels

The golf grip market is a mature industry and, therefore, manufacturing methods have become fairly standardized. Golf grips manufacturers typically have facilities located in China, Taiwan, or Mexico and produce rubber and elastomeric products for a wide variety of industrial uses. While the production of grips is not particularly complex, usually involving some injection or extrusion molding process, it is important that they can be manufactured in large batches and with a high degree of consistency. It is also necessary to have the flexibility to manufacture grips of a variety of materials, qualities, sizes, and even colors to meet the myriad tastes of golfers of differing sexes, ages, and skill levels. The company will become a supplier to golf equipment retailers and, eventually, to several major golf club OEMs. Most major OEMs demand high standards of quality and service from all suppliers and require reliable second sources for most components, including grips. The company's success with OEMs will be dependent upon its ability to supply high quality grips and provide a high level of service.

Strategy

ProGrip will outsource all phases of production and distribution for the foreseeable future. This strategy eliminates the need for extensive fixed assets while maintaining flexibility in design and production. In addition, this strategy allows the company to best meet the needs of its OEM customers, which are projected to collectively account for 20 percent of sales by year five. It will also allow the company to better establish initial market acceptance by focusing its attention on product development, marketing, and sales. Sourced products will be manufactured according to ProGrip's strict quality control specifications. To assure the quality of its sourced products, the company will work closely with third-party manufacturers, emphasizing product reliability, performance standards, and strict quality controls to which all producers must adhere. ProGrip will monitor its sourced products to improve quality. We will establish product specifications, select the materials to be used to produce the grips, and test the specifications of all grips received by the company. In addition, ProGrip will maintain redundant sources of supply for each of its grips.

ProGrip is currently negotiating with Freightliners to provide for all of the company's warehousing and distribution needs and with Calypso, one of the leading manufacturers in Indonesia, to supply the company's initial products. In addition, ProGrip is in discussions with Advance Elastic Corporation, a wholly owned subsidiary of Dow Chemical, to provide the company with premium materials to use in the manufacture of the Impress grip.

MANAGEMENT

Management Team

The management team of ProGrip is one of the company's greatest strengths. The members collectively have more than 31 years of real world experience in the areas of entrepreneurship, finance, marketing, and operations. The individual members of the management team and their positions are listed below.

Martin Roland, Chief Executive Officer and Chief Financial Officer—Martin has more than four years of experience as a small business owner and six years of financial experience. He currently works as an Associate with Brooks Company, an Atlanta-based venture capital firm. Prior to this, Martin was an Associate with Benz Willow & Dodd where he completed over $25 million in private equity and debt placements for Georgia-based companies. In addition, he completed $550 million in public equity and debt offerings and over $1 billion in M&A transactions as an analyst in the Atlanta office of Friedman, Smitherman & Flip Securities Corp. Martin received a B.F.A. from the University of North Carolina, a B.B.A. from North Georgia College, and is currently pursuing his M.B.A. from Georgia State University.

James Martow, Vice President of Operations—James has a background in industrial management and manufacturing, with a particularly strong record of process improvements and change management. As a U.S. Army lieutenant, James' weapons department consistently achieved the highest performance ratings. He saved the Army hundreds of thousands of dollars through cost-savings measures in training and in maintenance procedures. After receiving a Master of Science from the Massachusetts Institute of Technology, James joined CNN, where he identified over $60,000 in annual savings in manufacturing processes. Later, he led a 24,000-member volunteer organization through a challenging organizational transition while meeting all operational objectives. While working toward his M.B.A. at Georgia State University, James remained active in practicum and ancillary work, identifying over $700,000 in process savings to a single client.

Govinder Rama, Vice President of Sales and Marketing—Govinder Rama has a B.A. in economics from the University of Massachusetts, a master's degree in Public Health from the University of Missouri, and is currently a candidate for an M.B.A. from Georgia State University. Professionally, he has experience in business development and marketing in the pharmaceutical industry, first for Global Pharmaceuticals and most recently Pfizer. Govinder has experience developing strategic marketing plans, establishing joint ventures, evaluating business plans, and negotiating contracts.

ProGrip will supplement its management team with individuals possessing product development and sales experience in the sports industry.

Advisory Group

ProGrip has selected a number of individuals to advise management. The advisors were chosen because of their excitement about our product and its potential and their valuable experience in areas critical to the company's success. Each member has been instrumental in advising ProGrip through its initial development, and management is confident that the board of advisors will continue to play a valuable role in the company's growth. Our advisors include:

Aaron Zhender—Managing Director, Project Ventures—Mr. Zhender is a venture capitalist with extensive hands-on experience in starting and growing new ventures. Mr. Zhender was founder and President of CyberWays Company, acting COO for Online Solutions, and interim CEO of 1PC, Inc. and Jazz IT. Mr. Zhender currently serves on the Boards of OmniWare, Design Group, Flatter, and e-Zine.

Patrick Andrews—Principal, Project Ventures—Mr. Andrews is a venture capitalist with many years of project management and operational experience. Mr. Andrews also served for over seven years as a pilot in the United States Army, earning the rank of Lieutenant. Mr. Andrews received his M.B.A. and a B.S. in Electrical Engineering from Georgia State University.

Dr. William Ames—Management Department Chairman, Georgia State University—Dr. Ames is a professor of entrepreneurship and has conducted extensive research in the areas of organizational design, entrepreneurship, small business, and venture capital. Dr. Ames is extensively involved with various corporate and public sector organizations and his research has been widely published. He is the recipient of grants from the Wiseman Foundation, the Sun Foundation, the Donald Frommer, and the National Science Foundation.

Les Flack—Former Director of Marketing, Golf Authority—Mr. Flack played a vital role in the rapid growth of Golf Authority, a designer and manufacturer of premium quality, technologically innovative golf clubs with revenues of approximately $86 million in 2000. In addition, Mr. Flack was instrumental in the success of Adam Golf's initial public offering and in making the company the third largest seller of fairway woods in the U.S.

Dr. Dennis Williams—Chief Scientist, SuperTech—Dr. Williams is the inventor of the technology behind the Impress grip and holds an S.B. in Physics from DeVry Institute of Technology and a Ph.D. in Physics from Georgia State University. He has 12 years of experience in plasma physics and pulsed power and has worked for industry, government, and academia.

THE OFFERING

Deal Structure

ProGrip is seeking $750,000 in equity capital. ProGrip's management is open to negotiating an appropriate investment strategy. As the company's initial products prove successful, we want to quickly expand the availability of the Impress grip and introduce new products. Accordingly, ProGrip will need the financial resources to aggressively move forward and capture the golf grip opportunity and will seek additional financing if and when necessary in the future.

Use of Funds

ProGrip intends to outsource all manufacturing of its premium grips. Thus, the primary use of funds generated from the private placement will be financing the company's initial launch and working capital requirements.

Investor Return

ProGrip's management is open to negotiating an appropriate investment strategy. Staged entries are possible given our current projection framework. Note, however, that such staging may result in lower aggregate returns. The following tables illustrate the calculation of the investor's internal rate of return (IRR) given the projected financial results.

Investment Opportunity

Investment required	$750,000
Assumed equity ownership	50.00%
EBITDA multiple	5.0x
Year 5 EBITDA	$3,609,155
Terminal value in year 5	$18,045,777
Value of investment in year 5	$9,022,888
Internal rate of return	64.50%
Multiple of original investment	12.0x

Sensitivity Analysis
Projected Internal Rate of Return for a $750,000 Investment

		Assumed EBITDA Multiple						
		2	**3**	**4**	**5**	**6**	**7**	**8**
Year 5 EBITDA	$2,500,000	27.20%	38.00%	46.10%	52.80%	58.50%	63.50%	67.90%
	$3,000,000	32.00%	43.10%	51.60%	58.50%	64.40%	69.50%	74.10%
	$3,500,000	36.10%	47.60%	56.30%	63.50%	69.50%	74.80%	79.60%
	$4,000,000	39.80%	51.60%	60.50%	67.90%	74.10%	79.60%	84.40%
	$4,500,000	43.10%	55.20%	64.40%	71.90%	78.30%	83.80%	88.80%
	$5,000,000	46.10%	58.50%	67.90%	75.50%	82.10%	87.80%	92.80%

Holistic Health Center

BUSINESS PLAN

HOLISTIC CHOICES, LLC

1437 Springdale Drive
Rockford, Illinois 61108

The mission of Holistic Choices is to bring preventative and restorative lifelong health solutions to the whole consumer. We believe in providing essentials for a healthy body, both on the inside and the outside, using natural methods that are chemical-free and allow the consumer to take responsibility for their health.

- EXECUTIVE SUMMARY
- PROGRAMS
- MARKETING
- COMPETITION
- BACKGROUND ON PRINCIPAL PARTNERS
- OPERATING PROCEDURES
- PERSONNEL
- BREAK-EVEN ANALYSIS

HOLISTIC HEALTH CENTER BUSINESS PLAN

EXECUTIVE SUMMARY

Description of the Business

Holistic Choices, LLC, is a wellness studio. The partners, Joanne Fuller and Mary Smart, are both professionals in a health/wellness field and they are teaming up to put several health/wellness services under one roof. Holistic Choices will offer holistic skin/personal grooming care services, personal fitness training, nutrition classes and counseling, Yoga/Pilates classes, and therapeutic massage. We feel these are a good combination of services because as a person becomes interested in one aspect of a healthier lifestyle, it naturally leads to interest in other phases, and we feel the components we offer are part of a larger healthy lifestyle continuum.

Mission Statement

The mission of Holistic Choices is to bring preventative and restorative lifelong health solutions to the whole consumer. We believe in providing essentials for a healthy body, both on the inside and the outside, using natural methods that are chemical-free and allow the consumer to take responsibility for their health.

PROGRAMS

Group Personal Training
(Mary Smart)

While individual personal training appointments will be offered, we will be encouraging most people to participate in a group setting, as it is more effective both in health/physical results as well as cost. The program we facilitate emphasizes a general high quality-of-life fitness level for the total body approach. While some programs encourage different body part work on different days, we are trying to reach a larger audience by inciting a workout that targets the whole body and is therefore less intimidating to many levels of consumers. In addition to being less intimidating, it also is more effective because participants tend to adhere to their fitness program longer, bringing about lasting results.

Yoga and Pilates
(Mary Smart)

Holistic Choices will be offering Yoga and mat Pilates classes (Pilates done without a piece of equipment called a Reformer). These types of classes are quickly gaining in popularity as more is being understood about deep muscle tissue work and its benefits.

Nutrition Counseling
(Mary Smart)

Holistic Choices will be offering nutrition consultations and guidance. We will work with the general public to improve their health through their diet. We will help them sort through the diet information portrayed through all modes of media and give solid scientific information as well as make individual allowances to bring about weight management success. As for special populations (such as diabetics, etc.), Mary Smart is qualified to work within a dietician/doctor's recommended diet. This would mean finding ways to make the diet restrictions more palatable to the tastes of the individual. Holistic Choices also will offer nutrition classes where groups of people can come to our studio for cooking demonstrations, to taste food, and get useful information to use for making better nutritional choices.

Skin Care
(Joanne Fuller)

Holistic Choices will be offering several skin-care services directed by Joanne Fuller. Our licensed estheticians will specialize in treating various skin disorders with a holistic approach. In addition to our facials, we also will offer waxing, makeup, and full-body treatments. Holistic Choices will offer the consumer an alternative to conventional skin-care methods. Chronic skin-care disorders, such as rosacea, are generally treated by masking the symptoms with harmful chemicals and prescription drugs. Holistic Choices believes in treating the core of the problem for long-lasting results. Our state-of-the-art equipment, superior skin-care products, and innovative anti-aging facials will put Holistic Choices in a class all by itself.

Manicures/ Pedicures
(Sherry Forman)

Sherry Forman has been a licensed nail technician for over ten years. During that time, she has been actively working at various salons in the Rockford area. She has continued her education through regularly-scheduled classes and classes she created herself with other professional nail technicians. Anyone who knows her knows she has a passion for doing nails. Holistic Choices will offer natural nail services, such as manicures, pedicures, and natural wraps as opposed to nail tips and acrylics. Manicure and pedicure services are all about the "work" that has to be done. People seek these services so they don't have to do the work themselves. In the past ten years, she has learned how to do this work in a professional and timely manner and has built up a loyal clientele. She looks forward to being a part of and participating in the success of Holistic Choices.

Massage Therapy
(Beatrice Whitman)

Massage Therapy, as a non-invasive, holistic approach to maintain the body's natural functions, is an essential component of the wellness continuum. Direct and indirect manipulation of the body supports general physical and emotional well-being. Massage Therapy promotes and extensive range of benefits, which include:

- Increasing circulation
- Decreasing pain
- Restoring balance in musculature
- Decreasing muscle fatigue and soreness
- Boosting immune function
- Aiding the body's natural healing process
- Decreasing stress

Performing massage therapy without completing comprehensive training can potentially do more harm than good. Beatrice Whitman is a graduate of the Health Enrichment Center, an accredited massage therapy program located in Freeport, Illinois. In addition, Beatrice is a member of the American Massage Therapy Association, a national organization that is limited to certified massage therapists. She has held a private practice in Rockford and has nearly tripled her clientele base since she first began two and a half years ago. With a high client retention rate, her business shows promising signs of continued exponential growth.

Beatrice's services include full-body massage, aromatherapy and essential oil treatments, and hot stone therapy. As Beatrice furthers her continuing education in other modalities of body work, more services will be available for the Holistic Choices clientele.

MARKETING

The principal partners, Joanne Fuller and Mary Smart, are both established in their health/ wellness fields as are the rest of the contracted professionals. We have comprehensive clientele that we are confident will be following us into our new venture. Most of our business thus far has grown by word-of-mouth. However, to inform our clients as to our new location and additional services, we plan to advertise in the local papers such as the *Observer*, the *Journal* and the *Community Crier* with a photo of us and a description of the services we offer. We also will have brochures describing Holistic Choices as a whole, as well as each individual service that we provide. They will give an overview of the professional providing the service and a description of the amenities their service entails as well as the cost. We also plan to speak in front of and run clinics for various groups, such as PTA/O groups, the Rotary club, MOPS (Mothers of Preschoolers) groups, Scouts, and other similar groups.

COMPETITION

Our major competitors would be local health clubs, such as Curves. We believe we are set apart from the "health club" scene by several factors, such as: an inviting, relaxed, warm atmosphere–our location is a commercially zoned house as opposed to an industrial "building," our desire to educate and treat the consumer as a whole to provide lifelong healthy habits as opposed to "diet plans," makeup, and "spa" packages. We believe that our wellness studio does and will attract the large percentage of people who are intimidated by a big health club because of the smaller scale and more personal approach. We also believe that our (the principal partners as well as the contracted professionals) individual education and professional experience(s) help to set us apart from any of our competitors. We are all dedicated to our own education in an attempt to bring excellence and health to ourselves and our clientele.

BACKGROUND ON PRINCIPAL PARTNERS

Mary Smart

I was certified as a group fitness instructor through the American Council on Exercise (ACE) in February 1991. I taught group fitness classes, a.k.a. "aerobic" classes, in the Schaumburg area at several health clubs and facilities as well as for a few corporate and community education programs. When we moved to Elmhurst in early 1996, I obtained jobs teaching group fitness at a couple local fitness facilities, including Fitness Strategies. In all of these facilities, I taught classes such as High/Low and Step Aerobics, Kickboxing, Cycling, Pregnancy and Postpartum fitness, Circuit Training, children's and family fitness classes, Yoga, Pilates, and many more. In 1997, I was certified as a personal trainer through ACE and began taking on individual and groups as clients. Some clients that started with me then are still my clients today. In March of 1998, I was promoted to the Land Fitness Coordinator (in charge of all fitness instructors and programs not taking place in water).

The program grew to a point where the Fitness Coordinator position went from a part-time job to a fulltime Health and Wellness Specialist assignment in 2001. With a comprehensive group of personal training clients at the time and the mother of four children, I didn't feel the position suited me. The new Health and Wellness Specialist for the Summit contracted me to teach a course in Women's Weight Training, a two-night course discussing and demonstrating many weight-training techniques for women. The class was so successful, it has been repeated several times. It has attracted many women that are intimidated to go into a fitness center and who aren't knowledgeable about weight lifting and weight lifting machines.

In July of 2003, I was contracted by the American Heart Association to be a coach/trainer for the "Train to End Stroke" program. I am currently training the largest of the four central Rockford teams going to either Walt Disney World, Florida, or Phoenix, Arizona, for a half or full marathon in January 2004. I also have been re-contracted for the next marathon season. I train participants to either walk or run a half or full marathon and oversee their progress for five months. As a coach I have run clinics for the participants on proper form, shoe wear, clothing, nutrition, breathing techniques, hydration, and cross training.

In July 2003, I was certified as a Lifestyle and Weight Management Consultant through ACE, which requires a previous certification of either group fitness instructor or personal trainer. With this certification, I am able to offer nutrition counseling for my clientele. Fitness Strategies has contracted me to teach a Lifestyle and Weight Management class where participants learn proper nutrition techniques, including recipes, as well as exercise instruction and guidance. As part of the recertification process, instructors (trainers and consultants) are required to attend 15 hours of continuing education classes every 2 years. Since my first certification in 1991, I have consistently attended 12-15 hours of continuing education classes/workshops every single year in an effort to strive for excellence in my chosen field of health and fitness. I am a current member of the non-profit health and fitness organization, PULSE, and have been since 1998. I receive several different publications that offer articles on scientific breakthroughs, programming, and implementation as well as consumer information on fitness equipment.

Since 1996, I have been accumulating fitness equipment for use with clients including a treadmill, stair machine, stationary bikes, weight benches, hex weights, exercise therapy balls, medicine balls, and a balance trainer, among other things. I plan to use this equipment as well as a couple additional things for clients at Health-E-essentials. I also have believed in our duty to use our talents to give back to the community. I was on the committee of the Winnebago County "Fulfill a Dream"—a workout to raise funds for AIDS and related cancers research for the years 1993, 1994, and1995. I helped facilitate FIT (Fitness in Time), a workout to benefit a local charitable endowment fund in Winnebago County that started after "Fulfill a Dream" was discontinued. I have been a "Friend of the Cure" fundraiser for several years raising money for the Barbara Karmanos Cancer Institute as well as taking clients to the Race for the Cure in Rockford. I have hosted "Cooking for the Cure," "Training for the Cure," and (aerobic) "Workout for the Cure" as health and fitness fundraisers. My job at the American Heart Association does not require me to fundraise. However, I fundraised for my team as they are required to raise $3,500 /person as part of their program participation. Since the health of the community is very important to me, I plan to continue health-related fundraising through Holistic Choices for worthy causes.

Joanne Fuller

I have been in the skin-care profession for six years. In this time I have learned a great deal about the personal needs of my clients. My extensive knowledge of the service industry I attribute to the experience I gained at the places I have worked. I started my career at a busy full-service salon called Beautiful You, in old town Rockford. I worked as a receptionist, while I was in school to become an esthetician. Scheduling clients, taking inventory, ordering products, and answering the phones were my daily tasks. When I finished school I had already become familiar with the clients in the salon and many of them became my skin-care clients. After working there for three years, I had outgrown my small facial room. I was recommended to the owner of a skin-care studio called Skin Care Professionals. She approached me with a job offer, which I readily accepted. I worked directly with the owner who had been an esthetician for about fourteen years. It was an excellent learning experience. With the use of quality products and state-of-the-art equipment, I was able to triple my clientele. With Skin Care Professionals being a smaller scale operation, I was able to learn a lot about the business and the operating procedures. I scheduled my own clients, developed marketing techniques, placed product orders, and researched new equipment. I also am an advocate of continuing education and attend seminars and conventions often. My mission is to educate my clients on how to live a healthier lifestyle.

OPERATING PROCEDURES

Hours of operation: Monday through Friday we will open at 5:30A.M. for either personal training group sessions or Yoga/Pilates classes. There will be appointments all day for all departments and the last class/appointment will be at 7:30P.M. We will have a daytime receptionist/office manager working Tuesday through Thursday 10:00A.M. to 6:00P.M. She will answer phones, greet clients, do inventory, order retail, and run the cash register. Joanne and Mary will alternate covering the receptionist position on Friday, Saturday, and Monday until we hire an additional part-time receptionist. All other personnel (massage therapist, nail tech, and esthetician) will be independent contractors and will be responsible for their own accounting and taxes. They will contribute an additional fee in addition to their monthly rent to gain services from the receptionist and process any credit card fees. All independent contractors have had previous experience managing their own business/clientele.

PERSONNEL

The personnel for Holistic Choices will consist of two working partners and three independent contractors. Additional staff will consist of a receptionist/office manager. One partner, Joanne Fuller, is an Esthetician and the other partner, Mary Smart, is a Personal Trainer and Nutrition

Counselor. The independent contractors will be a massage therapist, nail technician, and an additional esthetician. Each will be responsible for their equipment and supplies. They each will have a suitable space available to them for which they will pay monthly rent and additional fees for use of the receptionist services and credit card processing fees. Joanne and Mary will be paid commission on their individual sales/appointments and the rest will go toward the operation of Holistic Choices and the profit to be split by the partners. The ability to work for yourself and build your own clientele is very motivational. Holistic Choices is very interested in building lasting relationships both with the professionals contracted to work there and the clientele it services. This format will allow that relationship to grow and flourish under the common goal of providing exceptional services for a healthy lifestyle. We are confident that the natural referral process will activate itself under this type of operation and permit all professionals to benefit from growth that comes from recommending clients to one another. All of the professionals working at Holistic Choices specialize in different yet related fields and are committed to the health and well-being of all clientele, whether theirs or their colleagues'.

BREAK-EVEN ANALYSIS

Monthly Operating Costs: (Fixed costs)

Rent	$1,800	
Utilities	$250	
Insurance	$250	
Receptionist	$1,000	
Loan payment	$1,200	
Miscellaneous	$500	(Internet, phones, etc.)
TOTAL	**$5,000**	

Monthly Sales Revenue: (Projected)

Rental (Nail tech, massage)	$1,100
Retail sales (Skin-care products, etc.)	$4,200
Skin-care services (Joanne)	$6,000
(20 people/week x $75.00)	
Personal Training (Mary)	$4,480
(112 people/week x $10.00)	
TOTAL	**$15,780**

Average Gross Profit for each sale:

Rental	$1,100	(100%)
Retail	$2,100	(50%)
Skin Care	$4,800	(80%)
Personal Training	$4,390	(98%)
TOTAL	**$12,390**	

Start-up Costs/Needs:

Retail product	
Pevonia	$4,000
Miscellaneous products	$6,000
Facial Equipment	
Bed	$1,500
Steamer	$1,000
Light Therapy	$7,000
Ultra Sound	$3,500
Office Supplies	
Furniture	$2,500
Paint	$500
Towels, sheets, gown	$300
Computer	$3,000
Software	$250
Refrigerator, kitchen supplies	$500
Exercise Equipment	
Ellyptical	$3,000
Rubber flooring	$500
Miscellaneous (tubing, balls, etc.)	$200
Mirrors	$2,500
Website	
Original setup	$250
Grand Opening Party	$1,000
Advertising	$500
Sign out front	$750
Security Deposit	$3,600
Security System	$500
Brochures	$250
TOTAL	**$43,100**

Current equipment list and replacement value:

Trotter 510 treadmill	$3495.00
Tectrix Climbmax Climber	$1999.99
Keys Pro Spinner Bike *(2 @ 799.99 ea.)*	$1599.98
Body Solid Linear Bearing Smith	$999.99
Lat Pulldown option w/285 lb.	$499.99
Olympic weight set	$149.99
Body Solid Flat/Inc. bench	$219.99
Dick's weight bench	$100.00
BOSU-BOth Sides Up balance trainer	$110.00
Exercise tubes, various tensions *(8 @ $7.00 ea.)*	$56.00
Flexiballs *(3 @ $30.00 ea.)*	$90.00
Body bars *(3 @ $35.00 ea.)*	$105.00
Rubber flooring	$1,000.00
Hex weights *(634 lbs. @ .49/lb.)*	$310.66
Watercooler	$120.00
TOTAL	**$10,856.59**

Home Décor Products Manufacturer

BUSINESS PLAN

BURTON DECOR, INC.

14275 Washington Avenue
Skokie, Illinois 60077

Burton Décor manufactures high-quality specialty home décor products for the mass market, specifically items designed for the Christmas season. This plan raised more than $1 million in capital for the company's owners.

- DESCRIPTION OF BUSINESS
- PRODUCTS & SERVICES OFFERED
- MARKET ANALYSIS
- LOCATION OF BUSINESS
- COMPETITION
- MANAGEMENT
- PERSONNEL
- APPLICATION & EXPECTED EFFECT OF INVESTMENT
- FINANCIAL DATA

DESCRIPTION OF BUSINESS

Burton Décor, Inc., designs and develops specialty Christmas and soft (also known as "cut and sewn") home décor products manufactured in India. India's extraordinary fabrics and handiwork are not readily available in other countries and stand out from the typical mass-produced product currently available. These unique, value-priced products will be targeted to U.S.-based mass merchants such as Sears, Target, and Wal-Mart. Specifically, Burton Décor will bring a high-end look to the mass market.

Burton Décor aims to offer unusual, unique specialty items at competitive prices. Beautiful handiwork such as beading, embroidery, and weaving will help merchants stand out from their competitors and draw in shoppers. Although Burton Décor will offer narrow product lines as compared to their competitors, the company will produce in high volumes to meet the demands of mass merchants. In addition, Burton Décor can customize products to suit individual buyers' tastes.

John Smith, the man behind Burton Décor, has the product development experience, design talent, and established relationships necessary to meet those demands. Along with his 20 years of retailing and interior design experience, John spent the last two-and-a-half years working for Tuppi, one of the nation's leading gift product importers to mass merchants. His sourcing, product development, and production experience, in combination with his design talent and people skills, has allowed him to develop the know-how and relationships necessary to understand and meet the needs of mass merchants.

Business Model

As a direct importer, Burton Décor products will be shipped from the factory directly to the retailer. As such, Burton Décor will carry no inventory, with production beginning only when a purchase order is received. Payments between retailers and Burton Décor, and between Burton Décor and its factories will be made by letter-of-credit, resulting in minimal financial exposure.

PRODUCTS & SERVICES OFFERED

Burton Décor develops the designs, samples, and packaging for specialty Christmas and soft home décor products manufactured in India. Its product lines are meant to broaden the offerings of mass merchants, with unique handiwork such as beading, embroidery, and weaving in beautiful silks, velvets, and pashmina. In order for buyers to review the product lines, samples of each product are displayed in Burton Décor's Chicago showroom.

Product Lines

Burton Décor's product lines will be narrow and focused on the unique fabrics, colors, and beautiful handiwork typical of India. The lines will have a specific point of view and, as such, will not try to be all things to all buyers. The product categories for which Burton Décor will design products are:

Christmas
Gift bags
Ornaments
Stockings
Table linens
Table runners
Tree skirts
Wire-edged ribbon

Home Décor
Bedding
Pillows
Ready-made draperies
Shower curtains
Soft picture frames
Table linens
Throws
Wire-edged ribbon

Burton Décor's philosophy is that it is possible to feature well-designed, fashion-forward, high-quality products at competitive prices. The four cornerstones of that philosophy are:

- Design: Well-designed, fashion-forward products for the mass market
- Quality: High-quality products produced in a quality-controlled environment
- Value: Offering well-designed, quality products at affordable prices
- Relationships: Listening to our buyers and building trusting relationships with them

The product lines will feature a distinct point of view, yet products can be customized to suit individual buyers' tastes. Burton Décor will work closely with buyers to build their businesses because they want the merchants to succeed. Burton Décor does that by listening and responding to their needs. As a mass merchant buyer recently told John Smith, "You're the only person I trust because you're the only one who doesn't try to sell me something I don't want or need." This sentiment is the underpinning of Burton Décor's philosophy.

Benefits

Mass merchants want high-quality, fashion-forward products at competitive prices because they want to offer their customers a high-end look at an affordable price. India is an untapped geographic resource.

In the current marketplace, China is India's biggest competitor. While China offers good quality and great prices, the level of creativity and craftsmanship is limited. China's strength is in setting up factories to do mass runs. India offers great creativity, great quality, and great prices. The drawback has been their inability to offer mass merchants a way to buy consistently well-designed and well-produced products in one centralized location.

Burton Décor offers mass merchants the opportunity to draw in customers with products heretofore unavailable at these price points. Mass merchants can:

1. Bring high-end looks to the mass market, by offering their customers well-designed, fashion-forward products at affordable prices
2. Buy unique products with unusual handiwork at competitive prices
3. Round out and add depth to their departments
4. Stand out from their competitors
5. Buy products of India in a centralized buying location
6. Enjoy the security of knowing they are buying well-designed, quality-controlled products
7. Benefit from Burton Décor's retailing, design, and production experience

Pricing

Burton Décor products are developed within the context of mass merchant price points. Burton Décor wants to provide great design and great quality at a great value. The standard industry markup on Christmas and home décor products is 30 to 40 percent. Burton Décor is structured in such a way that overhead is kept low and the markup is 25 percent. Burton Décor is able to do this because of two cost-effective differences from their competitors: (i) no warehouse and (ii) no inventory.

Production

Burton Décor will be working with a new, Wal-Mart-approved factory located in India not far from Mumbai (Bombay). This factory will be the primary production facility for Burton Décor products. The factory owner, Bob Davidson, is a local businessman who has had a close working relationship with John Smith for several years and will also act as the agent for Burton Décor.

The production cycle will be as follows:

1. Once the factory receives an order, the factory, in turn, places the orders for fabric—which takes 7 to 10 days, depending on the specific fabric used.
2. The fabric is then delivered on the 15th day from the order date, at which point the fabric is cut. Overall, the first 30 days from the order date go into procuring fabric and cutting.
3. Once the pieces are cut, they are sent for embroidery and stitching, and then sent back to the factory for final production.
4. Fabric and work quality are inspected at each stage. Sign-off samples for Burton Décor will be used for quality control.
5. Orders will require a lead time of 90 to 150 days, depending on the work and quantities involved.
6. The ICD ("Inland Container Depot") is 2 to 3 kilometers away from the factory site. Containers will be packed in the factory.
7. All customs clearance formalities will be handled at the ICD, after which the containers will be sealed for inland transportation to the port in Mumbai. From there it will be shipped to the customer. Payment will be made by letter-of-credit.
8. Transit time to the East Coast is 30 days and to the West Coast is 45 days.

Timeline

Burton Décor will enter the marketplace by developing its Christmas line for the Christmas 2003 buying season, as outlined below. Buyers typically fly to Hong Kong in October and/or January in order to buy their overseas merchandise for the Christmas season at least one year in advance.

- Spring/Summer 2002: John Smith will design the Burton Décor Christmas line
- September 2002: Burton Décor's Chicago showroom will have samples and begin bringing in buyers to introduce them to the company and the Christmas line

MARKET ANALYSIS

"Today, Christmas is part of the gift industry, part of the home décor industry and even part of the fashion industry. Christmas décor...is being reinterpreted through the same prisms of style and culture and self-expression that influence other consumer categories."

— Mary Ford, Editor, *Selling Christmas Décorations,* March 2002

Burton Décor's target markets are the Christmas and home décor departments of mass merchants. The synergy between the two is clear, as illustrated in the quote above. By targeting both markets, Burton Décor can reduce the seasonal earnings fluctuations typical of Christmas-only vendors. Both markets are fashion-driven, with buyers always looking for the next new thing—in terms of design and resources.

Today's mass merchants want to offer broader looks in their Christmas and home décor departments. They want to offer products and looks from more than one country in order to:

- Round out product selection by offering unusual, unique specialty items
- Add eye-catching products to draw in customers
- Appeal to the growing ethnic diversity of their customer base
- Stand out from competitors

Consumer tastes are becoming more sophisticated as their exposure to global influences increases. Television shows such as "Martha Stewart," "Oprah," and those on HGTV have broadened the horizons of consumers. Add to this the "bargain as fashion" message of Target stores, and you've got consumers who want high style, but at an affordable price.

The country's trend toward cocooning at home has increased the demand for decorative home accessories in rich colors and fabrics. Combine this trend with the more cost-conscious consumer and you've got the mass merchant customer who wants it all: high style at an affordable price. Buyers understand these trends and want to exploit them. They understand that accessories can change the look of a room without refurnishing—tapping into the consumer's fashion and budget demands.

Current trends demonstrate another important factor at work in the marketplace: Consumers are more ethnically diverse than ever, and they want to embrace their cultural differences. Mass merchants want sources that can tap into the ethnic diversity that is their customer base. Buyers are looking for new resources with fresh design ideas, and India is an untapped geographic resource.

Why India?

Retail merchants and their customers are increasingly demanding the handcrafted, detailed look typical of India's artisans. Trend-setting merchants such as Pottery Barn, Crate & Barrel, and Z Gallerie have been sourcing India for the last several years. They manufacture and import their own products from their own India-based resources. These retailers have invested in their own product development departments, which allows them to successfully source new markets.

Mass merchants, however, are not able to dedicate such substantial financial resources and still maintain their low price points. They want to follow the trends and offer their customers similar looks, but at affordable prices. However, India does not have the infrastructure in place to service them. Mass merchants want to find resources ready to produce high volumes of desired items upon demand.

Below is a brief geographic analysis of the Christmas and home décor marketplace, specifically focusing on countries manufacturing cut and sewn products.

- **Philippines:** Although they do intricate, incredibly beautiful work, their prices are very high. In addition, their manufacturing is set up as a cottage industry and, as such, is too small to handle the volume mass merchants demand.

- **China:** The quality, details, and types of materials used are good, not great. They do not have the creativity and handiwork abilities that are available in India. China's strength is in setting up factories to do mass production runs. Although the prices for their product have been very low, that pricing strategy has come under increasing pressure as the Chinese government cracks down on manufacturers' "flexible" accounting, resulting in higher tax payments.

- **India:** They are known for their fabrics (silks, velvets, pashmina), and their handiwork (beading, embroidery, weaving). Currently, India has no infrastructure for large production runs. The Wal-Marts of the world don't have the time, design capabilities, know-how or ability to control the process from afar—it's too much of a headache for them to go to India, and they do not have the contacts necessary to make it work.

Burton Decor's Comparative Advantage

India is a difficult country to work with due to cultural and legal issues. There are no copyright laws in India, and while agents and manufacturers will promise almost anything, having them deliver on those promises is anything but reliable. The key to success in India is finding a resource that understands design and production requirements while also being trustworthy and reliable—difficult qualities to find in India. John Smith has developed just such a relationship, which is the key to Burton Décor's ability to service U.S.-based mass merchants. Burton Décor's agent and primary manufacturer, Bob Davidson, states, "Remember, this is India and there are no copyright laws. Business is based purely on trust, which is a very rare commodity."

Sales Strategy

Burton Décor will establish itself by building on the strong buyer relationships John Smith developed during his years at Tuppi. Based on those relationships, Burton Décor can arrange meetings with the Christmas buyers, and then leverage those relationships to arrange for meetings with home décor buyers.

The key to Burton Décor's sales strategy is showing the product lines to the right buyers. Burton Décor understands that cross-selling among the departments within a store is an overlooked, yet strategic advantage in retailing. Cross-selling will set Burton Décor apart from their competition. For example, gift bags and wire-edged ribbon are product categories sold in both Christmas and stationery/gift departments. Each department has separate buyers with different budgets. Typically, vendors only target one department's buyer, thereby missing out on sales opportunities within the same organization. Burton Décor will not let those strategic opportunities slip away.

Most vendors participate in trade shows, which can cost $10,000 per show. However, these shows target smaller retailers. Since Burton Décor is targeting mass merchants, the company can use their marketing dollars more effectively by flying in buyers who might not otherwise come to Chicago. It is important to note that Burton Décor will attend trade shows in order to keep abreast of the trends and competitors' product lines.

Target Markets

Burton Décor is specifically targeting high-volume retailers serving the value-conscious consumer. These retailers fall into numerous categories. Several of these categories, along with examples of specific retailers, are listed below.

- Mass Merchants: Wal-Mart, Target, Sears
- Catalogue: Spiegel, Lillian Vernon, Fingerhut
- Craft/Garden: Frank's Nursery, Garden Ridge, Michael's
- Drug/Hardware: Walgreen's, Rite Aid, Ace Hardware
- Warehouse: Sam's Club, Lowe's, Costco
- Bed/Bath: Linens 'n Things, Bed Bath & Beyond

LOCATION OF BUSINESS

Burton Décor will lease 3,000 square feet of office and showroom space (2,000 for office and 1,000 for showroom). Rent is approximately $22/square feet annually, totaling $66,000/year or $5,500/month. For budgeting purposes Burton Décor is assuming an annual increase of 3 to 5 percent.

The space will be located in or near the Chicago suburbs of Lincolnwood, Skokie, or Des Plaines because they are conveniently located near O'Hare Airport and the rent is lower than in Chicago.

COMPETITION

There are literally thousands of design and manufacturing companies in the Christmas and home décor marketplace. Typically, competitors fall into one of two categories: (1) The vast majority offer a product assortment that is too broad and lacks an appealing point of view or look. The price point may be attractive, but the product is mundane and the same as what their competitors are showing, or (2) the products are designed well and offer an exciting look, but the price point is too high.

As a result, the competition for mass merchant buying dollars is not especially competitive. Vendors consistently target the high-end buyers at merchants such as department stores and specialty stores. No one is thinking both "fashion forward" and "volume," which leaves the market open for Burton Décor. An analysis of Burton Décor's four nearest competitors follows.

Competitor #1

Who They Are

Competitor #1 designs and develops Christmas-related products. They have direct import and domestic product lines. The company is based in Illinois and is privately owned by Loonis-X Corp. Competitor #1 has been in business for more than 20 years. Estimated annual revenues are $300 million.

Products

Product categories include: lights, trees, mouth-blown glass ornaments, table linens, animation, tree skirts, stockings, ribbon and bows, wreaths and garland, and bead garland. The company imports primarily from China. Competitor #1 offers a domestic line, requiring them to warehouse inventory domestically. This allows them to sell to smaller shops and to sell smaller quantities to customers buying less than a container-load.

Strengths

- Marketing/merchandising. They put together beautiful, eye-catching presentations in showrooms located at prime addresses. They display the showroom like a high-end department store; i.e., products are not just thrown on a shelf. Detail-oriented.
- Offer better product for the price. Competitor #1 spots high-end trends and develops knock-offs at affordable prices.
- If one category is not selling well in a particular year, Competitor #1 will adapt quickly by jumping into another category to make up the dollars lost for that year.

Weaknesses

- They do not build their business from year to year. When a particular category starts doing well for a competitor, Competitor #1 changes direction and chases the business in that same category while ignoring the categories that they had been building. As in a plate spinning circus act, they let plates drop as they run to spin others.
- Inventory risk—by offering a domestic line and warehousing the product.

What Was Learned from Watching Their Operation

- The importance of presentation
- Offer a good product for the price
- Always demand more from the manufacturer—design for the high-end first and adjust manufacturing and design details affecting the price at a later stage.

Competitor #2

Who They Are
Competitor #2 designs and manufactures holiday items for six holidays: Halloween, Thanksgiving, Christmas, St. Patrick's Day, Easter, and July Fourth. They have direct import and domestic product lines. The company is based in New York and is privately owned by Alan Brown, an Israeli-born engineer. Competitor #2 has been in business for approximately 15 years. Estimated annual revenues are $100 million.

Products
Competitor #2 designs their own fabrics. They focus primarily on wire-edged ribbons and bows, although their product line also includes glass ball ornaments. Competitor #2 has begun to enter the home décor market with products using fabric matching their ribbon, e.g., table linens, table runners, and gift bags. The company manufactures its products in Guatemala—they are the largest employer there. Until Christmas 2002, Competitor #2 has been Kmart's largest Christmas supplier (now it will be Martha Stewart).

Strengths

- Lowest price point on ribbon (because they are the manufacturer).
- Owner is very analytical; he's very good at analyzing his business.
- Year to year he knows what items are selling and helps buyers choose their assortments.

Weaknesses

- Poor people skills; inflexible and unaccommodating with buyers, resulting in lost business.
- Not creative. They offer the same looks year after year, with very similar fabrics. They do not develop "looks," so what they offer looks mundane, boring. Alan thinks the fabrics make a look when, in fact, it's the application that makes a look.
- Inventory risk—by offering a domestic line and warehousing the product.

What Was Learned from Watching Their Operation
Competitor #2 controls the design and manufacture process from beginning to end, so they are able to control costs. (However, John can accomplish the same thing with close working relationships.)

Competitor #3

Who They Are
Competitor #3 designs and manufactures Christmas and holiday items for Halloween, Christmas, Valentine's, and Easter as well as home textile products. The family-owned company is based in Mumbai, India, and has an office in New Jersey. It has been exporting its products for more than 15 years. Exports are estimated to be $20 million annually.

Products
Product categories include: tree skirts, stockings, mantel scarves, table linens, gift bags, napkin rings, kitchen textiles, bath, bedding, and window accessories. They have been building their Christmas and holiday business for the last three years.

Strengths

- Nice looking designs, but not fine-tuned for the western market (gaudy, overdone).
- Offices, showroom, and development room in India were very impressive.
- Very impressive operation; very organized and methodical, clean (rare in India), like offices in the U.S. Their research department has everything categorized and filed. Workflow, paperwork is very organized. The division of responsibilities is very thorough so nothing falls through the cracks.

Weaknesses

- Their factory is primitive, set up as a cottage industry
- No quality control
- Poor marketing skills

Competitor #4

Who They Are
Competitor #4 is the Christmas products division of a metallic yarn manufacturer based in Mumbai, India. Competitor #4 designs and manufactures Christmas-related products. The parent company has been in business since 1962, while Competitor #4 has been in business since 1999. Exports are estimated to be $2 million annually.

Products
Product categories include: tree skirts, stockings, wire-edged ribbon, table linens, table runners, and gift bags.

Strengths

- Incredible design talent for fabrics; great creativity.
- They have very good quality and nicely designed products, based on their samples; however, it's hard to tell whether that can be maintained in production.
- They have fabulous raw materials and know-how of handiwork techniques.

Weaknesses

- Their designs are not fully developed; they don't fully understand design concepts (creating a "look") or scale. They have no idea how to put their creativity to its best use.
- They do not have enough business to sustain a factory, so they outsource by using a cottage industry setup.
- Poor marketing skills.

What Was Learned from Watching Their Operation
They have an operation with wonderful potential. Burton Décor would like to take them over.

MANAGEMENT

History of Principals

John Smith has put together a team with years of industry-specific experience and demonstrated talent. The professionals listed below cover the four functional areas critical to Burton Décor's success:

1. design and product development
2. management
3. manufacturing
4. sales

John Smith—John is a seasoned design and retailing professional with more than 20 years of experience. His educational background includes degrees in both retail management and interior design. His professional experience includes:

- Product development for Tuppi, including design, international sourcing and production
- Department store and specialty store retailing for 10 years
- Interior design for 10 years

John's product development experience encompasses the process from start to finish, i.e., from putting the design on paper to production to packaging to putting it on a retailer's shelves. In addition, he has successfully managed a staff of 10 and regularly managed multiple time-sensitive projects simultaneously.

Bob Davidson—Bob and his family own and run three factories in Nepal and India. Their manufacturing experience dates back to 1974. Bob has substantial experience in managing both the manufacturing and exporting functions of their businesses in India, most recently for Octagon Textile Industries. Prior to that he managed production and quality control for a division of Mip Plastic Industries.

Bob's factories have been exporting garments and textiles to the U.S. since 1989. They provide in-house product development and research facilities for their production and marketing, and they maintain consistent quality control and sound financial practices. Their factories are experienced in working with top U.S. retailers such as Wal-Mart and Kmart. All their factories meet international standards and U.S. regulations.

Bob has a bachelor's in Commerce degree from Bombay University, and spent an additional year studying Business Administration at the International University of America in San Francisco, California.

Jane Doe—Jane has more than 15 years of product design, graphic arts, and supervisory experience. Specifically, she has 15 years of computer design experience; 20 years of traditional design, rendering, and illustration experience; and 15 years of experience working with overseas vendors in Europe, Asia, and India in producing graphics and products.

Jane has built in-house product design and graphics departments for three companies. In addition, her professional experience includes:

- **Product Design:** Giftware/collectibles/decorative, tins/bath and body/pet; gifts/decorative design/seasonal and holiday items/leather (and fabric) goods, e.g., business cases, men's accessories, luggage, and gift items.

- **Graphic Design:** Graphics incorporated with product, package design, decorative design, catalog, and photography. Concept, design, and production for products, packaging, and graphics.
- **Management:** Supervised designers, retouchers, and freelancers. Managed employees, workflow, clients, and budgets for graphics/multimedia studios consisting of 12-15 employees.

PERSONNEL

Management Team

John Smith, CEO—John will oversee the sales and design functions of Burton Décor. He will work directly with the factories and the agent in India by overseeing their performance and negotiating the first cost of the products. Until a CFO can be hired, John will also handle all financial issues. Salary: $130,000.

Bob Davidson, Agent—Bob will be Burton Décor's primary contact and agent in India, and Bob's factory will be the primary manufacturer of Burton Décor products. He will oversee production at his factory and the outside factories by monitoring and coordinating production, quality control, packaging, customs paperwork, and transportation until the release of goods at the port. Salary: Compensation will be included in Burton Décor's cost of goods sold (first cost).

Jane Doe, Vice President of Design—Jane will be responsible for all graphic design and product development, i.e., packaging, presentations to buyers, as well as the Burton Décor showroom display. Jane will handle the product lines from conception through packaging, which includes developing themes and keeping abreast of marketplace trends. Long-term, Jane will build and manage the art department, including in-house and freelance artists. Salary: $80,000 + bonus.

Elizabeth Brown, Vice President of Sales: Elizabeth will be responsible for developing the marketing plan to meet sales objectives, as well as establishing/maintaining customer relationships. Elizabeth will make initial contact with buyers, handle day-to-day contact and follow-up with buyers, i.e., she will manage the process from the time the order is placed to the time the merchandise is off the retailer's shelves. Long-term, Elizabeth will build and manage the sales department, including outside sales reps. Salary: $80,000 + bonus.

Additional Personnel

Office Manager: Reports to VP of Design. Responsible for day-to-day office operations; will assist CEO and VP of Design. Must be highly organized and have the ability to multi-task. Attention to detail a must. Salary: $50,000.

Graphic Designer: Reports to VP of Design. Responsible for designing packaging for each product as well as for private label merchandise. Must be fluent in design software for the Mac, excel in conceptual design, and have experience in marketing trends and working with overseas vendors. Experience also required in working on product/decorative design and working with printers and production files. Salary: $40,000.

Artist: Reports to VP of Design. Responsible for conceiving, designing, and producing artwork for home décor and Christmas product lines. Must be fluent in design software for the Mac, excel in conceptual design, and have experience in marketing trends and working with overseas vendors. Experience also required in working on product/decorative design and working with printers and production files. Salary: $30,000.

Import Manager: Reports to VP of Sales. Responsible for building product database, putting together price quotes for buyers, issuing purchase orders and following through on sales, delivery, and payment approval. Must be highly organized and have the ability to multi-task. Attention to detail a must. Salary: $30,000.

Sales Assistant: Reports to VP of Sales. Responsible for supporting Sales Department. Must be highly organized and have the ability to multi-task. Attention to detail a must. Salary: $28,000.

Order Expediter: Reports to Import Manager. Responsible for assisting in putting together price quotes for buyers, issuing purchase orders, and following through on sales and delivery. Must be highly organized and have the ability to multi-task. Attention to detail a must. Salary: $25,000.

Staffing Plan

Title	Year 1*	Year 2	Year 3
CEO/President	1	1	1
VP of Design	1	1	1
VP of Sales	1	1	1
Office Manager	1	1	1
Import Manager	1	1	1
Order Expediter	0	2	4
Artist	0	1	2
Graphic Designer	0	1	2
Sales Assistant	0	2	2
Sales Representative	0	1	1
TOTAL	**5**	**12**	**16**

** last 6 months of 2002*

Organization Chart

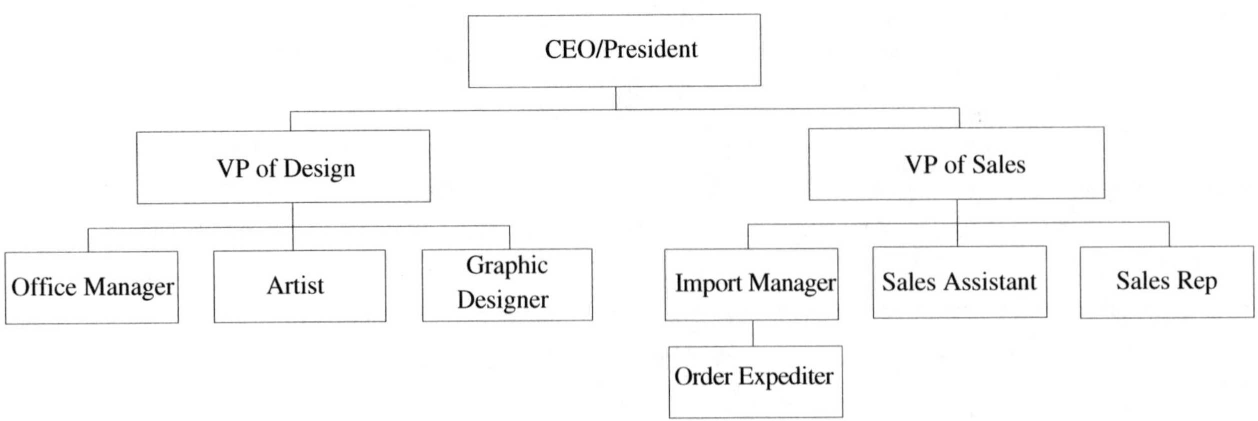

Human Resources Administration

Burton Décor will outsource the human resources administration function to a Professional Employer Organization ("PEO"). A PEO provides cost effective HR management and administration, and takes on the related employment risks of its clients. Through an operating agreement, the PEO and Burton Décor will create a co-employer relationship between them in reference to their co-employees. Thus, the PEO establishes itself as the "employer of record," responsible for administrative functions associated with the employment of co-employees, while the client is established as the "workplace employer," responsible for directing the manner in which co-employees deliver their work efforts, as well as hiring, disciplining, compensating, reviewing, and terminating such co-employees. More specifically, the PEO will:

- Pay wages, employment taxes, and benefits expenses out of its own accounts
- Report, collect, and deposit employment taxes with State and Federal authorities

In addition, the PEO will act as negotiating agent for Burton Décor in order to secure an attractive employee benefit plan, including some or all of the following benefits: medical, dental, life and long-term disability insurance, 401(k) plan, Section 125 cafeteria plan, and employee assistance plan.

By using a PEO, growing companies such as Burton Décor are able to capitalize on economies-of-scale and offer their employees significantly better benefits—typically equal to those of larger corporations, but at a price a smaller firm can afford. This is particularly important when trying to attract the most qualified and talented employees.

The end result is that a PEO removes the majority of employer-related paperwork from Burton Décor's desk, eliminates the time it takes to shop around for benefits packages, and helps reduce Burton Décor's liabilities by assuming and/or sharing some of the liabilities of being an employer.

APPLICATION & EXPECTED EFFECT OF INVESTMENT

Burton Décor is seeking a $650,000 loan and a $650,000 credit line. The funds will allow Burton Décor to:

1. Build its management team and personnel infrastructure
2. Design, sell, and produce its products for Burton Décor's first selling season
3. Purchase the required computer hardware, software, and office equipment
4. Set up its office and showroom space

The loan will allow Burton Décor to establish itself in its first selling season. Burton Décor is paid only when the merchant takes possession of the goods at the port in India. The sales cycle—the time from product design to the merchant taking possession—can be as long as twelve months. As such, the loan will enable Burton Décor to make the necessary up-front investment. The credit line will allow Burton Décor to pay off the loan and accommodate the sales cycle on a ongoing basis. Cash flow projections illustrate that the loan is scheduled to be repaid in the third quarter of Year 3.

FINANCIAL DATA

Sources and Uses of Funding

Sources:	
Principal's Contribution	$10,000
Investment	1,800,000
Total Sources	**$1,810,000**
Uses:	
Purchase of Assets	
Computer and Other Equipment (includes installation and support)	$75,000
Leasehold Improvements	40,000
Furniture and Fixtures	40,000
Total Purchase of Assets	**155,000**
Cash Needs for first 12 months of Operations	
1st 6 months of Year 1	600,000
1st 6 months of Year 2	680,000
Total Cash Needs for first 12 months of Operations	**1,280,000**
Cash Reserve for contingencies	375,000
Total Uses	**$1,810,000**

Computer and Other Equipment

Qty	Model	RAM	HD	Processor	Price	Ext Price	Purpose
1	Nortel Phone System				$8,500	$8,500	Company-wide
3	Palm M515				$399	$1,197	Operations
6	iMac	256MB	40GB	700 MHz	$1,599	$9,594	Operations
3	G4—w/17" Studio Display	1.5GB	80GB	Dual 1GHz	$4,400	$13,200	Design
1	G4 Server	1GB	2-80GB	Dual 1GHz	$3,900	$3,900	Server
1	Display—17" monitor				$300	$300	Server
12	AppleCare Extended Warranty				$249	$2,988	Company-wide
2	iBook	384MB	20GB	600 MHz	$1,649	$3,298	Operations/Sales
3	Adobe Design Suite				$1,000	$3,000	Design
3	Extensis Suitcase				$170	$510	Design
1	Extensis Portfolio—server/clients				$1,200	$1,200	Design
1	MYOB				$230	$230	Operations
1	Retrospect Workgroup: 20-client license				$499	$499	Company-wide
9	Microsoft Office				$440	$3,960	Company-wide
1	VXA Autoloader (1x15)				$4,500	$4,500	Company-wide
2	10-pk Media				$620	$1,240	Company-wide
3	HP Inkjet Printer				$200	$600	Operations
1	GCC Elite XL 20/1200, 20PPM				$2,200	$2,200	Design
1	HP Color Laser 4550 10/100				$2,400	$2,400	Company-wide
1	Nikon Coolpix 995				$500	$500	Design
1	Panasonic Fax Machine				$300	$300	Company-wide
1	Lights and Backdrop				$200	$200	Design
1	Netopia R9100 Router				$430	$430	Company-wide
1	8 port 10/100 ethernet hub				$80	$80	Company-wide
Equipment Subtotal						**$64,826**	
Ongoing Support						$4,500	
Labor (5 days)					$1,000	$5,000	
Total						**$74,326**	

Projected Balance Sheet as of July 1, 2002

Assets		Liabilities	
Current Assets		**Current Liabilities**	
Cash	$1,655,000	Accounts Payable	$ -
Accounts Receivable (net)	-	Other	-
Prepaid Expenses[1]	10,000	**Total Current Liabilities**	**-**
Total Current Assets	**$1,665,000**		
Fixed Assets		**Total Long-Term Liabilities**	
Computer and Other Equipment	65,000		
Furniture and Fixtures	40,000	**TOTAL LIABILITIES**	**$ -**
Leasehold Improvements	40,000		
Total Fixed Assets	**$145,000**	Stockholders' Equity	
		Paid-in Capital	1,810,000
		Total Stockholders' Equity	**1,810,000**
TOTAL ASSETS	**$1,810,000**	**TOTAL LIABILITIES AND NET WORTH**	**$1,810,000**

Footnotes:

[1]Prepaid expenses include computer support, licenses, insurance.

Income Projection: Five-Year Summary

	Year 1[1]	Year 2	Year 3	Year 4	Year 5
Sales	$ -	$6,000,000	$10,000,000	$12,000,000	$15,000,000
Cost of Goods Sold (75%)	0	4,500,000	7,500,000	9,000,000	11,250,000
Gross Margin	0	1,500,000	2,500,000	3,000,000	3,750,000
Operating Expenses					
Computer[2]	2,844	5,258	5,460	6,006	6,607
Freelance Artists	83,333	200,000	208,000	220,000	242,000
HR Administration	3,450	17,222	17,885	19,674	21,641
Insurance	5,000	10,000	10,000	11,000	12,100
Legal and Accounting	5,000	10,400	10,800	11,880	13,068
Licenses	750	1,500	1,560	1,650	1,815
Maintenance and Cleaning	3,125	7,500	7,800	8,250	9,075
Office Supplies	20,540	8,000	8,320	8,800	9,680
Payroll	185,004	606,000	756,300	794,115	833,821
Payroll Taxes and Benefits	16,428	58,116	74,300	78,015	81,916
Postage/Shipping	30,000	66,000	72,600	79,860	87,846
Printing	30,000	66,000	72,600	79,860	87,846
Rent	33,000	66,000	66,000	66,000	66,000
Samples[3]	10,000	20,000	20,800	22,000	24,200
Subscriptions	3,000	6,000	6,240	6,600	7,260
Telephone	10,000	22,000	24,200	26,620	29,282
Travel and Entertainment[4]	130,000	250,000	275,000	302,500	332,750
Utilities	3,000	6,240	6,480	6,864	7,550
Miscellaneous	10,000	20,000	20,000	20,000	20,000
Total Operating Expenses	**584,474**	**1,446,237**	**1,664,345**	**1,769,694**	**1,894,457**
Net Income (Loss) from Operations	**-584,474**	**53,763**	**835,655**	**1,230,307**	**1,855,543**
Depreciation	16,000	32,000	32,000	32,000	32,000
Net Income (Loss) Before Taxes	-600,474	21,763	803,655	1,198,307	1,823,543
State Replacement Tax—1.5%[5]	0	326	12,055	10,047	10,047
Net Income (Loss)	**($600,474)**	**$21,437**	**$791,600**	**$659,772**	**$659,772**
Cumulative Profit (Loss)	**($600,474)**	**($579,037)**	**$212,562**	**$1,109,921**	**$1,234,685**

Footnotes:

[1]Last 6 months of 2002.

[2]Computer includes DSL, maintenance, and prepaid support.

[3]Samples include showroom samples, buyer samples, and items sent to India for design inspiration/clarification.

[4]Travel includes FMA travel to India and buyers traveling to Chicago showroom.

[5]Organized as LLC, which is not liable for federal and state (of Illinois) income taxes.

Income Projection

Year 1[1] (by month)	Jul	Aug	Sep	Oct	Nov	Dec	Total
Sales	-	-	-	-	-	-	-
Cost of Goods Sold (75%)	-	-	-	-	-	-	-
Gross Profit Margin	**-**	**-**	**-**	**-**	**-**	**-**	**-**
Operating Expenses							
Computer[2]	474	474	474	474	474	474	2,844
Freelance Artists	16,667	13,333	13,333	13,333	13,333	13,333	83,333
HR Administration	575	575	575	575	575	575	3,450
Insurance	833	833	833	833	833	833	5,000
Legal and Accounting	833	833	833	833	833	833	5,000
Licenses	125	125	125	125	125	125	750
Maintenance and Cleaning	625	500	500	500	500	500	3,125
Office Supplies[3]	10,540	2,000	2,000	2,000	2,000	2,000	20,540
Payroll	30,834	30,834	30,834	30,834	30,834	30,834	185,004
Payroll Taxes and Benefits	2,738	2,738	2,738	2,738	2,738	2,738	16,428
Postage/Shipping	5,000	5,000	5,000	5,000	5,000	5,000	30,000
Printing	5,000	5,000	5,000	5,000	5,000	5,000	30,000
Rent	5,500	5,500	5,500	5,500	5,500	5,500	33,000
Samples[4]	1,667	1,667	1,667	1,667	1,667	1,667	10,000
Subscriptions and Dues	500	500	500	500	500	500	3,000
Telephone	1,667	1,667	1,667	1,667	1,667	1,667	10,000
Travel and Entertainment[5]	21,667	21,667	21,667	21,667	21,667	21,667	130,000
Utilities	500	500	500	500	500	500	3,000
Miscellaneous	1,667	1,667	1,667	1,667	1,667	1,667	10,000
Total Operating Expenses	**107,411**	**95,413**	**95,413**	**95,413**	**95,413**	**95,413**	**584,474**
Net Income (Loss) from Operations	**-107,411**	**-95,413**	**-95,413**	**-95,413**	**-95,413**	**-95,413**	**-584,474**
Depreciation	2,667	2,667	2,667	2,667	2,667	2,667	16,000
Net Income (Loss) Before Taxes	-110,078	-98,079	-98,079	-98,079	-98,079	-98,079	-600,474
State Replacement Tax—1.5%[6]	-	-	-	-	-	-	-
Net Income (Loss)	**($110,078)**	**($98,079)**	**($98,079)**	**($98,079)**	**($98,079)**	**($98,079)**	**($600,474)**
Cumulative Profit (Loss)	($110,078)	($208,157)	($306,236)	($404,316)	($502,395)	($600,474)	

Footnotes:

[1]Last 6 months of 2002.

[2]Computer includes DSL, maintenance, and prepaid support.

[3]Office supplies include Pantone books at a cost of $6,540.

[4]Samples include showroom samples, buyer samples, and items sent to India for design inspiration/clarification.

[5]Travel includes FMA travel to India and buyers traveling to Chicago showroom.

[6]Organized as LLC, which is not liable for federal and state (of Illinois) income taxes.

Income Projection: Year 2 (by quarter)

	Q1	Q2	Q3	Q4	Total	%
Sales	$1,500,000	$1,500,000	$1,500,000	$1,500,000	$6,000,000	100.00%
Cost of Goods Sold (75%)	1,125,000	1,125,000	1,125,000	1,125,000	4,500,000	75.00%
Gross Profit Margin	**375,000**	**375,000**	**375,000**	**375,000**	**1,500,000**	**25.00%**
Operating Expenses[1]						
Computer[2]	1,315	1,315	1,315	1,315	5,258	0.10%
Freelance Artists	50,000	50,000	50,000	50,000	200,000	3.30%
HR Administration	4,306	4,306	4,306	4,306	17,222	0.30%
Insurance	2,500	2,500	2,500	2,500	10,000	0.20%
Legal and Accounting	2,600	2,600	2,600	2,600	10,400	0.20%
Licenses	375	375	375	375	1,500	0.00%
Maintenance and Cleaning	1,875	1,875	1,875	1,875	7,500	0.10%
Office Supplies	2,000	2,000	2,000	2,000	8,000	0.10%
Payroll	151,500	151,500	151,500	151,500	606,000	10.10%
Payroll Taxes and Benefits	14,529	14,529	14,529	14,529	58,116	1.00%
Postage/Shipping	16,500	16,500	16,500	16,500	66,000	1.10%
Printing	16,500	16,500	16,500	16,500	66,000	1.10%
Rent	16,500	16,500	16,500	16,500	66,000	1.10%
Samples[3]	5,000	5,000	5,000	5,000	20,000	0.30%
Subscriptions	1,500	1,500	1,500	1,500	6,000	0.10%
Telephone	5,500	5,500	5,500	5,500	22,000	0.40%
Travel and Entertainment[4]	62,500	62,500	62,500	62,500	250,000	4.20%
Utilities	1,560	1,560	1,560	1,560	6,240	0.10%
Miscellaneous	5,000	5,000	5,000	5,000	20,000	0.30%
Total Operating Expenses	**361,559**	**361,559**	**361,559**	**361,559**	**1,446,237**	**24.10%**
Net Income (Loss) from Operations	**13,441**	**13,441**	**13,441**	**13,441**	**53,763**	**0.90%**
Depreciation	8,000	8,000	8,000	8,000	32,000	0.50%
Net Income (Loss) Before Taxes	5,441	5,441	5,441	5,441	21,763	0.40%
State Replacement Tax—1.5%[5]	82	82	82	82	326	0.00%
Net Income (Loss)	**$5,359**	**$5,359**	**$5,359**	**$5,359**	**$21,437**	**0.40%**
Cumulative Profit (Loss)	($595,115)	($589,756)	($584,397)	($579,037)		

Footnotes:

[1]4% increase from Year 1 assumed for computer, HR administration, legal/accounting, utilities; 10% increase from Year 1 based on increased sales for shipping, printing, and telephone.

[2]Computer includes DSL, maintenance, and prepaid support.

[3]Samples include showroom samples, buyer samples, and items sent to India for design inspiration/clarification.

[4]Travel includes FMA travel to India and buyers traveling to Chicago showroom.

[5]Organized as LLC, which is not liable for federal and state (of Illinois) income taxes.

Income Projection: Year 3 (by quarter)

	Q1	Q2	Q3	Q4	Total	%
Sales	$2,500,000	$2,500,000	$2,500,000	$2,500,000	$10,000,000	100.00%
Cost of Goods Sold (75%)	1,875,000	1,875,000	1,875,000	1,875,000	7,500,000	75.00%
Gross Profit Margin	**625,000**	**625,000**	**625,000**	**625,000**	**2,500,000**	**25.00%**
Operating Expenses[1]						
Computer[2]	1,365	1,365	1,365	1,365	5,460	0.10%
Freelance Artists	52,000	52,000	52,000	52,000	208,000	2.10%
HR Administration	4,471	4,471	4,471	4,471	17,885	0.20%
Insurance	2,500	2,500	2,500	2,500	10,000	0.10%
Legal and Accounting	2,700	2,700	2,700	2,700	10,800	0.10%
Licenses	390	390	390	390	1,560	0.00%
Maintenance and Cleaning	1,950	1,950	1,950	1,950	7,800	0.10%
Office Supplies	2,080	2,080	2,080	2,080	8,320	0.10%
Payroll	189,075	189,075	189,075	189,075	756,300	7.60%
Payroll Taxes and Benefits	18,575	18,575	18,575	18,575	74,300	0.70%
Postage/Shipping	18,150	18,150	18,150	18,150	72,600	0.70%
Printing	18,150	18,150	18,150	18,150	72,600	0.70%
Rent	16,500	16,500	16,500	16,500	66,000	0.70%
Samples[3]	5,200	5,200	5,200	5,200	20,800	0.20%
Subscriptions	1,560	1,560	1,560	1,560	6,240	0.10%
Telephone	6,050	6,050	6,050	6,050	24,200	0.20%
Travel and Entertainment[4]	68,750	68,750	68,750	68,750	275,000	2.80%
Utilities	1,620	1,620	1,620	1,620	6,480	0.10%
Miscellaneous	5,000	5,000	5,000	5,000	20,000	0.20%
Total Operating Expenses	**416,086**	**416,086**	**416,086**	**416,086**	**1,664,345**	**16.60%**
Net Income (Loss) from Operations	**208,914**	**208,914**	**208,914**	**208,914**	**835,655**	**8.40%**
Depreciation	8,000	8,000	8,000	8,000	32,000	0.30%
Net Income (Loss) Before Taxes	200,914	200,914	200,914	200,914	803,655	8.00%
State Replacement Tax—1.5%[5]	3,014	3,014	3,014	3,014	12,055	0.10%
Net Income (Loss)	**$197,900**	**$197,900**	**$197,900**	**$197,900**	**$791,600**	**7.90%**
Cumulative Profit (Loss)	($381,137)	($183,237)	$14,663	$212,562		

Footnotes:

[1]4% increase from Year 2 assumed for computer, freelancers, HR administration, licenses, legal/accounting, maintenance, office supplies, subscriptions, and utilities; 0% increase from Year 2 based on increased sales for shipping, printing, telephone, and travel.

[2]Computer includes DSL, maintenance, and prepaid support.

[3]Samples include showroom samples, buyer samples, and items sent to India for design inspiration/clarification.

[4]Travel includes FMA travel to India and buyers traveling to Chicago showroom.

[5]Organized as LLC, which is not liable for federal and state (of Illinois) income taxes.

Cash Flow Projection: Year 1 (by month)

	Jul	Aug	Sep	Oct	Nov	Dec	Total
Sales	-	-	-	-	-	-	-
Cost of Goods Sold (75%)	-	-	-	-	-	-	-
Gross Profit Margin	**-**	**-**	**-**	**-**	**-**	**-**	**-**
Operating Expenses							
Computer	4,599	99	99	99	99	99	5,094
Freelance Artists	16,667	13,333	13,333	13,333	13,333	13,333	83,333
HR Administration	575	575	575	575	575	575	3,450
Insurance	10,000	-	-	-	-	-	10,000
Legal and Accounting	833	833	833	833	833	833	5,000
Licenses	1,500	-	-	-	-	-	1,500
Maintenance and Cleaning	625	625	625	625	625	625	3,750
Office Supplies	10,540	2,000	2,000	2,000	2,000	2,000	20,540
Payroll	30,834	30,834	30,834	30,834	30,834	30,834	185,004
Payroll Taxes and Benefits	2,738	2,738	2,738	2,738	2,738	2,738	16,428
Postage/Shipping	5,000	5,000	5,000	5,000	5,000	5,000	30,000
Printing	-	-	5,000	5,000	5,000	5,000	20,000
Rent	5,500	5,500	5,500	5,500	5,500	5,500	33,000
Samples	1,667	1,667	1,667	1,667	1,667	1,667	10,000
Subscriptions	500	500	500	500	500	500	3,000
Telephone	1,667	1,667	1,667	1,667	1,667	1,667	10,000
Travel and Entertainment	21,667	21,667	21,667	21,667	21,667	21,667	130,000
Utilities	500	500	500	500	500	500	3,000
Miscellaneous	1,667	1,667	1,667	1,667	1,667	1,667	10,000
Total Operating Expenses	**117,078**	**89,204**	**94,204**	**94,204**	**94,204**	**94,204**	**583,099**
Net Cash Flow	($117,078)	($89,204)	($94,204)	($94,204)	($94,204)	($94,204)	($583,099)
Beginning Cash Balance	0	-117,078	-206,282	-300,486	-394,691	-488,895	
Projected Ending Cash Balance	**-117,078**	**-206,282**	**-300,486**	**-394,691**	**-488,895**	**-583,099**	

Cash Flow Projection: Year 2 (by quarter)

	Q1	Q2	Q3	Q4	Total
Sales[1]	$ -	$ -	$1,500,000	$1,500,000	$3,000,000
Cost of Goods Sold (75%)	-	-	1,125,000	1,125,000	2,250,000
Gross Profit Margin	**-**	**-**	**375,000**	**375,000**	**750,000**
Operating Expenses					
Computer	1,315	1,315	1,315	1,315	5,258
Freelance Artists	50,000	50,000	50,000	50,000	200,000
HR Administration	4,306	4,306	4,306	4,306	17,222
Insurance	-	-	10,000	-	10,000
Legal and Accounting	2,600	2,600	2,600	2,600	10,400
Licenses	-	-	1,500	-	1,500
Maintenance and Cleaning	1,875	1,875	1,875	1,875	7,500
Office Supplies	2,000	2,000	2,000	2,000	8,000
Payroll	151,500	151,500	151,500	151,500	606,000
Payroll Taxes and Benefits	14,529	14,529	14,529	14,529	58,116
Postage/Shipping	16,500	16,500	16,500	16,500	66,000
Printing	16,500	16,500	16,500	16,500	66,000
Rent	16,500	16,500	16,500	16,500	66,000
Samples	5,000	5,000	5,000	5,000	20,000
Subscriptions	1,500	1,500	1,500	1,500	6,000
Telephone	5,500	5,500	5,500	5,500	22,000
Travel and Entertainment	62,500	62,500	62,500	62,500	250,000
Utilities	1,560	1,560	1,560	1,560	6,240
Miscellaneous	5,000	5,000	5,000	5,000	20,000
Total Operating Expenses	**358,684**	**358,684**	**370,184**	**358,684**	**1,446,237**
Net Cash Flow	**($358,684)**	**($358,684)**	**$4,816**	**$16,316**	**($696,237)**
Beginning Cash Balance	-583,099	-1,166,199	-1,524,883	-1,520,067	
Projected Ending Cash Balance	-1,166,199	-1,524,883	-1,520,067	-1,503,751	

Footnotes:

[1]Sales based on 6 month lag from time purchase order received to the time cash is received.

Cash Flow Projection: Year 3 (by quarter)

	Q1	Q2	Q3	Q4	Total
Sales	$2,500,000	$2,500,000	$2,500,000	$2,500,000	$10,000,000
Cost of Goods Sold (75%)	1,875,000	1,875,000	1,875,000	1,875,000	7,500,000
Gross Profit Margin	**625,000**	**625,000**	**625,000**	**625,000**	**2,500,000**
Operating Expenses					
Computer	1,365	1,365	1,365	1,365	5,460
Freelance Artists	52,000	52,000	52,000	52,000	208,000
HR Administration	4,471	4,471	4,471	4,471	17,885
Insurance	-	-	10,000	-	10,000
Legal and Accounting	2,700	2,700	2,700	2,700	10,800
Licenses	-	-	1,500	-	1,500
Maintenance and Cleaning	1,950	1,950	1,950	1,950	7,800
Office Supplies	2,080	2,080	2,080	2,080	8,320
Payroll	189,075	189,075	189,075	189,075	756,300
Payroll Taxes and Benefits	18,575	18,575	18,575	18,575	74,300
Postage/Shipping	18,150	18,150	18,150	18,150	72,600
Printing	18,150	18,150	18,150	18,150	72,600
Rent	16,500	16,500	16,500	16,500	66,000
Samples	5,200	5,200	5,200	5,200	20,800
Subscriptions	1,560	1,560	1,560	1,560	6,240
Telephone	6,050	6,050	6,050	6,050	24,200
Travel and Entertainment	68,750	68,750	68,750	68,750	275,000
Utilities	1,620	1,620	1,620	1,620	6,480
Miscellaneous	5,000	5,000	5,000	5,000	20,000
Total Operating Expenses	**413,196**	**413,196**	**424,696**	**413,196**	**1,664,285**
Net Cash Flow	**$211,804**	**$211,804**	**$200,304**	**$211,804**	**$835,715**
Beginning Cash Balance	-1,503,751	-1,291,947	-1,080,144	-879,840	
Projected Ending Cash Balance	-1,291,947	-1,080,144	-879,840	-668,036	

Projected Rates of Return for Investors

	Year 1*	Year 2	Year 3	Year 4	Year 5
Net Income (Loss) from Operations	($584,474)	$53,763	$835,655	$1,230,307	$1,855,543
Less: Debt Service	0	0	0	0	0
Net Cash Flow before Taxes	**-584,474**	**53,763**	**835,655**	**1,230,307**	**1,855,543**
Provision for Taxes					
Net Income before Taxes	-600,474	21,763	803,655	1,198,307	1,823,543
Less: NOL Provision	0	-42,763	-548,711	0	0
Add: T&E—50%	9,000	21,000	27,000	36,000	45,000
Taxable Income	-591,474	0	281,944	1,234,307	1,868,543
Income Tax Rate—Federal and State	0	0	0	0	0
Net Provision for Income Taxes	0	0	0	0	0
Add: State Replacement Tax—1.5%	0	0	4,229	18,515	28,028
Total Provision for Taxes	**0**	**0**	**4,229**	**18,515**	**28,028**
Net Cash Flow After Taxes	**-584,474**	**53,763**	**831,426**	**1,211,792**	**1,827,515**
Less: 30% of Cash Flow retained in business	0	-16,129	-249,428	-363,538	-548,254
Cash Available for Distribution	-584,474	37,634	581,998	848,254	1,279,260
Less: 1/3 to Founders/Key Employees	0	-12,545	-193,999	-282,751	-426,420
Balance of Distribution to Investors (2/3)	-584,474	25,090	387,999	565,503	852,840
Total Equity from Investors	1,810,000	1,810,000	1,810,000	1,810,000	1,810,000
Pre-Tax Rate of Return to Investors	**0**	**1.39%**	**21.44%**	**31.24%**	**47.12%**

*6 months

Housing Rehabilitation Company

BUSINESS PLAN

MADISON BUILDERS, LLC

147 Middleton Street
Kansas City, Missouri 64109

The mission of Madison Builders, LLC, is to capitalize on supply shortages and vacant land to provide quality, affordable housing for the city's middle class.

- EXECUTIVE SUMMARY
- COMPANY
- MARKET
- ORGANIZATION
- FINANCIALS

EXECUTIVE SUMMARY

Madison Builders, LLC, will construct 10 single-family market rate dwellings in Kansas City Circle. The current site of this development, to be called Jackson Place, consists of vacant lots owned by the Land Reutilization Authority (LRA). These homes will maintain the aesthetic appeal and characteristics of typical dwellings found within Kansas City, featuring brick facades and detached garages.

Potential customers include those currently living in the city and those wishing to return to new construction in familiar neighborhoods. A licensed real estate broker with an understanding and successful track record in the city market will assist in the marketing/selling of these homes. Jackson Place lies within a predominantly African American neighborhood, thus the target market will be African Americans who are able to spend about $190,000 for a house.

Madison Builders will capitalize on supply shortages and vacant land to provide quality, affordable housing for the city's middle class. Because of shortages of prime housing on the city's north side, many residents choose to move to surrounding counties to find the house of their dreams. The LRA land has been vacant for years, not creating any tax revenue for the city. Madison Builders will create value for both the city and the consumers.

Madison Builders has been rehabilitating distressed properties in the city since 2001 and wants to shift its focus to develop and build new residential dwellings, following in the footsteps of the great-grandfather of Madison Builders's founder. Each project has brought new challenges that have been met, with profit margins increasing from 10.9 percent to 21.4 percent. A stable of qualified subcontractors has been assembled and will be able to bid on this development. Outside legal counsel and accountants are being used to provide Madison Builders with the expert advice necessary for success.

Madison Builders is currently working with the Kansas City Development Corporation (KCDC) and the Land Clearance for Redevelopment Authority (LCRA) to purchase a single-family residence for rehab and sale in the southern part of the city. This small-scale project will enable Madison Builders to develop a working understanding of the various agencies, people, and processes involved in city redevelopment. Because of the growing number of new home starts in the area, Madison Builders will work with the 3rd Ward Alderwoman Roxanne Mulberry and the LRA in the coming weeks to acquire the necessary parcels of land.

Madison Builders will seek a combination of private and public funding for the land acquisition, development, and construction costs. A portion of the public funding will be in the form of free land, with the LRA assigning the parcels of land to Madison Builders. The remaining $300,000 in public funding will help offset development and construction costs. Development costs, estimated to be $128,675, will be financed with a 2-year, interest-only loan. Madison Builders wants to break ground on Jackson Place in February 2005, with the construction of a display home. The remaining nine homes will be built in a 3-phase period, with the final homes being sold in June 2006. Total construction costs for Jackson Place will be $1,596,000.

COMPANY

Company Description

Vision Statement

Madison Builders, LLC—bringing old world pride and craftsmanship to Kansas City neighborhoods, one development at a time.

Mission Statement

The mission of Madison Builders, LLC, is to capitalize on supply shortages and vacant land to provide quality, affordable housing for the city's middle class.

Objectives

- Acquire the land for the development.
- Secure financing for the project.
- Develop relationships with Kansas City Aldermen and other influential people/ associations to assist in this and future developments.
- Construct a display home to help drive sales of the remaining homes.
- Sell the remaining nine units prior to their groundbreaking.
- Adhere to project timeline and budget.
- Provide consumers with living accommodations that they will be proud of through the end of their ownership period.

Company Background

Madison Builders, LLC, began in 2001 to rehabilitate distressed properties in Kansas City. Madison Builders is currently working with the Kansas City Development Corporation (KCDC) and the Land Clearance for Redevelopment Authority (LCRA) to purchase a single-family residence for rehab and sale in the southern part of the city. This small-scale project will enable Madison Builders to develop a working understanding of the various agencies, people, and processes involved in city redevelopment. Madison Builders will contact the 3rd Ward Alderwoman Roxanne Mulberry and the Land Reutilization Authority (LRA) in the coming weeks to negotiate a deal for the vacant lots necessary for this development proposal.

Madison Builders wants to make the switch to new residential construction to carry on the tradition set forth by the founder's great-grandfather. Joseph Schmidt, a German immigrant, came to America and settled in Kansas City in the early 1900s. He built many homes in what is now known as the Dutchtown neighborhood, a community founded by German immigrants located in the southern part of the city. The legal descriptions of these homes refer to the area as Schmidt Subdivision. There was even a street named after him, Schmidt Place, which had its name changed to Prosper in 1918 due to the anti-German sentiment during World War I.

Product & Industry

Product Description

Name

The name Jackson Place comes from one of the greatest boxers to ever come out of Kansas City, Marvin Jackson. Jackson moved to Kansas City as a young boy and graduated from Central High School as an honor student. He is one of the only boxers to hold world titles in two weight classes at the same time: featherweight and welterweight. Jackson retired from boxing in 1952, amassing 99 wins, 15 losses and 7 draws, with 85 KOs. Just nine years later, Jackson became one of the first inductees into the International Boxing Hall of Fame. Many boxing experts rank Jackson as one of the three top boxers of all-time. During retirement, Jackson became a minister and devoted much of his time training young boxers and running the Downtown Boys' Club in Kansas City.

Location

The proposed site for Jackson Place is within the boundaries of Kansas City Circle. Kansas City Circle is rectangular in shape and is bordered by Morrison Avenue, Mark Avenue, North Washington, and Willow Street. Kansas City Circle Park, one of the only linear parks in Kansas

City, runs between Maple Lane, Hoover Avenue, Johnson Street, and North 23rd Street. There are many vacant lots and buildings that are in disrepair owned by the LRA within this neighborhood.

There are a couple of developments within Kansas City Circle that makes Jackson Place a viable idea. The first is Kansas City Circle Estates, a 16-home single-family development created by the Flatterly Development Company. The homes are adjacent to Kansas City Circle Park on North 23rd Street, with square footage ranging from 1,700 to 1,900. Almost all of the homes have been sold, with sales prices near $225,000. The former Gregg-Stine Site, located at 1700 Mark Avenue, is being offered through a Request for Proposal (RFP). Although the exact use of this 34-acre site has yet to be determined, there is a high likelihood that market rate housing will occupy a large percentage of it.

Madison Builders's initial proposal was to build Jackson Place in the 2200 block of North Faust Street. On Friday, April 9, 2004, Gerard White facilitated a meeting with 3rd Ward Alderwoman Roxanne Mulberry, 3rd Ward Alderman Cornell J. Huxley, Sr., and Madison Builders's founder, George Schmidt. Alderwoman Mulberry stated that the initial site is part of a much larger area that will be offered through an RFP. This means that a sizeable amount of land will be developed on a much larger scale than a 10-home development. Alderwoman Mulberry is open to the concept of Jackson Place and has other parcels of land available in her ward, but wants to know that Madison Builders can secure financing prior to allocating that land.

Number of Units

There will be a total of ten, single-family units built.

Appearance

Each of the ten units will be a detached, single-family dwelling. All of the units built in Jackson Place will be constructed with brick facades and siding on the remaining exterior walls. There will be fences installed around the backyards of each home. There will not be curb cuts for driveways because each home will have a detached garage with an alley entrance. There are many beautiful homes within Kansas City Circle and the concept is to compliment the existing dwellings. Other neighborhoods in the city have had infill properties built, usually consisting of frame construction, vinyl siding, and lacking any of the architectural detail that makes the city a great place to live. Different brick and siding colors will be available.

Amenities

Standard Features

Brick Facade	Front Porch
Copper Plumbing	200 Amp Electric
Circuit Breakers	Vinyl Siding
Gas Water Heater	Six Panel Interior Doors
Insulated Front Entry Door	Wire Shelving
2 Phone Jacks	2 Cable Jacks
Smoke Detectors	Wood Window Sills
R-30 Ceiling Insulation	Vinyl Insulated Windows
Double Bowl Vanity/2nd Floor Bathroom	Electric Range
Microwave	Dishwasher
Plain Front Cabinets	Fiberglass Tubs and Showers
Seeded Lawn	Ceramic Tile Entry and Baths
Vinyl Floor in Kitchen	Carpeting in Remaining Rooms
Lighting Fixtures	Garage Door Opener

Optional Features

Crown Moldings	Gas Hookups for Stove and Dryer
Maple Kitchen Cabinets	Hardwood Floors
Security Systems	Jacuzzi Tub
Sump Pump	Fireplace
Plumbing Rough-In-Lower Level	Lighting Upgrade
Sod	Additional Phone/Cable Jacks

Workforce

Madison Builders will do its best to make sure that no less than 25 percent minority-owned businesses and 5 percent female-owned businesses will build Jackson Place. A female minority will not count towards both categories.

Concerns

There are two main concerns at this point in the development process. The first is financing and the second is environmental. Financing is crucial to any development. Acquisition and development costs, although fairly low due to the number of parcels owned by the LRA, will be recognized early in the process. Gap financing might need to be established to protect Madison Builders if the homes do not sell, and these sunk costs have already been recognized. Another financing concern is that of the consumers. Programs are available through the Board of Aldermen that can cover the majority of closing costs and some other incidentals when purchasing a home. Madison Builders must negotiate with Alderwoman Mulberry to make these funds available for the purchasers of Jackson Place.

Environmental issues are abundant throughout the entire city. Many of the buildings that have been torn down over the years were simply dumped into the existing foundations and covered with dirt. Many sites have oil and gas tanks that have ruptured, causing leaks into the soil and water supply. The cost to clean up these sites is very high and could possibly halt the progress of this development. Any agreement that Madison Builders enters into will have an escape clause in case such environmental hazards are found on the site.

Industry Description

The Kansas City Development Corporation (KCDC) is an umbrella, not-for-profit corporation with the goal of fostering economic development and growth in the city through increased job and business opportunities and expansion of the city's tax base. Its own Board of Directors governs KCDC and its employees serve as staff support for the city's seven economic development authorities, two of them being the Land Clearance for Redevelopment Authority (LCRA) and the Land Reutilization Authority (LRA). LCRA recommends development incentives such as tax abatement, tax-exempt revenue bonds, and eminent domain for commercial, industrial, and residential projects in redevelopment areas approved by the Kansas City Board of Aldermen. LRA receives title to all tax delinquent properties not sold at the Sheriff's sale. They also receive title to properties through donations.

According to the 2002 North American Industry Classification System (NAICS), code number 236115, which is New Single-Family Housing Construction, provides the most accurate code. According to the 1997 Economic Census Data, Missouri had a total of 3,204 companies in New Single-Family Housing Construction, consisting of 14,220 employees with sales of more than $2.5 billion.

A promising sign for this industry is the growing number of building permits issued during 2003. According to the U.S. Census Bureau, Kansas City issued 171 single-family permits in 2003. These permits had associated construction costs of over $25 million. This would average $146,199 in construction costs for each new home. Including overruns, Jackson Place would incur $149,625 in construction costs per home. In 2002, the city issued 150 single-family permits, accounting for over $22 million in construction costs. In 2001, these numbers were even lower, as 126 single-family permits were issued, with construction costs of just over $18 million.

Revenue is realized when a residence is sold. Proceeds from the sale of a house must cover the construction expenses for that house, plus the various fixed costs associated with the land acquisition, development, and overhead costs associated with running the company. A prominent Kansas City developer says that his company recognizes a 12 percent profit margin on its sales. This is what Madison Builders will strive for with Jackson Place.

MARKET

Market & Target Customer

The market for Jackson Place consists of middle class African Americans in the Kansas City Metropolitan area who desire new homes in the city. Unlike most consumer goods, every person does not want, or need, a new home. For this reason, it is difficult to place a definitive figure on the number of consumers interested in Jackson Place. Assumptions can be made, based on other homes being built in the area, namely Kansas City Circle Estates development located on North 23rd Street, adjacent to Kansas City Circle Park. The Flatterly Development Company is building the 16-home single-family dwellings, with square footage ranging from 1,700 to 1,900. Construction began in July 2003 and to date, all of the lots have been sold, with each new home selling for around $225,000. The exteriors of these homes remind consumers of a typical city-style dwelling with garage access via the alley. Interior upgrades include everything found in most suburban home developments, including decorative moldings, flooring upgrades and kitchen and bath improvements. Phase 2 of this development will begin once additional parcels can be acquired. Based on the price point and amenities offered, demand for Jackson Place should far exceed the supply of homes.

There are three main groups of target customers for Jackson Place. The first group consists of African American families currently residing in Kansas City Circle. The parents range in age from early 30s to mid 50s with at least one child. These are the residents who appreciate city living and what it offers, but want to move up and out of their current living accommodations. At least one of the parents works, probably in an office or other professional capacity. This group will be called "local families."

The second group consists of younger African Americans, mid 20s to 30s, who are looking for their first house. These consumers are either recently married or desire a larger living space to accommodate children in the future. Much like the "local families," this group works in a professional capacity, probably in the city, and views this development as providing convenient access to their jobs. This group will be called "upstarts."

The third and final group of target customers represents the African Americans who want to return to the city after living in surrounding counties. This group, similar in age to the "local families," also work in professional jobs. Some in this group might be married with children, others are single. The common bond is a love of the city. This group will be called "transplants." Because two thirds of the target audience is coming from outside the boundaries of Kansas City Circle, the average income level of $25,000 should not raise a flag to Madison Builders.

Competition & Competitive Advantage

There are several new home developments being built in the city. Flatterly Development Company has sold out of lots in her Kansas City Circle Estates development. Flatterly is looking to secure additional parcels for Phase 2 of the development. There are other infill projects occurring, where one home is built among existing homes. This might satisfy some people, but the sense of community might be gone considering infill homes usually look nothing like their neighbors. Another competitor to Jackson Place is the various loft developments in the city. These are the three main sources of competition. Within Kansas City Circle, Madison Builders could not find other developments of new single-family detached dwellings with similar characteristics for under $200,000. Two things will help sell the homes at Jackson Place—their price point, and the fact that some people prefer a detached dwelling to that of an attached townhouse or loft.

Marketing Strategy

Overall Strategy

The overall strategy relates to the mission of Madison Builders, LLC; that of capitalizing on supply shortages and vacant ground to provide quality, affordable housing for the city's middle class. The city does not offer many new single-family homes for middle class African Americans. Because the LRA wants to promote development, they will offer their vacant lots for free to Madison Builders. These savings will ultimately be passed along to the consumer.

Once Alderwoman Mulberry sees that Madison Builders can secure financing, she will allocate the parcels necessary for Jackson Place. Madison Builders hopes to have the parcels no later than June 2004. From July 2004 to January 2005, Madison Builders will work with architects and the city planners to finalize the home plans. The display home will break ground in February 2005, with a scheduled completion of early June 2005. Once this home is complete, potential consumers (namely the local families, upstarts, and transplants mentioned earlier) will see the value that Madison Builders offers. Although prices will start at $190,000, additional features and square footage options could increase prices closer to the $200,000 threshold.

Contracts will be accepted before, during, and after the construction of the display home. The remaining nine homes will be built in three, three-home phases. Homes will be built in the order contracts were accepted.

Sales Plan

Before the first house of Jackson Place is built, Madison Builders will work to notify the various media outlets in the Kansas City area about the new development. This PR effort will specifically target the *Kansas City Star*, both from a real estate and a special interest story. The PR effort will also notify local real estate agents of the development. Special publications, those targeting the local families, upstarts, and transplants, will also be utilized. This will create interest in the homes and lead to the successful completion of one of the objectives, that of selling each home before construction begins.

The responsibility of selling these homes will be awarded to a local real estate broker who understands and has a successful track record with the city market. This broker will be responsible for placing the homes of Jackson Place in the computerized MLS system for other agents to obtain information about them. Madison Builders has allocated $1,500 per home to pay for the necessary advertising, i.e., newspaper, real estate show on cable access, flyers, etc. In exchange, the broker will receive a 5 percent commission. No broker has been retained as of yet, but a company such as Flatterly, or the contacts that Mr. White can provide, would be viable options.

Madison Builders must sell the Jackson Place development to potential brokers. With the strong family ties that the company has in new home construction, this development will be the first of many to come. Future sites can and will be developed, not only in Kansas City Circle, but in the surrounding neighborhoods as well. Once Madison Builders proves itself as a new home builder and gains the increasing confidence in the lending institutions and local politicians, the size and quality of its developments will improve exponentially.

Competitive Plan

This is an area where Madison Builders might request the assistance of the hired broker. Whether through mailings or other correspondence, Madison Builders can get a leg up on the competition by listening to what consumers have to say. A questionnaire pertaining to the preferences of consumers can go a long way in deciding which fixtures or cabinets to place in a display home. Once the display home is built, face time at the home will help Madison Builders in understanding the needs and desires of those prospects making the big decision of purchasing a new home. Flyers can also be left at the home in order for these prospects to answer questions regarding what they thought about the home, not only from an aesthetic sense, but also from a quality perspective. Once the homes are sold, Madison Builders will conduct 6-month and 1-year follow-ups to determine the satisfaction of each consumer in Jackson Place. These follow-ups will provide Madison Builders with the information to improve their product and service in the future.

ORGANIZATION

Legal & Organizational Structures

Madison Builders, LLC, was established in January 2001 and registered its Articles of Organization with the Missouri Secretary of State.

The mailing address of Madison Builders, LLC, is 147 Middleton Street, Kansas City, MO 64109.

George Schmidt is the sole member of this limited liability company. As such, there are no employees; other services are contracted with various organizations.

Key Personnel

George Schmidt started Madison Builders, LLC, and is looking to transform the company and develop vacant lots into new residential dwellings. The key for Madison Builders is to continue its tradition of building and maintaining relationships. As Madison Builders ventures into this new territory, new relationships must be formed—a strongpoint of the company's founder.

The founder's background includes three years of rehabilitating homes and three years of marketing experience. Profit margins have increased on the properties from 10.9 percent to 21.4 percent. The founder will complete his Master's of Business Administration in May 2005, improving his analytical skills to make wiser decisions with regards to prospective developments. Madison Builders's current process of working with the KCDC and LCRA to acquire a property in the southern part of the city is beneficial, as it provides a real-life example of working with government agencies in the city.

Related Services

Accounting	Attorney
Banking	Concrete
Electrical	Flooring
HVAC	Insurance
Plumbing	Windows

Location

The physical location of the office for Madison Builders, LLC, is the home of its president. This is key when determining costs associated with this particular project. Large sums of cash could be spent for office rent and equipment during the time period to negotiate terms with the city. By operating out of the house, costs are significantly reduced. At this point, there is no plan to change the current system.

FINANCIALS

Critical Risks

There are three main risks when accessing the Jackson Place development. The first is the risk that the market for new homes could decline. Although new home starts continue to climb, there will come a time when that production begins to level off, and eventually fall. The second risk lies in the interest rates. Mortgage rates are beginning to increase, albeit at a slow pace. Once the display home is under construction in February 2005, there's no telling where the rates might be. The third risk is costs. One example is the current steel situation, where China is retaining almost all of their supply in order to build for the Olympics, thus causing shortages and higher prices in the U.S. Similar pricing could occur on other items and cause construction costs to soar, or possibly, shut down the job.

The following section presents a cost breakdown by home and a cash flow statement. This is typical for housing developments as cash flow is the most important aspect of the financial section. This is why balance sheets and income statements have been omitted from the plan.

Cost Breakdown by Home

Total Sources		**$392,468**
Overhead	$915	
Acquisition and Development Costs	$12,895	
Insurance	$2,067	
Sales and Marketing Costs	$11,000	
Construction Costs and Overruns	$159,600	
Total Uses		**$186,477**
Loans and Interest		$183,746
Profit		**$22,245**

Assumptions

- Total sources include sales price, development loan, construction loan, and public financing.
- Overhead includes administrative, tax preparation, and attorney's fees.
- Acquisition and development costs include title, soil tests, civil engineer, architect, surveys, rubble removal, and utility connections.
- Insurance includes general liability and builders risk.
- Sales and marketing costs include all marketing, advertising, and commission.
- Construction costs are $95 per square foot and overruns are 12% of construction costs.
- Loans and interest include the construction and development loans.

Cash Flow—July 2004 to June 2005

	Jul	Aug	Sep	Oct	Nov
Total Sources	**$0**	**$128,675**	**$0**	**$0**	**$0**
Uses					
Overhead	$400	$100	$100	$400	$100
Acquisition and Development	0	13,992	13,992	13,992	13,992
Insurance	0	0	0	0	0
Interest	0	1,598	1,598	1,598	1,598
Sales and Marketing	0	0	0	0	0
Construction and Overruns	0	0	0	0	0
Loan Payoff	0	0	0	0	0
Total Uses	**$400**	**$15,690**	**$15,690**	**$15,990**	**$15,690**
Net Cash Flow	**-$400**	**$112,985**	**-$15,690**	**-$15,990**	**-$15,690**
Beginning Cash	**$5,500**	**$5,100**	**$118,085**	**$102,395**	**$86,405**
End Cash	**$5,100**	**$118,085**	**$102,395**	**$86,405**	**$70,715**

Cash Flow—July 2005 to June 2006

	Jul	Aug	Sep	Oct	Nov
Total Sources	**$133,380**	**$114,570**	**$95,760**	**$76,950**	**$628,140**
Uses					
Overhead	$100	$550	$100	$100	$550
Acquisition and Development	0	0	0	0	0
Insurance	1,140	1,515	1,140	1,140	1,515
Interest	5,236	6,658	7,847	8,803	9,525
Sales and Marketing	1,250	1,250	1,250	1,250	29,750
Construction and Overruns	133,380	114,570	95,760	76,950	58,140
Loan Payoff	0	0	0	0	553,800
Total Uses	**$154,606**	**$124,543**	**$106,097**	**$88,243**	**$653,280**
Net Cash Flow	**-$21,226**	**-$9,973**	**-$10,337**	**-$11,293**	**-$25,140**
Beginning Cash	**$129,236**	**$108,010**	**$98,037**	**$87,700**	**$76,407**
End Cash	**$108,010**	**$98,037**	**$87,700**	**$76,407**	**$51,267**

Dec	Jan	Feb	Mar	Apr	May	Jun
$0	**$120,000**	**$44,460**	**$38,190**	**$31,920**	**$25,650**	**$19,380**
$100	$400	$550	$100	$850	$550	$100
13,992	13,992	4,500	0	0	0	0
0	0	660	285	285	660	285
1,598	1,598	2,150	2,624	3,021	3,349	3,580
0	0	1,250	1,250	1,250	1,250	1,250
0	0	44,460	38,190	31,920	25,650	19,380
0	0	0	0	0	0	0
$15,690	**$15,990**	**$53,570**	**$42,449**	**$37,326**	**$31,459**	**$24,595**
-$15,690	**$104,010**	**-$9,110**	**-$4,259**	**-$5,406**	**-$5,809**	**-$5,215**
$70,715	**$55,025**	**$159,035**	**$149,925**	**$145,666**	**$140,260**	**$134,451**
$55,025	**$159,035**	**$149,925**	**$145,666**	**$140,260**	**$134,451**	**$129,236**

Dec	Jan	Feb	Mar	Apr	May	Jun
$0	**$180,000**	**$133,380**	**$114,570**	**$95,760**	**$76,950**	**$818,140**
$100	$100	$550	$100	$1,100	$550	$100
0	0	13,500	0	0	0	0
285	285	1,515	1,140	1,140	1,515	1,140
2,648	1,237	2,893	4,315	5,504	6,460	7,182
1,250	1,250	0	0	0	0	38,000
0	0	133,380	114,570	95,760	76,950	58,140
0	113,675	0	0	0	0	578,400
$4,283	**$116,547**	**$151,838**	**$120,125**	**$103,504**	**$85,475**	**$682,962**
-$4,283	**$63,453**	**-$18,458**	**-$5,555**	**-$7,744**	**-$8,525**	**$135,178**
$51,267	**$46,984**	**$110,437**	**$91,979**	**$86,424**	**$78,680**	**$70,155**
$46,984	**$110,437**	**$91,979**	**$86,424**	**$78,680**	**$70,155**	**$205,333**

Cash Flow—July 2006 to November 2006

	Jul	Aug	Sep	Oct	Nov
Total Sources	**$133,380**	**$114,570**	**$95,760**	**$76,950**	**$628,140**
Uses					
Overhead	$100	$550	$100	$100	$550
Acquisition and Development	13,500	0	0	0	0
Insurance	855	1,230	855	855	1,230
Interest	1,656	3,079	4,268	5,223	5,945
Sales and Marketing	0	0	0	0	28,500
Construction and Overruns	133,380	114,570	95,760	76,950	58,140
Loan Payoff	0	0	0	0	478,800
Total Uses	**$149,491**	**$119,429**	**$100,983**	**$83,128**	**$573,165**
Net Cash Flow	**-$16,111**	**-$4,859**	**-$5,223**	**-$6,178**	**$54,975**
Beginning Cash	**$205,333**	**$189,222**	**$184,363**	**$179,140**	**$172,962**
End Cash	**$189,222**	**$184,363**	**$179,140**	**$172,962**	**$227,937**

Assumptions

- Construction will begin on the first home in February 2005.
- The display home will not be sold until June 2006.
- No more than three homes will be under construction at any one time.
- Ground breaking will only occur once a sales contract has been received, with the exception of the display home.
- Development loan consists of development costs and architect fees.
- Construction loan includes 12% overrun charge.

Totals
$3,924,675
$9,150
128,952
20,670
112,781
110,000
1,596,000
1,724,675
$3,702,228
$222,447
$51
$46,984

Internet & Network Security Solution Provider

BUSINESS PLAN

SAFETY NET CANADA, INC.

8789 Elk Avenue
Vancouver, British Columbia V3N 4E9
Canada

Safety Net Canada wants to become the dominant provider of a reliable, impervious, easy-to-use Internet and network security solution to corporate and retail customers worldwide. This plan raised over $5 million (U.S.) for the company and was written by Concord Business Development Inc. of Vancouver, British Columbia.

- HIGHLIGHTS
- EXECUTIVE SUMMARY
- COMPANY OVERVIEW
- PRODUCTS
- MARKET ANALYSIS
- MARKETING PLAN
- COMPETITION
- FINANCE
- EXHIBITS

HIGHLIGHTS

Mission Statement

Safety Net Canada will be the dominant provider of a reliable, impervious, easy-to-use, and cost-effective hardware- and software-based, Internet and network security solution to corporate and retail customers worldwide.

Industry: Technology—Internet and network security.

Singular Features

Safety Net Canada will be the first network security company to introduce an information security solution that meets all criteria for reliability, compatibility, ease-of-use and scalability.

Target Market

Safety Net Canada identifies four target market segments for its Security™ line of network security products: large organizations, small and medium enterprises, and individual consumers.

Regional Expansion

Safety Net Canada will build its market share by gradually entering all major international markets by the end of the planning period subject to this plan.

Revenue Streams

The revenue model of Safety Net Canada comprises a primary and a secondary revenue category, with each category containing multiple revenue streams derived from the different Security™ models.

Capital Requirements: US $5 million.

Use of Proceeds

To complete product development and pre-launch testing, build and launch the website, launch marketing and promotion programs, build an administrative infrastructure, and acquire human resources.

EXECUTIVE SUMMARY

Corporate Vision

Safety Net Canada is based on the philosophy of growth. The company is dedicated to continuously innovating and expanding its line of security products in order to meet the needs of a dynamic and rapidly growing networked population. The management's vision for long-term sustainable growth incorporates the creation of a stimulating and creative corporate environment. Within such an environment, the members of Safety Net's talented team have the opportunity to continually enhance their individuality and creativity while contributing to the growth and long-term success of the company.

Products

Safety Net Canada will be the first network security company to introduce an information security solution that meets all criteria for reliability, compatibility, ease-of-use, and scalability. The flagship product line is comprised of two components: the Security™, a hardware device that protects computers from intruders, and the Security Guard™, complementary firewall and anti-virus software to protect the operating system and applications. By working in compliance and complementing each other, these two products amalgamate into a bulletproof network security solution that is resistant to currently known loopholes in security hardware appliances and software.

Market Opportunity

The Internet and network security industry is a rapidly growing segment of the high-tech business sector, as businesses and individual consumers become more aware of the security threats caused by conducting transactions and exchanging information in a networked environment. Internet and network security is currently a US $5 billion business, growing two-fold from its 1998 level of US $2.3 billion. North America and Western Europe account for 84 percent of all 1999 network security sales, with North America at more than two thirds of total sales worldwide. Network security sales revenue is expected to grow even faster over the next three years, as Internet and broadband adoption, as well as e-commerce, continue expanding worldwide.

Security is not just for insurance purposes anymore but is an important part of corporate policy and strategy. The Internet is a source for increased profitability, and companies need sophisticated security solutions to expand trusted relationships with their customers, partners, suppliers, and channels. This need is the vehicle of the network security market. According to IDC, its worldwide revenue will jump from less than $4 billion in 1999 to more than $11 billion in 2004.

Safety Net Canada will take advantage of the vast profit and market share potential in the industry by being the first-to-market supplier of a complete network and Internet security solution, targeted at both organizational and individual clients.

Marketing Plan

Building a strong corporate and retail customer base and developing a high industry image and profile are corporate-level objectives subject to the company's marketing and promotional efforts. Each of these goals will be pursued and achieved through the implementation of an array of marketing and promotional actions geared towards fulfilling the directives of Safety Net Canada's marketing plan.

The Security™ product line will be rolled out into all four target market segments simultaneously. Different blends of distribution channels and marketing techniques will be used to reach the various market segments.

Safety Net will build its market share by gradually entering all major international markets by the end of the planning period subject to this plan.

Strategic Alliances

Safety Net plans to form strategic alliances with large hardware equipment manufacturers and anti-virus software companies as part of its plan to pursue an expansionary corporate level strategy through vertical integration.

Competition Summary

As the Internet and network security industry is projected to grow, the competitive environment will become more heated. Competition will ensue from both incumbent companies and new entrants. Established technologies, such as firewall software, will be subject to downward price pressure and low-cost competition. The competitive rules for newer information security technologies, such as Gap Technology appliances, will continue to be derived from product innovation rivalry and differentiation.

Safety Net Canada has no direct and two close indirect competitors for its complete Security™ solution. None of the company's other industry rivals offer a software and hardware-integrated, off-the-shelf, and easy-to-use security product.

Competitive Advantage

Safety Net Canada's competitive advantage is two-dimensional. One aspect of it is the company's ability to differentiate its products based on core competencies—innovation in product development and superior customer service. The second source of competitive advantage is cost-efficiency, with Safety Net Canada being the sole player in the Internet and network industry able to deliver a multi-faceted, reliable security solution at nominal cost. Long-term sustainability will be achieved through continuous innovation and customer service improvement.

Management Team

Safety Net Canada's management team is composed of skilled executives and Information Technology experts with previous experience in the Internet and network security industry. Other areas of expertise include market assessment, hi-tech research and development, as well as business venture formation and development. These individuals possess the superior determination, clear vision, and exceptional experience key to the success of the company.

Revenue Streams

The revenue model of Safety Net Canada comprises a primary and a secondary revenue category, with each category containing multiple revenue streams derived from the different Security™ models:

- **Sales through Distributors**—Revenues derived from distribution network sales contributes up to 70% of total revenue.
- **Direct Sales**—Revenues derived through the direct sales channel comprises approximately 30% of total revenue.

Capital Requirements

To deliver on its business proposition and take advantage of the existing opportunities in the marketplace, Safety Net Canada is seeking to raise US $5 million. Proceeds will be used to complete flagship product line development and pre-launch testing, build and launch the website, launch preliminary marketing and promotion programs, build an administrative infrastructure, and acquire human resources.

COMPANY OVERVIEW

Vision

Today, the increasing volume and speed of information exchange is accompanied by an increased potential for data to be manipulated in various ways including illegal tampering, altering, theft, or destruction. Safety Net Canada has been created out of the vital need of consumers and business users to have complete and reliable protection of information exchanged via public and private networks. The company is dedicated to continuously innovate and expand its line of security products in order to meet the needs of a dynamic and rapidly growing networked population.

Safety Net Canada is based on the philosophy of growth. The management's vision for long-term, sustainable growth incorporates the creation of a stimulating and creative corporate environment. Within such an environment, the members of Safety Net Canada's talent team have the opportunity to continually enhance their individuality and creativity while contributing to the growth and long-term success of the company.

Goals

Safety Net Canada resolves to treat customers, stakeholders, and the community with fairness and respect. These groups see the company as providing a sound financial return on investment, a robust, state-of-the-art Internet and network security solution, customer service and support, and a commitment to economic growth within the community.

Corporate Objectives

Management believes that following a preset strategic course, leading to a clearly defined set of enterprise-wide objectives, will result in increased shareholder and stakeholder value and foster revenue and organizational growth. In line with its corporate mission, vision, and long-term growth strategy, Safety Net Canada will pursue the following fundamental corporate objectives:

- To position Safety Net Canada as a predominant leader in the Internet and network security industry
- To maximize shareholder and stakeholder value by growing the company and its revenue
- To keep innovating and testing new technologies in order to keep pace with the global demand for security

Short-Term Functional Objectives

Successful implementation of the company's business model requires accomplishment of the following short-term functional-level goals:

Product Development

- Creation and maintenance of an effective distribution system with sales of up to 70% of total revenue
- Successful launch of the Security™ flagship product line by the end of Q1 2001
- Initial design of fingerprint authentication technology and prototype development of the 1020 Security™ scrambler by the end of year 2001

Marketing and Sales

- To dominate the North American market, develop the Asian market, and penetrate the European and South American market by the end of year 2003
- To grow sales revenue from US $5.4 million in year 1 to US $62.5 million in year 3
- To develop a worldwide brand name by the end of year 3

Business Development

- To secure corporate allies for the manufacturing and distribution of the Security™ by mid-Q1 2001
- To utilize and sustain long-term competitive advantage based on differentiation through product and service innovation

Strategies

To accomplish the objectives of its short-term and long-term planning periods, Safety Net Canada will follow a predetermined set of strategies at the corporate and business levels.

Corporate-Level Strategy

Safety Net Canada will pursue an expansionary enterprise strategy, based on vertical integration through strategic partnerships with large hardware OEMs and leading security software companies. Through these partnerships, the company has the opportunity to explore the profit potential of its trademarked technology while limiting competitors' access to international distribution networks.

Business-Level Strategy

With its patent-pending status, Safety Net Canada's competitive advantage is rooted in differentiation through innovation. The patent pending allows the company to harvest profits from commercializing the technology. To sustain its competitive edge in the long run, Safety Net Canada will continue investing in new product development. To lock out competitors, the company will trademark all new and unique technologies developed in the future.

Corporate Data

Date of Incorporation	June 16, 2000
Name of Incorporation	Safety Net Canada Incorporated
State of Incorporation	Nevada, USA
Principal Place of Business	8789 Elk Avenue Vancouver, BC V3N 4E9
Telephone	(604) 588-7565
Fax	(604) 575-6415
E-mail	info@safetynet.com
Website	www. safetynet.com
Fiscal Year End	September 30
Corporate Accountant	Samual Tom
Corporate Attorney	Jensen Devil Barristers and Solicitors

Proprietary Technology

The company has a granted patent pending in North America and has applied to trademark its Security™ technology under the Patent Co-operation Treaty (PCT). Under this treaty, Safety Net Canada maintains exclusive rights to sell manufacturing rights for profit in North America and more than 90 other countries worldwide.

Management Team

Safety Net Canada's management team is composed of skilled executives and information technology experts with previous experience in the Internet and network security industry. Other areas of expertise include market assessment, hi-tech research and development, as well as business venture formation and development. These individuals possess the superior determination, clear vision, and exceptional experience key to the success of the company.

Safety Net Canada will continue acquiring new and creative individuals in order to complete the personnel requirements of its managerial and corporate structure. The company's management team will be gradually completed as new executives are interviewed and appointed to fitting positions, according to the company's hiring procedures.

Vicki Smith—President and CEO

Ms. Smith has extensive experience in business development in the Internet and network security industry. Before coming on board with Safety Net Canada, she was the active leader of New Wave Technologies—a network administration and support consulting company. During her four years of involvement with New Wave Technologies, Ms. Smith managed to build a substantial client base composed of small, medium, and large corporate customers throughout North America.

Ms. Smith wrote her first computer program at the age of 14, has a B.Sc. degree in Computer Science, and possesses in-depth knowledge and understanding of network security violations (hacking). She is an expert of network security and has an in-depth understanding of the information security industry dynamics.

As President and Chief Executive Officer of Safety Net Canada, Ms. Smith brings the essential technical and business expertise, as well as the advanced people and managerial skills critical for the company's success. Furthermore, she has the vision and technological and business insight to lead the company to success.

Kathy Bronco—Vice President Corporate Development

As a co-founder of Safety Net Canada, Ms. Bronco brings superior skills and experience in customer service management and client relations. Ms. Bronco's background is in marketing and promotional initiatives. Safety Net Canada benefits highly from Ms. Bronco's superior organizational and people management skills.

Ms. Bronco has successfully planned and implemented advertising and media buying campaigns for a number of businesses in the British Columbia hospitality industry. Hotel Vancouver and the Executive Plaza Hotel are among the client accounts under her management and supervision.

As a Vice President of Corporate Development for Safety Net Canada, Ms. Bronco is responsible for managing and co-ordinating all advertising, promotional, and public relations activities. Her outstanding dedication, energy, and personal drive guarantee flawless execution of her role in the organization and make an excellent addition to the Safety Net Canada team.

Michael Adams—Vice President Business Development

Mr. Adams brings to Safety Net Canada more than 10 years of experience in the information technology and business development fields. He is an accomplished Senior Consultant and, for the past four years, has been the project manager for the implementation of an array of IT applications such as mySAP.com, SAP, BAAN, and DDC. Through these and other technology development and project management assignments, Mr. Adams has acquired valuable knowledge and experience in business process re-engineering and customer relationship management.

Before mySAP.com, Mr. Adams spent six years with Dynapro in the capacity of Senior Product Consultant. During his contract with Dynapro, Mr. Adams implemented an ERP system, was responsible for product materials management, and consulted senior management, vendors, and external stakeholders on business processes and project management deliverables.

Mr. Adams has an extensive technical and business education background. As the Vice President of Business Development for Safety Net Canada, he brings to the company exceptional organizational, logistics, and people skills essential to establishing a flawless and efficient business entity.

Shannon Aims—Vice President Distribution

Ms. Aims brings to the Safety Net Canada talent pool 10 years of experience in senior-level marketing and sales. She has worked as a Senior Account Manager for renowned Canadian and Australian corporations, including Honeywell International, BGE Service & Supply Ltd., and Nuchem Australia.

Ms. Aims is a multi-talented Sales and Marketing professional with a solid background of training and experience to support solution-based, business-to-business projects. She is highly skilled in evaluating operations and introducing efficiencies, as well as assessing the feasibility of product line innovations in relation to client-specific needs.

Ms. Aims' strengths are deeply rooted in efficient project management and superior service delivery, communication, and client relations (including management of high-profile accounts), innovation, and problem solving, as well as technology and business operations. She brings to Safety Net Canada the confidence, know-how, and determination necessary to successfully establish and manage client and partner relations.

Dean Martin—Investor Relations

Mr. Martin has more than 15 years of experience in the real estate industry and with global corporate and project financing. As a Vice President to Codwell Banker Commercial, he has been involved in corporate real estate investment projects valued in the tens of millions of dollars. Mr. Martin's affiliation with the real estate investment firm Century 21 has resulted in the successful completion of multiple company mergers and joint ventures in the area of commercial real estate acquisitions.

Mr. Martin has been actively involved in the funding and financial management of a variety of large real estate investment projects, including fundraising for an investment project in the cemetery industry—which raised $6 million dollars investment capital—and participation in "Burns Bog"—a project valued at $2 billion. Currently, Mr. Martin is actively working on several joint venture opportunities in the entertainment, recreation, and hospitality industry. His background is in business administration, marketing, and sales, and he is a member of the Master Medallion Club (top 1% of industry professionals).

Mr. Martin is a significant addition to the Safety Net Canada's management team, as his business development expertise and years of investment experience are invaluable assets to the company's financial division.

Organizational Support

Safety Net Canada is planning to rapidly build its management team and functional divisions to reflect revenue and organizational growth. The increase in staff will correspond to revenue growth.

Safety Net Canada, Inc. Organizational Chart

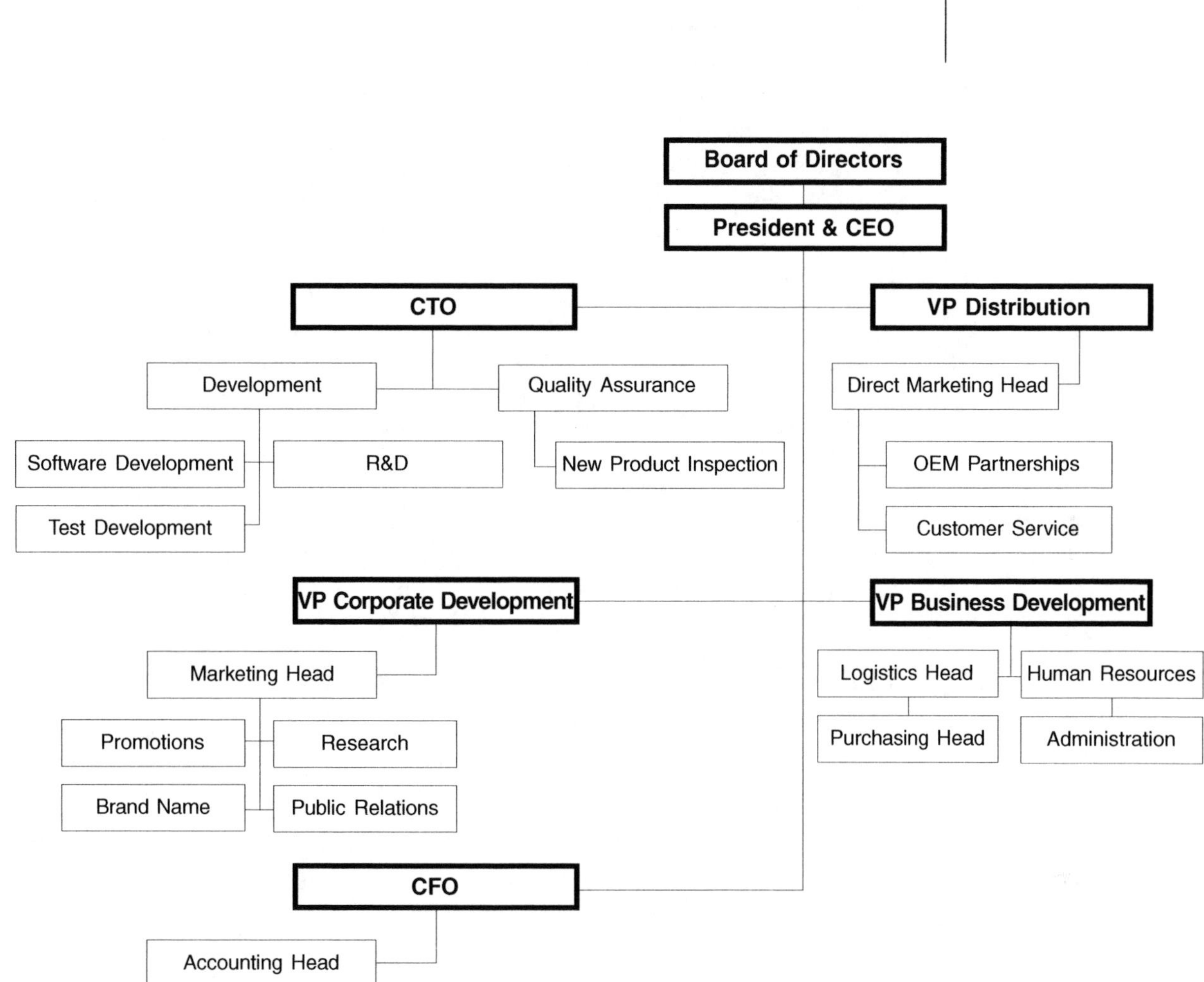

Strategic Alliances

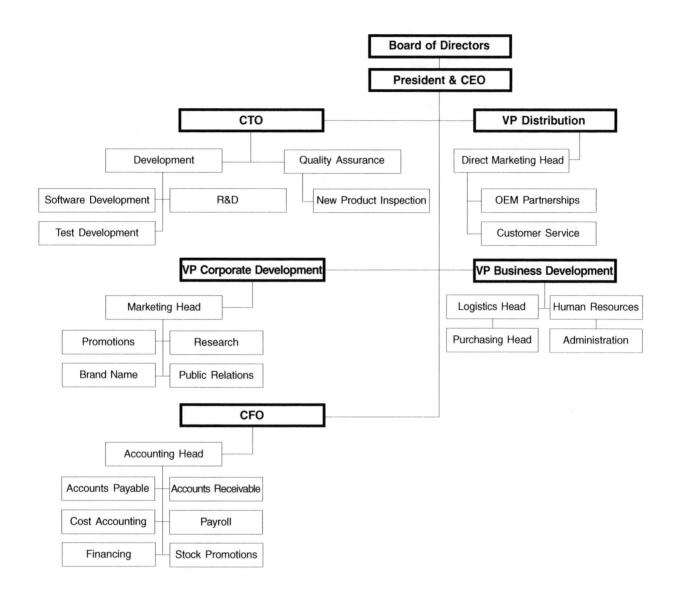

Safety Net Canada plans to form strategic alliances with large hardware equipment manufacturers and software companies as part of its plan to pursue an expansionary corporate level strategy through vertical integration.

Hardware OEMs

Safety Net Canada will seek to enter into licensed manufacturing agreements with hardware equipment manufacturers for the production and bundling of security products. Large computer hardware and network equipment makers, such as IBM and Hewlett Packard, will be considered as potential strategic alliance targets. Under these licensing agreements, the company will benefit from expedited market penetration and access to a large and committed installed base.

Software Companies

Forming an alliance with leading software companies will benefit Safety Net Canada in two directions. Potential exchange of technological know-how will provide the company with the product and technology infrastructure to deliver the finest Internet and network security solutions. Moreover, through this strategic alliance, Safety Net Canada will seek access to a robust and ubiquitous distribution system to reach retail customers. Safety Net Canada is currently in the process of evaluating potential strategic partnership opportunities with leaders in the anti-virus and firewall segment of the Internet and network security industry.

Outsourcing Partnerships

Safety Net Canada is a research and development company. Manufacturing, marketing, and other functions will be outsourced to third parties. The rationale behind the outsourcing decision is to focus on the company's core competencies—innovation and product development. Management considers that Safety Net Canada will benefit from outsourcing the following functions:

Advertising and Promotion

Safety Net Canada will examine prospective advertising agencies to outsource its marketing and promotion functions. Criteria in choosing a suitable advertising partner include:

- Global reach and resource sharing
- Client base and successful brands
- Experience managing hi-tech accounts

Web Development

A complete e-commerce enabled website is an integral part of Safety Net Canada's sales strategy through the direct channel. The company will contract out a web development team to build, implement, and maintain the e-commerce website. Key factors of choosing a web development outsourcing partner include uniqueness and functionality of the e-commerce technology and cost of development and maintenance.

Exit Strategy

Through its development of superior technology over existing network security solutions and by being first-to-market with a complete, off-the-shelf network security product, Safety Net Canada will explore the revenue potential to its full potential. If, as the company grows, a suitable bidder emerges, Safety Net Canada will consider the possibility of being acquired by a larger Internet and network security company.

PRODUCTS

Overview of Security Products

Network security is a multi-faceted technology field incorporating four different aspects of information security: Authentication, Administration and Audit, Access Control, and Encryption. The first two building blocks of information security—Authentication, Administration and Audit—are commonly conceptualized and referred to as the 3As of information security. Most companies involved in the network security industry manufacture products applicable to one of these four information security fields. Some of the currently available product groups and technologies, as well as their underlying functionalities are listed below. A more detailed description of these technologies is provided in the Exhibits section.

Available Technologies and Products

Authentication Products

Authentication tools manage user, host, and message verification. Primary authentication technologies include:

- Passwords
- Tokens
- Smart Cards
- Biometrics

Administration and Audit Products

Security administration and audit tools allow network managers to control and document which users get access to which resources. Principal components of security administration and audit are:

- Policy Management Services
- Database/File Management
- Auditing Software
- Virtual Private Networks (VPNs)

Access Control Product Group

Access control tools enable network managers to restrict access and filter the data traveling across the network. Chief data access technologies include:

- Firewalls (hardware appliances and software applications)
- Proxy servers
- Security Monitoring and Intrusion Detection Tools
- Gap Technology Devices

Encryption Product Group

Encryption and decryption technologies, such as Public/Private Key Infrastructure (PKI) and digital signatures, are used to guard data transmitted over the network. Within this product group, VPN, encryption enablers, and e-mail encryption are the key areas of product development.

Multi-Functionality Solutions

Most off-the-shelf security products address a single aspect of network security, which allows for vulnerabilities at one or more of the remaining three levels of information security. The trend toward increasing frequency and damage of security attacks has boosted demand for complete and bulletproof information security solutions. A number of industry players and individual security consultants have taken advantage of this opportunity by offering customized security solutions, addressing all four aspects of network security, at premium prices.

Stateful multilayer inspection firewalls filter packets at the network layer, determine whether session packets are legitimate and evaluate contents of packets at the application layer. They allow direct connection between client and host, alleviating the problem caused by the lack of transparency of application level gateways. They rely on algorithms to recognize and process application layer data instead of running application-specific proxies. Stateful multilayer inspection firewalls offer a high level of security, good performance, and transparency to end-users. They are expensive, however, and due to their complexity are potentially less secure than simpler types of firewalls if not administered by highly competent personnel.

Safety Net Security Solutions

Dial-up Internet accounts, even with their changing IP (Internet Protocol) address are easy targets for hackers, especially with security breaches in browsers and operating systems being discovered all the time. Network access via an "always on" connection, such as cable modem or xDSL, is particularly vulnerable to malicious and unauthorized intrusion due to its static IP address. Safety Net Canada will be the first network security company to introduce an information security solution that meets all criteria for reliability, compatibility, ease-of-use, and scalability. The flagship product line is comprised of two components: the Security™, a hardware appliance that protects hardware from intruders, and the Security Guard™, complementary firewall and anti-virus software applications to protect the operating system and applications. By working in compliance and complementing each other, these two products amalgamate into a bulletproof network security solution that is resistant to currently known loopholes in security hardware appliances and software. Safety Net Canada is dedicated to continue innovating its products by incorporating new research and technology in information security into its existing and future products.

Security™

Introduction

The Safety Net Canada proprietary Security™ is a hardware security device, based on the Gap Technology principle (see Exhibits for detailed explanation of gap technology), that resides on the connection between a computer and a modem. It monitors the inbound and outbound transmission pattern between these two devices to determine activity levels. If the device detects inactivity or idle connection for a pre-set amount of time (set by the user), it physically disconnects the computer from the network. Once the user resumes networking (i.e., requests a page on the Internet by following a link on their currently open browser), the Security™ detects the user input and re-establishes the network connection through the modem to the networked server in order to fulfill the request. Since the Security™ is placed in front of previously installed firewalls, the physical disconnection prevents outside access to the firewall itself (and anything behind it). If an intruder cannot access the firewall, he/she cannot break it.

The Security™ provides complete protection to hardware unsecured by firewall. Moreover, it closes the hardware vulnerability gap of existing firewalls by breaking the network connection physically and seamlessly to the user.

Hardware Specifications

The Security™ is a hardware security device—a micro gateway component on the network connection. It consists of:

- Chasis
- AC Power Supply
- Circuit Board
- Activation Switch
- Input and Output (for data transfer wiring)
- LEDs

Functionality

The Security™ provides the following functions and customizable options:

- Automatic Activation
- Artificial Intelligence Infrastructure
- Adjustable Re-connection Timer
- Signal Recognition
- Stand Alone Micro Gateway

- Category 5, Modular and 75-ohm coaxial cable compatibility
- Fingerprint Technology Option
- Remote Access Option

Features

The above Security™ specifications and functionality encompass a number of considerable features:

- Security™ will protect:
  –Privacy of personal information and correspondence
  –Financial information
  –Medical records
  –Proprietary business information
  –All levels of users
- Security™ is compatible with all existing firewalls
- Security™ gives the user complete control of their networking (LAN) and Internet use
- Security™ provides the user with bulletproof privacy
- Security™ prevents unauthorized server access and information transfer without interfering with e-mail
- Security™ supports multiple connectivity infrastructures, including "always on" broadband, dial-up, wireless, and satellite-connected computers
- Artificial Intelligence Infrastructure provides for background functioning and seamlessness for the user. It notifies the user of browser inactivity and enables Automatic Activation within an adjustable time frame
- Security™ stops intruders from accessing the computer system, including hardware, software, and data
- Optional Fingerprint Technology protects the computer/network from local unauthorized access
- Easily customizable interface puts the user in control of activated security level
- Security™ monitors all inbound and outbound traffic to detect unauthorized intruders
- Optional Remote Access provides Security™ security functionality from virtually anywhere

Security™ Product Line

The Security™ product line supports both high-speed and dial-up connections, as well as wireless access. The different models comprising the company's Security™ product line are distinguished based on type of connectivity they support. Safety Net Canada will support every type of Internet and network connectivity—dial-up access and "always on" high-speed connections through high-speed modems, cable, and Ethernet cards, as well as wireless access. (The Security™ product mix is broken down by type of connectivity later on in the plan.)

Security™ Models

Security™ 1000 (External)	Modular Line	High technology security device designed for dial-up connections.
Security™ 2000 (External)	Category 5	High technology security device designed for "always on" connection such as RHDSL, SDSL, DSL, ADSL, Cable Modem, and Fiber Optic.
Security™ 3000 (Internal—self-installation)	Category 5	High technology security device designed for "always on" connection such as ADSL, Cable Modem, and Fiber Optic. This self-installation device takes a 5.25 slot in front and a regular slot at the back of your computer.
Security™ 4000 (Internal—built-in)	Category 5	This specific product will be licensed out to different computer manufacturers such as Compaq, Gateway, Hewlett Packard, IBM, etc. This model will be licensed out to Cable and ADSL Modem Manufacturers and also to Ethernet Networking Card Manufacturers.
Security™ 5000 (Internal)	USB	Designed for USB Modems. Meets and exceeds 300bits per second.

Security Guard™

The Security Guard™ is an anti-virus and firewall software program that complements the Security™ to create a comprehensive and unbreakable security solution for corporate networks and the home computer. The Security Guard™ will be bundled with Security™ devices that are sold through the industry distribution and re-seller networks. With the addition of these software applications, Safety Net Canada's Security™ becomes a reliable and seamless solution to the end-user security problem.

Accomplishments to Date

Initial design, prototype development, and testing of all hardware and software products in the Safety Net Canada flagship product line (Security™ 1000, 2000, 3000, and Security Guard™) have been completed. The company is currently involved in the final phase of design and testing of the final Security™ and Security Guard™ products. The projected release date for the Security™ line of products, including the Security Guard™ firewall and anti-virus software components, is scheduled to be available for distribution and sale by the end of Q1 2001. The e-commerce website and other marketing and sales strategies are under development and negotiations are underway to secure strategic partnerships with manufacturers and distributors.

Future Products

To maintain its leadership in the Internet and network security market, Safety Net Canada will continually improve its products and services in order to reflect and meet the needs of the dynamic and constantly changing hi-tech industry. Safety Net Canada's product mix will be an area of continuous multi-dimensional expansion, with new products developed in all four areas of network security and new technologies integrated into the existing product line.

Wireless Accessibility

Safety Net Canada has finished preliminary conceptualization of a wireless accessory to the Security™ device. Users of any Security™ desktop model will have the ability to communicate to their desktop (or corporate LAN) via a wireless access device. The wireless accessory will incorporate into a wireless access device (such as a cell phone or a handheld) seamlessly to the user.

Encryption and Access Control

Currently, research and development is focused on technologies in all four areas of network security, which can be successfully integrated with Safety Net Canada's existing product mix. Fingerprint authentication and encryption protection, as well as optical scanning technology are the fields of future development and product integration with Safety Net Canada's existing product line. Safety Net Canada is currently evaluating potential partnerships and product development opportunities with existing anti-virus software companies to expand the Security Guard™ component of its existing product line.

Satellite Scrambler Shield

Safety Net Canada plans to expand its Security™ product line to include a satellite scrambler shield device that protects satellite-connected computers from security vulnerabilities. Preliminary conceptual designs for the satellite scrambler shield are currently being generated.

Manufacturing

The manufacturing cost associated with producing the Security™ product line is competitive and low. This cost structure combined with the ownership of an exclusive patent-pending status provides for an optimal profit maximization environment for an extended period of time (14 years under the technology patent). Safety Net Canada is currently investigating potential manufacturers for the company's Security™ hardware devices. Criteria in selecting a suitable manufacturer include:

- Access to inputs at competitive prices
- Manufacturing capacity
- Delivery network
- Production time

Service and Support

Safety Net Canada will outsource the development of a highly secure, scalable, database-driven e-commerce website as part of its high-quality, streamlined Customer Relationship Management (CRM) program. The site will be capable of supporting high-volume sales and will provide 24/7/365 support for a worldwide customer base. All online sales will be fully integrated with the manufacturing and fulfillment processes for seamless sales processing and inventory management.

Online Sales

Direct credit card sales of the complete Security™ line of products (bundled with the Security Guard™ firewall and anti-virus software) will be available to retail customers. Customers will have a choice of delivery options, such as delivery times and shipping methods. An international and reliable shipping company (such as FedEx) will be chosen to deliver Safety Net Canada's products to customers worldwide.

Product Registration

Through the website, customers will be able to register Safety Net Canada products upon purchase. Product registration will be the basis for customer tracking, support, and warranty service, as well as marketing.

Customer Support

Safety Net Canada Technology and Customer Support Center

This area of the website will be the central gateway for technical support to all customers of Safety Net Canada. It will provide account management support to corporate and retail customers. Implementation of single customer touch points will provide for superior long-term customer service. Unique customer IDs will be assigned to customers with registered Safety Net Canada products. The company will provide lifetime technical support to registered customers, with unique customers instantly identified through querying the customer database and seamless support provided via all means of communication (e.g. phone, e-mail, etc.).

General Support

This area will contain a product knowledge library, including FAQ, technical documentation and security issues and resolutions. In addition, the company's sales and support staff will receive general enquiries about Safety Net Canada products and additional product information (i.e., brochures). These requests will be processed via e-mail and potential clients recorded in the database. This area will also feature firmware configuration and installation instructions, as well as product updates and upgrades.

Warranty Service

A warranty service link will provide initiation of warranty service, generation of warranty tracking, and shipping instructions.

Intellectual Property

The company's Security™ technology process is protected by an exclusive patent-pending status that gives Safety Net Canada a worldwide advantage. The Security™ has an approved methodology patent pending in North America and a Patent Co-operation Treaty (PCT) applied. The PCT approval will provide the company with exclusive proprietary rights to the Security™ technology in more than 90 countries. Under these intellectual property agreements, no other business or entity can legally create or imitate the Security™ security device. Safety Net Canada maintains the privilege and power to sell manufacturing rights for a profit.

MARKET ANALYSIS

Global Need for Security

Vulnerability Factors and Risks

Internet Adoption

The *Computer Industry Almanac* predicts that the number of Internet users worldwide will grow to 766 million in 2005, more than double the online population in 2000. Internet adoption is largely saturated in North America, with the user base approaching 42% of the total North American population and 43% of the total online population worldwide. Most of the future growth of the Internet is predicted to take place overseas, with European users accounting for 30% and Asia-Pacific representing 25% of total worldwide users.

E-Commerce Growth

Increasing use of the Internet is beneficial to e-commerce and more businesses are migrating online to boost revenues and lower costs. While Internet adoption will grow overseas, e-commerce revenues will remain largely within the United States and amount to more than US $1.3 trillion worldwide by 2003. The business-to-business (B2B) sector is expected to contribute more than 85 percent of total global e-commerce revenue and add up to US $1.1 trillion in 2003. The business-to-consumer (B2C) sector will more than double and total US $178 billion in 2003.

In their Global Security Survey for 1999, PriceWaterhouseCoopers and *Information Week* report that e-commerce companies are one of the most vulnerable targets for security breaches. Compared to businesses that do not sell over the Internet, e-commerce companies are more pre-disposed to information and revenue loss as a result of security intrusions.

E-Commerce Firms at Higher Risk

Result of Security Breach	Firm Sells Online	No Online Sales
Information loss	22%	13%
Theft of data/trade secrets	12%	4%
Revenue loss	7%	1%

Broadband Adoption

Broadband access is expected to become one of the most explosive segments of the online economy as Internet users are starting to prefer the faster and reliable cable and DSL services to the slower and inconsistent dial-up connections. Worldwide broadband access will grow to 70 million high-speed Internet subscribers by the end of 2003. Broadband access is expected to grow from 14 percent to 40 percent of total Internet connections.

Broadband connections not only provide increased bandwidth to users but also establish a 24-hour-a-day connection to the Internet. A Forrester Research survey of high-speed Internet subscribers confirms that constant connectivity and faster download are the top reasons for choosing broadband access. However, these two features of high-speed Internet access expose users to the serious threat of security attacks. Constant connection and broader bandwidth increase the idle time for which a computer is connected to the Internet and, thus, open the door to intruder attacks.

Escalating Security Concerns

Explosive adoption of the Internet and e-commerce, as well as rapid commercialization of faster access technologies worldwide, have resulted in increased awareness of the importance of information security tools. Numerous instances of corporate security breaches have not only resulted in vulnerability to security attacks but also caused large monetary and reputation damages to renowned online businesses. As the frequency and magnitude of security attacks climbs, consumers become more concerned about invasion of their privacy and grow averse to shopping and conducting other transactions over the Internet.

Security Breaches

Globally, the number of companies reporting security breaches has surged from 53 percent in 1998 to 64 percent in 1999 (Source: *Information Week* Global Security Survey). Among the 2,700 executives and corporate security managers polled by the survey, 48 percent report hackers and terrorists as the probable cause of the breach (up from 14 percent in 1998) and 41 percent name authorized employees as the likely intruder.

Security Intrusion Costs

The fifth annual survey of computer crime and security, conducted by the FBI and the San Francisco-based Computer Security Institute, polled 640 corporations, banks, and government organizations about the state of their computer systems. Of the 90 percent reporting a security breach, only 42 percent could quantify the damage from the attacks. Nonetheless, the dollar figure losses as a result of security intrusion in 1999 are more than double the average annual total over the previous two years.

While information theft and financial fraud are causing the most severe financial losses, US $60 million and $58 million respectively, denial of service or server downtime, such as the ones that temporarily paralyzed Yahoo!, eBay, Buy.com, and several other websites in February 2000, are also a growing problem. The survey, which reports on numbers taken before the high-profile February strikes, quantifies the losses from denial of service attacks climbing from only US $77,000 in 1998 to US $8.2 million by the end of 1999. Loss of customers and public relations damage control are some of the intangible costs companies incur in association with security breaches.

Consumer Concerns

According to the 2000 American Express Global Internet Survey, which polled 11,410 Internet users and non-users across ten countries, four out of five people (79% of respondents) cited security and privacy issues as a concern when purchasing or making financial transactions online. A poll from Gallup and @Plan, taken shortly after the February denial of service attacks on major websites, reports that over 70 percent of online shoppers are concerned about privacy on the Internet in light of the attacks. The survey reveals that over 30 percent of online shoppers will be less likely to buy from e-commerce sites in the future and 85 percent of the respondents have privacy as their main concern regarding the Internet.

Security Market Overview

Industry Description and Size

The Internet and network security industry is a rapidly growing segment of the high-tech business sector, as businesses and individual consumers become more aware of the security threats caused by conducting transaction and exchanging information in a networked environment. Internet and network security is currently a US $5 billion business, growing two-fold from its 1998 level of US $2.3 billion. North America and Western Europe account for 84 percent of all 1999 network security sales, with North America at more than two thirds of total sales worldwide. Network security sales revenue is expected to grow even faster over the next three years, as Internet and broadband adoption, as well as e-commerce, continue expanding worldwide.

Growth Forecast

Security is not just for insurance purposes anymore but is an important part of corporate policy and strategy. The Internet is a source for increased profitability and companies need sophisticated security solutions to expand trusted relationships with their customers, partners, suppliers, and channels. This need is the vehicle of the network security market. According to IDC, its worldwide revenue will jump from less than $4 billion in 1999 to more than $11 billion in 2004.

IDC predicts that Authentication, Authorization, and Administration (3A) technology will be the leading sub-segments behind this industry growth. 3A technology is the largest segment of the network security industry and accounts for US $2.1 billion of total 1999 market revenues. IDC estimates that it will also be the fastest growing segment, at a compound annual growth rate (CAGR) of 28 percent from 1999 to 2004. The next nearest segments—firewall and anti-virus technologies—will each increase at CAGRs of 17 percent.

Safety Net Canada will take advantage of the vast profit and market share potential in the industry by being the first-to-market supplier of a complete network and Internet security solution to corporate and individual clients.

Industry Dynamics

There are more than 50 public companies operating in the network security industry. A growing industry and a large revenue potential indicate the presence of hundreds of other industry players—private companies involved in the development of new security technologies and products.

The industry is relatively fragmented and moving toward consolidation, as major players in the market are expanding into niche markets of the network security industry and rapidly gaining market share. Consolidation is expected to take two forms: research and development purchases for faster access to niche markets and diversification of revenue streams, and vertical integration through partnerships with software vendors (e.g., bundling with browsers and other software packages).

Regardless of consolidation trends, the network security industry will continue growing and attracting new participants within the next few years. The high revenue potential will provide for a competitive climate without an indication of market saturation in the short- to medium-term.

Distribution Channels

The network security industry has an established distribution network incorporating three main channels: distributors and re-sellers, licensing, and direct sales. Network security product manufacturers use these channels individually or in a combination depending on the product. Safety Net Canada intends to use an applicable combination of distribution channels for its network security products in order to reach a larger customer base and build market share.

Distributors and Re-sellers
Large computer components wholesalers, such as TechData (NASD:TECD) and Ingram Micro (NYSE:IM) are major distributors of network security hardware appliances and software products. These specific distributors deliver products to hundreds of thousands of re-sellers and reach customers in more than fifty countries worldwide. Safety Net Canada will investigate potential opportunities with a major computer components distributor in order to rapidly and efficiently rollout its products worldwide. Re-seller connectivity, global outreach and wholesale price will be among the top considerations in choosing a distributor.

Licensing
Licensing through Original Equipment Manufacturer (OEM) partnerships is a premiere distribution channel for security software products. Some hardware appliances are also licensed out and sold through network equipment manufacturers. Safety Net Canada will license its line of network security solutions to hardware and software manufacturers in order to reach the small business and home user market segments.

Direct Sales
Most manufacturers of network security products employ a full-service direct sales and support force to distribute their products, since a large portion of their revenue streams (in some cases up to 70%) is captured via support services. Direct sales channels usually comprise both an offline and an online channel, with most companies in the industry offering real-time 24/7/365 support and fully functional e-commerce websites.

Safety Net Canada will build an aggressive direct sales force in order to secure the enterprise target segment. The company will implement a complete total quality Customer Relationship Management (CRM) technical support program in order to build a loyal enterprise client base.

Target Markets

Safety Net Canada identifies the following four target market segments for its Security™ line of network security products.

1. Government and Non-Profit Organizations
Government agencies are a particularly lucrative market for the information security industry since they are major directories of highly sensitive information from personal data to military technology. A congressional subcommittee investigating the ability of federal agencies to protect computer systems from terrorists and hackers recently released a report card on

government information security practices. Not one federal agency received an A, and the overall grade for the largest federal agencies and departments was D-minus. In response to these facts, the current administration is seeking $2 billion for information security in next year's budget, a 15 percent increase.

The Government is one of the largest spenders in the economy and Safety Net Canada will take advantage of the opportunity presented by detected vulnerabilities of government information systems. The company will aggressively market its budget-conscious Security™ security solution to all levels of government administration and non-profit organizations in order to capitalize on this vast revenue opportunity.

2. Large Corporations

Enterprise customers are a high priority target market for the network security industry since a substantial volume of sensitive information and e-commerce transactions is exchanged over corporate networks and the Internet daily. Large corporations over 10,000 employees are expected to be top network security spenders, with security budgets increasing proportionately to company sizes.

Safety Net Canada will respond to the growing needs for security of larger corporations by providing a complete security solution, resistant to hacker attacks and internal security breaches.

3. Small and Medium Enterprises (SMEs)

SMEs are the primary market for cost-efficient high-speed Internet access. Growing broadband adoption among SMEs indicates increased vulnerability to security attacks of this market segment. As businesses become more exposed to networking and the Internet, they become a substantial target market for the network and Internet security industry.

U.S. Business Broadband Users 1999-2003 (Millions)

	1999	**2000**	**2001**	**2002**	**2003**
Fiber	1.71	2.36	3.15	4.07	5.07
DSL	0.15	0.42	0.73	0.93	1.1
Cable	NA	NA	NA	NA	NA
Satellite	NA	NA	0.02	0.04	0.25
Wireless	0.04	0.15	0.57	1.59	3.09
Copper T-1	1.6	1.9	2	1.9	1.8
Total	**3.49**	**4.83**	**6.47**	**8.53**	**11.3**

Safety Net Canada will target SMEs by offering "easy to install and use" and complete network security products at reasonable prices.

4. Individual Home Computing

Broadband adoption among home users will grow even faster than business users, with residential subscribers reaching 20.73 million across all broadband channels.

U.S. Residential Broadband Users 1999-2003 (Millions)

	1999	2000	2001	2002	2003
Fiber	0.05	0.1	0.17	0.24	0.32
DSL	0.39	1.42	3.35	5.69	9.85
Cable	1.47	2.94	4.99	7.27	9.78
Satellite	NA	NA	NA	NA	NA
Wireless	0.02	0.08	0.24	0.53	0.77
Copper T-1	NA	NA	NA	NA	NA
Total	**1.94**	**4.54**	**8.75**	**13.73**	**20.73**

Another trend in residential Internet access is the development and commercialization of home-based local area networks (LANs). The growth of home LANs is being driven both by multi-PC households and by high-speed Internet access. By 2004, 67.7 million American homes (63.4%) will have PCs, with 30.4 million of these housing more than one. Of the multi-PC households, 58 percent will be networking their devices by 2004.

Increased residential broadband access and a growing number of home-based LANs create a substantial security threat to home users. Safety Net Canada intends to aggressively target this segment in order to secure market share and realize the revenue potential offered by the home user market.

Buyer Trends

International Broadband Adoption

Western Europe will mirror the U.S. broadband industry development, with European high-speed Internet subscribers reaching 18 percent of households (or 27 million) from a minute 0.2 percent of households in 1999. Scandinavia and the Netherlands, with their traditionally high penetration rates, will take the lead with Germany and the United Kingdom following closely.

Another booming region for the broadband industry is Asia-Pacific. The number of broadband subscribers in the Asia-Pacific region is predicted to surge from 452,900 at year-end 1999 to 11.3 million by the end of 2003. Cable modem and ASDL will be the most popular forms of access, taking 46 percent and 42 percent of the market respectively by year-end 2003. Competing broadband providers across the region are focusing on SMEs and home offices as an entry strategy into this market. Further commercialization of broadband services will lead to increased competition, as international companies, such as Global Crossing and Level 3, have launched their services into the market.

Preferences for Security Solutions

Corporations would like to have one network security package that solves all of their security needs including:

Products that employ all 4 areas of network security:

- User ID/Authentication
- Encryption
- Access Control and Privilege Management
- Administration and Audit

Products that meet the following criteria:

- Ease-of-use
- Interoperability
- Scalability

- Ease of administration
- Integration with existing customer applications
- System reliability and availability

Strategic Opportunities

The complexity of competing information and network solutions—both software and hardware-based—provides a significant opportunity to the company in marketing its complete, off-the-shelf, user-friendly network security solution. Safety Net Canada's Security™/ Security Guard™ product line provides a high-level of reliability and matches client requirements for compatibility and ease-of-use.

Safety Net Canada will be the first mover in providing an all-inclusive security solution, incorporating all four segments of the network and Internet security industry. The current level of dial-up accessibility (more than 80% of Internet subscribers in 2000) will allow for quick market penetration of the Security™ 1000 model and rapidly growing market share and revenue for Safety Net Canada. Beneficial broadband adoption trends will ensure success for the company's Security™ 2000 and 3000 models, with market share and revenue increasing in parallel to the popularization of high-speed access.

Environmental Issues

Trends in most exogenous market variables, applicable to Safety Net Canada's business model, will have a positive impact on the company. Technology developments, social attitudes, and regulation are the external market factors that will potentially influence the development and success of Safety Net Canada.

Technology Development
The hi-tech industry is subject to constant fluctuations, as the life cycle of technology is short and it becomes obsolete every 18 months. Safety Net Canada welcomes the challenges of rapidly evolving technology and, through utilizing its strategic partners and internal team of tech-savvy and innovative individuals, the company will become a trendsetter for new technology adoption and implementation.

Social Attitudes toward Security
As more people become connected through computer networks and the Internet, security concerns are inevitably on the rise. This would only benefit the company in the long term, as the team of Safety Net Canada is dedicated to continue innovating and bringing the best security products and services to the wired (and wireless) population.

Regulatory Issues
Strictly enforced information security standards could become an obstacle for vendors of software applications (firewall and anti-virus software). For Safety Net Canada, such standards would only encourage sales of the Security™ product line, since it is highly reliable and independent of any hardware and/or software platform.

MARKETING PLAN

Marketing Objectives

Building a strong corporate and retail customer base and developing a high industry image and profile are corporate-level objectives subject to the company's marketing and promotional efforts. Each of these goals will be pursued and achieved through the implementation of an array of marketing and promotional actions geared towards fulfilling the directives of Safety Net Canada's marketing plan.

Build Customer Base

Building a loyal customer base of corporate and retail clients involves implementation of the following strategic marketing actions:

- Implement an effective and competitive product mix strategy to successfully position the Security™ product line as the leading Internet and network security solution on the market.
- Development of an e-commerce website with well-documented and displayed inventory and effective, efficient, and hassle-free retail and corporate service and support.
- Aggressive advertising in print and electronic media to create brand awareness and educate the public of the risks associated with broadband access and incomplete corporate security solutions.
- Sales strategies implementation including reseller networks, affiliate programs, corporate sales development, and direct marketing campaigns (including co-marketing).
- Exhibiting at business and computer industry conferences and trade shows and high-visibility consumer home and computer shows.

Develop a High Industry Profile

The company recognizes the importance of developing and maintaining a prominent place and a positive image in the Internet and network security community in order to sustain credibility, attract the highest quality of strategic partnerships and alliances, and position the company for successful execution of its exit strategy. Safety Net Canada's brand and image will positively benefit from:

- Publicity through news releases and announcements
- Participation in industry trade shows
- Membership and active participation in industry associations, initiatives, and studies

Security Marketing Mix

The Security™ marketing mix features competitive pricing, mass customized packaging, and creative distribution and promotional tactics to guarantee target market reach and revenue growth.

Flagship Product Line

The Security™ flagship product line comprises the Security™ 1000, 2000, and 3000 models, complemented by the Security Guard™ software. These three models meet the security needs of an established (dial-up) and a growing (broadband) market, which will allow Safety Net Canada to acquire market share in the current market and grow its market presence in the future.

Product Pricing

The Security™ product line is competitively priced at US $110 at the retail level. Distributor price is set at US $45.

Product Packaging

Safety Net Canada will employ separate product packaging strategies for its two general groups of customers:

- **Corporate Users**—Default packaging for corporate users will exclude the Security Guard™ from the product bundle. The rationale behind this is that most corporate users have already installed firewall and anti-virus software solutions on their corporate network. The Security™ can match corporate users' requirement for compatibility by seamlessly integrating into existing security software applications.

- **Small Business and Home Users**—A large number of home and small business users do not have anti-virus and firewall applications on their computers. Therefore, small business and home users will be provided with the Security™ device and the Security Guard™ as a bundled package. This form of packaging offers to the target customer group of home and small business users a unified, plug-and-play security solution that solves all incompatibility and vulnerability problems.

Product Sales Strategy

Safety Net Canada will incorporate a combination of distribution channels in order to pursue an aggressive and effective product sales strategy. Safety Net Canada considers the integration of direct sales and industry distribution as the fastest and most cost-efficient approach to penetrating the Internet and network security market. In order to generate superior sales results and meet unit and dollar sales targets, Safety Net Canada will provide special sales training programs to intermediaries and sales incentives to the direct sales force.

Industry Distribution Channel—70%

Safety Net Canada will gain access to a robust worldwide distribution network via partnering with international distributor of computer components. Prices to intermediaries afford them reasonable profits that will encourage intermediary flexibility. The Security™ 1000 and 2000 external devices, supplemented with the Security Guard™ software applications will be distributed primarily through this channel. Through the OEM manufacturing license agreements, Safety Net Canada will gain access to the international distribution network of a large hardware manufacturer. This industry distribution channel is best suited for the Security™ 3000 internal device with the corresponding version of the Security Guard™.

Direct Sales—30%

Direct sales will account for 30 percent of total Security™ sales and will be administered through the e-commerce website and by the Safety Net Canada direct sales force. The direct sales channel will accommodate management of most corporate accounts and large corporation purchases. All three flagship models of the Security™ device will be sold directly, with the option of adding the Security Guard™ software.

Advertising and Promotion

Safety Net Canada will utilize an abundant assortment of online and offline advertising and promotion tactics to build a solid global brand name and establish a high corporate profile in the technology industry.

Online Marketing

A comprehensive and consistent online marketing campaign is crucial to any company in the technology sector. Creating a robust, multi-functional, easy-to-use, and appealing website is a vital component of a successful online marketing program. Driving traffic to the website and closing the sale online are fundamental to securing the corresponding revenue stream.

Safety Net Canada E-Commerce website

The company will contract a team of professional web developers to build its e-commerce website. Anticipated features and components of the site include:

- Product presentations and technical information
- Library of knowledge on Internet and network security, including latest industry and technology news
- Multi-level technical support 24/7/365, with password-protected areas for large clients, partners, and affiliates

- Fully-functional e-commerce and inventory control back-end, supporting worldwide demand for Safety Net Canada products

Driving Traffic

This will be accomplished by a variety of online marketing tactics, with a portion of the advertising budget allocated but not limited to:

- **Search Engine Registration**—The company will register with top search engines using selected keywords (meta tags), such as security, anti-virus, firewall, etc.
- **Banners and Buttons**—The company will investigate link and banner exchange options compatible with Safety Net Canada. In addition to affiliate website advertisements, button and banner ads will be placed on selected hardware, network security, and other industry-related websites.
- **E-zines**—The targeting capabilities of e-mail newsletters, or e-zines, transform this into one of the best marketing tools that the Internet offers. The newsletter for Safety Net Canada will notify registered members of new and upcoming product updates and upgrades and keep in touch with the opt-in client community. Safety Net Canada will be featured in the top independent e-zines currently on the Internet. The company will feature in e-zines geared towards MIS and IT managers and corporate network professionals.
- **E-mail Marketing**—The success rate of opt-in e-mail broadcasts is approximately 17 percent (quite high for any form of direct marketing). The purchase or acquisition of targeted consumer lists, as well as targeted e-mail harvesting, will be used to source out prospects in lieu of Safety Net Canada's direct sales strategy. The company will use only targeted lists and e-mails to eliminate spam.

Offline Promotion

Complementary to its online marketing program, Safety Net Canada will employ a number of offline advertising and promotional actions to publicize the brand name, attract re-sellers, and reach customers. Safety Net Canada will promote itself through the following specific offline media:

Trade Shows

Safety Net Canada will lease exhibition space at some of the largest and most popular hi-tech industry trade show events. The following annual, nationwide hi-tech, and information security events will be considered as potential venues: Comdex, InfoSec World, and Annual Computer Security Conference and Exhibition (Computer Security Institute). These specific trade shows attract a large number of information security exhibitors, as well as a mass of wholesale and retail customers.

Print Publications

Much like e-zines, offline magazines dedicated to information security will be carefully chosen to promote Safety Net Canada. The rationale is that online and offline media combined reach a larger customer base than each medium separately.

Public Relations

A successful public relations campaign requires a close partnership with the media. Safety Net Canada will seek allies among publishers and columnists and will use website reviews and news releases as vital promotional techniques. Promotional channels to be considered include technology television and radio shows, publications for IT professionals, etc.

Target Market Penetration

The Security™/Security Guard™ product line will be rolled out into all four target market segments simultaneously. Different blends of distribution channels and marketing techniques will be used to reach the various market segments.

Large Organizations
This target segment encompasses large corporations, government agencies, and non-profit organizations. Safety Net Canada will market to this target segment through both the distribution network and direct sales channel. Trade events and online corporate account management will be the tools for reaching this market.

Small Business Customers
Small businesses are the fastest organizational units adopting broadband Internet access. The need for high-speed access echoes a need for better security solutions and Safety Net Canada will match this requirement by reaching small enterprises primarily via the industry distribution network. Print publications, trade shows, and opt-in e-mails are among the techniques the company will use to market its products to small businesses.

Home Users
Strategic banner advertising and advertising through distribution intermediaries will be used to attract home users. Home users will be provided with an off-the-shelf, easy-to-install and use, and complete security solution. Safety Net Canada products will be sold to home users predominantly through the intermediary distribution networks.

Global Rollout Strategy

Safety Net Canada will build its market share by gradually entering all major international markets by the end of the planning period subject to this plan. While all products will be available worldwide through the Safety Net Canada website, initial marketing and reseller network building will be focused on North America. The United States and Canada will be the opening markets for the Security™/Security Guard™ product line. Within six months of North American market entry, the company will move quickly towards entering Asia. Hong Kong will be the entry point for China and Asia overall, with the Korean, Taiwanese, and Japanese markets penetrated by the end of year two. Initial entry into Europe will also commence in year two, with the United Kingdom being the entry point. By the end of year three, Safety Net Canada expects to have a substantial market share in all of North America, Asia, Europe, and Latin America.

COMPETITION

Competitive Climate

As the Internet and network security industry is projected to grow, the competitive environment will become more heated. Competition will ensue from both incumbent companies and new entrants. Established technologies, such as firewall software, will be subject to downward price pressure and low-cost competition. The competitive rules for newer information security technologies, such as Gap technology appliances, will continue to be derived from product innovation rivalry and differentiation.

Direct Competition

Safety Net Canada has no close direct competitors for its complete Security™/Security Guard™ security solution. None of the company's industry rivals offers a software- and hardware-integrated, off-the-shelf, and easy-to-use security product.

Indirect Competition

There are indirect competitors to individual components of Safety Net Canada's product line. Indirect competitors are classified according to type of security product and described below. Safety Net Canada's differentiators are explained after each competitor classification group.

Gap Technology Devices

Gap technology allows for a physical "disconnection" between two logically connected networks. The physical disconnection prevents security intrusion while the logical connection allows the two networks to share resources. (A discussion on Gap Technology is located in the Exhibits). Most Gap Technology devices are designed for protection of the internal corporate network. The key players in this industry segment are described below.

Market Central Switch

Switch is the core product in Market Central's suite of security offerings. It is a network switcher in its most straightforward implementation. It is designed similar to the common keyboard/video/mouse (KVM) switches, except that it deals exclusively with network connections.

Switch has two knobs on the front connected by a crossbar that forces them to be turned simultaneously. The rear of the switch has four Ethernet outlets, two for each network the user wishes to connect to. The host PC must have two network interfaces to allow it to connect to the two networks. The network cables from the PC's interfaces are connected to the network interface card (NIC) ports on the switch, leaving the other two connections for the individual LAN cables. The network cards should be attached to the same side of the switch as their corresponding LAN cables, to ensure that there is no accidental crossover. Once the four cables are attached correctly, the user must turn either knob to switch from network "A" to network "B" (hence the crossbar). The flagship SecureSwitch™ costs US $399 to the consumer.

Beyond the basic network-switching model, the user can upgrade Switch to include keyboard/video/mouse-switching capabilities for a fee. In this case, all services switch at once. This allows the use of two workstations with a single keyboard, monitor, and mouse. When one system is active (and on the network), the other is not. The retail price of the Switch is US $528.

The next step up is the Switch Information Security System, which is designed to limit and log access to restricted systems. It does this via a hardware token, which must be presented before network connectivity or AC power is enabled on the PC. This allows administrators to grant access to a system while limiting some users to "offline" work if network privileges are not included.

Exhibits

Market Central also sells Data Bolts (US $59), simple and inexpensive switches meant to disconnect your local LAN when you connect to the Internet.

Differentiator: While Market Central's Switch allows for physical disconnection between desktop and network or two networks, it requires manual intervention from the user every time the connection needs to be broken or re-established. Safety Net Canada's Security™ is seamless to the user and is more cost-effective compared to Switch, retailing at $110 and $399 respectively.

RVT Stop-IT®

RVT Technologies is a Lilburn, Georgia, based company producing the Stop-IT® Internet and network security solution. The Stop-IT® product line functions on the principles of gap technology and currently consists of two form factors: one is an internal PC card and the second is an external device that is situated in front of the modem. Both devices intercept incoming network traffic before it reaches the personal computer and monitor it based on an internally stored signature.

The target market for Stop-IT® is ADSL and cable modem users, who are continuously connected to the Internet. Stop-IT® is a single-user device, and employs an upgradeable EPROM to store its virus signature library. It makes use of an optical isolator to introduce the air gap as required. Any information that is sent to the PC must pass through the device, where it is scanned before it reaches the system. If any of the data matches any virus signature, the light signal is cut, and the data is dropped. The signal is automatically resumed once the identified threat ends, causing minimal disruption to the end user.

Differentiator: Although within the price range of the Security™ models, RVT Stop-IT® is essentially a sophisticated virus filtering hardware card. RVT Technologies has scheduled product launch for the Stop-IT® line to commence in January 2001. The Stop-IT® product line will not offer the high level of protection of Safety Net Canada's Security™ line.

Whale Communications

Whale Communications is a privately-held New Jersey company that manufactures Shuttle—a hardware device that is placed between two endpoint servers, creating an air gap. The servers are on different networks that are not otherwise connected. Each server is configured to be the gateway from its network to the other, funneling all inter-network traffic through the gap. Shuttle is a non-programmable unit consisting of an analog switch and a SCSI-based memory bank. The switch is designed to connect to one or the other host, but never both. It uses short-circuit detection to ensure that it is functioning as designed. The function is to connect to one network, read any awaiting information, switch over, and push the data onto the second network. It alternates between the networks at speeds that allow a theoretical transfer rate of 130 Mbps. The system is comprised of the appliance and two PC hosts—one external and one internal.

Differentiator: Although Whale Communications claims that the system provides bulletproof security, it does not protect against denial-of-service attacks, configuration errors, internal attacks, or fraudulent transactions. It must be used in conjunction with other measures (such as firewalls and internal access authorization policies) in order to provide 100 percent security. The cost is US $43,000.

SpearHead Technologies Ltd.

Privately-held, SpearHead Technologies Ltd. is an Israel-based network security company manufacturing and distributing the AirGAP hardware device. Similar to AirGAP is a hardware network appliance that shuttles data between two mutually exclusive connections. However, whereas e-Gap™ is designed to connect (or disconnect) two machines, AirGAP is meant to connect two full-scale networks.

The AirGAP solution is a combination of hardware and software that comes in three models: AG100, AG200, and AG300. The hardware component contains three controllers: a master, a slave, and a content-inspection board. The gap lies between the slave and the content-inspection board, and there is no live session between the two networks at any given time.

With a hardware speed of 800 Mbps, the AG300 can sustain an average user base of about 5,000 to 10,000 (or about 1,000 concurrent sessions). The AG100 can handle smaller workgroups of approximately 1,000 users.

Differentiator: While AirGap security appliances can protect stand-alone personal computers, they are too expensive to appeal to the general consumer market. Safety Net Canada will target the corporate market segment by providing an exceptionally cost-effective and bulletproof corporate PC security solution.

Hardware Firewall Appliances

Hardware firewalls are the predecessor Gap Technology devices. There are two key players in the hardware security appliances industry segment, with their products geared towards different buyer segments.

WatchGuard Technologies Firebox

Founded in 1996, WatchGuard Technologies produces the Firebox—a hardware based network security appliance. The Firebox product line caters to corporate users including small business and large corporations. WatchGuard's enterprise products start at $4,990 to a high of $12,990. For the SOHO user (small office/home office), the base cost of WatchGuard (10 users) is $449 to a high of $1,000 for 50 users and an additional $449 to include the virtual private network (VPN) option. Other products include the WatchGuard VPN Manager at $995 for up to 4 Fireboxes to $7,005 for unlimited Fireboxes.

Cisco Secure PIX Firewall

The Cisco Secure PIX Firewall is the dedicated firewall appliance in Cisco's firewall family and holds the top ranking in both market share and performance. The Cisco Secure PIX Firewall delivers strong security and creates little to no network performance impact. The product line enforces secure access between an internal network and Internet, extranet, or intranet links. The Cisco Secure PIX Firewall scales to meet a range of customer requirements and network sizes and currently consists of four models:

1. The new Cisco Secure PIX 525 is the latest and largest addition to the PIX 500 series and is intended for Enterprise and Service Provider use. It has a throughput of 370 Mbps with the ability to handle as many as 280,000 simultaneous sessions. The 600 MHz CPU of the PIX 525 can enable it to deliver an additional 25-30 percent increase capacity for firewall services.
2. Cisco Secure PIX 520 is intended for large enterprise organizations and complex, high-end traffic environments. It also has a throughput of up to 370 Mbps with the ability to handle 250,000 simultaneous sessions.
3. Cisco Secure PIX 515 is intended for Small/Medium Businesses and remote office deployments and has throughput measured at 120 Mbps with the ability to handle up to 125,000 simultaneous sessions.
4. Cisco Secure PIX 506 is intended for high-end Small Office/Home Office organizations and has throughput measured at 10 Mbps (3DES of 7 Mbps).

All four Cisco Secure PIX Firewall models have IPSEC encryption built-in, permitting both site-to-site and remote access VPN deployments, and operate on a hardened operating system focused on protecting both the security of the device and the networks it protects. In addition to having the ability to be managed by the PIX Configuration Manager, the Cisco Secure PIX Firewalls also may be centrally managed by the Cisco Secure Policy Manager, which can manage up to 500 PIX Firewalls, Cisco Secure Integrated Software deployments, and site-to-site VPN installations.

As a dedicated appliance, the Cisco Secure PIX Firewall is easy to install and stable. The average price for this product line is approximately US $8,000.

Differentiator: Hardware firewall appliance manufacturers are not outfitted to respond to the needs of the small business/individual user. These are expensive server protection devices that are targeted at large corporate networks. Safety Net Canada will protect the desktop within the corporate network.

Firewall and Anti-Virus Software

The firewall and anti-virus software segment of the industry is highly competitive. There are more than 50 public and hundreds more private companies producing information security software. The top four players (all of them are public enterprises) and their security products are described below.

Symantec Norton Anti-Virus and Firewall Software

Symantec is a Cupertino, California, based company with 2,600 employees worldwide. Symantec is the producer of the extensive Norton line of security products. The product mix includes an enterprise, a small business, and a home-user solution. The software has four main functions:

1. **Virus Protection**—Symantec's anti-virus solutions protect computers and networks at multiple entry points from known and unknown threats.
2. **Mobile Code Protection**—Symantec's mobile code solutions protect customers from the malicious attack by legitimate technologies such as Java applets, Active X controls, auto-executable plug-ins and push-clients which can be used to deny service to customers, modify data, steal passwords and files, or even redirect modem dial-ins without a user being aware they are running a program.
3. **E-Mail Content Filtering**—Symantec's e-mail content scanning and filtering solutions help protect proprietary information, reduces liability exposure, and improves productivity for e-mail applications.
4. **Internet Content Filtering**—Symantec's Internet content filtering and management allows individuals and organizations to control and focus Internet usage for increased productivity and decreased liability.

Network Associates McAfee VirusScan

Suitable for individual users, small businesses, and large companies, McAfee VirusScan is a virus detection and removal solution for a major source of infection: the desktop machine. VirusScan has a broad platform coverage (PC, Mac, Unix, and Wireless) and fits seamlessly into any networked environment, with a wide array of proactive manageability and visibility features, ensuring an effective virus security solution for users.

Check Point Software

Check Point Software, an Israel-headquartered developer of security software, produces FireWall-1—an enterprise firewall solution for large organizations.

The FireWall Module is deployed on Internet gateways and other network access points. The Management Server downloads the Security Policy to the FireWall Module, which protects the network. The FireWall Module can be installed on a broad range of operating system platforms (Windows NT, Solaris, HP-UX, and IBM AIX). The FireWall Module includes the Inspection Module and the FireWall-1 Security Servers. The Security Servers provide the following authentication and content security features:

- **Authentication**—The Security Servers provide authentication for users of FTP, HTTP, TELNET, and RLOGIN. If the Security Policy specifies authentication for any of these services, the Inspection Module diverts the connection to the appropriate Security Server. The Security Server performs the required authentication. If the authentication is successful, the connection proceeds to the target server.

- **Content Security**—Content Security is available for HTTP, FTP, and SMTP. The HTTP Security Server provides content security based on schemes (HTTP, FTP, GOPHER, etc.), methods (GET, POST, etc.), hosts (for example, "*.com"), paths, and queries. A file containing a list of IP addresses and paths to which access will be denied or allowed can be used. The FTP Security Server provides content security based on FTP commands (PUT/GET), file name restrictions, and anti-virus checking for files transferred. The SMTP Security Server provides content security based on "From" and "To" fields in the mail envelope and header and attachment types. In addition, it provides a secure send mail application that prevents direct online connection attacks. The SMTP Security Server also serves as an SMTP address translator, that is, it can hide real user names from the outside world by rewriting the "From" field, while maintaining connectivity by restoring the correct addresses in the response.

Differentiator: Unless used with additional devices and security monitoring, firewall and anti-virus software (although inexpensive) is insufficient in preventing security breaches from outside. Moreover, none of the existing security software applications can prevent insider security breaches—a major concern for organizations online. Safety Net Canada combines a hardware and software component to offer organizational and individual users an off-the-shelf, competitively priced product impervious to both insider and outsider attacks.

Competitive Advantage

Safety Net Canada's competitive advantage is two-dimensional. One aspect of it is the company's ability to differentiate its products, based on core competencies—innovation in product development and superior customer service. The second source of competitive advantage is cost-efficiency, with Safety Net Canada being the sole player in the Internet and network industry able to deliver a multi-faceted reliable security solution at nominal cost. Long-term sustainability will be achieved through continuous innovation and customer service improvement.

Barriers to Entry

Safety Net Canada intends to lock out competitors via employing the exclusive manufacturing rights to the Security™ technology worldwide. Utilizing alliances with large hardware OEMs will allow for rapid market penetration and raise the barriers for new entrants in the industry.

FINANCE

Revenue Streams

The revenue model of Safety Net Canada comprises a primary and a secondary revenue category, with each category containing multiple revenue streams.

Sales through Distributors

Revenue derived from distribution network sales contributes up to 70% of total revenue and is composed of:

- Security™ 1000 Sales—26% of distribution network revenue and 13.4% of total revenue from all channels
- Security™ 2000 Sales—35% of distribution network revenue and 20.3% of total revenue from al channels
- Security™ 3000 Sales—39% of distribution network revenue and 35.6% of total revenue from all channels

Direct Sales

Revenue derived through the direct sales channel comprises approximately 30% of total revenue and consists of:

- Security™ 1000 Sales—26% of direct sales revenue and 7.9% of total revenue from all channels
- Security™ 2000 Sales—35% of direct sales revenue and 10.9% of total revenue from all channels
- Security™ 3000 Sales—39% of direct sales revenue and 11.9% of total revenue from all channels

EXHIBITS

Information Security Products

Authentication Products

Authentication tools manage user, host, and message verification. Primary authentication technologies include:

Passwords

Most operating systems and software applications have built-in password functionality. Passwords can limit access and protect hardware devices (such as hard drives and printers), user accounts, files, corporate network data, etc. The disadvantage of passwords is that they can be deciphered or stolen if made available to outsiders.

Tokens

Tokens are computer-generated authentication tools (such as numeric or alphanumeric keys) that authorize access for the computer, as opposed to the individual. A considerable fault of tokens is their inability to protect the individual from internal security attacks (as in corporate scenarios).

Smart Cards

Smart cards are physical plastic cards that carry original information, such as a unique number or a unique combination of data about their owner. Similar to credit cards, smart cards allow for seamless purchasing transactions and are applicable to online shopping as a shopper authentication tool. The drawbacks of smart cards are that they are easy to lose, inconvenient to carry, and require additional investment in smart card reading hardware devices.

Biometrics

All individuals are unique and this is what biometrics authentication technologies rely on to identify unique users. Fingerprint, voice, and retina scans are the currently available methods of differentiating individuals. These authentication technologies are implemented in two stages. First, a user needs to register his biometric information into the authentication system. This involves scanning and creating an image of a person's fingerprints or eye retina, or recording a sample of a person's voice. Associated with these samples are the user ID and other information. During authentication, the user's fingerprint is scanned or his/her voice recorded into the system and compared to the sample stored in the database. The matching result, by minutiae or template pattern comparison, confirms if the user is pre-registered or not.

Biometrics authentication is not yet widely commercialized but its numerous industrial applications are an indicator of future for this technology.

Administration and Audit Products

Security™ administration and audit tools allow network managers to control and document which users get access to which resources. Principal components of security administration and audit are:

- **Policy Management Services**—These are applicable primarily to the corporate environment and involve: devising of security strategy, security implementation procedures, hiring of qualified network security professionals, etc. These services provide for the generation of custom-tailored security solutions and are effective in combating security crimes. The disadvantage of these services is that they are usually expensive and beyond the purchasing capabilities of small businesses and individuals.
- **Database/File Management**—These products are usually components of the database or operating system. They allow network administrators to set different levels of access and control to different users or user groups. Major flaws of these products and/or network administration features is their inability to protect the user from virus attacks.
- **Auditing Software**—Auditing software records and stores logs on server and data access. Auditing software is a powerful network management tool for detecting weak spots and security loopholes on the private network.
- **Virtual Private Networks (VPNs)**—VPNs are an amalgamation of intranet and extranet technologies to allow remote access by employees and lock out public network intruders (i.e., hackers). VPN security is crucial, as sensitive data is transmitted to remote corporate users.

Access Control Product Group

Access control tools enable network managers to restrict access and filter the data traveling across the network. Chief data access technologies include:

Firewalls

Firewalls are the most popular security product, with applications ranging from home desktop protection to worldwide corporate network protection. A firewall protects networked computers from intentional hostile intrusion that could compromise confidentiality or result in data corruption or denial of service. It may be a hardware device or a software program running on a secure host computer. In either case, it must have at least two network interfaces, one for the network it is intended to protect, and one for the network it is exposed to. A firewall sits at the junction point or gateway between the two networks, usually a private network and a public network such as the Internet.

A firewall examines all traffic routed between the two networks to see if it meets certain criteria. If it does, data is routed between the networks; otherwise it is stopped. A firewall filters both inbound and outbound traffic. It can also manage public access to private networked resources such as host applications. It can be used to log all attempts to enter the private network and trigger alarms when hostile or unauthorized entry is attempted. Firewalls can filter packets based on their source and destination addresses and port numbers—address filtering, by specific types of network traffic—protocol filtering, or by packet attribute or state.

Some users object to the fact that hardware firewall appliances eliminate access to the operating system. Significant disadvantage of software firewalls is that even high-end sophisticated multi-layer firewalls can be penetrated.

Proxy servers

When a user on the internal network attempts to connect to a server on the Internet, the proxy server sets up the connection and is the only system publicly advertised. Proxy servers should be used in conjunction with some form of packet filtering, or else clients and attackers alike might be able to go around the server.

Security Monitoring and Intrusion Detection Tools

These are software products that reside on gateway servers and constantly monitor for unauthorized access attempts. If a security intruder is detected, the application sends an intrusion alert message to potentially vulnerable users. These tools are effective in protecting a corporate network from external intruders and/or limiting the damage from the attack by immediately warning users.

Gap Technology Devices

Gap technology allows for a "disconnection" between two networks while allowing them to share resources or information. The difference between a firewall and a gap technology device is the following: a firewall is the logical disconnection of two physically connected networks, while a gap is a physical disconnection of two logically connected networks. Currently, there are three main categories of gap technology:

- **Real-Time Switch**—in a real-time switch architecture, two networks that are physically disconnected can share data as if they were connected. This seeming contradiction is achieved by adding a gap device that shuttles information back and forth between the two networks. In this case, the gap device is a hardware switch that can be physically connected to only one of the networks at a time. On a very basic level, the switch connects to one network, reads the waiting data, switches to the other network, and pushes the information onto it. This switching happens at very high speeds, allowing for functional operation in a real-time environment.
- **One-Way Link**—a one-way link is the most straightforward gap configuration. It creates what is essentially a "read-only" network connection, which doesn't allow data to cross back into the source network. Like a real-time switch, it must be implemented in a hardware solution that physically prevents data from going the wrong way.
- **Network Switcher**—a network switcher is similar to a real-time switch, with the notable difference that it does not work in real time. A network switcher is typically implemented as a card with dual interfaces. Each interface is connected to a separate network, with only one interface active at a time. A proper implementation will segment all system resources, assigning some to each interface, with none belonging to both. In this way, storage that is assigned to one network is never accessible to the other network. This means that files and information retrieved from one network cannot inadvertently be put out on the other. If these files contain sensitive information, viruses, or malicious code, they cannot traverse this boundary.

Encryption Product Group

Encryption and decryption technologies, such as public/private key (PKP) and digital signatures, are used to guard data transmitted over the network. Within this product group, VPN, encryption enablers, and e-mail encryption are the key areas of product development.

PKI and Digital Signatures

PKI encryption works in relation to digital signatures. When the sender encrypts a message with his/her private key, any receiver with a sender public key can read it. When a digital signature is attached by a sender to a message encrypted in the receiver's public key, the receiver is the only one that can read the message and, at the same time, he/she is assured that the message was indeed sent by the sender.

PKI cryptography and digital signatures are applicable and widely available encryption/decryption technologies. They are mostly used when information is sent by e-mail and protect data as it travels through public networks (i.e. the Internet).

Litigation Services Company

BUSINESS PLAN

ACME LITIGATION COMPANY

4700 11 Mile Road
Royal Oak, Michigan 48067

ALC provides general and specialized business support and process services for the legal and engineering business community. ALC's services are centered on the need for clear, concise communication and research needs legal and engineering firms face when experiencing and/or responding to litigation in relation to employee performance, injury, or product safety and use.

- COMPANY OVERVIEW
- BUSINESS MODEL & SERVICE DELIVERY PRACTICES
- PRICING STRATEGY
- BUSINESS CHALLENGES
- SALES & MARKETING PLAN
- FINANCIALS

COMPANY OVERVIEW

Acme Litigation Company is an independently operated company located in Southeastern Michigan, founded by Mrs. Lyn Kondrako in the summer of 1999, and is now entering its third year of profitability. ALC provides general and specialized business support and process services for the legal and engineering business community. ALC's services are centered on the need for clear, concise communication and research needs legal and engineering firms face when experiencing and/or responding to litigation in relation to employee performance, injury, or product safety and use.

This business summary does not go into detail of all of ALC's individual capabilities and services provided, but they are described categorically in the following three areas:

Deposition summarization
Providing clients with deposition summarization services and legal support for expert witness testimony. These clients include cases and development for plaintiff, defendant, and expert witness clients. Thus providing the greatest value for ALC's current client base. This service set makes up ALC's largest client base and revenue stream.

Ergonomic and product use compliance
Providing clients with analysis and data study services for ergonomic issues including injury data, product effectiveness, and common use serves clients with specialized information in support of product development and litigation support documentation.

Product safety and product use research
Providing clients with product safety compliance and regulation research and litigation trend data brings value to clients in the form of real-world intelligence on common use of products, product effects on common consumer and industrial users, as well as providing a "window" into alternative uses for products initially intended for another use.

Client Profile

ALC's typical client is specialized, by profile and historical industry capability, particularly the industrial and transportation industries. Our target client profile is primarily expert witnesses and leaders in the engineering and ergonomic/human factors business community with considerable emphasis on those also servicing individual law firms, attorney groups, and to a lesser extent, product manufacturers and service providers. Our client profile is a dynamic driven by market forces and client need. We do not have a "specific" client profile other than the loose framework mentioned above. Our services and capabilities, although concentrated at times to a specific industry, are leveragable across multiple industries and legal communities.

Employee Profile

ALC's employees are its strength. ALC's business is all about employee experiences, education, flexibility, and relationships. ALC's employees are handpicked by the owner and are experienced in a wide breadth of legal and business areas. Our employees bring industry relationships and the opportunity to leverage those relationships to bring growth to the company. First and foremost, the legal community builds its business on relationships and trust. We must operate successfully within those relationships to maintain a successful enterprise.

BUSINESS MODEL & SERVICE DELIVERY PRACTICES

ALC's business and service delivery model can be summed up in one sentence. We are a small company operating on a contractor-type operating model. We manage and leverage a network of subcontractors across the continental U.S. to provide a suite of services at the project level for immediate and longer-term client support. Our services and relationships to clients results in an environment of mutual trust for on-time delivery and client satisfaction. We are only as good as our employees can deliver on a day-to-day basis. Each project must exceed client expectations.

ALC provides services to its clients on a per hour, per project basis. The constant flow of growing client requests enables us to manage our growth as desired and as we choose to manage. Our business model is based on leveraging a closely held network of individuals, all acting in a subcontractor business capacity to the enterprise with direct responsibility to meeting client expectations and direct responsibility to ALC for business management. ALC retains the responsibility for payment for hours worked and employee training and development needs.

We make extensive use of client based pass-through billing practices. It is our belief that the fewer the amount of line item expenses and unnecessary complexity in our accounting and business processes the smoother our operations will run. We establish trust-based relationships with our clients to leverage THEIR organization and operational business processes to pass through the largest percentage of cost and operating expenses without directly impacting our accounting and business procedures. For example, by leveraging client administrative resources, communications, package shipping, and sundry practices, our expense line grows "thinner," thus avoiding additional cost structure for an internal administrative support structure.

PRICING STRATEGY

Our pricing strategy is based on competitive, market-oriented pricing models for a nationally blended, non-city, industry or client specific rate. We use services industry norms in establishing our strategies and policies. Our basic rate structure is outlined below:

• Per hour based on level of experience and pages per hour	$30-40.00/hour
• Per hour based on expectations of project completion date, i.e. rush	$37.50-45.00/hour [variable to schedule]
• Per hour based on specialized client requirements	$40-55.00/hour [variable to client and project]

The average blend of hourly revenue is $35-$45.00 for deposition summarization and rush services. Special rates are developed at a higher level on a project-by-project basis for advanced service offering sets, typically $40-$50.00/hour. While our pricing norms are highly competitive, we are not considered the low-cost provider on an actual rate-basis, nor on a service-delivery basis. Our service pricing is squarely positioned in the "middle" amongst our competitors.

Negotiation Strategies

Preferred clients may receive blended rates and/or negotiated discounts off market rack rates. Typically, discounts on hourly rates result in a discount of 10 to 15 percent. More often than not, when discounts are given they are in the form of negotiating rush deadlines and/or accommodating specialized or advanced client requirements, i.e. using basic rate range for expert opinion summary requirements in exchange for first right of refusal on larger upcoming project or agreeing to extended completion timeline.

BUSINESS CHALLENGES

In summary, our business challenges are similar to all people/hour based businesses, particularly the legal industry. In this summary plan I have provided a list of challenges that have significant positive impact if overcome but also carry the ability to cripple our long-term growth and success if unchecked.

- Maintaining employee/subcontractor network
- Flexibility to client demands (projects and dates are always changing)
- Revenue growth
- Managing cash-flow for short and long-term investment/expense requirements
- Managing growth to delivery capability

SALES & MARKETING PLAN

ALC intends to grow for the next two years at a growth rate conservatively estimated at 30 to 40 percent. Current market conditions relating to client demand and work availability will enable us to achieve this goal with moderate effort. However, we will only be able to achieve this by sticking to what we do best and enabling the employee network to grow and flourish. This creates some unique situations for managing growth within our current business and revenue model. To get there we must stick to the basics and be successful at the following three marketing principles:

- Establish a position within target market as a trusted partner to provide process outsourcing and supplemental legal and research services.
- Use a highly focused, targeting strategy based on existing relationships in region, industry, and national level.
- Experiment and innovate to acquire clients, but stick to what works. Things change, but not that much.

Miscellaneous

Employee Operating and Pay Policies

Each subcontract employee is expected to and/or has signed a nondisclosure agreement intended to protect ALC and its clients from public discussion and negative exposure of previous and pending business.

Each employee provides services to ALC on a subcontract basis and will be issued pay per hours worked, per project basis. Frequency of project payment for hours worked is without established frequency. Each employee is paid within 7-10 business days of ALC receiving payment from client for each completed project.

FINANCIALS

ALC's Financial Request

It is my intent in submitting this business plan to attain a commercial transaction account with Second Bank of America and establish a credit transaction facility in support of Acme Litigation Company's operations.

The following table illustrates a financial summary of 2001 operations.

2001 Summary Financial Operations

Total billed revenue	$84,700.00	2,420 billed hours—estimate based on conservative assumption of $35.00/hour billing average
Total Expense	**59,810.00**	
Operating profit	22,890.00	

Summary MarginEst. 26-28%

Costs Summary
Administrative

Accounting, legal, misc.		$1,000.00	Per year estimate
Office Supplies		$780.00	$65.00/month
Delivery/Package shipment services		$900.00	$75.00/month
Communications and equipment		$1,320.00	Includes cell phone and e-mail [$110.00/month]
Facilities		$1,620.00	Includes utilities and space in home office [electricity $25/month, gas $10/month, space $100/month]
Office Equipment		$750.00	Per year [software upgrades, computer hardware maintenance expense]
Transportation/Entertainment			
Business vehicle		$1,200.00	$100.00/month
Fuel, maintenance, etc.		$750.00	Per year
Client entertainment/out-of-office business discussions			$1,250.00 Per year
Labor			
Partner One	$30.00/hour	$21,600.00	Average of 15 billable hours/ week x 48 weeks/year [720 hrs/year]
Northeast resource	$18.00/hour	$12,960.00	Average of 15 billable hours/ week x 48 weeks/year [720 hrs/year]
Pacific Northwest resource	$16.00/hour	$7,680.00	Average of 10 billable hours/ week x 48 weeks/year [480 hrs/year]
Midwest resource	$15.00/hour	$7,500.00	Average of 10 billable hours/ week x 50 weeks/year [500 hrs/year]
Employee Recognition			$500.00
Total Summary Costs			**$57,440.00**

Medical Equipment Producer

BUSINESS PLAN

PREMIUM THERAPY, LLC

7500 Miller Street
Cambridge, Massachusetts 02142

Premium Therapy, LLC is a medical device company focused on the field of rehabilitation medicine. It has designed and developed a patented technology to deliver ElectroMagnetic Induction Therapy (EMIT) in large markets that include the treatment of arthritis, pain, and muscular atrophy.

MEDICAL EQUIPMENT PRODUCER BUSINESS PLAN

EXECUTIVE SUMMARY

Premium Therapy, LLC is a medical device company focused on the field of rehabilitation medicine. It has designed and developed a patented technology to deliver ElectroMagnetic Induction Therapy (EMIT) in large markets that include the treatment of arthritis, pain, and muscular atrophy.

Technology

Pulsed electromagnetic stimulation is a well-established technique with a long history of use in medical applications. The scientific principle behind this technology is that an electric current passed through a coil will generate an electromagnetic field. These fields, in turn, have been shown to induce current within conductive materials placed within the field. When applied to the human body, pulsed electromagnetic stimulation has been scientifically proven to be effective in: 1) causing muscles to contract, 2) altering nerve signal transmission to decrease experienced pain, and 3) causing new cell growth in cartilage.

Harnessing these benefits, the company has developed EMIT as a new and improved, patented delivery technology. Using this technology, Premium Therapy plans to treat a variety of medical conditions. A full utility patent that provides protection for Premium Therapy's technology has been filed in the U.S. and is currently pending approval.

Market

Premium Therapy will target market segments comprised of persons desiring treatment for muscular atrophy, neurogenic bladder/bowel (a form of paralysis of the muscles in the bladder/bowel), musculoskeletal pain and/or arthritis. Together, the several market segments yield an initial potential U.S. market of greater than 200 million customers.

In a recent survey of individuals suffering from these conditions, a large percentage of them were found to be completely dissatisfied with current therapies. In fact, almost half of all respondents indicated that they would be willing to try new treatments and would spend more on a treatment if they knew it would work. Based on this data, and Premium Therapy's calculations, over 97 million of the greater than 200 million potential customers are completely dissatisfied with all current therapies and suffer from intractable disease (see Market Segmentation). It is this group of poorly-managed patients that Premium Therapy expects to be the earliest adopters of its technology.

Product

Premium Therapy's new device, the EMIT system, consists of two components: a programmable Logic Controller (LC), which generates the required current, and an Array of Overlapping Coils (AOC), through which the current is channeled in generating the pulsed electromagnetic fields. Premium Therapy's novel technology is embodied in the patented form of its AOC, which contains a series of overlapping coils encased within an ergonomic, body-contoured wrap. The ergonomic wraps have been designed for the multiple applications of EMIT and are easily placed by any untrained user around the lower back, knee, shoulder, and other regions of the body to deliver targeted, therapeutic pulses of electromagnetic stimuli. For example, the ergonomic AOC wrap developed for the knee contains strategically placed coils designed to produce therapeutic magnetic fields within the knee.

Premium Therapy's technology is incorporated into the two models of the EMIT system: EMIT MX and EMIT SX. The two models of this system each target a number of different market segments. The EMIT MX model generates a powerful maximal (MX) current stimulus sufficient to cause contraction in targeted muscle groups and is intended for persons desiring the prevention/treatment of muscular atrophy and/or the treatment of neurogenic bladder and bowel. The EMIT SX model, on the other hand, has been designed to generate a less powerful, submaximal (SX) stimulus which will not cause muscles to contract, but which will alter pain sensations and enhance cartilage growth through the modulation of cell signaling pathways.

The competitive advantages of the EMIT system include:

- Unique therapeutic application of EMIT
- Patented delivery device with multiple user-friendly applicators
- Two models for multiple applications in the treatment of a variety of diseases
- Reduction of healthcare costs with home healthcare applications

Development Status

Research involving the EMIT system has produced encouraging laboratory results and a formal request to perform human clinical trials has been filed. Once this approval is obtained, several leading U.S. medical institutions, including Harvard University, University of California - Berkeley, the Therapeutic Institute, and the University of Arizona, have expressed interest in participating in collaborative research and clinical trials. Given encouraging results, each has also indicated an interest in purchasing the EMIT system.

Competition

Currently, the two main technologies competing with the EMIT system are Electrical Stimulation (ES) and existing Pulsed Electromagnetic Stimulation (PES). While each of these technologies attempts to treat the same conditions as the EMIT system, both have severe limitations. ES devices, for example, are unable to penetrate tissues to reach deep muscles without causing skin burns and irritation. PES devices, on the other hand, can penetrate deeply and painlessly, but have been developed exclusively for diagnostic applications, such as nerve or muscle testing. As a result, these devices, while effective in a diagnostic setting, make ineffective therapeutic tools and currently are not available in any form that is appropriate for home healthcare.

Leading products in this field include Rehabilitation Center's ES device, which grossed over $62 million in revenues last year, and Top Line Stimulus's Model 500 PES device which sells for $12,500 and has grossed $32.5 million in revenues since its market entrance in 1998. While these technologies are currently among Premium Therapy's main competitors, the company believes that the focus of competition in the future will be between the different technologies, with a paradigm shift to more effective therapy.

Strategy

Premium Therapy will initially market its technology to healthcare providers through established medical device specialty distributors. The specialty distributors will provide sales, support, and distribution functions. Premium Therapy will complement the distributors' sales force with an internal program focused on highlighting the increased efficacy of the EMIT system in research publications and journals in order to encourage adoption of its technology. Premium Therapy expects those involved in the distribution and sales of the EMIT system to be able to charge a sustainable premium for providing patients with access to this breakthrough technology. Premium Therapy will also market its technology to patient/consumers once healthcare providers have begun to adopt the EMIT system.

Regulatory Issues

Medical devices such as the company's EMIT system are subject to regulatory review and approval by the U.S. Food and Drug Administration (FDA). While it is expected that full FDA approval will be gained quickly based on the approval of similar devices, Premium Therapy will seek an expedited market entrance by obtaining an Investigational Device Exemption

(IDE) and clearly labeling the device "For Investigational Use Only." IDE approvals are typically obtained within an average of 3 months including necessary revisions. This strategy has been successful with a similar device, Leetonus' LeeTone, where an IDE was obtained and devices were sold prior to full FDA approval.

Despite this accelerated market entrance, Premium Therapy is cognizant of the fact that full FDA approval will be necessary in order to claim therapeutic efficacy of the EMIT system for each of its indications.

Management Team

Premium Therapy's management team includes founders with extensive experience in rehabilitative medicine and in the design and development of novel technology. Credentials include two M.B.A.s, two B.S.E.s in Biomedical Engineering, two M.D.s and a B.S.E. in Electrical Engineering. Furthermore, active consultation is being provided by a serial entrepreneur and technology development expert, an FDA specialist, the director of clinical studies for Harvard University's Physical Therapy Department, and a patent agent specializing in biomedical devices.

Financial

Premium Therapy's principals are heavily invested in the company's success with a planned $100,000 worth of capital input prior to any external funding. Assuming a product diffusion that parallels comparable technology in the medical field and receipt of an additional $1,000,000 in funding, Premium Therapy anticipates profitable operations by year four with a net profit of $1.3 million. International populations were not included in the financial analysis, as global expansion is not anticipated until late in the business plan.

Financial Highlights	**2002**	**2003**	**2004**	**2005**	**2006**
Revenues	-	962,747	2,691,544	10,104,497	32,985,773
Cost of Sales	-	383,301	1,023,188	3,625,288	11,550,243
Gross Margin	-	579,446	1,668,356	6,479,209	21,435,530
Capital Input	1,100,000	-	1,500,000	-	-
Net Profit	**-322,810**	**-493,222**	**-889,512**	**1,342,427**	**8,809,331**

COMPANY SUMMARY

Premium Therapy will develop biomedical devices, including the EMIT system, to aid in the treatment of a variety of medical conditions. Premium Therapy has developed patented technology to employ ElectroMagnetic Induction Therapy (EMIT) in delivering stimuli to targeted anatomic regions of the human body. While this will be Premium Therapy's initial focus, the company expects to leverage its medical device expertise in capitalizing on other opportunities as they arise.

TECHNOLOGY

Pulsed electromagnetic stimulation (PES) technologies have been developed and refined over the course of several decades of scientific research. These technologies found relatively early application in the setting of medical diagnostics with the commercialization of several devices that have been utilized since the early 1990s at medical centers throughout the United States for the diagnosis of nerve and muscle disorders.

The results of emerging scientific trials, however, have demonstrated the dramatic potential for PES to painlessly and non-invasively treat, rather than simply diagnose, a variety of medical conditions. Studies have shown PES to be effective in: 1) causing muscles to contract, 2) altering nerve signal transmission to decrease experienced pain, and 3) causing new cell growth in cartilage. A number of additional therapeutic effects are postulated and being researched extensively.

It is on this well-established base of research that Premium Therapy has developed and patented an innovative medical device to deliver ElectroMagnetic Induction Therapy (EMIT). Premium Therapy's technology is a further advance in this field designed to effectively treat muscular atrophy, neurogenic bladder/bowel, musculoskeletal pain and arthritis through the use of electromagnetic stimulation in a highly user-friendly format.

Background

The renowned scientist Michael Faraday first observed the concept of pulsed electromagnetic stimulation in 1831. Faraday was able to demonstrate that time varying, or pulsed electromagnetic fields, have the potential to induce current in a conductive object. Faraday's experimental setup was simple. He found that by passing strong electric current through a coil of wire he was able to produce pulsed electromagnetic stimuli. This pulsed electromagnetic stimulus was able to induce the flow of current in a nearby electrically conductive body.

In the years since the discoveries of Faraday, pulsed electromagnetic stimulators have found application in countless areas of scientific investigation. In 1965, the scientists Bickford and Freming demonstrated the use of pulsed electromagnetic stimulation to induce conduction within nerves of the face. Later, in 1982 Polson et al. produced a device capable of stimulating peripheral nerves of the body. This group of investigators was able to stimulate peripheral nerves of the body sufficiently to cause muscle activity, recording the first evoked potentials from pulsed electromagnetic stimulation.

The ability of pulsed electromagnetic stimulation to induce electrical currents within tissues of the human body has prompted medical research in recent years with respect to the diagnosis, monitoring, and therapy of a variety of important conditions.

Technologic Advances

Since the days of Bickford, Freming, and Polson, magnetic fields have been clinically applied to both central and peripheral nerves through the utilization of a single, large coil. Repetitive electromagnetic stimulation of the brain, for instance, has been utilized as an alternative to electroconvulsive "shock" therapy in treating depression, and as a means to trigger seizure activity in locating the source of epilepsy. Peripherally, magnetic stimulation has been used for pain syndromes, for improving neuromuscular function in the setting of chronic progressive multiple sclerosis and for the stimulation of peripheral nerves in the diagnostic detection of nerve conduction abnormalities.

Due to the promise of electromagnetic stimulation in painlessly and non-invasively treating a variety of diseases, research in this field is progressing rapidly. New indications for treatment with electromagnetic stimulation are arising every year with strong, scientifically-supported results. Premium Therapy's technology is a further advance in this field designed to effectively treat muscular atrophy, neurogenic bladder/bowel, musculoskeletal pain and arthritis through the use of electromagnetic stimulation in a user-friendly format appropriate for home healthcare applications.

MARKET

The different models of the EMIT system each target a number of different market segments consisting of persons desiring therapy for multiple conditions, including: muscular atrophy, neurogenic bladder and bowel, musculoskeletal pain and/or arthritis. Together, the several market segments yield a total potential U.S. market for the EMIT system of greater than 223 million customers with over 97 million customers falling into the category of dissatisfied patients.

A recent survey of patients suffering from these conditions found that nearly half were so dissatisfied with current therapies that they would be willing to both try new treatments and pay a premium for these treatments if they were effective. These dissatisfied populations, that are both unable to find relief with current therapies and willing to pay more for an effective new therapy, are expected to be the earliest adopters of EMIT.

Market Segmentation

The United States will serve as Premium Therapy's initial target market for both models of the EMIT system. The potential market for each device was extrapolated using data from reputable, referenced sources. In determining the percentage of patients that Premium Therapy expects to be early adopters, estimates of the percentages of persons in the United States currently suffering from chronic, poorly managed medical conditions in each of the various market segments were used based upon the assumption that individuals who have already used existing therapies without significant success would be most likely to try a novel medical device. Thus, it is expected that the earliest adopters of the EMIT system will be those patients afflicted with muscular atrophy, neurogenic bladder and bowel, musculoskeletal pain and/or arthritis for whom all other therapies have failed.

The number of patients that are not being well managed with current therapies, though, is significant. Premium Therapy's principals estimate that in patients with fractures, paralysis, and immobilization (including mechanical ventilation and Guillain-Barre disease), the percentages that subsequently develop long-term complications of atrophy that could be avoided through the use of the EMIT system are 41 percent, 75 percent and 90 percent respectively. In neurogenic bladder and bowel, virtually half of all patients have found no relief through any of the existing therapies. For musculoskeletal pain and arthritis sufferers it was found that "78% are willing to try new treatments, and 43% would spend more on a treatment if they knew it would work." Further supporting these figures, a study published by the *Society of Pain Sufferers* found that, "56% of pain sufferers have had their pain for more than 5 years and 41% of them described their pain as 'out of control'." These numbers have been factored into the "Intractable Disease" column in the tables below and have been used to calculate the dissatisfied population of patients most likely to try a novel therapy listed under "Early Adopters."

EMIT Market Segments

For a sense of scope, both the total potential market and expected early adopter market are listed in the tables below for all of the indications of the EMIT system.

Prevention and Treatment of Muscular Atrophy:

Muscular Atrophy Patients Treatable with the EMIT system in the U.S.

Condition	Total Potential Market	Intractable Disease	Early Adopter Market
All Fractures	9,600,000	41%	3,936,000
Paralysis	2,430,000	75%	1,822,500
Mechanical Ventilation	963,000	90%	866,700
Guillain-Barre	3,000	90%	2,700
Total	**12,996,000**		**6,627,900**

Treatment of Neurogenic Bladder and Bowel:

Neurogenic Bladder/Bowel Patients Treatable with the EMIT system in the U.S.

Condition	Total Potential Market	Intractable Disease	Early Adopter Market
Multiple Sclerosis	200,000	25%	50,000
Spinal Cord Injury	300,000	50%	150,000
Total	**500,000**		**200,000**

Treatment of Musculoskeletal Pain:

Musculoskeletal Pain Patients Treatable with the EMIT system in the U.S.

Condition	Total Potential Market	Intractable Disease	Early Adopter Market
Low Back Pain	132,300,000	43%	56,889,000
Neck Pain	33,000,000	43%	14,190,000
Total	**165,300,000**		**71,079,000**

Treatment of Arthritis:

Arthritis Patients Treatable with the EMIT system in the U.S.

Condition	Total Potential Market	Intractable Disease	Early Adopter Market
Arthritis	45,000,000	43%	19,350,000
Total	**45,000,000**		**19,350,000**

TOTAL U.S. Market

The total potential and expected early adopter markets in the United States for the Premium Therapy EMIT system are projected to be the following:

Total U.S. Market for the EMIT system

Device Model	Total Potential Market	Intractable Disease	Early Adopter Market
EMIT MX	Muscular Atrophy	12,996,000	6,627,900
	Neurogenic Bladder and Bowel	500,000	200,000
	Model MX Subtotal	**13,496,000**	**6,827,900**
EMIT SX	Musculoskeletal Pain	165,300,000	71,079,000
	Arthritis	45,000,000	19,350,000
	Model SX Subtotal	**210,300,000**	**90,429,000**
All Models	**Total**	**223,796,000**	**97,256,900**

Assuming the entire market were able to be tapped, with pricing, cost schedules, and component use as indicated, the revenues associated with the total potential market and expected early adopter market are $132.4 billion and $57.8 billion respectively.

Industry Analysis

The industry for electromagnetic stimulating technologies is both growing and evolving rapidly. In the 1990s, more than 250,000 prescriptions were written each year in the United States for electrical and electromagnetic stimulating medical devices. As scientific data surrounding PES technology has grown in recent years, trends in both neuromuscular stimulation and pain control have pushed towards the use of this powerful new technology.

The forces driving this trend towards increasing use of PES technology include: 1) the ability to be applied painlessly without the adverse side effects found with electrical technologies, and 2) the demonstrated capability to effectively treat conditions that electrical stimulating technologies fail to adequately address. The problem with PES devices currently in use is that because of design limitations they are either relegated solely to diagnostic purposes or require the constant manipulation of trained personnel for use. Industry product developers have not taken the necessary steps to develop devices that are easily applied in the treatment of medical conditions that have been shown to respond to this form of stimulation.

It is on this stage of emerging demand that the Premium Therapy EMIT system has been created. The proprietary position of Premium Therapy protects the ability to employ EMIT with the use of an ergonomic, body-contoured wrap containing strategically placed induction coils. This protection allows Premium Therapy to assert a unique position within its industry, and helps to support the expectation that those involved with the propagation of EMIT system will be able to charge a sustainable premium and realize economic profits for at least the duration of the patent.

Reimbursement Patterns

Intimate knowledge of third-party payer reimbursement is essential to the marketing plans for any medical device. In the case of the Premium Therapy EMIT system, acceptance of the technology is already demonstrated in the establishment of appropriate billing codes and charge histories for related technologies. Current Procedural Terminology (CPT) for the American Medical Association provides for Category III coding of a number of different forms of magnetic stimulation under the rubric of "investigational treatments". This classification of PES devices as "investigational" becomes an important issue in reimbursement patterns.

In a broader sense, reimbursement plans for pulsed electromagnetic stimulation devices can be supported by established billing practices for related technologies such as electric neurostimulation devices, TENS units, and a host of other electrical stimulation devices. While traditionally the market has been highly sensitive to reimbursement patterns, the fact cannot be ignored that consumers will seek therapeutic intervention with or without third party payor acceptance if they believe a device to be effective.

Experts have estimated that Americans spent $13.7 billion for devices that would fall into the category of "investigational treatments" in 1990 alone. Of these expenditures, $10.3 billion was spent as out-of-pocket, nonreimbursable expenses. These figures highlight the fact that while reimbursement is expected to expand our potential market, a large market exists for medical treatments that are paid out-of-pocket without reimbursement. It is this market that Premium Therapy will target in the early years of the business plan prior to full FDA approval and insurance reimbursement.

Purchasing Patterns

As with most significant investments in medical technology, large-scale adoption of the Premium Therapy EMIT technology will require an executive-level decision at the purchasing institution. In order to convince the decision-making unit at the purchasing institution, Premium Therapy must first prove the efficacy of its EMIT system. This is especially true of the MX system, which requires a larger investment, and much of Premium Therapy's initial efforts will be focused on scientifically proving the efficacy of its technology. Once this has been established, and marketing efforts begin to take effect, demand will be generated among healthcare providers and patients, and institutions and practices will begin investing in the EMIT system.

Typically, individual departments within an institution are held financially accountable and, if they decide to purchase a new technology, the decision is reviewed by the hospital administration. If the department is profitable, the decision is rarely overturned. Therefore, the most important market to consider in targeting sales will be the decision-making unit of the medical department. Premium Therapy's management recognizes that decision-making processes vary at different institutions, and the sales team, in cooperation with the specialty distributors, will consider each institution individually.

Distribution Patterns

While direct distribution was traditionally an option in the medical field, there have been multiple changes in the last decade including intense consolidation and increasing use of purchasing agreements in the industry that have made this an impractical option for most novel technologies. This is especially true of highly specialized, truly innovative technologies such as Premium Therapy's EMIT system. Due to the importance of utilizing existing distribution channels in the highly developed medical device arena, selecting an appropriate distributor will be one of the keys to Premium Therapy's success.

As illustrated in the table below, medical device distributors vary greatly in services provided, ranging from strictly distribution to warehousing, billing, customer service, shipping, and selling functions. With greater services, though, comes greater cost. Medical device companies that opt for direct distribution incur only the cost of the freight while at the opposite end, use of specialty distributors typically will result in a 35-50 percent markup.

Medical Device Distribution Options

Type	Services Provided	Markup
Direct Distributor	None	3-5%
General Distributor	Distribution only, no sales or support	10%
Specialty Distributor	Shipping, warehousing, billing, service/support, and sales	35-50%

In light of Premium Therapy's highly specialized market, and in order to minimize initial costs and develop robust distribution rapidly, Premium Therapy intends to utilize specialty distributors focused on the physical medicine and rehabilitation market. Premium Therapy anticipates conversion to general distribution and a direct sales team when the opportunity arises, but for the timeline of this business plan, specialty distribution will be utilized.

In order to tap the full potential of the market, Premium Therapy intends to utilize the services of regional specialty distributors. Premium Therapy has contacted multiple potential distributors, including Parker Doyle of Medical Products and Barnard Smithson of Applied Medical, and is in the process of developing working relationships with select distributors.

PRODUCTS

Premium Therapy plans on targeting this large and growing market with its innovative EMIT system. Designed to deliver ElectroMagnetic Induction Therapy (EMIT), the EMIT system consists of two components: a programmable Logic Controller (LC), which generates the required current, and an Array of Overlapping Coils (AOC) through which the current is channeled in generating the electromagnetic field. Premium Therapy's novel technology is embodied in the patented form of its AOC, which contains overlapping coils in an ergonomic, body-contoured wrap designed for the lower back, knee, shoulder, and other targeted regions of the body.

Premium Therapy's true innovation resides in its use of electromagnetic stimulation technology in a therapeutic setting along with its patented delivery device and multiple user-friendly applicators. In order to treat a wide range of diseases, Premium Therapy has developed two different models of the EMIT system, both of which are cost-effective with multiple home healthcare applications.

Product Description

The Premium Therapy EMIT system, a powerful therapeutic device created for the purpose of stimulating tissues of the human body, utilizes the revolutionary EMIT technology to deliver pulsed electromagnetic stimuli to targeted regions of the body. This patented technology is embodied in the form of ergonomic, body-contoured wraps containing a series of overlapping coils. A number of different ergonomic wraps have been developed for the lower back, knee, shoulder, and other regions targeted by the various applications of the EMIT MX and SX models. The wraps are designed to be easy to apply, with simple attachments and clear markings in order to ensure correct placement of the wrap by an untrained user. The coils housed within the ergonomic wraps, when placed over targeted areas of the human body, create stimuli powerful enough to cause muscles to contract, alter pain sensations, and/or enhance cell growth.

The EMIT system will be sold in two parts: a programmable logic controller and an array of overlapping coils.

- **Programmable logic controller (LC):** The logic controller is a sophisticated, but easy-to-use device designed to provide pulses of current, which create electromagnetic fields when channeled through the coils located in the various wraps. The electromagnetic field generated by the LC is capable of being adjusted in terms of amplitude and frequency in order to meet specific patient needs.
- **Array of overlapping coils (AOC):** The overlapping coils have technological advantages in that they effectively blanket the therapeutic area with electromagnetic stimulation, thus making therapies consistent, rapid, and easy to administer. A flexible, ergonomic wrap has been designed to position the coils over key regions targeted by each specific application. The design of the wrap will be such that markings on the material of the wrap will indicate correct alignment of the device over the intended area of the body. The wraps will also be contoured and fit to the region targeted making application even more consistent and effortless. Every design is available in multiple sizes to accommodate patients of various dimensions. Multiple wraps have been designed including knee, shoulder, pelvic, lower back, etc.

Product Applications

The EMIT MX system generates a maximal (MX) current stimulus sufficient to cause contraction in targeted muscle groups and is used in applications requiring large currents including the treatment and prevention of muscular atrophy and the treatment of neurogenic bladder and bowel. The treatment of musculoskeletal pain and arthritis, though, requires relatively lower levels of current. In order to satisfy this market, the EMIT SX model has been tailored to generate a submaximal (SX) stimulus that will not cause muscular contraction.

EMIT MX Applications

Prevention and Treatment of Muscle Atrophy: The Premium Therapy EMIT MX system addresses the unanswered need for atrophy prevention and treatment in conditions resulting in patient immobilization for greater than two weeks, such as in the case of hip, knee, and shoulder surgery; spinal cord injury; and a number of other cases. In animal models, the average muscle loss after just two weeks of immobilization was noted to be greater than 30 percent of the total pre-immobilization mass. This loss of muscle mass results in increased times to complete recovery and, with prolonged immobilization, in permanent disability. Studies have shown that inactive muscle stimulated by pulsed electromagnetism has better function and reduced loss of mass subsequent to immobilization.

Treatment of Neurogenic Bowel and Bladder: The EMIT MX system also offers a simple, noninvasive solution to the problem of neurogenic bladder and rectum causing retention of urine and bowel contents in persons with spinal cord injuries, Multiple Sclerosis, and various other disorders. Similar to the paralysis of the arms or legs in a patient with spinal cord injuries, patients with neurogenic bladder and bowel have "paralysis" of their bowel and bladder leading to difficulties with defecation and urination. The complications that can arise from neurogenic bladder and bowel are significant. In mortality studies of persons with spinal cord injuries, after a period of high mortality at the time surrounding the initial injury, neurogenic bladder has been shown to be the primary cause of death.

Invasive methods have been attempted to address this problem but without significant success and with multiple side effects. In both human and animal models, pulsed electromagnetic stimulation has been shown to increase bladder and bowel pressures, and to thereby effect evacuation. This technique is simple, safe, noninvasive, and has no known adverse effects. Using a lumbosacral wrap with coils targeting key nerves and muscles, Premium Therapy's EMIT MX system will provide effective, easy-to-use therapy for patients with neurogenic bowel and bladder.

EMIT SX Applications

Treatment of Musculoskeletal Pain: The Premium Therapy EMIT SX system offers the capability to reduce and/or eliminate pain in persons with localized musculoskeletal processes. A number of scientific studies have clearly demonstrated the power of pulsed electromagnetic coil stimulators to control pain. In one study, patients reported a 59 percent decrease in a subjective pain score after a single treatment with pulsed electromagnetic stimulation. The pain relief attained regularly persisted for several days. Additional studies have demonstrated consistent production of analgesia in subjects receiving pulsed electromagnetic stimulation, with long-lasting pain relief occurring in over half of the subjects.

Specifically in the treatment of back pain, the placement of a pulsed electromagnetic stimulator over muscles surrounding the spine consistently demonstrated a significant decrease in patient-reported scores of lower back pain. In addition to its demonstrated efficacy with lower back pain, pulsed electromagnetic stimulation has been found to be beneficial for musculoskeletal pain of all types, including neck, knee, and chronic and acute localized pain conditions.

Treatment of Arthritis: The Premium Therapy EMIT SX system also has applications in the treatment of arthritis where it has been shown that low frequency pulsed electromagnetic field stimulation results in the growth of cartilage cells. This ability to stimulate new cartilage growth creates a tremendous potential to reverse the degenerative changes of arthritis, a disease characterized by the destruction of existing cartilage in and around joint spaces.

In addition to the potential benefits of cartilage repair and growth, pulsed electromagnetic devices have also been shown to be cost-effective in reducing pain, including chronic knee pain, and improving function in osteoarthritis. Due to both its increased efficacy and lack of adverse side effects, pulsed electromagnetic stimulation may prove useful in forestalling joint replacements.

Proprietary Position

A full utility patent has been authored, filed, and is currently pending for "Method and Apparatus for Electromagnetic Stimulation of Nerve, Muscle, and/or Body Tissues." This patent takes into account both offensive and defensive postures in its claims and represents an extension of Provisional Patent No. 60/266,455. Opinions of legal counsel are confident that Premium Therapy's patent applications are enforceable and defensible. Care has been taken to file all potential claims of the invention in order to protect it from possible competition from other technologies. All patent application documents will be made available for examination by potential investors. Trademark applications are in process on the names Premium Therapy and EMIT. No conflicts or other use of these names has been found in an initial search. There are no third party claims for any interest in Premium Therapy technology, as none of the technology was developed using the facilities of any other institution and the developers were not employed by any other institution prior to the filing of their provisional patent.

Development Status

Premium Therapy's technology is currently in the bench-testing stage of development, the results of which have been highly encouraging. An Investigational Review Board (IRB) application has been filed to conduct human clinical studies and rapid approval is expected based on approval of similar studies.

Premium Therapy has contacted leading medical institutions in the U.S., many of which have expressed interest in participating in collaborative research and, given encouraging research results, purchasing the EMIT system. Investigators expressing strong interest include Dr. Henry Dillard of Harvard University, Dr. Floyd Marcus of University of California - Berkeley, Dr. Josh Williamson of the Therapeutic Institute, and Dr. Jason Martinez of the University of Arizona. It is expected that once Premium Therapy's IRB application has been approved, clinical studies will commence at each of these institutions.

Future Products

Premium Therapy anticipates future product development in profitable markets in the medical industry in the form of both the expansion of indications for the EMIT system and the development of novel technologies.

An example of a potentially profitable new indication for the EMIT system is found in the treatment of the major cause of stress urinary incontinence—a condition referred to as "idiopathic detrusor instability." Detrusor instability describes the unstable contractions of the detrusor muscle (a muscle controlling the release of urine from the bladder), which can cause sufferers to unexpectedly release urine. More than 20 million Americans are affected by this condition in which traditional therapies, such as dietary manipulation, surgical procedures, medications, and physical therapy, have been poorly tolerated and ineffective. Studies have shown that electromagnetic stimulation of sacral (an area of the lower spine) nerve roots acutely abolishes unstable contractions in patients with this condition making this a condition that will likely be treatable with the EMIT system.

In addition to researching new uses for the EMIT system, Premium Therapy will also explore novel technologies. To this end, the patent process has been initiated for a device designed to teach correct posture. This device is designed to train the user in maintenance of a healthy posture in order to treat the back and neck problems often associated with incorrect posture. In contrast to current devices that simply hold the spine in the correct position and then allow resumption of incorrect posture upon discontinuation, this device will actually train the user to maintain the correct posture by developing the musculature required for permanent correction of the problem.

While future product development is planned, Premium Therapy will concentrate, for the time being, on the ability of the EMIT system to treat muscular atrophy, neurogenic bladder and bowel, musculoskeletal pain and arthritis. Once success has been demonstrated in these markets, expansion to other markets, such as the treatment of stress incontinence, will be considered and new product development will be explored.

COMPETITION

Competition in the field of electromagnetic stimulating devices is developing rapidly. Established modalities such as electrical stimulation, physical therapy, and pharmacologic therapies have been used for a number of years in the treatment of conditions that are now gaining exposure to the potential of pulsed electromagnetic stimulating devices. Direct competition takes the form of two main technologies: Electrical Stimulation (ES) and existing Pulsed Electromagnetic Stimulation (PES). While each of these technologies attempts to treat the same conditions as the EMIT system, both have severe limitations. ES devices, for example, are unable to penetrate tissues to reach deep muscles without causing skin burns and irritation. PES devices, on the other hand, can penetrate deeply and painlessly, but have been developed exclusively for diagnostic applications, such as nerve or muscle testing. As a result, these devices, while effective in a diagnostic setting, make ineffective therapeutic tools.

Competitive Advantage

Premium Therapy's proprietary position allows for the patented use of an ergonomic, body-contoured wrap and overlapping coils. These proprietary elements allow targeted anatomic regions to be blanketed with pulsed electromagnetic stimulation in a format that is user-friendly and capable of being employed by untrained users including patients in their homes. In this way, Premium Therapy's EMIT technology creates a solution to the most significant limitations of existing pulsed electromagnetic stimulating technologies—namely the difficult nature of manipulating a single coil and the cost-intensive requirement of using highly-skilled medical personnel for operation.

The competitive advantages of the EMIT system can be summarized as follows:

- Unique therapeutic application of pulsed electromagnetic stimulation
- Patented delivery device with multiple user-friendly applicators
- Two models for multiple applications in the treatment of a variety of diseases
- Reduction of healthcare costs due to home healthcare applications

Competition

To date, the company is not currently aware of any product that provides as cost-effective, user-friendly, therapeutic care as the EMIT system. The EMIT system Models MX and SX target distinct market segments. For a more detailed description of competitive technologies, see Appendix A. The main competitors within each of the market segments are listed below (see Appendix B for competitive pricing chart).

EMIT MX Market Segments

Prevention and Treatment of Muscular Atrophy: In the large market for the treatment/prevention of atrophy, existing therapeutic devices have to date involved primarily electrical muscle stimulators. The different competitors include:

- **Electrical Stimulating Devices (ES):** ES units, often referred to as functional electrical stimulators, employed in large clinic and physical therapy centers cost approximately $15,000. Smaller ES units for home use can cost from $3,000 to $5,000.

Important manufacturers include:

- Electrolite Products, Inc.: A manufacturer of the StimOne device, a modified exercise type cycle used by persons with spinal cord injuries in order to prevent atrophy and spasms, and to increase range of motion.

- Electro Med Services, Inc.: A provider of a range of devices and electrodes for functional electrical stimulation.

- **Pulsed Electromagnetic Stimulating Devices (PES):** The only significant competitors currently in the field of therapeutic functional PES are Leetonus and Top Line Stimulus. These companies have focused solely on products that involve the use of a single stimulatory coil. The use of these products requires expensive, highly-skilled operator involvement. Even with the highly-skilled operator, treatments are lengthy (greater than 15 minutes per muscle group) and inconsistent due to the constant manipulation required to achieve the desired result. As a result of these limitations, existing functional pulsed electromagnetic stimulation devices are not well tailored for therapeutic applications. Instead, they are primarily suited for the diagnostic field, in which Top Line Stimulus has captured the greatest market share.

Important manufacturers include:

- **Leetonus:** The LeeTone model base cost is $20,000. This unit is designed for a trained operator, such as a physical therapist or physician, to hold the stimulating coil over a specific area of the body in treatments for atrophy, muscle spasms, and decreased blood flow. The Leetonus Company is currently directing marketing focus around the LeeControl device, which is employed in the treatment of urological conditions, and the LeePulse device, which uses transcranial stimulation in the treatment of psychiatric conditions. Leetonus recently received $7.3 million in a second round of venture capital funding, bringing its total to $12.2 million.

- **Top Line Stimulus Corporation:** Top Line Stimulus' main offering is a hand held coil similar to the Leetonus LeeTone product for the stimulation of specific nerves and nearby tissue. Top Line Stimulus' devices find application primarily in areas of diagnostic evaluation of brain or central motor disorders and spinal injuries. The Top Line Stimulus Model 500 has a base cost of $12,500. Other models range in price from $20,000 to $30,000. As of November 2001, Top Line Stimulus had sold approximately 2,500 units worldwide.

- **Electronic Medicals, SupraTimer, and Beingarden GmbH** are also involved in the pulsed electromagnetic stimulation business but have only produced devices for diagnostic purposes to date.

Treatment of Neurogenic Bladder and Bowel: There are currently no devices that offer noninvasive treatment for the conditions of neurogenic bladder and bowel. Pulsed electromagnetic stimulation offers the opportunity to effectively treat these conditions without the adverse side effects. Current care options include intermittent catheterization, surgery, and functional electrical stimulation, the latter of which is still in the experimental stage and not commercially available.

EMIT SX Market Segments

Treatment of Musculoskeletal Pain: In the vast market for the treatment of musculoskeletal pain there are numerous therapeutic options available, the majority of which are based solely on pain control. There are few, if any, direct competitors with the noninvasive therapeutic potential embodied in the EMIT system. Therapies currently available, which compete only indirectly with EMIT, include pharmacologic and physical therapies.

- **Electrical Stimulating Devices (ES):** ES technologies have primarily been employed in the form of transcutaneous electrical nerve stimulation (TENS units). At present, there are well over 100 different models of transcutaneous electrical nerve stimulators (TENS) devices in the marketplace and an increasing number of other electrical devices.

The major manufacturer of TENS devices is:

- **Rehabilicare Inc.:** A manufacturer and provider of electrotherapy devices for rehabilitation, as well as products for chronic and acute pain management, consisting of small, portable, battery-powered electrical pulse generators. For the fiscal year ended 6/30/01, total revenues rose 5 percent to $62 million. Net income rose 51 percent to $3.3 million. Rehabilicare has a market capitalization of $34.8 million.

Treatment of Arthritis: In the vast market for the treatment of arthritis, existing therapies have focused on pain control issues. No therapy, aside from EMIT, has demonstrated the ability to reverse the wear-and-tear degenerative changes that cause such significant pain for osteoarthritis sufferers. A number of different therapies involved in the treatment of this condition that compete only indirectly with Premium Therapy include: nutritional supplements, hyaluronic acid injections, and pharmacologic therapy.

STRATEGY & IMPLEMENTATION SUMMARY

Premium Therapy's strategy will be to target both the market for the EMIT MX as well as the market for the lower power EMIT SX. The models will be promoted separately in each of their disparate markets and specialty distributors will be utilized in order to rapidly form robust distribution and sales networks.

An important step will be the establishment of the EMIT system at key medical institutions throughout the country. A strategic partnership has already been formed with the Physical Therapy department at Harvard University. Once an IDE has been obtained and pending investigational review board applications are approved, clinical studies will commence with the assistance of Dr. Henry Dillard, Director of Clinical Services in the Physical and Occupational Therapy department at Harvard University. Dr. Dillard is excited to begin the studies and to be a part of a technology that he feels has the potential to revolutionize the industry. Additional institutions expressing interest in collaborative studies include: University of California - Berkeley, the Therapeutic Institute, and the University of Arizona.

Value Proposition

The true value of Premium Therapy's ElectroMagnetic Induction Therapy (EMIT) technology lies with the patient. In using the EMIT system, the patient stands to gain unparalleled, scientifically proven, therapeutic benefits including: improved treatment of muscular atrophy, effective therapy for neurogenic bowel and bladder, consistent production of analgesia in arthritis and musculoskeletal pain, and reversal of the degenerative changes found in arthritis.

Not only will the EMIT system treat multiple, previously poorly-managed diseases, it will do so in a user-friendly manner with cost-effective, home-healthcare applications. Compared to existing technologies that require trained healthcare professionals to operate the complex machinery, the EMIT system is incredibly user-friendly. In fact, once the patient is shown how to use the EMIT system, there will be no need for continued healthcare provider input other than routine follow-up. Thus, with decreased healthcare professional requirements and home healthcare applications, use of the EMIT system will result in an overall decrease in healthcare costs for the patient while providing superior clinical results.

The value proposition for institutions and healthcare providers to adopt the technology is threefold: 1) Premium Therapy's proprietary position will allow a sustainable premium to be charged for the EMIT system; 2) Even with this sustainable premium, assuming only a 20 percent reduction in requirement for existing therapies with the use of the EMIT system, overall treatment costs will decline (see Appendix 1) and 3) Use of the EMIT system will result in superior patient care.

Marketing Strategy

Marketing efforts for Premium Therapy's technology will involve the targeting of two different populations: 1) healthcare providers treating muscular atrophy, neurogenic bowel and bladder, musculoskeletal pain and/or arthritis, and 2) patients suffering from muscular atrophy, neurogenic bowel and bladder, musculoskeletal pain and/or arthritis.

Premium Therapy's success is dependent first upon demonstrating scientific support for the efficacy of the device and then on creating acceptance among health care providers and patients. Promotional strategies will be reflective of this fact. Of course, acceptance by either patients or providers will provide an impetus for the other group to follow suit.

Sales/marketing will be directed in coordination with specialty distributors contracted by Premium Therapy, thus significantly reducing the company's own required sales/marketing expenditures. The efforts of Premium Therapy's internal sales/marketing forces will be focused on marketing the EMIT system, developing educational tools, and training the specialty distributor sales representatives.

Promotion Strategy

Premium Therapy has already worked closely with physicians to design its products. The importance of working with physicians in developing novel therapies is well known. Initiation of clinical studies with the eager assistance of Dr. Henry Dillard, Director of Clinical Services in the Physical and Occupational Therapy department at Harvard University will be invaluable in the promotion of EMIT as a viable medical therapy. It is expected that once the device is found to be effective, Harvard University will use it as a high-profile example of its technological advancement.

Promotion efforts for Premium Therapy's technology will focus on its two target populations, namely: 1) healthcare providers treating muscular atrophy, neurogenic bowel and bladder, musculoskeletal pain and/or arthritis, and 2) patients suffering from muscular atrophy, neurogenic bowel and bladder, musculoskeletal pain and/or arthritis.

- **Healthcare Providers:** Acceptance among the more than 550,000 healthcare providers who treat muscular atrophy, neurogenic bowel and bladder, musculoskeletal pain and/or arthritis will be one of the keys to Premium Therapy's success. Even with strong patient demand, if the healthcare providers are unwilling to recommend Premium Therapy's technology, then the market will remain largely untapped. Furthermore, healthcare providers are persuasive in consulting patients concerning novel therapies and those healthcare providers who have embraced Premium Therapy's technology will be powerful advocates.

  In marketing the procedure to healthcare providers, the main consideration will be the efficacy of Premium Therapy's technology and its superiority over existing technologies. First and foremost, Premium Therapy will utilize the competent, trained sales force of the specialty distributors to create a demand push for its technology. These efforts will be complemented by Premium Therapy's internal sales force, which will engage in direct calling or visiting in order to encourage trials.

  Furthermore, Premium Therapy intends to promote its technology through publications and advertisements in reputable medical journals along with presentations at national conventions. Using this sales/marketing strategy, along with the promise of sustainable premiums for healthcare providers involved with the EMIT system, Premium Therapy expects to generate demand among healthcare providers.

- **Patients:** Premium Therapy will also market its technology to patient-consumers once healthcare providers have begun to adopt the EMIT system. In promoting Premium Therapy's technology to this population, the most important factor will be concrete research results displaying the superior efficacy of the EMIT system compared to existing technologies. Once these data have been acquired, Premium Therapy will embark on a large-scale, national advertising campaign focusing on television and print media. Using these channels, along with intentionally facilitating publicity, Premium Therapy will be able to generate a demand pull from individuals with conditions treatable with the EMIT system.

Pricing Strategy

The EMIT MX and EMIT SX systems are priced in two components, both in keeping with industry standards. EMIT MX will require more complex, expensive circuitry and will need greater functionality than EMIT SX due to its higher power requirements. Based on these much higher costs, the retail and wholesale price for EMIT MX will be significantly higher than for EMIT SX, but will fall well within the range of industry standards.

Premium Therapy expects to lease the EMIT MX system much more frequently than the SX system, so estimates of one logic controller (LC) per ten patients and one LC per two patients were used for the MX and SX systems respectively. The Arrays of Overlapping Coils (AOCs) are single-patient devices, as they are not designed to withstand the harsh resterilization procedures.

It is expected that the specialty distributor selected for Premium Therapy's technology will use a markup of approximately 50 percent in determining retail price. This is the upper end of estimates received from specialty distributors with quotes ranging from 35 percent to 50 percent. Prices are inclusive of both customer service and technical support as the specialty distributor will provide these functions.

Wholesale and Retail Prices

Component	**Wholesale Price**	**Expected Retail**
EMIT MX Logic Controller	$13,000	$20,000
EMIT SX Logic Controller	$2,000	$3,000
Arrays of Overlapping Coils	$250	$350

Sales Strategy

The key step in generating sales will be to initiate the investment in Premium Therapy's technology after which initial sales efforts are expected to decrease significantly. Therefore, the sales force will be relied on heavily for the initial demand push for the adoption of the EMIT system, then to a much lesser extent for the additional components. While Premium Therapy will maintain a small internal sales force in order to encourage adoption of its technology at select medical centers and to train specialty distributor sales personnel, the bulk of all selling will be accomplished through the use of specialty distributors. The specialty distributors to be utilized have well-established distribution networks and widespread sales contacts, which will prove invaluable in promoting Premium Therapy's innovative technology in the early years of the business plan.

Premium Therapy's internal sales force will initially consist of two personnel in Year 2. This number is expected to increase to approximately twelve by Year 5 with expected dramatic increases in sales. This number is remarkably low as a percentage of sales due to the role of the specialty distributor in providing many sales functions.

Milestones

The following are the key milestones for Premium Therapy's operations:

1. Patent process and business plan have been completed.
2. Investigational Device Exemption Application filed by June 2002.

3. Specialty Distributors selected by June 2002.
4. Start-up capital will be raised by August 2002.
5. First round of human clinical trials completed by June 2003.
6. Full FDA approval obtained by June 2005.
7. All other milestones are currently on schedule in accordance with the business plan.

Regulatory Issues

The FDA classifies new devices into one of two categories: experimental or investigational. Experimental devices are innovative devices for which "absolute risk" has not been established, meaning that the initial questions of safety and efficacy have not been resolved. Investigational devices are those for which "incremental risk" is the primary risk in question, meaning that questions of safety and efficacy have been resolved to the satisfaction of the FDA. Due to the precedent set by existing pulsed electromagnetic stimulators as "investigational" devices, Premium Therapy expects its EMIT technology to also be granted the preferable "investigational" status in the form of an Investigational Device Exemption (IDE).

Furthermore, while it is expected that full FDA approval will be gained quickly based on the approval of similar devices, the EMIT system will be produced and marketed prior to this approval. Once the IDE has been granted, Premium Therapy will be able to market and sell the device to interested parties prior to FDA approval with the label "For Investigational Use Only." An example of such expedited market entrance can be seen with Leetonus' LeeTone in which an IDE was obtained and devices were sold prior to full FDA approval. Only minimal delay in market entrance is expected as IDE approvals are typically obtained within an average of 3 months including required revisions.

Once full FDA approval is obtained for therapeutic use of the EMIT system, the market is expected to expand dramatically and entrance into foreign markets will be possible. At this stage, as well, it is expected that insurance companies will begin reimbursing for pulsed electromagnetic therapy, greatly increasing demand for Premium Therapy's products. Full FDA approval will be necessary in order to claim therapeutic efficacy of the EMIT system for each of its indications.

MANAGEMENT TEAM

The founders of Premium Therapy are Dr. Julius Nestor, Mr. Pi Long Su, Dr. Sherman MacDonald, and Ivan Astov. Dr. Nestor will serve the company as interim CEO, Mr. Su will serve as interim CFO, Mr. Astov will serve as interim COO, and Dr. MacDonald will serve as Director of Research and Development.

Several key people, including a CEO, are being sought.

Founders and Principals

Julius Nestor, M.D./M.B.A.: Dr. Nestor has a long history of biomedical device design and testing. During his undergraduate career at the University of Arkansas, Dr. Nestor concentrated in Biomedical Engineering with a cumulative GPA of 4.0 in his major. While pursuing his undergraduate degree, he led a team that designed toys for children with cerebral palsy and was subsequently awarded the Excellence in Senior Design Award by the Department of Bioengineering. To augment his academic experience, Dr. Nestor spent a total of 10 months at the Arkansas Department of Health and Safety both testing devices and writing congressional reports on the current state-of-the-art devices. Dr. Nestor is the inventor of Premium Therapy's patented EMIT system as well as multiple other devices including a myringotomy tube insertion device (patent pending), a non-invasive corneal sculpting device (patent pending), and a peritoneovesicular shunt (patent pending). Dr. Nestor is currently a first-year resident at the Therapeutic Institute in Cambridge, Massachusetts.

Pi Long Su, M.B.A.: Mr. Su was previously involved in several Initial Public Offerings and Mergers and Acquisitions as an investment banker, and is a Certified Public Accountant with extensive experience in the U.S., Asia, and Australia. He is also a founding director of a successful start-up company in Hong Kong involved in organizing round-table conferences for senior bankers, publishing banking journals, and creating banking intelligence and proprietary research reports. Mr. Su is currently employed by National Bank as an investment banker.

Sherman MacDonald, M.D.: Dr. MacDonald is highly involved in the improvement of function in people's lives. With the focus of his training in the specialty of Physical Medicine and Rehabilitation, Dr. MacDonald's areas of interest include chronic pain, musculoskeletal and back pain, as well as sports medicine. He received his training in medicine at the University of Arizona School of Medicine. Prior to entering the field of medicine, Dr. MacDonald received his undergraduate education at Harvard University, where he graduated with honors with a degree in Organismic and Evolutionary Biology. Dr. MacDonald is currently a physician at the Therapeutic Institute in Cambridge, Massachusetts.

Ivan Astov: Mr. Astov has an extensive background in general management, finance and research. As an undergraduate at the University of Arkansas, Mr. Astov researched both the pressure distributions in the human microvasculature and the genetically determined temperature sensitivity of the high molecular weight, low copy number pRts1 plasmid. Mr. Astov's commitment to science while pursuing a dual degree in Electrical and Bioengineering was recognized by admission to the University Scholars program. Having worked with Walters Consulting, StockPrice, and later Chase Manhattan, Mr. Astov has over four years of experience in helping American corporate clients to maximize shareholder value by streamlining operations, reengineering systems, and implementing new business strategies. Mr. Astov is currently completing his M.B.A. degree at the Harvard Business School.

Consultants

Morton S. Biddley, J.D.: Mr. Sheldon's background includes over thirty years of experience in business, law, and education. For 12 years, he was one of two principals in MedTech Group, Inc., a Cambridge-based venture development firm. Two public companies, MedTechlex and MedSys, resulted from MedTech's efforts. Prior to founding MedTech, Mr. Biddley was a principal in or consultant to several high technology start-up companies in Cambridge Research Park. These included venture capital-backed firms such as MedFlex,BMG Data, Healthwise Corporation, and Cambridge Biomedical Sciences. In addition, Mr. Biddley has held a faculty position with the Harvard Business School for 24 years. He has served as a member of the Business Review Board of the Department of Technology, Massachusetts Department of Commerce, and the Massachusetts Biotechnology Center Task Force on University-Industry Technology Transfer. Mr. Biddley currently is a founder and principal of Technology Foundations Consulting, an international consulting firm.

Howard Melton: After graduating from Wesleyan University with a degree in Biomedical Engineering, Mr. Melton joined the Medical Device Company where he spent a total of five years. His duties with the Medical Device Company included research in the Hydrodynamics and Acoustics Branch and new device evaluation in the Office of Device Evaluation. He then spent two years with Blue Cross Research prior to his current position with the Radiology Department at Harvard University where he has been employed for one year.

Dr. Henry Dillard: Dr. Dillard is currently the Director of Clinical Services in the Physical and Occupational Therapy department at Harvard University. He has assisted in the launch and management of multiple clinical trials, which have set the standard for physical therapy care. Dr. Dillard will be assisting Premium Therapy in the management of its research.

Dennis MacDonald, J.D./MSCE: Mr. MacDonald's background includes experience in the field of structural engineering and the practice of law. He has worked with Johnson Structural Engineers and then later with Ford in structural engineering positions. He has pursued the practice of law for the past 28 years, with a focus of expertise in the area of intellectual property protection.

Management Team Gaps

The founders of Premium Therapy are actively seeking both an experienced CEO and a VP of Business Development. The desired profile for a CEO is an individual experienced in the medical device arena, ideally who was part of a previous successful start-up venture. The ideal VP of Business Development is an individual with experience in distributing and marketing products based on innovative biomedical technologies. Once recruited, the CEO and VP of Business Development will assist the management team in the search for a COO, a CFO, sales/ marketing personnel, and technical personnel.

Dr. Nestor will serve as interim CEO, Mr. Su will serve as interim CFO, Dr. MacDonald will serve as Director of Research and Development, and Mr. Astov will serve as interim COO.

Personnel Plan

The Personnel Plan chronicles the growth of the organization to thirty employees in the first five years. Each year could require a few additional people besides those indicated, based on the growth of the company in accordance with the Business Plan.

Prior to funding, the four principals will be the sole employees and salaries will not be paid unless outside grants are secured. Once funded, the company will hire additional personnel and the principals will begin to earn salaries. See Appendix H for total payroll and headcount.

OPERATIONAL PLAN

Premium Therapy's products will initially consist of manufactured goods. The strategic operational plan is to minimize overhead through the outsourcing of production, distribution, sales and support for both the EMIT MX and SX. Premium Therapy will also decrease required start-up capital through the rental of necessary equipment whenever possible.

Manufacturing

Premium Therapy has arranged to outsource production to Schmidt Scientific, Inc. in Boston, Massachusetts. Schmidt Scientific, Inc., is part of the Schmidt Magnetics Group which has been in magnetics since the late 1800s. Throughout the previous century, Schmidt Scientific, Inc. has gained experience in the production of electromagnetic devices for a variety of applications, including both medical and industrial. The manufactured components will be stored and distributed by specialty distributors contracted for such purposes.

Products

In order to manufacture both the MX and SX models of the EMIT system, three components will need to be produced:

- **Logic Controller MX:** This device will send powerful currents through the Arrays of Overlapping Coils, causing stimulation of the underlying motor neurons and contraction of the targeted muscle. Due to the requirement for increased power over the SX model, the Logic Controller for the MX model will be significantly more expensive to produce.

- **Logic Controller SX:** This device will send less powerful pulses of electrical current through the Arrays of Overlapping Coils, stimulating the underlying tissue without contracting the underlying muscle.
- **Arrays of Overlapping Coils:** This last component will require much more variability than the previous components. Not only will it be necessary to effectively target different regions of the body, but it will also be necessary to accommodate different body sizes. Premium Therapy will initially produce arrays targeting 6 different regions, each with 3 different sizes.

Production Costs

Production costs for each component were estimated using initial price quotes from Schmidt Scientific, Inc. Upon realization of its projected level of sales, Premium Therapy will investigate the feasibility of manufacturing facilities of its own to improve on its cost structure and increase its profitability.

Through outsourcing production, Premium Therapy will be able to keep initial capital requirements lower with the trade-off of higher production costs. It is estimated that the total cost of manufacture for each of the components will be:

- **EMIT MX Logic Controller:** $5,000.00 per unit
- **EMIT SX Logic Controller:** $925.00 per unit
- **Array of Coils (for models MX and SX):** $95.00 per unit

It is estimated, as well, that production costs will drop 3 percent per year as volume increases and experience with manufacturing techniques is gained.

Sourcing

Primary raw materials needed are as follows:

- Electrical components (capacitor, wiring, etc.) for Logic Controller and Arrays of Coils.
- Molds for external console of Logic Controller.
- Material for wraps in which overlapping coils will be placed.

All of these components are easily sourced and multiple suppliers have been identified. Premium Therapy will establish business relationships with these suppliers to be negotiated for preferred pricing structures without compromising quality standards.

Product Support

In the early years, trained employees of the specialty distributors will provide product support for the EMIT systems MX and SX. Once the EMIT system gains acceptance, Premium Therapy will consider adopting the responsibility of product support.

Facilities and Properties

The company will initially be based in Cambridge Research Park, Massachusetts. This location will facilitate research and testing opportunities at Harvard University to be conducted in coordination with the University of Arizona Health Sciences Center.

In view of the strategic plan to contract with third parties for all manufacturing and distribution requirements, the only necessary facilities will be offices for personnel. After Year 5, when the company has reached its anticipated milestones, the company will explore the feasibility of constructing its own manufacturing and distribution facilities.

FINANCIAL PLAN

Premium Therapy intends to raise approximately US $1,000,000 worth of seed capital. Founders and principals have already committed $100,000.

Current Capital Structure:

Stock Type	Shares Authorized	Shares Issued
Common	20,000,000	1,500,000
Preferred	2,000,000	-

Current Shareholders:

Owner	Common Shares Granted	Percentage Ownership
Julius Nestor	825,000	55%
Sherman MacDonald	450,000	35%
Pi Long Su	150,000	10%

For $1,000,000, the investing party will receive convertible, preferred shares with an ownership interest, liquidation preference, and anti-dilution provisions as negotiated.

The proceeds from the offer will be used to fund the working capital requirements including employee compensation, research and development, initial operations facilities, and patent and trademark registration. Premium Therapy has no intention to purchase land, building, or plant, and will attempt to leverage its current assets with lease and rental whenever economical. Premium Therapy intends to issue equity options for subscription of common shares up to 20 percent of the capital as employee incentives, which will result in dilution of current shareholdings.

Liquidity for Investors and Equity Valuation:

Premium Therapy's management intends to grow Premium Therapy into the market leader with its innovative, therapeutic devices. With the attainment of each of its milestones, Premium Therapy's potential will accelerate and its enterprise value will grow accordingly. With consistently strong performance, it is likely that private investors will continue to show interests in Premium Therapy's common and preferred shares, creating market liquidity for current investors even without the benefit of an initial public offering.

To the extent that actual operational results materially exceed those projected herein, the probability of an initial public offering increases dramatically. Alternatively, the medical instrument industry has been experiencing significant consolidation for more than a decade. The company will be receptive to any appropriate merger opportunities, and investors may achieve liquidity through this vehicle.

Projected Profit and Loss

Barring any unforeseen circumstances, Premium Therapy anticipates profitability by Year 4 of operations and expects profits in subsequent years to accelerate with the increase in anticipated sales volume, yielding approximately $1.3 million in net profit in Year 4 and $8.8 million in Year 5. See Appendix D for detailed projections.

Projected Cash Flow

In Year 1 of the business plan, Premium Therapy expects to raise $1,000,000 in working capital. While Premium Therapy has planned for additional capital raising of $1,500,000 in Year 3 of the business plan, it is expected that many of the research grants for which Premium Therapy has applied, collectively totaling over $2,500,000, will have been secured by this point and that the actual required capital will be significantly less. The potential for securing grants will be greatly enhanced due to Premium Therapy's relationships with multiple renowned investigators at the nations leading universities. See Appendix E for detailed Pro-forma Cash Flow projections.

Projected Balance Sheet

In order to minimize required capital in the early years of the business plan, Premium Therapy will lease and rent equipment and supplies whenever possible. This effort will be further complemented by the use of a specialty distributor, which will greatly decrease initial capital requirements. See Appendix F for a detailed Pro-forma Balance Sheet.

APPENDIX

Appendix A: Competitive Technology

The current industry for Premium Therapy's EMIT system is rapidly evolving. Analysis of the current state of the industry surrounding these products must first consider the sum in terms of its parts. The several industry segments for the EMIT system Models MX and SX are outlined below.

EMIT MX Industry Segments

Prevention and Treatment of Muscular Atrophy: The industry for atrophy prevention and treatment currently involves primarily electrical stimulating technologies. Other technologies have made small inroads in the industry, but the bulk of therapeutic intervention consists of traditional exercise and physical therapy-based activities.

- **Electrical Stimulating Devices (ES):** Commonly referred to as functional electrical stimulators, these devices utilize the direct application of electric potentials in order to excite nerves. There are hundreds of different devices available for ES of muscle. The use of these devices has encountered several significant obstacles in the treatment of atrophy, though. While effective in stimulating superficial muscles, ES technology is limited by the fact that it is not able to penetrate tissues to reach deep muscles without causing skin burns and irritation. As a result, this form of stimulation has found very limited success in the treatment of atrophy for large muscle groups, such as those found in the legs, shoulder, back, and other areas.
- **Existing Pulsed Electromagnetic Stimulating Devices (PES):** PES has been shown to overcome a number of the limitations of electrical stimulating technology. Significantly, PES has been shown to penetrate much more deeply and to do so much less painfully. What is more, PES has potential indications that do not overlap those of ES. Due to its painless nature, PES can be used more frequently and over a larger area of the body without significant discomfort. Despite these scientifically proven advantages, no competitor, to date, has developed a user-friendly, consistently-effective therapeutic device employing PES technology.

Neurogenic Bladder and Bowel Treatments: The present industry for the treatment of neurogenic bladder and bowel involves principally invasive therapies that are associated with high risks of complications. The treatment options for persons with this condition have, to date, included the following therapies:

- **Intermittent Catheterization:** Catheters, or hollow tubes, can be inserted into the bladder in order to provide evacuation at regular intervals. While simple and effective, long-term use of catheterization is associated with a number of significant complications, including: bladder and kidney infections, chronic kidney inflammation, kidney stones, and bladder stones.
- **Surgery:** The alternative to intermittent catheterization for treating these conditions for many patients has been surgical intervention. Surgical procedures can involve the

placement of an artificial sphincter around the neck of the bladder or manipulation of the outflow tracts to assist with bladder emptying. Surgical intervention is invasive, and thus associated with long-term complications including infection and continued need for catheterization or similar procedures. In addition, surgical management has failed to demonstrate significant improvements in the quality of life of persons affected with these conditions.

- **Electrical Stimulation (ES):** This technology has been used on a limited basis for the facilitation of voiding with neurogenic bladder. Application of ES technology in this field has remained largely experimental to date, and has failed to translate into a viable treatment option for patients.

EMIT SX Market Segments

Treatment of Musculoskeletal Pain: The market for the treatment of musculoskeletal pain is staggering in size, with estimates of greater than 100 million pain sufferers in the U.S. alone. Treatment options include:

- **Pharmacologic Therapy:** Medications are used widely in the treatment of musculoskeletal-related pain. The mechanisms by which the numerous medications function in the treatment of musculoskeletal pain include: the modulation of pain signals received in the brain, alteration of the transmission of pain signals along nerves, and the production of pain-reducing chemicals in the body. While pharmacologic treatments of musculoskeletal pain can be effective, they can also have highly significant side effects. These side effects can be of great consequence, especially in the elderly who account for the bulk of musculoskeletal pain sufferers.

- **Electrical Stimulating Devices (ES):** ES technologies, primarily in the form of transcutaneous electrical nerve stimulation (TENS units), have been used in the treatment of musculoskeletal pain for decades. ES technology is now a widely used modality for the treatment of general acute and chronic pain syndromes. The primary disadvantages of ES technologies relate to the fact that this form of stimulation is associated with risk of tissue damage at the interface between the electrodes and the skin. In addition, ES is associated with frequent reports of "uncomfortable sensations or pain" and requires an invasive approach to target regions that are deeper than the surface of the skin.

- **Existing Pulsed Electromagnetic Stimulating Technology (PES):** PES devices have made only limited inroads in the industry of musculoskeletal pain treatment. PES technologies, though, have demonstrated efficacy in treating musculoskeletal pain in a number of different studies. Despite this fact, to date, existing PES industry forces have failed to create a user-friendly application for the treatment of musculoskeletal pain.

Treatment of Arthritis: The market for the treatment of arthritis is also quite large, approximately 90 percent of which is osteoarthritis. This form of arthritis involves degenerative changes in the cartilage lining the joint surfaces. To date, there are no therapies that have demonstrated the ability to reverse the wear-and-tear degenerative changes that cause such significant pain for osteoarthritis sufferers.

- **Nutritional Supplements:** Glucosamine and chondroitin are the principle players in the $330 million joint health supplement market. These supplements are used widely in Europe and are becoming increasingly popular in the U.S. There has, however, been very little in the way of scientific evidence to support any claims of efficacy. Dr. Daniel Clegg, the director of a National Institutes of Health supplement study, reports that research to date "has not proven that the supplements work... The lure of glucosamine and chondroitin is that there isn't really any good treatment for degenerative arthritis."

- **Hyaluronic Acid Injections:** Intra-articular hyaluronic acid injections have also been used to treat degenerative arthritis. The use of these injections is based on the premise that the replenishment of hyaluronan, an important substance for cartilage growth, can alleviate pain in the knee joint and possibly even repair cartilage damage in early osteoarthritis. Several studies, though, have failed to show a statistical difference in symptomatic improvement between intra-articular hyaluronic acid injections and the placebo, intra-articularly introduced saline. In addition, the injection of any foreign substance into the body is associated with increased risks of infection and other adverse side effects.

- **Pharmacologic Therapy:** Pharmacologic therapies are used widely in the treatment of arthritis pain. Drug-based therapies used for this type of pain are similar to those used for the treatment of musculoskeletal pain (as outlined above) and involve primarily narcotics and nonsteroidal anti-inflammatory drugs (NSAIDS). Pharmacologic treatments of arthritis pain can be effective, but as noted earlier, can also have significant side effects. These side effects are of greatest consequence to the elderly who are the most likely to suffer from arthritis.

- **Existing Pulsed Electromagnetic Stimulation Devices (PES):** PES devices have not yet gained a significant foothold in the market for arthritis treatment. The power of PES to reduce pain, improve function, and enhance the growth of cartilage producing cells, though, offers a promising opportunity for future growth in this field.

Appendix B: Main Competitors

Premium Therapy Competitors

Technology	Company	Application	Model Price
ES	Electrologic of America	Atrophy	$15,000
	ElectroStim Medical Devices	Atrophy	$3,000-$5,000
	Rehabilicare	Pain	$500-$1,000
PES	Leetonus	Atrophy	$20,000
	Magstim	Diagnostic Testing	$12,500-$30,000

Appendix C: Sales Forecasts

In compiling sales forecasts, Premium Therapy used another innovative technology, vacuum-assisted closure (VAC), as an analogy in estimating diffusion of the EMIT system. Much like Premium Therapy's EMIT technology, VAC entered the medical device market as an innovative extension of existing technology. Also much like EMIT, VAC offered a novel solution to an otherwise poorly-managed disease. VAC was quickly proven to be highly effective in the treatment of chronic wounds and sales increased exponentially over the first five years of company operation.

Premium Therapy extrapolated the diffusion of EMIT SX and MX using the historical diffusion of the VAC device. Using this information, Premium Therapy was able to compile sales forecasts for the five-year horizon of the business plan. These forecasts do not take into account the fact that the diffusion rate will likely be accelerated due to increased acceptance of precedent pulsed electromagnetic technologies.

Appendix C: Sales Forecasts

Continued...

Dollar Sales	**2002**	**2003**	**2004**	**2005**	**2006**
EMIT SX - Logic Controller	-	428,568	1,249,459	4,249,828	18,430,229
EMIT SX - Array of Coils	-	107,142	312,365	1,062,457	4,607,557
EMIT MX - Logic Controller	-	358,160	947,507	4,019,275	8,343,473
EMIT MX - Array of Coils	-	68,877	182,213	772,937	1,604,514
Total Dollar Sales	**-**	**962,747**	**2,691,544**	**10,104,497**	**32,985,773**
Direct Cost of Sales					
EMIT SX - Logic Controller	-	188,592	523,141	1,693,012	6,985,729
EMIT SX - Array of Coils	-	38,738	107,456	347,754	1,434,907
EMIT MX - Logic Controller	-	131,068	329,909	1,331,531	2,629,922
EMIT MX - Array of Coils	-	24,903	62,983	252,991	499,685
Total Unit Costs	**-**	**383,301**	**1,023,188**	**3,625,288**	**11,550,243**

Unit Sales	**2002**	**2003**	**2004**	**2005**	**2006**
EMIT SX - Logic Controller	-	210	600	2,000	8,500
EMIT SX - Array of Coils	-	420	1,200	4,000	17,000
EMIT MX - Logic Controller	-	27	70	291	592
EMIT MX - Array of Coils	-	270	700	2,910	5,920
Total Unit Sales	**-**	**927**	**2,570**	**9,201**	**32,012**
Unit Sale Prices					
EMIT SX - Logic Controller	$2,000.00	$2,040.80	$2,082.43	$2,124.91	$2,168.26
EMIT SX - Array of Coils	$250.00	$255.10	$260.30	$265.61	$271.03
EMIT MX - Logic Controller	$13,000.00	$13,265.20	$13,535.81	$13,811.94	$14,093.70
EMIT MX - Array of Coils	$250.00	$255.10	$260.30	$265.61	$271.03
Unit Costs					
EMIT SX - Logic Controller	$925.00	$898.06	$871.90	$846.51	$821.85
EMIT SX - Array of Coils	$95.00	$92.23	$89.55	$86.94	$84.41
EMIT MX - Logic Controller	$5,000.00	$4,854.37	$4,712.98	$4,575.71	$4,442.44
EMIT MX - Array of Coils	$95.00	$92.23	$89.55	$86.94	$84.41

Appendix D: Income Statement

	2002	**2003**	**2004**	**2005**	**2006**
Total Revenues	**-**	**962,747**	**2,691,544**	**10,104,497**	**32,985,773**
Direct Cost of Sales	-	383,301	1,023,188	3,625,288	11,550,243
Gross Margin	-	579,446	1,668,356	6,479,209	21,435,530
Gross Margin %	-	60%	62%	64%	65%
Operating Expenses:					
Advertising and Promotion	-	48,137	134,577	505,225	1,649,289
Travel	4,500	30,000	100,000	200,000	300,000
Research and Development	150,000	250,000	1,100,000	1,350,000	2,750,000
Regulatory Expenses	10,000	25,000	80,000	120,000	135,000
Payroll	222,000	696,000	119,200	1,615,280	2,396,446
Payroll Burden	46,620	146,160	235,032	339,209	503,254
Depreciation and Amortization	500	1,000	3,000	6,000	11,000

	2002	2003	2004	2005	2006
Utilities	-	24,069	67,289	252,612	824,644
Insurance	25,000	35,000	45,000	65,000	105,000
Rent	24,000	26,000	28,000	48,000	88,000
Contract Workforce/Consultants	-	15,000	35,000	75,000	135,000
Total Operating Expenses	**482,620**	**1,296,366**	**2,947,098**	**4,576,326**	**8,897,633**
Earnings Before Interest and Taxes	**(482,620)**	**(716,920)**	**(1,278,742)**	**1,902,883**	**12,537,897**
Net Interest Expense (Income)	(15,024)	(8,622)	(5,607)	(10,409)	(32,803)
Provision for Taxes	(144,786)	(215,076)	(383,623)	570,865	3,761,369
Net Profit	**(322,810)**	**(493,222)**	**(889,512)**	**1,342,427**	**8,809,331**
Net Profit Margin %	-	51.20%	33.00%	13.30%	26.70%
Dividends Paid	-	-	-	-	3,000,000

Appendix E: Cash Flow

	2002	2003	2004	2005	2006
Net Profit:	**(322,810)**	**(493,222)**	**(889,512)**	**1,342,427**	**8,809,331**
Plus:					
Depreciation and Amortization	500	1,000	3,000	6,000	11,000
Working Capital Changes:					
Accounts Receivable	-	(118,695)	(213,139)	(913,926)	(2,820,979)
Inventory	-	(92,318)	(165,775)	(710,831)	(2,194,095)
Other Short-Term Assets	-	(5,000)	(1,000)	(20,000)	(40,000)
Accounts Payable	-	63,008	105,187	427,742	1,302,732
Long-Term Debt	-	-	-	-	-
Long-Term Liabilities	-	10,000	20,000	40,000	80,000
Capital Expenditures	(5,000)	(5,000)	(20,000)	(30,000)	(50,000)
Financing Activities:					
Capital Infusion	1,078,500	-	1,500,000	-	-
Dividends Paid	-	-	-	-	(3,000,000)
Net Cash Flow	**751,191**	**(640,227)**	**338,760**	**141,412**	**2,097,989**
Beginning Cash Balance	-	751,190	110,963	449,723	591,135
Ending Cash Balance	751,190	110,963	449,723	591,135	2,689,124

Appendix F: Balance Sheet

ASSETS	**2002**	**2003**	**2004**	**2005**	**2006**
Current Assets					
Cash	751,190	110,963	449,723	591,135	2,689,124
Accounts Receivable	-	118,695	331,834	1,245,760	4,066,739
Inventory	-	92,318	258,093	968,924	3,163,019
Other Short-Term Assets	-	5,000	6,000	26,000	66,000
Total Current Assets	**751,190**	**326,976**	**1,045,650**	**2,831,820**	**9,984,883**
Long-Term Assets					
Net Property, Plant and Equipment	4,500	8,500	25,500	49,500	88,500
Total Long-Term Assets	**4,500**	**8,500**	**25,500**	**49,500**	**88,500**
TOTAL ASSETS	**755,690**	**335,476**	**1,071,150**	**2,881,320**	**10,073,383**
LIABILITIES AND CAPITAL					
Accounts Payable	-	63,008	168,195	595,938	1,898,670
Bank Revolving Facility	-	-	-	-	-
Current Liabilities	**-**	**63,008**	**168,195**	**595,938**	**1,898,670**
Long-Term Debt	-	-	-	-	-
Long-Term Liabilities	-	10,000	30,000	70,000	150,000
Total Liabilities	**-**	**73,008**	**198,195**	**665,938**	**2,048,670**
Paid-in Capital	1,100,000	1,100,000	2,600,000	2,600,000	2,600,000
Retained Earnings	(21,500)	(344,310)	(837,532)	(1,727,045)	(3,384,618)
Proft/(Loss) for the year	(322,810)	(493,222)	(889,512)	1,342,427	8,809,331
Total Shareholders' Equity	**755,690**	**262,468**	**872,955**	**2,215,382**	**8,024,712**
TOTAL LIABILITIES AND EQUITY	**755,690**	**335,476**	**1,071,150**	**2,881,320**	**10,073,383**

Appendix G: Business Ratios

Profitability Ratios:	**2002**	**2003**	**2004**	**2005**	**2006**
Gross Margin (%)	-	60.0%	62.0%	64.0%	65.0%
Net Profit Margin (%)	-	-51.0%	-33.0%	13.0%	27.0%
Return on Average Assets	-85.4%	-90.4%	126.5%	67.9%	136.0%
Return on Average Equity	-85.4%	96.9%	-156.7%	86.9%	172.1%
Activity Ratios:					
AR Turnover	-	8.1 x	8.1 x	8.1 x	8.1 x
Collection Days	-	45.0	45.0	45.0	45.0
Inventory Payable Turnover Days	-	35.0	35.0	35.0	35.0
Accounts Payable Turnover Days	-	60.0	60.0	60.0	60.0
Total Asset Turnover	**-**	**0.3 x**	**0.4 x**	**0.3 x**	**0.3 x**
Debt Ratios:					
Debt to Equity	0.0 x	0.0 x	0.0 x	0.0 x	0.0 x
Short-Term Liabilities to Total Liabilities	**-**	**0.9 x**	**0.8 x**	**0.9 x**	**0.9 x**
Liquidity Ratios:					
Current Ratio	-	5.2 x	6.2 x	4.8 x	5.3 x
Quick Ratio	-	3.6 x	4.6 x	3.1 x	3.6 x
Net Working Capital	$751,190	$263,968	$877,455	$2,235,882	$8,086,212
Interest	-	-	-	-	-

Appendix H: Personnel Plan

	2002	2003	2004	2005	2006
CEO	48,000	115,000	126,500	139,150	153,065
CFO	32,000	115,000	126,500	139,150	153,065
COO	16,000	100,000	110,000	121,000	133,100
Director of R&D	36,000	100,000	110,000	121,000	133,100
Research Engineers	40,000	50,000	165,000	302,500	532,400
Sales and Marketing	42,000	120,000	330,000	580,800	958,320
Administrative	8,000	96,000	151,200	211,680	333,396
Total Payroll	**222,000**	**696,000**	**1,119,200**	**1,615,280**	**2,396,446**
Total Headcount	**7**	**9**	**15**	**21**	**30**
Payroll Burden	**46,620**	**146,160**	**235,032**	**339,209**	**503,254**
Total Payroll Expense	**268,620**	**842,160**	**1,354,232**	**1,954,489**	**2,899,700**

Appendix I: Important Assumptions

Market

- Vacuum-assisted closure (VAC) was used as an analogy in estimating diffusion of the EMIT system. For further explanation, see Appendix C.

Sales/Revenues

- The Low Power (SX) model will be leased less frequently than the High Power (MX) model and thus the total potential market for logic controllers (LC) will be one for every two potential customers for the SX model. The MX model will frequently be owned by hospitals and leased more routinely, so the total potential market for LCs will be one for every ten potential customers.
- The potential market for the arrays of overlapping coils (AOC) will be: one AOC per potential customer for the SX and MX systems as the AOCs will not be designed to withstand sterilization.
- Insurance company reimbursement will be approved by year 3.

Cost/Pricing Factors

- Assume 5 percent annual decrease in costs/unit and a 3 percent annual increase in price.
- Specialty Distributor Markup will be approximately 50 percent of wholesale price.
- Average Cost to treat arthritis, atrophy, and pain per patient per year is approximately $2,400.
- Use of the EMIT system will result in a 20 percent reduction in consumption of current therapies.

	2002	2003	2004	2005	2006
Interest Earned on Cash Balances	2.0%	2.0%	2.0%	2.0%	2.0%
Interest Rates on Bank Revolver	12.0%	12.0%	12.0%	12.0%	12.0%
Long-term Debt Interest Rate	10.0%	10.0%	10.0%	10.0%	10.0%
Accounts Payable Days	60	60	60	60	60
Accounts Receivable Days	45	45	45	45	45
Inventory Turnover Days	35	35	35	35	35
Short-term Assets ($)	-	5,000	1,000	20,000	40,000
Capital Expenditures (CapEx)	5,000	5,000	20,000	30,000	50,000
Long-term Liabilities	-	10,000	20,000	40,000	80,000
Tax Rate Estimated	30.0%	30.0%	30.0%	30.0%	30.0%
Personnel/Payroll Burden	21.0%	21.0%	21.0%	21.0%	21.0%

Mural Company

BUSINESS PLAN

SMITH RAY DESIGN

5300 Market Street
Cincinnati, Ohio 45216

Smith Ray Design specializes in murals, faux finishing, and fine arts for residential and commercial spaces. The owner has successfully created a niche for herself, in that her work is recognizable for its festive color, attention to detail, and often whimsical children's subjects.

- EXECUTIVE SUMMARY
- COMPANY SUMMARY
- INDUSTRY ANALYSIS
- COMPETITION
- SERVICES
- OPERATIONS
- MARKETING PLAN
- HUMAN RESOURCES
- FINANCIAL HISTORY & PLAN

MURAL COMPANY BUSINESS PLAN

EXECUTIVE SUMMARY

The Company

My name is Janine Smith Ray. I began Smith Ray Design mid-year of 2000 specializing in murals, faux finishing, and fine arts for residential and commercial spaces. I have successfully created a niche for myself, in that my work is recognizable for its festive color, attention to detail, and often whimsical children's subjects.

I am a graduate of the Cincinnati Museum of Art, where I received a Bachelor of Fine Arts degree. I painted theater sets after graduation, simulating many styles of architecture, stone, landscape, and portraiture.

Mission

"Art for All"—I believe that every home is a haven and should reflect the passions of its inhabitants; In this cookie-cutter society, I can help a home become a unique expression of its owners.

Businesses strive to distinguish themselves from the herd, and I believe I can help them make a unique and creative setting for their workplace and a memorable experience for their clients.

Industry, Market & Competition

The greater Cincinnati area supports approximately a dozen companies that offer some or all of what I offer. Approximately six of them are in direct competition with me.

There is a target audience of over 50,000 enthusiasts who subscribe to *Cincinnati Bright Interiors,* a glossy lifestyle magazine that features many services for home design and remodeling, and lists professional resources regionally available.

The area supports several hundred licensed interior designers, most of whom would find my skills and services useful to their client base.

Services Offered

1. I offer free, in-home design consultation, portfolio review, and initial sketches.
2. I custom-design murals or hand-painted subjects in a variety of styles, most often painted directly on a client's walls, ceilings, furniture, and also as framed fine art.
3. I custom design faux finishes, which are painting techniques that imply stone, aging or pattern, while maintaining hand-painted, custom color mixing and matching, as opposed to wallpaper or commercially mixed and applied pattern and color.

Marketing & Sales Strategy

I have produced a professionally printed full-color brochure for distribution to a mailing list of over 300, and an e-mail list of over 200, including former clients, art exhibit patrons, and interior designers. I have designed and placed two, full-color, one-third page ads in *Cincinnati Bright Interiors* in 2001, and have been featured in *Cincinnati Magazine*, *Southern Ohio Live*, *Cincinnati Times*, the nationally produced and distributed *Artists' Magazine*, and on HGTV's "Room by Room," where I was interviewed while painting a large-scale mural for Cincinnati's American Cancer Society Designer Show House.

I plan to target future advertisement to these publications as well as arts programs for the Cincinnati Orchestra, Playhouse Square, and other performing arts venues, to focus on the arts patron demographic, who tend to spend disposable income on multiple arts events.

Management

Smith Ray Design is owned and operated by me, with financial advising by my husband, John Ray, a professional painter who owned and operated his own painting business from 1996 to 2000.

I subcontract the financial assistance of Abe Farnsworth, CPA, in Hamilton, Ohio. I have had start-up legal work done by an attorney who specializes in intellectual property and copyright law, Seymour Florelli, with the firm of Janes, Brightmoore & Falcon, in downtown Cincinnati.

I am currently searching for database entry and phone sales/office assistance.

Status of Operations

Smith Ray Design is in its third year of operation, with future plans of incorporation as the budget increases.

Financials

1. In my first complete year of 2001, Smith Ray Design's Gross Income was just over $18,000 with Net Profit (before taxes) of over $6,000 (see Financial History & Plan for specific numbers).
2. In 2002 Gross Income was just over $17,000, Total Expenses were over $18,000 with a Net Loss of about $1,000.
3. My 2003 year-to-date Gross Income is $23,806, Total Expenses $15,550, Net Profit (before taxes) is $8,256.
4. I project an estimated need of $20,000 over the next year in seed capital to properly approach marketing, staffing, and to update needed equipment.

COMPANY SUMMARY

My vividly colorful paintings and drawings are inspired by a multicultural view of life, having grown up in a diverse neighborhood in Fairfield, Ohio, and attending diverse primary and secondary schools. My experiences traveling to India, after graduation from Cincinnati Museum of Art, energized my world view and color palette.

My early experience working in theater set painting led me to desire a more long-term venue for my large paintings—personal and custom murals in people's homes and businesses—right on their walls!

After graduating from the Cincinnati Museum of Art with a Bachelor of Fine Arts degree, and upon returning from India, I freelanced with a custom art company in downtown Cincinnati's City Hall from 1988 to 1991.

I won top prize from the Cincinnati Museum of Art's "Parade the Circle" Poster and T-shirt Design Competition in 1993, and was featured in an article by Florence Meininger titled "Painting to a Creative Beat" on the front page of the Living/Arts section, in June 1993.

I attended University of Cincinnati from 1991 to 1993 in Art Education, and I attended Cincinnati Community College in Ceramics from 2000 to 2002.

I worked for over six years, from 1994 to mid-2000, with a Fairfield mural and faux finishing company, as a Senior Design Associate, where I designed and painted hundreds of murals, and was featured in *Southern Ohio Live*, in a special pull-out Interiors section in March 2000.

In the latter half of the year 2000, I began my own mural and custom faux finishing company and have successfully created a niche for myself, in that my work is recognizable for its festive color, attention to detail, and often whimsical children's subjects.

Major works or exhibits at the following venues:

- Uptown Club, downtown Cincinnati, 2002
- First Presbyterian, downtown Cincinnati, 1999
- Cincinnati Public Theater, 1995
- Cincinnati Botanical Garden, downtown Cincinnati, 1994
- Michaels Gallery of the Cincinnati Museum of Natural History, 1993
- Cincinnati Center for Contemporary Art, 1993
- Strong Center, Sharonville, Ohio 1993
- Rhythm Shoes Dance Company, Cincinnati, 1991
- Cincinnati Orchestra, 1985
- Cincinnati Hall, 1982 to 1984

Featured in the following media:

1. *Cincinnati Bright Interiors*, Autumn 2002 issue, where one of my murals was featured on page 25.

2. *Cincinnati Magazine* "Best of..." issue, October 2001, on page 114—where I was included in their "Home & Garden Guide."

3. *Artists' Magazine*, a nationally distributed, full-color, glossy publication, in which one of my pieces was included in an article, in August 1995, page 28.

4. CIN TV (a Cincinnati CBS Cable Affiliate) "Interior Elements," an interior design program, where I appeared as their first guest artist on the premiere episode, in a ten-minute segment, displaying selections from my portfolio and demonstrating a faux finish technique.

5. I received national media exposure on HGTV's program "Room by Room," an interior design program, where I was interviewed while painting a mural for the American Cancer Society's Designer Show House in 1998, which is currently on rotation in re-runs.

Company Facilities

I created a studio in the basement of my home and share a second floor office with my husband.

Mission

My motto, "Art for All," expresses my desire to make available the arts to those who are intrigued by creativity, but may not think they are able to afford art or are creative enough to express themselves through art. I not only target a wealthy demographic, but also try to make my work available for modest income families and businesses, and have done "pro bono" work for a select group of lower-income residents and businesses.

I believe that every home is a haven and should reflect the passions of its inhabitants; in this cookie cutter society, I can help a home to be a unique expression of its owners.

Businesses strive to distinguish themselves from the rest, and I believe I can help them make a unique and creative setting for their workplace and a memorable experience for their clients.

Objectives

I have set the following objectives for 2004:

1. Achieve sales of $50,000 (Net Profit of $30,000, before taxes)
2. Achieve distribution of promotional materials to 100 area interior designers
3. Achieve distribution of promotional materials to 100 area builders
4. Achieve media recognition for at least one major mural project

Keys to Success

1. Press releases to promote my major projects via media documentation
2. Promotional mailings to interior designers and builders
3. Telephone contact for appointments and sales with mailing recipients

INDUSTRY ANALYSIS

The Local View

There are a handful of small companies in the greater Cincinnati area that offer custom murals and faux finishing. They all have a particular field of expertise, and there seems to be a large enough market in the region to provide a sustainable living for all.

The Regional/National View

I have been hired to design and paint murals from California to Maine, and am excited with the prospect of travel for interesting projects. While there are qualified artists in each city, I have a distinctive style and welcome the opportunity to lend my particular vision to a project, regardless of location. The availability of digital scanning and access to e-mailed images keeps costs low and protects original documents during the design process, as well.

Target Market

1. Local and regional interior designers and builders
2. Recipients of interior design publications
3. Patrons of fine arts performances and events
4. Private children's care facilities and retail businesses
5. Selected art galleries

Market Size & Trends

I have noticed that in the financial climate of recovery from the recession, many home and business owners are rehabilitating present locations as opposed to relocating or investing in new constructions.

The trend I have observed is that of families and businesses sprucing up their existing spaces, where I am brought in to help nurture their ideas.

Purchase Patterns/ Process

Often a client approaches me through three channels:

1. Interior designers
2. Referrals from contacts that have purchased or have seen my work
3. Individuals who have seen my advertisements, brochures, or media

I allow for a commission for interior designers, and often reward individual clients with a referral fee as an incentive to sell my work to their contacts.

COMPETITION

Currently, there are about six companies in my region that are in direct competition, but it seems that all of us have a specific area of expertise.

There are a limited amount of projects a small team can paint at a time, and it's not unheard of for one company to recommend one or two of the better companies to bid a project that they are unable to fit into a busy schedule (if a client can't wait).

My experience is that if I feel that another artist can tackle a subject that I am uncomfortable with, I will refer the client, with either a finder's fee required, or expressly stated return referrals expected back. Other artists may have projects they are not as adept at, which may fit into my area of expertise. All of which can engender goodwill and more work in a competitive market.

SWOT (Strengths, Weaknesses, Opportunities, Threats) Analysis

Company Strengths

My education, technical skill, and over twenty years of experience include:

1. Elegant line quality
2. Complex composition
3. Layered and energetic use of color
4. Meticulous attention to detail
5. Whimsical and unique children's subjects
6. Wide range of expertise in creative techniques and historical references
7. Strong graphic design background for promotional opportunities

I foster a good reputation for my professional attention in regards to:

1. Punctuality and promptness in appointments and contact
2. Clean and reliable job site maintenance
3. Honesty and consistency in quotes and billing
4. Dedication to delivering more than the client expects, facilitating excitement with their creative experience, resulting in enthusiastic referrals
5. Due to my location, I have very low overhead, and do not foresee the need for an off-site studio in the future

Company Weaknesses/Barriers to Entry

1. Lack of time to pursue new contacts
2. Inexperienced in website maintenance resulting in lag time for updates
3. Inexperienced at phone sales cold contact

Needs Analysis

Unmet/Incompletely Met Needs

1. Marketing capital for magazine advertising
2. Capital for staffing to accomplish mailings and phone contact
3. Capital for exclusive use of a larger, reliable vehicle to transport equipment safely
4. Capital for a DSL (a dedicated line for a modem) for e-transmission of larger scanned files in a more timely manner
5. Capital for larger format full-color scanner and printer

Market Opportunities

1. A national organization called the American Society of Interior Designers (ASID) that I have yet to approach, where I could join as a professional resource member. This would give me access to all licensed interior designers in my region, and possible advertising in their quarterly publications.

2. I also have access to a regional retail furniture chain and a regional retail paint outlet chain that may allow me to hold painting demonstrations and workshops in return for distribution of my promotional materials and referrals to their customers.

3. Very few artists' mural companies have the resources or interest to advertise, and if they have, the design and layout has been unimpressive, in my opinion. I have the motivation to be recognizable as a high quality resource in the regional media, budget permitting.

4. I have yet to explore the market of home improvement due to property damage, in which insurance awards would pay for renovations.

Market Threats

1. The economy has curtailed business and home improvement spending by 50 percent in my experience and observation over the last year. As a new business, I rely on a good economy for disposable income to support the luxury of home improvement.

2. There is a small, slow upturn in the economy, but layoffs have affected about a third of my clients' ability to follow through with scheduled projects which have been delayed until the climate improves.

3. The newly available resources of home improvement cable television and workshops at outlets such as Home Depot, have slightly altered my client base, as people are more emboldened to try faux finishes and stenciling patterns on their own. Lately I am more often approached to fix their attempts, and improve on them.

SERVICES

I am skilled in and offer the following services:

1. Free, in-home portfolio design consultation with initial sketches
2. Mural styles ranging from classical to whimsical—drawn and painted samples
3. A wide variety of faux finish techniques—samples available
4. Custom color matching—samples available for project options
5. Maintenance and touch-up services
6. Custom portrait painting and drawing
7. Portable works on canvas or paper, for exhibit and purchase
8. Workshops in skills and technique
9. Group and private fine arts instruction
10. Flexible hours and calendar

Products

Competitive Comparison

1. I have been repeatedly told by clients and designers that I offer a wider variety of styles than many of my competitors.

2. I have researched the fact that I am moderately priced in comparison to my competitors, and have been told this by designers and clients alike.

3. I have noticed that when my clients have received quotes from other companies, they choose my company due to my rapport with them and my willingness to utilize their ideas and vision, as well as my professional and flexible approach to their design needs and schedule.

Sourcing

1. Clyde's, paint supply, Montgomery, Ohio, where I receive a discount on my account
2. Wynan's, art supply, Hamilton, Ohio, where I receive 50% discounts
3. Home Depot, Greenhills, Ohio, where I receive skilled instruction and advice
4. Xacto Printing, Cincinnati, Ohio, for full-color offset printing
5. Gerard's Design Shop, Cincinnati, Ohio, graphic design of stationary and first brochure
6. #1 Photo Labs, Sharonville, Ohio, for inexpensive, high quality prints
7. Southern Insured Group, Business Liability Insurance, Forestville, Ohio
8. Abe Farnsworth, Certified Public Accountant, Hamilton, Ohio
9. Seymour Florelli, Attorney, Janes, Brightmoore & Falcon, Cincinnati, Ohio
10. Michael Bailey, Cincinnati, Ohio, website designer

I am a member of the following:

- Art Beat, Old Cincinnati, Ohio, Self-Employed Artists Network
- Arts District, Cincinnati, founding member, Steering Committee
- Northwestern Development Corporation, Cincinnati, visual art consultant
- Cincinnati Museum of Art, general member and volunteer

I have contacts at:

- Cincinnati Museum of Art
- University of Cincinnati, art department
- Cincinnati Community College, art and interior design departments

These provide a pool of qualified artists for part-time employment.

I currently exhibit my work at:

- Design House, Loveland, Ohio
- Zeke's Restaurant, Forestville, Ohio
- Winding Road Books & Art, downtown Cincinnati
- Ginetti Gallery, Cincinnati

These promote my business through referrals, sales, and brochure distribution.

I am actively represented by 5 local interior designers and am on file at more than 20 establishments for referral purposes. I also have donated time/work to numerous businesses for promotional purposes, including Cincinnati Museum of Art; Cincinnati Zoo; Cincinnati Botanical Gardens; and Cincinnati chapters of Habitat for Humanity, Big Brothers/Big Sisters, and the American Cancer Society.

These raise my visibility to my key demographic with little or no expense.

OPERATIONS

Plant and Facilities

1. Basement studio is used for painting and drying samples. Lighting has been increased by 75% in 2001.

2. Expansion of lighting, storage, and restroom facilities is planned as capital increases.
3. The upstairs office is utilized for computer access, mailing preparation, phone sales, and follow-up contact.
4. Improved storage of records in the office is scheduled for 2004.

Equipment & Technology

1. Primary use of an iMac (2000 Model) equipped with Quicken financial software, Quark graphic design and Dreamweaver HTML software for website design
2. Shared use of a Lexmark Z23 color printer
3. Shared use of one land telephone line
4. Shared use of a Sharp UX P1000 fax machine
5. Shared use of an HP Scanjet 4400C color scanner
6. Sole access to a Verizon cell phone
7. Shared use of two VCRs to duplicate footage for use in initial contact of new interior designers
8. Approximately 30 gallons of latex paint, in a variety of colors
9. Approximately 100 paintbrushes, in a variety of sizes and quality
10. Approximately 200 pounds of mat board for painted samples
11. Three photo albums of portfolio history
12. Approximately 200 Prismacolor pencils in a variety of colors
13. Approximately 100 pounds of heavy, white drawing paper
14. Two large portfolio cases for full-sized samples
15. 5' x 4' x 5' wood flat file for storage
16. Four-foot aluminum ladder
17. Four-foot fiberglass ladder
18. Six-foot aluminum ladder
19. 18-foot aluminum extension ladder
20. 16-foot Multimatic aluminum folding ladder
21. Shared use of a leased 2000 Subaru Forrester (a small SUV)

Production Plan

1. After receipt of a design fee deposit, I schedule time to create painted samples or black and white/color drawn samples, according to the agreed and received fee.
2. Using previously prepared cut heavy mat board, I paint at least two faux finish samples for each project. The client retains the one they choose to proceed with and I either recycle the extra board or use it in my portfolio.
3. I then contact the client for an appointment to review samples within a couple of weeks, and repeat the design process (for the original fee) until the client is happy and agrees to a sample.
4. I present a quote and contract for signature—copy for client, copy for me, and schedule a begin date, with half of the quote due as deposit and calendar commitment.
5. At the completion of the project, I photograph the work for promotional use, and receive the remaining half of the fee.
6. I give the client a handful of brochures for promotional use, and discuss referral fee incentive opportunities.

Inventory Management

1. I utilize the best of the painted samples in a large portfolio case for interviews with new designers and clients, and constantly update smaller photograph portfolios to display a large variety of styles available, to spark ideas if the client is unsure of the desired work.
2. I update my website with the best of the scanned photos and send copies of enlargements to the media for press releases.
3. I use the best of the scanned photos in advertisements and brochures.

Order Fulfillment and Customer Service

1. At the in-home consultation, I take notes and do some sketches, free of charge, then send a quote by mail on letterhead. After a week I call and determine willingness to move forward, or negotiate their concerns.
2. If they agree to continue with the design process, I try to honestly assess my schedule and hold to my estimated time frame for creation of samples, appointments and projects, but am flexible to client needs, and can delay or hasten projects accordingly, with phone contact in either event.
3. Within six months after a project is completed, I call a client to see if they need any touch-up or are concerned with anything.
4. I include clients in promotional mailings for upcoming exhibit events or bi-annual promotional mailings for updates on my latest work.
5. I call a year after their completed project to remind clients that I am available for their next project.

MARKETING PLAN

Product

1. I pride myself in helping my clients realize their creative vision for their home or business, and work to accomplish it in reality. I will go the extra mile, even at no extra fee, to create samples until they are excited about the project.

2. I retain reproduction copyrights to all of my work, signed, dated, and photographed for my portfolio use.

3. I require any changes to the work be done with permission, since my designs are unique and artists usually don't allow others to add to or change their work.

Price

A rough estimate for an average eight-foot by ten-foot mural on a smooth, prepared wall would range from:

1. $1,000 to $1,200, depending on subject and complexity.

2. Two walls $2,000 to $2,200, depending on subject and complexity.

3. All four walls would range from $3,000 to $4,000, depending on subject and complexity.

4. A smooth ceiling would range from $1,000 to $2,000 depending on size, subject, and complexity.

5. $100 design fee covers an 8 1/2" x 11" color drawing that the client would keep, even if they decided not to continue with the project.

Estimates include materials and a variety of touch-up paints.

Faux finishing estimates begin at:

1. $500 for a small eight-foot by ten-foot room—four smooth walls, depending on complexity of technique, can rise to $2,000 or more taking into account scaffold and/or daily breakdown needs for high traffic areas.

2. $100 design fee will cover two color faux samples.

Upon receipt of the first half payment to begin the project, the remaining half is due upon completion. I usually give a range for the quote in the event of unforeseen difficulty, and most of the time, come in under budget for goodwill, but in the event of great difficulty, I will not exceed the high end of the quote.

I'm often asked to add details later, or touch-up if work is damaged. After the project is completed, I make touch-up appointments at the rate of $50 per hour (includes drive time if in excess of 30 minutes).

Place (Distribution)

1. I provide an average of a dozen brochures to each client, more if they entertain often, or if their project is included in the newer printings of brochures.

2. I place my brochures in stand-up boxes in the galleries where I exhibit, or they display them as they wish.

3. I have placed brochures in private schools and daycare centers where my work appears, libraries that allow promotional display, as well as health food stores and coffee shops in mid- to high-income neighborhoods that allow display.

Promotion

1. I have utilized the graphic design software Quark to create a professionally printed, glossy, full-color brochure, and have updated them each year since I launched my business—three to date; 3,000 copies each printing for mailing and distribution.

2. I have a two-color professionally designed and printed business card, letterhead, and envelopes, and can generate color stickers of the same for special mailing or packaging needs.

3. I have a professionally designed website, with multiple pages and sections for in-depth display of the variety of work offered, and maintain it as I continue to learn the Dreamweaver HTML software.

4. In 2002, I designed and placed two, one-third page, full-color ads in *Cincinnati Bright Interiors*, a quarterly, glossy, regional interior design magazine with a 50,000 plus subscription target audience. The package cost $1,400, and included extra full-color photo coverage. This directly resulted in new representation by two interior designers, resulting in six major projects. I foresee the need to repeat this package each year.

5. I have permission to reproduce the video footage from CTN's Design Elements in which I appear, for distribution to new interior designer contacts.

6. Projected need to place an ad package in the Cincinnati Orchestra, Museum, and Opera program guide books to target the arts patron audience.

7. Projected need to be installed onto a few web search engines, as budget increases.

8. Projected need to join the American Society of Interior Designers as a professional resource member.

9. Projected need to create and submit slides for an Ohio Arts Council Individual Artist Grant, and submit a full array of slides to their Resource Slide Library.

10. HGTV's "Room by Room" is locally based—I intend to present a proposal for an appearance as a featured guest for a major project in 2004 or 2005.

Promotional Products Distributors

1. As my budget increases, I will actively recruit new interior designers for promotion for our mutual profit.

2. I plan to create new print ads for promotion as budget increases.

Educators, Catalog Merchants, Retail Stores

1. I plan to target children's educational resources and retail for promotional events and mailings, as budget and staffing allows.

2. I will target interior design outlets, upscale furniture outlets and showrooms, through display as well as offering workshops to the public.

HUMAN RESOURCES

1. I am the primary designer and on-site artist. My husband, John Ray—a professionally trained painter, is skilled in small plaster repair, base-coat work, and faux-finishing—assists me when the schedule allows (as a nationally touring musician/performer he's not always available).

2. I have six part-time, skilled assistants for large on-site projects, available in rotation as scheduling allows. Hourly pay starts at $10/hour for simple faux work and increases to $15/hour for more complex work. These subcontractors sign an agreement for clarity in requirements and expectations, and are responsible for their own taxes and liability insurance.

3. I am currently looking for office assistance in creating a database for new designer/builder contacts through web search, mailing, phone inquiry, and sales.

FINANCIAL HISTORY & PLAN

1. 2001 Gross Income $18,364
   Total Expenses **$11,651**
   Net Profit, Before Taxes $6,713

2. 2002 Gross Income $17,613
   Total Expenses **$18,709**
   Net Loss $(1,096)

3. 2003 Year-to-Date
   Gross Income $23,806
   Total Expenses **$15,550**
   Net Profit, Before Taxes $8,256

4. Projected 2003
   Gross Income $35,000
   Total Expenses **$20,000**
   Net Profit, Before Taxes $15,000

5. I project an estimated need of $20,000 in seed capital for 2004, to properly approach marketing, staffing, and updating equipment.

Projected Sales

1. 2004—Achieve Sales of $50,000, Net Profit of $30,000, before taxes

2. 2005—Achieve Sales of $75,000, Net Profit of $50,000, before taxes

3. 2006—Achieve Sales of $100,000, Net Profit of $75,000, before taxes

Network Game Centers

BUSINESS PLAN

POWERPLAY GAMING, LLC

11007 Woodworth Avenue, Suite 101
Portland, Oregon 97209

This business proposal seeks to set up Network Game Centers, called PowerPlay Gaming, throughout the United States. By setting up networks of computers or consoles that are able to truly capture and show off the programming expertise and high quality of presentation produced by game software, gamers will be able to enjoy playing a new and exciting game without having to purchase the equipment and software associated with a high quality gaming experience.

NETWORK GAME CENTERS BUSINESS PLAN

EXECUTIVE SUMMARY

Background

The worldwide video gaming industry generates in excess of $50 billion per year according to the "Executive Interview Series: The State of the Game Market 2001" report published by DFC Intelligence. Most of this revenue is through the sale of hardware and software associated with video games.

A new avenue of additional income connected with the video games industry that has remained largely unexplored throughout the world is that of Network Game Centers (NGC). Our NGC will be named PowerPlay Gaming.

In essence, an NGC's business model exploits the fact that gamers can enjoy playing a new and exciting game without having to purchase the equipment and software associated with a high quality gaming experience. A computer or console that is able to truly capture and show off the programming expertise and high quality of presentation produced by game software developers these days requires a high-end machine with special graphics and sound components as well as other costly hardware prerequisites. These machines are therefore prohibitively expensive and the video gaming fan is relegated to a sub-optimal gaming experience on his affordable but medium to low-end computer at home.

Another factor that is key to the success of the NGC model is the fact that all games, whether computers or otherwise, are vastly more enjoyable when played in groups. Group dynamics is a field of psychology that has been studied endlessly and will not be mentioned in detail here, but it is suffice to say the following: The "challenge" factor that is evident in group games and sports is by far one of the most powerful of driving forces. The camaraderie and sense of satisfaction and achievement that is derived from playing a team sport or group game is not comparable to any other feeling and is now a well established form of entertainment in the world. The NGC business model exploits exactly this group dynamic, resulting in a proven, profit-generating business with a low investment/low operating cost.

The huge market potential and virtually instant return on investment for these entertainment venues is evident from its phenomenal growth rate in both the United States and abroad.

This business proposal therefore seeks to set up NGCs, called PowerPlay Gaming, throughout the United States with an aim to be the best in each selected city and therefore maximizing the profits earned from it.

The main objectives of the development of these new venues are:

- Capitalize on excellent opportunity to extract maximum revenue in a competitor-less market.
- To launch the NGC with a highly targeted publicity campaign in the summer of 2003.
- To maintain tight control of costs, operations, and cash flow through diligent management and automated computer control.
- To maintain a high standard of product and service provided in the NGC.
- To exceed $150,000 in annual sales by the third year of plan implementation.

The keys to success in achieving our goals are:

- Be the first in the market to provide a new entertainment service that has broad appeal.
- Provide an exceptional service and product that leaves an impression.
- Consistent entertainment atmosphere and product quality.
- Managing our internal finances and cash flow to enable upward capital growth.
- Strict control of all costs at all times, without exception.

COMPANY SUMMARY

The key elements of PowerPlay Gaming's concept are as follows:

1. "War Games" based themes—The company will focus on themes that have mass appeal. A variety of games will be available though.
2. Distinctive design features—The NGC will be characterized by elaborate interior decoration that simulates a "Control Center" as can be seen in any Hollywood movie based on military or Space Travel themes.
3. Location, location, location—One of the major strengths that the NGC will have is its careful choice of location in a high visibility area with plenty of parking as well as complementary businesses close by, such as restaurants.
4. Variety—The NGC will provide a variety of games in its software portfolio to cater to the diverse tastes of people.
5. Quality Hardware—The NGC will provide high-end hardware on which the network and its components will run, to ensure a first-class entertainment experience.
6. Exceptional service—In order to reach and maintain a unique image of quality, the NGC will provide attentive and friendly service through the careful selection of service personnel, and will also invest in the training and supervision of its employees. We estimate two to three staff for an NGC unit to be sufficient and will ensure that their needs are well looked after.

Company Ownership

PowerPlay Gaming will be a privately held LLC, the details of which have not been solidified as of the date of this publication.

Start-up Summary

The company will seek a loan from either a local bank or a venture capitalist for start-up purposes for PowerPlay Gaming.

Funds needed to accomplish goal referenced above will be $50,000. The applicants will require the entire $50,000 to finish project build-out.

We will utilize the anticipated loans in the amount of $50,000 to build out the approximate 500-square-foot space and purchase and set up equipment necessary for start-up of the company. It also will pay for miscellaneous expenses associated with key personnel for the first couple of months. The following tables and charts illustrate the capital requirements.

Start-up Requirements	
Start-up Expenses	
Cabling	$500
Interior Decoration	$2,500
Advertising	$1,000
Legal	$1,000
Rent for 6 Months in Advance	$12,000
Total Start-up Expense	**$17,000**
Start-up Assets Needed	
Cash Balance on Starting Date	$500
Salaries Deposit	$5,000
Total Short-term Assets	**$5,500**

Start-up Summary

Continued...

Long-term Assets	
Computer Equipment	$22,000
Network Switches	$2,500
F&F	$3,000
Total Long-term Assets	**$27,500**
Total Assets	**$33,000**
Total Requirements	**$50,000**
Funding	
Investment	
Bank or Venture Capitalist	$50,000
Total Investment	**$50,000**
Short-term Liabilities	
Accounts Payable	$0
Current Borrowing	$0
Other Short-term Liabilities	$0
Subtotal Short-term Liabilities	**$0**
Long-term Liabilities	**$0**
Total Liabilities	**$0**
Loss at Start-up	($17,000)
Total Capital	**$33,000**
Total Capital and Liabilities	**$33,000**

BUSINESS DESCRIPTION

With the emergence of new network technology and high-speed infrastructure around the world, more and more game developers are realizing the huge demand for multiplayer network-based games and have been channeling funds into developing games that can meet this unprecedented demand. These developments have brought a unique opportunity to capitalize on the nature of these games through the model of an NGC. The fact that Internet speed is largely dependent on expensive infrastructure means that a local area network will still be the fastest network available for game playing. This translates into faster and smoother game-play with no jerkiness or delays.

PowerPlay Gaming will provide an exciting environment in which people can play games competitively against each other. The challenge of going up against one's friends in the same place is a far more enjoyable experience than playing against a computer's artificial intelligence or against an anonymous player on the Internet. In the NGC environment, a customer is able to see his opponents as well as converse with them during the game, making for a much more "interactive" environment as opposed to the confines of their PC at home. The gamer also will be able to enjoy the camaraderie that goes with any group activity that usually is not available at home.

MARKET ANALYSIS SUMMARY

The concept and management of PowerPlay Gaming has been well received in the Portland, Oregon, area where hundreds of customers regularly come to engage in a battle of wits against their friends and other NGC customers.

The NGC phenomenon is due to the fact that the challenge factor proves to be very addictive as in any sport or game, and the fact that there are no physical limitations on the players opens up the market for players of all ages, sizes, physical and mental ability to play against one another. A ten-year-old child can easily be the best player in a match against other players much older and wiser. The same goes for players less fit and less physically active than other "sporty" competitors. PowerPlay Gaming provides a level playing field for all.

The fact that this is a new and exciting form of entertainment is especially attractive in cities that are limited in the variety of entertainment that is available for the young generation.

The demographics and entertainment market in Portland, Oregon, appear to be ripe for which PowerPlay Gaming to flourish. No doubt that with the right set-up and marketing, it will prove to be so.

Market Segmentation

We see PowerPlay Gaming as appealing to three major market segments. Fortunately, the long hours of operation help the company lend itself to multiple segment appeal. Our market segmentation scheme allows some room for estimates and nonspecific definitions.

1. **Childless Young Professionals**—Due to the nature of the games, PowerPlay Gaming will appeal to primarily single young males that will enjoy a group activity after working hours to blow away the stresses of the day. Video games are certainly not the domain of children anymore as evident in the demographics of people who have purchased the Sony Playstation consoles (I and II) as well as more recently, Microsoft's X-Box. Up to 75% of NGC customers are single adult males between the ages of 18 and 35. This segment also spends the most amount of time (and money) in the NGCs (10 - 20 hours a week).

2. **College Students**—Although less affluent than young professionals, college and high school students also make up a significant portion of an NGC's customer base. These are people that are just starting to enjoy social activities that were not available to them as youngsters. Their spending power may be less than our first group but makes up a significant portion of revenues since they are able to visit the NGC at earlier times than members of our first group due to their working hours. This segment makes up roughly 20% of the NGC's patronage.

3. **Children**—Although at first glance it would seem that children would have the most significant part to play in the success of PowerPlay Gaming, the reality is that children's time in an NGC is limited largely due to the restrictions placed on them by parents as well as a lack of money available to spend on a daily basis. Parents would rather buy their child a console to play within the safety of their homes where they can "keep an eye" on them. Having said that, this segment does prove to be useful in revenue terms to fill PowerPlay Gaming for a short time after school hours when the parents allow their children some flexibility to meet with their friends for some harmless fun. A variety of games are available to meet the needs of these younger customers that make up roughly 5% of an NGC's customer base.

Target Market Segment Strategy

Our strategy is based on serving our niche markets exceptionally well. The pure gaming enthusiast, the group activity buffs, as well as children, can all enjoy the NGC experience.

The marketing strategy is essential to the main strategy:

- Emphasize exceptional service.
- Create awareness of PowerPlay Gaming's high quality hardware.
- Focus on our target markets.

We must charge appropriately for the high-end, high-quality service we offer as well as take advantage of the fact that we will be the best in the market. Our revenue structure will be higher (but not prohibitively so) than Internet Cafés (the closest comparison to this kind of business) due to the fact that our computers and network will be of a much higher quality and specification than that required in Internet Cafés.

Part of the superior experience we will offer will be the ease of use of the computers since the software we will use to manage the center will store all the customer's customized setups of the keyboard and multimedia features. Customers will not have to go through the hassle of setting up their computers to their exact requirements every time they come back to us. Logging into the system with their user name and password will set their computer back exactly to their previously stored settings. The software also will ensure that they can pick up their previously saved games exactly where they left off since most games require several hours to complete.

Special pricing structures also will exist to accommodate groups of players and "off peak" days of the week and hours of the day. This will ensure that the maximum revenue can be obtained from each working day of PowerPlay Gaming and will be an added incentive for customers to utilize the center to its fullest.

Tournaments will be held on a regular basis with sponsored prizes to appeal to the competitive streaks of groups and individuals as well as a "Top Ten Players" list that will be analyzed using specialized software. A prizes and incentives scheme will be associated with this list. These elements will further ensure that customers come back to our establishment repeatedly.

Service Business Analysis

Video games have significantly impacted young peoples' lifestyles and the economy in every developed country in the 1990s. Entrancing players with fantasy, visual effects, and addictive game play, video games are still one of the highest cash flow businesses in the world. The average gamer will spend three to four hours every day in this type of activity and will spend an average of $9 to $15 every time. As we move further into the new millennium, this trend shows no signs of declining.

The typical NGC of our style is open from 12:00P.M. to 12:00A.M., and within this time frame, the NGC can achieve gross revenues anywhere from $500 to $1,000 daily. The primary sources of revenue in an NGC of this type are high volume traffic and regular, long-staying customers who play for 4 to 5 hours every day. In addition to gaming revenues, we also have an option to generate substantial revenues from food and beverage sales should the right environment be attained and a customer need perceived.

Additionally, the NGC industry is shifting towards a more entertainment-oriented concept. Customers of these venues are not only offered a unique gaming experience, but also a place to participate in additional exciting events through interactive contests, theme nights, and other events. We intend to heavily utilize entertainment-oriented marketing in an effort to withstand the perpetual shift in trends and cater to as large a client base as possible.

NGCs are extremely self-sufficient with little support required from outside suppliers. Aside from the occasional maintenance of computer equipment and replacement of breakables (such as keyboards, mice, and headphones), the only regular supply that is required for the normal and profitable operation of the NGC is electricity.

In Portland, Oregon, all major brands of computer equipment and peripherals are readily available at ever cheapening prices due to heavy competition. In addition, preferential pricing can be obtained for breakables from local suppliers due to the fact that our business has a higher than normal rate of peripheral damage and therefore replacement requirement.

Business Participants

The NGC will be part of the audiovisual entertainment industry, which includes several kinds of businesses:

- **Cinema and Rented Movies**—This genre usually appeals to the same demographic clientele as an NGC. This same client base dictates that the average price structure be comparable in order to create "regulars."
- **Home-based Console and Computer Games**—Although on paper a significant competitor, an NGC provides a form of entertainment not available to the home gamer. This stems from the fact that home gaming is a solitary or at best small group activity whereas in an NGC, gaming can be enjoyed with groups of up to 20 in our proposed venture.
- **Internet Cafés**—Primarily used for more passive activities such as E-Mail, information gathering and "chatting," an NGC's main customer base will come from those people that are already quite used to paying for their computer time and are familiar to the concept of Computer Cafés.

Main Competitors

Manhunt—Cedar Hills 30+ PCs
Space Raiders—Walnut Grove 30+ PCs
Rivenated—Metzger 30+ PCs

PowerPlay Gaming's competition lies mainly with other forms of audiovisual entertainment as well as group activities such as sports. We need to effectively market our concept and ensure word-of-mouth advertising by providing a first-class entertainment experience, while maintaining the idea that playing computer games in groups can be a lot of fun. Our polling has indicated that consumers think of quality, reliability, atmosphere, and price respectively. Additionally, price was frequently mentioned by pointing out that if the former concerns are present then they are willing to pay more for the experience.

The main indirect competitors of the NGC will be:

Cinema & Video Rentals
Not as regular an activity as going to an NGC since new movies are shown at a minimum of every week and therefore a customer may spend on average two to four hours every two weeks or so going to the cinema.

Home Video Games
A solitary activity and one which is easily surpassed in terms of appeal by hardware at an NGC that is far superior to that affordable by the normal gamer. Further, the group element of an NGC proves to be far more appealing than playing by oneself.

Internet Cafés
A very indirect competitor since the services offered are very different to those at a dedicated gaming establishment.

STRATEGY & IMPLEMENTATION SUMMARY

In order to place emphasis on exceptional, reliable entertainment quality, our main tactics are bi-monthly servicing of computers, including the replacement of faulty peripherals as needed. We also will upgrade computers as required according to the recommended specifications of game publishing companies.

Our second strategy is emphasizing customer satisfaction. We will ensure that the customer is never allowed to be bored with the activities available at PowerPlay Gaming. Not only will he always have the latest and most popular games available to play, but he will be able to take part in competitions. A close eye will be kept on gaming magazines and Internet sites to ensure that we are always first to market with new and exciting games that are released in the United States and Europe.

Our promise fulfillment strategy may be our most important. The necessary tactics are friendliness of staff, long-lasting relationships, ongoing maintenance, and attention to detail, especially after popularity has been established and new competitors enter the market. Through empowerment of service employees to solve problems and reward regular customers without waiting for management consultation, we create a win-win situation for the customer and the NGC.

Continuous and never-ending improvement is the order of the day through our "on the job" training sessions and regular meetings. Since value is equal to service rendered minus the price charged, it is crucial to go beyond the mere supplying of computers and games—you have to create a long-lasting impression.

- Emphasize reliability—We MUST prove to our customers that perfectly functioning computers and associated equipment should be expected as part of the gaming experience. We will differentiate ourselves from the mediocre NGCs when they surely arrive in the market.
- Emphasize an entertaining experience—By assuring that all guests will enjoy themselves every time without a lapse in reliability, we will be securing market share through repeat business.
- Focus on a variety of rewarding activities—Our marketing, promotions, group activities, and competitions will ensure that people do not get bored with our service.
- Differentiate and fulfill the above promises.

We cannot just market and sell a new entertainment concept; we must actually *deliver* on our promise of quality, service, and a unique gaming experience. We need to make sure we have the fun and service-intensive staff that we claim to have.

Marketing Strategy

Through friendly and courteous service, we will build relationships with our regular customers to ensure that when competition does arrive, our regulars will be reluctant to go to them due to their personal ties with us.

Advertising budgets, tournaments, and promotions are ongoing processes of management geared to promote the brand name and keep at the forefront of the NGC industry in Portland, Oregon.

We will depend on newspaper advertising as well as leaflet distribution at places of gathering of our customer base to promote our establishment. Our strategies and practices will remain constant, as will the way we promote ourselves:

- Advertising—We will be developing a core-positioning message.
- Grand Opening—We will concentrate a substantial portion of our early advertising budget towards the "Grand Opening Event."
- Direct Marketing—We will directly market in areas of high traffic for our main market segment such as cinemas and restaurants.

PowerPlay Gaming will create an identity-oriented marketing strategy with executions particularly in print media, in-store promotions at supermarkets and video stores.

A grand opening event will be held to launch PowerPlay Gaming in the summer of 2003. A newspaper advertising blitz will precede the event for two weeks, with ambiguous teasers about an "event like no other" in the city's history and the forthcoming opening date. Contests will be held through the newspaper and handouts, giving away V.I.P. passes (coupons) to the event while at the same time creating excitement about the opening. The opening date is tentative at this point and dependent upon network set-up completion. The budget for the event will be $500, and the milestone date will parallel the available opening date.

Achievement of the following campaigns will be measured by the polling of customers as to how they heard of PowerPlayGaming for the first ninety days of operation. Future advertising budget adjustments will be made as the results dictate.

We will be running regular newspaper ads and direct-mail campaigns to create brand awareness. Our newspaper ads will be concentrated strongly in Portland's major newspapers. Through attractive design, a teaser campaign, and the use of catchy phrases, we hope to obtain intellectual ownership of our target market segments.

We will advertise directly to our regular customers through e-mail and normal post as well as in areas where our customers regularly gather, such as the cinema through the use of fliers and leaflets. Promos such as "introduce a new customer and get an hour free" would be relatively inexpensive from an advertising standpoint and require limited ongoing maintenance and expense. Ads also will go into the college newspapers for the local campuses.

Jessica Miller will be responsible for all advertising and promotions activities with consultation from Mark Stafford. The monthly budget for advertising and promotions activities will be set once the levels of "word-of-mouth" advertising and business levels are assessed.

Shirts, baseball caps, and bumper stickers bearing the NGC's logo also will be eventually marketed, as well as given away as prizes, in order to further spread brand awareness. All the partners will approve artistic design but Jessica Miller will negotiate the supply.

Sales Forecast

Our forecast for income for the first year of operation is based on an NGC with 20 PCs and the lowest hourly sales price of $3.00.

Competitive Pricing

The price will be brought down from a relatively high price of $5 per hour to $4.50 to $4 per hour in order to maximize revenue during the process of lowering the prices to market norms. The lowest price will be maintained at $3 per hour with any additional cut in prices by competitors battled with an aggressive marketing strategy.

The time frame for the price reductions will be decided upon after analyzing the situation at the time and will be done so with every resistance tactic including the sales of packages for bulk purchase, group discounts, and other such promotions that will keep us competitive, but maintain a higher average price for hours sold.

MANAGEMENT SUMMARY

The company will have two managers with a common passion for this business and a firm commitment to realizing the vision, and share a common goal: to provide a unique and entertaining experience through state-of-the-art technology and exceptional service.

Management Team

Mark Stafford, Operations Manager
Stafford's specific responsibilities will lie primarily with the coordination of events and oversight of the operations as well as technical support and development of the NGC.

Jessica Miller, General Manager
Miller primarily will be responsible for the marketing and publicity with a view to developing the business in other areas. Specific responsibilities will be to manage the reinvestment of funds and coordinate marketing activities with Mark Stafford.

The positions of operations support staff, technical assistants, cleaners, etc. will be openly sought from the market nearer to the opening of the NGC.

Management Team Gaps

We believe we have a solid team constructed in order to cover the main points of the business plan for the first NGC. Management growth through training and exposure will be an ongoing component of PowerPlay Gaming's priorities.

However, we do realize that as we expand to other NGCs in the region (as is the long-term plan), we will require other managers and technicians to whom we can entrust the operations of this cash-based business. The candidates will be carefully chosen due to their backgrounds and personalities and through personal recommendations of their character.

The process of identifying suitable candidates for the General Manager's position will be ongoing as we expand our operations and any candidates identified will be hired as assistants and trained according to our requirements while under perpetual assessment as to their suitability for the job.

Personnel Requirements

The Personnel Requirements reflect the dual objective of providing an ample amount of service personnel to run the day-to-day operations of PowerPlay Gaming as well as to develop staff for future setups. Our headcount will remain at two to three employees (including the General Manager) at each NGC unless any unforeseen demands dictate otherwise.

General Manager	Salary	Technical/ Operations Manager	Salary	Part-Time Cleaner/ Assistant	Salary
1	$2,000	1	$2,000	1	$1,000

FINANCIAL PLAN

The financial projections for this plan are presented in the tables and charts of the following subtopics.

Important Assumptions

The financial plan depends on important assumptions. The key underlying assumptions are:

- We assume a slow-growth economy of five percent the first year, and three percent thereafter, without major recession.
- We assume that price will be a key competitive element in the first three years of operations where competitors in the business will seek to cut into our business through price cutting.
- We assume continued popularity of NGCs and the growing demand for high-energy, high-tech entertainment venues.
- We assume that average daily customer usage of PCs is 3 hours per customer.
- We assume that the NGC will be open daily between the hours of 12:00P.M. to 12:00A.M.

Break-even Analysis

The NGC Break-even Analysis formulas are presented in the text below.

Fixed Costs = $7,500 /month
Debt Repayment = $1,000 /month (approximate)

Break Even Point = $8,500
Average Daily Revenue Required = **$283.33**
Minimum Daily Hours Sold Required = 283.33 / 3 = **94.44 hours**
Minimum Daily Hours Sold/PC Required = 94.44 / 20 = **4.72 hours**
Minimum Daily Customers Required = 94.44 / 3 = **31.48**

Fixed Costs	$7,500.00
Debt Repayment	1,000.00
Total	**$8,500.00**

Minimum Calculations	
Average Daily Revenue Required	283.33
Average Daily Hours Required	94.44
Average Daily Hours/PC Required	4.72
Average Daily Customers Required	31.48
Total Hours Available for Daily Sale	240.00
Percentage of Utilization Required	39%

Projected Profit and Loss

The table presents expected Profit and Loss figures for the coming years, based on the first year figures and a 10 percent growth in the market. The expenses have been overestimated for the table for the sake of remaining conservative and a drop in hourly price to reflect competition also has been incorporated in the calculation. We expect though, that the market will stabilize by the end of the third year of operation.

Sales	160,000	158,400	154,880
Expenses	101,500	100,500	100,000
Profit	58,500	57,900	54,880

Revenue Estimates	**Year 1**	**Year 2**	**Year 3**
Total Hours Sold/Day/PC	4.44	4.89	5.38
Total Hours Sold/Month/PC	133	147	161
Total Hours Sold/Month	2,667	2,933	3,227
Revenue/Month	**160,000**	**158,400**	**154,880**

Expenses Estimates	**Year 1**	**Year 2**	**Year 3**
Rent	24,000	24,000	24,000
Salaries	60,000	60,000	60,000
Utilities	2,500	2,500	2,500
Maintenance	2,000	1,500	1,000
Debt Repayment	12,000	12,000	12,000
Other	1,000	500	500
Total	**101,500**	**100,500**	**100,000**

Online Customer Service Support

BUSINESS PLAN

LIVE E-CARE, INC.

801 North Main Street
Ann Arbor, Michigan 48104

live e-care is an outsource provider of online customer service support. We guarantee personalized e-mail management and live text chat response at a cost 30 to 50 percent lower than our customers' cost for an in-house alternative. The company plans to add revenue streams from ancillary services, including enhanced knowledge management and consulting services. Our goal is to become the leading outsourcer of web-based customer service support in the United States.

ONLINE CUSTOMER SERVICE SUPPORT BUSINESS PLAN

EXECUTIVE SUMMARY

The Company

live e-care is an outsource provider of online customer service support, one of the critical customer-retention services for e-business. We guarantee personalized e-mail management and live text chat response at a cost 30 to 50 percent lower than our customers' cost for an in-house alternative. As we amass customer and company information, live e-care will add revenue streams from ancillary services, including enhanced knowledge management and consulting services. Our goal is to become the leading outsourcer of web-based customer service support in the United States.

Operations will be located in the Philippines to draw on an educated, highly skilled, English-fluent workforce with labor costs substantially lower than in the U.S. Sales, marketing, client contact, and billing will be handled through U.S. offices.

The Opportunity

The Internet technologies which created the opportunity for e-business have also destroyed the traditional switching costs on which businesses relied for customer retention. With switching costs for online customers nearly negligible—the competitor's site is just one click away—customer service is becoming the key to developing and maintaining online customer loyalty and to managing online customer repurchase, recommendation, and retention.

Although e-businesses are becoming aware of this critical need, few have developed a plan, much less an infrastructure, to respond adequately to the volume or the specificity of customer service requests. Online requests for customer service come, overwhelmingly, via e-mail: IT consultants the Gartner Group predict that 25 percent of all customer communications will be via e-mail and web form by 2001. In surveying 125 major websites, however, marketing communications firm Jupiter Communications found that 42 percent either took too long to respond, or entirely failed to respond to customer inquiries. The business outcomes are tangible: Andersen Consulting found that over the 1999 holiday season, 88 percent of online customers left behind their virtual shopping carts without completing a purchase.

Meanwhile, total revenues flowing through online retailing channels continue to grow about 53 percent annually—1999's total of $36 billion is expected to stretch to $84 billion by 2001—increasing the pressure on online retailers to sharpen their core competencies in the manufacture and supply of retail goods. Retailers who have turned the responsibility for online customer service over to automated, immediate solutions, such as auto reply applications, have found these applications do not truly address the specifics of customer inquiries, and are therefore of little help in building customer loyalty.

The core competence of live e-care is bridging this gap. We guarantee a personalized response to each online customer service request our clients receive; we guarantee response time of less than twelve hours; we make the online shopping experience pleasant and personal for our clients' customers; and we allow our clients to refocus all their energies on their own core competitive competencies.

Key Success Factors

Because the market for our services is still so young, the key success factors for developing market share involve the ability to deliver service quickly and reliably, and to scale operations quickly without loss of quality. live e-care will succeed by delivering:

1. Quality, consistent, and timely service to our clients' customers
2. Rapid implementation of customized web-based support solutions

3. Timely and insightful analysis (trends, etc.) of customer service transactions
4. Accurate and reliable customer service at costs 30 to 50 percent lower than the costs our clients would bear in supporting these capabilities in-house.

Sustainable Competitive Advantages

There is no clear dominant provider of outsourced online customer service support. What is clear is that there are not enough providers in the market to handle the increasing demand. Competitors, correspondingly, have focused on grabbing early market share, rather than developing a long-term strategy for maintaining share as the market matures.

live e-care's operational competencies are built around two long-term competitive advantages:

1. A labor cost advantage of 30 percent or greater, without compromising quality. By basing operations in the Philippines, we have access to an educated, literate, English-speaking workforce of 35 million people which commands salaries 80 to 90 percent lower than their counterparts in the U.S. Because the Philippines and the U.S. have strong historical ties, moreover, this workforce is more culturally attuned to U.S. jargon, brands, and attitudes than workforces in other low-labor-cost locations.
2. A 4- to 8-year tax holiday, followed by a 5 percent income tax rate. The nature of the services we offer qualify us as a Philippine Export Zone Association (PEZA) company. In addition to the tax incentives, we are granted duty-free import of capital equipment.

Management Team

These structural advantages are bolstered by a management team which brings together practical experience in all aspects of live e-care's operations, as well as business training and experience in the U.S. and the Philippines.

Board of Advisors

live e-care has assembled a Board of Advisors with background in the business cultures of both the U.S. and the Philippines, and with functional experience in sales, marketing, finance, and private equity.

Marketing Strategy

live e-care will position itself as a highly-reliable, competitively-priced outsource provider of online customer service, and target:

- the new breed of successful e-tailers
- the traditional brick-and-mortar retailers rushing to go online

Our target clients will have estimated e-mail volume of at least 250 e-mails per day. Our marketing efforts will be a combination of direct sales force outreach and strategic advertising.

Sales Strategy

Our sales strategy relies on a direct sales force building relationships with U.S.-based businesses. We will recruit strong, experienced salespeople with backgrounds in industries reliant on customer relationships. A substantial portion (30-40%) of total cash compensation will be commission keyed to measures of customer satisfaction.

To allow our salespeople to focus on new business, and to help drive our projected increase in closing rates, account managers will service clients after the sale and will be responsible for generating prospective client lists. To ensure seamless, high-quality service we will assign a Client Relationship Team, composed of a salesperson, a sales account assistant, and dedicated customer service representatives in the Philippines, to each client account.

Pricing Strategy

E-mail management services will be billed at a fixed monthly rate of $5,000, with a variable fee of $1 for each e-mail transaction beyond the standard account quota of 5,000/month. Chat support services will be billed $10,000 per month for one 24/7 operator.

Human Resource Strategy

The ability to recruit high-quality customer service representatives in the Philippines will be critical to our success. Our recruiting will focus primarily on top Philippine universities and on identifying and hiring experienced talent. We will also work to reduce turnover, promote creativity, and attract quality talent through design of the physical and social work environments.

Operations Strategy

Operations will be located in the Philippines' Subic Bay Freeport, the former site of the largest U.S. Naval Base outside the United States. The infrastructure, of unusually high quality, includes office buildings, redundant electrical power, and access to high-speed data/telecommunications lines managed through a joint venture of AT&T.

Our IT operations will use current software to manage customer inquiry flow, skills-based routing of e-mails, chat sessions, and (eventually) voice calls. Strict quality assurance procedures and statistically valid sampling will ensure accurate and timely responses to inquiries. As we further develop expertise in the business needs and data of our clients, we will develop proprietary, state-of-the-art customer inquiry management software. We anticipate this software will become a sustainable advantage over our competitors.

Financial Forecasts

live e-care anticipates that revenues will grow from $370,497 in Year 1 to $72,442,250 by Year 3, with a Net Loss in Year 1 of $820,640 and Net Income reaching $18,777,841 by Year 3. Our ability to convert clients at a rate of 5 percent in Year 1, 7 percent in Year 2, and 10 percent in Year 3 and beyond, as well as an 80 percent adoption rate for our live chat and telephony service, will drive this revenue growth. Less certain revenues, such as those for consulting or FAQ database management, are not expected until late in Year 2 or 3 and are not included in these projections.

Return on Invested Equity (ROE)—based on projected capital needs of $350,000 at the start of operations, $2,500,000 in Q3 of Year 1, and $20,000,000 in Q2 of Year 2—will be 82 percent at the end of Year 3. The ROE will further increase in future years as Net Income grows.

live e-care will realize economies of both scale and scope as the number of clients increases. This is reflected in projections of annual costs per operator seat. Chat operator per-seat costs will drop from $63,087 in Year 1 to $16,058 in Year 3, and e-mail operator per-seat costs will decrease from $1.95 in Year 1 to $0.61 in Year 3. As these costs decrease, the Net Income margin will increase to 40 percent at the end of Year 3.

Use of Funds

The company has summarized a series of detailed pro-forma financial statements outlining the capital needs of the company over its first three years. The company intends to seek $350,000 for working capital needs at the start of the business. The majority of this capital will be needed to fund the purchase/licensing of hardware and software, as well as human resource needs. An additional $2,500,000 of capital will be needed approximately 6 to 9 months later in the project and $20,000,000 approximately 18 months after start-up. These funds will primarily be used for expansion of the sales force, infrastructure, and marketing.

BACKGROUND

The Opportunity—A Large and Growing Market

The market for outsourced, web-based customer support service is currently estimated at $18.4 million, out of a total teleservices market of $101 million, and is expected to grow to $1 billion in 3 years. Online buyers overwhelmingly rely on e-mail for customer service support: Forrester Research reports that 71 percent turn to e-mail to resolve their issues, and 51 percent use the telephone.

As online retailing activity increases, the need for web-based customer support, especially interactive online service providers, will continue to grow. Jae Kim of Paul Kagen Associates, an Internet consulting firm, estimates that less than 5 percent of retail websites now offer immediate customer assistance, but that 90 percent will offer the service within 3 years.

...which is turning toward an outsourcing solution. Yet the infrastructure of online customer service support is not, and will never become, the core competence of most retail firms. This is especially true of middle-market firms, for whom the resources required to develop and manage an effective, efficient online support center are a comparatively large and uncertain investment. Since online retailing eliminates many traditional switching costs for retail consumers, moreover, large and small firms alike must increasingly build their strategies for customer retention around tactics for customer satisfaction. As information technologies available for these purposes improve, these firms face an ongoing and expensive commitment to continuous improvement of infrastructure to support their continuous improvements in customer retention.

While online customer service support is both increasingly costly and necessary to these firms, it is unlikely to be a sustainable competitive advantage for any of them.

Outsourcing provides an ideal solution, especially for middle-market companies which will never achieve the economies of scale necessary to make an effective in-house operation cost competitive. Outsourcing allows these firms to maintain a substantial online competitive presence with minimal fixed investment in overhead and physical infrastructure.

...in which demand already outstrips the supply of quality service. Although outsourcing is increasing, web-based customer support is still often inadequate. Many companies have turned to autoreply software to meet the deluge of e-mail inquiries. These responses may prove worse than ignoring an e-mail: *Business 2.0* found that 40 percent of automated responses did not even answer the customer's question. Surveying 125 sites supported by autoreply, in-house or outsourced customer response systems, Jupiter Communications found that 42 percent either ignored e-mail inquiries entirely or took longer than 5 days to respond.

Service Offerings

Focusing on providing a high level of service, exceptional reliability, and competitive pricing, live e-care will initially offer clients three support services:

1. **E-mail management**
   E-mail support will be the heart of the live e-care system. State-of-the-art hardware and skills-based software routing will direct e-mails to appropriate customer service representatives (CSRs) who will review every reply to customer inquiries prior to sending a response. This will ensure a reply that answers the customer's question, and increases the probability of issue resolution at the first point of contact. Leveraging our knowledge and resources across multiple clients, moreover, we will achieve operational efficiencies, allowing us to provide the latest technologies as well as personalized, superior customer support to our clients.

2. **Real-Time Text Chat Support**
   A newer customer support tool, chat support provides a pop-up text window on the customer's monitor through which the customer and the CSR "chat" about the customer's

questions or concerns. Like e-mail, live chat allows a CSR to answer the customer's actual question directly; it also allows the CSR to act as a virtual salesperson, driving customer sales.

Chat support is currently being used, in fact, primarily as a sales tool. The majority of online customers end their purchasing efforts partway through the process: Jupiter Communications reports that 27 percent of web shoppers give up on their purchases when faced with online forms. Live chat services allow CSRs to walk the customer through the buying process, increasing the likelihood of an online sale.

3. Customer Information Analysis and Reporting

Using data gathered through these e-mail and chat transactions, live e-care can also analyze, summarize, and develop timely reports on customer trends which our clients can use to better adapt their businesses to the changing marketplace. This ability to develop, mine, and analyze customer databases has powered the growth of Amazon.com, among others. live e-care will offer our clients this ability to develop meaningful, real-time customer insights without the substantial expense of developing that ability in-house.

Future Offerings

As Internet and telecommunications technologies continue to converge, the blurring of their distinctions will present new opportunities to improve customer satisfaction and retention. live e-care will develop two additional service offerings to take advantage of these opportunities.

Voiceover I/P (VoIP)

VoIP allows a consumer to speak with a website representative directly over the Internet connection, without disconnecting from the website or purchasing a second phone line. Used effectively, VoIP can be even more valuable than live chat in helping firms close an online sale. Our CSRs will be well positioned to migrate to this new technology. The strong Americanization of Filipinos, combined with their excellent English speaking skills, make them ideal knowledge workers for this emerging medium.

Teleservices

live e-care will begin offering telephone and fax communications, a natural extension of our product line and a strong fit with our highly-skilled English speaking Filipino workforce, by the third quarter of Year 1.

MANAGEMENT TEAM & ORGANIZATION

The Management Team brings together practical experience in all aspects of live e-care's operations, as well as business training and experience in the U.S. and the Philippines:

Jeff Russell, CEO, managed technical infrastructure upgrades for call centers and telecommunications switching facilities in the U.S. and the Philippines. He has also worked as a quality assurance consultant to U.S. companies which outsource their data entry operations to overseas contractors. He holds an M.B.A. from the University of Michigan Business School.

Dax Almendras, COO, created and managed his own firm to resell long distance communication services to small and medium-sized Philippine businesses. He was previously a financial auditor for Arthur Andersen in the Philippines and is a member of the Philippine Institute of Certified Public Accountants. He holds an M.B.A. from the University of Michigan Business School.

Ken Hung, Director of Information Technology, holds three master's degrees (Industrial and Operations Engineering, Systems Science and Engineering, and Financial Engineering) and a bachelor's degree (Electrical Engineering and Computer Science) from the University of Michigan. He has worked extensively as a Web Master, Systems Administrator, and Web Programmer.

Board of Advisors

live e-care has assembled a Board of Advisors with background in the business cultures of both the U.S. and the Philippines, and with functional experience in sales, marketing, finance, and private equity:

John Siverling has worked with Frank Russell Capital, a private equity firm, and currently consults with Sloan Ventures, a venture development company, on venture market potential and financial projection sensitivities. His previous experience includes a variety of sales and customer service management positions with General Motors' Cadillac Motor Car Division. He holds an M.B.A. from the University of Michigan Business School.

Timothy Renn, who is based in Manila, is actively involved in the development of the Subic Bay Economic Development Center. He was previously the marketing communications executive for Nike in Southeast Asia, and has served as Associate Dean at Northwestern University's Kellogg School of Management.

Marshall Kiev is a founding partner of Colt Capital Group. Prior to that, he spent 13 years at FH Capital, a $500 million asset management firm, most recently as a Managing Director. He brings to live e-care extensive knowledge of the private equity industry. Marshall received his B.A. from New York University and his M.B.A. from NYU's Stern School of Business.

Board of Directors

Initially the Board of Directors will also serve as the management team of the company. However, the founders recognize that the Board of Directors will need to be developed into a separate body (although one or two management team members will have seats on the board). The founders plan to recruit directors and executives in the customer care industry who can aid the team in attracting large clients in the future.

Job Descriptions and Qualifications

live e-care will fill several additional positions within the first few months of operations:

Regional Sales Managers
Sales Managers will identify and acquire customers for the company, represent live e-care and its services to prospective clients, and cultivate business relationships with current and prospective customers.

Sales Account Assistants
The Sales Account Assistants will provide after-sales support to the sales managers. He or she will work closely with U.S. clients to determine their online customer service needs. The sales account assistant will also work closely with the Customer Sales Representative Manager in the Philippines to provide performance feedback to the CSRs.

Chief Technology Officer (CTO)
The CTO will oversee the growth and development of the company's IT department. In addition, the CTO will develop the company's internal technological capabilities to augment third party vendors' existing customer service software.

Chief Financial Officer (CFO)

The CFO will provide the financial leadership necessary to manage the rapid growth of the company. In addition, the CFO shall be responsible for the implementation of formal accounting control policies within the organization and manage the sources and uses of company funds.

Philippine Operations Manager

The Philippine Operations Manager will report directly to the COO and will oversee the execution of customer service operations in the Philippines.

Information Technology Manager (Philippines)

The Philippine IT Manager will assist the Philippine Operations Manager in the maintenance of the software and web-based systems of the Philippine operations. In addition, the IT manager will continuously update Philippine activities in order to help the CTO develop the company's internal technological capabilities in order to augment the use of third party vendors' existing customer service software.

CSR Manager (Philippines)

The CSR Manager will oversee the hiring, training, and retention strategies of CSRs and personally handle complex customer inquiry transactions.

CSR (Philippines)

The CSR will handle the processing and editing of customer e-mail and provide live chat support for client customers.

MARKET ANALYSIS

Definition and Size

The market for outsourced customer service support can be categorized into several sub-markets or industries. One way of segmenting this market is by dividing it into the web-based outsourcing industry, the customer support outsourcing industry, and the teleservices industry. Many of these segments overlap due to the current convergence of technologies. live e-care has further segmented our market within the web-based outsourcing industry into the web-based customer support e-mail and the live chat market.

E-tailing has legs and is running quickly. Online sales are expected to reach $36 billion this year, up from $15 billion in 1998, according to the Boston Consulting Group. It is estimated that e-commerce will grow to $84 billion by 2004. Lehman Brothers reports that Internet sales will eventually equal 5 to10 percent of retail sales.

As previously mentioned, the online customer service market is predicted to be $1 billion in 3 years. The table below indicates that the number of web users is expected to increase by 143 percent in the next three years.

Estimated Internet Users—United States

	1998	**1999**	**2000**	**2001**	**2002**
U.S. Households (mm)	100.7	101.5	102.7	103.8	104.8
% with PCs	42%	45%	47%	49%	52%
% Online	55%	63%	74%	82%	95%
Total Online	**26**	**34**	**42**	**52**	**67**
www Users (mm)	97.3	131.6	170	227.7	319.8

Target Markets

Segmentation and Critical Trends

Most of the Internet's estimated 650,000 existing sites (63 percent are dot coms) currently provide some means for visitors to contact a web manager by e-mail for further support. However, given our existing capabilities and resources, we plan to direct our efforts at two specific industries. We have chosen to focus on (1) currently successful e-tailers and (2) traditional brick-and-mortar retailers who are rushing to go online.

Successful e-tailers. A critical trend in this industry is the rapid rate of e-commerce growth. Internet-based retailers have gotten a head start over their bricks-and-mortar competitors and the traditional retailers are attempting to catch up. Amazon.com became a behemoth in the book world in a few short years, selling over $1 billion in books and other merchandise over the Internet in 1999. Barnes and Noble ($3.8 billion 1999 sales), the market leader of traditional book sales, has since scrambled to compete in the retail online business with Barnesandnoble.com. Of the top ten Internet revenue earners, nine are dot coms. As these revenues are predicted to increase, Lehman Brothers reports that the e-commerce movement will affect established brick-and-mortar retailers. To remain competitive, most broadline retailers have launched websites or revamped existing ones.

Top 10 Internet Money Makers (in millions)

1.	Amazon.com	$1,000
2.	Onsale	$266
3.	Priceline.com	$189
4.	eBay	$125
5.	uBid	$119
6.	Barnesandnoble.com	$113
7.	Cyberian Outpost	$106
8.	Value America	$98
9.	CDnow	$92
10.	Beyond.com	$68

Traditional bricks-and-mortar retailers rushing to go online. Traditional retailers are speeding to compete on the Internet but web-based customer support services will be critical to their online success. In a survey conducted by PRTM management consulting, 97 percent of sales and marketing executives plan to offer online service support by 2000, and another 88 percent believe customer service will be the most important long-term e-business objective. Given these Internet customer care predictions, live e-care is well positioned to target traditional retailers in addition to the fast-growing e-tail companies. Our ideal client will receive a minimum of 4,500 messages per month but will be generally ill equipped to handle the rapid surge of e-mail inquiries to their site.

Based on initial market analysis involving calls to target clients who have recently launched websites, many new sites are receiving an average of 500 e-mails a day, yet have only 1 to 5 people responding to customers (Nordstrom's, Williams-Sonoma, Crate and Barrel, Pottery Barn, and furniture.com). In fact, a recent survey of 91 companies on the Internet showed that:

- 38 percent did not have a dedicated customer support mechanism
- 16 percent never bothered to answer e-mails
- 12 percent took more than 48 hours to respond and their replies were rated "poor"
- 18 percent answered within 48 hours, but their responses were still rated "poor"

Of the 91 companies, only 16 percent responded with a satisfactory and prompt reply. live e-care's goal is to ensure that our clients are viewed by their customers as exceptionally proactive, responsive e-companies.

Target Customers

We have identified an initial list of target customers within our two target market segments. All target retailers, whether traditional brick-and-mortar companies or modern e-tailers, have websites, receive a high volume of e-mail, and need to maintain a strong positive relationship with their customers. Our target client will have an average of 250-350 e-mails per day; our minimum acceptable number will be 150 e-mails a day. live e-care will initially focus on mid-sized companies to help establish our reputation.

Having secured a number of mid-sized, satisfied clients to testify to our quality and effectiveness, live e-care will focus on attracting larger and more established clients. Serving a few large clients instead of many smaller clients will allow for greater efficiencies and higher quality customer service (based on the assumption that it will be easier to answer 500 e-mails for one client than 50 e-mails for 10 clients). Our target customers either have poor e-mail support—they did not respond to test e-mails sent—or have indicated that they are overwhelmed and unprepared to handle the volume of e-mail they are receiving. These companies currently do not outsource their e-mail nor do they provide an online chat service to their customers.

Critical Needs

The retailers within live e-care's initial target market need swift implementation of customer support solutions. Our target market defines online quality customer service as the ability to answer inquiries in a timely and accurate manner at a low cost. These clients need to get their websites up and running quickly and often need third party vendors to assist them. However, only 1 percent of cybershops currently provide live chat customer support, and 5 percent or less outsource their customer support.

E-mail management is not a core competency of these companies. Our target companies would rather devote their efforts to developing company brand equity and selling merchandise. live e-care allows them to focus their attention on their core business functions by handling, and responding effectively, to their e-mail, engaging their customers in online chat sessions to support sales initiatives, and providing them with concise reports on customer trends and preferences. In addition, live e-care CSRs will be exceptional and of direct benefit to our clients, yet we will deliver our clients from the burden of recruitment and training. From our initial search on Monster.com, there are a number of companies frantically searching for people to fill positions as Internet CSRs. Retention is also an issue—the average annual industry turnover in the U.S. can be high as 100 percent. With live e-care our clients can be assured of continuity in customer relations personnel and service, without undue distraction from their core business functions.

Marketing Challenges

One of the main challenges to live e-care will be convincing retailers, especially traditional brick-and-mortar businesses trying to quickly ramp up their online presence, of the benefits and advantages of outsourcing their customer support. In a survey of companies that currently outsource, the top three reasons for deciding to outsource were to:

- reduce and control operating costs
- improve company focus
- gain access to world-class capabilities

The top three factors for vendor selection were:

1. commitment to quality
2. price
3. references/reputation

Competitors

The primary competition will be the client's own internal customer support departments and a few existing niche market players. PriceWaterhouseCoopers reports that 80 to 90 percent of call centers are still in-house. Our target customers will be those companies who are unsuccessfully handling their e-mail support in-house.

There are five important oursource competitors in the e-mail customer support industry:

E-mail and Chat Support Providers

Brigade Solutions
Brigade is live e-care's most direct competitor. They have a similar business model in that they offer e-mail customer support using third party software vendors and focus solely on web-based customer support. They were founded in late 1997 as an Internet customer support company and have received their first round of venture capital funding early this year. They have not gone public to date. They, too, employ "cyberreps" who respond to 95 percent of e-mail queries within 24 hours. Their corporate headquarters in San Francisco has about 80 people (including reps). They also have a center in Madras, India, where 80 more cyberreps are located. At each location there are two shifts providing round-the-clock coverage. Brigade has focused on Fortune 500 clients and currently provides service to clients such as Excite, Compaq, and GTE.

PeopleSupport
PeopleSupport is based in Los Angeles, California, and currently employs 360 customer reps. They offer outsourced Internet customer care through e-mail response services, knowledge management reporting, and recently, voiceover IP. However, they specialize in live chat support. They believe that they provide superior quality customer care. Their customer focus is e-commerce companies—both traditional and Internet. Customers include Nokia, MGM, CarParts.com, and GE Capital.

Live Chat Support Only

LiveAssistance
LiveAssistance is owned by International Business Systems, Inc., and is based in Chantilly, Virginia. Founded in 1986 as a traditional customer call center, it currently focuses its Internet initiatives on providing live chat assistance. Its customers include 3buddies.com, HomeAuction.com, Department of Veteran Affairs, Bureau of Census, and HomeGain. Their site seems to be one of the most professional of the live chat competitors. The site provides a live demo chat and does not require any information from the site visitor. There was no waiting time for a chat operator, and the demo effectively illustrated the value of their service.

Finali.com
Finali.com is a new entrant in the live chat market, based in Broomfield, Colorado. They have focused on three market sectors: retail, financial services, and business-to-business chat. Their website live demo requires more visitor information than the LiveAssistance website, and requires a wait to get to an operator.

e-Assist.net
e-Assist.net is also a new entrant to the live chat Internet industry. They are based out of San Diego, California, and have the least impressive website of all competitors. They provide live chat, customer support management, and reports on customer data. The wait for an operator was over 7 minutes during their demo. These findings exemplify the critical need to provide potential clients access to a live demo with minimal wait time without having to divulge significant personal information.

MARKETING PLAN

Overview

In the Philippines, which posted an unemployment rate greater than 10 percent in 1998 and an underemployment rate double that, we have the ability to attract higher level CSRs than our customers or competitors in the United States. live e-care's customer service agents, recruited from the top universities in the Philippines, will provide superior care for our clients' customers. Additionally, the low cost of doing business in the Philippines will enable us to support various pricing levels without compromising our quality.

Although the retail customer operations will be located in the Philippines, live e-care will establish a physical sales and marketing presence in the U.S., whose direct sales efforts will be supplemented by print and other media advertising. live e-care will attend six to eight trade shows a year; each sales representative will contact an average of 20 new potential customers a month.

live e-care will also maintain an interactive website, through which potential customers will be able to demo our e-mail and live chat services and learn more about the company and its product offerings.

Value to Our Clients

Greater customer loyalty through better customer service
Websites currently spend an average of $40 apiece to attract customers, but they dedicate few resources to ensuring customer satisfaction and return visits. live e-care will provide the exceptional customer service to online retailer consumers that will help our clients build stronger customer relationships and generate bankable customer loyalty. Because attracting a new customer is 10 times more costly than retaining an existing one, live e-care's services will both save our clients money and give them a means to increase future revenues.

Competent, dedicated CSRs
Our customer service agents will be recruited from the top universities in the Philippines and encouraged to bring their considerable initiative and creativity to bear in solving customer dilemmas. Every CSR will have excellent written and spoken English skills. We will supplement an initial, comprehensive training with regular sessions keeping them abreast of the latest trends and developments of our business. Our human resources strategy includes retention incentives to ensure that our CSR teams enjoy continuity and satisfaction.

Intimate understanding of retail customers needs and concerns
live e-care will help clients better understand their customers' needs by providing trend-summarized information of customer feedback and comments. These reports will allow them to scale their website capabilities, adjust their merchandise offerings, and improve their appeal to potential customers on numerous indices.

Increased online revenues
As many as 62 percent of online shoppers give up on a purchase because of the difficulty they encounter navigating the website. As many as 20 percent of potential online shoppers report they would purchase online if the site had a live chat CSR to talk them through the process. HomeTownStores.com, a home improvement site, increased online sales 30 percent in four weeks by introducing a live chat service. live e-care's services will help our clients leap from a static website to a live, friendly, interactive, customer-oriented site which encourages browsers to become buyers.

Allow clients to focus on their retailing operations
live e-care helps free up clients' managerial and financial resources by intercepting the flood of e-mail messages and undertaking all service rep training sessions.

Improved cycle time for implementation
live e-care will enable its clients to handle dramatic increases in customer inquiry volume more quickly and more efficiently than they could be managed in-house. This capability is especially valuable to companies that experience high volatility in online sales, such as retailers in the Christmas season. The flexibility of live e-care's operations will also give clients the option of adding or subtracting live chat services and operators as necessary.

Cost savings through outsourcing
PriceWaterhouseCoopers estimates that the average company will save up to 30 percent by outsourcing customer service centers. live e-care's low cost structure and pricing strategy allow us to match or beat that savings benchmark.

Pricing Strategy

Competitors' strategies. Most e-mail outsourcing firms price per transaction, either in a multi-tiered pricing structure or by desired turnaround time. Pricing strategies for live chat services range from a fixed monthly fee based on the number of dedicated operators to a variable rate based on some metric of productivity, such as number of transactions handled or minutes spent chatting to a live operator.

Our e-mail pricing. live e-care clients will pay $5,000 per month for a monthly quota of 5,000 e-mails, and $1 apiece for e-mail in excess of that quota. Our quality assurance program will ensure that 95 percent of all client e-mails will be serviced within 24 hours. This fixed fee is based on the expected minimum number of e-mail inquiries we expect an average client to receive in a month, and the labor and training costs that client would incur to create this service in-house. This fixed fee is competitive with, or lower than, what competitors charge. Our inherent labor cost advantage allows live e-care to discount this price by as much as 35 percent and still meet profit margin goals.

Our live-chat pricing. live e-care will pay a fixed monthly fee of $10,000 per operator seat, which will guarantee them one chat operator 24/7. Because each operator seat requires a team of four CSRs on four shift cycles, this pricing strategy will be difficult for competitors to match using the U.S. labor market for their CSRs.

Long- and short-term quotes. Traditional call center contracts, which extend for one year or more, are unrealistic for a web-based business model. live e-care will initially offer six-month to one-year contracts, along with a free, one-month, "live" trial period beginning at service implementation. Payment terms will include an initial deposit covering one month's services, to be paid before the consultation process begins. The payment will be immediately applied to the first month of the actual customer service operations. Upon completion of the consultation and testing process, the client will pay the next two months' fees before the operation goes live. Thereafter, client payments will be made at the start of every quarter of the service period covered. The contract will also provide live e-care and its clients the flexibility to add other value-added services, such as competitive intelligence research and Internet marketing.

It is expected that as live e-care continues to understand and serve clients more effectively, it will become easier to cross-sell a variety of services, and that—after gaining the necessary expertise in serving clients on the Internet—it will be possible to negotiate longer contract terms, ensuring a more stable cash flow stream for the company.

Market Positioning: Unequaled Quality, Competitive Prices

live e-care will guarantee response rates of 95 percent within 24 hours or less. Our CSRs will be fully trained in e-customer service as well as cognizant of the issues most important to our clients and their customers. live e-care will be able to offer these services at competitive prices because of lower labor rates in the Philippines, lower costs due to lower rates of employee training and turnover, and special tax and legal advantages enjoyed as a PEZA-registered company. Price is one of the critical decision points in determining an outsourcing vendor: live e-care will clearly be able to offer customers cost savings in comparison to their in-house customer care centers and other outsourcing competitors.

Advertising

While our marketing strategy does not focus on advertising promotion, resources are earmarked for the second and third year's advertising expenses. Advertisement is planned on the *Wall Street Journal* national edition twice a year in the first year (half page) and three times a year in the third year (also half page). This may be supplemented with trade journal print ads. The goal for advertising is reach rather than frequency, to broaden the awareness of our company in our target market.

Alliance Strategy

Participation in alliances is a key industry trend. Brigade Communications, which handles just e-mail support, is partnered with both Egain and Kana for software. New companies entering the market, such as PeopleSupport, provide more alliance possibilities.

As a provider of strategic outsourcing services to clients, live e-care will focus on alliances which can offer as seamless a relationship with the client as possible. We are currently in discussions with several e-mail management software providers as well as newer chat room management software developers. The most attractive operating and software systems would be browser-based, and will also use products that run on Unix, Linux, or Windows NT. live e-care will seriously consider the use of newer start-up companies as partners, since most established firms already have developed numerous alliances that may not serve the best interests of the company.

SALES STRATEGY

Tactics

Sales force effectiveness. Our sales strategy is based on a direct model, utilizing experienced salespeople to make sales calls and build client relationships. Because of the importance of the client relationship, live e-care will have a secondary layer of account support personnel working in conjunction with the sales force. Finally, live e-care will coordinate specific client sales teams with their corresponding CSR teams in the Philippines in order to maintain a cohesive, consistent client interface.

Geographic organization. Initially, live e-care will have three salespeople, each one having geographic responsibilities. One will be responsible for the Eastern part of the U.S., one the Midwest, and one the West. They will work out of home offices, allowing them the flexibility to develop their markets.

Management, compensation, and recruitment. The Vice President-Marketing and Sales will oversee the performance of the sales force but the keys to success will be the selection and compensation structure. First, the selection of experienced salespeople is important. Their experience need not be, specifically, in customer support sales, but should be in a service sector and heavily focused on customer relationships. Successful individuals could be recruited from the likes of Xerox or IBM, where they have learned about business-to-business sales calls and customer focus. The attraction of live e-care will be the opportunity to run their own region, potentially greater compensation, and involvement with a growing start-up.

Compensation will be a key driver of the success of the sales force and, ultimately, the company. Consequently, live e-care will focus on a complete compensation package with competitive salary and commission, averaging about $60 thousand in total cash compensation. At the same time, live e-care will offer the upside potential of any start-up, stock options.

Compensation will be tied to sales and the retention of customers as well as individual goals. Naturally, each salesperson will be allocated a car allowance, travel and entertainment budget, and home office equipment. The VP-Marketing and Sales will be responsible for developing the overall training and review process, but will also help each salesperson develop an individual sales strategy.

Account support assistants for each salesperson. While we are planning to ramp up additional sales personnel as we gain clients, it is critical that the sales force has the time to seek new clients without live e-care losing the key relationship proximity to current clients. Therefore, each salesperson will have an account support individual working in tandem with him or her. The account support position will be a junior position to the salesperson but will report directly to the VP-Marketing and Sales rather than to the salesperson in order to ensure company-wide continuity. This position can also be used as a tool to develop future sales managers. Account support personnel will be compensated similarly to the salespeople, but on a somewhat lower scale, averaging $40,000 in total cash compensation. Their job description will not contain the same level of prerequisites of the salespeople. Their compensation will rely more heavily on client retention than attraction.

Developing client relationship teams. Finally, live e-care will develop client relationship teams within the organization. These teams will include the original salesperson and the related account support person, as well as the team of customer representatives in the Philippines. As a team, they will be responsible for a seamless, high quality relationship with the client. The salesperson and account support person will be able to keep the Philippine team informed of key issues with the client and product or service updates. Likewise, the Philippine team will be able to provide critical information and reports to the account support person and the salesperson.

Developing leads. live e-care will take a number of routes to develop leads for the sales force that will be managed by the VP-Marketing and Sales. Among the approaches will be trade show displays, reviews of trade journals and industry events, advertising, and Internet searches. All members of the team will be recruited to develop all leads whenever they notice an opportunity, such as a website without e-mail support, or sites with poor responses to e-mail. In addition, account support assistants and staff in the Philippines will be tasked with surfing the net, searching for retail sites with e-mail support facility. He or she will test the reliability of the e-mail support facility by sending numerous e-mails and checking the speed and quality of responses. Sites with poor response speed or quality will be marked as leads.

Identifying client's key decision-makers. Determining the key decision-makers at each potential client is critical to sales success. live e-care will use industry networks and expertise to find the right person within each organization. live e-care will also utilize a companywide customer contact database, so that anyone can add information to a client record as they come across information.

OPERATIONS

Strategy

live e-care will utilize the best of available technology and human resources to provide clients with seamless, prompt, and accurate web-based customer support. Locating the bulk of the operations in the Philippines will allow live e-care to offer these services at lower costs.

U.S. Operations

U.S. operations will consist mainly of regional sales and account management staff who will initially work out of home offices. Customer billing will be outsourced and overseen by the accounting staff in the Philippines, as well as account management staff in the U.S., until regional offices are established. Sales coverage will be maintained by staff located in the Eastern mid-Atlantic, Midwest, and West Coast regions.

Philippines Operations

The bulk of operations will be located in the Subic Bay Freeport (SBF), an Economic Zone managed by the Subic Bay Metropolitan Authority. Subic Bay was formerly a U.S. Naval base, the largest outside the U.S. When the U.S. vacated the base in 1992, most of the infrastructure was left relatively intact. Over the years it has been upgraded and further developed to suit commercial and business purposes. This area is near several technical universities and is known for the progressive mindset of its inhabitants.

Office space will be leased within Subic Bay which provides:

Dedicated, reliable, high speed T-1 and T-3 series data communications lines
Telecommunications are managed by Subic Telecom—a joint venture between AT&T and the Philippine Long Distance Telephone company, the largest telephone company in the Philippines. State-of-the-art 5ESS digital switches provide seamless connections to international telecommunications networks.

Reliable power supply (in-house redundancy will be installed—Uninterrupted Power Supply units will back up computer systems)
Power infrastructure was left behind by the U.S. Navy. The generating capacity far exceeds current as well as expected future demand. Power generation is managed by Enron and the Subic Power Corporation.

24 hours/day 7 days/week access
Nearly 2,000 residential homes were left behind by U.S. Navy personnel in the surrounding residential areas.

Access to transportation
Natural deep water ports, a newly renovated international airport, and a newly completed highway provide easy access to SBF.

Provisions for accommodating rapid growth
Sufficient capacity exists to accommodate our projected growth for the first 5 years of operation and well beyond.

Web-based Customer Support Systems

A general description of the systems needed to offer e-mail management, live text chat, or VoIP services follows.

With each type of service there are generally two options available. **Option 1:** Pay the application provider a fee to host the application and client data on in-house servers. This option usually requires a per client fee as well as a monthly fee based on the number of CSRs servicing that particular client. **Option 2:** Purchase the application and the necessary servers to host the application in-house. This entails a much higher fee up front for the purchase of the application software and a set number of "seat licenses." Usually the minimum fee includes 5-10 seat licenses. The seat license entitles a client to one CSR, 24 hours a day, 7 days a week. Option 1 is preferable until we have grown sufficiently to warrant the purchase of the application.

E-mail Management System

Currently, e-mail is the most common form of online customer service. Nearly 100 percent of businesses active on the Internet offer customer service via e-mail. E-mail message management applications manage customer e-mails generated from these client websites. They allow businesses to prioritize, categorize, route, track, respond to, and learn from their customer inquiries.

The following explains the online e-mail process:

1. An e-mail message is received from a customer via an address given on the client's website.
2. The e-mail is routed through the e-mail response management server.
3. An automated response is sent to the customer acknowledging the receipt of the e-mail and possibly providing an estimated response time.
4. The e-mail management server decides how to handle the e-mail based on categories designated by the client. The server will search for key phrases and then determine the appropriate action for the e-mail.
5. If the e-mail falls into a predetermined category, the server will search the response database for an appropriate response and automatically respond to the customer. If it does not match the e-mail message with an existing category, the message is routed to the next available CSR.
6. The CSR can then look up the customer's history and/or browse the response library for the appropriate response. Depending on the nature of the e-mail, the CSR may need to consult a client representative.
7. Once a response is generated, either automatically or by a CSR, the response is routed to the e-mail response server which archives the message, and sends it back to the mail server to be forwarded to the customer.

Live Text Chat

This form of online customer service is becoming more popular as customers demand human contact from e-businesses. Text Chat generally takes the form of a button on the client's website. When the customer activates this button, a chat box is opened and a signal is sent to the CSR notifying him or her of the customer's request for assistance. CSRs can then respond using preformatted responses or customized responses, depending on the nature of the inquiry.

Most text chat applications provide the ability to transfer the chat to a more knowledgeable CSR or supervisor as necessary. They also provide tracking of CSR performance and customer profiling and survey capabilities.

Voiceover Internet Protocal (VoIP)

VoIP is similar to live text chat except that the exchange occurs using voice data. When the service request button is activated on the client's website, a call is initiated to an available CSR. Instead of a chat box, an actual voice call is made using the Internet as the medium. Because very few customers have the technology required to initiate these types of calls, and because the quality of the voice transmission is not high, developments surrounding VoIP technology will be monitored in order to best integrate this, at the right time, into the existing line of web-based customer support services being offered.

Quality Assurance (QA)

QA will be performed using the administrative features included in the various customer service application packages. In addition, the QA process will be designed to randomly sample and analyze responses to customer inquiries. These responses will be checked for accuracy, clarity, and timeliness. Automatic and categorized responses will be continuously updated to reflect the latest available information. Weekly QA meetings will address client concerns and update CSRs on new client promotions and product offerings.

Disaster Recovery and Business Continuity

live e-care is committed to providing seamless, continuous service to our clients in the event of a natural disaster or technology failure. We are currently devising a disaster recovery strategy which includes a combination of alternate sites, network recovery, and offsite storage initiatives.

HUMAN RESOURCES STRATEGY

Attract, develop, retain the best. One of the key success factors identified in the customer support industry is the ability of a company to attract, develop, and retain the best CSRs. The founders' familiarity with the cultural, social, and business conditions in the Philippines will give the company a competitive advantage in this respect.

Benchmark existing best practices. As part of the human resource strategy, research was done to benchmark existing best practices used in similar companies that have been effective in attracting the best talent in the Philippines. Based on research, Infosys and Cisco have been identified as companies whose human resource strategies have been both successful and best suited to the companies' Philippine operations. Infosys, an Indian software company based in Bangalore, India, is one of India's leading IT services companies. It utilizes an extensive offshore infrastructure to provide managed software solutions to clients worldwide. live e-care realizes that our success will also largely depend upon the ability to recruit, train, deploy, and retain highly talented professionals.

Recruiting—Philippines

Focus on campus recruitment, supplemented by experienced hires. The recruiting strategy will be targeted towards two sets of applicants. The first part will involve visiting the top universities and colleges throughout the Philippines in search of the brightest and most talented students. The company will use a series of interviews and tests to identify the best applicants. In an effort to attract the most highly qualified candidates, the founders sent out a survey to the top universities in the Philippines designed to help live e-care understand and create a quality work environment. Initially, our objective will be to create a campus-like environment in order to foster the culture of a learning organization where ideas will flow freely irrespective of title or tenure. The results of the survey (still pending) will be used in designing the ideal workplace for employees in terms of employment.

To supplement the college recruiting efforts, another hiring strategy involves hiring CSRs away from existing e-mail centers. At this moment, AOL is the only company that has been identified as having such a facility set up in the Philippines. Based on recent reports, AOL is currently paying their CSRs an average of $5.50 a day. This is approximately 35 percent above the existing minimum wage laws. We believe that live e-care can easily double or even triple the amount they are earning without significantly affecting the profit margins of the company. By attracting the best people, live e-care will have the basis to serve the U.S. e-mail market with unparalleled excellence.

Skill profile sought in recruitment. From a skill perspective, it imperative that all CSRs be able to comprehend and communicate effectively in both written and spoken English. In addition, the ideal CSR will have excellent problem-solving skills and a superb customer relations approach. Basic computer and Internet-related skills such as sending and receiving e-mail and surfing the World Wide Web are also desirable.

Focus on Metro Manila, Cebu, and Davao. The skills needed for CSRs can be found in many of the colleges and universities around the Philippines, particularly universities based in the cities of Metro Manila, Cebu, and Davao. These are the three largest urban cities in the Philippines that have a combined population of almost 20 million people. These are also the regions with the highest concentration of universities in the country and whose medium of instruction, at all levels, is English in both education and business.

Training

Two-step training process. Based on interviews with an existing competitor, the training of CSRs is a two step process. The first period of training begins when they join the company. The training focuses on the roles and responsibilities of a CSR while teaching them the tools of the job, including how to handle inquiries using the existing technologies. This process is estimated to take about 1-2 weeks. The second part of the training begins once a company has signed on as a client and the information transfer between the client and the personnel in the U.S. office is complete. The nature of this part of the training focuses more on helping the CSR understand the exact nature of the client's business, how to classify, respond, and deliver responses to customers, as well as how to handle questions requiring a higher level of expertise. This portion of the training takes between 2-6 weeks depending on the level of complexity of the business, customer requirements, and information gathered.

Retention

Relationship-oriented atmosphere. The Filipino culture, like many Asian cultures, is very relationship-oriented. So it comes as no surprise that the core strategy for retaining workers in the Philippines is to cultivate a friendly and relationship-building atmosphere.

To build this atmosphere, the company will encourage existing employees to attract friends who may possess the skills needed by giving financial incentives to "successful referees." It was discovered during the course of research that Cisco Systems uses the referral method (called the Friends program) as a critical component to their recruitment and retention strategy. The principle of encouraging referrals to recruit quality talent is a key strategy in the relationship-oriented culture of Filipinos, and does not add any significant cost to the company.

Stock Options. The company plans to use stock options to reward employees, an almost unheard of practice among private companies, not only in the Philippines, but the rest of Asia as well. Infosys Systems of Bangalore, India, was one of the first companies in India to offer such an incentive scheme to all their key employees from the management down to the staff level. It has proven successful in maintaining their low turnover rate. Given their intimate understanding of the Filipino people, the founders believe that live e-care can apply the same strategy as Infosys and achieve the same results by using stock options or some alternate form of equity participation as a way of retaining and motivating employees.

Continuous learning. Finally, the third component of the company's retention strategy is to ensure that employees are continuously learning new skills and being rewarded with promotions and career advancement within the company. One tactic would be to reward and train the Filipino CSRs by sending them for work-related seminars abroad. live e-care will also tie opportunities to travel abroad to their time with the company. For example, the employment contract can be written in such a way that an employee is required to work for the company for a certain number of months or years in return for such an opportunity. This is a strategy used by Arthur Andersen Philippines to retain its employees and it has served the company well in retaining top talent within the firm despite the low salaries allocated to its entry-level employees. Their average turnover rate is about 20 percent annually and their employees stay on average two years.

FINANCIAL PLAN

Projections and Pro-forma Statements

live e-care anticipates that revenues will grow from $370,497 in Year 1 to $72,442,250 by Year 3, with a Net Loss in Year 1 of ($820,640) but reaching Net Income of $18,777,841 by Year 3. Driving this revenue model and growth will be our ability to gain customers at a rate of 5 percent in Year 1, 7 percent in Year 2, and 10 percent in Year 3 and stabilizing. In addition, future revenues will in part be driven by customers' adoption of live chat services and telephony on top of the e-mail support. We project that 80 percent of our customers will adopt this service. Revenues for additional products or services, such as consulting or FAQ database management have not been included in these projections since they are less certain and not expected until late in Year 2 or 3. Based on these revenue and earnings estimates as well as the required investment capital, Return on Invested Equity (ROE) will be 82 percent at the end of Year 3. The ROE will continue to increase substantially in future years as Net Income grows.

	End of Year 1	End of Year 2	End of Year 3
# of Customers	6	93	384
Average Daily volume of e-mail	984	23,250	153,600
Net Revenues	$370,497	$11,639,875	$72,442,250
Net Income	($820,640)	($2,358,677)	$18,777,841
Net Margin	-221%	-20%	26%
Return on Invested Equity	-29%	-10%	82%
Total Costs per e-mail	**$1.95**	**$0.83**	**$0.61**
Total Costs per Operator Seat	**$63,087**	**$20,584**	**$16,058**

Revenues

Revenues will come from e-mail and live chat services in the beginning, growing from $370,497 in Year 1 to $72,442,250 by Year 3. The key drivers of revenue are the ability to close on potential customers and the adoption of the additional live chat services by customers.

The customer closing rate is forecast at 5 percent in Year 1 and is expected to increase to 7 percent in Year 2 and 10 percent in Year 3. These rates are based on an estimated 15 new sales calls per salesperson per month. The increased closing rate will result from increased experience of the salespeople with live e-care services and an expectation they will be able to showcase the historical performance of live e-care for its clients. E-mail services will be priced at a fixed fee of $15,000 for the first 15,000 e-mails per quarter. Additional e-mails handled will be priced at $1.00 per e-mail. These prices are between the prices quoted by competitors, from $.75 to $1.50 per e-mail. The fixed price will provide live e-care with a consistent cash flow and provide the customers with a similarly consistent expense to more easily budget for the services. It is expected that pricing will be negotiated with customers individually and live e-care may give discounts to some early adopters to gain a foothold in the industry.

Customer adoption of live chat and telephony services is forecast at 80 percent. For the pro-forma financials, this adoption is forecast to come 9 months after initial sign-up. It is expected that as technology improves and the Internet develops, the number of customers that adopt these live chat services will be even higher in order to be competitive on customer services in the marketplace. The timing of adoption may also decrease as customers sign up immediately for both services. Live chat services are priced at $30,000 per operator seat per month for 24/7 service. Both fees were determined by evaluating competitors and estimating the cost for clients to perform the same services in-house.

Costs

As a service support company, the majority of the costs associated with the company is variable costs, to set-up and staff the center in the Philippines. As noted earlier, the hiring and training of the Customer Support Representatives is currently only about 20 percent of the costs for a similar operation in the U.S. Since the staffing is a significant portion of the total costs, live e-care can be price competitive and maintain strong margins. In our projections, CSR costs are 26 percent of total operating costs at the end of Year 1, but grow to be 55 percent of total operating costs by the end of Year 3. We also will be licensing the software for both e-mail and live chat at the start. The costs are an initial charge of $15,000, monthly fixed fee of about of $1,200. Longer term, we plan to develop our own software for competitive reasons, but licensing allows for much faster ramp-up and client acquisition. Sales and Marketing costs are semi-variable with the number of customers, but reduces as a percentage of total operating costs. It is 36 percent of operating costs at the end of Year 1, but shrinks to 13 percent by the end of Year 3. Initially, overhead costs are a sizable 26 percent of total operating costs, but scalability reduces these costs to only 8 percent by the end of Year 3.

Earnings Growth

Using the revenue and cost assumptions as stated above, live e-care will show net operating losses through Q4 of Year 2. Once operating profits begin in Q1 of Year 3, cumulative losses are forecast to total $3,179,317. Net Income for the remainder of Year 2 and Year 3 will result in cumulative breakeven in Q2 of Year 3.

Based on the net income forecasts, the return on the invested capital is 82 percent at the end of Year 3, from (20%) in Year 1 and (10%) in Year 2. These figures are based on the capital needs of $350,000 initially, $2,500,000 after 6-9 months and $20,000,000 after approximately 18 months after the start of operations.

Funding Requirements

The company has summarized a series of detailed pro-forma financial statements outlining the capital needs of the company over its first three years. The company intends to seek $350,000 for working capital needs at the start of the business. The majority of this capital will be needed to fund the purchase/licensing of hardware and software, as well as human resource needs. An additional $2,500,000 of capital will be needed approximately 6 to 9 months later into the project and $20,000,000 approximately 18 months after start-up. These funds will primarily be used for expansion of the sales force, infrastructure and marketing. The anticipated use of funds for the first three months of operation is shown below.

Use of Funds: First Three Months

Hardware	$80,000
Software	70,000
Infrastructure	80,000
Training	20,000
Salaries	100,000
Total	**$350,000**

Painting Company

BUSINESS PLAN

KO-BAS PAINTING COMPANY

1700 West State Street
Hartland, Michigan 48353

The focus of Ko-Bas Painting Company is to provide high-quality surface preparation, finished painting, and refinishing services to residential, commercial, municipal building, and facilities clients primarily in the most-populated area within the tri-county communities defined as Wayne, Oakland, and Washtenaw counties.

INTRODUCTION

Ko-Bas Painting Company was formed to meet the growing demand and ongoing need for professional-grade painting and refinishing services in Southeastern Michigan.

The focus of Ko-Bas Painting Company is to provide high-quality surface preparation, finished painting, and refinishing services to residential, commercial, municipal building, and facilities clients primarily in the most-populated area within the tri-county communities defined as Wayne, Oakland, and Washtenaw counties.

MISSION & PRINCIPLES

Ko-Bas Painting will be known for providing a high-quality service product. We will become known as a premium provider of custom and commercial painting and finishing services, operating at multiple levels within our prospect and existing client community.

To achieve our mission, Ko-Bas Painting will have to succeed at doing the following:

- Provide unique, practical, and professional services to our clients on a timely basis, applying and leveraging time-tested, and state-of-the-art techniques and practices. To succeed at meeting our goals, our first responsibility is to our customers.
- Maintain a strong financial environment to allow us to establish ourselves as a multi-faceted service provider in the regional market we serve.
- Behave with the philosophy that our customers are entitled to a professional service that performs to above expectation satisfaction, in a reasonable, agreed-to amount of time and at a competitive, attractive price.
- Treat our partners, employees, and customers with fairness and consideration.
- Bring value to our business operations community and client community.

We expect that through the effective application of these philosophies and principles we will succeed in achieving our mission.

GROWTH, MARKET, & CLIENTS WE SERVE

Market factors have indicated a current trend of moderately increasing income and commercial budgets with a pent-up demand for convenience and beautification services. It will not be unreasonable for the number of potential residential and commercial customers to increase 10 to 30 percent each year.

Market and Prospect Client Base

Who: Ko-Bas Painting Company serves a marketplace made up of commercial and residential clients. Our ongoing focus is to develop and serve the correct blend of work to ensure ongoing revenue requirements. Our market focus is typically made up of an even split of residential and commercial clients. Our commercial clients are made up of municipal buildings, school buildings, and private businesses (manufacturing and/or retail).

Where and Why

We choose our clients in this market to ensure that we do not extend our operations beyond reasonable areas of service, primarily, to manage and moderate costs in drive time, customer follow-up servicing, quoting, and inspections.

SERVICE DELIVERY EXPECTATIONS

In order for Ko-Bas to attain its business objective, the following goals must be achieved:

- Acquire proper number of prospect clients for manageable growth
- Complete service at or below the price forecasted in the client financial quote
- Complete above-expectation service for the home or commercial client on or before the agreed-to deadline
- Leverage the customer as a reference for the next potential customer
- Utilize the recognition of the quality work to develop a demand for continued revenue growth

ABOUT THE COMPANY

Ko-Bas Painting Company was founded in 1997 by Karen and Ken Ko-Bas. The Ko-Bas Company sprang out of an idea—"We should make a go of this on our own!" Five years later, Ko-Bas is a highly successful, growing concern with all the unique business challenges faced by a locally owned, expanding business.

The founders of Ko-Bas Painting Company, Ken and Karen Ko-Bas, have served the Southeast Michigan business and residential community for a combined total of more than 18 years. Their experience and dedication to the service industry has provided a positive force on multiple levels.

Ken Ko-Bas has brought value to customers as a paint and surface-coating consultant at the retail management level as well as commercial coatings applications sales management. Karen has achieved multiple certifications in custom and commercial finishing and designer coating applications. She provides operational expertise and leadership to the company.

Ko-Bas Painting Company manages a focused team of highly experienced, professional painters and coating specialists to execute on any level of service required by a client. We select and manage our team to satisfy our ultimate goal, to treat each project as if it was our own. We pride ourselves on our legacy and service provided and intend to ensure ongoing satisfaction through quality service, operational management, and relationships with our employees, partners, and clients. We will continue to develop and leave behind a reputation nothing short of first class.

BUSINESS OBJECTIVE

Grow the company to a targeted achievement of more than 15 to 20 percent operating margin year-to-year.

We've maintained an objective view and take a conservative approach in developing and attempting to achieve our business goals. The financial data and business model provided is based on a year-to year running operational and growth plan that is developed on an as-needed basis, typically by quarterly review. Thus, the numbers provided are based on a blend of real and approximated costs using the most conservative expense expectations available (and are based on our considerable experience).

BUSINESS CHALLENGES & ECONOMIC RISKS

The basic risks that Ko-Bas faces on a day-to-day basis are not unique to the average small business owner. However, when considering local economic pressures we may need to change our mix of business to "flex" to market demands and fill market needs.

The following list outlines many of our ongoing tactical and strategic concerns:

- Maintaining client base to sustain growth
- Significant changes in the market demand for high-quality, premium services
- Ongoing ability to attract and retain qualified, dependable employees
- Significant unforeseen insurance event beyond reasonable expectations for on-the-job related injury

COMPETITION & MARKET POSITION

The competitive environment and the upswing of local and national economies put us in an enviable position for the last two years in terms of the demand for convenience services and client custom/commercial coatings requirements. This created a positive competitive environment, as there were not enough service providers to satisfy the body of available work. Needless to say, time changes everything, the economic downswing as of late has put moderate competitive pressures on the painting services provider community at large, creating a developing environment of cutthroat pricing and job leverage.

It is our position that by changing our mix of business, competitive client pursuit, and pricing practices we have been able to remain competitive and most importantly growing. Ko-Bas competes on service and price. We gather market-based information on an ongoing basis and develop our pricing and cost strategies based on market norms specific to our client profile and geographic considerations.

Our competitors range from the small independent 1-2 man painting service for residential and light commercial work to the medium-size 10-20 man commercial-only shops. To find out who to beat and who's getting the work, we need not look further than the local Yellow Pages and more importantly, by having those tough discussions with our client prospects that select another provider and asking them "Why weren't we chosen?"

We have found that dealing with reality and modifying our tactics with reality has helped us keep an edge when it comes to beating the competition.

On any given day, in our particular market segment we have to keep an eye out for an average of 10-15 competitors in our market, particularly in the commercial and municipal service sector.

MARKETING STRATEGY

Our marketing strategy is simple—use the available channels appropriately to impact growth, gaining considerable name recognition through word of mouth. Contracting for painting and finishing services in our commercial and municipal markets is not an impulse decision, so the primary thrust of the marketing strategy is to inform our prospective clients of reference work similar to the services they require.

In rank order we have identified where our priorities lie in developing market presence to acquire clients.

1. Word of mouth
2. Client testimonials
3. Local business associations
4. Traditional print media, Internet advertising, and miscellaneous promotion techniques

Market Perception & Positioning Strategy

Our marketing, advertising, and promotion strategy is to differentiate Ko-Bas Painting as a premium provider. The Ko-Bas Company's marketing strategy incorporates plans to educate and recruit potential homeowners and commercial prospects through several proven channels:

- Newspaper advertising targeting specific local buyers
- Direct reference channels from satisfied current and previous clients
- Direct sales contact with property management and municipal property portfolio managers
- Small business network community

KEY PARTNERS

We view our partners and network of business contacts as a reflection how we get business done. Without the partners and business contacts we could not operate as an operationally lean company and most importantly, leverage this network for continued sales and business growth. The following list provides a window into the depth and breadth of engagement required to make our business go.

- Paint product and supply manufacturers
- Commercial/retail suppliers at large
- Financial institutions
- Community-based business network
- Business associations
- Better Business Bureau
- Michigan Economic Development Corporation (MEDC)

LEGAL CONSIDERATIONS

Ko-Bas Painting is a Michigan company, based in Hartland, Michigan. Ko-Bas retains and maintains relationships with legal representation experienced in contracting and building service provider industries. Our company is organized to minimize risk to our operations while providing for maximum safety and security to our employees, their families, and client community.

CONCLUSION

The future looks bright for Ko-Bas Painting and we fully expect to be recognized in the marketplace and we will be able to achieve growth and sustain profitable operations through reputation and adherence to our most basic operating philosophies for maximum competitive advantage.

Routing/Navigation Software Company

BUSINESS PLAN

PATH SYSTEMS, INC.

36000 Washington Street
Pittsburgh, Pennsylvania 15219

This business plan outlines the strategies for the development and sales of routing /navigation software that allows vehicles to travel faster, safer, and more predictably. PATH Systems, Inc., provides transportation companies with routes optimized to avoid accidents (vs. shortest-path routes). Using a simulation model we have projected that we can reduce involvement in accidents by over 40 percent.

ROUTING/NAVIGATION SOFTWARE COMPANY BUSINESS PLAN

EXECUTIVE SUMMARY

PATH Systems, Inc., provides transportation companies with routes optimized to avoid accidents (vs. shortest-path routes). Using a simulation model we have projected that we can reduce involvement in accidents by over 40 percent. Accidents and their associated financial liabilities are an acute problem for large trucking companies. Recently jury awards have skyrocketed, sending up the cost of insurance by over 50 percent per year, and threaten many trucking companies—large and small—with bankruptcy. We are assembling an industry alliance of transportation companies, insurance companies, and logistics firms to prove on the road what we have shown in the lab. We will use the PATH system with thought-leader trucking firms large enough to rack up the necessary miles to statistically document the system's efficacy.

Philip M. Moon, CEO, founded PATH Systems in 2001 to take advantage of a significant market opportunity to build a road condition database and next-generation routing/navigation software to move vehicles through increasing road congestion more safely, profitably, and with fewer delays. PATH builds road condition databases and next-generation routing software. PATH's technology measures road speeds under a variety of conditions using GPS and other sensors, and combines it with other dynamic road attributes to create future road speed estimates based on proprietary databases and analytics. We then provide directions to the vehicles through next-generation routing software that we have developed in conjunction with several technology partners.

PATH answers the question, "How long will it take to get there?" and extends that knowledge into more efficient and safer routes. PATH meticulously catalogs the traffic patterns associated with everyday incidents so that future trips can be routed to best navigate around trouble spots. We gather the following data:

- Actual Road Speeds—by time of day, from participating partner vehicles
- Accident Data—from DOT, insurance, and state agencies
- Construction Data—from State transportation departments
- Weather Data—from National agencies

Objectives

- Form a loose alliance of companies to jointly develop, road test, and document our products, obviating the need to raise large amounts of capital
- Provide alliance companies full access to the developed products
- Integrate PATH's next-generation navigation software with existing routing software vendors' and tracking companies' solutions
- Market the navigation software solution to large transportation companies
- Promote the accident avoidance benefits of the database solution to insurance companies who benefit from reduced accidents, claims, and lawsuits

Mission

PATH Systems was founded to make road travel safer, more profitable, and more efficient. We have studied the problem and have begun implementing a solution that models the considerable complexity of the traveling world, based on empirical data gathered automatically, which is then stored, processed, and redistributed in a format that a traveler can use to make timely navigation decisions.

Keys to Success

- PATH's competitive advantage lies in the ability to generate dynamic routes by time of day that also consider external attributes such as high-accident areas, construction zones, and weather. Our routes are superior to those that are calculated solely on shortest path.
- PATH's core asset is our intellectual property protected by three pending patents. Those technologies include knowledge of how to precisely gather data in complex networks, how to store that data, how to make that data available for high-speed applications, and how to optimize future trips under a very flexible set of conditions.
- By relocating the company to Pittsburgh, Pennsylvania, PATH will reside in the heart of the Midwest transportation routes, with quick access to the major trucking carriers' headquarters. With seven major Interstate highways (I-70, 71, 75, 76, 77, 80, and 90) and being situated in a primary East-West commercial traffic corridor, Pennsylvania is a showcase of commercial highway transportation.

Timeline

- Gather "alliance of the willing" with representation from insurance, transportation and logistics/consulting industries to form the Accident Avoider Alliance
- Form Implementation Teams for Individual Companies
- Develop Specs (overall, database, business integration, I/O)
- Alliance Covers PATH's Operating Expenses During Field Trial
- Once Savings/Benefits Are Documented:
    - Transportation companies roll out solution fleet-wide
    - Insurance companies introduce to client-base and new customers reduced premium insurance product
    - PATH co-markets with insurance and logistics companies

COMPANY OVERVIEW

PATH Systems, Inc., is a California C-Corporation formed in September 2001. Philip M. Moon founded the company to take advantage of a significant market opportunity presented by combining the precision of passive tracking services with next-generation routing software.

PATH moved its headquarters to Pittsburgh, Pennsylvania, in August 2003, signing a lease for space in a building on the corner of Main and Washington streets. The city of Pittsburgh and the Pittsburgh investment community have proven to be a receptive locale for PATH, providing a $250,000 regional loan/grant package.

Pittsburgh is an ideal location for servicing transportation companies: it is centrally located in the nation's Texas to Mid-Atlantic transportation nexus. Major customer sites are just a short trip away. Also, real estate and labor is much more reasonably priced.

In addition to providing a headquarters facility, the Pittsburgh office will focus on the transportation/logistics opportunity while a California office will be maintained to further develop our suite of intellectual property.

Company History

In a previous position at IBM, Philip Moon had a chance to work with the early GPS prototypes. While early GPS applications were focused on the military and consumer retail markets, Philip felt there was an untapped business market broadly defined as trucking and delivery. In 2001 he founded PATH Systems, Inc., with the goal of bringing location-based services to the world using GPS, wireless, and Internet technologies.

Early interviews with trucking/delivery companies suggested the industry penetration of these technologies was still shallow, and implementations were piecemeal. The transportation field had yet to experience the systemization that occurred when ERP systems transformed manufacturing over the last two decades. There was an opportunity to use tracking devices to provide input to transportation planning software, allowing it to reflect the realities of the transportation world.

Philip returned to his alma mater, Harvard, and in particular, Harvard's legendarily prolific Electrical Engineering and Computer Science departments. Students from these departments have created past engineering miracles such as Alta Vista, Reuters, and most recently, Yahoo! Philip assembled a team of Ph.D. engineering candidates, software specialists, wireless communication gurus, and mathematical algorithm wizards to develop and code the new PATH platform.

In spring 2002, PATH launched the first of several products into the tracking segment of the market. During the development and marketing of these products, we developed a deep understanding of the capabilities and limitations of tracking technologies, the varying capabilities of wireless technologies, and the unit economics of the value propositions. We also learned that the tracking business was a poor fit for PATH's strategic competencies, so we refocused the company towards using the data that tracking systems generate to provide higher order benefits.

The first embodiment of that strategy was the creation of the Driver-base, a comprehensive set of road speeds and road conditions automatically rolled into our master file, leveraging the latest tracking, wireless, and database technologies. We felt the Driver-base was the breakthrough development necessary to create and maintain dynamic or time-expanded networks (networks where road speed assumptions change by time of day). Dynamic networks necessarily produce more accurate and precise vehicle location estimates, thus allowing transportation firms to remove dead time out of their schedules and dramatically improve return on assets.

We chose to go to market by partnering with existing routing software vendors who would license our database via an ASP model to enhance the functionality of their products. However, subsequent industry discussions revealed that many routing algorithms currently in use are ill-suited to handle the demands of time-expanded networks under any commercially reasonable processing time requirement.

This insight led us back to the labs where we researched and worked the algorithm issues aggressively. The result was our patent pending EP (Estimate-Pruning) algorithm. EP provides two important contributions: 1) It allows for quick optimization in networks where road speed estimates change by time of day, and 2) it creates a practical solution for optimization based on a new set of routing characteristics, such as accident avoidance, standard deviation reduction, and profitability optimization in operations where random, spontaneous pick-ups have highly variable prices. In 2003, PATH received important validation for EP from the IEEE who refereed and published our first seminal paper describing the algorithm.

In early fall 2003, PATH moved its headquarters to Pittsburgh, Pennsylvania, from California to be closer to our client base and to leverage the vibrant logistics and transportation communities of Pennsylvania and the Midwest.

We are currently assembling an industry alliance of transportation companies, insurance companies and logistics firms to prove on the road what we have shown in the lab. We will use the PATH System with thought-leader trucking firms large enough to rack up the necessary miles to statistically document the efficacy of the PATH system.

PRODUCTS & SERVICES

PATH's core product is the database that allows users to a) predict a series of trip durations under a variety of conditions and b) identify and document operational inefficiencies. Depending on the type of client and their particular needs, the information database can be packaged in a number of ways:

Accident Avoider

Problems Addressed	High jury awards against trucking companies have caused loss exposure and commercial insurance rates to skyrocket. Insurance company clients are going bankrupt.
Product Description	PATH's system provides routes optimized for accident avoidance (vs. shortest path) based on historical accident records.
Target Customers	Fleets with annual road-miles over 100 million where losses are evident. Self-insured transportation companies. Thought-leader insurance companies.
Value Proposition	Computer simulation models indicate the Accident Avoider can reduce fleet accidents by 40% Fewer accidents, fewer claims, fewer lawsuits, saved lives.

Routing Calibration

Problems Addressed	Routing software today generates many planned routes that don't consider road conditions. Planned routes quickly become inconsistent with true road conditions, forcing planners to abandon planned routes and scramble, causing missed stops, last minute changes, and overtime.
Product Description	We track client vehicles traversing their routes. At end of day, we compare actual routes taken to planned routes, giving an objective measure of calibration. We then perform diagnostics, assigning reasons for variation so planners can tune their systems for optimal performance.
Target Customers	Transportation companies already using routing software (by definition, early technology adopters) and routing software companies as resellers.
Value Proposition	Provides tools to improve planning for less missed stops and afternoon chaos. Routes that save time and money are delivered without the administrative hassles. With better road knowledge, planners can tighten up their schedules, reducing overtime while improving on-time performance.

Dynamic Route Navigation (time-expanded routes)

Problems Addressed	As roads and customers change and new drivers are added, the old routes lose efficiency by the month. The task of gathering current road condition information is tedious, expensive, inaccurate and rarely done.
Product Description	PATH automatically gathers road condition data from GPS-based tracking systems and effortlessly enters that into a database. We then model future road speeds and integrate this with next-generation routing software.
Target Customers	Transportation companies already using routing software. Routing software companies as resellers.
Value Proposition	With better road knowledge, planners can tighten up their schedules, reducing overtime while improving on-time performance.

Routing Services

Problems Addressed	As roads and customers change and new drivers are added, the old routes lose efficiency by the month. The task of gathering current road condition information is tedious, expensive, inaccurate, and rarely done.
Product Description	PATH automatically gathers road condition data from GPS-based tracking systems and effortlessly enters that into a database. We then model future road speeds and integrate this with next-generation routing software. Re-routing can happen annually, quarterly, even weekly.
Target Customers	Delivery companies and private fleets that run regular routes.
Value Proposition	Provides tools to improve planning for less missed stops and afternoon chaos. Routes that save time and money are delivered without the administrative hassles. With better road knowledge, planners can tighten up their schedules, reducing overtime while improving on-time performance.

All of the above will be priced based on a monthly revenue per rig model. In addition, PATH charges fees for installation, consulting, and engineering customization at an hourly rate.

Products & Services Description

PATH is introducing the next generation in routing and navigation software. PATH's technology measures road speeds under a variety of conditions using GPS and other sensors to create future road speed estimates based on proprietary databases and analytics. We then relay directions to the vehicles using next-generation routing software that we have developed in conjunction with several technology partners.

PATH answers the question, "How long will it take to get there?" and extends that knowledge into more efficient and safer routes. We measure actual road speeds under a variety of conditions using GPS and other devices to create future road speed estimates based on a set of protected, proprietary databases and analytics. We then feed those estimates into our next-generation routing software to generate an optimal route based on the conditions the vehicle is expected to encounter. In so doing, we are codifying all the traffic information that humans have imperfectly tried to keep in their heads and are providing significantly more route choices by giving access to other drivers' trip experiences.

Routing software today grossly simplifies road condition assumptions: road speeds are assumed to be the same across all roads in a "class," the road speed assumptions don't change by the time of day, and all intersections are assumed to clear at the same rate. For example, if a delivery vehicle is routed to make 15 drop-offs per day using standard routing software, the routes will become grossly uncalibrated with road conditions by sometime mid-morning. The estimated times of arrivals do not take into account the time of day/evening the vehicle is traveling, road construction, weather delays, or traffic accidents. As a result, they are rarely calibrated with the actual events on the road, and they are only optimized for sequential considerations such as distance and time versus more randomly occurring events such as safety, standard deviation, and profitability. PATH meticulously catalogs the traffic patterns associated with such everyday incidents, so that future trips can be routed to best navigate around trouble spots.

PATH has solved the problem by developing a set of algorithms that 1) optimize in consideration of a large set of road conditions that change by time of day ("time-expanded networks"), and 2) optimize based on user preference including nonsequential events such as safety. PATH meticulously catalogs the traffic patterns associated with such everyday incidents so that future trips can be routed to best navigate around trouble spots.

Networks where the road speeds change by time of day—called dynamic networks—have long enjoyed acceptance at academic logistics citadels such as Georgia Tech, Virginia Polytechnic, and others. Yet, there are few real-world implementations due to 1) the complexity of gathering the huge amount of data required, and 2) the computer science challenges of generating optimized routes within reasonable computer run times. To solve the run-time problem, routing companies have resorted to a simplifying assumption referred to as FIFO (First-In, First-Out), which allows run times to be short, but disallows optimization of variables such as accident avoidance, standard deviation of road speeds and profitability of jobs. PATH Systems has solved both of these problems:

> 1) our patent pending method of automatically gathering, storing, and integrating road condition data with next-generation routing software allows for practical implementation of time expanded networks, and 2) our EP algorithm (also patent pending) solves the computer science problem of quick run-time solutions for large, time-expanded networks without the imposition of the FIFO simplification.

With non-FIFO algorithms, the following optimization routines are possible:

- Routes with fewest incidence of accidents
- Routes with lowest overall standard deviation
- Routes that avoid speed traps
- Routes that consider variable dock times by time of day
- Multi-stop routes that optimize on overall profitability
- Inter-modal planning problems where the cost of transit changes by time of day

While the concept of easily implemented time-expanded networks under non-FIFO conditions had great appeal among the logistic elite, such language sent many practicing transportation managers packing for the hills. We reduced that large concept down to two bite-sized products: 1) Accident Avoider and 2) Routing Calibration.

Product Benefits

Implementing PATH's vehicle routing and navigation solution provides a variety of benefits:

Boost Productivity

- Serve more customers in less time
- Increase your bottom line by better utilizing your fleet assets
- Increase the number of profitable turns on your vehicles each day
- Send your drivers on the most efficient, safest, and most predictable routes available
- Reduce the number of hours your drivers spend being unloaded and loaded

Reduce Operating and Maintenance Costs

- Reduce fuel costs through improved scheduling
- Cut down on wear and tear of your vehicles

Improve Safety

- Reduce accidents, claims, lawsuits
- Save lives

Enhance Customer Service

- Increase on-time deliveries
- Provide more accurate predictions of arrival time
- Dispatch closest vehicle for faster pickups and deliveries

Key characteristics of PATH Next-Generation Routes:

- Routes reflect actual road conditions
- Road speeds and recommended routes change by:
  - Time of day
  - Day of week/year
  - Known construction zones
  - Weather
- Routes can be optimized to:
  - Deliver safer routes, avoiding accident areas
  - Reduce travel times (without speeding)
  - Reduce variations in trip length (lower standard deviation of route times)

Professional Services

PATH's deep team of transportation industry veterans and business professionals can help solve transportation problems. Our senior team has over 215 years of combined management and transportation experience.

Services include:

- Analysis of current routing software and routing processes
- Evaluation/analysis of your fleet's operations
- Integration of mobile resource management tools with legacy applications

- Develop a mobile asset management program that is right for you
- Implementation of the specially-designed technology solution

TECHNOLOGY

The PATH technology platform is highly reliable, scalable, and flexible. PATH combines proven technologies with proprietary, innovative processes to deliver unparalleled service.

Key Characteristics of the PATH Technology Platform:

Easy-to-Use

- Digital maps that are easy to read and navigate

Flexible

- PATH software and services are built on industry-leading and open standards
- Linux operating system, JAVA-based software, Internet protocol communication standards
- Integrates easily with existing software applications and legacy systems
- Agnostic approach to wireless networks and GPS hardware—PATH works with any network or device

Reliable

- PATH leverages multiple data center server facilities to ensure 24x7x365 service
- Industry-leading data storage and management practices
- Data is protected through redundant locations and automatic backup twice per day

Scalable

- State-of-the-art database software to manage diverse data collection and analysis
- Industry-leading data storage and data management practices

PATH is Network Agnostic

While networks and standards change continually, PATH retains the flexibility to work with any wireless data network available. We are not tied to one technology, platform or data network.

The combustive growth in the technology sector during the late 1990s delivered several powerful new tools that have yet to be harnessed together for the Geographic Information Systems (GIS) task:

- Global Positional Satellites (GPS) allow us to track the paths and speeds of individual vehicles
- Wireless communication networks allow us to communicate those paths and speeds in fast and economical ways
- Database and storage technologies allow us to warehouse and retrieve terabytes of information with little manual intervention
- Internet technologies provide a universal platform through which we may communicate broadly

PATH Systems was founded to make road travel more efficient, safer, and more predictable. We studied the problem and began implementing a solution that models the considerable complexity of the traveling world, using empirical data that is gathered automatically, stored, processed, and redistributed in a format that a traveler can use to make timely navigation decisions.

Specifically, the innovations we introduce are:

- Concept of systematically gathering voluminous quantities of precise road and trip history data
- Cross referencing and building that data record to enhance its explanatory power using, for example, weather conditions, vehicle profile, driver profile, emergency conditions, etc.
- Maintaining a complete record of actual observations as well as creating a highly available predictive layer of data for use in time-expanded optimization systems
- A set of stochastic models that translate historical observations into expected road conditions
- The creation of optimized routes using today's CPU processing power, that can realistically handle time-expanded routes
- The creation of optimized routes that consider nonsequential (a.k.a. post-FIFO) events, such as the incidence of accidents, standard deviation, and the preponderance of different drivers traveling across the same road at different speeds
- The development of preference profiles where drivers can choose to optimize routes based on a weighting of efficiency, distance, safety, standard deviation, avoidance of speed traps, and other considerations
- The gathering of a subset of road condition data in real time that has proven to have significant and far-reaching impact (so-called "Flashpoint" data) using satellite and other technologies
- The re-processing of expected navigation paths based on the flashpoint data and the communication of updated navigation suggestions to drivers in real time

These solutions are protected with three pending patents.

Patented Technology

- *Business Process*—Gathering, managing, and analyzing event-based data on road conditions/experiences
- *Optimization Algorithms*—Multi-variable optimization algorithms for routing decisions
- *Database Technology*—Storing large volumes of road condition data and making that data available for high-speed applications

COMPETITION

PATH's competitive advantage lies in the ability to generate dynamic routes by time of day that also consider external attributes such as high-accident areas, construction zones, and weather. Our routes are superior to those that are calculated solely on shortest-path.

PATH's core asset is our intellectual property protected by three pending patents. Those technologies include knowledge of how to precisely gather data in complex networks, how to store that data, how to make that data available for high-speed applications and how to optimize future trips under a very flexible set of conditions.

We know of no other company building a database using GPS devices to be integrated with routing software. There are two sets of competitors in adjacent industries: 1) Tracking companies and 2) Routing software companies. PATH retains the flexibility to compete with these companies or partner with them. Each set of competitors can benefit from the PATH database service.

Although tracking isn't the core focus of PATH, we do compete with many companies to provide fleet management and tracking solutions. These companies are focused on reliable tracking and communication with drivers. These competitors typically lack the capability to do database analysis, and none possess the expertise to deliver next-generation routes.

The leading tracking companies are Magellan, Garmin, Altec, TravelWell, and StreetWise. None of these companies has decided to build a database necessary for this application and we are in discussions with them and their customers regarding appending our services onto theirs to deliver our higher order benefits.

We are decidedly not in the GPS tracking business although our products use the data gathered from such products. Rather we will get finders' fees from placing their units into service.

Likewise, we know of no other company offering routing calibration services or routes optimized to avoid accidents. Conceivably a routing software company could acquire a tracking system and develop such a service, but they would be in violation of our first patent, and we would seek a royalty stream from them. The leading routing software companies are Smithson, Philips, and Panasonic. We are in discussions with them as well.

There are two commercial companies who understand dynamic networks and could potentially develop a product: UPS/Roadway and BMT Systems. We've discussed our method of building dynamic networks with UPS. They have provided strong validation saying they are in the process of developing a similar system and have invited us in to discuss these kinds of systems. We also have had discussions with BMT Systems about our range of services. They have the understanding, expertise, and desire to create a calibration product and possibly an Accident Avoider product in violation of our pending patents. We are attempting to partner with them versus compete.

There are scores of small logistics re-routing services consulting outfits that offer re-routes for $250,000 to $600,000 using highly labor intensive methods. We feel our tracking services will allow us to significantly undercut their pricing while maintaining high margins.

Finally, there are numerous Geographical Information System (GIS) software vendors that provide visual maps for use in navigation, including GDT, iiMap, Navtech, Telcontar, and Tele Atlas. PATH's technology can interface with any of them, and we are in discussions with several of the vendors.

THE MARKET

Two broad application markets are targeted by PATH: the logistics/transportation market and the data packet/networking market. PATH's core has been in the transportation space, and this plan primarily covers transportation. Still, we have identified opportunities to apply our collection methods and optimization algorithms to the data packet market as well. That opportunity will be pursued by a dedicated division and will be the focus of an additional forthcoming business plan.

Market Needs

Why the need for Next-Generation Routing and Navigation Software? Congestion—both on the road and at the dock—is a major problem...and it's getting worse.

Road Congestion

- Traffic jams have increased by 350% in the last 16 years (source: 1999 Mobility Report)
- Trucking traffic will grow by 83% by 2020 (source: 10/3/02 DOT Study)
- Road congestion annually costs U.S. business $72 billion (source: 1999 Mobility Report)
- 6.6 billion gallons in wasted fuel
- Cost per driver in Los Angeles is $1,370 per year

Dock Congestion

- Average driver spends 37.5 hours per week waiting to be loaded or unloaded (source: TCA Study 2000)
- Docks at port are in crisis. California legislature is countering with the Lowenthal Bill, assessing $250 for each incidence of a 30+ minute wait
- Unpredictable trips make backhauls difficult. 24% of trucks on road are rolling empty (source: The Logistics Institute at Georgia Tech—January 2002 Study)

Congestion is a serious problem for freight transportation. It contributes to making transit times longer and more unpredictable. Unpredictability can hamper just-in-time inventory management and hinder some production processes. As a result, shippers and carriers assign a value to increases in travel time, ranging from $25 to almost $200 per hour, depending on the product carried. The value of reliability (i.e., the cost of unexpected delay) for trucks is another 50 percent to 250 percent higher (2001 USDOT FHWA). Hence, congestion increases the cost of freight and therefore has an effect on the U.S. economy.

Market Trends

The market for PATH's services is developing very rapidly, as the transportation/trucking industry rushes to reap the benefits of technology that manufacturing has already demonstrated. U.S. trucking revenues total more than $550 billion annually (~6% of GDP), yet the market remains highly fragmented. No trucking company has captured more than 1 percent of the market. The main reason for this is that operations remain primarily manual and there has been under-investment in automation and value-added software applications. We anticipate this being a large and growing market for the next 10 to 15 years. If the Trucking Industry would invest like other more efficient industries, then the potential market for external software could total approximately $24 billion:

Industry	Industry Revenue	Current External Software Expenditures	Penetration	Potential Market*
Manufacturing	$1,566 Bn	$66.6 Bn	4.3%	
Trucking	$566 Bn	$1.9 Bn	0.3%	$23.7 Bn

**assumes trucking industry spends 4.3% of revenue on external software*

The Manufacturing vertical spent $804 million on Transportation Management Systems (TMS) in 2001, and that is projected to increase to $1.7 billion by 2006 (source: ARC Advisory Group).

Every day in the U.S. an estimated—

- 21 million trucks,
- make 245 million stops,
- delivering 750,000 tons of product,
- after traveling 2 billion miles,
- under constantly changing conditions.

Yet, trucking operations are primarily manual. 72 percent of route planning operations are still done manually (source: The Logistics Institute at Georgia Tech—January 2002). Key reasons for this phenomenon are that it is too difficult to gather trip data accurately and organize for computerized planning, and it is easier to just rely on the experience base of dispatchers. Current software for the trucking market simply does not work.

Current Routing Software

Current routing and navigation software was developed to reduce congestion, but it has several limitations:

Current Routing/Navigation Software

Does Do	**Doesn't Do**
Roads are defined	No knowledge of actual road speeds or conditions
Cross reference roads with addresses and zip codes	Cross reference with accident data and standard deviations of travel times
Better viewing and manipulation tools	Consider most popular paths traveled between nodes by time of day

Early software usefulness has been limited:

- Primary impact has been to reduce amount of time planning for a trip before initiating
- Travel time hasn't been significantly reduced

How is PATH different from other vehicle tracking services?

- PATH delivers faster, safer, and more predictable routes for your fleet
- PATH utilizes event-based data to create an ever-growing, road history database
- PATH databases and analytics grow and improve with your enterprise; PATH data is never out of date
- We create custom solutions for unique requirements, such as providing objective, detailed location reports when required for law enforcement and dispute resolution, or exception reports that flag speeding vehicles, errant vehicles, and detained vehicles

MANAGEMENT & BOARD

PATH has assembled a world-class team of experienced senior-level personnel with proven track records for innovation, product marketing, Internet operations, and sales to business customers.

Key Executives

Philip Moon, Founder, Chairman and CEO

Philip is a seasoned general manager with speed-oriented, entrepreneurial expertise built on a solid traditional foundation. Most recently Philip served as Chairman and Chief Executive Officer for Fairways.com, the leading online golf retailer and manufacturer of mass customized clubs. There he managed a team of 200 people, raised $30 million, recruited a senior management team, acquired a subsidiary, and created an award-winning website. Prior to Fairways.com, he was General Manager, Consumer Division and Vice President of Marketing at Skye.com, the leading online software retailer. There he created the Skye brand and built the core disciplines and team that grew the company from $16 million in sales to $120 million in sales. Prior positions include Vice President of Sales and Marketing at CNN, launched BlueDress.com, and Vice President of Marketing and Sales, IBM Corporation, where he pioneered IBM's handheld product line and launched IBM's first website. He has also served as Brand Manager at Pfizer and MIS Director for Boeing Corporation. Philip received his M.B.A. from Harvard Graduate School of Business and his M.A. in Economics from the University of Michigan.

Daniel O'Day, Vice President of Client Services and Administration

Daniel is a Certified Public Accountant with a broad financial, retail, and consulting career. Daniel has extensive experience with business systems and applications involving large scale ERP systems design and implementation for mid- to large-sized organizations. As Vice President of BMI Group, a retail management consulting firm, he directed numerous systems projects, managing project teams comprised of consultants, vendors, and client resources.

Consulting clients included: Heartfelt Greetings, Coleman, Adidas, Trek, and Apple Corporation. Prior to BMI, Daniel consulted for Peters & James's management consulting division. Prior positions include Business Analyst at State Farm Insurance, and Financial Systems Analyst/Accountant at Ryder Transportation. Daniel received his Master's in Accounting and Information Systems from the University of Virginia and his B.S. in Accounting from Columbia University.

Board Members

Philip Moon, Chairman

Michael Belle, Director

Michael Belle is experienced in logistics and supply chain efficiency, having served thirty-one years with UPS. Among other jobs, he served as President and CEO of Consolidated Freightways, Trailways Freight, and General Trucking Industries, where he successfully implemented a dramatic turnaround. He led the strategic planning effort resulting in the creation of Roadway, one of the world's most profitable trucking companies. He also participated in the creation of and served as the first president of Jordan Logistics, one of the world's fastest growing and most profitable logistics companies.

Jane Smith, Director

Jane Smith has almost 30 years of experience in the trucking industry, representing the trucking industry in Washington, D.C., both as a Senior Vice President for the General Truck Associations and the president of the Semitruck Association. She is currently the Principal in Smith and Associates, a transportation consulting firm that specializes in bringing new technology products to the trucking industry. Ms. Smith earned a B.A. in Political Science from the University of Wyoming and an M.A. in Politics and Public Affairs from the University of North Carolina. She has been president of the Transportation Research Forum and was named Person of the Year by the Women's Transportation Seminar. She serves on the Board of Directors of TravelWays, Truckitonline, TravelWell Communications, and the Cost-Effective Transport.

Borden Jackson, Director

Mr. Jackson has more than 30 years of experience as CFO, consultant, and serial entrepreneur. He spent the first 18 years of his career with Johnson and Marks, serving for seven years as Partner-in-Charge of the San Francisco office's Emerging Business Department. In that role, he assisted scores of start-up companies from inception to IPO. Grant was Senoir Vice President and CFO at Finders, Inc., a publicly traded company. He was one of the first employees at the Arena Management Corporation. In addition, he has held senior roles in a variety of companies, including Morningstar, Financial Times, Yahoo!, and Fairways.com. He has participated in over $700 million of corporate financings. Grant holds a B.B.A. in accounting from St. Louis University and an M.B.A. in finance from Bowling Green University. He also is the author of a seminal book on international trade.

Technical Team

Our technical team is largely drawn from Harvard's legendarily prolific Electrical Engineering and Computer Science departments. Students from these departments have created past engineering miracles such as Alta Vista, Reuters, and most recently, Yahoo! There, we met Jason Schmidt, a Ph.D. candidate in Electrical Engineering. Jason liked Philip's vision and signed on immediately. Shortly after, Philip found Monty Fresard, a seasoned software wizard whose resume includes the Amiga operating system, the first SIMS launch, and several Internet platforms. Monty attracted Kevin Stringer, a seasoned web author versed in the ways of Velocity, to join PATH as well. The team developed code and created the new PATH platform. In February 2002, the Harvard team recruited several other trusted Harvard classmates to pick up the mantle. Over the next six months, Sanja Patel and Ali Ulakonda joined PATH. In addition to writing code, each new member brought some cutting-edge talent to PATH. Sanja is a wireless communications expert; Ali's special insight lies in optimization.

Advisory Board

Joseph Tuber	Vice President Logistics Operations, Palm. Director of Delivery Operations for NavMan. Transportation and logistics consultant for Busways and Delphi.
John Roen	CEO Freightways, West
Abe Noble	COO Toyota Research Labs
Sanford Stein	VP Logistics and Operations, NavMan, Skye.com, Busways, Philips, MIT
Walter Bond	Partner, Merchant Travellers International. Former president, Roadway.

Personnel Resources

PATH plans to staff the following positions to round out our development and management team. Hiring will be at market rates, and we don't anticipate any shortage of marketable candidates in the region.

Position	**Quarter of Hire**	**Person/Source**
CEO	filled	Philip Moon
VP Client Services	filled	Daniel O'Day
Controller	1	tbd/Pennsylvania
CTO	1	tbd/Pennsylvania
Office Administrator	1	tbd/Pennsylvania
VP Sales	1	tbd/Pennsylvania
Product Manager	1	tbd/Pennsylvania
Sales Engineers	2	tbd/Pennsylvania
Database Engineers	2	tbd/Pennsylvania
Director, Corp. Development	2	tbd/Pennsylvania
Programmer	2	tbd/Pennsylvania
VP Engineering	2	tbd/Pennsylvania
Consultants	2	tbd/Pennsylvania
Director, Training	4	tbd/Pennsylvania
Salespeople	4	tbd/Pennsylvania
Dir. Marketing	7	tbd/Pennsylvania
Other Staff (finance, etc.)	8	tbd/Pennsylvania
CFO	8	tbd/Pennsylvania
Architect	3	tbd/California
Network Administrator	3	tbd/California
Designer	5	tbd/California

Project Management

The most important component of a successful engagement is a clearly defined plan. A good plan that is achievable and understood by individual participants can serve as the "roadmap" to enhance communication and gain consensus in defining how the group anticipates achieving its goals. In addition, it can facilitate improved understanding of coordination of roles, interdependency of responsibilities, and the importance of completion dates.

PATH will work with our alliance members in developing the detailed development plan for the initial phases of the engagement and measuring progress against the plan. The plan will outline the engagement activities and tasks, responsibilities, start date, end date, and deliverables. PATH will also lead the alliance team in developing a summary-level work plan for the rollout phases of the project.

PATH will direct the alliance team in producing the following:

- Confirmation of Project Scope (i.e., features to be developed, interfaces required, phases, etc.)
- Detailed Engagement Plan for the initial project development and testing phases
- Summary-Level Project Plan for remainder of the engagement rollout
- Status Reports (produced bi-weekly, outlining progress against the Engagement Plan, issues, etc.)

PATH Systems will act as the project lead for all phases. Specifically, Daniel O'Day will perform as Project Director, directing project management, identifying and resolving issues, maintaining project work plans, conducting management and status meetings, and reviewing all important work product.

SALES STRATEGY & MARKETING PLAN

PATH Systems provides two products: 1) an Accident Avoider product which generates routes optimized to avoid accident times/areas (versus shortest-path routes), and 2) a Routing Calibration product that allows existing users of routing software to easily tune their operations to significantly higher levels of efficiency.

We intend to commercialize our Accident Avoider technology by forming an industry alliance of top transportation companies who will split the development costs during a field test period. We will then use those companies as reference accounts as we introduce the proven product though insurance companies and logistics providers.

To date, PATH has developed the Accident Avoider product using computer simulation models. At Harvard's EE/Computer Science department we invented the EP algorithm which uniquely optimizes routes to be the safest possible using past accident times/locations as predictors of future trouble areas. We have filed three patents on various aspects of this technology and have submitted our academic paper describing the EP algorithm to IEEE/ITS (Institute of Electrical and Electronics Engineers; the division we're working with is the Intelligent Transportation Systems group) and have been invited to publish it and present it at their worldwide conference in Hong Kong in the fall of 2005. This provides strong validation.

In order to prove on the road what we've proven in the lab, we are joining leading transportation, logistics, and insurance companies into an industry alliance to test the product. As part of the PSAASA (PATH System Accident Avoider Safety Alliance), the member companies will pool their safety and speed data to create routes to guide the member trucking companies away from known trouble times/locations. Together we will measure the rate of accidents during the trial period compared to 1) previous years and 2) where the vehicles would have gone without our routes. The alliance members will subsidize PATH's costs during the trial period. In exchange the trucking companies will get the product at cost for a 3-5 year period of time after the field trials, and insurance/logistics companies will receive a 3-year exclusive on marketing the product in conjunction with a reduced insurance rate. Following the exclusivity period, we continue to license the product to aggressive resellers and will consider expanding our own sales force as well.

We have identified several target industries that can immediately benefit from our products:

Target Market	Industry Revenue	PATH Product
Commercial Transportation	$600 Bn	Routing Calibration, Accident Avoider
Commercial Vehicle Insurance	$100 Bn	Accident Avoider
Routing Software Vendors	$2 Bn	Routing Calibration

We have approached over 20 companies regarding partnership opportunities to develop, road test, and introduce these products:

- *Routing Software*—We have strong interest from Trailways, Telecommute, GLOBAL, and the Travellers regarding the Routing Calibration product.
- *Insurance*—We have strong interest from Mutual of Omaha and Progressive Insurance for the Accident Avoider product.
- *Transportation*—Collier's National (one of the largest trucking companies in the U.S.) has agreed to become our first charter member in the alliance. We have strong interest from Freightways Custom Critical in the Accident Avoider product.
- *Tracking Companies*—We have strong interest from Magellan, Altec, and TravelWell about co-marketing PATH's extensions to their platforms.

We are scheduling meetings to follow up with this broad set of leads and others over the next few months. This is a great deal for them, as they get a compelling money saver/earner for some fraction of the development costs, while PATH avoids the need to raise large amounts of capital.

Beyond the industry categories above, we also are targeting the following:

- Leverage our database product with established Third Party Logistics (3PL) providers who already have established relationships with medium and large trucking companies. Companies such as Smithson Systems Group, Penske Logistics, and Ryder logistics already have large customer bases. Here, PATH is another value-added product to sell to these customers to further improve their operations. Further, those logistics companies typically have the large staffs required to effect a complicated installation.

- Form technology partnerships with the smartest people in the transportation business. PATH's EP algorithm is a true scientific breakthrough in network management. Transportation companies with large fleets such as UPS and Federal Express will disproportionately benefit from employing it. We are in discussions with these companies about structuring a technology enhancement project that will build out the capabilities of EP.

The PATH marketing plan will focus on trade advertising, industry conferences, and public relations activities. These tactics have the greatest impact in generating sales leads and pre-qualifying the early adopters in the commercial market.

BUSINESS/PRICING MODEL

PATH's core product is the database that allows users to a) predict a series of trip durations under a variety of conditions and b) identify and document operational inefficiencies. Depending on the type of client and their particular needs, the information database can be packaged in a number of ways:

PATH Product Type	Product Services Description	Typical Client
Routing Calibration	We track client vehicles traversing their routes; at the end of the day, we compare actual routes taken to planned routes, giving an objective measure of calibration. We then perform diagnostics, assigning reason for variation so planners can tune their systems for optimal performance.	Transportation companies already using routing software Routing software companies as resellers Tracking software companies as resellers
Routing Services	PATH automatically gathers road condition data using GPS sensors and effortlessly enters that into a database. Re-routing can happen annually, quarterly, even weekly.	Delivery companies and private fleets that run regular routes
Dynamic Route Navigation	PATH automatically gathers road speed information from GPS-based tracking systems. We then model future road speeds and integrate this with next-generation routing software.	Transportation companies already using routing software Routing software companies as resellers
Accident Avoider	PATH's system provides routes optimized for accident avoidance (vs. shortest path) based on historical accident records.	Fleets with annual road-miles over 100 million where losses are evident Self-insured transportation companies Thought-leader insurance companies

All of the above will be priced based on a monthly revenue per rig model. In addition, PATH charges fees for installation, consulting, and engineering customization at an hourly rate.

INVESTMENT & FINANCING STRATEGY

PATH Systems has achieved its current position with internal financing from Philip Moon and sweat equity from the employees and option holders who have contributed services at rates well below their value. We are seeking wherever possible to minimize dilution by leveraging government funding. We are in the process of closing a $250,000 loan from the city of Pittsburgh and have applied to several state programs.

There is a need and an appetite for equity financing in the near term to supplement the other sources while we drive the company toward cash flow break-even. Those funds—ranging from $250,000-$750,000—will be used to finish prototypes and fund sales call activities with customers. Since we feel our early customers will get us to cash flow break-even and we don't intend to grow any faster than we can internally finance, this may be the last time we seek financing. There is a possibility, however, that following a successful trial and the expiration of the exclusivity of our charter partners that we may return for financing in the $5 million range to build a sales force and sell our proven products into the industry. This is only one of several options we will consider and isn't expected to occur until 2008 when we will likely have a significant valuation to support such an offering with minimal dilution.

This investment shares many of the qualities of a venture capital investment:

- We can enjoy high growth potential in a large overlooked market
- We are introducing new proprietary technology with significant value add
- As an enterprise software provider, we expect to enjoy high levels of profit

We also have two areas where we differ from traditional venture investments:

- We are not designed for a quick liquidity event (or a "flip"). We are slavishly devoted to creating the best value for our customers. We will not roll out a product until our beta customers tell us it's ready for the market.
- We do not have voracious cash needs. Unlike many venture-funded companies that require $15-$25 million or more to break even, we expect to do so with $1 million.

As such we are seeking an investor who is knowledgeable about transportation, technology, and logistics who can comfortably invest $100,000-$250,000. This investor will consider a $25 million company with 80 percent gross margins a success. Regarding liquidity, we may choose to pursue some traditional methods such as an Initial Public Offering or a sale to a number of large strategic partners, but we also intend to keep dividend payments as an option as well. In any event, the earliest an investor should expect a return is following the field trials (in Q4 2005).

Exit Strategy

We expect to offer investors a liquidity event through a sale of the company, probably to one of the key partners with whom we will build the business. It also is possible the IPO market will recover in a reasonable time frame, providing an alternative liquidity vehicle.

FINANCIAL PLAN

PATH Systems was developed with a sound business model and efficient capital use in mind. The primary goal of the business is to make money. Each PATH product and service line is designed and priced to generate profits for the business. The PATH Financial Plan includes detailed financial projections for the first two years and summary information/assumptions for years three through five.

Key Financial Characteristics

- Recurring Revenues
- Attractive and Sustainable Gross Profit Margins

- Scalable Sales and Distribution Plan
- Low labor and capital requirements

Assets Required

The majority of our assets are technology-based, such as database servers and communications equipment. Where it makes sense for control and security purposes, we will purchase and host the necessary equipment which is easily sourced. For database and web server facilities, PATH plans to lease equipment and hosting services from reputable providers.

Accounts Receivables

Our budget calculates accounts receivables being paid within 45 days.

Management Compensation

Per the Headcount spreadsheet in the financial statement section below, PATH will gradually ramp up management salaries, from 50 percent in year one to 100 percent by the end of year two.

Cash Strategy

To cover any short-term cash shortfalls, PATH will look to personal funds from the owner and/or refinancing of any current debt agreements.

Financial Statements

- Model Drivers, Assumptions
- Income Statement
- Balance Sheet
- Cash Flow
- Breakeven Analysis

This page left intentionally blank to accommodate tabular matter following.

Model Drivers, Assumptions

Model Drivers

Revenue Related	**2003**	**2004**	**2005**	**2006**	**2007**
Returned Units per month	0%	0%	0%	0%	0%
% of Customers Needing Sales Engineer	50%	40%	33%	33%	25%
Tune-up Fees—4 times per year	$10,000	$10,000	$10,000	$10,000	$10,000
Professional Fee per partner per month	$15,000	$15,000	$10,000	$10,000	$10,000
Average Referral Size (in units)	250	500	750	1,000	1,250
Cost Related					
Finder's Fee Costs—commissions	10%	0%	10%	10%	10%
Servers/Website Hosting/month	$2	$10	$30	$90	$180
Data Management Costs—% of Database Service Revenues	15%	15%	15%	15%	15%
Partner—Database Services Costs					
Non-Recurring Engineer Costs per new partner ($000's)	$25				
Sales Engineers per partner	1.0				
Engineers per partner	1.0				
Research & Development/Product Development Schedule					
Database Development	$15	$60	$500	$3,500	$7,500
Projects—Customer Related Work	$15	$60	$500	$3,500	$7,500
New Product Ideas/Innovation	$0	$0	$250	$500	$2,000
Total R&D (excluding Salaries)	**$30**	**$120**	**$1,250**	**$7,500**	**$17,000**
R&D as % of Revenue	7%	3%	7%	14%	15%
Sales & Marketing Budget (excluding Salaries)					
Trade Show	$2	$20	$200	$1,000	$2,000
Public Relations	$1	$20	$200	$1,500	$3,000
Trade ads	$1	$20	$200	$1,000	$3,000
Promotion	$1	$10	$100	$200	$1,500
Research	$1	$10	$50	$100	$500
Total Sales & Marketing	**$6**	**$80**	**$750**	**$3,800**	**$10,000**
Sales & Marketing as % of Revenues	1%	2%	4%	7%	9%
General Expenses					
Salaries					
Rent per month ($000's)	$1	$2	$4	$6	$8
Benefits (% of total salary expense)	5%	15%	25%	30%	30%
Bad Debts Expense (% of Revenue)	1.00%	1.00%	1.00%	1.00%	1.00%
IT—Servers, computers, etc. (per person)	$1,000	$1,000	$2,000	$2,500	$3,000
Travel Expenses (per salesperson per month)	$3,000	$3,000	$4,000	$4,000	$4,000
Miscellaneous—Office Expenses (per month)	$1,000	$1,500	$3,000	$5,000	$6,000
Professional Fees/Expenses (per year)	$25,000	$40,000	$75,000	$100,000	$200,000
Telecom Expenses (per salesperson & executive)/month	$150				
Telecom Expenses (per engineer, etc.)/month	$40				
Tax Rate	40%				

Cash Related		
Inventory—months of volume	1	months
A/P on Hardware Units	0	days
A/P on general items (AT&T, etc.)	35	days
A/R	45	days
Bank Revolver	5%	interest rate
A/R Financing—Factored Receivables	0%	
Inventory Financing—% of Inventory Financed	50%	

	2003	**2004**	**2005**	**2006**	**2007**
Investment in Fixed Assets	$20	$40	$200	$500	$1,000
Average Life	5				
Depreciation Schedule per month	$0.30	$0.30	$0.30	$0.30	$0.30
		$0.70	$0.70	$0.70	$0.70
			$3.30	$3.30	$3.30
				$8.30	$8.30
					$16.70
	$0.30	$1.00	$4.30	$12.70	$29.30

Income Statement 2003

Detailed Income Statement	**Jan**	**Feb**	**Mar**	**1Q**	**Apr**	**May**	**Jun**
(Dollars in thousands)							
Revenue							
Finder's Fee—Referrals	0.00	0.00	0.00	0.00	0.00	0.00	0.00
Software License & Maintenance	0.00	0.00	0.00	0.00	0.00	2.50	2.50
Training/Implementation	0.00	0.00	0.00	0.00	0.00	0.00	10.00
Professional Services	0.00	0.00	0.00	0.00	0.00	15.00	15.00
Software Maintenance Fees	0.00	0.00	0.00	0.00	0.00	0.00	0.00
Installation Fees	0.00	0.00	0.00	0.00	0.00	0.00	0.00
Additional Network Usage Fees	0.00	0.00	0.00	0.00	0.00	0.00	0.00
Total Revenue	**0.00**	**0.00**	**0.00**	**0.00**	**0.00**	**17.50**	**27.50**
Cost of Goods Sold							
Finder's Fee Costs	0.00	0.00	0.00	0.00	0.00	0.00	0.00
Packaging	0.00	0.00	0.00	0.00	0.00	0.00	0.00
Customer Support	0.00	0.00	0.00	0.00	0.00	0.00	7.90
Servers & Hosting	0.00	0.00	0.00	0.00	0.00	2.00	2.00
Sales Engineering	0.00	0.00	0.00	0.00	0.00	0.00	0.00
Consultant Salaries	0.00	0.00	0.00	0.00	0.00	0.00	5.20
Data Storage & Management	0.00	0.00	0.00	0.00	0.00	0.40	0.40
Partner Startup Costs	0.00	0.00	0.00	0.00	0.00	0.00	0.00
Network Charges	0.00	0.00	0.00	0.00	0.00	0.00	0.00
Initiation Charges	0.00	0.00	0.00	0.00	0.00	0.00	0.00
Subtotal	**0.00**	**0.00**	**0.00**	**0.00**	**0.00**	**2.40**	**15.50**
Gross Profit	**0.00**	**0.00**	**0.00**	**0.00**	**0.00**	**15.10**	**12.00**
	N/A	N/A	N/A	N/A	N/A	86%	44%
Operating Expenses							
Engineering Salaries	1.60	1.60	1.60	4.70	1.60	1.60	11.90
Product Development	0.00	0.00	0.00	0.00	0.00	0.00	2.00
Sales & Marketing	0.00	0.00	0.00	0.00	0.00	0.00	0.00
General & Administration							
Rent	0.00	0.00	0.00	0.00	0.00	1.00	1.00
Salaries	0.00	0.00	0.00	0.00	0.00	0.00	20.20
Benefits, Insurance, etc.	0.00	0.00	0.00	0.00	0.00	0.10	2.30
Bad Debts Expense	0.00	0.00	0.00	0.00	0.00	0.20	0.30
Depreciation	0.30	0.30	0.30	1.00	0.30	0.30	0.30
IT Equipment—Staff & Headquarters	0.00	0.00	0.00	0.00	0.00	2.00	2.00
Travel Expenses	0.00	0.00	0.00	0.00	0.00	0.00	2.00
Telecom	0.00	0.00	0.00	0.00	0.00	0.00	0.30
Professional Fees	0.00	0.00	0.00	0.00	0.00	5.00	0.00
Miscellaneous	1.00	1.00	1.00	3.00	1.00	1.00	1.00
Total General & Administration	**1.30**	**1.30**	**1.30**	**4.00**	**1.30**	**9.60**	**29.40**
Total Operating Expenses	**2.90**	**2.90**	**2.90**	**8.70**	**2.90**	**11.10**	**43.30**
Operating Income	**-2.90**	**-2.90**	**-2.90**	**-8.70**	**-2.90**	**4.00**	**-31.30**
Operating Margin	N/A	N/A	N/A	N/A	N/A	23%	-114%
Interest Income	0.00	0.00	0.00	0.10	0.00	0.00	0.00
Interest Expense	0.00	0.00	0.00	0.00	0.00	0.00	0.00
Pretax Income	-2.90	-2.90	-2.90	-8.60	-2.90	4.00	-31.30
Income Taxes	0.00	0.00	0.00	0.00	0.00	1.60	0.00
Net Income	**-2.90**	**-2.90**	**-2.90**	**-8.60**	**-2.90**	**2.40**	**-31.30**

2Q	Jul	Aug	Sep	3Q	Oct	Nov	Dec	4Q	Fiscal 2003
0.00	3.70	3.90	4.10	11.70	8.00	8.40	8.80	25.20	36.90
5.00	9.00	9.00	9.00	27.00	15.00	15.00	15.00	45.00	77.00
10.00	10.00	10.00	10.00	30.00	10.00	20.00	20.00	50.00	90.00
30.00	30.00	30.00	30.00	90.00	45.00	45.00	45.00	135.00	255.00
0.00	0.00	0.00	0.00	0.00	0.00	0.00	0.00	0.00	0.00
0.00	0.00	0.00	0.00	0.00	0.00	0.00	0.00	0.00	0.00
0.00	0.00	0.00	0.00	0.00	0.00	0.00	0.00	0.00	0.00
45.00	**52.70**	**52.90**	**53.10**	**158.70**	**78.00**	**88.40**	**88.80**	**255.20**	**458.90**
0.00	0.40	0.40	0.40	1.20	0.80	0.80	0.90	2.50	3.70
0.00	0.00	0.00	0.00	0.00	0.00	0.00	0.00	0.00	0.00
7.90	7.90	7.90	7.90	23.80	7.90	7.90	7.90	23.80	55.40
4.00	2.00	2.00	2.00	6.00	2.00	2.00	2.00	6.00	16.00
0.00	1.90	1.90	1.90	5.60	3.00	3.00	3.00	9.00	14.60
5.20	5.20	5.20	5.20	15.60	5.20	5.20	5.20	15.60	36.50
0.80	1.40	1.40	1.40	4.10	2.30	2.30	2.30	6.80	11.60
0.00	4.20	4.20	4.20	12.50	6.30	6.30	6.30	18.80	31.30
0.00	0.00	0.00	0.00	0.00	0.00	0.00	0.00	0.00	0.00
0.00	0.00	0.00	0.00	0.00	0.00	0.00	0.00	0.00	0.00
17.90	**22.90**	**22.90**	**22.90**	**68.70**	**27.40**	**27.50**	**27.50**	**82.40**	**169.00**
27.10	**29.80**	**30.00**	**30.20**	**90.00**	**50.60**	**60.90**	**61.30**	**172.80**	**289.90**
60%	57%	57%	57%	57%	65%	69%	69%	68%	63%
15.00	18.10	18.10	18.10	54.40	29.90	29.90	29.90	89.70	163.80
2.00	4.00	4.00	5.00	13.00	5.00	5.00	5.00	15.00	30.00
0.00	1.00	1.00	1.00	3.00	1.00	1.00	1.00	3.00	6.00
2.00	1.00	1.00	1.00	3.00	1.00	1.00	1.00	3.00	8.00
20.20	24.40	24.40	24.40	73.10	27.50	27.50	27.50	82.50	175.80
2.30	2.90	2.90	2.90	8.60	3.70	3.70	3.70	11.00	22.00
0.50	0.50	0.50	0.50	1.60	0.80	0.90	0.90	2.60	4.60
1.00	0.30	0.30	0.30	1.00	0.30	0.30	0.30	1.00	4.00
4.00	2.00	2.00	2.00	6.00	2.00	2.00	2.00	6.00	16.00
2.00	2.00	2.00	2.00	6.00	2.00	2.00	2.00	6.00	14.00
0.30	0.30	0.30	0.30	0.90	0.30	0.30	0.30	0.90	2.10
5.00	0.00	5.00	0.00	5.00	10.00	0.00	0.00	10.00	20.00
3.00	1.00	1.00	1.00	3.00	1.00	1.00	1.00	3.00	12.00
40.30	**34.40**	**39.40**	**34.40**	**108.20**	**48.60**	**38.70**	**38.70**	**126.00**	**278.50**
57.30	**57.50**	**62.50**	**58.50**	**178.60**	**84.50**	**74.60**	**74.60**	**233.70**	**478.30**
-30.20	**-27.70**	**-32.50**	**-28.40**	**-88.60**	**-33.90**	**-13.70**	**-13.30**	**-60.90**	**-188.40**
-67%	-53%	-62%	-53%	-56%	-43%	-15%	-15%	-24%	-41%
0.00	0.00	0.00	0.00	0.00	0.00	0.00	0.00	0.00	0.10
0.00	0.00	0.00	0.00	0.00	0.00	0.00	0.00	0.00	0.00
-30.10	-27.70	-32.50	-28.40	-88.60	-33.90	-13.70	-13.30	-60.90	-188.20
1.60	0.00	0.00	0.00	0.00	0.00	0.00	0.00	0.00	1.60
-31.70	**-27.70**	**-32.50**	**-28.40**	**-88.60**	**-33.90**	**-13.70**	**-13.30**	**-60.90**	**-189.80**

Income Statement 2004

Detailed Income Statement	**Jan**	**Feb**	**Mar**	**1Q**	**Apr**	**May**	**Jun**	**2Q**	**Jul**
(Dollars in thousands)									
Revenue									
Finder's Fee—Referrals	15.30	16.30	17.30	48.90	31.80	33.80	35.80	101.40	46.00
Software License & Maintenance	41.30	41.30	41.30	123.80	86.30	86.30	86.30	258.80	153.80
Training/Implementation	20.00	20.00	20.00	60.00	20.00	20.00	20.00	60.00	20.00
Professional Services	60.00	60.00	60.00	180.00	75.00	75.00	75.00	225.00	105.00
Software Maintenance Fees	0.00	0.00	0.00	0.00	0.00	0.00	0.00	0.00	0.00
Installation Fees	0.00	0.00	0.00	0.00	0.00	0.00	0.00	0.00	0.00
Additional Network Usage Fees	0.00	0.00	0.00	0.00	0.00	0.00	0.00	0.00	0.00
Total Revenue	**136.60**	**137.60**	**138.60**	**412.70**	**213.10**	**215.10**	**217.10**	**645.20**	**324.80**
Cost of Goods Sold									
Finder's Fee Costs	1.50	1.60	1.70	4.90	3.20	3.40	3.60	10.10	4.60
Packaging	0.00	0.00	0.00	0.00	0.00	0.00	0.00	0.00	0.00
Customer Support	17.90	17.90	17.90	53.80	22.70	22.70	22.70	68.00	27.50
Servers & Hosting	10.00	10.00	10.00	30.00	10.00	10.00	10.00	30.00	10.00
Sales Engineering	3.80	3.80	3.80	11.30	7.50	7.50	7.50	22.50	15.00
Consultant Salaries	7.80	7.80	7.80	23.40	10.40	10.40	10.40	31.30	20.80
Data Storage & Management	6.20	6.20	6.20	18.60	12.90	12.90	12.90	38.80	23.10
Partner Startup Costs	8.30	8.30	8.30	25.00	10.40	8.30	8.30	27.10	10.40
Network Charges	0.00	0.00	0.00	0.00	0.00	0.00	0.00	0.00	0.00
Initiation Charges	0.00	0.00	0.00	0.00	0.00	0.00	0.00	0.00	0.00
Subtotal	**55.50**	**55.60**	**55.70**	**166.90**	**77.10**	**75.20**	**75.40**	**227.80**	**111.40**
Gross Profit	**81.00**	**81.90**	**82.80**	**245.80**	**135.90**	**139.80**	**141.60**	**417.40**	**213.30**
	59%	60%	60%	60%	64%	65%	65%	65%	66%
Operating Expenses									
Engineering Salaries	36.70	36.70	38.30	111.80	51.00	51.00	53.50	155.60	62.30
Product Development	10.00	10.00	10.00	30.00	10.00	10.00	10.00	30.00	10.00
Sales & Marketing	12.90	12.90	12.90	38.80	16.70	16.70	16.70	50.00	22.90
General & Administration									
Rent	2.00	2.00	2.00	6.00	2.00	2.00	2.00	6.00	2.00
Salaries	33.30	33.30	33.30	100.00	44.60	44.60	44.60	133.80	49.60
Benefits, Insurance, etc.	15.90	15.90	16.10	47.80	21.90	21.90	22.30	66.20	28.70
Bad Debts Expense	1.40	1.40	1.40	4.10	2.10	2.20	2.20	6.50	3.20
Depreciation	1.00	1.00	1.00	3.00	1.00	1.00	1.00	3.00	1.00
IT Equipment—Staff & HQ	4.00	0.00	1.00	5.00	4.00	0.00	1.00	5.00	7.00
Travel Expenses	3.00	3.00	3.00	9.00	4.50	4.50	4.50	13.50	7.50
Telecom	0.80	0.80	0.90	2.60	1.20	1.20	1.20	3.50	1.60
Professional Fees	3.30	3.30	3.30	10.00	3.30	3.30	3.30	10.00	3.30
Miscellaneous	1.50	1.50	1.50	4.50	1.50	1.50	1.50	4.50	1.50
Total General & Administration	**66.20**	**62.20**	**63.50**	**192.00**	**86.10**	**82.20**	**83.60**	**251.90**	**105.50**
Total Operating Expenses	**125.90**	**121.90**	**124.70**	**372.50**	**163.80**	**159.90**	**163.80**	**487.50**	**200.70**
Operating Income	**-44.90**	**-40.00**	**-41.90**	**-126.80**	**-27.90**	**-20.10**	**-22.20**	**-70.20**	**12.70**
Operating Margin	-33%	-29%	-30%	-31%	-13%	-9%	-10%	-11%	4%
Interest Income	0.00	0.00	0.00	0.00	0.00	0.00	0.00	0.00	0.00
Interest Expense	0.00	0.00	0.00	0.00	0.00	0.00	0.00	0.00	0.00
Pretax Income	-44.90	-40.00	-41.90	-126.80	-27.90	-20.10	-22.20	-70.20	12.70
Income Taxes	0.00	0.00	0.00	0.00	0.00	0.00	0.00	1.60	5.10
Net Income	**-44.90**	**-40.00**	**-41.90**	**-126.80**	**-27.90**	**-20.10**	**-22.20**	**-70.20**	**7.60**

Aug	Sep	3Q	Oct	Nov	Dec	4Q	Fiscal 2004	Fiscal 2005	Fiscal 2006	Fiscal 2007
49.20	52.40	147.60	64.40	68.40	72.40	205.20	801.00	2,333.40	4,307.40	7,566.00
153.80	153.80	461.30	243.80	243.80	243.80	731.30	2,418.80	11,565.00	44,220.00	101,820.00
20.00	20.00	60.00	30.00	30.00	30.00	90.00	450.00	920.00	1,400.00	1,800.00
105.00	105.00	315.00	135.00	135.00	135.00	405.00	1,845.00	2,040.00	3,240.00	4,440.00
0.00	0.00	0.00	0.00	0.00	0.00	0.00	0.00	0.00	0.00	0.00
0.00	0.00	0.00	0.00	0.00	0.00	0.00	0.00	0.00	0.00	0.00
0.00	0.00	0.00	0.00	0.00	0.00	0.00	0.00	0.00	0.00	0.00
328.00	**331.20**	**983.90**	**473.20**	**477.20**	**481.20**	**1,431.50**	**5,514.80**	**16,858.40**	**53,167.40**	**115,626.00**
4.90	5.20	14.80	6.40	6.80	7.20	20.50	50.30	233.30	430.70	756.60
0.00	0.00	0.00	0.00	0.00	0.00	0.00	0.00	0.00	0.00	0.00
27.50	27.50	82.50	30.80	30.80	30.80	92.50	296.80	850.00	1,250.00	1,650.00
10.00	10.00	30.00	10.00	10.00	10.00	30.00	120.00	360.00	1,080.00	2,160.00
15.00	15.00	45.00	15.00	15.00	15.00	45.00	123.80	450.00	900.00	1,350.00
20.80	20.80	62.50	31.30	31.30	31.30	93.80	210.90	1,125.00	1,750.00	2,375.00
23.10	23.10	69.20	36.60	36.60	36.60	109.70	236.30	1,734.80	6,633.00	15,273.00
10.40	10.40	31.30	12.50	12.50	12.50	37.50	120.80	200.00	250.00	250.00
0.00	0.00	0.00	0.00	0.00	0.00	0.00	0.00	0.00	0.00	0.00
0.00	0.00	0.00	0.00	0.00	0.00	0.00	0.00	0.00	0.00	0.00
111.70	**112.10**	**335.20**	**142.60**	**143.00**	**143.40**	**429.00**	**1,158.80**	**4,953.10**	**12,293.70**	**23,814.60**
216.20	**219.10**	**648.70**	**330.60**	**334.20**	**337.80**	**1,002.50**	**2,314.30**	**11,905.30**	**40,873.70**	**91,811.40**
66%	66%	66%	70%	70%	70%	70%	42%	71%	77%	79%
62.30	62.30	186.90	71.00	71.00	71.00	213.10	667.40	1,250.00	2,210.00	3,020.00
10.00	10.00	30.00	10.00	10.00	10.00	30.00	120.00	1,250.00	7,500.00	17,000.00
22.90	22.90	68.80	22.90	22.90	22.90	68.80	226.30	1,155.00	4,280.00	10,555.00
2.00	2.00	6.00	2.00	2.00	2.00	6.00	24.00	48.00	72.00	96.00
49.60	49.60	148.80	49.60	49.60	49.60	148.80	531.30	865.00	1,115.00	1,355.00
28.70	28.70	86.20	32.10	32.10	32.10	96.30	296.40	1,236.30	2,311.50	3,091.50
3.30	3.30	9.80	4.70	4.80	4.80	14.30	34.70	168.60	531.70	1,156.30
1.00	1.00	3.00	1.00	1.00	1.00	3.00	12.00	52.00	152.00	352.00
0.00	0.00	7.00	3.00	0.00	0.00	3.00	20.00	32.00	38.00	36.00
7.50	7.50	22.50	7.50	7.50	7.50	22.50	67.50	192.00	240.00	288.00
1.60	1.60	4.80	1.70	1.70	1.70	5.10	16.00	40.50	60.10	78.70
3.30	3.30	10.00	3.30	3.30	3.30	10.00	40.00	75.00	100.00	200.00
1.50	1.50	4.50	1.50	1.50	1.50	4.50	18.00	36.00	60.00	72.00
98.50	**98.50**	**302.50**	**106.50**	**103.50**	**103.50**	**313.50**	**1,059.90**	**2,745.30**	**4,680.20**	**6,725.40**
193.70	**193.70**	**588.10**	**210.40**	**207.50**	**207.50**	**625.40**	**2,073.50**	**6,400.30**	**18,670.20**	**37,300.40**
22.50	**25.40**	**60.50**	**120.20**	**126.70**	**130.30**	**377.10**	**240.70**	**5,505.00**	**22,203.40**	**54,511.00**
7%	8%	6%	25%	27%	27%	26%	4%	33%	42%	47%
0.00	0.00	0.00	0.00	0.00	0.00	0.00	0.00	0.00	42.30	245.20
0.00	0.00	0.00	0.00	0.00	0.00	0.00	0.00	0.00	0.00	0.00
22.50	25.40	60.50	120.20	126.70	130.30	377.10	240.70	5,505.00	22,245.80	54,756.20
9.00	10.10	24.20	48.10	50.70	52.10	150.90	175.10	2,202.00	8,898.30	21,902.50
13.50	**15.20**	**36.30**	**72.10**	**76.00**	**78.20**	**226.30**	**65.70**	**3,303.00**	**13,347.50**	**32,853.70**

Balance Sheet

Balance Sheet

(Dollars in thousands)

	1Q 2003	2Q 2003	3Q 2003	4Q 2003	Fiscal 2003	1Q 2004
Cash	12.40	-41.60	-120.20	-186.80	-186.80	-311.90
Accounts Receivable	0.00	36.30	79.60	133.00	133.00	207.30
Inventory	0.00	0.00	0.00	0.00	0.00	0.00
Other Current Assets	0.00	0.00	0.00	0.00	0.00	0.00
Total Current Assets	**12.40**	**-5.30**	**-40.70**	**-53.80**	**-53.80**	**-104.60**
P, P & E	2.40	5.30	13.80	22.40	22.40	32.40
Less: Accumulated Depreciation	2.20	3.20	4.20	5.20	5.20	8.20
Net P, P & E	0.20	2.10	9.60	17.20	17.20	24.20
Other Assets				0.00		
Total Assets	**12.60**	**-3.30**	**-31.00**	**-36.60**	**-36.60**	**-80.40**
Accounts Payable	0.00	15.90	26.70	32.10	32.10	65.00
Accrued Liabilities	0.00	0.00	0.00	0.00	0.00	0.00
Other Current Liabilities	0.00	0.00	0.00	0.00	0.00	0.00
Total Current Liabilities	**0.00**	**15.90**	**26.70**	**32.10**	**32.10**	**65.00**
Bank Revolver	0.00	0.00	0.00	0.00	0.00	0.00
Long-term Debt (Loans)	0.00	0.00	50.00	100.20	100.20	150.50
Note Payable	470.00	470.00	470.00	470.00	470.00	470.00
Total Debt	**470.00**	**470.00**	**520.00**	**570.20**	**570.20**	**620.50**
Other Liabilities				0.00		
Total Liabilities	**470.00**	**485.90**	**546.80**	**602.30**	**602.30**	**685.50**
Convertible Preferred Stock	0.00	0.00	0.00	0.00	0.00	0.00
Common Stock & APIC	4.50	4.50	4.50	4.50	4.50	4.50
Retained Earnings	-461.90	-493.60	-582.30	-643.40	-643.40	-770.40
Total Equity	**-457.40**	**-489.10**	**-577.80**	**-638.90**	**-638.90**	**-765.90**
Total Liabilities & Equity	**12.60**	**-3.30**	**-31.00**	**-36.60**	**-36.60**	**-80.40**
Balance Check	0.00	0.00	0.00	0.00	0.00	0.00
Balance Sheet Ratios						
Accounts Receivable Turnover	N/A	9.10	8.00	8.00	8.00	8.00
Accounts Payable Turnover	N/A	11.70	10.30	10.30	10.30	10.30

2Q 2004	**3Q 2004**	**4Q 2004**	**Fiscal 2004**	**Fiscal 2005**	**Fiscal 2006**	**Fiscal 2007**
-433.40	-481.90	-450.70	-450.70	2,117.20	12,258.80	39,538.50
324.60	495.10	719.70	719.70	1,621.00	5,112.30	11,117.90
0.00	0.00	0.00	0.00	0.00	0.00	0.00
0.00	0.00	0.00	0.00	0.00	0.00	0.00
-108.80	**13.20**	**269.10**	**269.10**	**3,738.20**	**17,371.00**	**50,656.40**
42.40	52.40	62.40	62.40	262.40	762.40	1,762.40
11.20	14.20	17.20	17.20	69.20	221.20	573.20
31.20	38.20	45.20	45.20	193.20	541.20	1,189.20
				0.00	0.00	
-77.60	**51.40**	**314.30**	**314.30**	**3,931.40**	**17,912.20**	**51,845.60**
88.00	130.70	167.20	167.20	481.40	1,194.70	2,314.40
0.00	0.00	0.00	0.00	0.00	0.00	0.00
0.00	0.00	0.00	0.00	0.00	0.00	0.00
88.00	**130.70**	**167.20**	**167.20**	**481.40**	**1,194.70**	**2,314.40**
0.00	0.00	0.00	0.00	0.00	0.00	0.00
200.90	251.50	252.10	252.10	254.60	177.20	138.90
470.00	470.00	470.00	470.00	470.00	470.00	470.00
670.90	**721.50**	**722.10**	**722.10**	**724.60**	**647.20**	**608.90**
			0.00	0.00	0.00	0.00
758.90	**852.10**	**889.30**	**889.30**	**1,206.00**	**1,841.90**	**2,923.30**
0.00	0.00	0.00	0.00	0.00	0.00	0.00
4.50	4.50	4.50	4.50	4.50	4.50	4.50
-841.00	-805.20	-579.60	-579.60	2,720.90	16,065.80	48,917.70
-836.50	**-800.70**	**-575.10**	**-575.10**	**2,725.40**	**16,070.30**	**48,922.20**
-77.60	**51.40**	**314.30**	**314.30**	**3,931.40**	**17,912.20**	**51,845.60**
0.00	0.00	0.00	0.00	0.00	0.00	0.00
8.00	8.00	8.00	8.00	10.40	10.40	10.40
10.30	10.30	10.30	10.30	10.30	10.30	10.30

Cash Flow Statement 2003

Cash Flow Statement *(Dollars in thousands)*	**Jan**	**Feb**	**Mar**	**Apr**	**May**	**Jun**
Cash Flow from Operating Activities						
Net Income	-2.90	-2.90	-2.90	-2.90	2.40	-31.30
Depreciation	0.30	0.30	0.30	0.30	0.30	0.30
Amortization	0.00	0.00	0.00	0.00	0.00	0.00
(Increase) Decrease in Accounts Receivable	0.00	0.00	0.00	0.00	-17.50	-18.80
(Increase) Decrease in Inventory	0.00	0.00	0.00	0.00	0.00	0.00
(Increase) Decrease in Other Current Assets	0.00	0.00	0.00	0.00	0.00	0.00
(Increase) Decrease in Other Assets	0.00	0.00	0.00	0.00	0.00	0.00
(Increase) Decrease in Accounts Payable	0.00	0.00	0.00	0.00	2.40	13.50
(Increase) Decrease in Accrued Liabilities	0.00	0.00	0.00	0.00	0.00	0.00
(Increase) Decrease in Other Current Liabilities	0.00	0.00	0.00	0.00	0.00	0.00
(Increase) Decrease in Other Liabilities	0.00	0.00	0.00	0.00	0.00	0.00
Cash Provided (Used) in Operations Activities	**-2.50**	**-2.50**	**-2.50**	**-2.50**	**-12.40**	**-36.10**
Capital Expenditures	0.00	0.00	0.00	0.00	0.00	-2.90
Cash Provided (Used) in Investing Activities	**0.00**	**0.00**	**0.00**	**0.00**	**0.00**	**-2.90**
Net Proceeds (Payments) of Revolver	0.00	0.00	0.00	0.00	0.00	0.00
Net Proceeds (Payments) of Loans	0.00	0.00	0.00	0.00	0.00	0.00
Net Proceeds (Payments) of Equity Issuance	0.00	0.00	0.00	0.00	0.00	0.00
Net Proceeds (Payments) of Note Payable	10.00	0.00	0.00	0.00	0.00	0.00
Cash Provided (Used) in Financing Activities	10.00	0.00	0.00	0.00	0.00	0.00
Net Increase (Decrease) in Cash	**7.50**	**-2.50**	**-2.50**	**-2.50**	**-12.40**	**-39.00**
Cash at Beginning of Period	**10.00**	**17.50**	**14.90**	**12.40**	**9.80**	**-2.60**
Cash at End of Period	**17.50**	**14.90**	**12.40**	**9.80**	**-2.60**	**-41.60**
Cash Burn—Operations & Investments (pre-finance)	-2.50	-2.50	-2.50	-2.50	-12.40	-39.00
Cumulative Cash Burn	-2.50	-5.10	-7.60	-10.20	-22.60	-61.60
Cash Burn—Including Revolver	-2.50	-2.50	-2.50	-2.50	-12.40	-39.00
Cumulative Cash Burn—Including Revolver	-2.50	-5.10	-7.60	-10.20	-22.60	-61.60
Loan from City of Cleveland						
Beginning Balance				0.00	0.00	0.00
Capital Call				0.00	0.00	0.00
Accrued Interest				0.00	0.00	0.00
Principal Payment				0.00	0.00	0.00
Principal Forgiven under terms				0.00	0.00	0.00
Ending Balance			0.00	0.00	0.00	0.00

Jul	Aug	Sep	Oct	Nov	Dec	Fiscal 2003
-27.70	-32.50	-28.40	-33.90	-13.70	-13.30	-189.80
0.30	0.30	0.30	0.30	0.30	0.30	4.00
0.00	0.00	0.00	0.00	0.00	0.00	0.00
-30.20	-12.80	-0.30	-25.00	-22.90	-5.60	-133.00
0.00	0.00	0.00	0.00	0.00	0.00	0.00
0.00	0.00	0.00	0.00	0.00	0.00	0.00
0.00	0.00	0.00	0.00	0.00	0.00	0.00
9.60	1.30	0.00	4.50	0.80	0.00	32.10
0.00	0.00	0.00	0.00	0.00	0.00	0.00
0.00	0.00	0.00	0.00	0.00	0.00	0.00
0.00	0.00	0.00	0.00	0.00	0.00	0.00
-48.00	**-43.80**	**-28.30**	**-54.10**	**-35.40**	**-18.50**	**-286.80**
-2.90	-2.90	-2.90	-2.90	-2.90	-2.90	-20.00
-2.90	**-2.90**	**-2.90**	**-2.90**	**-2.90**	**-2.90**	**-20.00**
0.00	0.00	0.00	0.00	0.00	0.00	0.00
0.00	50.00	0.00	0.00	50.00	0.00	100.00
0.00	0.00	0.00	0.00	0.00	0.00	0.00
0.00	0.00	0.00	0.00	0.00	0.00	10.00
0.00	50.00	0.00	0.00	50.00	0.00	110.00
-50.90	**3.40**	**-31.20**	**-56.90**	**11.80**	**-21.40**	**-196.80**
-41.60	**-92.40**	**-89.00**	**-120.20**	**-177.10**	**-165.40**	**10.00**
-92.40	**-89.00**	**-120.20**	**-177.10**	**-165.40**	**-186.80**	**-186.80**
-50.90	-46.60	-31.20	-56.90	-38.20	-21.40	-306.80
-112.40	-159.00	-190.20	-247.10	-285.40	-306.80	-306.80
-50.90	-46.60	-31.20	-56.90	-38.20	-21.40	-306.80
-112.40	-159.00	-190.20	-247.10	-285.40	-306.80	-306.80
0.00	0.00	50.00	50.04	50.08	100.13	0.00
0.00	50.00	0.00	0.00	50.00	0.00	100.00
0.00	0.00	0.04	0.04	0.04	0.08	0.21
0.00	0.00	0.00	0.00	0.00	0.00	0.00
0.00	0.00	0.00	0.00	0.00	0.00	0.00
0.00	50.00	50.04	50.08	100.13	100.21	100.21

Cash Flow Statement 2004

Cash Flow Statement *(Dollars in thousands)*	**Jan**	**Feb**	**Mar**	**Apr**	**May**	**Jun**
Cash Flow from Operating Activities						
Net Income	-44.90	-40.00	-41.90	-27.90	-20.10	-22.20
Depreciation	1.00	1.00	1.00	1.00	1.00	1.00
Amortization	0.00	0.00	0.00	0.00	0.00	0.00
(Increase) Decrease in Accounts Receivable	-48.00	-24.90	-1.50	-75.00	-39.30	-3.00
(Increase) Decrease in Inventory	0.00	0.00	0.00	0.00	0.00	0.00
(Increase) Decrease in Other Current Assets	0.00	0.00	0.00	0.00	0.00	0.00
(Increase) Decrease in Other Assets	0.00	0.00	0.00	0.00	0.00	0.00
(Increase) Decrease in Accounts Payable	28.00	4.80	0.10	21.40	1.70	-0.10
(Increase) Decrease in Accrued Liabilities	0.00	0.00	0.00	0.00	0.00	0.00
(Increase) Decrease in Other Current Liabilities	0.00	0.00	0.00	0.00	0.00	0.00
(Increase) Decrease in Other Liabilities	0.00	0.00	0.00	0.00	0.00	0.00
Cash Provided (Used) in Operations Activities	**-63.80**	**-59.10**	**-42.30**	**-80.50**	**-56.60**	**-24.30**
Capital Expenditures	-3.30	-3.30	-3.30	-3.30	-3.30	-3.30
Cash Provided (Used) in Investing Activities	**-3.30**	**-3.30**	**-3.30**	**-3.30**	**-3.30**	**-3.30**
Net Proceeds (Payments) of Revolver	0.00	0.00	0.00	0.00	0.00	0.00
Net Proceeds (Payments) of Loans	0.00	50.00	0.00	0.00	50.00	0.00
Net Proceeds (Payments) of Equity Issuance	0.00	0.00	0.00	0.00	0.00	0.00
Net Proceeds (Payments) of Note Payable	0.00	0.00	0.00	0.00	0.00	0.00
Cash Provided (Used) in Financing Activities	**0.00**	**50.00**	**0.00**	**0.00**	**50.00**	**0.00**
Net Increase (Decrease) in Cash	**-67.10**	**-12.40**	**-45.60**	**-83.80**	**-10.00**	**-27.60**
Cash at Beginning of Period	**-186.80**	**-253.90**	**-266.30**	**-311.90**	**-395.80**	**-405.70**
Cash at End of Period	**-253.90**	**-266.30**	**-311.90**	**-395.80**	**-405.70**	**-433.40**
Cash Burn—Operations & Investments (pre-finance)	-67.10	-62.40	-45.60	-83.80	-60.00	-27.60
Cumulative Cash Burn	-373.90	-436.30	-481.90	-565.80	-625.70	-653.40
Cash Burn—Including Revolver	-67.10	-62.40	-45.60	-83.80	-60.00	-27.60
Cumulative Cash Burn—Including Revolver	-373.90	-436.30	-481.90	-565.80	-625.70	-653.40
Loan from City of Cleveland						
Beginning Balance	100.21	100.29	150.38	150.50	150.63	200.75
Capital Call	0.00	50.00	0.00	0.00	50.00	0.00
Accrued Interest	0.08	0.08	0.13	0.13	0.13	0.17
Principal Payment	0.00	0.00	0.00	0.00	0.00	0.00
Principal Forgiven under terms	0.00	0.00	0.00	0.00	0.00	0.00
Ending Balance	100.29	150.38	150.50	150.63	200.75	200.92

Jul	Aug	Sep	Oct	Nov	Dec	Fiscal 2004	Fiscal 2005	Fiscal 2006	Fiscal 2007
7.60	13.50	15.20	72.10	76.00	78.20	65.70	3,303.00	13,347.50	32,853.70
1.00	1.00	1.00	1.00	1.00	1.00	12.00	52.00	152.00	352.00
0.00	0.00	0.00	0.00	0.00	0.00	0.00	0.00	0.00	0.00
-108.70	-57.10	-4.80	-143.60	-75.00	-6.00	-586.70	-901.30	-3,491.30	-6,005.60
0.00	0.00	0.00	0.00	0.00	0.00	0.00	0.00	0.00	0.00
0.00	0.00	0.00	0.00	0.00	0.00	0.00	0.00	0.00	0.00
0.00	0.00	0.00	0.00	0.00	0.00	0.00	0.00	0.00	0.00
36.00	6.30	0.40	30.60	5.50	0.50	135.10	314.10	713.40	1,119.60
0.00	0.00	0.00	0.00	0.00	0.00	0.00	0.00	0.00	0.00
0.00	0.00	0.00	0.00	0.00	0.00	0.00	0.00	0.00	0.00
0.00	0.00	0.00	0.00	0.00	0.00	0.00	0.00	0.00	0.00
-64.10	**-36.20**	**11.80**	**-39.90**	**7.50**	**73.60**	**-373.90**	**2,767.90**	**10,721.60**	**28,319.70**
-3.30	-3.30	-3.30	-3.30	-3.30	-3.30	-40.00	-200.00	-500.00	-1,000.00
-3.30	**-3.30**	**-3.30**	**-3.30**	**-3.30**	**-3.30**	**-40.00**	**-200.00**	**-500.00**	**-1,000.00**
0.00	0.00	0.00	0.00	0.00	0.00	0.00	0.00	0.00	0.00
0.00	50.00	0.00	0.00	0.00	0.00	150.00	0.00	-80.00	-40.00
0.00	0.00	0.00	0.00	0.00	0.00	0.00	0.00	0.00	0.00
0.00	0.00	0.00	0.00	0.00	0.00	10.00	0.00	0.00	0.00
0.00	**50.00**	**0.00**	**0.00**	**0.00**	**0.00**	**150.00**	**0.00**	**-80.00**	**-40.00**
-67.40	**10.40**	**8.50**	**-43.30**	**4.20**	**70.30**	**-263.90**	**2,567.90**	**10,141.60**	**27,279.70**
-433.40	**-500.80**	**-490.40**	**-481.90**	**-525.20**	**-521.00**	**-186.80**	**-450.70**	**2,117.20**	**12,258.80**
-500.80	**-490.40**	**-481.90**	**-525.20**	**-521.00**	**-450.70**	**-450.70**	**2,117.20**	**12,258.80**	**39,538.50**
-67.40	-39.60	8.50	-43.30	4.20	70.30	-413.90	2,567.90	10,221.60	27,319.70
-720.80	-760.40	-751.90	-795.20	-791.00	-720.70	-720.70	1,847.20	12,068.80	39,388.50
-67.40	-39.60	8.50	-43.30	4.20	70.30	-413.90	2,567.90	10,221.60	27,319.70
-720.80	-760.40	-751.90	-795.20	-791.00	-720.70	-720.70	1,847.20	12,068.80	39,388.50
200.92	201.09	251.25	251.46	251.67	251.88	100.21	252.09	254.61	177.16
0.00	50.00	0.00	0.00	0.00	0.00	150.00	0.00	0.00	0.00
0.17	0.17	0.21	0.21	0.21	0.21	1.88	2.52	2.55	1.77
0.00	0.00	0.00	0.00	0.00	0.00	0.00	0.00	-30.00	-40.00
0.00	0.00	0.00	0.00	0.00	0.00	0.00	0.00	-50.00	0.00
201.09	251.25	251.46	251.67	251.88	252.09	252.09	254.61	177.16	138.93

Breakeven Analysis

	4Q 2003	1Q 2004	2Q 2004	3Q 2004	4Q 2004	1Q 2005	2Q 2005	3Q 2005
Fixed Costs	300.00	372.50	487.50	588.10	625.40	1,600.10	1,600.10	1,600.10
Average Fixed Costs	3,808.50	3,808.50	3,808.50	3,808.50	3,808.50	3,808.50	3,808.50	3,808.50
Variable Costs	82.40	166.90	227.80	335.20	429.00	1,238.30	1,238.30	1,238.30
Variable and Average Fixed	3,890.90	3,975.40	4,036.30	4,143.70	4,237.50	5,046.80	5,046.80	5,046.80
Revenues	255.20	412.70	645.20	983.90	1,431.50	4,214.60	4,214.60	4,214.60
Breakeven Revenues	**345.10**	**625.50**	**753.60**	**892.10**	**892.90**	**2,265.80**	**2,265.80**	**2,265.80**

4Q 2005	1Q 2006	2Q 2006	3Q 2006	4Q 2006	1Q 2007	2Q 2007	3Q 2007	4Q 2007	Average
1,600.10	4,667.60	4,667.60	4,667.60	4,667.60	9,325.10	9,325.10	9,325.10	9,325.10	3,808.50
3,808.50	3,808.50	3,808.50	3,808.50	3,808.50	3,808.50	3,808.50	3,808.50	3,808.50	
1,238.30	3,073.40	3,073.40	3,073.40	3,073.40	5,953.70	5,953.70	5,953.70	5,953.70	
5,046.80	6,881.90	6,881.90	6,881.90	6,881.90	9,762.20	9,762.20	9,762.20	9,762.20	
4,214.60	13,291.90	13,291.90	13,291.90	13,291.90	28,906.50	28,906.50	28,906.50	28,906.50	
2,265.80	**6,071.40**	**6,071.40**	**6,071.40**	**6,071.40**	**11,743.90**	**11,743.90**	**11,743.90**	**11,743.90**	**4,931.40**

APPENDIX

Systems Overview

This section provides an overview of the PATH Systems processes. First is the construction of the predictive database which is built and characterized by gathering empirical observations in a quasi-batch mode as those events occur. At the other end of the process, end users request routes through the website or other means. Such requests are handled on a very fast, real-time basis.

a) **GPS**—U.S. Department of Defense network of 28 Global Positioning Satellites in geosynchronous orbit 11,000 miles above the earth. Global Positioning Satellites shower the earth with precise time stamps. When three or more are within range, those signals can be triangulated to calculate precise speed, location, heading, and altitude observations. The satellites were launched for military purposes by the U.S. government, but they've become available for reliable civilian use in May 2000 when SA (Selective Availability) scrambling was stopped. These signals are free and one-way; it isn't possible to transmit to a GPS satellite.

b) **Hardware Tracking/Communication Unit**—There are a variety of tracking devices employed, many requiring no driver interaction, featuring a GPS receiver, wireless transponder, memory cache, and RAM processor attached to the vehicle's 12-volt power supply. PATH can harvest data from a wide variety of tracking vendors. Popular tracking systems are offered by Magellan, StreetWise, Garmin, TravelWell, and Altec. We also anticipate many more sources of data coming online very soon, e.g., every cell phone will soon be a location-aware, data-gathering device to be captured.

c) **Wireless, Communication Methods**—A key component to making the database accumulation process feasible is effortlessly communicating large sets of data back to our Operations Centers. PATH is wireless-agnostic, meaning we utilize whatever the best wireless solution is at the time. We have practical experience with LMPD (our current platform) and Microblast (from NetComm). We are exploring GPRS, satellite (as needed) and other flavors of the WiFi.

d) **External, 3rd Party Data**—Historical accident data, current construction data, and current/predicted weather data can be obtained from DOT, FARS, MCMAS, individual States' speed, accident, and construction data, and National weather data.

e) **PATH's Driver-base**—However acquired, the raw observation data is then stored in PATH's large database dubbed the Driver-base. The raw observations including latitude/longitude, vehicle identity, speed, heading, altitude, and timestamp are recorded. We will never discard a valid observation from this database.

f) **Translation to Road Segments**—On some regular schedule, the raw latitude/longitude data will be translated to road segment data for the purposes of updating the stochastic model. Map vendors describe the roads using defined "road segments" or "links." The two broad classes of links are intersections and road segments between intersections. North America has about 30 million links. Links are pieced together to form a path in the algorithm/routing process.

g) **Stochastic Modeling**—The stochastic model considers the history of road conditions to generate predictions of what speeds and other cost elements are expected to be under the conditions projected for the roads in the planning period.

h) **Creation of the NOW-base**—The real-time demands of a responsive routing system require a highly available simplified database describing the conditions of each road segment under the possible conditions expected to be encountered during the planning process. Although smaller than the Driver-base, the NOW-base is still scoped to be approximately 4 terabytes in size. Availability is maintained by segmenting it into logical geographic modules.

i) **Post-FIFO, Time Expanded Algorithm**—PATH has developed the next-generation optimization algorithm.

j) **GIS**—There are numerous Geographical Information System software vendors that provide visual maps for use in navigation, including GDT, iiMap, Navtech, Telcontar, and Tele Atlas. PATH's technology can interface with any of them, and we are in discussions with several of the vendors.

k) **Input/Output Methods**—Finally, we have a variety of ways to deliver the route information to the end user. Our initial implementation is web-based using PCs. In addition to web delivery, PATH anticipates several delivery modules when they're commercially available including in-vehicle displays, in-vehicle voice commands, and server-resident application to name just three. It is not our intent to create the means for delivering these platforms, but rather to use them as they emerge.

Structural Genomics Software Provider

BUSINESS PLAN

PHARMATECH GENOMICS

14001 South Lincoln Boulevard
San Diego, California 92101

Pharmatech Genomics is a license provider and application service provider (ASP) of structural genomics software. Structural genomics software helps scientists turn data from the Human Genome Project into drugs and cures for disease. Specifically, our technology enables the biotechnology industry to rapidly discover patentable lead compounds from unclassified gene sequences. We intend to capture a dominant market share by supplying an economical, yet powerful, analysis platform.

STRUCTURAL GENOMICS SOFTWARE PROVIDER BUSINESS PLAN

MISSION

Pharmatech Genomics is a license provider and application service provider (ASP) of structural genomics software. Structural genomics software helps scientists turn data from the Human Genome Project into drugs and cures for disease. Specifically, our technology enables the biotechnology industry to rapidly discover patentable lead compounds from unclassified gene sequences. The platform consists of an online computing environment designed specifically to address every step of the post-genomic drug development path, from data visualization to structural analysis and protein engineering. We intend to capture a dominant market share by supplying an economical, yet powerful, analysis platform.

BUSINESS MODEL

Pharmatech Genomics has a technology platform for structural genomics research that can be deployed within an enterprise network, over the Internet, or in a Virtual Private Network (VPN). Structural genomics is a field of research that is integral to the drug discovery and development process and promises to reduce the cost and time to market for drugs. However, the problem of maintaining and using the existing solutions is costly and time consuming. Pharmatech Genomics has a unique, cost-effective, integrative, and easy-to-use platform to address this problem. The platform consists of an "operating environment" and integrated software modules. Users can either license or subscribe to our technology and services in the following ways:

- The platform will be licensed as an integrative operating environment with software modules (primarily for enterprise networks or VPNs in biotech/pharmacuetical companies)
- The core operating environment can be licensed to customers wishing to integrate proprietary software (primarily for enterprise networks or VPNs in biotech/pharmaceutical companies with proprietary software)
- Users can subscribe to use the platform over the Internet (primarily small to mid-sized biotech/pharmaceutical companies desiring ASP service, i.e., lacking informatics infrastructure and personnel)
- Users can subscribe to use the core operating environment with integrated proprietary software over the Internet (primarily small to mid-sized biotech/pharmaceutical companies desiring ASP service with proprietary software)

Our structural genomics platform will attract customers for the following reasons:

- Integrative "operating environment" will allow interoperability between previously disparate software
- Easy-to-use interface will solve usability issues with software
- Internet-deployed platform will allow users to access previously platform-dependent software through any Internet browser, regardless of client platform
- Secure application and data hosting will free the customer from:
  - needing to build a costly informatics infrastructure and personnel
  - needing expensive servers and storage arrays to run software
  - maintenance of software, hardware, and upgrades
- Flexible and customizable subscription rates
- Competitive pricing

We will attract corporate partnerships for the following reasons:

- We make their software available to a wider market through low-cost pricing (small to mid-sized biotech companies with limited resources or informatics expertise)

- We will train novice users on our easy-to-use platform and retain them with powerful licensed software modules
- We host and integrate their proprietary software and data

Similar to how the now multi-billion-dollar, electronic CAD industry began, Pharmatech Genomics provides a way for cryptic, unfriendly, yet powerful software tools to reach a mass audience in the biotech industry. Many of these tools reside in university labs, where once developed, do not reach the biotech industry. Pharmatech Genomics provides interfaces to unfriendly structural analysis software and creates a channel of distribution for the software to reach a mass audience of users. We have first-to-market advantage in this area of biotechnology.

Revenue flows from direct subscription to online services including access to the technology platform and data hosting services. As an application service provider, Pharmatech Genomics prices services according to each user, enabling them to balance their financial and scientific needs. The base subscription includes use of the structural genomics platform, its core software modules, and basic data-hosting services. Upgrades are available for use of additional software modules and data-hosting. As integration experts, we work closely with customers should they prefer to use their own "in-house" software in an integrative platform. For a nominal integration and consulting fee, Pharmatech Genomics will integrate and host the customer's proprietary software within our "operating environment" for the sole use of the customer. Additional revenue streams include licensing fees for use of the platform in-house, custom consulting services, and Internet banner advertising. Pharmatech Genomics markets services through a direct sales force, focusing first on under-served sectors of the market. Long term, we have the domain expertise to develop proprietary software modules for use within the operating environment or for licensing outside. Through ongoing research, Pharmatech Genomics will remain at the forefront of structural genomics.

WHY STRUCTURAL GENOMICS IS IMPORTANT

The Human Genome Project is nearly complete. Scientists are "mining" vast amounts of genetic information to identify disease-related genes. Sequencing the data, however, is only a small part of the research process. Once a gene has been identified, researchers are faced with the task of determining the structure and function of the protein product(s) encoded by the gene. It is the behavior of these proteins within the body that ultimately affects a person's health, and understanding its 3-D structure and function is the key to structural genomics. This "post-mining" phase is, and will continue to be, the bottleneck of most drug development efforts. By 2002, this process will cost pharmaceutical companies $32 billion per year, a 25 percent increase in spending from 1998 (Burrill & Company annual report, 1999).

The field of structural genomics describes the relationship between genomic sequences and 3-D protein structure and function. Using structural genomics software will significantly reduce the time and costs of development of new therapeutics by drug companies. Pharmatech Genomics' goal is to provide a computing environment that gives scientists the tools to efficiently and seamlessly go from sequence to lead compound.

Services Description

- Custom Integration and Consulting Services
- Secure Application Service, Data Storage, and Archiving
- Online Training Environment and Technical Support

The Pharmatech Genomics' platform offers researchers a very high degree of flexibility in analysis tools and service. This flexibility enables customers to balance their scientific and financial needs. We will work with customers to integrate their proprietary software into our operating environment, thus allowing interoperability among proprietary and available software modules. The proprietary platform can be installed and maintained on an enterprise network or a virtual private network (VPN). Custom consulting services are available to organizations that request specific changes to the standard platform to meet internal infrastructure needs.

Pharmatech Genomics' customers have the option to securely perform analyses and then store the data on our systems. We have partnered with a software company whose unique approach to the ASP market space offers ASPs a privately-branded, turnkey solution that enables them to deliver applications over the Internet through any web browser. The company's proprietary, state-of-the-art technologies provide the ASP infrastructure and application service capabilities required for creating and launching application-service businesses in weeks. As an ASP hosting service, New Moon provides us with the following abilities:

- Network directory servers
- Load-balancing servers
- Powerful ASP management tools
- Secure network services

These services remove the burden of having to maintain an in-house database, eases the flow of data from one site to another, and allows the users to access their data from any geographic location.

Through our online training environment, a technical support staff will be available to answer user questions at any time. Technical support and consultants will be available to customers using our platform or operating environment offline.

Technology Description

Our company's technology platform consists of a computing environment designed specifically to address every step of this post-genomic drug development path. The environment will perform the following tasks through integrated software modules.

- Data Visualization (sequence, structure, and pathway information)
- Discovering Similarities to Known Sequences (homology modeling and multiple alignment)
- Developing a 3-dimensional Model (threading, secondary, and tertiary prediction)
- Pathway (Functional) Analysis
- Structural Analysis
- Discovering Lead Compounds (searching of virtual drug libraries, de novo drug design)
- Protein Engineering

A key feature is an integrated visualization interface to our operating environment deployable through a web browser. This interface allows the user to view multiple data types, provides necessary instruction and assistance, seamlessly connects the currently disjointed aspects of structural genomics analysis, and provides computer platform independence for the user. Further, our system allows the user to define the work environment according to their level of expertise by offering a variety of individual programs and interfaces. If the user is a neophyte to structural genomics analysis, the system will "walk" them through all the steps, setting defaults for noncritical variables and coaching them on how to set the critical variables in their analyses. If a user is an experienced structural genomicist, the system will provide them all the comfort of being able to manipulate every variable in the environment to their content.

The interface will also be highly customizable to meet the personalized demands of individual users. For example, an X-ray crystallographer might be interested in predicting potential lead compounds from a solved structure. For example, they may not need tools for building multiple alignments, so these tools, while available, would not maintain a high profile in their personal interface.

We are building an Internet-deployable operating environment that facilitates communication between independent software applications, the interface, and the user. The user is seamlessly provided with the tools needed to perform structural genomics research and will be free from the burdens of software, hardware, and database management. Building the packages into modules obviates the need to move between different file formats, interfaces, and platforms—increasing the overall efficiency of the drug development timeline and eliminating the need to build and maintain a large in-house bioinformatics infrastructure.

Not until recently did technology exist that enabled researchers to perform each of these individual steps. Currently, each step is independent and tenuously linked, using disparate interfaces and data output. Visualization of the module output is a key component of the user interface. The interface will be tailored for all ability levels from the novice to the expert.

Pharmatech Genomics' user interface will communicate with independent software modules developed by and licensed from various industrial and academic institutions. Tools will translate each module's data requirements into a common language and present them to the user through a single interface. With tools that translate the software's proprietary interface into a common language, the modules will be harnessed together to perform powerful structural genomic analysis. For example, starting from a DNA sequence, the interface will find related sequences from genomic data, model the structure of the resulting protein, and predict lead drug compounds using the modeled structure. Pharmatech Genomics' environment will have all the modules necessary for performing the tasks outlined in the previous section.

The environment has the following key features:

- Users enter any data format (sequence, multiple alignment, structure, etc.) into the system
- The technology offers a platform independent of visualization and analysis tools
- The tool set covers every step in the drug development pathway
- Users enter and exit at any stage of the pathway, leaving with a data format supported by the entire biotechnology industry

INTELLECTUAL PROPERTY

Our intellectual property revolves around the ability to seamlessly integrate the independent programs into a single package, as well as build a common language that allows module technologies to communicate with each other. While the environment is built around the idea of developing a sequence of unknown function into a profitable drug or something else of patentable value, the user can enter the analysis pathway at any point in the process with the guarantee that their needs will be met with our environment.

LICENSING & CORPORATE PARTNERSHIP

During discussions with the Office of Technology Management (OTM) at UCSD, Pharmatech Genomics has established favorable, but informal, licensing terms for our "core" software modules. Once a formal agreement is reached, Pharmatech Genomics expects to deploy the platform on the Internet in six to eight months. The licensing of these "core" modules from UCSD is necessary for a timely launch. Additionally, we will actively pursue strategic partnerships with commercial software vendors to obtain mutually agreeable licensing terms for their software modules.

MARKET

We estimate the total number of people employed in biological research to be 1 million worldwide, with an active user base of 200,000. Research and Development personnel constitute roughly 40 percent of the total employees. Of all employees in R&D, about 50 percent will use structural genomics software. These users include protein engineers, computational biologists and chemists, structural biologists, chemists, organic chemists, geneticists, biophysicists, and bioinformaticists. These figures were obtained from the California Healthcare Institute's 1999 Report on Biotechnology and by directly polling the bioinformatics directors at several large pharmaceutical and biotech companies.

The revenue potential from this user base is $1.2 to $1.8 billion. This figure is derived by multiplying the cost of current applications (approximately $6,000/user/year; cost of a comparable software/service package) by the total estimated potential user base. Another measure of the market size was determined by evaluating the total amount spent on bioinformatics technologies by large pharmaceutical companies. In 1998, these large organizations spent $1.8 billion on enabling technologies (1998 Burrill & Company Biotechnology Report).

Market Segmentation

Our target market consists of biotechnology, pharmaceutical, and university organizations actively engaged in developing patentable drug-like compounds from unclassified gene sequences. The market can be divided into three sectors based on the number of employees per organization (these values are averages from five different biotech industry reports). Stratification according to the number of employees allows us to value the market and project our growth values according to the growth of the estimated user base. The figure below illustrates the current potential user base.

1) Large pharmaceutical and biotechnology companies (> 2,000 employees): These companies are often publicly traded and have large ($30-40 billion) R&D budgets—significant fractions of which are spent on enabling technologies. Percentage of R&D spending on outsourced technologies is steadily increasing ($15 billion in 1998). These companies demand cutting-edge and efficient applications. While the financial resources are usually not a constraining factor, location, number of concurrent users, security, maintenance, and upgrading are critical issues. The user base in this sector is projected to grow at a rate of 20 percent annually.

2) Small to medium-sized companies (< 2,000 employees): This market segment is currently underserved and is one of our primary target segments. Approximately 90 percent of all U.S. biotechnology companies (1,500 companies in 1999) lie in this sector. Seventy-five percent of all U.S. companies are private and have less than 50 employees. They represent a sizable potential market because of the increasing use of genetic data to find promising drug targets. While implementation issues do not necessarily constrain these users, the need for consistent access to economical yet functional analytical tools is important to these companies. Due to the increased need for visualization and analysis software in this segment, as well as the increase in the number of employees trained in structural genomics, it is expected that this sector will grow at 35 percent annually until 2005.

3) Educational Institutions: The educational sector is a key to Pharmatech Genomics' success. Universities train and influence a large number of potential researchers but lack the unlimited funding of pharmaceutical companies. This situation demands that we meet their special needs for education and low-cost solutions. This sector will greatly benefit from a service that provides flexibility in the choice of analytical tools and pricing structures. The increased dependence and emphasis on structural genomics in both research and education will cause this sector to grow at a rapid rate (40% annually) until 2005.

Market Trends

The growing need for structural genomics applications is driven by several factors:

- The Genome project will provide companies with many putative drug targets. However, the rapid growth of potential targets causes a bottleneck in the development pipeline. Downstream processes have not been optimized to fully handle the deluge of information. Structural genomics will play a crucial role in optimizing downstream development processes, and increasing the flow of products through the drug development pipeline.

- Structural genomics is becoming part of every biologist's training, routinely used to analyze a protein at the structure and function level. They will expect that the analytical tools they use are customizable, easily deployable, and intuitive. By 2020, structural genomics analysis and molecular visualization is expected to be a routine aspect of research (from Base4 Informatics, Inc.). Structural genomics will become emphasized in the training of future generations of biologists. Structure—function analyses of genes, proteins, and pathways—will become part of the core skill sets in biologists.

- Genetic sequencing of infectious diseases is, and will continue to be, a focal point for drug development research. Structural genomics research is an essential aspect of developing drugs specific to certain infectious organisms.

We expect an overall growth of approximately 29 percent annually until 2005; this was estimated based on the United States Labor and Statistics Department and the California Healthcare Institute's growth projections for employment in the biotechnology and pharmaceutical sectors until 2004. In that year our total potential user base will be 720,000 users with a projected value of $4.4 billion.

Marketing Strategy

- Our first goal is to rapidly secure a significant market share of the under-served segments. We will focus our efforts on emphasizing the value our platform can add to the R&D pipeline relative to their costs.
- We will effectively compete in the larger market segment composed of large organizations.
- Through focused advertising in scientific journals, conferences, research institutions, and industry specific websites, we will target the structural genomics community.
- Direct sales staff will contact, recruit, and convert researchers to the Pharmatech Genomics' platform.
- Online training will ensure the Pharmatech Genomics' platform is easy-to-use and retained among future generations of researchers—meeting a serious need for bioinformatics education.

Distribution

Pharmatech Genomics will deploy over the Internet with universal browser compatibility. For in-house use of our platform or operating environment, software will be available via down-load or CD-ROM. Custom integration services will require on-site technical support and consulting. Our direct sales staff will contact interested researchers and negotiate the fee for services.

Competitive Analysis

The structural genomics applications industry is composed of several key corporations that provide competing software solutions. These providers sell their products to companies and university laboratories that can afford them or establish other types of cooperative agreements. More established solutions providers often partner, or are acquired by, pharmaceutical companies in order to obtain exclusive rights to critical software solutions, typified by Warner-

Lambert's recent agreement to use Evos' discovery platform, or by U.S. Pharmacopeia's acquisition of Scientific Simulations, Inc. There is a substantial range in how these products are priced, and how cooperative research agreements are structured. At the simplest level, a customer can license copies of the software for their own use. Conversely, a software provider can allow a pharmaceutical or biotechnology company to license their software solution in exchange for shared royalties or intellectual property rights on commercially viable products that are discovered through its use.

Our competitors can be classified as non-ASP or ASP companies. Non-ASP competitors consist of companies that have an enterprise around building and distributing visualization and analysis software using traditional (softcopy) methods. These companies have necessary domain expertise to compete with us, but lack of flexibility in their software platforms, the inability to offer users economical and effective tools, and infrastructures incapable of supporting universal platform compatibility. ASP competitors have the necessary infrastructure to provide solutions, but lack the domain expertise to rapidly develop, market, and deploy a structural genomics platform. The table below illustrates each competitor's available toolset.

Service/Toolset	Pharmatech Genomics	Evos	MSG	ABC	SSI	ST	Akmer	EGI
ASP = 0 Non-ASP=X	0	X	0	0	0	0	0	0
Offsite Data Hosting	0	X	0	0	0	0	0	0
Homology Building	0	X	X	X	0	X	X	0
3-D Visualization	0	0	X	X	X	X	X	X
Model Building	0	0	X	X	X	X	X	X
Compound Libraries	0	0	0	X	X	X	X	X
Lead Compound Refinement	0	0	0	0	X	X	X	X
Functional Analysis	0	0	0	0	X	X	X	X
Pathway Visualization	0	0	0	0	0	0	X	X
Protein Engineering	0	0	0	0	0	X	X	X
Custom Integration Services	0	X	0	0	0	X	X	X
Platform Independence	0	X	0	0	0	X	0	0
Low Cost	0	X	0	0	0	X	X	0

EGI = eGenomics, Inc.; SSI = Scientific Simulations, Inc.; MSG = Molecular Science Group; ST = SuperTech.com

Competitive Edge

- **Rapid Time to Market:** Because all the modules for the computational backbone are built, we can release our system in six to eight months after obtaining the appropriate licenses.
- **Unique Technology:** Pharmatech Genomics' toolset contains key analysis tools which cannot be found in any other application.
- **Universal Platform Compatibility:** Unlike currently available software solutions, Pharmatech Genomics' technology is designed to deploy on any platform. We achieve universal compatibility by delivering our solutions over the Internet. With either Netscape 4+ or Internet Explorer 5+ anyone can use the software as they research.
- **Flexible Pricing:** As an ASP, Pharmatech Genomics' prices services in unique ways based on the individual module structure. We meet the needs of budget conscious start-ups, large pharmaceutical companies, and every researcher in between.
- **Domain Expertise:** With expertise in structural biology, computer science, drug development, and artificial intelligence, our team has the scientific and technical background to develop a platform that meets the needs of scientists of all levels.

- **Flexibility and Scaleability of the ASP Model:** As an ASP, our platform supports a variety of future services including collaborative teleconferencing, banner advertisments, and online informatics training and educational services.

Barriers to Entry

There are two dominant threats to Pharmatech Genomics' business model:

Current companies (SSI, Evos, etc.) might develop Internet deployable versions of their existing platforms.

1. Pharmatech Genomics' built-in diversity of analytic tools gives users far more choices than any single competitor. As founding members of this project, we will develop many of these applications at the University of California, San Diego. As authors, we have first rights to license these applications for industry purposes. It is unlikely, therefore, that our competitors will be able to obtain these applications.
2. There is significant first-mover advantage in this market. Our competitive edge (above) establishes natural barriers to secondary entrant into the market. In particular, the scaleability of the technology, the uniqueness of Pharmatech Genomics' toolset, and the short development times give the ability to rapidly adapt to any potential competitors. By the time a competitor moves into the space, Pharmatech Genomics will have obtained a dominant market share, established service-quality branding, and will retain it by continuously providing customers with the highest degree of flexibility in their choice of analysis tools.
3. This is a scaleable business model in a number of ways. Pharmatech Genomics can rapidly increase its ability to serve larger numbers of users without incurring any redevelopment or infrastructure costs. We can also easily expand our service platform to include community-focused services (collaborative research portals, etc.) that would increase value to our users.
4. All of the current systems are OS specific and are dependent on local hardware resources. It would require a large investment of time and personnel to re-engineer these systems to be web deployable.
5. These competitors lack the infrastructure to develop themselves into an ASP. Current companies are built around systems that require local hardware support. Hence their sales, R&D, manufacturing, and support structures are built around distributing software in compact disc form, rather than deploying them over the Internet. We are not arguing that a shift from a traditional model to an ASP model is impossible, only that such a shift would require a significant restructuring and redevelopment time. Further, the company would have to split its resources into maintaining its legacy- based customer base and to attracting a new Internet user base.

New ASP competitors arise or current ASPs attempt to move into our space.

1. Some of the applications included in this platform have been in development for over 20 years, while others have taken less than 2 or 3 years to develop. Once deployed, it would take a new entrant a long time to develop similar or stronger applications. Pharmatech Genomics would be the dominant application provider.
2. We have an established domain expertise and the ability to rapidly update and develop user specific applications.

FINANCE

Pharmatech Genomics is seeking $5.1 million in first round funding. The majority of the funds would go toward developing proprietary technology, acquiring software licenses, and setting up infrastructure to deliver our services over the Internet. The following table details how the funds will be spent. Additional funding will be raised in the future.

Operating Expenses (in thousands)

Sales and Marketing	
Print	100.00
Public Relations	200.00
Banner Advertising	100.00
Strategic Advertising	300.00
Total	**$700.00**
Office	
Computers	100.00
Utilities	30.00
Furniture	40.00
Total	**170.00**
Personnel	
CEO	120.00
Controller	80.00
CTO	100.00
VP Sales and Marketing	100.00
Sales and Marketing 1	60.00
Sales and Marketing 2	60.00
VP Business Development	100.00
Business Development 1	60.00
Business Development 2	60.00
VP of Engineering	100.00
Software Engineer (4)	320.00
Senior Scientist	100.00
Scientific Programmer (5)	400.00
Webmaster	60.00
Web Programmer	50.00
Database Administrator	90.00
Database Programmer 1	80.00
Database Programmer 2	80.00
Database Programmer 3	80.00
Systems Administrator 1	80.00
Systems Administrator 2	80.00
Admin 1	40.00
Admin 2	40.00
Q.A. 1	45.00
Q.A. 2	45.00
Total	**$2,430.00**
Technology	
Storage Databases (ORCL)	400.00
Computation Servers (DEC)	400.00
Total Technology	**$800.00**
Licensing and Legal	$1,000.00
Total Capital	**$5,100.00**

General Financial Assumptions

Our assumptions are listed in the following table.

Revenue Buildup Assumption **assume software beta testing in 2000, year-to-date	**2000****	**2001**	**2002**	**2003**	**2004**
Sales and Marketing Team	2	5	10	15	20
Accounts per Manager					
Large Corp	1	3	4	5	5
Small to Mid	2	10	15	15	15
Academic	5	15	20	20	20
Users per Account					
Large Corp	10	20	25	28	30
Small to Mid	2	8	10	12	15
Academic	20	40	60	65	70
Corporate Users	28	700	2,500	4,800	7,500
Past Users		28	728	3,228	8,028
Total	**28**	**728**	**3,228**	**8,028**	**15,528**
Academic Users	200	3,000	12,000	19,500	28,000
Past Users		200	3,200	15,200	34,700
Total	**200**	**3,200**	**15,200**	**34,700**	**62,700**
Pricing (including ASP, Data Hosting and Consulting)					
Corporation	-	$2,000	$2,500	$3,000	$3,500
Academic	-	$200	$250	$300	$350
Revenue					
Corporation	-	$1,456,000	$8,070,000	$24,084,000	$54,348,000
Academic	-	$640,000	$3,800,000	$10,410,000	$21,945,000
Total	**-**	**$2,096,000**	**$11,870,000**	**$34,494,000**	**$76,293,000**

Key Assumptions

- Current market size is 200,000 users worldwide and will grow 29% annually through 2005
- Our market penetration will be 1% for year 1, 5% for year 2, 15% for year 3, 25% for year 4
- Our company will market aggressively in response to the demand growth
- Our income projections only reflect costs incurred from licensing academic software; we assume that we will establish strategic positioning with the corporate software developers

Financial Highlights

Based on the assumptions stated in the previous section, we note the following financial highlights. Please refer to the pro forma income statements, balance sheets, and cash flow statements for further detail.

- We expect to be RPI positive in 2003
- We expect to break even in 2005
- By Q4 2005, we expect to have earned $19.2 million

Pro Forma Balance Sheet

Asset	**2000**	**2001**	**2002**	**2003**	**2004**
Cash	$2,773,944	$10,384,852	$9,040,367	$13,680,908	$32,699,802
Total Short-term Assets	**$2,773,944**	**$10,384,852**	**$9,040,367**	**$13,680,908**	**$32,699,802**
Long-term Assets					
Capital Assets	$600,000	$1,200,000	$2,200,000	$3,200,000	$4,200,000
Accumulated Depreciation	($120,000)	($360,000)	($800,000)	($1,440,000)	($2,280,000)
Total Long-term Assets					
Total Assets	**$3,253,944**	**$11,224,852**	**$10,440,367**	**$15,440,908**	**$34,619,802**
Liabilities and Capital	-	-	-	-	-
Short-term Notes	-	-	-	-	-
Long-term Liabilities	-	-	-	-	-
Total Liabilities	**-**	**-**	**-**	**-**	**-**
Earnings	($1,746,056)	($3,775,148)	($4,559,633)	$440,908	$19,619,802
Shareholders' Equity	$5,000,000	$10,000,000	$10,000,000	$10,000,000	$10,000,000
Total Equity	**$3,253,944**	**$6,224,852**	**$5,440,367**	**$10,440,908**	**$29,619,802**
Total Liabilities and Equity	**$3,253,944**	**$6,224,852**	**$5,440,367**	**$10,440,908**	**$29,619,802**

Pro Forma Income Statement

	2000	**2001**	**2002**	**2003**	**2004**
Revenue	$0	$2,096,000	$11,870,000	$34,494,000	$76,293,000
Cost of Goods Sold	$0	$628,800	$3,561,000	$10,348,200	$22,887,900
Gross Profit	$0	$1,467,200	$8,309,000	$24,145,800	$53,405,100
Marketing and Sales Expenses	$350,000	$838,400	$1,424,400	$3,104,460	$5,340,510
% of Total Revenue	n/a	40%	12%	9%	7%
Marketing dollars spent per Business Development person	$175,000	$167,680	$142,440	$206,964	$267,026
Development and Technology Expenses	$900,000	$1,048,000	$4,154,500	$8,623,500	$11,443,950
% of Total Revenue	n/a	50%	35%	25%	15%
General and Administration					
Expenses (including salaries)	$1,300,000	$2,430,000	$2,750,000	$3,000,000	$3,300,000
% of Total Revenue	n/a	22%	10%	4%	4%
Other	$136,240	$272,480	$1,187,000	$1,724,700	$3,814,650
% of Total Revenue	n/a	13%	10%	5%	5%
Operating Profit	**($2,686,240)**	**($3,121,680)**	**($1,206,900)**	**$7,693,140**	**$29,505,990**
	n/a	-149%	-10%	22%	39%
Taxes (assume 35%)	$0	$0	$0	$2,692,599	$10,327,097
Net Income	**($2,686,240)**	**($3,121,680)**	**($1,206,900)**	**$5,000,541**	**$19,178,894**

	2000	2001	2002	2003	2004
Capital Expenditure	$600,000	$600,000	$1,000,000	$1,000,000	$1,000,000
Depreciation					
Year 1	$120,000	$120,000	$120,000	$120,000	$120,000
Year 2		$120,000	$120,000	$120,000	$120,000
Year 3			$200,000	$200,000	$200,000
Year 4				$200,000	$200,000
Year 5					$200,000
Total Depreciation	**$120,000**	**$240,000**	**$440,000**	**$640,000**	**$840,000**

Pro Forma Cash Flow Tables

Cash Flow from Operating Activities	2000	2001	2002	2003	2004
Net Income (loss)	($2,686,240)	($3,121,680)	($1,206,900)	$5,000,541	$19,178,894
Depreciation and Amoritization	($120,000)	($240,000)	($440,000)	($640,000)	($840,000)
Decrease (increase) in assets:					
Accounts receivable	$0	$0	$0	$0	$0
Prepaid Inventory	$0	$0	$0	$0	$0
Inventory	$0	$0	$0	$0	$0
Increase (decrease) in liabilities					
Accounts payable	$0	$0	$0	$0	$0
Net cash provided by (used in) operating activities	**($2,806,240)**	**($3,361,680)**	**($1,646,900)**	**$4,360,541**	**$18,338,894**
Cash Flow from Investing Activities					
Capital expenditures	($600,000)	($600,000)	($1,000,000)	($1,000,000)	($1,000,000)
Investments	$0	$0	$0	$0	$0
Net cash used in investing activities	**($600,000)**	**($600,000)**	**($1,000,000)**	**($1,000,000)**	**($1,000,000)**
Cash Flow from Investing Activities					
Borrow (repayments)	$0	$0	$0	$0	$0
Issuance of preferred stock	$5,000,000	$10,000,000	$0	$0	$0
Net cash (used in) provided by financing activities	**$5,000,000**	**$10,000,000**	**$0**	**$0**	**$0**
Increase (decrease) in cash	($3,406,240)	($3,961,680)	($2,646,900)	$3,360,541	$17,338,894
Cash beginning of period	$0	$1,593,760	$7,632,080	$4,985,180	$8,345,721
Cash end of period	$1,593,760	$7,632,080	$4,985,180	$8,345,721	$25,684,615

FOUNDER PROFILES

Eugene R. Mantella

Mr. Mantella is a doctoral candidate and member of the Laboratory for Molecular Studies at UCSD. He is one of the primary architects behind the GAECS algorithm, and has a significant amount of experience working in the pharmaceutical and bioinformatics industries. He is a co-founder of the non-profit organization "Entrepreneurs in Healthcare and Biotechnology" at UCSD, and regularly acts as a domain consultant to several leading life science investment firms in New York and the San Diego area.

F. Ray Smythe

F. Ray Smythe is a doctoral candidate in bioinformatics at UCSD. As a member of the BioT Group at Harvard University, Mr. Smythe develops novel algorithms and visualization tools for analysis of macromolecular structure and function. Mr. Smythe received a B.A. in Biochemistry and Molecular Cell Biology from U.C. Irvine. He has worked for large pharmaceutical companies, biotech start-ups, as well as a government-backed research effort focusing on the genetics of multiple sclerosis. He is a co-founder of the "Entrepreneurs in Healthcare and Biotechnology" at UCSD.

Beverly Johnson

Beverly Johnson is in the UCSD Graduate Group in Biophysics. She has a significant amount of experience in structural biology and enzymology. She has recently completed the X-ray crystallographic structure of granzyme B, a serine protease involved in T-cell immune response. She graduated with a degree in physics from the University of California at San Diego. Ms. Johnson is a founding member of the "Entrepreneurs" and has served as the student representative planning UCSD's newest course—From Idea to IPO...and Beyond. Her perspective regarding the needs of experimental research will be a driving force behind the implementation of our technology platform.

George Jamison

George Jamison is the 2002 American Cancer Society Joseph P. Henry Postdoctoral Fellow at Harvard University in the Departments of Medicine and Genetics. He holds a Ph.D. in Pharmaceutical Chemistry from the University of California, San Diego, and a B.S. with distinction from the University of Michigan. He is a member of the Phi Kappa Phi and Phi Beta Kappa national honor societies and has won several awards for his work, including the Jacob N. Napier award for research in physical chemistry and the ARCS award for student scientists. As a researcher, he has worked at the National NMR Center in Madison, Wisconsin, the Computer Graphics Laboratory (now the Resource for Biocomputing, Visualization, and Informatics) at UCSD, and the Section on Medical Informatics at Harvard University.

KEYS TO SUCCESS

- Establish strategic partnerships with key software firms, and license necessary technology from universities
- Develop and deploy software tools through the Internet in six to eight months after obtaining the software licenses
- Target small- to medium-sized biotechnology and pharmaceutical companies and universities to establish a dominant market share in currently under-served sectors
- Target the growing use of outsourcing in the biotechnology industry to meet the needs of companies of all sizes

Why We Will Succeed

Pharmatech Genomics has proven domain expertise in developing structural genomics software. Our team members have advanced backgrounds in computer science, structure-based drug design, and structural biology. Software tools in our technology suite were developed by several of our team members. We have the necessary relationships within the structural genomics community to identify and license or build relevant technologies.

Pharmatech Genomics' scientific advisors include faculty at the University of California Irvine, the University of California, San Diego, and Harvard University. Other advisors include prominent venture capitalists, a seasoned equity analyst with a leading investment bank, and the CEO and CFO of a mid-sized biotechnology company. These individuals will continue to guide the development of this company through all stages of its growth.

Appendix A - Business Plan Template

Business Plan Template

USING THIS TEMPLATE

A business plan carefully spells out a company's projected course of action over a period of time, usually the first two to three years after the start-up. In addition, banks, lenders, and other investors examine the information and financial documentation before deciding whether or not to finance a new business venture. Therefore, a business plan is an essential tool in obtaining financing and should describe the business itself in detail as well as all important factors influencing the company, including the market, industry, competition, operations and management policies, problem solving strategies, financial resources and needs, and other vital information. The plan enables the business owner to anticipate costs, plan for difficulties, and take advantage of opportunities, as well as design and implement strategies that keep the company running as smoothly as possible.

This template has been provided as a model to help you construct your own business plan. Please keep in mind that there is no single acceptable format for a business plan, and that this template is in no way comprehensive, but serves as an example.

The business plans provided in this section are fictional and have been used by small business agencies as models for clients to use in compiling their own business plans.

GENERIC BUSINESS PLAN

Main headings included below are topics that should be covered in a comprehensive business plan. They include:

Business Summary

Purpose
Provides a brief overview of your business, succinctly highlighting the main ideas of your plan.

Includes

- ❍Name and Type of Business
- ❍Description of Product/Service
- ❍Business History and Development
- ❍Location
- ❍Market
- ❍Competition
- ❍Management
- ❍Financial Information
- ❍Business Strengths and Weaknesses
- ❍Business Growth

Table of Contents

Purpose
Organized in an Outline Format, the Table of Contents illustrates the selection and arrangement of information contained in your plan.

Includes

- ❍Topic Headings and Subheadings
- ❍Page Number References

Business History and Industry Outlook

Purpose
Examines the conception and subsequent development of your business within an industry specific context.

Includes

- ❍Start-up Information
- ❍Owner/Key Personnel Experience
- ❍Location
- ❍Development Problems and Solutions
- ❍Investment/Funding Information
- ❍Future Plans and Goals
- ❍Market Trends and Statistics
- ❍Major Competitors
- ❍Product/Service Advantages
- ❍National, Regional, and Local Economic Impact

Product/Service

Purpose
Introduces, defines, and details the product and/or service that inspired the information of your business.

Includes

- ❍Unique Features
- ❍Niche Served
- ❍Market Comparison
- ❍Stage of Product/Service Development
- ❍Production
- ❍Facilities, Equipment, and Labor
- ❍Financial Requirements
- ❍Product/Service Life Cycle
- ❍Future Growth

Market Examination

Purpose
Assessment of product/service applications in relation to consumer buying cycles.

Includes

❍Target Market
❍Consumer Buying Habits
❍Product/Service Applications
❍Consumer Reactions
❍Market Factors and Trends
❍Penetration of the Market
❍Market Share
❍Research and Studies
❍Cost
❍Sales Volume and Goals

Competition

Purpose
Analysis of Competitors in the Marketplace.

Includes

❍Competitor Information
❍Product/Service Comparison
❍Market Niche
❍Product/Service Strengths and Weaknesses
❍Future Product/Service Development

Marketing

Purpose
Identifies promotion and sales strategies for your product/service.

Includes

❍Product/Service Sales Appeal
❍Special and Unique Features
❍Identification of Customers
❍Sales and Marketing Staff
❍Sales Cycles
❍Type of Advertising/Promotion
❍Pricing
❍Competition
❍Customer Services

Operations

Purpose
Traces product/service development from production/inception to the market environment.

Includes

- ❍Cost Effective Production Methods
- ❍Facility
- ❍Location
- ❍Equipment
- ❍Labor
- ❍Future Expansion

Administration and Management

Purpose
Offers a statement of your management philosophy with an in-depth focus on processes and procedures.

Includes

- ❍Management Philosophy
- ❍Structure of Organization
- ❍Reporting System
- ❍Methods of Communication
- ❍Employee Skills and Training
- ❍Employee Needs and Compensation
- ❍Work Environment
- ❍Management Policies and Procedures
- ❍Roles and Responsibilities

Key Personnel

Purpose
Describes the unique backgrounds of principle employees involved in business.

Includes

- ❍Owner(s)/Employee Education and Experience
- ❍Positions and Roles
- ❍Benefits and Salary
- ❍Duties and Responsibilities
- ❍Objectives and Goals

Potential Problems and Solutions

Purpose
Discussion of problem solving strategies that change issues into opportunities.

Includes

❍Risks
❍Litigation
❍Future Competition
❍Economic Impact
❍Problem Solving Skills

Financial Information

Purpose
Secures needed funding and assistance through worksheets and projections detailing financial plans, methods of repayment, and future growth opportunities.

Includes

❍Financial Statements
❍Bank Loans
❍Methods of Repayment
❍Tax Returns
❍Start-up Costs
❍Projected Income (3 years)
❍Projected Cash Flow (3 Years)
❍Projected Balance Statements (3 years)

Appendices

Purpose
Supporting documents used to enhance your business proposal.

Includes

❍Photographs of product, equipment, facilities, etc.
❍Copyright/Trademark Documents
❍Legal Agreements
❍Marketing Materials
❍Research and or Studies
❍Operation Schedules
❍Organizational Charts
❍Job Descriptions
❍Resumes
❍Additional Financial Documentation

Food Distributor

FICTIONAL BUSINESS PLAN

COMMERCIAL FOODS, INC.

3003 Avondale Ave.
Knoxville, TN 37920

October 31, 1992

This plan demonstrates how a partnership can have a positive impact on a new business. It demonstrates how two individuals can carve a niche in the specialty foods market by offering gourmet foods to upscale restaurants and fine hotels. This plan is fictional and has not been used to gain funding from a bank or other lending institution.

FOOD DISTRIBUTOR BUSINESS PLAN

STATEMENT OF PURPOSE

Commercial Foods, Inc. seeks a loan of $75,000 to establish a new business. This sum, together with $5,000 equity investment by the principals, will be used as follows:

Merchandise inventory	$25,000
Office fixture/equipment	12,000
Warehouse equipment	14,000
One delivery truck	10,000
Working capital	39,000
Total	**$100,000**

DESCRIPTION OF THE BUSINESS

Commercial Foods, Inc. will be a distributor of specialty food service products to hotels and upscale restaurants in the geographical area of a 50 mile radius of Knoxville. Richard Roberts will direct the sales effort and John Williams will manage the warehouse operation and the office. One delivery truck will be used initially with a second truck added in the third year.

We expect to begin operation of the business within 30 days after securing the requested financing.

MANAGEMENT

A. Richard Roberts is a native of Memphis, Tennessee. He is a graduate of Memphis State University with a Bachelor's degree from the School of Business. After graduation, he worked for a major manufacturer of specialty food service products as a detail sales person for five years, and, for the past three years, he has served as a product sales manager for this firm.

B. John Williams is a native of Nashville, Tennessee. He holds a B.S. Degree in Food Technology from the University of Tennessee. His career includes five years as a product development chemist in gourmet food products and five years as operations manager for a food service distributor.

Both men are healthy and energetic. Their backgrounds complement each other, which will ensure the success of Commercial Foods, Inc. They will set policies together and personnel decisions will be made jointly. Initial salaries for the owners will be $1,000 per month for the first few years. The spouses of both principals are successful in the business world and earn enough to support the families.

They have engaged the services of Foster Jones, CPA, and William Hale, Attorney, to assist them in an advisory capacity.

PERSONNEL

The firm will employ one delivery truck driver at a wage of $8.00 per hour. One office worker will be employed at $7.50 per hour. One part-time employee will be used in the office at $5.00 per hour. The driver will load and unload his own trucks. Mr. Williams will assist in the warehouse operation as needed to assist one stock person at $7.00 per hour. An additional delivery truck and driver will be added the third year.

LOCATION

The firm will lease a 20,000 square foot building at 3003 Avondale Ave., in Knoxville, which contains warehouse and office areas equipped with two-door truck docks. The annual rental is $9,000. The building was previously used as a food service warehouse and very little modification to the building will be required.

PRODUCTS AND SERVICES

The firm will offer specialty food service products such as soup bases, dessert mixes, sauce bases, pastry mixes, spices, and flavors, normally used by upscale restaurants and nice hotels. We are going after a niche in the market with high quality gourmet products. There is much less competition in this market than in standard run of the mill food service products. Through their work experiences, the principals have contacts with supply sources and with local chefs.

THE MARKET

We know from our market survey that there are over 200 hotels and upscale restaurants in the area we plan to serve. Customers will be attracted by a direct sales approach. We will offer samples of our products and product application data on use of our products in the finished prepared foods. We will cultivate the chefs in these establishments. The technical background of John Williams will be especially useful here.

COMPETITION

We find that we will be only distributor in the area offering a full line of gourmet food service products. Other foodservice distributors offer only a few such items in conjunction with their standard product line. Our survey shows that many of the chefs are ordering products from Atlanta and Memphis because of a lack of adequate local supply.

SUMMARY

Commercial Foods, Inc. will be established as a foodservice distributor of specialty food in Knoxville. The principals, with excellent experience in the industry, are seeking a $75,000 loan to establish the business. The principals are investing $25,000 as equity capital.

The business will be set up as an "S" Corporation with each principal owning 50% of the common stock in the corporation.

Attached is a three year pro forma income statement we believe to be conservative. Also attached are personal financial statements of the principals and a projected cash flow statement for the first year.

PRO FORMA INCOME STATEMENT

	1st Year	2nd Year	3rd Year
Gross Sales	300,000	400,000	500,000
Less Allowances	1,000	1,000	2,000
Net Sales	299,000	399,000	498,000
Cost of Goods Sold	179,400	239,400	298,800
Gross Margin	119,600	159,600	199,200
Operating Expenses			
Utilities	1,200	1,500	1,700
Salaries	76,000	79,000	102,000
Payroll Taxes/Benefits	9,100	9,500	13,200
Advertising	3,000	4,500	5,000
Office Supplies	1,500	2,000	2,500
Insurance	1,200	1,500	1,800
Maintenance	1,000	1,500	2,000
Outside Services	3,000	3,000	3,000
Whse Supplies/Trucks	6,000	7,000	10,000
Telephone	900	1,000	1,200
Rent	9,000	9,500	9,900
Depreciation	2,500	2,000	3,000
Total Expenses	114,400	122,000	155,300
Other Expenses			
Bank Loan Payment	15,000	15,000	15,000
Bank Loan Interest	6,000	5,000	4,000
Total Expenses	**120,400**	**142,000**	**174,300**
Net Profit (Loss)	**(800)**	**17,600**	**24,900**

FINANCIAL STATEMENT I

Assets		**Liabilities**	
Cash	15,000		
1991 Olds	11,000	Unpaid Balance	8,000
Residence	140,000	Mortgage	105,000
Mutual Funds	12,000	Credit Cards	500
Furniture	5,000	Note Payable	4,000
Merck Stock	10,000		
	182,200		117,500
Net Worth			**64,700**
	182,200		**182,200**

FINANCIAL STATEMENT II

Assets		**Liabilities**	
Cash	5,000		
1992 Buick Auto	15,000	Unpaid Balance	12,000
Residence	120,000	Mortgage	100,000
U.S. Treasury Bonds	5,000	Credit Cards	500
Home Furniture	4,000	Note Payable	2,500
AT&T Stock	3,000		
	147,000		115,000
Net Worth			**32,000**
	147,000		**147,000**

Hardware Store

FICTIONAL BUSINESS PLAN

OSHKOSH HARDWARE, INC.

123 Main St.
Oshkosh, WI 54901

June 1994

The following plan outlines how a small hardware store can survive competition from large discount chains by offering products and providing expert advice in the use of any product it sells. This plan is fictional and has not been used to gain funding from a bank or other lending institution.

HARDWARE STORE BUSINESS PLAN

EXECUTIVE SUMMARY

Oshkosh Hardware, Inc. is a new corporation that is going to establish a retail hardware store in a strip mall in Oshkosh, Wisconsin. The store will sell hardware of all kinds, quality tools, paint, and housewares. The business will make revenue and a profit by servicing its customers not only with needed hardware but also with expert advice in the use of any product it sells.

Oshkosh Hardware, Inc. will be operated by its sole shareholder, James Smith. The company will have a total of four employees. It will sell its products in the local market. Customers will buy our products because we will provide free advice on the use of all of our products and will also furnish a full refund warranty.

Oshkosh Hardware, Inc. will sell its products in the Oshkosh store staffed by three sales representatives. No additional employees will be needed to achieve its short and long range goals. The primary short range goal is to open the store by October 1, 1994. In order to achieve this goal a lease must be signed by July 1, 1994 and the complete inventory ordered by August 1, 1994.

Mr. James Smith will invest $30,000 in the business. In addition, the company will have to borrow $150,000 during the first year to cover the investment in inventory, accounts receivable, and furniture and equipment. The company will be profitable after six months of operation and should be able to start repayment of the loan in the second year.

THE BUSINESS

The business will sell hardware of all kinds, quality tools, paint, and housewares. We will purchase our products from three large wholesale buying groups.

In general our customers are homeowners who do their own repair and maintenance, hobbyists, and housewives. Our business is unique in that we will have a complete line of all hardware items and will be able to get special orders by overnight delivery. The business makes revenue and profits by servicing our customers not only with needed hardware but also with expert advice in the use of any product we sell. Our major costs for bringing our products to market are cost of merchandise of 36%, salaries of $45,000, and occupancy costs of $60,000.

Oshkosh Hardware, Inc.'s retail outlet will be located at 1524 Frontage Road, which is in a newly developed retail center of Oshkosh. Our location helps facilitate accessibility from all parts of town and reduces our delivery costs. The store will occupy 7500 square feet of space. The major equipment involved in our business is counters and shelving, a computer, a paint mixing machine, and a truck.

THE MARKET

Oshkosh Hardware, Inc. will operate in the local market. There are 15,000 potential customers in this market area. We have three competitors who control approximately 98% of the market at present. We feel we can capture 25% of the market within the next four years. Our major reason for believing this is that our staff is technically competent to advise our customers in the correct use of all products we sell.

After a careful market analysis, we have determined that approximately 60% of our customers are men and 40% are women. The percentage of customers that fall into the following age categories are:

Under 16:	0%
17-21:	5%
22-30:	30%
31-40:	30%

41-50:	20%
51-60:	10%
61-70:	5%
Over 70:	0%

The reasons our customers prefer our products is our complete knowledge of their use and our full refund warranty.

We get our information about what products our customers want by talking to existing customers. There seems to be an increasing demand for our product. The demand for our product is increasing in size based on the change in population characteristics.

SALES

At Oshkosh Hardware, Inc. we will employ three sales people and will not need any additional personnel to achieve our sales goals. These salespeople will need several years experience in home repair and power tool usage. We expect to attract 30% of our customers from newspaper ads, 5% of our customers from local directories, 5% of our customers from the yellow pages, 10% of our customers from family and friends, and 50% of our customers from current customers. The most cost effect source will be current customers. In general our industry is growing.

MANAGEMENT

We would evaluate the quality of our management staff as being excellent. Our manager is experienced and very motivated to achieve the various sales and quality assurance objectives we have set. We will use a management information system that produces key inventory, quality assurance, and sales data on a weekly basis. All data is compared to previously established goals for that week, and deviations are the primary focus of the management staff.

GOALS IMPLEMENTATION

The short term goals of our business are:

1. Open the store by October 1, 1994
2. Reach our breakeven point in two months
3. Have sales of $100,000 in the first six months

In order to achieve our first short term goal we must:

1. Sign the lease by July 1, 1994
2. Order a complete inventory by August 1, 1994

In order to achieve our second short term goal we must:

1. Advertise extensively in Sept. and Oct.
2. Keep expenses to a minimum

In order to achieve our third short term goal we must:

1. Promote power tool sales for the Christmas season
2. Keep good customer traffic in Jan. and Feb.

The long term goals for our business are:

1. Obtain sales volume of $600,000 in three years
2. Become the largest hardware dealer in the city
3. Open a second store in Fond du Lac

The most important thing we must do in order to achieve the long term goals for our business is to develop a highly profitable business with excellent cash flow.

FINANCE

Oshkosh Hardware, Inc. Faces some potential threats or risks to our business. They are discount house competition. We believe we can avoid or compensate for this by providing quality products complimented by quality advice on the use of every product we sell. The financial projections we have prepared are located at the end of this document.

JOB DESCRIPTION: GENERAL MANAGER

The General Manager of the business of the corporation will be the president of the corporation. He will be responsible for the complete operation of the retail hardware store which is owned by the corporation. A detailed description of his duties and responsibilities is as follows:

Sales

Train and supervise the three sales people. Develop programs to motivate and compensate these employees. Coordinate advertising and sales promotion effects to achieve sales totals as outlined in budget. Oversee purchasing function and inventory control procedures to insure adequate merchandise at all times at a reasonable cost.

Finance

Prepare monthly and annual budgets. Secure adequate line of credit from local banks. Supervise office personnel to insure timely preparation of records, statements, all government reports, control of receivables and payables, and monthly financial statements.

Administration

Perform duties as required in the areas of personnel, building leasing and maintenance, licenses and permits, and public relations.

QUARTERLY FORECASTED BALANCE SHEETS

	Beg. Bal.	1st Qtr	2nd Qtr	3rd Qtr	4th Qtr
Assets					
Cash	30,000	418	(463)	(3,574)	4,781
Accounts Receivable	0	20,000	13,333	33,333	33,333
Inventory	0	48,000	32,000	80,000	80,000
Other Current Assets	0	0	0	0	0
Total Current Assets	30,000	68,418	44,870	109,759	118,114
Land	0	0	0	0	0
Building & Improvements	0	0	0	0	0
Furniture & Equipment	0	75,000	75,000	75,000	75,000
Total Fixed Assets	0	75,000	75,000	75,000	75,000
Less Accum. Depreciation	0	1,875	3,750	5,625	7,500
Net Fixed Assets	0	73,125	71,250	69,375	67,500
Intangible Assets	0	0	0	0	0
Less Amortization	0	0	0	0	0
Net Intangible Assets	0	0	0	0	0
Other Assets	0	0	0	0	0
Total Assets	**30,000**	**141,543**	**116,120**	**179,134**	**185,614**

	Beg. Bal.	1st Qtr	2nd Qtr	3rd Qtr	4th Qtr
Liabilities and Shareholders' Equity					
Short-Term Debt	0	0	0	0	0
Accounts Payable	0	12,721	10,543	17,077	17,077
Dividends Payable	0	0	0	0	0
Income Taxes Payable	0	(1,031)	(2,867)	(2,355)	(1,843)
Accrued Compensation	0	1,867	1,867	1,867	1,867
Other Current Liabilities	0	0	0	0	0
Total Current Liabilities	0	13,557	9,543	16,589	17,101
Long-Term Debt	0	110,000	110,000	160,000	160,000
Other Non-Current Liabilities	0	0	0	0	0
Total Liabilities	0	123,557	119,543	176,589	177,101
Common Stock	30,000	30,000	30,000	30,000	30,000
Retained Earnings	0	(12,014)	(33,423)	(27,455)	(21,487)
Shareholders' Equity	30,000	17,986	(3,423)	2,545	8,513
Total Liabilities & Shareholders' Equity	30,000	141,543	116,120	179,134	185,614

QUARTERLY FORECASTED STATEMENTS OF EARNINGS AND RETAINED EARNINGS

	Beg. Actual	1st Qtr	2nd Qtr	3rd Qtr	4th Qtr	Total
Total Sales	0	60,000	40,000	100,000	100,000	300,000
Goods/Services	0	21,600	14,400	36,000	36,000	108,000
Gross Profit	0	38,400	25,600	64,000	64,000	192,000
Operating Expenses	0	47,645	45,045	52,845	52,845	198,380
Fixed Expenses						
Interest	0	1,925	1,925	2,800	2,800	9,450
Depreciation	0	1,875	1,875	1,875	1,875	7,500
Amortization	0	0	0	0	0	0
Total Fixed Expenses	0	3,800	3,800	4,675	4,675	16,950
Operating Profit (Loss)	0	(13,045)	(23,245)	6,480	6,480	(23,330)

	Beg. Actual	1st Qtr	2nd Qtr	3rd Qtr	4th Qtr	Total
Other Income (Expense)	0	0	0	0	0	0
Interest Income	0	0	0	0	0	0
Earnings (Loss) Before Taxes	0	(13,045)	(23,245)	6,480	6,480	(23,330)
Income Taxes	0	(1,031)	(1,836)	512	512	(1,843)
Net Earnings	0	(12,014)	(21,409)	5,968	5,968	(21,487)
Retained Earnings, Beginning	0	0	(12,014)	(33,423)	(27,455)	0
Less Dividends	0	0	0	0	0	0
Retained Earnings, Ending	0	(12,014)	(33,423)	(27,455)	(21,487)	(21,487)

QUARTERLY FORECASTED STATEMENTS OF CHANGES IN FINANCIAL POSITION

	Beg. Bal.	1st Qtr	2nd Qtr	3rd Qtr	4th Qtr	Total
Sources (Uses) of Cash						
Net Earnings (Loss)	0	(12,014)	(21,409)	5,968	5,968	(21,487)
Depreciation & Amortization	0	1,875	1,875	1,875	1,875	7,500
Cash Provided by Operations	0	(10,139)	(19,534)	7,834	7,834	(13,987)
Dividends	0	0	0	0	0	0
Cash Provided by (Used For) Changes in						
Accounts Receivable	0	(20,000)	6,667	(20,000)	0	(33,333)
Inventory	0	(48,000)	16,000	(48,000)	0	(80,000)
Other Current Assets	0	0	0	0	0	0
Accounts Payable	0	12,	721	(2,178)	6,534 0	17,077
Income Taxes	0	(1,031)	(1,836)	512	512	(1,843)
Accrued Compensation	0	1,867	0	0	0	1,867
Dividends Payable	0	0	0	0	0	0
Other Current Liabilities	0	0	0	0	0	0

	Beg. Bal.	1st Qtr	2nd Qtr	3rd Qtr	4th Qtr	Total
Other Assets	0	0	0	0	0	0
Net Cash Provided by (Used For)						
Operating Activities	0	(54,443)	18,653	(60,954)	512	(96,233)
Investment Transactions						
Furniture & Equipment	0	(75,000)	0	0	0	(75,000)
Land	0	0	0	0	0	0
Building & Improvements	0	0	0	0	0	0
Intangible Assets	0	0	0	0	0	0
Net Cash from Investment Transactions	0	(75,000)	0	0	0	(75,000)
Financing Transactions						
Short-Term Debt	0	0	0	0	0	0
Long-Term Debt	0	110,000	0	50,000	0	160,000
Other Non-Current Liabilities	0	0	0	0	0	0
Sale of Common Stock	30,000	0	0	0	0	0
Net Cash from Financing Transactions	30,000	110,000	0	50,000	0	160,000
Net Increase (Decrease) in Cash	30,000	(29,582)	(881)	(3,111)	8,355	(25,219)
Cash, Beginning of Period	0	30,000	418	(463)	(3,574)	30,000
Cash, End of Period	30,000	418	(463)	(3,574)	4,781	4,781

FINANCIAL RATIO ANALYSIS

	Beg. Actual	1st Qtr	2nd Qtr	3rd Qtr	4th Qtr
Overall Performance					
Return on Equity	0.00	(66.80)	625.45	234.50	70.10
Return on Total Assets	0.00	(8.49)	(18.44)	3.33	3.22
Operating Return	0.00	(9.22)	(20.02)	3.62	3.49
Profitability Measures					
Gross Profit Percent	0.00	64.00	64.00	64.00	64.00
Profit Margin (AIT)	0.00	(20.02)	(53.52)	5.97	5.97
Operating Income per Share	0.00	0.00	0.00	0.00	0.00
Earnings per Share	0.00	0.00	0.00	0.00	0.00
Test of Investment Utilization					
Asset Turnover	0.00	0.42	0.34	0.56	0.54
Equity Turnover	0.00	3.34	(11.69)	39.29	11.75
Fixed Asset Turnover	0.00	0.82	0.56	1.44	1.48
Average Collection Period	0.00	30.00	30.00	30.00	30.00
Days Inventory	0.00	200.00	200.00	200.00	200.00
Inventory Turnover	0.00	0.45	0.45	0.45	0.45
Working Capital Turns	0.00	1.09	1.13	1.07	0.99
Test of Financial Condition					
Current Ratio	0.00	5.05	4.70	6.62	6.91
Quick Ratio	0.00	1.51	1.35	1.79	2.23
Working Capital Ratio	1.00	0.43	0.33	0.57	0.60
Dividend Payout	0.00	0.00	0.00	0.00	0.00
Financial Leverage					
Total Assets	1.00	7.87	(33.92)	70.39	21.80

	Beg. Actual	1st Qtr	2nd Qtr	3rd Qtr	4th Qtr
Debt/Equity	0.00	6.87	(34.92)	69.39	20.80
Debt to Total Assets	0.00	0.87	1.03	0.99	0.95
Year-End Equity History					
Shares Outstanding	0	0	0	0	0
Market Price per Share (@20x's earnings)	0.00	0.00	0.00	0.00	0.00
Book Value per Share	0.00	0.00	0.00	0.00	0.00
Altman Analysis Ratio					
1.2x (1)	1.20	0.47	0.37	0.62	0.65
1.4x (2)	0.00	(0.12)	(0.40)	(0.21)	(0.16)
3.3x (3)	0.00	(0.35)	(0.72)	0.07	0.07
0.6x (4)	0.00	0.00	0.00	0.00	0.00
1.0x (5)	0.00	0.42	0.34	0.56	0.54
Z Value	1.20	.042	(.041)	1.04	1.10

DETAILS FOR QUARTERLY STATEMENTS OF EARNINGS

	Beg. Act.	1st Qtr	2nd Qtr	3rd Qtr	4th Qtr	Total	%Sales	Fixed
Sales								
Dollars Sales Forecasted								
Product 1	0	60,000	40,000	100,000	100,000	300,000		
Product 2	0	0	0	0	0	0		
Product 3	0	0	0	0	0	0		
Product 4	0	0	0	0	0	0		
Product 5	0	0	0	0	0	0		
Product 6	0	0	0	0	0	0		
Total Sales	0	60,000	40,000	100,000	100,000	300,000		

DETAILS FOR QUARTERLY STATEMENTS OF EARNINGS

...continued

	Beg. Act.	1st Qtr	2nd Qtr	3rd Qtr	4th Qtr	Total	%Sales	Fixed
Cost of Sales								
Dollar Cost Forecasted								
Product 1	0	21,600	14,400	36,000	36,000	108,000	36.00%	0
Product 2	0	0	0	0	0	0	0.00%	0
Product 3	0	0	0	0	0	0	0.00%	0
Product 4	0	0	0	0	0	0	0.00%	0
Product 5	0	0	0	0	0	0	0.00%	0
Product 6	0	0	0	0	0	0	0.00%	0
Total Cost of Sales	0	21,600	14,400	36,000	36,000	108,000		
Operating Expenses								
Payroll	0	12,000	12,000	12,000	12,000	48,000	0.00%	12,000
Paroll Taxes	0	950	950	950	950	3,800	0.00%	950
Advertising	0	4,800	3,200	8,000	8,000	24,000	8.00%	0
Automobile Expenses	0	0	0	0	0		0.00%	0
Bad Debts	0	0	0	0	0	0	0.00%	0
Commissions	0	3,000	2,000	5,000	5,000	15,000	5.00%	0
Computer Rental	0	1,200	1,200	1,200	1,200	4,800	0.00%	1,200
Computer Supplies	0	220	220	220	220	880	0.00%	220
Computer Maintenance	0	100	100	100	100	400	0.00%	100
Dealer Training	0	1,000	1,000	1,000	1,000	4,000	0.00%	1,000
Electricity	0	3,000	3,000	3,000	3,000	12,000	0.00%	3,000
Employment Ads and Fees	0	0	0	0	0	0	0.00%	0
Entertainment: Business	0	1,500	1,500	1,500	1,500	6,000	0.00%	1,500
General Insurance	0	800	800	800	800	32,000	0.00%	800
Health & W/C Insurance	0	0	0	0	0	0	0.00%	0
Interest: LT Debt	0	2,500	2,500	2,500	2,500	10,000	0.00%	2,500
Legal & Accounting	0	1,500	1,500	1,500	1,500	6,000	0.00%	1,500
Maintenance & Repairs	0	460	460	460	460	1,840	0.00%	460

DETAILS FOR QUARTERLY STATEMENT OF EARNINGS

...continued

	Beg. Act.	1st Qtr	2nd Qtr	3rd Qtr	4th Qtr	Total	%Sales	Fixed
Office Supplies	0	270	270	270	270	1,080	0.00%	270
Postage	0	85	85	85	85	340	0.00%	85
Prof. Development	0	0	0	0	0	0	0.00%	0
Professional Fees	0	1,000	1,000	1,000	1,000	4,000	0.00%	1,000
Rent	0	8,000	8,000	8,000	8,000	2,000	0.00%	8,000
Shows & Conferences	0	0	0	0	0	0	0.00%	0
Subscriptions & Dues	0	285	285	285	285	1,140	0.00%	285
Telephone	0	1,225	1,225	1,225	1,225	4,900	0.00%	1,225
Temporary Employees	0	0	0	0	0	0	0.00%	0
Travel Expenses	0	750	750	750	750	3,000	0.00%	750
Utilities	0	3,000	3,000	3,000	3,000	12,000	0.00%	3,000
Research & Development	0	0	0	0	0	0	0.00%	0
Royalties	0	0	0	0	0	0	0.00%	0
Other 1	0	0	0	0	0	0	0.00%	0
Other 2	0	0	0	0	0	0	0.00%	0
Other 3	0	0	0	0	0	0	0.00%	0
Total Operating Expenses	0	47,645	45,045	52,845	52,845	198,380		
Percent of Sales	0.00%	79.41	112.61	52.85	52.85	66.13		

Appendix B - Organizations, Agencies and Consultants

Organizations, Agencies, & Consultants

A listing of Associations and Consultants of interest to entrepreneurs, followed by the 10 Small Business Administration Regional Offices, Small Business Development Centers, Service Corps of Retired Executives offices, and Venture Capital & Finance companies.

ASSOCIATIONS

This section contains a listing of associations and other agencies of interest to the small business owner. Entries are listed alphabetically by organization name.

American Association of Family Businesses
PO Box 547217
Surfside, FL 33154
Phone: (305)864-1184
Fax: (305)864-1187
Craig Gordon, Pres.

American Small Businesses Association
8773 IL Rte. 75E.
Rock City, IL 61070
Free: (800)942-2722
E-mail: gavazzi.1@osu.edu
Website: http://www.asbaonline.org/
Vernon Castle, Exec. Dir.

American Society of Independent Business
c/o Keith Wood
777 Main St., Ste. 1600
Fort Worth, TX 76102
Phone: (817)870-1880
Keith Wood, Pres.

American Women's Economic Development Corporation
216 East 45th St.
New York, NY 10017
Phone: (917)368-6120
Fax: (212)786-7114
E-mail: info@awed.org
Website: http://www.awed.org
Suzanne Israel Tufts, Pres. & CEO

Association for Enterprise Opportunity
70 E Lake St., Ste. 1120
Chicago, IL 60601
Phone: (312)357-0177
Fax: (312)357-0180
E-mail: aeochicago@ad.com
Christine M. Benuzzi, Exec. Dir.

Association of Small Business Development Centers
c/o Don Wilson
8990 Burke Lake Rd.
Burke, VA 22015
Phone: (703)764-9850
Fax: (703)764-1234
E-mail: don@asbdc-us.org
Website: http://www.asbdc-us.org
Don Wilson, Pres.

BEST Employers Association
2505 McCabe Way
Irvine, CA 92614
Phone: (714)756-1000
Free: (800)433-0088
Fax: (714)553-0883
Donald R. Lawrenz, Exec. Sec.

Business Market Association
4131 N. Central Expy., Ste. 720
Dallas, TX 75204
R. Mark King, Pres.

Coalition of Americans to Save the Economy
1100 Connecticut Ave. NW, Ste. 1200
Washington, DC 20036-4101
Phone: (202)293-1414
Fax: (202)293-1702
Barry Maloney, Treas.

Employers of America
520 S Pierce, Ste. 224
Mason City, IA 50401
Phone: (641)424-3187
Free: (800)728-3187
Fax: (641)424-1673
E-mail: employer@employerhelp.org
Website: http://
www.employerhelp.org
Jim Collison, Pres.

Family Firm Institute
221 N. Beacon St.
Boston, MA 02135-1943
Phone: (617)789-4200
Fax: (617)789-4220
E-mail: ffi@ffi.org
Website: http://www.ffi.org
Judy L. Green, Ph.D., Exec. Dir.

Group Purchasing Association
Plaza Tower, 35th Fl.
1001 Howard Ave.
New Orleans, LA 70113-2002
Phone: (504)529-2030
Fax: (504)558-0929
E-mail: lenn@firstgpa.com

Independent Business Alliance
111 John St.
New York, NY 10038
Free: (800)559-2580
Fax: (212)285-1639
Robert J. Levine, CEO

International Association of Business
701 Highlander Blvd., Ste. 500
Arlington, TX 76015-4332
Paula Rainey, Pres.

International Association for Business Organizations
PO Box 30149
Baltimore, MD 21270
Phone: (410)581-1373
Rudolph Lewis, Exec. Officer

International Council for Small Business
c/o Jefferson Smurfit Center for Entrepreneurial Studies
St. Louis University
3674 Lindell Blvd.
St. Louis, MO 63108
Phone: (314)977-3628
Fax: (314)977-3627
E-mail: icsb@slu.edu
Website: http://www.icsb.org
Sharon Bower, Sec.

National Alliance for Fair Competition
3 Bethesda Metro Center, Ste. 1100
Bethesda, MD 20814
Phone: (410)235-7116
Fax: (410)235-7116
E-mail: ampesq@aol.com
Tony Ponticelli, Exec. Dir.

National Association of Business Leaders
PO Box 766
Bridgeton, MO 63044
Phone: (314)344-1111
Fax: (314)298-9110
E-mail: nabl@nabl.com
Website: http://www.nabl.com/
John Weigel, Contact

National Association for Business Organizations
PO Box 30220
Baltimore, MD 21270
Phone: (410)581-1373
Website: http://www.ameribiz.com/quicklink.htm
Rudolph Lewis, Pres.

National Association of Government Guaranteed Lenders
c/o Tony Wilkinson
PO Box 332
Stillwater, OK 74076
Phone: (405)377-4022
Fax: (405)377-3931
E-mail: twilkinson@naggl.com
Website: http://www.naggl.com/
Tony Wilkinson, Pres./CEO

National Association of Private Enterprise
7819 Shelburne Cir.
Spring, TX 77379-4687
Phone: (281)655-5412
Free: (800)223-6273
Fax: (281)257-3244
E-mail: info@nape.org
Laura Squiers, Exec. Dir.

National Association for the Self-Employed
PO Box 612067
DFW Airport
Dallas, TX 75261-2067
Free: (800)232-NASE
Fax: (800)551-4446
Website: http://www.nase.org
Robert Hughes, Pres.

National Association of Small Business Investment Companies
666 11th St. NW, No. 750
Washington, DC 20001
Phone: (202)628-5055
Fax: (202)628-5080
E-mail: nasbic@nasbic.org
Website: http://www.nasbic.org
Lee W. Mercer, Pres.

National Business Association
PO Box 700728
Dallas, TX 75370
Phone: (972)458-0900
Free: (800)456-0440
Fax: (972)960-9149
E-mail: p.archibald@nationalbusiness.org
Website: http://www.nationalbusiness.org
Pat Archibald, Pres.

National Business Owners Association
820 Gibbon St. Ste. 204
Alexandria, VA 22314
Phone: (202)737-6501
Free: (888)755-NBOA
Fax: (877)626-2329
E-mail: govaffairs@nboa.org
Thomas Rumfelt, Chm.

National Center for Fair Competition
8421 Frost Way
Annandale, VA 22003
Phone: (703)280-4622
Fax: (703)280-0942
E-mail: kentonp1@aol.com
Kenton Pattie, Pres.

National Federation of Independent Business
53 Century Blvd., Ste. 300
Nashville, TN 37214
Phone: (615)872-5800
Free: (800)NFIBNOW
Fax: (615)872-5353
Website: http://www.nfib.org
Jack Faris, Pres. and CEO

National Small Business Benefits Association
2244 N. Grand Ave. E.
Springfield, IL 62702
Phone: (217)753-2558
Fax: (217)753-2558
Les Brewer, Exec. VP

National Small Business United
1156 15th St. NW, Ste. 1100
Washington, DC 20005
Phone: (202)293-8830
Free: (800)345-6728
Fax: (202)872-8543
E-mail: nsbu@nsbu.org
Website: http://www.nsbu.org
Todd McCraken, Pres.

Network of Small Businesses
5420 Mayfield Rd., Ste. 205
Lyndhurst, OH 44124
Phone: (216)442-5600
Fax: (216)449-3227
Irwin Friedman, Chm.

Research Institute for Small and Emerging Business
722 12th St. NW
Washington, DC 20005
Phone: (202)628-8382
Fax: (202)628-8392
E-mail: info@riseb.org
Website: http://www.riseb.org
Mark Schultz, CEO/Pres.

Score Association - Service Corps of Retired Executives
c/o Service Corps of Retired Executives Association
409 3rd St. SW, 6th Fl.
Washington, DC 20024
Phone: (202)205-6762
Free: (800)634-0245
Fax: (202)205-7636
Website: http://www.score.org
W. Kenneth Yancey, Jr., CEO

Small Business Legislative Council
1010 Massachusetts Ave. NW
Washington, DC 20001
Phone: (202)639-8500
Fax: (202)296-5333
Website: http://www.sblc.org
John Satagaj, Pres.

Small Business Network
PO Box 30149
Baltimore, MD 21270
Phone: (410)581-1373
E-mail: natibb@ix.netcom.com
Rudolph Lewis, CEO

Small Business Service Bureau
554 Main St.
PO Box 15014
Worcester, MA 01615-0014
Phone: (508)756-3513

Fax: (508)770-0528
Francis R. Carroll, Pres.

Small Business Service Bureau
554 Main St.
PO Box 15014
Worcester, MA 01608
Phone: (508)756-3513
Free: (800)343-0939
Fax: (508)770-0528
E-mail: membership@sbsb.com
Website: http://www.sbsb.com
Francis R. Carroll, Pres.

Small Business Support Center Association
c/o James S. Ryan
8811 Westheimer Rd., No. 210
Houston, TX 77063-3617
James S. Ryan, Admin.

Small Business Survival Committee
1920 L St., NW, Ste. 200
Washington, DC 20036
Phone: (202)785-0238
Fax: (202)822-8118
E-mail: membership@sbsc.org
Website: http://www.sbsc.org
Christopher Wysocki, Pres.

Support Services Alliance
PO Box 130
Schoharie, NY 12157-0130
Phone: (518)295-7966
Free: (800)836-4772
Fax: (518)295-8556
E-mail: comments@ssainfo.com
Website: http://www.ssainfo.com
Gary Swan, Pres.

CONSULTANTS

This section contains a listing of consultants specializing in small business development. It is arranged alphabetically by country, then by state or province, then by city, then by firm name.

CANADA

Alberta

Common Sense Solutions
3405 16A Ave.
Edmonton, AB, Canada
Phone: (403)465-7330
Fax: (403)465-7380
E-mail: gcoulson@comsensesolutions.com
Website: http://www.comsensesolutions.com

Varsity Consulting Group
School of Business
University of Alberta
Edmonton, AB, Canada T6G 2R6
Phone: (780)492-2994
Fax: (780)492-5400
Website: http://www.bus.ualberta.ca/vcg

Viro Hospital Consulting
42 Commonwealth Bldg., 9912 - 106 St. NW
Edmonton, AB, Canada T5K 1C5
Phone: (403)425-3871
Fax: (403)425-3871
E-mail: rpb@freenet.edmonton.ab.ca

British Columbia

SRI Strategic Resources Inc.
4330 Kingsway, Ste. 1600
Burnaby, BC, Canada V5H 4G7
Phone: (604)435-0627
Fax: (604)435-2782
E-mail: inquiry@sri.bc.ca
Website: http://www.sri.com

Andrew R. De Boda Consulting
1523 Milford Ave.
Coquitlam, BC, Canada V3J 2V9
Phone: (604)936-4527
Fax: (604)936-4527
E-mail: deboda@intergate.bc.ca
Website: http://www.ourworld.compuserve.com/homepages/deboda

The Sage Group Ltd.
980 - 355 Burrard St.
744 W Haistings, Ste. 410
Vancouver, BC, Canada V6C 1A5
Phone: (604)669-9269
Fax: (604)669-6622

Tikkanen-Bradley
1345 Nelson St., Ste. 202
Vancouver, BC, Canada V6E 1J8
Phone: (604)669-0583
E-mail: webmaster@tikkanenbradley.com
Website: http://www.tikkanenbradley.com

Ontario

The Cynton Co.
17 Massey St.
Brampton, ON, Canada L6S 2V6
Phone: (905)792-7769
Fax: (905)792-8116
E-mail: cynton@home.com
Website: http://www.cynton.com

Begley & Associates
RR 6
Cambridge, ON, Canada N1R 5S7
Phone: (519)740-3629
Fax: (519)740-3629
E-mail: begley@in.on.ca
Website: http://www.in.on.ca/~begley/index.htm

CRO Engineering Ltd.
1895 William Hodgins Ln.
Carp, ON, Canada K0A 1L0
Phone: (613)839-1108
Fax: (613)839-1406
E-mail: J.Grefford@ieee.ca
Website: http://www.geocities.com/WallStreet/District/7401/

Task Enterprises
Box 69, RR 2 Hamilton
Flamborough, ON, Canada L8N 2Z7
Phone: (905)659-0153
Fax: (905)659-0861

HST Group Ltd.
430 Gilmour St.
Ottawa, ON, Canada K2P 0R8
Phone: (613)236-7303
Fax: (613)236-9893

Harrison Associates
BCE Pl.
181 Bay St., Ste. 3740
PO Box 798
Toronto, ON, Canada M5J 2T3
Phone: (416)364-5441
Fax: (416)364-2875

TCI Convergence Ltd. Management Consultants
99 Crown's Ln.
Toronto, ON, Canada M5R 3P4
Phone: (416)515-4146
Fax: (416)515-2097
E-mail: tci@inforamp.net
Website: http://tciconverge.com/index.1.html

Ken Wyman & Associates Inc.
64B Shuter St., Ste. 200

Toronto, ON, Canada M5B 1B1
Phone: (416)362-2926
Fax: (416)362-3039
E-mail:
kenwyman@compuserve.com

JPL Business Consultants
82705 Metter Rd.
Wellandport, ON, Canada L0R 2J0
Phone: (905)386-7450
Fax: (905)386-7450
E-mail:
plamarch@freenet.npiec.on.ca

Quebec

The Zimmar Consulting Partnership Inc.
Westmount
PO Box 98
Montreal, QC, Canada H3Z 2T1
Phone: (514)484-1459
Fax: (514)484-3063

Saskatchewan

Trimension Group
No. 104-110 Research Dr.
Innovation Place, SK, Canada S7N 3R3
Phone: (306)668-2560
Fax: (306)975-1156
E-mail: trimension@trimension.ca
Website: http://www.trimension.ca

UNITED STATES

Alabama

Business Planning Inc.
300 Office Park Dr.
Birmingham, AL 35223-2474
Phone: (205)870-7090
Fax: (205)870-7103

Tradebank of Eastern Alabama
546 Broad St., Ste. 3
Gadsden, AL 35901
Phone: (205)547-8700
Fax: (205)547-8718
E-mail: mansion@webex.com
Website: http://www.webex.com/~tea

Alaska

AK Business Development Center
3335 Arctic Blvd., Ste. 203
Anchorage, AK 99503
Phone: (907)562-0335
Free: (800)478-3474
Fax: (907)562-6988
E-mail: abdc@gci.net
Website: http://www.abdc.org

Business Matters
PO Box 287
Fairbanks, AK 99707
Phone: (907)452-5650

Arizona

Carefree Direct Marketing Corp.
8001 E Serene St.
PO Box 3737
Carefree, AZ 85377-3737
Phone: (480)488-4227
Fax: (480)488-2841

Trans Energy Corp.
1739 W 7th Ave.
Mesa, AZ 85202
Phone: (480)827-7915
Fax: (480)967-6601
E-mail: aha@clean-air.org
Website: http://www.clean-air.org

CMAS
5125 N 16th St.
Phoenix, AZ 85016
Phone: (602)395-1001
Fax: (602)604-8180

Comgate Telemanagement Ltd.
706 E Bell Rd., Ste. 105
Phoenix, AZ 85022
Phone: (602)485-5708
Fax: (602)485-5709
E-mail: comgate@netzone.com
Website: http://www.comgate.com

Moneysoft Inc.
1 E Camelback Rd. #550
Phoenix, AZ 85012
Free: (800)966-7797
E-mail: mbray@moneysoft.com

Harvey C. Skoog
PO Box 26439
Prescott Valley, AZ 86312
Phone: (520)772-1714
Fax: (520)772-2814

LMC Services
8711 E Pinnacle Peak Rd., No. 340
Scottsdale, AZ 85255-3555
Phone: (602)585-7177
Fax: (602)585-5880
E-mail: louws@earthlink.com

Sauerbrun Technology Group Ltd.
7979 E Princess Dr., Ste. 5
Scottsdale, AZ 85255-5878
Phone: (602)502-4950
Fax: (602)502-4292
E-mail: info@sauerbrun.com
Website: http://www.sauerbrun.com

Gary L. McLeod
PO Box 230
Sonoita, AZ 85637
Fax: (602)455-5661

Van Cleve Associates
6932 E 2nd St.
Tucson, AZ 85710
Phone: (520)296-2587
Fax: (520)296-3358

California

Acumen Group Inc.
Phone: (650)949-9349
Fax: (650)949-4845
E-mail: acumen-g@ix.netcom.com
Website: http://pw2.netcom.com/~janed/acumen.html

On-line Career and Management Consulting
420 Central Ave., No. 314
Alameda, CA 94501
Phone: (510)864-0336
Fax: (510)864-0336
E-mail: career@dnai.com
Website: http://www.dnai.com/~career

Career Paths-Thomas E. Church & Associates Inc.
PO Box 2439
Aptos, CA 95001
Phone: (408)662-7950
Fax: (408)662-7955
E-mail: church@ix.netcom.com
Website: http://www.careerpaths-tom.com

Keck & Co. Business Consultants
410 Walsh Rd.
Atherton, CA 94027
Phone: (650)854-9588
Fax: (650)854-7240
E-mail: info@keckco.com
Website: http://www.keckco.com

Ben W. Laverty III, PhD, REA, CEI
4909 Stockdale Hwy., Ste. 132
Bakersfield, CA 93309
Phone: (661)283-8300

Free: (800)833-0373
Fax: (661)283-8313
E-mail: cstc@cstcsafety.com
Website: http://www.cstcsafety.com/cstc

Lindquist Consultants-Venture Planning
225 Arlington Ave.
Berkeley, CA 94707
Phone: (510)524-6685
Fax: (510)527-6604

Larson Associates
PO Box 9005
Brea, CA 92822
Phone: (714)529-4121
Fax: (714)572-3606
E-mail: ray@consultlarson.com
Website: http://www.consultlarson.com

Kremer Management Consulting
PO Box 500
Carmel, CA 93921
Phone: (408)626-8311
Fax: (408)624-2663
E-mail: ddkremer@aol.com

W and J PARTNERSHIP
PO Box 2499
18876 Edwin Markham Dr.
Castro Valley, CA 94546
Phone: (510)583-7751
Fax: (510)583-7645
E-mail: wamorgan@wjpartnership.com
Website: http://www.wjpartnership.com

JB Associates
21118 Gardena Dr.
Cupertino, CA 95014
Phone: (408)257-0214
Fax: (408)257-0216
E-mail: semarang@sirius.com

House Agricultural Consultants
PO Box 1615
Davis, CA 95617-1615
Phone: (916)753-3361
Fax: (916)753-0464
E-mail: infoag@houseag.com
Website: http://www.houseag.com/

3C Systems Co.
16161 Ventura Blvd., Ste. 815
Encino, CA 91436
Phone: (818)907-1302
Fax: (818)907-1357
E-mail: mark@3CSysCo.com
Website: http://www.3CSysCo.com

Technical Management Consultants
3624 Westfall Dr.
Encino, CA 91436-4154
Phone: (818)784-0626
Fax: (818)501-5575
E-mail: tmcrs@aol.com

RAINWATER-GISH & Associates, Business Finance & Development
317 3rd St., Ste. 3
Eureka, CA 95501
Phone: (707)443-0030
Fax: (707)443-5683

Global Tradelinks
451 Pebble Beach Pl.
Fullerton, CA 92835
Phone: (714)441-2280
Fax: (714)441-2281
E-mail: info@globaltradelinks.com
Website: http://www.globaltradelinks.com

Strategic Business Group
800 Cienaga Dr.
Fullerton, CA 92835-1248
Phone: (714)449-1040
Fax: (714)525-1631

Burnes Consulting
20537 Wolf Creek Rd.
Grass Valley, CA 95949
Phone: (530)346-8188
Free: (800)949-9021
Fax: (530)346-7704
E-mail: kent@burnesconsulting.com
Website: http://www.burnesconsulting.com

Pioneer Business Consultants
9042 Garfield Ave., Ste. 312
Huntington Beach, CA 92646
Phone: (714)964-7600

Beblie, Brandt & Jacobs Inc.
16 Technology, Ste. 164
Irvine, CA 92618
Phone: (714)450-8790
Fax: (714)450-8799
E-mail: darcy@bbjinc.com
Website: http://198.147.90.26

Fluor Daniel Inc.
3353 Michelson Dr.
Irvine, CA 92612-0650
Phone: (949)975-2000
Fax: (949)975-5271
E-mail: sales.consulting@fluordaniel.com
Website: http://www.fluordanielconsulting.com

MCS Associates
18300 Von Karman, Ste. 710
Irvine, CA 92612
Phone: (949)263-8700
Fax: (949)263-0770
E-mail: info@mcsassociates.com
Website: http://www.mcsassociates.com

Inspired Arts Inc.
4225 Executive Sq., Ste. 1160
La Jolla, CA 92037
Phone: (619)623-3525
Free: (800)851-4394
Fax: (619)623-3534
E-mail: info@inspiredarts.com
Website: http://www.inspiredarts.com

The Laresis Companies
PO Box 3284
La Jolla, CA 92038
Phone: (619)452-2720
Fax: (619)452-8744

RCL & Co.
PO Box 1143
737 Pearl St., Ste. 201
La Jolla, CA 92038
Phone: (619)454-8883
Fax: (619)454-8880

Comprehensive Business Services
3201 Lucas Cir.
Lafayette, CA 94549
Phone: (925)283-8272
Fax: (925)283-8272

The Ribble Group
27601 Forbes Rd., Ste. 52
Laguna Niguel, CA 92677
Phone: (714)582-1085
Fax: (714)582-6420
E-mail: ribble@deltanet.com

Norris Bernstein, CMC
9309 Marina Pacifica Dr. N
Long Beach, CA 90803
Phone: (562)493-5458
Fax: (562)493-5459
E-mail: norris@ctecomputer.com
Website: http://foodconsultants.com/bernstein/

Horizon Consulting Services
1315 Garthwick Dr.
Los Altos, CA 94024
Phone: (415)967-0906
Fax: (415)967-0906

Brincko Associates Inc.
1801 Avenue of the Stars, Ste. 1054
Los Angeles, CA 90067
Phone: (310)553-4523
Fax: (310)553-6782

Rubenstein/Justman Management Consultants
2049 Century Park E, 24th Fl.
Los Angeles, CA 90067
Phone: (310)282-0800
Fax: (310)282-0400
E-mail: info@rjmc.net
Website: http://www.rjmc.net

F.J. Schroeder & Associates
1926 Westholme Ave.
Los Angeles, CA 90025
Phone: (310)470-2655
Fax: (310)470-6378
E-mail: fjsacons@aol.com
Website: http://www.mcninet.com/GlobalLook/Fjschroe.html

Western Management Associates
5959 W Century Blvd., Ste. 565
Los Angeles, CA 90045-6506
Phone: (310)645-1091
Free: (888)788-6534
Fax: (310)645-1092
E-mail: gene@cfoforrent.com
Website: http://www.cfoforrent.com

Darrell Sell and Associates
Los Gatos, CA 95030
Phone: (408)354-7794
E-mail: darrell@netcom.com

Leslie J. Zambo
3355 Michael Dr.
Marina, CA 93933
Phone: (408)384-7086
Fax: (408)647-4199
E-mail: 104776.1552@compuserve.com

Marketing Services Management
PO Box 1377
Martinez, CA 94553
Phone: (510)370-8527
Fax: (510)370-8527
E-mail: markserve@biotechnet.com

William M. Shine Consulting Service
PO Box 127
Moraga, CA 94556-0127
Phone: (510)376-6516

Palo Alto Management Group Inc.
2672 Bayshore Pky., Ste. 701
Mountain View, CA 94043
Phone: (415)968-4374
Fax: (415)968-4245
E-mail: mburwen@pamg.com

BizplanSource
1048 Irvine Ave., Ste. 621
Newport Beach, CA 92660
Free: Free: 888-253-0974
Fax: (800)859-8254
E-mail: info@bizplansource.com
Website: http://www.bizplansource.com
Adam Greengrass, President

The Market Connection
4020 Birch St., Ste. 203
Newport Beach, CA 92660
Phone: (714)731-6273
Fax: (714)833-0253

Muller Associates
PO Box 7264
Newport Beach, CA 92658
Phone: (714)646-1169
Fax: (714)646-1169

International Health Resources
PO Box 329
North San Juan, CA 95960-0329
Phone: (530)292-1266
Fax: (530)292-1243
Website: http://www.futureofhealthcare.com

NEXUS - Consultants to Management
PO Box 1531
Novato, CA 94948
Phone: (415)897-4400
Fax: (415)898-2252
E-mail: jimnexus@aol.com

Aerospcace.Org
PO Box 28831
Oakland, CA 94604-8831
Phone: (510)530-9169
Fax: (510)530-3411
Website: http://www.aerospace.org

Intelequest Corp.
722 Gailen Ave.
Palo Alto, CA 94303
Phone: (415)968-3443
Fax: (415)493-6954
E-mail: frits@iqix.com

McLaughlin & Associates
66 San Marino Cir.
Rancho Mirage, CA 92270
Phone: (760)321-2932
Fax: (760)328-2474
E-mail: jackmcla@msn.com

Carrera Consulting Group, a division of Maximus
2110 21st St., Ste. 400
Sacramento, CA 95818
Phone: (916)456-3300
Fax: (916)456-3306
E-mail: central@carreraconsulting.com
Website: http://www.carreraconsulting.com

Bay Area Tax Consultants and Bayhill Financial Consultants
1150 Bayhill Dr., Ste. 1150
San Bruno, CA 94066-3004
Phone: (415)952-8786
Fax: (415)588-4524
E-mail: baytax@compuserve.com
Website: http://www.baytax.com/

California Business Incubation Network
101 W Broadway, No. 480
San Diego, CA 92101
Phone: (619)237-0559
Fax: (619)237-0521

G.R. Gordetsky Consultants Inc.
11414 Windy Summit Pl.
San Diego, CA 92127
Phone: (619)487-4939
Fax: (619)487-5587
E-mail: gordet@pacbell.net

Freeman, Sullivan & Co.
131 Steuart St., Ste. 500
San Francisco, CA 94105
Phone: (415)777-0707
Free: (800)777-0737
Fax: (415)777-2420
Website: http://www.fsc-research.com

Ideas Unlimited
2151 California St., Ste. 7
San Francisco, CA 94115
Phone: (415)931-0641
Fax: (415)931-0880

Russell Miller Inc.
300 Montgomery St., Ste. 900
San Francisco, CA 94104
Phone: (415)956-7474
Fax: (415)398-0620
E-mail: rmi@pacbell.net
Website: http://www.rmisf.com

PKF Consulting
425 California St., Ste. 1650
San Francisco, CA 94104
Phone: (415)421-5378
Fax: (415)956-7708
E-mail: callahan@pkfc.com
Website: http://www.pkfonline.com

Welling & Woodard Inc.
1067 Broadway
San Francisco, CA 94133
Phone: (415)776-4500
Fax: (415)776-5067

Highland Associates
16174 Highland Dr.
San Jose, CA 95127
Phone: (408)272-7008
Fax: (408)272-4040

ORDIS Inc.
6815 Trinidad Dr.
San Jose, CA 95120-2056
Phone: (408)268-3321
Free: (800)446-7347
Fax: (408)268-3582
E-mail: ordis@ordis.com
Website: http://www.ordis.com

Stanford Resources Inc.
20 Great Oaks Blvd., Ste. 200
San Jose, CA 95119
Phone: (408)360-8400
Fax: (408)360-8410
E-mail: sales@stanfordsources.com
Website: http://
www.stanfordresources.com

Technology Properties Ltd. Inc.
PO Box 20250
San Jose, CA 95160
Phone: (408)243-9898
Fax: (408)296-6637
E-mail: sanjose@tplnet.com

Helfert Associates
1777 Borel Pl., Ste. 508
San Mateo, CA 94402-3514
Phone: (650)377-0540
Fax: (650)377-0472

Mykytyn Consulting Group Inc.
185 N Redwood Dr., Ste. 200
San Rafael, CA 94903
Phone: (415)491-1770
Fax: (415)491-1251
E-mail: info@mcgi.com
Website: http://www.mcgi.com

Omega Management Systems Inc.
3 Mount Darwin Ct.
San Rafael, CA 94903-1109
Phone: (415)499-1300
Fax: (415)492-9490
E-mail: omegamgt@ix.netcom.com

The Information Group Inc.
4675 Stevens Creek Blvd., Ste. 100
Santa Clara, CA 95051
Phone: (408)985-7877
Fax: (408)985-2945
E-mail: dvincent@tig-usa.com
Website: http://www.tig-usa.com

Cast Management Consultants
1620 26th St., Ste. 2040N
Santa Monica, CA 90404
Phone: (310)828-7511
Fax: (310)453-6831

Cuma Consulting Management
Box 724
Santa Rosa, CA 95402
Phone: (707)785-2477
Fax: (707)785-2478

The E-Myth Academy
131B Stony Cir., Ste. 2000
Santa Rosa, CA 95401
Phone: (707)569-5600
Free: (800)221-0266
Fax: (707)569-5700
E-mail: info@e-myth.com
Website: http://www.e-myth.com

Reilly, Connors & Ray
1743 Canyon Rd.
Spring Valley, CA 91977
Phone: (619)698-4808
Fax: (619)460-3892
E-mail: davidray@adnc.com

Management Consultants
Sunnyvale, CA 94087-4700
Phone: (408)773-0321

RJR Associates
1639 Lewiston Dr.
Sunnyvale, CA 94087
Phone: (408)737-7720
E-mail: bobroy@rjrassoc.com
Website: http://www.rjrassoc.com

Schwafel Associates
333 Cobalt Way, Ste. 21
Sunnyvale, CA 94085
Phone: (408)720-0649
Fax: (408)720-1796
E-mail: schwafel@ricochet.net
Website: http://www.patca.org

Staubs Business Services
23320 S Vermont Ave.
Torrance, CA 90502-2940
Phone: (310)830-9128
Fax: (310)830-9128
E-mail: Harry_L_Staubs@Lamg.com

Out of Your Mind...and Into the Marketplace
13381 White Sands Dr.
Tustin, CA 92780-4565
Phone: (714)544-0248
Free: (800)419-1513
Fax: (714)730-1414
E-mail: lpinson@aol.com
Website: http://www.business-plan.com

Independent Research Services
PO Box 2426
Van Nuys, CA 91404-2426
Phone: (818)993-3622

Ingman Company Inc.
7949 Woodley Ave., Ste. 120
Van Nuys, CA 91406-1232
Phone: (818)375-5027
Fax: (818)894-5001

Innovative Technology Associates
3639 E Harbor Blvd., Ste. 203E
Ventura, CA 93001
Phone: (805)650-9353

Grid Technology Associates
20404 Tufts Cir.
Walnut, CA 91789
Phone: (909)444-0922
Fax: (909)444-0922
E-mail: grid_technology@msn.com

Ridge Consultants Inc.
100 Pringle Ave., Ste. 580
Walnut Creek, CA 94596
Phone: (925)274-1990
Fax: (510)274-1956
E-mail: info@ridgecon.com
Website: http://www.ridgecon.com

Bell Springs Publishing
PO Box 1240
Willits, CA 95490
Phone: (707)459-6372
E-mail: bellsprings@sabernet
Website: http://www.bellsprings.com

Hutchinson Consulting and Appraisal
23245 Sylvan St., Ste. 103
Woodland Hills, CA 91367
Phone: (818)888-8175
Free: (800)977-7548
Fax: (818)888-8220
E-mail: r.f.hutchinson-cpa@worldnet.att.net

Colorado

Sam Boyer & Associates
4255 S Buckley Rd., No. 136
Aurora, CO 80013
Free: (800)785-0485
Fax: (303)766-8740
E-mail: samboyer@samboyer.com
Website: http://www.samboyer.com/

Ameriwest Business Consultants Inc.
PO Box 26266
Colorado Springs, CO 80936
Phone: (719)380-7096
Fax: (719)380-7096
E-mail: email@abchelp.com
Website: http://www.abchelp.com

GVNW Consulting Inc.
2270 La Montana Way
Colorado Springs, CO 80936
Phone: (719)594-5800
Fax: (719)594-5803
Website: http://www.gvnw.com

M-Squared Inc.
755 San Gabriel Pl.
Colorado Springs, CO 80906
Phone: (719)576-2554
Fax: (719)576-2554

Thornton Financial FNIC
1024 Centre Ave., Bldg. E
Fort Collins, CO 80526-1849
Phone: (970)221-2089
Fax: (970)484-5206

TenEyck Associates
1760 Cherryville Rd.
Greenwood Village, CO 80121-1503
Phone: (303)758-6129
Fax: (303)761-8286

Associated Enterprises Ltd.
13050 W Ceder Dr., Unit 11
Lakewood, CO 80228
Phone: (303)988-6695
Fax: (303)988-6739
E-mail: ael1@classic.msn.com

The Vincent Company Inc.
200 Union Blvd., Ste. 210
Lakewood, CO 80228
Phone: (303)989-7271
Free: (800)274-0733
Fax: (303)989-7570
E-mail: vincent@vincentco.com
Website: http://www.vincentco.com

Johnson & West Management Consultants Inc.
7612 S Logan Dr.
Littleton, CO 80122
Phone: (303)730-2810
Fax: (303)730-3219

Western Capital Holdings Inc.
10050 E Applwood Dr.
Parker, CO 80138
Phone: (303)841-1022
Fax: (303)770-1945

Connecticut

Stratman Group Inc.
40 Tower Ln.
Avon, CT 06001-4222
Phone: (860)677-2898
Free: (800)551-0499
Fax: (860)677-8210

Cowherd Consulting Group Inc.
106 Stephen Mather Rd.
Darien, CT 06820
Phone: (203)655-2150
Fax: (203)655-6427

Greenwich Associates
8 Greenwich Office Park
Greenwich, CT 06831-5149
Phone: (203)629-1200
Fax: (203)629-1229
E-mail: lisa@greenwich.com
Website: http://www.greenwich.com

Follow-up News
185 Pine St., Ste. 818
Manchester, CT 06040
Phone: (860)647-7542
Free: (800)708-0696
Fax: (860)646-6544
E-mail: Followupnews@aol.com

Lovins & Associates Consulting
309 Edwards St.
New Haven, CT 06511
Phone: (203)787-3367
Fax: (203)624-7599
E-mail: Alovinsphd@aol.com
Website: http://www.lovinsgroup.com

JC Ventures Inc.
4 Arnold St.
Old Greenwich, CT 06870-1203
Phone: (203)698-1990
Free: (800)698-1997
Fax: (203)698-2638

Charles L. Hornung Associates
52 Ned's Mountain Rd.
Ridgefield, CT 06877
Phone: (203)431-0297

Manus
100 Prospect St., S Tower
Stamford, CT 06901
Phone: (203)326-3880
Free: (800)445-0942
Fax: (203)326-3890
E-mail: manus1@aol.com
Website: http://www.RightManus.com

Delaware

Focus Marketing
61-7 Habor Dr.
Claymont, DE 19703
Phone: (302)793-3064

Daedalus Ventures Ltd.
PO Box 1474
Hockessin, DE 19707
Phone: (302)239-6758
Fax: (302)239-9991
E-mail: daedalus@mail.del.net

The Formula Group
PO Box 866
Hockessin, DE 19707
Phone: (302)456-0952
Fax: (302)456-1354
E-mail: formula@netaxs.com

Selden Enterprises Inc.
2502 Silverside Rd., Ste. 1
Wilmington, DE 19810-3740
Phone: (302)529-7113
Fax: (302)529-7442
E-mail: selden2@bellatlantic.net
Website: http://www.seldenenterprises.com

District of Columbia

Bruce W. McGee and Associates
7826 Eastern Ave. NW, Ste. 30
Washington, DC 20012
Phone: (202)726-7272
Fax: (202)726-2946

McManis Associates Inc.
1900 K St. NW, Ste. 700
Washington, DC 20006
Phone: (202)466-7680
Fax: (202)872-1898
Website: http://www.mcmanis-mmi.com

Smith, Dawson & Andrews Inc.
1000 Connecticut Ave., Ste. 302
Washington, DC 20036
Phone: (202)835-0740
Fax: (202)775-8526
E-mail: webmaster@sda-inc.com
Website: http://www.sda-inc.com

Florida

BackBone, Inc.
20404 Hacienda Court
Boca Raton, FL 33498
Phone: (561)470-0965
Fax: 516-908-4038
E-mail: BPlans@backboneinc.com
Website: http://www.backboneinc.com
Charles Epstein, President

Whalen & Associates Inc.
4255 Northwest 26 Ct.
Boca Raton, FL 33434
Phone: (561)241-5950
Fax: (561)241-7414
E-mail: drwhalen@ix.netcom.com

E.N. Rysso & Associates
180 Bermuda Petrel Ct.
Daytona Beach, FL 32119
Phone: (386)760-3028
E-mail: erysso@aol.com

Virtual Technocrats LLC
560 Lavers Circle, #146
Delray Beach, FL 33444
Phone: (561)265-3509
E-mail: josh@virtualtechnocrats.com; info@virtualtechnocrats.com
Website: http://www.virtualtechnocrats.com
Josh Eikov, Managing Director

Eric Sands Consulting Services
6193 Rock Island Rd., Ste. 412
Fort Lauderdale, FL 33319
Phone: (954)721-4767
Fax: (954)720-2815
E-mail: easands@aol.com
Website: http://www.ericsandsconsultig.com

Professional Planning Associates, Inc.
1975 E. Sunrise Blvd. Suite 607
Fort Lauderdale, FL 33304
Phone: (954)764-5204
Fax: 954-463-4172
E-mail: Mgoldstein@proplana.com
Website: http://proplana.com
Michael Goldstein, President

Host Media Corp.
3948 S 3rd St., Ste. 191
Jacksonville Beach, FL 32250
Phone: (904)285-3239
Fax: (904)285-5618
E-mail: msconsulting@compuserve.com
Website: http://www.mediaservicesgroup.com

William V. Hall
1925 Brickell, Ste. D-701
Miami, FL 33129
Phone: (305)856-9622
Fax: (305)856-4113
E-mail: williamvhall@compuserve.com

F.A. McGee Inc.
800 Claughton Island Dr., Ste. 401
Miami, FL 33131
Phone: (305)377-9123

Taxplan Inc.
Mirasol International Ctr.
2699 Collins Ave.
Miami Beach, FL 33140
Phone: (305)538-3303

T.C. Brown & Associates
8415 Excalibur Cir., Apt. B1
Naples, FL 34108
Phone: (941)594-1949
Fax: (941)594-0611
E-mail: tcater@naples.net.com

RLA International Consulting
713 Lagoon Dr.
North Palm Beach, FL 33408
Phone: (407)626-4258
Fax: (407)626-5772

Comprehensive Franchising Inc.
2465 Ridgecrest Ave.
Orange Park, FL 32065
Phone: (904)272-6567
Free: (800)321-6567
Fax: (904)272-6750
E-mail: theimp@cris.com
Website: http://www.franchise411.com

Hunter G. Jackson Jr. - Consulting Environmental Physicist
PO Box 618272
Orlando, FL 32861-8272
Phone: (407)295-4188
E-mail: hunterjackson@juno.com

F. Newton Parks
210 El Brillo Way
Palm Beach, FL 33480
Phone: (561)833-1727
Fax: (561)833-4541

Avery Business Development Services
2506 St. Michel Ct.
Ponte Vedra Beach, FL 32082
Phone: (904)285-6033
Fax: (904)285-6033

Strategic Business Planning Co.
PO Box 821006
South Florida, FL 33082-1006
Phone: (954)704-9100
Fax: (954)438-7333
E-mail: info@bizplan.com
Website: http://www.bizplan.com

Dufresne Consulting Group Inc.
10014 N Dale Mabry, Ste. 101
Tampa, FL 33618-4426
Phone: (813)264-4775
Fax: (813)264-9300
Website: http://www.dcgconsult.com

Agrippa Enterprises Inc.
PO Box 175
Venice, FL 34284-0175
Phone: (941)355-7876
E-mail: webservices@agrippa.com
Website: http://www.agrippa.com

Center for Simplified Strategic Planning Inc.
PO Box 3324
Vero Beach, FL 32964-3324
Phone: (561)231-3636
Fax: (561)231-1099
Website: http://www.cssp.com

Georgia

Marketing Spectrum Inc.
115 Perimeter Pl., Ste. 440
Atlanta, GA 30346
Phone: (770)395-7244
Fax: (770)393-4071

Business Ventures Corp.
1650 Oakbrook Dr., Ste. 405
Norcross, GA 30093
Phone: (770)729-8000
Fax: (770)729-8028

Informed Decisions Inc.
100 Falling Cheek
Sautee Nacoochee, GA 30571
Phone: (706)878-1905
Fax: (706)878-1802
E-mail: skylake@compuserve.com

Tom C. Davis & Associates, P.C.
3189 Perimeter Rd.
Valdosta, GA 31602
Phone: (912)247-9801
Fax: (912)244-7704
E-mail: mail@tcdcpa.com
Website: http://www.tcdcpa.com/

Illinois

TWD and Associates
431 S Patton
Arlington Heights, IL 60005
Phone: (847)398-6410
Fax: (847)255-5095
E-mail: tdoo@aol.com

Management Planning Associates Inc.
2275 Half Day Rd., Ste. 350
Bannockburn, IL 60015-1277
Phone: (847)945-2421
Fax: (847)945-2425

Phil Faris Associates
86 Old Mill Ct.
Barrington, IL 60010
Phone: (847)382-4888
Fax: (847)382-4890
E-mail: pfaris@meginsnet.net

Seven Continents Technology
787 Stonebridge
Buffalo Grove, IL 60089
Phone: (708)577-9653
Fax: (708)870-1220

Grubb & Blue Inc.
2404 Windsor Pl.
Champaign, IL 61820
Phone: (217)366-0052
Fax: (217)356-0117

ACE Accounting Service Inc.
3128 N Bernard St.
Chicago, IL 60618
Phone: (773)463-7854
Fax: (773)463-7854

AON Consulting Worldwide
200 E Randolph St., 10th Fl.
Chicago, IL 60601
Phone: (312)381-4800
Free: (800)438-6487
Fax: (312)381-0240
Website: http://www.aon.com

FMS Consultants
5801 N Sheridan Rd., Ste. 3D
Chicago, IL 60660
Phone: (773)561-7362
Fax: (773)561-6274

Grant Thornton
800 1 Prudential Plz.
130 E Randolph St.
Chicago, IL 60601
Phone: (312)856-0001
Fax: (312)861-1340
E-mail: gtinfo@gt.com
Website: http://
www.grantthornton.com

Kingsbury International Ltd.
5341 N Glenwood Ave.
Chicago, IL 60640
Phone: (773)271-3030
Fax: (773)728-7080
E-mail: jetlag@mcs.com
Website: http://www.kingbiz.com

MacDougall & Blake Inc.
1414 N Wells St., Ste. 311
Chicago, IL 60610-1306
Phone: (312)587-3330
Fax: (312)587-3699
E-mail: jblake@compuserve.com

James C. Osburn Ltd.
6445 N. Western Ave., Ste. 304
Chicago, IL 60645
Phone: (773)262-4428
Fax: (773)262-6755
E-mail: osburnltd@aol.com

Tarifero & Tazewell Inc.
211 S Clark
Chicago, IL 60690
Phone: (312)665-9714
Fax: (312)665-9716

Human Energy Design Systems
620 Roosevelt Dr.
Edwardsville, IL 62025
Phone: (618)692-0258
Fax: (618)692-0819

China Business Consultants Group
931 Dakota Cir.
Naperville, IL 60563
Phone: (630)778-7992
Fax: (630)778-7915
E-mail: cbcq@aol.com

Center for Workforce Effectiveness
500 Skokie Blvd., Ste. 222
Northbrook, IL 60062
Phone: (847)559-8777
Fax: (847)559-8778
E-mail: office@cwelink.com
Website: http://www.cwelink.com

Smith Associates
1320 White Mountain Dr.
Northbrook, IL 60062
Phone: (847)480-7200
Fax: (847)480-9828

Francorp Inc.
20200 Governors Dr.
Olympia Fields, IL 60461
Phone: (708)481-2900
Free: (800)372-6244
Fax: (708)481-5885
E-mail: francorp@aol.com
Website: http://www.francorpinc.com

Camber Business Strategy Consultants
1010 S Plum Tree Ct
Palatine, IL 60078-0986
Phone: (847)202-0101
Fax: (847)705-7510
E-mail: camber@ameritech.net

Partec Enterprise Group
5202 Keith Dr.
Richton Park, IL 60471
Phone: (708)503-4047
Fax: (708)503-9468

Rockford Consulting Group Ltd.
Century Plz., Ste. 206
7210 E State St.
Rockford, IL 61108
Phone: (815)229-2900
Free: (800)667-7495
Fax: (815)229-2612
E-mail:
rligus@RockfordConsulting.com

Website: http://
www.RockfordConsulting.com

RSM McGladrey Inc.
1699 E Woodfield Rd., Ste. 300
Schaumburg, IL 60173-4969
Phone: (847)413-6900
Fax: (847)517-7067
Website: http://
www.rsmmcgladrey.com

A.D. Star Consulting
320 Euclid
Winnetka, IL 60093
Phone: (847)446-7827
Fax: (847)446-7827
E-mail: startwo@worldnet.att.net

Indiana

Modular Consultants Inc.
3109 Crabtree Ln.
Elkhart, IN 46514
Phone: (219)264-5761
Fax: (219)264-5761
E-mail: sasabo5313@aol.com

Midwest Marketing Research
PO Box 1077
Goshen, IN 46527
Phone: (219)533-0548
Fax: (219)533-0540
E-mail: 103365.654@compuserve

Ketchum Consulting Group
8021 Knue Rd., Ste. 112
Indianapolis, IN 46250
Phone: (317)845-5411
Fax: (317)842-9941

MDI Management Consulting
1519 Park Dr.
Munster, IN 46321
Phone: (219)838-7909
Fax: (219)838-7909

Iowa

McCord Consulting Group Inc.
4533 Pine View Dr. NE
PO Box 11024
Cedar Rapids, IA 52410
Phone: (319)378-0077
Fax: (319)378-1577
E-mail: smmccord@hom.com
Website: http://
www.mccordgroup.com

Management Solutions L.C.
3815 Lincoln Pl. Dr.
Des Moines, IA 50312
Phone: (515)277-6408
Fax: (515)277-3506
E-mail: wasunimers@uswest.net

Grandview Marketing
15 Red Bridge Dr.
Sioux City, IA 51104
Phone: (712)239-3122
Fax: (712)258-7578
E-mail: eandrews@pionet.net

Kansas

Assessments in Action
513A N Mur-Len
Olathe, KS 66062
Phone: (913)764-6270
Free: (888)548-1504
Fax: (913)764-6495
E-mail: lowdene@qni.com
Website: http://www.assessments-in-action.com

Maine

Edgemont Enterprises
PO Box 8354
Portland, ME 04104
Phone: (207)871-8964
Fax: (207)871-8964

Pan Atlantic Consultants
5 Milk St.
Portland, ME 04101
Phone: (207)871-8622
Fax: (207)772-4842
E-mail: pmurphy@maine.rr.com
Website: http://www.panatlantic.net

Maryland

Clemons & Associates Inc.
5024-R Campbell Blvd.
Baltimore, MD 21236
Phone: (410)931-8100
Fax: (410)931-8111
E-mail: info@clemonsmgmt.com
Website: http://
www.clemonsmgmt.com

Imperial Group Ltd.
305 Washington Ave., Ste. 204
Baltimore, MD 21204-6009
Phone: (410)337-8500
Fax: (410)337-7641

Leadership Institute
3831 Yolando Rd.
Baltimore, MD 21218
Phone: (410)366-9111
Fax: (410)243-8478
E-mail: behconsult@aol.com

Burdeshaw Associates Ltd.
4701 Sangamore Rd.
Bethesda, MD 20816-2508
Phone: (301)229-5800
Fax: (301)229-5045
E-mail: jstacy@burdeshaw.com
Website: http://www.burdeshaw.com

Michael E. Cohen
5225 Pooks Hill Rd., Ste. 1119 S
Bethesda, MD 20814
Phone: (301)530-5738
Fax: (301)530-2988
E-mail: mecohen@crosslink.net

World Development Group Inc.
5272 River Rd., Ste. 650
Bethesda, MD 20816-1405
Phone: (301)652-1818
Fax: (301)652-1250
E-mail: wdg@has.com
Website: http://www.worlddg.com

Swartz Consulting
PO Box 4301
Crofton, MD 21114-4301
Phone: (301)262-6728

Software Solutions International Inc.
9633 Duffer Way
Gaithersburg, MD 20886
Phone: (301)330-4136
Fax: (301)330-4136

Strategies Inc.
8 Park Center Ct., Ste. 200
Owings Mills, MD 21117
Phone: (410)363-6669
Fax: (410)363-1231
E-mail: strategies@strat1.com
Website: http://www.strat1.com

Hammer Marketing Resources
179 Inverness Rd.
Severna Park, MD 21146
Phone: (410)544-9191
Fax: (305)675-3277
E-mail: info@gohammer.com
Website: http://www.gohammer.com

Andrew Sussman & Associates
13731 Kretsinger
Smithsburg, MD 21783
Phone: (301)824-2943
Fax: (301)824-2943

Massachusetts

Geibel Marketing and Public Relations
PO Box 611
Belmont, MA 02478-0005
Phone: (617)484-8285
Fax: (617)489-3567
E-mail: jgeibel@geibelpr.com
Website: http://www.geibelpr.com

Bain & Co.
2 Copley Pl.
Boston, MA 02116
Phone: (617)572-2000
Fax: (617)572-2427
E-mail: corporate.inquiries@bain.com
Website: http://www.bain.com

Mehr & Co.
62 Kinnaird St.
Cambridge, MA 02139
Phone: (617)876-3311
Fax: (617)876-3023
E-mail: mehrco@aol.com

Monitor Company Inc.
2 Canal Park
Cambridge, MA 02141
Phone: (617)252-2000
Fax: (617)252-2100
Website: http://www.monitor.com

Information & Research Associates
PO Box 3121
Framingham, MA 01701
Phone: (508)788-0784

Walden Consultants Ltd.
252 Pond St.
Hopkinton, MA 01748
Phone: (508)435-4882
Fax: (508)435-3971
Website: http://www.waldenconsultants.com

Jeffrey D. Marshall
102 Mitchell Rd.
Ipswich, MA 01938-1219
Phone: (508)356-1113
Fax: (508)356-2989

Consulting Resources Corp.
6 Northbrook Park
Lexington, MA 02420
Phone: (781)863-1222
Fax: (781)863-1441
E-mail: res@consultingresources.net
Website: http://www.consultingresources.net

Planning Technologies Group L.L.C.
92 Hayden Ave.
Lexington, MA 02421
Phone: (781)778-4678
Fax: (781)861-1099
E-mail: ptg@plantech.com
Website: http://www.plantech.com

Kalba International Inc.
23 Sandy Pond Rd.
Lincoln, MA 01773
Phone: (781)259-9589
Fax: (781)259-1460
E-mail: info@kalbainternational.com
Website: http://www.kalbainternational.com

VMB Associates Inc.
115 Ashland St.
Melrose, MA 02176
Phone: (781)665-0623
Fax: (425)732-7142
E-mail: vmbinc@aol.com

The Company Doctor
14 Pudding Stone Ln.
Mendon, MA 01756
Phone: (508)478-1747
Fax: (508)478-0520

Data and Strategies Group Inc.
190 N Main St.
Natick, MA 01760
Phone: (508)653-9990
Fax: (508)653-7799
E-mail: dsginc@dsggroup.com
Website: http://www.dsggroup.com

The Enterprise Group
73 Parker Rd.
Needham, MA 02494
Phone: (617)444-6631
Fax: (617)433-9991
E-mail: lsacco@world.std.com
Website: http://www.enterprise-group.com

PSMJ Resources Inc.
10 Midland Ave.
Newton, MA 02458
Phone: (617)965-0055
Free: (800)537-7765
Fax: (617)965-5152
E-mail: psmj@tiac.net
Website: http://www.psmj.com

Scheur Management Group Inc.
255 Washington St., Ste. 100
Newton, MA 02458-1611
Phone: (617)969-7500
Fax: (617)969-7508
E-mail: smgnow@scheur.com
Website: http://www.scheur.com

I.E.E.E., Boston Section
240 Bear Hill Rd., 202B
Waltham, MA 02451-1017
Phone: (781)890-5294
Fax: (781)890-5290

Business Planning and Consulting Services
20 Beechwood Ter.
Wellesley, MA 02482
Phone: (617)237-9151
Fax: (617)237-9151

Michigan

Walter Frederick Consulting
1719 South Blvd.
Ann Arbor, MI 48104
Phone: (313)662-4336
Fax: (313)769-7505

Fox Enterprises
6220 W Freeland Rd.
Freeland, MI 48623
Phone: (517)695-9170
Fax: (517)695-9174
E-mail: foxjw@concentric.net
Website: http://www.cris.com/~foxjw

G.G.W. and Associates
1213 Hampton
Jackson, MI 49203
Phone: (517)782-2255
Fax: (517)782-2255

Altamar Group Ltd.
6810 S Cedar, Ste. 2-B
Lansing, MI 48911
Phone: (517)694-0910
Free: (800)443-2627
Fax: (517)694-1377

Sheffieck Consultants Inc.
23610 Greening Dr.
Novi, MI 48375-3130
Phone: (248)347-3545
Fax: (248)347-3530
E-mail: cfsheff@concentric.net

Rehmann, Robson PC
5800 Gratiot
Saginaw, MI 48605

Phone: (517)799-9580
Fax: (517)799-0227
Website: http://www.rrpc.com

Francis & Co.
17200 W 10 Mile Rd., Ste. 207
Southfield, MI 48075
Phone: (248)559-7600
Fax: (248)559-5249

Private Ventures Inc.
16000 W 9 Mile Rd., Ste. 504
Southfield, MI 48075
Phone: (248)569-1977
Free: (800)448-7614
Fax: (248)569-1838
E-mail: pventuresi@aol.com

JGK Associates
14464 Kerner Dr.
Sterling Heights, MI 48313
Phone: (810)247-9055
Fax: (248)822-4977
E-mail: kozlowski@home.com

Minnesota

Health Fitness Corp.
3500 W 80th St., Ste. 130
Bloomington, MN 55431
Phone: (612)831-6830
Fax: (612)831-7264

Consatech Inc.
PO Box 1047
Burnsville, MN 55337
Phone: (612)953-1088
Fax: (612)435-2966

Robert F. Knotek
14960 Ironwood Ct.
Eden Prairie, MN 55346
Phone: (612)949-2875

DRI Consulting
7715 Stonewood Ct.
Edina, MN 55439
Phone: (612)941-9656
Fax: (612)941-2693
E-mail: dric@dric.com
Website: http://www.dric.com

Markin Consulting
12072 87th Pl. N
Maple Grove, MN 55369
Phone: (612)493-3568
Fax: (612)493-5744
E-mail:
markin@markinconsulting.com
Website: http://
www.markinconsulting.com

Minnesota Cooperation Office for
Small Business & Job Creation Inc.
5001 W 80th St., Ste. 825
Minneapolis, MN 55437
Phone: (612)830-1230
Fax: (612)830-1232
E-mail: mncoop@msn.com
Website: http://www.mnco.org

Enterprise Consulting Inc.
PO Box 1111
Minnetonka, MN 55345
Phone: (612)949-5909
Fax: (612)906-3965

Amdahl International
724 1st Ave. SW
Rochester, MN 55902
Phone: (507)252-0402
Fax: (507)252-0402
E-mail: amdahl@best-service.com
Website: http://www.wp.com/
amdahl_int

Power Systems Research
1365 Corporate Center Curve, 2nd Fl.
St. Paul, MN 55121
Phone: (612)905-8400
Free: (888)625-8612
Fax: (612)454-0760
E-mail: Barb@Powersys.com
Website: http://www.powersys.com

Missouri

Business Planning and Development
Corp.
4030 Charlotte St.
Kansas City, MO 64110
Phone: (816)753-0495
E-mail: humph@bpdev.demon.co.uk
Website: http://
www.bpdev.demon.co.uk

CFO Service
10336 Donoho
St. Louis, MO 63131
Phone: (314)750-2940
E-mail: jskae@cfoservice.com
Website: http://www.cfoservice.com

Nebraska

International Management Consulting
Group Inc.
1309 Harlan Dr., Ste. 205
Bellevue, NE 68005
Phone: (402)291-4545
Free: (800)665-IMCG
Fax: (402)291-4343
E-mail: imcg@neonramp.com
Website: http://
www.mgtconsulting.com

Heartland Management Consulting
Group
1904 Barrington Pky.
Papillion, NE 68046
Phone: (402)339-2387
Fax: (402)339-1319

Nevada

The DuBois Group
865 Tahoe Blvd., Ste. 108
Incline Village, NV 89451
Phone: (775)832-0550
Free: (800)375-2935
Fax: (775)832-0556
E-mail: DuBoisGrp@aol.com

New Hampshire

Wolff Consultants
10 Buck Rd.
Hanover, NH 03755
Phone: (603)643-6015

BPT Consulting Associates Ltd.
12 Parmenter Rd., Ste. B-6
Londonderry, NH 03053
Phone: (603)437-8484
Free: (888)278-0030
Fax: (603)434-5388
E-mail: bptcons@tiac.net
Website: http://
www.bptconsulting.com

New Jersey

Bedminster Group Inc.
1170 Rte. 22 E
Bridgewater, NJ 08807
Phone: (908)500-4155
Fax: (908)766-0780
E-mail: info@bedminstergroup.com
Website: http://
www.bedminstergroup.com

Delta Planning Inc.
PO Box 425
Denville, NJ 07834
Phone: (913)625-1742
Free: (800)672-0762
Fax: (973)625-3531

E-mail: DeltaP@worldnet.att.net
Website: http://deltaplanning.com

Kumar Associates Inc.
1004 Cumbermeade Rd.
Fort Lee, NJ 07024
Phone: (201)224-9480
Fax: (201)585-2343
E-mail: mail@kumarassociates.com
Website: http://kumarassociates.com

John Hall & Company Inc.
PO Box 187
Glen Ridge, NJ 07028
Phone: (973)680-4449
Fax: (973)680-4581
E-mail: jhcompany@aol.com

Market Focus
PO Box 402
Maplewood, NJ 07040
Phone: (973)378-2470
Fax: (973)378-2470
E-mail: mcss66@marketfocus.com

Vanguard Communications Corp.
100 American Rd.
Morris Plains, NJ 07950
Phone: (973)605-8000
Fax: (973)605-8329
Website: http://www.vanguard.net/

ConMar International Ltd.
1901 US Hwy. 130
North Brunswick, NJ 08902
Phone: (732)940-8347
Fax: (732)274-1199

KLW New Products
156 Cedar Dr.
Old Tappan, NJ 07675
Phone: (201)358-1300
Fax: (201)664-2594
E-mail: lrlarsen@usa.net
Website: http://
www.klwnewproducts.com

PA Consulting Group
315A Enterprise Dr.
Plainsboro, NJ 08536
Phone: (609)936-8300
Fax: (609)936-8811
E-mail: info@paconsulting.com
Website: http://www.pa-
consulting.com

Aurora Marketing Management Inc.
66 Witherspoon St., Ste. 600
Princeton, NJ 08542
Phone: (908)904-1125
Fax: (908)359-1108
E-mail: aurora2@voicenet.com
Website: http://
www.auroramarketing.net

Smart Business Supersite
88 Orchard Rd., CN-5219
Princeton, NJ 08543
Phone: (908)321-1924
Fax: (908)321-5156
E-mail: irv@smartbiz.com
Website: http://www.smartbiz.com

Tracelin Associates
1171 Main St., Ste. 6K
Rahway, NJ 07065
Phone: (732)381-3288

Schkeeper Inc.
130-6 Bodman Pl.
Red Bank, NJ 07701
Phone: (732)219-1965
Fax: (732)530-3703

Henry Branch Associates
2502 Harmon Cove Twr.
Secaucus, NJ 07094
Phone: (201)866-2008
Fax: (201)601-0101
E-mail: hbranch161@home.com

Robert Gibbons & Company Inc.
46 Knoll Rd.
Tenafly, NJ 07670-1050
Phone: (201)871-3933
Fax: (201)871-2173
E-mail: crisisbob@aol.com

PMC Management Consultants Inc.
6 Thistle Ln.
Three Bridges, NJ 08887-0332
Phone: (908)788-1014
Free: (800)PMC-0250
Fax: (908)806-7287
E-mail: int@pmc-management.com
Website: http://www.pmc-
management.com

R.W. Bankart & Associates
20 Valley Ave., Ste. D-2
Westwood, NJ 07675-3607
Phone: (201)664-7672

New Mexico

Vondle & Associates Inc.
4926 Calle de Tierra, NE
Albuquerque, NM 87111
Phone: (505)292-8961
Fax: (505)296-2790
E-mail: vondle@aol.com

InfoNewMexico
2207 Black Hills Rd., NE
Rio Rancho, NM 87124
Phone: (505)891-2462
Fax: (505)896-8971

New York

Powers Research and Training
Institute
PO Box 78
Bayville, NY 11709
Phone: (516)628-2250
Fax: (516)628-2252
E-mail:
powercocch@compuserve.com
Website: http://
www.nancypowers.com

Consortium House
296 Wittenberg Rd.
Bearsville, NY 12409
Phone: (845)679-8867
Fax: (845)679-9248
E-mail: eugenegs@aol.com
Website: http://www.chpub.com

Progressive Finance Corp.
3549 Tiemann Ave.
Bronx, NY 10469
Phone: (718)405-9029
Free: (800)225-8381
Fax: (718)405-1170

Wave Hill Associates Inc.
2621 Palisade Ave., Ste. 15-C
Bronx, NY 10463
Phone: (718)549-7368
Fax: (718)601-9670
E-mail: pepper@compuserve.com

Management Insight
96 Arlington Rd.
Buffalo, NY 14221
Phone: (716)631-3319
Fax: (716)631-0203
E-mail:
michalski@foodserviceinsight.com
Website: http://
www.foodserviceinsight.com

Samani International Enterprises,
Marions Panyaught Consultancy
2028 Parsons
Flushing, NY 11357-3436
Phone: (917)287-8087

Fax: (800)873-8939
E-mail: vjp2@biostrategist.com
Website: http://
www.biostrategist.com

Marketing Resources Group
71-58 Austin St.
Forest Hills, NY 11375
Phone: (718)261-8882

Mangabay Business Plans & Development
Subsidiary of Innis Asset Allocation
125-10 Queens Blvd., Ste. 2202
Kew Gardens, NY 11415
Phone: (905)527-1947
Fax: 509-472-1935
E-mail: mangabay@mangabay.com
Website: http://www.mangabay.com
Lee Toh, Managing Partner

ComputerEase Co.
1301 Monmouth Ave.
Lakewood, NY 08701
Phone: (212)406-9464
Fax: (914)277-5317
E-mail: crawfordc@juno.com

Boice Dunham Group
30 W 13th St.
New York, NY 10011
Phone: (212)924-2200
Fax: (212)924-1108

Elizabeth Capen
27 E 95th St.
New York, NY 10128
Phone: (212)427-7654
Fax: (212)876-3190

Haver Analytics
60 E 42nd St., Ste. 2424
New York, NY 10017
Phone: (212)986-9300
Fax: (212)986-5857
E-mail: data@haver.com
Website: http://www.haver.com

The Jordan, Edmiston Group Inc.
150 E 52nd Ave., 18th Fl.
New York, NY 10022
Phone: (212)754-0710
Fax: (212)754-0337

KPMG International
345 Park Ave.
New York, NY 10154-0102
Phone: (212)758-9700
Fax: (212)758-9819
Website: http://www.kpmg.com

Mahoney Cohen Consulting Corp.
111 W 40th St., 12th Fl.
New York, NY 10018
Phone: (212)490-8000
Fax: (212)790-5913

Management Practice Inc.
342 Madison Ave.
New York, NY 10173-1230
Phone: (212)867-7948
Fax: (212)972-5188
Website: http://www.mpiweb.com

Moseley Associates Inc.
342 Madison Ave., Ste. 1414
New York, NY 10016
Phone: (212)213-6673
Fax: (212)687-1520

Practice Development Counsel
60 Sutton Pl. S
New York, NY 10022
Phone: (212)593-1549
Fax: (212)980-7940
E-mail: pwhaserot@pdcounsel.com
Website: http://www.pdcounsel.com

Unique Value International Inc.
575 Madison Ave., 10th Fl.
New York, NY 10022-1304
Phone: (212)605-0590
Fax: (212)605-0589

The Van Tulleken Co.
126 E 56th St.
New York, NY 10022
Phone: (212)355-1390
Fax: (212)755-3061
E-mail: newyork@vantulleken.com

Vencon Management Inc.
301 W 53rd St.
New York, NY 10019
Phone: (212)581-8787
Fax: (212)397-4126
Website: http://www.venconinc.com

Werner International Inc.
55 E 52nd, 29th Fl.
New York, NY 10055
Phone: (212)909-1260
Fax: (212)909-1273
E-mail: richard.downing@rgh.com
Website: http://www.wernertex.com

Zimmerman Business Consulting Inc.
44 E 92nd St., Ste. 5-B
New York, NY 10128
Phone: (212)860-3107
Fax: (212)860-7730
E-mail: ljzzbci@aol.com
Website: http://www.zbcinc.com

Overton Financial
7 Allen Rd.
Peekskill, NY 10566
Phone: (914)737-4649
Fax: (914)737-4696

Stromberg Consulting
2500 Westchester Ave.
Purchase, NY 10577
Phone: (914)251-1515
Fax: (914)251-1562
E-mail:
strategy@stromberg_consulting.com
Website: http://
www.stromberg_consulting.com

Innovation Management Consulting Inc.
209 Dewitt Rd.
Syracuse, NY 13214-2006
Phone: (315)425-5144
Fax: (315)445-8989
E-mail: missonneb@axess.net

M. Clifford Agress
891 Fulton St.
Valley Stream, NY 11580
Phone: (516)825-8955
Fax: (516)825-8955

Destiny Kinal Marketing Consultancy
105 Chemung St.
Waverly, NY 14892
Phone: (607)565-8317
Fax: (607)565-4083

Valutis Consulting Inc.
5350 Main St., Ste. 7
Williamsville, NY 14221-5338
Phone: (716)634-2553
Fax: (716)634-2554
E-mail: valutis@localnet.com
Website: http://
www.valutisconsulting.com

North Carolina

Best Practices L.L.C.
6320 Quadrangle Dr., Ste. 200
Chapel Hill, NC 27514
Phone: (919)403-0251
Fax: (919)403-0144
E-mail: best@best:in/class
Website: http://www.best-in-class.com

Norelli & Co.
Bank of America Corporate Ctr.
100 N Tyron St., Ste. 5160
Charlotte, NC 28202-4000
Phone: (704)376-5484
Fax: (704)376-5485
E-mail: consult@norelli.com
Website: http://www.norelli.com

North Dakota

Center for Innovation
4300 Dartmouth Dr.
PO Box 8372
Grand Forks, ND 58202
Phone: (701)777-3132
Fax: (701)777-2339
E-mail: bruce@innovators.net
Website: http://www.innovators.net

Ohio

Transportation Technology Services
208 Harmon Rd.
Aurora, OH 44202
Phone: (330)562-3596

Empro Systems Inc.
4777 Red Bank Expy., Ste. 1
Cincinnati, OH 45227-1542
Phone: (513)271-2042
Fax: (513)271-2042

Alliance Management International Ltd.
1440 Windrow Ln.
Cleveland, OH 44147-3200
Phone: (440)838-1922
Fax: (440)838-0979
E-mail: bgruss@amiltd.com
Website: http://www.amiltd.com

Bozell Kamstra Public Relations
1301 E 9th St., Ste. 3400
Cleveland, OH 44114
Phone: (216)623-1511
Fax: (216)623-1501
E-mail:
jfeniger@cleveland.bozellkamstra.com
Website: http://
www.bozellkamstra.com

Cory Dillon Associates
111 Schreyer Pl. E
Columbus, OH 43214
Phone: (614)262-8211
Fax: (614)262-3806

Holcomb Gallagher Adams
300 Marconi, Ste. 303
Columbus, OH 43215
Phone: (614)221-3343
Fax: (614)221-3367
E-mail: riadams@acme.freenet.oh.us

Young & Associates
PO Box 711
Kent, OH 44240
Phone: (330)678-0524
Free: (800)525-9775
Fax: (330)678-6219
E-mail: online@younginc.com
Website: http://www.younginc.com

Robert A. Westman & Associates
8981 Inversary Dr. SE
Warren, OH 44484-2551
Phone: (330)856-4149
Fax: (330)856-2564

Oklahoma

Innovative Partners L.L.C.
4900 Richmond Sq., Ste. 100
Oklahoma City, OK 73118
Phone: (405)840-0033
Fax: (405)843-8359
E-mail: ipartners@juno.com

Oregon

INTERCON - The International Converting Institute
5200 Badger Rd.
Crooked River Ranch, OR 97760
Phone: (541)548-1447
Fax: (541)548-1618
E-mail:
johnbowler@crookedriverranch.com

Talbott ARM
HC 60, Box 5620
Lakeview, OR 97630
Phone: (541)635-8587
Fax: (503)947-3482

Management Technology Associates Ltd.
2768 SW Sherwood Dr, Ste. 105
Portland, OR 97201-2251
Phone: (503)224-5220
Fax: (503)224-5334
E-mail: lcuster@mta-ltd.com
Website: http://www.mgmt-tech.com

Pennsylvania

Healthscope Inc.
400 Lancaster Ave.
Devon, PA 19333
Phone: (610)687-6199
Fax: (610)687-6376
E-mail: health@voicenet.com
Website: http://www.healthscope.net/

Elayne Howard & Associates Inc.
3501 Masons Mill Rd., Ste. 501
Huntingdon Valley, PA 19006-3509
Phone: (215)657-9550

GRA Inc.
115 West Ave., Ste. 201
Jenkintown, PA 19046
Phone: (215)884-7500
Fax: (215)884-1385
E-mail: gramail@gra-inc.com
Website: http://www.gra-inc.com

Mifflin County Industrial Development Corp.
Mifflin County Industrial Plz.
6395 SR 103 N
Bldg. 50
Lewistown, PA 17044
Phone: (717)242-0393
Fax: (717)242-1842
E-mail: mcide@acsworld.net

Autech Products
1289 Revere Rd.
Morrisville, PA 19067
Phone: (215)493-3759
Fax: (215)493-9791
E-mail: autech4@yahoo.com

Advantage Associates
434 Avon Dr.
Pittsburgh, PA 15228
Phone: (412)343-1558
Fax: (412)362-1684
E-mail: ecocba1@aol.com

Regis J. Sheehan & Associates
Pittsburgh, PA 15220
Phone: (412)279-1207

James W. Davidson Company Inc.
23 Forest View Rd.
Wallingford, PA 19086
Phone: (610)566-1462

Puerto Rico

Diego Chevere & Co.
Metro Parque 7, Ste. 204

Metro Office
Caparra Heights, PR 00920
Phone: (787)774-9595
Fax: (787)774-9566
E-mail: dcco@coqui.net

Manuel L. Porrata and Associates
898 Munoz Rivera Ave., Ste. 201
San Juan, PR 00927
Phone: (787)765-2140
Fax: (787)754-3285
E-mail:
m_porrata@manuelporrata.com
Website: http://manualporrata.com

South Carolina

Aquafood Business Associates
PO Box 13267
Charleston, SC 29422
Phone: (843)795-9506
Fax: (843)795-9477
E-mail: rraba@aol.com

Profit Associates Inc.
PO Box 38026
Charleston, SC 29414
Phone: (803)763-5718
Fax: (803)763-5719
E-mail: bobrog@awod.com
Website: http://www.awod.com/gallery/business/proasc

Strategic Innovations International
12 Executive Ct.
Lake Wylie, SC 29710
Phone: (803)831-1225
Fax: (803)831-1177
E-mail: stratinnov@aol.com
Website: http://www.strategicinnovations.com

Minus Stage
Box 4436
Rock Hill, SC 29731
Phone: (803)328-0705
Fax: (803)329-9948

Tennessee

Daniel Petchers & Associates
8820 Fernwood CV
Germantown, TN 38138
Phone: (901)755-9896

Business Choices
1114 Forest Harbor, Ste. 300
Hendersonville, TN 37075-9646
Phone: (615)822-8692
Free: (800)737-8382
Fax: (615)822-8692
E-mail: bz-ch@juno.com

RCFA Healthcare Management Services L.L.C.
9648 Kingston Pke., Ste. 8
Knoxville, TN 37922
Phone: (865)531-0176
Free: (800)635-4040
Fax: (865)531-0722
E-mail: info@rcfa.com
Website: http://www.rcfa.com

Growth Consultants of America
3917 Trimble Rd.
Nashville, TN 37215
Phone: (615)383-0550
Fax: (615)269-8940
E-mail: 70244.451@compuserve.com

Texas

Integrated Cost Management Systems Inc.
2261 Brookhollow Plz. Dr., Ste. 104
Arlington, TX 76006
Phone: (817)633-2873
Fax: (817)633-3781
E-mail: abm@icms.net
Website: http://www.icms.net

Lori Williams
1000 Leslie Ct.
Arlington, TX 76012
Phone: (817)459-3934
Fax: (817)459-3934

Business Resource Software Inc.
2013 Wells Branch Pky., Ste. 305
Austin, TX 78728
Free: (800)423-1228
Fax: (512)251-4401
E-mail: info@brs-inc.com
Website: http://www.brs-inc.com

Erisa Adminstrative Services Inc.
12325 Hymeadow Dr., Bldg. 4
Austin, TX 78750-1847
Phone: (512)250-9020
Fax: (512)250-9487
Website: http://www.cserisa.com

R. Miller Hicks & Co.
1011 W 11th St.
Austin, TX 78703
Phone: (512)477-7000
Fax: (512)477-9697
E-mail: millerhicks@rmhicks.com
Website: http://www.rmhicks.com

Pragmatic Tactics Inc.
3303 Westchester Ave.
College Station, TX 77845
Phone: (409)696-5294
Free: (800)570-5294
Fax: (409)696-4994
E-mail: ptactics@aol.com
Website: http://www.ptatics.com

Perot Systems
12404 Park Central Dr.
Dallas, TX 75251
Phone: (972)340-5000
Free: (800)688-4333
Fax: (972)455-4100
E-mail: corp.comm@ps.net
Website: http://www.perotsystems.com

ReGENERATION Partners
3838 Oak Lawn Ave.
Dallas, TX 75219
Phone: (214)559-3999
Free: (800)406-1112
E-mail: info@regeneration-partner.com
Website: http://www.regeneration-partners.com

High Technology Associates - Division of Global Technologies Inc.
1775 St. James Pl., Ste. 105
Houston, TX 77056
Phone: (713)963-9300
Fax: (713)963-8341
E-mail: hta@infohwy.com

MasterCOM
103 Thunder Rd.
Kerrville, TX 78028
Phone: (830)895-7990
Fax: (830)443-3428
E-mail:
jmstubblefield@mastertraining.com
Website: http://www.mastertraining.com

PROTEC
4607 Linden Pl.
Pearland, TX 77584
Phone: (281)997-9872
Fax: (281)997-9895
E-mail: p.oman@ix.netcom.com

Bastian Public Relations
614 San Dizier
San Antonio, TX 78232
Phone: (210)404-1839
E-mail: info@bastianpr.com

Website: http://www.bastianpr.com
Lisa Bastian CBC

Business Strategy Development Consultants
PO Box 690365
San Antonio, TX 78269
Phone: (210)696-8000
Free: (800)927-BSDC
Fax: (210)696-8000

Tom Welch, CPC
6900 San Pedro Ave., Ste. 147
San Antonio, TX 78216-6207
Phone: (210)737-7022
Fax: (210)737-7022
E-mail: bplan@iamerica.net
Website: http://www.moneywords.com

Utah

Business Management Resource
PO Box 521125
Salt Lake City, UT 84152-1125
Phone: (801)272-4668
Fax: (801)277-3290
E-mail: pingfong@worldnet.att.net

Virginia

Tindell Associates
209 Oxford Ave.
Alexandria, VA 22301
Phone: (703)683-0109
Fax: 703-783-0219
E-mail: scott@tindell.net
Website: http://www.tindell.net
Scott Lockett, President

Elliott B. Jaffa
2530-B S Walter Reed Dr.
Arlington, VA 22206
Phone: (703)931-0040
E-mail: thetrainingdoctor@excite.com
Website: http://www.tregistry.com/jaffa.htm

Koach Enterprises - USA
5529 N 18th St.
Arlington, VA 22205
Phone: (703)241-8361
Fax: (703)241-8623

Federal Market Development
5650 Chapel Run Ct.
Centreville, VA 20120-3601
Phone: (703)502-8930
Free: (800)821-5003
Fax: (703)502-8929

Huff, Stuart & Carlton
2107 Graves Mills Rd., Ste. C
Forest, VA 24551
Phone: (804)316-9356
Free: (888)316-9356
Fax: (804)316-9357
Website: http://www.wealthmgt.net

AMX International Inc.
1420 Spring Hill Rd. , Ste. 600
McLean, VA 22102-3006
Phone: (703)690-4100
Fax: (703)643-1279
E-mail: amxmail@amxi.com
Website: http://www.amxi.com

Charles Scott Pugh (Investor)
4101 Pittaway Dr.
Richmond, VA 23235-1022
Phone: (804)560-0979
Fax: (804)560-4670

John C. Randall and Associates Inc.
PO Box 15127
Richmond, VA 23227
Phone: (804)746-4450
Fax: (804)730-8933
E-mail: randalljcx@aol.com
Website: http://www.johncrandall.com

McLeod & Co.
410 1st St.
Roanoke, VA 24011
Phone: (540)342-6911
Fax: (540)344-6367
Website: http://www.mcleodco.com/

Salzinger & Company Inc.
8000 Towers Crescent Dr., Ste. 1350
Vienna, VA 22182
Phone: (703)442-5200
Fax: (703)442-5205
E-mail: info@salzinger.com
Website: http://www.salzinger.com

The Small Business Counselor
12423 Hedges Run Dr., Ste. 153
Woodbridge, VA 22192
Phone: (703)490-6755
Fax: (703)490-1356

Washington

Burlington Consultants
10900 NE 8th St., Ste. 900
Bellevue, WA 98004
Phone: (425)688-3060
Fax: (425)454-4383
E-mail: partners@burlingtonconsultants.com
Website: http://www.burlingtonconsultants.com

Perry L. Smith Consulting
800 Bellevue Way NE, Ste. 400
Bellevue, WA 98004-4208
Phone: (425)462-2072
Fax: (425)462-5638

St. Charles Consulting Group
1420 NW Gilman Blvd.
Issaquah, WA 98027
Phone: (425)557-8708
Fax: (425)557-8731
E-mail: info@stcharlesconsulting.com
Website: http://www.stcharlesconsulting.com

Independent Automotive Training Services
PO Box 334
Kirkland, WA 98083
Phone: (425)822-5715
E-mail: ltunney@autosvccon.com
Website: http://www.autosvccon.com

Kahle Associate Inc.
6203 204th Dr. NE
Redmond, WA 98053
Phone: (425)836-8763
Fax: (425)868-3770
E-mail: randykahle@kahleassociates.com
Website: http://www.kahleassociates.com

Dan Collin
3419 Wallingord Ave N, No. 2
Seattle, WA 98103
Phone: (206)634-9469
E-mail: dc@dancollin.com
Website: http://members.home.net/dcollin/

ECG Management Consultants Inc.
1111 3rd Ave., Ste. 2700
Seattle, WA 98101-3201
Phone: (206)689-2200
Fax: (206)689-2209
E-mail: ecg@ecgmc.com
Website: http://www.ecgmc.com

Northwest Trade Adjustment Assistance Center

900 4th Ave., Ste. 2430
Seattle, WA 98164-1001
Phone: (206)622-2730
Free: (800)667-8087
Fax: (206)622-1105
E-mail: matchingfunds@nwtaac.org
Website: http://www.taacenters.org

Business Planning Consultants
S 3510 Ridgeview Dr.
Spokane, WA 99206
Phone: (509)928-0332
Fax: (509)921-0842
E-mail: bpci@nextdim.com

Wisconsin

White & Associates Inc.
5349 Somerset Ln. S
Greenfield, WI 53221
Phone: (414)281-7373
Fax: (414)281-7006
E-mail: wnaconsult@aol.com

SMALL BUSINESS ADMINISTRATION REGIONAL OFFICES

This section contains a listing of Small Business Administration offices arranged numerically by region. Service areas are provided. Contact the appropriate office for a referral to the nearest field office, or visit the Small Business Administration online at www.sba.gov.

Region 1

U.S. Small Business Administration
10 Causeway St.
Boston, MA 02222-1093
Phone: (617)565-8415
Fax: (617)565-8420
Serves Connecticut, Maine, Massachusetts, New Hampshire, Rhode Island, and Vermont.

Region 2

U.S. Small Business Administration
26 Federal Plaza, Ste. 3108
New York, NY 10278
Phone: (212)264-1450
Fax: (212)264-0038
Serves New Jersey, New York, Puerto Rico, and the Virgin Islands.

Region 3

Serves Delaware, the District of Columbia, Maryland, Pennsylvania, Virginia, and West Virginia. For the nearest field office, visit the Small Business Administration online at www.sba.gov.

Region 4

U.S. Small Business Administration
233 Peachtree St. NE
Harris Tower 1800
Atlanta, GA 30303
Phone: (404)331-4999
Fax: (404)331-2354
Serves Alabama, Florida, Georgia, Kentucky, Mississippi, North Carolina, South Carolina, and Tennessee.

Region 5

U.S. Small Business Administration
500 W. Madison St., Ste. 1240
Chicago, IL 60661-2511
Phone: (312)353-5000
Fax: (312)353-3426
Serves Illinois, Indiana, Michigan, Minnesota, Ohio, and Wisconsin.

Region 6

U.S. Small Business Administration
4300 Amon Carter Blvd.
Dallas/Fort Worth, TX 76155
Phone: (817)885-6581
Fax: (817)885-6588
Serves Arkansas, Louisiana, New Mexico, Oklahoma, and Texas.

Region 7

U.S. Small Business Administration
323 W. 8th St., Ste. 307
Kansas City, MO 64105-1500
Phone: (816)374-6380
Fax: (816)374-6339
Serves Iowa, Kansas, Missouri, and Nebraska.

Region 8

U.S. Small Business Administration
721 19th St., Ste. 400
Denver, CO 80202
Phone: (303)844-0500
Fax: (303)844-0506
Serves Colorado, Montana, North Dakota, South Dakota, Utah, and Wyoming.

Region 9

U.S. Small Business Administration
455 Market St., Ste. 2200
San Francisco, CA 94105
Phone: (415)744-2118
Fax: (415)744-2119
Serves American Samoa, Arizona, California, Guam, Hawaii, Nevada, and the Trust Territory of the Pacific Islands.

Region 10

U.S. Small Business Administration
1200 6th Ave., Ste. 1805
Seattle, WA 98101-1128
Phone: (206)553-5676
Fax: (206)553-2872
Serves Alaska, Idaho, Oregon, and Washington.

SMALL BUSINESS DEVELOPMENT CENTERS

This section contains a listing of all Small Business Development Centers organized alphabetically by state/U.S. territory name, then by city, then by agency name.

Alabama

Auburn University
SBDC
108 College of Business
Auburn, AL 36849-5243
Phone: (334)844-4220
Fax: (334)844-4268
Garry Hannem, Dir.

Alabama Small Business Procurement System
University Of Alabama at Birmingham
SBDC
1717 11th Ave. S., Ste. 419
Birmingham, AL 35294-4410
Phone: (205)934-7260
Fax: (205)934-7645
Charles Hobson, Procurement Dir.

University of Alabama at Birmingham
Alabama Small Business Development Consortium
SBDC
1717 11th Ave. S., Ste. 419
Birmingham, AL 35294-4410
Phone: (205)934-7260
Fax: (205)934-7645
John Sandefur, State Dir.

University of Alabama at Birmingham
SBDC
1601 11th Ave. S.
Birmingham, AL 35294-2180
Phone: (205)934-6760
Fax: (205)934-0538
Brenda Walker, Dir.

University of North Alabama
Small Business Development Center
Box 5248, Keller Hall
Florence, AL 35632-0001
Phone: (205)760-4629
Fax: (205)760-4813

Alabama A & M University
University of Alabama at Huntsville
NE Alabama Regional Small Business Development Center
PO Box 168
225 Church St., NW
Huntsville, AL 35804-0168
Phone: (205)535-2061
Fax: (205)535-2050
Jeff Thompson, Dir.

Jacksonville State University
Small Business Development Center
114 Merrill Hall
700 Pelham Rd. N.
Jacksonville, AL 36265
Phone: (205)782-5271
Fax: (205)782-5179
Pat Shaddix, Dir.

University of West Alabama
SBDC
Station 35
Livingston, AL 35470
Phone: (205)652-3665
Fax: (205)652-3516
Paul Garner, Dir.

University of South Alabama
Small Business Development Center
College of Business, Rm. 8
Mobile, AL 36688
Phone: (334)460-6004
Fax: (334)460-6246

Alabama State University
SBDC
915 S. Jackson St.
Montgomery, AL 36104-5714
Phone: (334)229-4138
Fax: (334)269-1102
Lorenza G. Patrick, Dir.

Troy State University
Small Business Development Center
Bibb Graves, Rm. 102
Troy, AL 36082-0001
Phone: (205)670-3771
Fax: (205)670-3636
Janet W. Kervin, Dir.

University of Alabama
Alabama International Trade Center
Small Business Development Center
Bidgood Hall, Rm. 250
Box 870397
Tuscaloosa, AL 35487-0396
Phone: (205)348-7011
Fax: (205)348-9644
Paavo Hanninen, Dir.

Alaska

University of Alaska (Fairbanks)
Small Business Development Center
510 Second Ave., Ste. 101
Fairbanks, AK 99701
Phone: (907)474-6700
Fax: (907)474-1139
Billie Ray Allen, Dir.

University of Alaska (Juneau)
Small Business Development Center
612 W. Willoughby Ave., Ste. A
Juneau, AK 99801
Phone: (907)463-1732
Fax: (907)463-3929
Norma Strickland, Acting Dir.

Kenai Peninsula Small Business Development Center
PO Box 3029
Kenai, AK 99611-3029
Phone: (907)283-3335
Fax: (907)283-3913
Mark Gregory

University of Alaska (Matanuska-Susitna)
Small Business Development Center
201 N. Lucile St., Ste. 2-A
Wasilla, AK 99654
Phone: (907)373-7232
Fax: (907)373-7234
Timothy Sullivan, Dir.

Arizona

Central Arizona College
Pinal County Small Business Development Center
8470 N. Overfield Rd.
Coolidge, AZ 85228
Phone: (520)426-4341
Fax: (520)426-4363
Carol Giordano, Dir.

Coconino County Community College
Small Business Development Center
3000 N. 4th St., Ste. 25
Flagstaff, AZ 86004
Phone: (520)526-5072
Fax: (520)526-8693
Mike Lainoff, Dir.

Northland Pioneer College
Small Business Development Center
PO Box 610
Holbrook, AZ 86025
Phone: (520)537-2976
Fax: (520)524-2227
Mark Engle, Dir.

Mohave Community College
Small Business Development Center
1971 Jagerson Ave.
Kingman, AZ 86401
Phone: (520)757-0894
Fax: (520)757-0836
Kathy McGehee, Dir.

Yavapai College
Small Business Development Center
Elks Building
117 E. Gurley St., Ste. 206
Prescott, AZ 86301
Phone: (520)778-3088

Fax: (520)778-3109
Richard Senopole, Director

Cochise College
Small Business Development Center
901 N. Colombo, Rm. 308
Sierra Vista, AZ 85635
Phone: (520)515-5478
Fax: (520)515-5437
E-mail: sbdc@trom.cochise.cc.az.us
Shelia Devoe Heidman, Dir.

Arizona Small Business Development Center Network
2411 W. 14th St., Ste. 132
Tempe, AZ 85281
Phone: (602)731-8720
Fax: (602)731-8729
E-mail: york@maricopa.bitnet
Michael York, State Dir.

Maricopa Community Colleges
Arizona Small Business Development Center Network
2411 W. 14th St., Ste. 132
Tempe, AZ 85281
Phone: (602)731-8720
Fax: (602)731-8729
Michael York, Dir.

Eastern Arizona College
Small Business Development Center
622 College Ave.
Thatcher, AZ 85552-0769
Phone: (520)428-8590
Fax: (520)428-8462
Greg Roers, Dir.

Pima Community College
Small Business Development and Training Center
4905-A E. Broadway Blvd., Ste. 101
Tucson, AZ 85709-1260
Phone: (520)206-4906
Fax: (520)206-4585
Linda Andrews, Dir.

Arizona Western College
Small Business Development Center
Century Plz., No. 152
281 W. 24th St.
Yuma, AZ 85364
Phone: (520)341-1650
Fax: (520)726-2636
John Lundin, Dir.

Arkansas

Henderson State University
Small Business Development Center
1100 Henderson St.
PO Box 7624
Arkadelphia, AR 71923
Phone: (870)230-5224
Fax: (870)230-5236
Jeff Doose, Dir.

Genesis Technology Incubator
SBDC Satellite Office
University of Arkansas - Engineering Research Center
Fayetteville, AR 72701-1201
Phone: (501)575-7473
Fax: (501)575-7446
Bob Penquite, Business Consultant

University of Arkansas at Fayetteville
Small Business Development Center
Business Administration Bldg., Ste. 106
Fayetteville, AR 72701
Phone: (501)575-5148
Fax: (501)575-4013
Ms. Jimmie Wilkins, Dir.

Small Business Development Center
1109 S. 16th St.
PO Box 2067
Ft. Smith, AR 72901
Phone: (501)785-1376
Fax: (501)785-1964
Vonelle Vanzant, Business Consultant

University of Arkansas at Little Rock, Regional Office (Fort Smith)
Small Business Development Center
1109 S. 16th St.
PO Box 2067
Ft. Smith, AR 72901
Phone: (501)785-1376
Fax: (501)785-1964
Byron Branch, Business Specialist

University of Arkansas at Little Rock, Regional Office (Harrison)
Small Business Development Center
818 Hwy. 62-65-412 N
PO Box 190
Harrison, AR 72601
Phone: (870)741-8009
Fax: (870)741-1905
Bob Penquite, Business Consultant

University of Arkansas at Little Rock, Regional Office (Hot Springs)
Small Business Development Center
835 Central Ave., Box 402-D
Hot Springs, AR 71901
Phone: (501)624-5448
Fax: (501)624-6632
Richard Evans, Business Consultant

Arkansas State University
Small Business Development Center
College of Business
Drawer 2650
Jonesboro, AR 72467
Phone: (870)972-3517
Fax: (501)972-3868
Herb Lawrence, Dir.

University of Arkansas at Little Rock
SBDC
Little Rock Technology Center Bldg.
100 S. Main St., Ste. 401
Little Rock, AR 72201
Phone: (501)324-9043
Fax: (501)324-9049
Janet Nye, State Dir.

University of Arkansas at Little Rock, Regional Office (Magnolia)
Small Business Development Center
600 Bessie
PO Box 767
Magnolia, AR 71753
Phone: (870)234-4030
Fax: (870)234-0135
Mr. Lairie Kincaid, Business Consultant

University of Arkansas at Little Rock, Regional Office (Pine Bluff)
Small Business Development Center
The Enterprise Center III
400 Main, Ste. 117
Pine Bluff, AR 71601
Phone: (870)536-0654
Fax: (870)536-7713
Russell Barker, Business Consultant

University of Arkansas at Little Rock, Regional Office (Stuttgart)
Small Business Development Center
301 S. Grand, Ste. 101
PO Box 289
Stuttgart, AR 72160
Phone: (870)673-8707
Fax: (870)673-8707
Larry Lefler, Business Consultant

Mid-South Community College
SBDC
2000 W. Broadway
PO Box 2067
West Memphis, AR 72303-2067
Phone: (870)733-6767

California

Central Coast Small Business
Development Center
6500 Soquel Dr.
Aptos, CA 95003
Phone: (408)479-6136
Fax: (408)479-6166
Teresa Thomae, Dir.

Sierra College Small Business
Development Center
560 Wall St., Ste. J
Auburn, CA 95603
Phone: (916)885-5488
Fax: (916)823-2831
Mary Wollesen, Dir.

Weill Institute Small Business
Development Center
1706 Chester Ave., Ste. 200
Bakersfield, CA 93301
Phone: (805)322-5881
Fax: (805)322-5663
Jeffrey Johnson, Dir.

Butte College
Small Business Development Center
260 Cohasset Rd., Ste. A
Chico, CA 95926
Phone: (916)895-9017
Fax: (916)895-9099
Kay Zimmerlee, Dir.

Southwestern College
Small Business Development and
International Trade Center
900 Otay Lakes Rd., Bldg. 1600
Chula Vista, CA 91910
Phone: (619)482-6393
Fax: (619)482-6402
Mary Wylie, Dir.

Contra Costa SBDC
2425 Bisso Ln., Ste. 200
Concord, CA 94520
Phone: (510)646-5377
Fax: (510)646-5299
Debra Longwood, Dir.

North Coast Small Business
Development Center
207 Price Mall, Ste. 500
Crescent City, CA 95531
Phone: (707)464-2168
Fax: (707)465-6008
Fran Clark, Dir.

Imperial Valley Satellite SBDC
Town & Country Shopping Center
301 N. Imperial Ave., Ste. B
El Centro, CA 92243
Phone: (619)312-9800
Fax: (619)312-9838
Debbie Trujillo, Satellite Mgr.

Export SBDC/El Monte Outreach
Center
10501 Valley Blvd., Ste. 106
El Monte, CA 91731
Phone: (818)459-4111
Fax: (818)443-0463
Charles Blythe, Manager

North Coast
Small Business Development Center
520 E St.
Eureka, CA 95501
Phone: (707)445-9720
Fax: (707)445-9652
Duff Heuttner, Bus. Counselor

Central California
Small Business Development Center
3419 W. Shaw Ave., Ste. 102
Fresno, CA 93711
Phone: (209)275-1223
Fax: (209)275-1499
Dennis Winans, Dir.

Gavilan College Small Business
Development Center
7436 Monterey St.
Gilroy, CA 95020
Phone: (408)847-0373
Fax: (408)847-0393
Peter Graff, Dir.

Accelerate Technology Assistance
Small Business Development Center
4199 Campus Dr.
University Towers, Ste. 240
Irvine, CA 92612-4688
Phone: (714)509-2990
Fax: (714)509-2997
Tiffany Haugen, Dir.

Amador SBDC
222 N. Hwy. 49
PO Box 1077
Jackson, CA 95642
Phone: (209)223-0351
Fax: (209)223-5237
Ron Mittelbrunn, Mgr.

Greater San Diego Chamber of
Commerce
Small Business Development Center
4275 Executive Sq., Ste. 920
La Jolla, CA 92037
Phone: (619)453-9388
Fax: (619)450-1997
Hal Lefkowitz, Dir.

Yuba College SBDC
PO Box 1566
15145 Lakeshore Dr.
Lakeport, CA 95453
Phone: (707)263-0330
Fax: (707)263-8516
George McQueen, Dir.

East Los Angeles SBDC
5161 East Pomona Blvd., Ste. 212
Los Angeles, CA 90022
Phone: (213)262-9797
Fax: (213)262-2704

Export Small Business Development
Center of Southern California
110 E. 9th, Ste. A669
Los Angeles, CA 90079
Phone: (213)892-1111
Fax: (213)892-8232
Gladys Moreau, Dir.

South Central LA/Satellite
SBDC
3650 Martin Luther King Blvd., Ste.
246
Los Angeles, CA 90008
Phone: (213)290-2832
Fax: (213)290-7191
Cope Norcross, Satellite Mgr.

Alpine SBDC
PO Box 265
3 Webster St.
Markleeville, CA 96120
Phone: (916)694-2475
Fax: (916)694-2478

Yuba/Sutter Satellite
SBDC
10th and E St.
PO Box 262
Marysville, CA 95901
Phone: (916)749-0153
Fax: (916)749-0155
Sandra Brown-Abernathy, Dir.

Valley Sierra SBDC
Merced Satellite
1632 N St.
Merced, CA 95340
Phone: (209)725-3800
Fax: (209)383-4959
Nick Starianoudakis, Satellite Mgr.

Valley Sierra Small Business Development Center
1012 11th St., Ste. 300
Modesto, CA 95354
Phone: (209)521-6177
Fax: (209)521-9373
Kelly Bearden, Dir.

Napa Valley College Small Business Development Center
1556 First St., Ste. 103
Napa, CA 94559
Phone: (707)253-3210
Fax: (707)253-3068
Chuck Eason, Dir.

Inland Empire Business Incubator SBDC
155 S. Memorial Dr.
Norton Air Force Base, CA 92509
Phone: (909)382-0065
Fax: (909)382-8543
Chuck Eason, Incubator Mgr.

East Bay Small Business Development Center
519 17th. St., Ste. 210
Oakland, CA 94612
Phone: (510)893-4114
Fax: (510)893-5532
Napoleon Britt, Dir.

International Trade Office SBDC
3282 E. Guasti Rd., Ste. 100
Ontario, CA 91761
Phone: (909)390-8071
Fax: (909)390-8077
John Hernandez, Trade Manager

Coachella Valley SBDC
Palm Springs Satellite Center
501 S. Palm Canyon Dr., Ste. 222
Palm Springs, CA 92264
Phone: (619)864-1311
Fax: (619)864-1319
Brad Mix, Satellite Mgr.

Pasadena Satellite SBDC
2061 N. Los Robles, Ste. 106
Pasadena, CA 91104
Phone: (818)398-9031
Fax: (818)398-3059
David Ryal, Satellite Mgr.

Pico Rivera SBDC
9058 E. Washington Blvd.
Pico Rivera, CA 90660
Phone: (310)942-9965
Fax: (310)942-9745
Beverly Taylor, Satellite Mgr.

Eastern Los Angeles County Small Business Development Center
375 S. Main St., Ste. 101
Pomona, CA 91766
Phone: (909)629-2247
Fax: (909)629-8310
Toni Valdez, Dir.

Pomona SBDC
375 S. Main St., Ste. 101
Pomona, CA 91766
Phone: (909)629-2247
Fax: (909)629-8310
Paul Hischar, Satellite Manager

Cascade Small Business Development Center
737 Auditorium Dr., Ste. A
Redding, CA 96001
Phone: (916)247-8100
Fax: (916)241-1712
Carole Enmark, Dir.

Inland Empire Small Business Development Center
1157 Spruce St.
Riverside, CA 92507
Phone: (909)781-2345
Free: (800)750-2353
Fax: (909)781-2353
Teri Ooms, Dir.

California Trade and Commerce Agency
California SBDC
801 K St., Ste. 1700
Sacramento, CA 95814
Phone: (916)324-5068
Fax: (916)322-5084
Kim Neri, State Dir.

Greater Sacramento SBDC
1410 Ethan Way
Sacramento, CA 95825
Phone: (916)563-3210
Fax: (916)563-3266
Cynthia Steimle, Director

Calaveras SBDC
PO Box 431
3 N. Main St.
San Andreas, CA 95249
Phone: (209)754-1834
Fax: (209)754-4107

San Francisco SBDC
711 Van Ness, Ste. 305
San Francisco, CA 94102
Phone: (415)561-1890
Fax: (415)561-1894
Tim Sprinkles, Director

Orange County Small Business Development Center
901 E. Santa Ana Blvd., Ste. 101
Santa Ana, CA 92701
Phone: (714)647-1172
Fax: (714)835-9008
Gregory Kishel, Dir.

Southwest Los Angeles County Westside Satellite SBDC
3233 Donald Douglas Loop S., Ste. C
Santa Monica, CA 90405
Phone: (310)398-8883
Fax: (310)398-3024
Sue Hunter, Admin. Asst.

Redwood Empire Small Business Development Center
520 Mendocino Ave., Ste. 210
Santa Rosa, CA 95401
Phone: (707)524-1770
Fax: (707)524-1772
Charles Robbins, Dir.

San Joaquin Delta College Small Business Development Center
445 N. San Joaquin, 2nd Fl.
Stockton, CA 95202
Phone: (209)474-5089
Fax: (209)474-5605
Gillian Murphy, Dir.

Silicon Valley SBDC
298 S. Sunnyvale Ave., Ste. 204
Sunnyvale, CA 94086
Phone: (408)736-0680
Fax: (408)736-0679
Eliza Minor, Director

Southwest Los Angeles County Small Business Development Center
21221 Western Ave., Ste. 110
Torrance, CA 90501
Phone: (310)787-6466
Fax: (310)782-8607
Susan Hunter, Dir.

West Company SBDC
367 N. State St., Ste. 208
Ukiah, CA 95482
Phone: (707)468-3553

Fax: (707)468-3555
Sheilah Rogers, Director

North Los Angeles Small Business Development Center
4717 Van Nuys Blvd., Ste. 201
Van Nuys, CA 91403-2100
Phone: (818)907-9922
Fax: (818)907-9890
Wilma Berglund, Dir.

Export SBDC Satellite Center
5700 Ralston St., Ste. 310
Ventura, CA 93003
Phone: (805)658-2688
Fax: (805)658-2252
Heather Wicka, Manager

Gold Coast SBDC
5700 Ralston St., Ste. 310
Ventura, CA 93003
Phone: (805)658-2688
Fax: (805)658-2252
Joe Higgins, Satellite Mgr.

High Desert SBDC
Victorville Satellite Center
15490 Civic Dr., Ste. 102
Victorville, CA 92392
Phone: (619)951-1592
Fax: (619)951-8929
Janice Harbaugh, Business Consultant

Central California - Visalia Satellite SBDC
430 W. Caldwell Ave., Ste. D
Visalia, CA 93277
Phone: (209)625-3051
Fax: (209)625-3053
Randy Mason, Satellite Mgr.

Colorado

Adams State College
Small Business Development Center
School of Business, Rm. 105
Alamosa, CO 81102
Phone: (719)587-7372
Fax: (719)587-7603
Mary Hoffman, Dir.

Community College of Aurora
Small Business Development Center
9905 E. Colfax
Aurora, CO 80010-2119
Phone: (303)341-4849
Fax: (303)361-2953
E-mail: asbdc@henge.com
Randy Johnson, Dir.

Boulder Chamber of Commerce
Small Business Development Center
2440 Pearl St.
Boulder, CO 80302
Phone: (303)442-1475
Fax: (303)938-8837
Marilynn Force, Dir.

Pueblo Community College (Canon City)
Small Business Development Center
3080 Main St.
Canon City, CO 81212
Phone: (719)275-5335
Fax: (719)275-4400
Elwin Boody, Dir.

Pikes Peak Community College
Small Business Development Center
Colorado Springs Chamber of Commerce
CITTI Bldg.
1420 Austin Bluff Pkwy.
Colorado Springs, CO 80933
Phone: (719)592-1894
Fax: (719)533-0545
E-mail: sbdc@mail.uccs.edu
Iris Clark, Dir.

Colorado Northwestern Community College
Small Business Development Center
50 College Dr.
Craig, CO 81625
Phone: (970)824-7078
Fax: (970)824-1134
Ken Farmer, Dir.

Delta Montrose Vocational School
Small Business Development Center
1765 US Hwy. 50
Delta, CO 81416
Phone: (970)874-8772
Free: (888)234-7232
Fax: (970)874-8796
Bob Marshall, Dir.

Community College of Denver
Greater Denver Chamber of Commerce
Small Business Development Center
1445 Market St.
Denver, CO 80202
Phone: (303)620-8076
Fax: (303)534-3200
Tamela Lee, Dir.

Office of Business Development
Colorado SBDC
1625 Broadway, Ste. 1710
Denver, CO 80202
Phone: (303)892-3809
Free: (800)333-7798
Fax: (303)892-3848
Lee Ortiz, State Dir.

Fort Lewis College
Small Business Development Center
136-G Hesperus Hall
Durango, CO 81301-3999
Phone: (970)247-7009
Fax: (970)247-7623
Jim Reser, Dir.

Front Range Community College (Ft. Collins)
Small Business Development Center
125 S. Howes, Ste. 105
Ft. Collins, CO 80521
Phone: (970)498-9295
Fax: (970)204-0385
Frank Pryor, Dir.

Morgan Community College (Ft. Morgan)
Small Business Development Center
300 Main St.
Ft. Morgan, CO 80701
Phone: (970)867-3351
Fax: (970)867-3352
Dan Simon, Dir.

Colorado Mountain College (Glenwood Springs)
Small Business Development Center
831 Grand Ave.
Glenwood Springs, CO 81601
Phone: (970)928-0120
Free: (800)621-1647
Fax: (970)947-9324
Alisa Zimmerman, Dir.

Small Business Development Center
1726 Cole Blvd., Bldg. 22, Ste. 310
Golden, CO 80401
Phone: (303)277-1840
Fax: (303)277-1899
Jayne Reiter, Dir.

Mesa State College
Small Business Development Center
304 W. Main St.
Grand Junction, CO 81505-1606
Phone: (970)243-5242
Fax: (970)241-0771
Julie Morey, Dir.

Aims Community College
Greeley/Weld Chamber of Commerce

Small Business Development Center
902 7th Ave.
Greeley, CO 80631
Phone: (970)352-3661
Fax: (970)352-3572
Ron Anderson, Dir.

Red Rocks Community College Small Business Development Center
777 S. Wadsworth Blvd., Ste. 254
Bldg. 4
Lakewood, CO 80226
Phone: (303)987-0710
Fax: (303)987-1331
Jayne Reiter, Acting Dir.

Lamar Community College
Small Business Development Center
2400 S. Main
Lamar, CO 81052
Phone: (719)336-8141
Fax: (719)336-2448
Dan Minor, Dir.

Small Business Development Center
Arapahoe Community College
South Metro Chamber of Commerce
7901 S. Park Plz., Ste. 110
Littleton, CO 80120
Phone: (303)795-5855
Fax: (303)795-7520
Selma Kristel, Dir.

Pueblo Community College Small Business Development Center
900 W. Orman Ave.
Pueblo, CO 81004
Phone: (719)549-3224
Fax: (719)549-3338
Rita Friberg, Dir.

Morgan Community College (Stratton)
Small Business Development Center
PO Box 28
Stratton, CO 80836
Phone: (719)348-5596
Fax: (719)348-5887
Roni Carr, Dir.

Trinidad State Junior College
Small Business Development Center
136 W. Main St.
Davis Bldg.
Trinidad, CO 81082
Phone: (719)846-5645
Fax: (719)846-4550
Dennis O'Connor, Dir.

Front Range Community College (Westminster)
Small Business Development Center
3645 W. 112th Ave.
Westminster, CO 80030
Phone: (303)460-1032
Fax: (303)469-7143
Leo Giles, Dir.

Connecticut

Bridgeport Regional Business Council
Small Business Development Center
10 Middle St., 14th Fl.
Bridgeport, CT 06604-4229
Phone: (203)330-4813
Fax: (203)366-0105
Juan Scott, Dir.

Quinebaug Valley Community Technical College
Small Business Development Center
742 Upper Maple St.
Danielson, CT 06239-1440
Phone: (860)774-1133
Fax: (860)774-7768
Roger Doty, Dir.

University of Connecticut (Groton)
Small Business Development Center
Administration Bldg., Rm. 300
1084 Shennecossett Rd.
Groton, CT 06340-6097
Phone: (860)405-9009
Fax: (860)405-9041
Louise Kahler, Dir.

Middlesex County Chamber of Commerce
SBDC
393 Main St.
Middletown, CT 06457
Phone: (860)344-2158
Fax: (860)346-1043
John Serignese

Greater New Haven Chamber of Commerce
Small Business Development Center
195 Church St.
New Haven, CT 06510-2009
Phone: (203)782-4390
Fax: (203)787-6730
Pete Rivera, Regional Dir.

Southwestern Area Commerce and Industry Association (SACIA)
Small Business Development Center
1 Landmark Sq., Ste. 230
Stamford, CT 06901
Phone: (203)359-3220
Fax: (203)967-8294
Harvey Blomberg, Dir.

University of Connecticut
School of Business Administration
Connecticut SBDC
2 Bourn Place, U-94
Storrs, CT 06269
Phone: (860)486-4135
Fax: (860)486-1576
E-mail: oconnor@ct.sbdc.uconn.edu
Dennis Gruel, State Dir.

Naugatuck Valley Development Center
Small Business Development Center
100 Grand St., 3rd Fl.
Waterbury, CT 06702
Phone: (203)757-8937
Fax: (203)757-8937
Ilene Oppenheim, Dir.

University of Connecticut (Greater Hartford Campus)
Small Business Development Center
1800 Asylum Ave.
West Hartford, CT 06117
Phone: (860)570-9107
Fax: (860)570-9107
Dennis Gruel, Dir.

Eastern Connecticut State University
Small Business Development Center
83 Windham St.
Williamantic, CT 06226-2295
Phone: (860)465-5349
Fax: (860)465-5143
Richard Cheney, Dir.

Delaware

Delaware State University
School of Business Economics
SBDC
1200 N. Dupont Hwy.
Dover, DE 19901
Phone: (302)678-1555
Fax: (302)739-2333
Jim Crisfield, Director

Delaware Technical and Community College
SBDC
Industrial Training Bldg.
PO Box 610
Georgetown, DE 19947

Phone: (302)856-1555
Fax: (302)856-5779
William F. Pfaff, Dir.

University of Delaware
Delaware SBDC
Purnell Hall, Ste. 005
Newark, DE 19716-2711
Phone: (302)831-1555
Fax: (302)831-1423
Clinton Tymes, State Dir.

Small Business Resource & Information Center
SBDC
1318 N. Market St.
Wilmington, DE 19801
Phone: (302)571-1555
Fax: (302)571-5222
Barbara Necarsulmer, Mgr.

District of Columbia

Friendship House/Southeastern University
SBDC
921 Pennsylvania Ave., SE
Washington, DC 20003
Phone: (202)547-7933
Fax: (202)806-1777
Elise Ashby, Dir.

George Washington University
East of the River Community Development Corp.
SBDC
3101 MLK Jr. Ave., SE, 3rd Fl.
Washington, DC 20032
Phone: (202)561-4975
Howard Johnson, Accounting Specialist

Howard University
George Washington Small Business Legal Clinic
SBDC
2000 G St., NW, Ste. 200
Washington, DC 20052
Phone: (202)994-7463
Jose Hernandez, Counselor

Howard University
Office of Latino Affairs
SBDC
2000 14th St., NW, 2nd Fl.
Washington, DC 20009
Phone: (202)939-3018
Fax: (202)994-4946
Jose Hernandez, Gov. Procurement Specialist

Howard University
SBDC
Satellite Location
2600 6th St., NW, Rm. 125
Washington, DC 20059
Phone: (202)806-1550
Fax: (202)806-1777
Terry Strong, Acting Regional Dir.

Marshall Heights Community Development Organization
SBDC
3917 Minnesota Ave., NE
Washington, DC 20019
Phone: (202)396-1200
Terry Strong, Financing Specialist

Washington District Office
Business Information Center
SBDC
1110 Vermont Ave., NW, 9th Fl.
Washington, DC 20005
Phone: (202)737-0120
Fax: (202)737-0476
Johnetta Hardy, Marketing Specialist

Florida

Central Florida Development Council
Small Business Development Center
600 N. Broadway, Ste. 300
Bartow, FL 33830
Phone: (941)534-4370
Fax: (941)533-1247
Marcela Stanislaus, Vice President

Florida Atlantic University (Boca Raton)
Small Business Development Center
777 Glades Rd.
Bldg. T9
Boca Raton, FL 33431
Phone: (561)362-5620
Fax: (561)362-5623
Nancy Young, Dir.

UCF Brevard Campus
Small Business Development Center
1519 Clearlake Rd.
Cocoa, FL 32922
Phone: (407)951-1060

Dania Small Business Development Center
46 SW 1st Ave.
Dania, FL 33304-3607
Phone: (954)987-0100
Fax: (954)987-0106
William Healy, Regional Mgr.

Daytona Beach Community College
Florida Regional SBDC
1200 W. International Speedway Blvd.
Daytona Beach, FL 32114
Phone: (904)947-5463
Fax: (904)258-3846
Brenda Thomas-Ramos, Dir.

Florida Atlantic University
Commercial Campus
Small Business Development Center
1515 W. Commercial Blvd., Rm. 11
Ft. Lauderdale, FL 33309
Phone: (954)771-6520
Fax: (954)351-4120
Marty Zients, Mgr.

Minority Business Development Center
SBDC
5950 West Oakland Park Blvd., Ste. 307
Ft. Lauderdale, FL 33313
Phone: (954)485-5333
Fax: (954)485-2514

Edison Community College
Small Business Development Center
8099 College Pkwy. SW
Ft. Myers, FL 33919
Phone: (941)489-9200
Fax: (941)489-9051
Dan Regelski, Management Consultant

Florida Gulf Coast University
Small Business Development Center
17595 S. Tamiami Trail, Ste. 200
Midway Ctr.
Ft. Myers, FL 33908-4500
Phone: (941)948-1820
Fax: (941)948-1814
Dan Regleski, Management Consultant

Indian River Community College
Small Business Development Center
3209 Virginia Ave., Rm. 114
Ft. Pierce, FL 34981-5599
Phone: (561)462-4756
Fax: (561)462-4796
Marsha Thompson, Dir.

Okaloosa-Walton Community College
SBDC
1170 Martin Luther King, Jr. Blvd.
Ft. Walton Beach, FL 32547
Phone: (850)863-6543
Fax: (850)863-6564
Jane Briere, Mgr.

University of North Florida (Gainesville)
Small Business Development Center
505 NW 2nd Ave., Ste. D
PO Box 2518
Gainesville, FL 32602-2518
Phone: (352)377-5621
Fax: (352)372-0288
Lalla Sheehy, Program Mgr.

University of North Florida (Jacksonville)
Small Business Development Center
College of Business
Honors Hall, Rm. 2451
4567 St. John's Bluff Rd. S
Jacksonville, FL 32224
Phone: (904)620-2476
Fax: (904)620-2567
E-mail: smallbiz@unf.edu
Lowell Salter, Regional Dir.

Gulf Coast Community College
SBDC
2500 Minnesota Ave.
Lynn Haven, FL 32444
Phone: (850)271-1108
Fax: (850)271-1109
Doug Davis, Dir.

Brevard Community College (Melbourne)
Small Business Development Center
3865 N. Wickham Rd.
Melbourne, FL 32935
Phone: (407)632-1111
Fax: (407)634-3721
Victoria Peak, Program Coordinator

Florida International University
Small Business Development Center
University Park
CEAS-2620
Miami, FL 33199
Phone: (305)348-2272
Fax: (305)348-2965
Marvin Nesbit, Dir.

Florida International University (North Miami Campus)
Small Business Development Center
Academic Bldg. No. 1, Rm. 350
NE 151 and Biscayne Blvd.
Miami, FL 33181
Phone: (305)919-5790
Fax: (305)919-5792
Roy Jarrett, Regional Mgr.

Miami Dade Community College
Small Business Development Center
6300 NW 7th Ave.
Miami, FL 33150
Phone: (305)237-1906
Fax: (305)237-1908
Frederic Bonneau, Regional Mgr.

Ocala Small Business Development Center
110 E. Silver Springs Blvd.
PO Box 1210
Ocala, FL 34470-6613
Phone: (352)622-8763
Fax: (352)651-1031
E-mail: sbdcoca@mercury.net
Philip Geist, Program Dir.

University of Central Florida
Small Business Development Center
College of Business Administration, Ste. 309
PO Box 161530
Orlando, FL 32816-1530
Phone: (407)823-5554
Fax: (407)823-3073
Al Polfer, Dir.

Palm Beach Gardens
Florida Atlantic University
SBDC
Northrop Center
3970 RCA Blvd., Ste. 7323
Palm Beach Gardens, FL 33410
Phone: (407)691-8550
Fax: (407)692-8502
Steve Windhaus, Regional Mgr.

Procurement Technical Assistance Program
University of West Florida
Small Business Development Center
19 W. Garden St., Ste. 302
Pensacola, FL 32501
Phone: (850)595-5480
Fax: (850)595-5487
Martha Cobb, Dir.

University of West Florida
Florida SBDC Network
19 West Garden St., Ste. 300
Pensacola, FL 32501
Phone: (850)595-6060
Fax: (850)595-6070
E-mail: fsbdc@uwf.edu
Jerry Cartwright, State Dir.

Seminole Community College
SBDC
100 Weldon Blvd.
Sanford, FL 32773
Phone: (407)328-4722
Fax: (407)330-4489
Wayne Hardy, Regional Mgr.

Florida Agricultural and Mechanical University
Small Business Development Center
1157 E. Tennessee St.
Tallahassee, FL 32308
Phone: (904)599-3407
Fax: (904)561-2049
Patricia McGowan, Dir.

University of South Florida—CBA
SBDC Special Services
4202 E. Fowler Ave., BSN 3403
Tampa, FL 33620
Phone: (813)974-4371
Fax: (813)974-5020
Dick Hardesty, Procurement Mgr.

University of South Florida (Tampa)
Small Business Development Center
1111 N. Westshore Dr., Annex B, Ste. 101-B
Tampa, FL 33607
Phone: (813)554-2341
Free: (800)733-7232
Fax: (813)554-2356
Irene Hurst, Dir.

Georgia

University of Georgia
Small Business Development Center
230 S. Jackson St., Ste. 333
Albany, GA 31701-2885
Phone: (912)430-4303
Fax: (912)430-3933
E-mail: sbdcalb@uga.cc.uga.edu
Sue Ford, Asst. District Dir.

NE Georgia District
SBDC
1180 E. Broad St.
Athens, GA 30602-5412
Phone: (706)542-7436
Fax: (706)542-6823
Gayle Rosenthal, Mgr.

University of Georgia
Chicopee Complex
Georgia SBDC
1180 E. Broad St.
Athens, GA 30602-5412
Phone: (706)542-6762
Fax: (706)542-6776
E-mail: sbdcath@uga.cc.uga.edu
Hank Logan, State Dir.

Georgia State University
Small Business Development Center
University Plz.
Box 874
Atlanta, GA 30303-3083
Phone: (404)651-3550
Fax: (404)651-1035
E-mail: sbdcatl@uga.cc.uga.edu
Lee Quarterman, Area Dir.

Morris Brown College
Small Business Development Center
643 Martin Luther King, Jr., Dr. NW
Atlanta, GA 30314
Phone: (404)220-0205
Fax: (404)688-5985
Ray Johnson, Center Mgr.

University of Georgia
Small Business Development Center
1054 Claussen Rd., Ste. 301
Augusta, GA 30907-3215
Phone: (706)737-1790
Fax: (706)731-7937
E-mail: sbdcaug@uga.cc.uga.edu
Jeff Sanford, Area Dir.

University of Georgia (Brunswick)
Small Business Development Center
1107 Fountain Lake Dr.
Brunswick, GA 31525-3039
Phone: (912)264-7343
Fax: (912)262-3095
E-mail: sbdcbrun@uga.cc.uga.edu
David Lewis, Area Dir.

University of Georgia (Columbus)
Small Business Development Center
North Bldg., Rm. 202
928 45th St.
Columbus, GA 31904-6572
Phone: (706)649-7433
Fax: (706)649-1928
E-mail: sbdccolu@uga.cc.uga.edu
Jerry Copeland, Area Dir.

DeKalb Chamber of Commerce
DeKalb Small Business Development Center
750 Commerce Dr., Ste. 201
Decatur, GA 30030-2622
Phone: (404)373-6930
Fax: (404)687-9684
E-mail: sbdcdec@uga.cc.uga.edu
Eric Bonaparte, Area Dir.

Gainesville Small Business Development Center
500 Jesse Jewel Pkwy., Ste. 304
Gainesville, GA 30501-3773
Phone: (770)531-5681
Fax: (770)531-5684
E-mail: sbdcgain@uga.cc.uga.edu
Ron Simmons, Area Dir.

Kennesaw State University
Small Business Development Center
1000 Chastain Rd.
Kennesaw, GA 30144-5591
Phone: (770)423-6450
Fax: (770)423-6564
E-mail: sbdcmar@uga.cc.uga.edu
Carlotta Roberts, Area Dir.

Southeast Georgia District (Macon)
Small Business Development Center
401 Cherry St., Ste. 701
PO Box 13212
Macon, GA 31208-3212
Phone: (912)751-6592
Fax: (912)751-6607
E-mail: sbdcmac@uga.cc.uga.edu
Denise Ricketson, Area Dir.

Clayton State College
Small Business Development Center
PO Box 285
Morrow, GA 30260
Phone: (770)961-3440
Fax: (770)961-3428
E-mail: sbdcmorr@uga.cc.uga.edu
Bernie Meincke, Area Dir.

University of Georgia
SBDC
1770 Indian Trail Rd., Ste. 410
Norcross, GA 30093
Phone: (770)806-2124
Fax: (770)806-2129
E-mail: sbdclaw@uga.cc.edu
Robert Andoh, Area Dir.

Floyd College
Small Business Development Center
PO Box 1864
Rome, GA 30162-1864
Phone: (706)295-6326
Fax: (706)295-6732
E-mail: sbdcrome@uga.cc.uga.edu
Drew Tonsmeire, Area Dir.

University of Georgia (Savannah)
Small Business Development Center
450 Mall Blvd., Ste. H
Savannah, GA 31406-4824
Phone: (912)356-2755
Fax: (912)353-3033
E-mail: sbdcsav@uga.cc.uga.edu
Lynn Vos, Area Dir.

Georgia Southern University
Small Business Development Center
325 S. Main St.
PO Box 8156
Statesboro, GA 30460-8156
Phone: (912)681-5194
Fax: (912)681-0648
E-mail: sbdcstat@uga.cc.uga.edu
Mark Davis, Area Dir.

University of Georgia (Valdosta)
Small Business Development Center
Baytree W. Professional Offices
1205 Baytree Rd., Ste. 9
Valdosta, GA 31602-2782
Phone: (912)245-3738
Fax: (912)245-3741
E-mail: sbdcval@uga.cc.uga.edu
Suzanne Barnett, Area Dir.

University of Georgia (Warner Robins)
Small Business Development Center
151 Osigian Blvd.
Warner Robins, GA 31088
Phone: (912)953-9356
Fax: (912)953-9376
E-mail: sbdccwr@uga.cc.uga.edu
Ronald Reaves, Center Mgr.

Guam

Pacific Islands SBDC Network
UOG Station
303 University Dr.
Mangilao, GU 96923
Phone: (671)735-2590
Fax: (671)734-2002
Dr. Sephen L. Marder, Dir.

Hawaii

Kona Circuit Rider
SBDC
200 West Kawili St.
Hilo, HI 96720-4091
Phone: (808)933-3515

Fax: (808)933-3683
Rebecca Winters, Business Consultant

University of Hawaii at Hilo
Small Business Development Center
200 W. Kawili St.
Hilo, HI 96720-4091
Phone: (808)974-7515
Fax: (808)974-7683
Website: http://www.maui.com/~sbdc/hilo.html
Dr. Darryl Mleynek, State Director

University of Hawaii at West Oahu
SBDC
130 Merchant St., Ste. 1030
Honolulu, HI 96813
Phone: (808)522-8131
Fax: (808)522-8135
Laura Noda, Center Dir.

Maui Community College
Small Business Development Center
Maui Research and Technology Center
590 Lipoa Pkwy., No. 130
Kihei, HI 96779
Phone: (808)875-2402
Fax: (808)875-2452
David B. Fisher, Dir.

University of Hawaii at Hilo
Business Research Library
SBDC
590 Lipoa Pkwy., No. 128
Kihei, HI 96753
Phone: (808)875-2400
Fax: (808)875-2452

Kauai Community College
Small Business Development Center
3-1901 Kaumualii Hwy.
Lihue, HI 96766-9591
Phone: (808)246-1748
Fax: (808)246-5102
Randy Gringas, Center Dir.

Idaho

Boise State University
Small Business Development Center
1910 University Dr.
Boise, ID 83725
Phone: (208)385-3875
Free: (800)225-3815
Fax: (208)385-3877
Robert Shepard, Regional Dir.

Idaho State University (Idaho Falls)
Small Business Development Center
2300 N. Yellowstone
Idaho Falls, ID 83401
Phone: (208)523-1087
Free: (800)658-3829
Fax: (208)523-1049
Betty Capps, Regional Dir.

Lewis-Clark State College
Small Business Development Center
500 8th Ave.
Lewiston, ID 83501
Phone: (208)799-2465
Fax: (208)799-2878
Helen Le Boeuf-Binninger, Regional Dir.

Idaho Small Business Development Center
305 E. Park St., Ste. 405
PO Box 1901
McCall, ID 83638
Phone: (208)634-2883
Larry Smith, Associate Business Consultant

Idaho State University (Pocatello)
Small Business Development Center
1651 Alvin Ricken Dr.
Pocatello, ID 83201
Phone: (208)232-4921
Free: (800)232-4921
Fax: (208)233-0268
Paul Cox, Regional Dir.

North Idaho College
SBDC
525 W. Clearwater Loop
Post Falls, ID 83854
Phone: (208)769-3296
Fax: (208)769-3223
John Lynn, Regional Dir.

College of Southern Idaho
Small Business Development Center
315 Falls Ave.
PO Box 1238
Twin Falls, ID 83303
Phone: (208)733-9554
Fax: (208)733-9316
Cindy Bond, Regional Dir.

Illinois

Waubonsee Community College (Aurora Campus)
Small Business Development Center
5 E. Galena Blvd.
Aurora, IL 60506-4178
Phone: (630)801-7900
Fax: (630)892-4668
Linda Garrison-Carlton, Dir.

Southern Illinois University at Carbondale
Small Business Development Center
150 E. Pleasant Hill Rd.
Carbondale, IL 62901-4300
Phone: (618)536-2424
Fax: (618)453-5040
Dennis Cody, Dir.

John A. Logan College
Small Business Development Center
700 Logan College Rd.
Carterville, IL 62918-9802
Phone: (618)985-3741
Fax: (618)985-2248
Richard Fyke, Dir.

Kaskaskia College
Small Business Development Center
27210 College Rd.
Centralia, IL 62801-7878
Phone: (618)532-2049
Fax: (618)532-4983
Richard McCullum, Dir.

University of Illinois at Urbana-Champaign
International Trade Center
Small Business Development Center
428 Commerce W.
1206 S. 6th St.
Champaign, IL 61820-6980
Phone: (217)244-1585
Fax: (217)333-7410
Tess Morrison, Dir.

Asian American Alliance
SBDC
222 W. Cermak, No. 302
Chicago, IL 60616
Phone: (312)326-2200
Fax: (312)326-0399
Emil Bernardo, Dir.

Back of the Yards Neighborhood Council
Small Business Development Center
1751 W. 47th St.
Chicago, IL 60609-3889
Phone: (773)523-4419
Fax: (773)254-3525
Bill Przybylski, Dir.

Chicago Small Business Development Center
DCCA/James R. Thompson Center
100 W. Randolph, Ste. 3-400
Chicago, IL 60601-3219
Phone: (312)814-6111
Fax: (312)814-5247
Carson A. Gallagher, Mgr.

Eighteenth Street Development Corp.
Small Business Development Center
1839 S. Carpenter
Chicago, IL 60608-3347
Phone: (312)733-2287
Fax: (312)733-8242
Maria Munoz, Dir.

Greater North Pulaski Development Corp.
Small Business Development Center
4054 W. North Ave.
Chicago, IL 60639-5223
Phone: (773)384-2262
Fax: (773)384-3850
Kaushik Shah, Dir.

Industrial Council of Northwest Chicago
Small Business Development Center
2023 W. Carroll
Chicago, IL 60612-1601
Phone: (312)421-3941
Fax: (312)421-1871
Melvin Eiland, Dir.

Latin American Chamber of Commerce
Small Business Development Center
3512 W. Fullerton St.
Chicago, IL 60647-2655
Phone: (773)252-5211
Fax: (773)252-7065
Ed Diaz, Dir.

North Business and Industrial Council (NORBIC)
SBDC
2500 W. Bradley Pl.
Chicago, IL 60618-4798
Phone: (773)588-5855
Fax: (773)588-0734
Tom Kamykowski, Dir.

Richard J. Daley College
Small Business Development Center
7500 S. Pulaski Rd., Bldg. 200
Chicago, IL 60652-1299
Phone: (773)838-0319
Fax: (773)838-0303
Jim Charney, Dir.

Women's Business Development Center
Small Business Development Center
8 S. Michigan, Ste. 400
Chicago, IL 60603-3302
Phone: (312)853-3477
Fax: (312)853-0145
Joyce Wade, Dir.

McHenry County College
Small Business Development Center
8900 U.S. Hwy. 14
Crystal Lake, IL 60012-2761
Phone: (815)455-6098
Fax: (815)455-9319
Susan Whitfield, Dir.

Danville Area Community College
Small Business Development Center
28 W. North St.
Danville, IL 61832-5729
Phone: (217)442-7232
Fax: (217)442-6228
Ed Adrain, Dir.

Cooperative Extension Service
SBDC
Building 11, Ste. 1105
2525 E. Federal Dr.
Decatur, IL 62526-1573
Phone: (217)875-8284
Fax: (217)875-8288
Bill Wilkinson, Dir.

Sauk Valley Community College
Small Business Development Center
173 Illinois, Rte. 2
Dixon, IL 61021-9188
Phone: (815)288-5511
Fax: (815)288-5958
John Nelson, Dir.

Black Hawk College
Small Business Development Center
301 42nd Ave.
East Moline, IL 61244-4038
Phone: (309)755-2200
Fax: (309)755-9847
Donna Scalf, Dir.

East St. Louis Small Business Development Center
Federal Building
650 Missouri Ave., Ste. G32
East St. Louis, IL 62201-2955
Phone: (618)482-3833
Fax: (618)482-3859
Robert Ahart, Dir.

Southern Illinois University at Edwardsville
Small Business Development Center
Campus Box 1107
Edwardsville, IL 62026-0001
Phone: (618)692-2929
Fax: (618)692-2647
Alan Hauff, Dir.

Elgin Community College
Small Business Development Center
1700 Spartan Dr.
Elgin, IL 60123-7193
Phone: (847)888-7488
Fax: (847)931-3911
Craig Fowler, Dir.

Evanston Business and Technology Center
Small Business Development Center
1840 Oak Ave.
Evanston, IL 60201-3670
Phone: (847)866-1817
Fax: (847)866-1808
Rick Holbrook, Dir.

College of DuPage
Small Business Development Center
425 22nd St.
Glen Ellyn, IL 60137-6599
Phone: (630)942-2771
Fax: (630)942-3789
David Gay, Dir.

Lewis and Clark Community College
SBDC
5800 Godfrey Rd.
Godfrey, IL 62035
Phone: (618)466-3411
Fax: (618)466-0810
Bob Duane, Dir.

College of Lake County
Small Business Development Center
19351 W. Washington St.
Grayslake, IL 60030-1198
Phone: (847)223-3633
Fax: (847)223-9371
Linda Jorn, Dir.

Southeastern Illinois College
Small Business Development Center
303 S. Commercial
Harrisburg, IL 62946-2125
Phone: (618)252-5001
Fax: (618)252-0210
Becky Williams, Dir.

Rend Lake College
Small Business Development Center
Rte. 1
Ina, IL 62846-9801
Phone: (618)437-5321
Fax: (618)437-5677
Lisa Payne, Dir.

Joliet Junior College
Small Business Development Center
Renaissance Center, Rm. 312
214 N. Ottawa St.
Joliet, IL 60431-4097
Phone: (815)727-6544
Fax: (815)722-1895
Denise Mikulski, Dir.

Kankakee Community College
Small Business Development Center
River Rd., Box 888
Kankakee, IL 60901-7878
Phone: (815)933-0376
Fax: (815)933-0217
Kelly Berry, Dir.

Western Illinois University
Small Business Development Center
214 Seal Hall
Macomb, IL 61455-1390
Phone: (309)298-2211
Fax: (309)298-2520
Dan Voorhis, Dir.

Maple City Business and Technology Center
Small Business Development Center
620 S. Main St.
Monmouth, IL 61462-2688
Phone: (309)734-4664
Fax: (309)734-8579
Carol Cook, Dir.

Illinois Valley Community College
Small Business Development Center
815 N. Orlando Smith Ave., Bldg. 11
Oglesby, IL 61348-9692
Phone: (815)223-1740
Fax: (815)224-3033
Boyd Palmer, Dir.

Illinois Eastern Community College
Small Business Development Center
401 E. Main St.
Olney, IL 62450-2119
Phone: (618)395-3011
Fax: (618)395-1922
Debbie Chilson, Dir.

Moraine Valley Community College
Small Business Development Center
10900 S. 88th Ave.
Palos Hills, IL 60465-0937
Phone: (708)974-5468
Fax: (708)974-0078
Hilary Gereg, Dir.

Bradley University
Small Business Development Center
141 N. Jobst Hall, 1st Fl.
Peoria, IL 61625-0001
Phone: (309)677-2992
Fax: (309)677-3386
Roger Luman, Dir.

Illinois Central College
Procurement Technical Assistance Center
Small Business Development Center
124 SW Adams St., Ste. 300
Peoria, IL 61602-1388
Phone: (309)676-7500
Fax: (309)676-7534
Susan Gorman, Dir.

John Wood Community College
Procurement Technical Assistance Center
Small Business Development Center
301 Oak St.
Quincy, IL 62301-2500
Phone: (217)228-5511
Fax: (217)228-5501
Edward Van Leer, Dir.

Rock Valley College
Small Business Development Center
1220 Rock St.
Rockford, IL 61101-1437
Phone: (815)968-4087
Fax: (815)968-4157
Shirley DeBenedetto, Dir.

Department of Commerce & Community Affairs
Illinois SBDC
620 East Adams St., Third Fl.
Springfield, IL 62701
Phone: (217)524-5856
Fax: (217)524-0171
Jeff Mitchell, State Dir.

Lincoln Land Community College
Small Business Development Center
100 N. 11th St.
Springfield, IL 62703-1002
Phone: (217)789-1017
Fax: (217)789-9838
Freida Schreck, Dir.

Shawnee Community College
Small Business Development Center
Shawnee College Rd.
Ullin, IL 62992
Phone: (618)634-9618
Fax: (618)634-2347
Donald Denny, Dir.

Governors State University
Small Business Development Center
College of Business, Rm. C-3370
University Park, IL 60466-0975
Phone: (708)534-4929
Fax: (708)534-1646
Christine Cochrane, Dir.

Indiana

Batesville Office of Economic Development
SBDC
132 S. Main
Batesville, IN 47006
Phone: (812)933-6110

Bedford Chamber of Commerce
SBDC
1116 W. 16th St.
Bedford, IN 47421
Phone: (812)275-4493

Bloomfield Chamber of Commerce
SBDC
c/o Harrah Realty Co.
23 S. Washington St.
Bloomfield, IN 47424
Phone: (812)275-4493

Bloomington Area Regional Small Business Development Center
216 Allen St.
Bloomington, IN 47403
Phone: (812)339-8937
Fax: (812)335-7352
David Miller, Dir.

Clay Count Chamber of Commerce
SBDC
12 N. Walnut St.
Brazil, IN 47834
Phone: (812)448-8457

Brookville Chamber of Commerce
SBDC
PO Box 211
Brookville, IN 47012
Phone: (317)647-3177

Clinton Chamber of Commerce
SBDC

292 N. 9th St.
Clinton, IN 47842
Phone: (812)832-3844

Columbia City Chamber of Commerce
SBDC
112 N. Main St.
Columbia City, IN 46725
Phone: (219)248-8131

Columbus Regional Small Business Development Center
4920 N. Warren Dr.
Columbus, IN 47203
Phone: (812)372-6480
Free: (800)282-7232
Fax: (812)372-0228
Jack Hess, Dir.

Connerville SBDC
504 Central
Connersville, IN 47331
Phone: (317)825-8328

Harrison County Development Center
SBDC
405 N. Capitol, Ste. 308
Corydon, IN 47112
Phone: (812)738-8811

Montgomery County Chamber of Commerce
SBDC
211 S. Washington St.
Crawfordsville, IN 47933
Phone: (317)654-5507

Decatur Chamber of Commerce
SBDC
125 E. Monroe St.
Decatur, IN 46733
Phone: (219)724-2604

City of Delphi Community Development
SBDC
201 S. Union
Delphi, IN 46923
Phone: (317)564-6692

Southwestern Indiana Regional Small Business Development Center
100 NW 2nd St., Ste. 200
Evansville, IN 47708
Phone: (812)425-7232
Fax: (812)421-5883
Kate Northrup, Dir.

Northeast Indiana Regional Small Business Development Center
1830 Wayne Trace
Fort Wayne, IN 46803
Phone: (219)426-0040
Fax: (219)424-0024
E-mail: sbdc@mailfwi.com
Nick Adams, Dir.

Clinton County Chamber of Commerce
SBDC
207 S. Main St.
Frankfort, IN 46041
Phone: (317)654-5507

Northlake Small Business Development Center
487 Broadway, Ste. 201
Gary, IN 46402
Phone: (219)882-2000

Greencastle Partnership Center
SBDC
2 S. Jackson St.
Greencastle, IN 46135
Phone: (317)653-4517

Greensburg Area Chamber of Commerce
SBDC
125 W. Main St.
Greensburg, IN 47240
Phone: (812)663-2832

Hammond Development Corp.
SBDC
649 Conkey St.
Hammond, IN 46324
Phone: (219)853-6399

Blackford County Economic Development
SBDC
PO Box 43
Hartford, IN 47001-0043
Phone: (317)348-4944

Indiana SBDC Network
One North Capitol, Ste. 420
Indianapolis, IN 46204
Phone: (317)264-6871
Fax: (317)264-3102
E-mail: sthrash@in.net
Stephen Thrash, Exec. Dir.

Indianapolis Regional Small Business Development Center
342 N. Senate Ave.
Indianapolis, IN 46204-1708
Phone: (317)261-3030
Fax: (317)261-3053
Glenn Dunlap, Dir.

Clark County Hoosier Falls Private Industry Council Workforce
1613 E. 8th St.
Jeffersonville, IN 47130
Phone: (812)282-0456

Southern Indiana Regional Small Business Development Center
1613 E. 8th St.
Jeffersonville, IN 47130
Phone: (812)288-6451
Fax: (812)284-8314
Patricia Stroud, Dir.

Kendallville Chamber of Commerce
SBDC
228 S. Main St.
Kendallville, IN 46755
Phone: (219)347-1554

Kokomo-Howard County Regional Small Business Development Center
106 N. Washington
Kokomo, IN 46901
Phone: (317)454-7922
Fax: (317)452-4564
E-mail: sbdc5@holli.com
Kim Moyers, Dir.

LaPorte Small Business Development Center
414 Lincolnway
La Porte, IN 46350
Phone: (219)326-7232

Greater Lafayette Regional Area Small Business Development Center
122 N. 3rd
Lafayette, IN 47901
Phone: (765)742-2394
Fax: (765)742-6276
Susan Davis, Dir.

Union County Chamber of Commerce
SBDC
102 N. Main St., No. 6
Liberty, IN 47353-1039
Phone: (317)458-5976

Linton/Stockton Chamber of Commerce
SBDC
PO Box 208
Linton, IN 47441
Phone: (812)847-4846

Southeastern Indiana Regional Small Business Development Center
975 Industrial Dr.
Madison, IN 47250
Phone: (812)265-3127
Fax: (812)265-5544
E-mail: seinsbdc@seidata.com
Rose Marie Roberts, Dir.

Crawford County
Private Industry Council Workforce
SBDC
Box 224 D, R.R. 1
Marengo, IN 47140
Phone: (812)365-2174

Greater Martinsville Chamber of Commerce
SBDC
210 N. Marion St.
Martinsville, IN 46151
Phone: (317)342-8110

Lake County Public Library
Small Business Development Center
1919 W. 81st. Ave.
Merrillville, IN 46410-5382
Phone: (219)756-7232

First Citizens Bank
SBDC
515 N. Franklin Sq.
Michigan City, IN 46360
Phone: (219)874-9245

Mitchell Chamber of Commerce
SBDC
1st National Bank
Main Street
Mitchell, IN 47446
Phone: (812)849-4441

Mt. Vernon Chamber of Commerce
SBDC
405 E. 4th St.
Mt. Vernon, IN 47620
Phone: (812)838-3639

East Central Indiana Regional Small Business Development Center
401 S. High St.
PO Box 842
Muncie, IN 47305
Phone: (765)284-8144
Fax: (765)751-9151
Barbara Armstrong, Dir.

Brown County Chamber of Commerce
SBDC
PO Box 164
Nashville, IN 47448
Phone: (812)988-6647

Southern Indiana Small Business Development Center
Private Industry Council Workforce
4100 Charleston Rd.
New Albany, IN 47150
Phone: (812)945-0266
Fax: (812)948-4664
Gretchen Mahaffey, Dir.

Henry County Economic Development Corp.
SBDC
1325 Broad St., Ste. B
New Castle, IN 47362
Phone: (317)529-4635

Jennings County Chamber of Commerce
SBDC
PO Box 340
North Vernon, IN 47265
Phone: (812)346-2339

Orange County
Private Industry Council Workforce
SBDC
326 B. N. Gospel
Paoli, IN 47454-1412
Phone: (812)723-4206

Northwest Indiana Regional Small Business Development Center
Small Business Development Center
6100 Southport Rd.
Portage, IN 46368
Phone: (219)762-1696
Fax: (219)763-2653
Mark McLaughlin, Dir

Jay County Development Corp.
SBDC
121 W. Main St., Ste. A
Portland, IN 47371
Phone: (219)726-9311

Richmond-Wayne County Small Business Development Center
33 S. 7th St.
Richmond, IN 47374
Phone: (765)962-2887
Fax: (765)966-0882
Cliff Fry, Dir.

Rochester and Lake Manitou Chamber of Commerce
Fulton Economic Development Center
SBDC
617 Main St.
Rochester, IN 46975
Phone: (219)223-6773

Rushville Chamber of Commerce
SBDC
PO Box 156
Rushville, IN 46173
Phone: (317)932-2222

St. Mary of the Woods College
SBDC
St. Mary-of-the-Woods, IN 47876
Phone: (812)535-5151

Washington County
Private Industry Council Workforce
SBDC
Hilltop Plaza
Salem, IN 47167
Phone: (812)883-2283

Scott County
Private Industry Council Workforce
SBDC
752 Lakeshore Dr.
Scottsburg, IN 47170
Phone: (812)752-3886

Seymour Chamber of Commerce
SBDC
PO Box 43
Seymour, IN 47274
Phone: (812)522-3681

Minority Business Development
Project Future
SBDC
401 Col
South Bend, IN 46634
Phone: (219)234-0051

South Bend Regional Small Business Development Center
300 N. Michigan
South Bend, IN 46601
Phone: (219)282-4350
Fax: (219)236-1056
Jim Gregar, Dir.

Economic Development Office
SBDC
46 E. Market St.
Spencer, IN 47460
Phone: (812)829-3245

Sullivan Chamber of Commerce
SBDC
10 S. Crt. St.
Sullivan, IN 47882
Phone: (812)268-4836

Tell City Chamber of Commerce
SBDC
645 Main St.
Tell City, IN 47586
Phone: (812)547-2385
Fax: (812)547-8378

Terre Haute Area Small Business Development Center
School of Business, Rm. 510
Terre Haute, IN 47809
Phone: (812)237-7676
Fax: (812)237-7675
William Minnis, Dir.

Tipton County Economic Development Corp.
SBDC
136 E. Jefferson
Tipton, IN 46072
Phone: (317)675-7300

Porter County
SBDC
911 Wall St.
Valparaiso, IN 46383
Phone: (219)477-5256

Vevay/Switzerland Country Foundation
SBDC
PO Box 193
Vevay, IN 47043
Phone: (812)427-2533

Vincennes University
SBDC
PO Box 887
Vincennes, IN 47591
Phone: (812)885-5749

Wabash Area Chamber of Commerce
Wabash Economic Development Corp.
SBDC
67 S. Wabash
Wabash, IN 46992
Phone: (219)563-1168

Washington Daviess County
SBDC
1 Train Depot St.
Washington, IN 47501
Phone: (812)254-5262
Fax: (812)254-2550
Mark Brochin, Dir.

Purdue University
SBDC
Business & Industrial Development Center
1220 Potter Dr.
West Lafayette, IN 47906
Phone: (317)494-5858

Randolph County Economic Development Foundation
SBDC
111 S. Main St.
Winchester, IN 47394
Phone: (317)584-3266

Iowa

Iowa SBDC
137 Lynn Ave.
Ames, IA 50014
Phone: (515)292-6351
Free: (800)373-7232
Fax: (515)292-0020
Ronald Manning, State Dir.

Iowa State University
Small Business Development Center
ISU Branch Office
Bldg. 1, Ste. 615
2501 N. Loop Dr.
Ames, IA 50010-8283
Phone: (515)296-7828
Free: (800)373-7232
Fax: (515)296-6714
Steve Carter, Dir.

DMACC Small Business Development Center
Circle West Incubator
PO Box 204
Audubon, IA 50025
Phone: (712)563-2623
Fax: (712)563-2301
Lori Harmening, Dir.

University of Northern Iowa
Small Business Development Center
8628 University Ave.
Cedar Falls, IA 50614-0032
Phone: (319)273-2696
Fax: (319)273-7730
Lyle Bowlin, Dir.

Iowa Western Community College
Small Business Development Center
2700 College Rd., Box 4C
Council Bluffs, IA 51502
Phone: (712)325-3260
Fax: (712)325-3408
Ronald Helms, Dir.

Southwestern Community College
Small Business Development Center
1501 W. Townline Rd.
Creston, IA 50801
Phone: (515)782-4161
Fax: (515)782-3312
Robin Beech Travis, Dir.

Eastern Iowa Small Business Development Center
304 W. 2nd St.
Davenport, IA 52801
Phone: (319)322-4499
Fax: (319)322-8241
Jon Ryan, Dir.

Drake University
Small Business Development Center
2507 University Ave.
Des Moines, IA 50311-4505
Phone: (515)271-2655
Fax: (515)271-1899
Benjamin Swartz, Dir.

Northeast Iowa Small Business Development Center
770 Town Clock Plz.
Dubuque, IA 52001
Phone: (319)588-3350
Fax: (319)557-1591
Charles Tonn, Dir.

Iowa Central Community College
SBDC
900 Central Ave., Ste. 4
Ft. Dodge, IA 50501
Phone: (515)576-5090
Fax: (515)576-0826
Todd Madson, Dir.

University of Iowa
Small Business Development Center
108 Papajohn Business Administration Bldg., Ste. S-160
Iowa City, IA 52242-1000
Phone: (319)335-3742
Free: (800)253-7232
Fax: (319)353-2445
Paul Heath, Dir.

Kirkwood Community College
Small Business Development Center
2901 10th Ave.
Marion, IA 52302

Phone: (319)377-8256
Fax: (319)377-5667
Steve Sprague, Dir.

North Iowa Area Community College
Small Business Development Center
500 College Dr.
Mason City, IA 50401
Phone: (515)422-4342
Fax: (515)422-4129
Richard Petersen, Dir.

Indian Hills Community College
Small Business Development Center
525 Grandview Ave.
Ottumwa, IA 52501
Phone: (515)683-5127
Fax: (515)683-5263
Bryan Ziegler, Dir.

Western Iowa Tech Community College
Small Business Development Center
4647 Stone Ave.
PO Box 5199
Sioux City, IA 51102-5199
Phone: (712)274-6418
Free: (800)352-4649
Fax: (712)274-6429
Dennis Bogenrief, Dir.

Iowa Lakes Community College (Spencer)
Small Business Development Center
1900 N. Grand Ave., Ste. 8
Hwy. 71 N
Spencer, IA 51301
Phone: (712)262-4213
Fax: (712)262-4047
John Beneke, Dir.

Southeastern Community College
Small Business Development Center
Drawer F
West Burlington, IA 52655
Phone: (319)752-2731
Free: (800)828-7322
Fax: (319)752-3407
Deb Dalziel, Dir.

Kansas

Bendictine College
SBDC
1020 N. 2nd St.
Atchison, KS 66002
Phone: (913)367-5340
Fax: (913)367-6102
Don Laney, Dir.

Butler County Community College
Small Business Development Center
600 Walnut
Augusta, KS 67010
Phone: (316)775-1124
Fax: (316)775-1370
Dorinda Rolle, Dir.

Neosho County Community College
SBDC
1000 S. Allen
Chanute, KS 66720
Phone: (316)431-2820
Fax: (316)431-0082
Duane Clum, Dir.

Coffeyville Community College
SBDC
11th and Willow Sts.
Coffeyville, KS 67337-5064
Phone: (316)251-7700
Fax: (316)252-7098
Charles Shaver, Dir.

Colby Community College
Small Business Development Center
1255 S. Range
Colby, KS 67701
Phone: (913)462-3984
Fax: (913)462-8315
Robert Selby, Dir.

Cloud County Community College
SBDC
2221 Campus Dr.
PO Box 1002
Concordia, KS 66901
Phone: (913)243-1435
Fax: (913)243-1459
Tony Foster, Dir.

Dodge City Community College
Small Business Development Center
2501 N. 14th Ave.
Dodge City, KS 67801
Phone: (316)227-9247
Fax: (316)227-9200
Wayne E. Shiplet, Dir.

Emporia State University
Small Business Development Center
130 Cremer Hall
Emporia, KS 66801
Phone: (316)342-7162
Fax: (316)341-5418
Lisa Brumbaugh, Regional Dir.

Ft. Scott Community College
SBDC
2108 S. Horton
Ft. Scott, KS 66701
Phone: (316)223-2700
Fax: (316)223-6530
Steve Pammenter, Dir.

Garden City Community College
SBDC
801 Campus Dr.
Garden City, KS 67846
Phone: (316)276-9632
Fax: (316)276-9630
Bill Sander, Regional Dir.

Ft. Hays State University
Small Business Development Center
109 W. 10th St.
Hays, KS 67601
Phone: (785)628-6786
Fax: (785)628-0533
Clare Gustin, Regional Dir.

Hutchinson Community College
Small Business Development Center
815 N. Walnut, Ste. 225
Hutchinson, KS 67501
Phone: (316)665-4950
Free: (800)289-3501
Fax: (316)665-8354
Clark Jacobs, Dir.

Independence Community College
SBDC
Arco Bldg.
11th and Main St.
Independence, KS 67301
Phone: (316)332-1420
Fax: (316)331-5344
Preston Haddan, Dir.

Allen County Community College
SBDC
1801 N. Cottonwood
Iola, KS 66749
Phone: (316)365-5116
Fax: (316)365-3284
Susan Thompson, Dir.

University of Kansas
Small Business Development Center
734 Vermont St., Ste. 104
Lawrence, KS 66044
Phone: (785)843-8844
Fax: (785)865-8878
Randy Brady, Regional Dir.

Seward County Community College
Small Business Development Center
1801 N. Kansas

PO Box 1137
Liberal, KS 67901
Phone: (316)629-2650
Fax: (316)629-2689
Dale Reed, Dir.

Kansas State University (Manhattan)
Small Business Development Center
College of Business Administration
2323 Anderson Ave., Ste. 100
Manhattan, KS 66502-2947
Phone: (785)532-5529
Fax: (785)532-5827
Fred Rice, Regional Dir.

Ottawa University
SBDC
College Ave., Box 70
Ottawa, KS 66067
Phone: (913)242-5200
Fax: (913)242-7429
Lori Kravets, Dir.

Johnson County Community College
Small Business Development Center
CEC Bldg., Rm. 223
Overland Park, KS 66210-1299
Phone: (913)469-3878
Fax: (913)469-4415
Kathy Nadiman, Regional Dir.

Labette Community College
SBDC
200 S. 14th
Parsons, KS 67357
Phone: (316)421-6700
Fax: (316)421-0921
Mark Turnbull, Dir.

Pittsburg State University
Small Business Development Center
Shirk Hall
1501 S. Joplin
Pittsburg, KS 66762
Phone: (316)235-4920
Fax: (316)232-6440
Kathryn Richard

Pratt Community College
Small Business Development Center
Hwy. 61
Pratt, KS 67124
Phone: (316)672-5641
Fax: (316)672-5288
Pat Gordon, Dir.

Salina Area Chamber of Commerce
Small Business Development Center
PO Box 586
Salina, KS 67402
Phone: (785)827-9301
Fax: (785)827-9758
James Gaines, Regional Dir.

Kansas SBDC
214 SW 6th St., Ste. 205
Topeka, KS 66603-3261
Phone: (785)296-6514
Fax: (785)291-3261
E-mail: ksbdc@cjnetworks.com
Debbie Bishop, State Dir.

Washburn University of Topeka
SBDC
School of Business
101 Henderson Learning Center
Topeka, KS 66621
Phone: (785)231-1010
Fax: (785)231-1063
Don Kingman, Regional Dir.

Wichita State University
SBDC
1845 Fairmont
Wichita, KS 67260
Phone: (316)689-3193
Fax: (316)689-3647
Joann Ard, Regional Dir.

Kentucky

Morehead State University College of Business
Boyd-Greenup County Chamber of Commerce
SBDC
1401 Winchester Ave., Ste. 305
207 15th St.
Ashland, KY 41101
Phone: (606)329-8011
Fax: (606)324-4570
Kimberly A. Jenkins, Dir.

Western Kentucky University
Bowling Green Small Business Development Center
2355 Nashville Rd.
Bowling Green, KY 42101
Phone: (502)745-1905
Fax: (502)745-1931
Richard S. Horn, Dir.

University of Kentucky (Elizabethtown)
Small Business Development Center
133 W. Dixie Ave.
Elizabethtown, KY 42701
Phone: (502)765-6737
Fax: (502)769-5095
Lou Ann Allen, Dir.

Northern Kentucky University
SBDC
BEP Center 463
Highland Heights, KY 41099-0506
Phone: (606)572-6524
Fax: (606)572-6177
Sutton Landry, Dir.

Murray State University (Hopkinsville)
Small Business Development Center
300 Hammond Dr.
Hopkinsville, KY 42240
Phone: (502)886-8666
Fax: (502)886-3211
Michael Cartner, Dir.

Small Business Development Center
Lexington Central Library, 4th Fl.
140 E. Main St.
Lexington, KY 40507-1376
Phone: (606)257-7666
Fax: (606)257-1751
Debbie McKnight, Dir.

University of Kentucky
Center for Entrepreneurship
Kentucky SBDC
225 Gatton Business and Economics Bldg.
Lexington, KY 40506-0034
Phone: (606)257-7668
Fax: (606)323-1907
Janet S. Holloway, State Dir.

Bellarmine College
Small Business Development Center
School of Business
600 W. Main St., Ste. 219
Louisville, KY 40202
Phone: (502)574-4770
Fax: (502)574-4771
Thomas G. Daley, Dir.

University of Louisville
Center for Entrepreneurship and Technology
Small Business Development Centers
Burhans Hall, Shelby Campus, Rm. 122
Louisville, KY 40292
Phone: (502)588-7854
Fax: (502)588-8573
Lou Dickie, Dir.

Southeast Community College
SBDC
1300 Chichester Ave.
Middlesboro, KY 40965-2265
Phone: (606)242-2145
Fax: (606)242-4514
Kathleen Moats, Dir.

Morehead State University
Small Business Development Center
309 Combs Bldg.
UPO 575
Morehead, KY 40351
Phone: (606)783-2895
Fax: (606)783-5020
Keith Moore, District Dir.

Murray State University
West Kentucky Small Business Development Center
College of Business and Public Affairs
PO Box 9
Murray, KY 42071
Phone: (502)762-2856
Fax: (502)762-3049
Rosemary Miller, Dir.

Murray State University
Owensboro Small Business Development Center
3860 U.S. Hwy. 60 W
Owensboro, KY 42301
Phone: (502)926-8085
Fax: (502)684-0714
Mickey Johnson, District Dir.

Moorehead State University
Pikeville Small Business Development Center
3455 N. Mayo Trail, No. 4
110 Village St.
Pikeville, KY 41501
Phone: (606)432-5848
Fax: (606)432-8924
Michael Morley, Dir.

Eastern Kentucky University
South Central Small Business Development Center
The Center for Rural Development, Ste. 260
2292 S. Hwy. 27
Somerset, KY 42501
Phone: (606)677-6120
Fax: (606)677-6083
Kathleen Moats, Dir.

Louisiana

Alexandria SBDC
Hibernia National Bank Bldg., Ste. 510
934 3rd St.
Alexandria, LA 71301
Phone: (318)484-2123
Fax: (318)484-2126
Kathey Hunter, Consultant

Southern University
Capital Small Business Development Center
1933 Wooddale Blvd., Ste. E
Baton Rouge, LA 70806
Phone: (504)922-0998
Fax: (504)922-0024
Gregory Spann, Dir.

Southeastern Louisiana University
Small Business Development Center
College of Business Administration
Box 522, SLU Sta.
Hammond, LA 70402
Phone: (504)549-3831
Fax: (504)549-2127
William Joubert, Dir.

University of Southwestern Louisiana
Acadiana Small Business Development Center
College of Business Administration
Box 43732
Lafayette, LA 70504
Phone: (318)262-5344
Fax: (318)262-5296
Kim Spence, Dir.

McNeese State University
Small Business Development Center
College of Business Administration
Lake Charles, LA 70609
Phone: (318)475-5529
Fax: (318)475-5012
Paul Arnold, Dir.

Louisiana Electronic Assistance Program
SBDC
NE Louisiana, College of Business Administration
Monroe, LA 71209
Phone: (318)342-1215
Fax: (318)342-1209
Dr. Jerry Wall, Dir.

Northeast Louisiana University
SBDC
Louisiana SBDC
College of Business Administration, Rm. 2-57
Room 2-57
Monroe, LA 71209
Phone: (318)342-5506
Fax: (318)342-5510
Dr. John Baker, State Dir.

Northeast Louisiana University
Small Business Development Center
College of Business Administration, Rm. 2-57
Monroe, LA 71209
Phone: (318)342-1215
Fax: (318)342-1209
Dr. Paul Dunn, Dir.

Northwestern State University
Small Business Development Center
College of Business Administration
Natchitoches, LA 71497
Phone: (318)357-5611
Fax: (318)357-6810
Mary Lynn Wilkerson, Dir.

Louisiana International Trade Center
SBDC
World Trade Center, Ste. 2926
2 Canal St.
New Orleans, LA 70130
Phone: (504)568-8222
Fax: (504)568-8228
Ruperto Chavarri, Dir.

Loyola University
Small Business Development Center
College of Business Administration
Box 134
New Orleans, LA 70118
Phone: (504)865-3474
Fax: (504)865-3496
Ronald Schroeder, Dir.

Southern University at New Orleans
Small Business Development Center
College of Business Administration
New Orleans, LA 70126
Phone: (504)286-5308
Fax: (504)286-5131
Jon Johnson, Dir.

University of New Orleans
Small Business Development Center
1600 Canal St., Ste. 620
New Orleans, LA 70112
Phone: (504)539-9292

Fax: (504)539-9205
Norma Grace, Dir.

Louisiana Tech University
Small Business Development Center
College of Business Administration
Box 10318, Tech Sta.
Ruston, LA 71272
Phone: (318)257-3537
Fax: (318)257-4253
Tracey Jeffers, Dir.

Louisiana State University at Shreveport
Small Business Development Center
College of Business Administration
1 University Dr.
Shreveport, LA 71115
Phone: (318)797-5144
Fax: (318)797-5208
Peggy Cannon, Dir.

Nicholls State University
Small Business Development Center
College of Business Administration
PO Box 2015
Thibodaux, LA 70310
Phone: (504)448-4242
Fax: (504)448-4922
Weston Hull, Dir.

Maine

Androscoggin Valley Council of Governments
Small Business Development Center
125 Manley Rd.
Auburn, ME 04210
Phone: (207)783-9186
Fax: (207)783-5211
Jane Mickeriz, Counselor

Coastal Enterprises Inc.
SBDC
Weston Bldg.
7 N. Chestnut St.
Augusta, ME 04330
Phone: (207)621-0245
Fax: (207)622-9739
Robert Chiozzi, Counselor

Eastern Maine Development Corp.
Small Business Development Center
1 Cumberland Pl., Ste. 300
PO Box 2579
Bangor, ME 04402-2579
Phone: (207)942-6389
Free: (800)339-6389
Fax: (207)942-3548
Ron Loyd, Dir.

Belfast Satellite
Waldo County Development Corp.
SBDC
67 Church St.
Belfast, ME 04915
Phone: (207)942-6389
Free: (800)339-6389
Fax: (207)942-3548

Brunswick Satellite
Midcoast Council for Business Development
SBDC
8 Lincoln St.
Brunswick, ME 04011
Phone: (207)882-4340

Northern Maine Development Commission
Small Business Development Center
2 S. Main St.
PO Box 779
Caribou, ME 04736
Phone: (207)498-8736
Free: (800)427-8736
Fax: (207)498-3108
Rodney Thompson, Dir.

East Millinocket Satellite
Katahdin Regional Development Corp.
SBDC
58 Main St.
East Millinocket, ME 04430
Phone: (207)746-5338
Fax: (207)746-9535

East Wilton Satellite
Robinhood Plaza
Rte. 2 & 4
East Wilton, ME 04234
Phone: (207)783-9186
Fax: (207)783-9186

Fort Kent Satellite
SBDC
Aroostook County Registry of Deeds
Elm and Hall Sts.
Fort Kent, ME 04743
Phone: (207)498-8736
Free: (800)427-8736
Fax: (207)498-3108

Houlton Satellite
SBDC
Superior Court House
Court St.
Houlton, ME 04730
Phone: (207)498-8736
Free: (800)427-8736
Fax: (207)498-3108

Lewiston Satellite
Business Information Center (BIC)
SBDC
Bates Mill Complex
35 Canal St.
Lewiston, ME 04240
Phone: (207)783-9186
Fax: (207)783-5211

Machias Satellite
Sunrise County Economic Council (Calais Area)
SBDC
63 Main St.
PO Box 679
Machias, ME 04654
Phone: (207)454-2430
Fax: (207)255-0983

University of Southern Maine
Maine SBDC
96 Falmouth St.
PO Box 9300
Portland, ME 04104-9300
Phone: (207)780-4420
Fax: (207)780-4810
E-mail: msbdc@portland.maine.edu
Charles Davis, Dir.

Rockland Satellite
SBDC
331 Main St.
Rockland, ME 04841
Phone: (207)882-4340
Fax: (207)882-4456

Rumford Satellite
River Valley Growth Council
Hotel Harris Bldg.
23 Hartford St.
Rumford, ME 04276
Phone: (207)783-9186
Fax: (207)783-5211

Biddeford Satellite
Biddeford-Saco Chamber of Commerce and Industry
SBDC
110 Main St.
Saco, ME 04072
Phone: (207)282-1567
Fax: (207)282-3149

Southern Maine Regional Planning Commission
Small Business Development Center
255 Main St.
PO Box Q
Sanford, ME 04073
Phone: (207)324-0316
Fax: (207)324-2958
Joseph Vitko, Dir.

Skowhegan Satellite
SBDC
Norridgewock Ave.
Skowhegan, ME 04976
Phone: (207)621-0245
Fax: (207)622-9739

South Paris Satellite
SBDC
166 Main St.
South Paris, ME 04281
Phone: (207)783-9186
Fax: (207)783-5211

Waterville Satellite
Thomas College
SBDC
Administrative Bldg. - Library
180 W. River Rd.
Waterville, ME 04901
Phone: (207)621-0245
Fax: (207)622-9739

Coastal Enterprises, Inc. (Wiscasset)
Small Business Development Center
Water St.
PO Box 268
Wiscasset, ME 04578
Phone: (207)882-4340
Fax: (207)882-4456
James Burbank, Dir.

York Satellite
York Chamber of Commerce
SBDC
449 Rte. 1
York, ME 03909
Phone: (207)363-4422
Fax: (207)324-2958

Maryland

Anne Arundel, Office of Economic Development
SBDC
2666 Riva Rd., Ste. 200
Annapolis, MD 21401
Phone: (410)224-4205
Fax: (410)222-7415
Mike Fish, Consultant

Central Maryland
SBDC
1420 N. Charles St., Rm 142
Baltimore, MD 21201-5779
Phone: (410)837-4141
Fax: (410)837-4151
Barney Wilson, Executive Dir.

Hartford County Economic Development Office
SBDC
220 S. Main St.
Bel Air, MD 21014
Phone: (410)893-3837
Fax: (410)879-8043
Maurice Brown, Consultant

Maryland Small Business Development Center
7100 Baltimore Ave., Ste. 401
College Park, MD 20740
Phone: (301)403-8300
Fax: (301)403-8303
James N. Graham, State Dir.

University of Maryland
SBDC
College of Business and Management
College Park, MD 20742-1815
Phone: (301)405-2144
Fax: (301)314-9152

Howard County Economic Development Office
SBDC
6751 Gateway Dr., Ste. 500
Columbia, MD 21044
Phone: (410)313-6552
Fax: (410)313-6556
Ellin Dize, Consultant

Western Maryland Small Business Development Center
Western Region, Inc.
3 Commerce Dr.
Cumberland, MD 21502
Phone: (301)724-6716
Free: (800)457-7232
Fax: (301)777-7504
Sam LaManna, Exec. Dir.

Cecil County Chamber of Commerce
SBDC
135 E. Main St.
Elkton, MD 21921
Phone: (410)392-0597
Fax: (410)392-6225
Maurice Brown, Consultant

Frederick Community College
SBDC
7932 Opossumtown Pike
Frederick, MD 21702
Phone: (301)846-2683
Fax: (301)846-2689
Website: http://SBDC
Mary Ann Garst, Program Dir.

Arundel Center N.
SBDC
101 Crain Hwy., NW, Rm. 110B
Glen Burnie, MD 21061
Phone: (410)766-1910
Fax: (410)766-1911
Mike Fish, Consultant

Community College at Saint Mary's County
SBDC
PO Box 98, Great Mills Rd.
Great Mills, MD 20634
Phone: (301)868-6679
Fax: (301)868-7392
James Shepherd

Hagerstown Junior College
SBDC
Technology Innovation Center
11404 Robinwood Dr.
Hagerstown, MD 21740
Phone: (301)797-0327
Fax: (301)777-7504
Tonya Fleming Brockett, Dir.

Landover SBDC
7950 New Hampshire Ave., 2nd Fl.
Langley Park, MD 20783
Phone: (301)445-7324
Fax: (301)883-6479
Avon Evans, Consultant

Charles County Community College
Southern Maryland SBDC
SBDC
Mitchell Rd.
PO Box 910
LaPlata, MD 20646-0910
Phone: (301)934-7580
Free: (800)762-7232
Fax: (301)934-7681
Betsy Cooksey, Exec. Dir.

Garrett Community College
SBDC
Mosser Rd.

McHenry, MD 21541
Phone: (301)387-6666
Fax: (301)387-3096
Sandy Major, Business Analyst

Salisbury State University
Eastern Shore Region Small Business Development Center
Power Professional Bldg., Ste. 170
Salisbury, MD 21801
Phone: (410)546-4325
Free: (800)999-7232
Fax: (410)548-5389
Marty Green, Exec. Dir.

Baltimore County Chamber of Commerce
SBDC
102 W. Pennsylvania Ave., Ste. 402
Towson, MD 21204
Phone: (410)832-5866
Fax: (410)821-9901
John Casper, Consultant

Prince George's County Minority Business Opportunities Commission
Suburban Washington Region Small Business Development Center
1400 McCormick Dr., Ste. 282
Upper Marlboro, MD 20774
Phone: (301)883-6491
Fax: (301)883-6479
Avon Evans, Acting Executive Dir.

Carrol County Economic Development Office
SBDC
125 N. Court St., Rm. 101
Westminster, MD 21157
Phone: (410)857-8166
Fax: (410)848-0003
Michael Fish, Consultant

Eastern Region - Upper Shore SBDC
PO Box 8
Wye Mills, MD 21679
Phone: (410)822-5400
Free: (800)762SBDC
Fax: (410)827-5286
Patricia Ann Marie Schaller, Consultant

Massachusetts

International Trade Center
University of Massachusetts Amherst
SBDC
205 School of Management
Amherst, MA 01003-4935
Phone: (413)545-6301
Fax: (413)545-1273

University of Massachusetts
Massachusetts SBDC
205 School of Management
Amherst, MA 01003-4935
Phone: (413)545-6301
Fax: (413)545-1273
John Ciccarelli, State Dir.

Massachusetts Export Center
World Trade Center, Ste. 315
Boston, MA 02210
Phone: (617)478-4133
Free: (800)478-4133
Fax: (617)478-4135
Paula Murphy, Dir.

Minority Business Assistance Center
SBDC
University of Massachusetts (Boston)
College of Management, 5th Fl.
Boston, MA 02125-3393
Phone: (617)287-7750
Fax: (617)287-7767
Hank Turner, Dir.

Boston College
Capital Formation Service
SBDC
Rahner House
96 College Rd.
Chestnut Hill, MA 02167
Phone: (617)552-4091
Fax: (617)552-2730
Don Reilley, Dir.

Metropolitan Boston Small Business Development Center Regional Office
Rahner House
96 College Rd.
Chestnut Hill, MA 02167
Phone: (617)552-4091
Fax: (617)552-2730
Dr. Jack McKiernan, Regional Dir.

Southeastern Massachusetts Small Business Development Center Regional Office
200 Pocasset St.
PO Box 2785
Fall River, MA 02722
Phone: (508)673-9783
Fax: (508)674-1929
Clyde Mitchell, Regional Dir.

North Shore Massachusetts Small Business Development Center Regional Office
197 Essex St.
Salem, MA 01970
Phone: (508)741-6343
Fax: (508)741-6345
Frederick Young, Regional Dir.

Western Massachusetts Small Business Development Center Regional Office
101 State St., Ste. 424
Springfield, MA 01103
Phone: (413)737-6712
Fax: (413)737-2312
Dianne Fuller Doherty, Regional Dir.

Clark University
Central Massachusetts Small Business Development Center Regional Office
Dana Commons
950 Main St.
Worcester, MA 01610
Phone: (508)793-7615
Fax: (508)793-8890
Laurence March, Regional Dir.

Michigan

Lenawee County Chamber of Commerce
SBDC
202 N. Main St., Ste. A
Adrian, MI 49221-2713
Phone: (517)266-1488
Fax: (517)263-6065
Sally Pinchock, Dir.

Allegan County Economic Alliance
SBDC
Allegan Intermediate School Bldg.
2891 M-277
PO Box 277
Allegan, MI 49010-8042
Phone: (616)673-8442
Fax: (616)650-8042
Chuck Birr, Dir.

Ottawa County Economic Development Office, Inc.
Small Business Development Center
6676 Lake Michigan Dr.
PO Box 539
Allendale, MI 49401-0539
Phone: (616)892-4120
Fax: (616)895-6670
Ken Rizzio, Dir.

Gratiot Area Chamber of Commerce
SBDC
110 W. Superior St.
PO Box 516
Alma, MI 48801-0516
Phone: (517)463-5525

Alpena Community College
SBDC
666 Johnson St.
Alpena, MI 49707
Phone: (517)356-9021
Fax: (517)354-7507
Carl Bourdelais, Dir.

MMTC SBDC
2901 Hubbard Rd.
PO Box 1485
Ann Arbor, MI 48106-1485
Phone: (313)769-4110
Fax: (313)769-4064
Bill Loomis, Dir.

Huron County Economic Development Corp.
Small Business Development Center
Huron County Bldg., Rm. 303
250 E. Huron
Bad Axe, MI 48413
Phone: (517)269-6431
Fax: (517)269-7221
Carl Osentoski, Dir.

Battle Creek Area Chamber of Commerce
SBDC
4 Riverwalk Centre
34 W. Jackson, Ste. A
Battle Creek, MI 49017
Phone: (616)962-4076
Fax: (616)962-4076
Kathy Perrett, Dir.

Bay Area Chamber of Commerce
SBDC
901 Saginaw
Bay City, MI 48708
Phone: (517)893-4567
Fax: (517)893-7016
Cheryl Hiner, Dir.

Lake Michigan College
Corporation and Community Development Department
Small Business Development Center
2755 E. Napier
Benton Harbor, MI 49022-1899
Phone: (616)927-8179
Fax: (616)927-8103
Milton E. Richter, Dir.

Ferris State University
Small Business Development Center
330 Oak St.
West 115
Big Rapids, MI 49307
Phone: (616)592-3553
Fax: (616)592-3539
Lora Swenson, Dir.

Northern Lakes Economic Alliance
SBDC
1048 East Main St.
PO Box 8
Boyne City, MI 49712-0008
Phone: (616)582-6482
Fax: (616)582-3213
Thomas Johnson, Dir.

Livingston County Small Business Development Center
131 S. Hyne
Brighton, MI 48116
Phone: (810)227-3556
Fax: (810)227-3080
Dennis Whitney, Dir.

Buchanan Chamber of Commerce
SBDC
119 Main St.
Buchanan, MI 49107
Phone: (616)695-3291
Fax: (616)695-4250
Marlene Gauer, Dir.

Tuscola County Economic Development Corp.
Small Business Development Center
194 N. State St., Ste. 200
Caro, MI 48723
Phone: (517)673-2849
Fax: (517)673-2517
James McLoskey, Dir.

Branch County Economic Growth Alliance
SBDC
20 Division St.
Coldwater, MI 49036
Phone: (517)278-4146
Fax: (517)278-8369
Joyce Elferdink, Dir.

University of Detroit-Mercy
Small Business Development Center
Commerce and Finance Bldg., Rm. 105
4001 W. McNichols
PO Box 19900
Detroit, MI 48219-0900
Phone: (313)993-1115
Fax: (313)993-1052
Ram Kesavan, Dir.

Wayne State University
Michigan SBDC
2727 Second Ave., Ste. 107
Detroit, MI 48201
Phone: (313)964-1798
Fax: (313)964-3648
E-mail: stateoffice@misbdc.wayne.edu
Ronald R. Hall, State Dir.

First Step, Inc.
Small Business Development Center
2415 14th Ave., S.
Escanaba, MI 49829
Phone: (906)786-9234
Fax: (906)786-4442
David Gillis, Dir.

Community Capital Development Corp.
SBDC
Walter Ruether Center
711 N. Saginaw, Ste. 123
Flint, MI 48503
Phone: (810)239-5847
Fax: (810)239-5575
Kim Yarber, Dir.

Center For Continuing Education-Macomb Community College
SBDC
32101 Caroline
Fraser, MI 48026
Phone: (810)296-3516
Fax: (810)293-0427

North Central Michigan College
SBDC
800 Livingston Blvd.
Gaylord, MI 49735
Phone: (517)731-0071

Association of Commerce and Industry
SBDC
1 S. Harbor Ave.
PO Box 509
Grand Haven, MI 49417
Phone: (616)846-3153
Fax: (616)842-0379
Karen K. Benson, Dir.

Grand Valley State University
SBDC
Seidman School of Business, Ste. 718S
301 W. Fulton St.
Grand Rapids, MI 49504
Phone: (616)771-6693
Fax: (616)458-3872
Carol R. Lopucki, Dir.

The Right Place Program
SBDC
820 Monroe NW, Ste. 350
Grand Rapids, MI 49503-1423
Phone: (616)771-0571
Fax: (616)458-3768
Raymond P. DeWinkle, Dir.

Oceana County Economic Development Corp.
SBDC
100 State St.
PO Box 168
Hart, MI 49420-0168
Phone: (616)873-7141
Fax: (616)873-5914
Charles Persenaire, Dir.

Hastings Industrial Incubator
SBDC
1035 E. State St.
Hastings, MI 49058
Phone: (616)948-2305
Fax: (616)948-2947
Joe Rahn, Dir.

Greater Gratiot Development, Inc.
Small Business Center
136 S. Main
Ithaca, MI 48847
Phone: (517)875-2083
Fax: (517)875-2990
Don Schurr, Dir.

Jackson Business Development Center
SBDC
414 N. Jackson St.
Jackson, MI 49201
Phone: (517)787-0442
Fax: (517)787-3960
Duane Miller, Dir.

Kalamazoo College
Small Business Development Center
Stryker Center for Management Studies
1327 Academy St.
Kalamazoo, MI 49006-3200
Phone: (616)337-7350
Fax: (616)337-7415
Carl R. Shook, Dir.

Lansing Community College
Small Business Development Center
Continental Bldg.
333 N. Washington Sq.
PO Box 40010
Lansing, MI 48901-7210
Phone: (517)483-1921
Fax: (517)483-9803
Deleski Smith, Dir.

Lapeer Development Corp.
Small Business Development Center
449 McCormick Dr.
Lapeer, MI 48446
Phone: (810)667-0080
Fax: (810)667-3541
Patricia Crawford Lucas, Dir.

Midland Chamber of Commerce
SBDC
300 Rodd St.
Midland, MI 48640
Phone: (517)839-9901
Fax: (517)835-3701
Sam Boeke, Dir.

Genesis Center for Entrepreneurial Development
SBDC
111 Conant Ave.
Monroe, MI 48161
Phone: (313)243-5947
Fax: (313)242-0009
Dani Topolski, Dir.

Macomb County Business Assistance Network
Small Business Development Center
115 S. Groesbeck Hwy.
Mt. Clemens, MI 48043
Phone: (810)469-5118
Fax: (810)469-6787
Donald L. Morandi, Dir.

Central Michigan University
Small Business Development Center
256 Applied Business Studies Complex
Mt. Pleasant, MI 48859
Phone: (517)774-3270
Fax: (517)774-7992
Charles Fitzpatrick, Dir.

Muskegon Economic Growth Alliance
Small Business Development Center
230 Terrace Plz.
PO Box 1087
Muskegon, MI 49443-1087
Phone: (616)722-3751
Fax: (616)728-7251
Mert Johnson, Dir.

Harbor County Chamber of Commerce
SBDC
3 W. Buffalo
New Buffalo, MI 49117
Phone: (616)469-5409
Fax: (616)469-2257

Greater Niles Economic Development Fund
SBDC
1105 N. Front St.
Niles, MI 49120
Phone: (616)683-1833
Fax: (616)683-7515
Chris Brynes, Dir.

Huron Shores Campus
SBDC
5800 Skeel Ave.
Oscoda, MI 48750
Phone: (517)739-1445
Fax: (517)739-1161
Dave Wentworth, Dir.

St. Clair County Community College
Small Business Development Center
800 Military St., Ste. 320
Port Huron, MI 48060-5015
Phone: (810)982-9511
Fax: (810)982-9531
Todd Brian, Dir.

Kirtland Community College
SBDC
10775 N. St. Helen Rd.
Roscommon, MI 48653
Phone: (517)275-5121
Fax: (517)275-8745
John Loiacano, Dir.

Saginaw County Chamber of Commerce
SBDC
901 S. Washington Ave.
Saginaw, MI 48601
Phone: (517)752-7161
Fax: (517)752-9055
James Bockelman, Dir.

Saginaw Future, Inc.
Small Business Development Center
301 E. Genesee, 3rd Fl.
Saginaw, MI 48607
Phone: (517)754-8222
Fax: (517)754-1715
Matthew Hufnagel, Dir.

Washtenaw Community College
SBDC
740 Woodland
Saline, MI 48176
Phone: (313)944-1016
Fax: (313)944-0165
Kathleen Woodard, Dir.

West Shore Community College
Small Business Development Center
Business and Industrial Development Institute
3000 N. Stiles Rd.
PO Box 277
Scottville, MI 49454-0277
Phone: (616)845-6211
Fax: (616)845-0207
Mark Bergstrom, Dir.

South Haven Chamber of Commerce
SBDC
300 Broadway
South Haven, MI 49090
Phone: (616)637-5171
Fax: (616)639-1570
Larry King, Dir.

Downriver Small Business Development Center
15100 Northline Rd.
Southgate, MI 48195
Phone: (313)281-0700
Fax: (313)281-3418
Paula Boase, Dir.

Arenac County Extension Service
SBDC
County Bldg.
PO Box 745
Standish, MI 48658
Phone: (517)846-4111

Sterling Heights Area Chamber of Commerce
Small Business Development Center
12900 Hall Rd., Ste. 110
Sterling Heights, MI 48313
Phone: (810)731-5400
Fax: (810)731-3521
Lillian Adams-Yanssens, Dir.

Northwest Michigan Council of Governments
Small Business Development Center
2200 Dendrinos Dr.
PO Box 506
Traverse City, MI 49685-0506
Phone: (616)929-5000
Fax: (616)929-5017
Richard J. Beldin, Dir.

Northwestern Michigan College
Small Business Development Center
Center for Business and Industry
1701 E. Front St.
Traverse City, MI 49686
Phone: (616)922-1717
Fax: (616)922-1722
Cheryl Troop, Dir.

Traverse Bay Economic Development Corp.
Small Business Development Center
202 E. Grandview Pkwy.
PO Box 387
Traverse City, MI 49684
Phone: (616)946-1596
Fax: (616)946-2565
Charles Blankenship, Dir.

Traverse City Area Chamber of Commerce
Small Business Development Center
202 E. Grandview Pkwy.
PO Box 387
Traverse City, MI 49684
Phone: (616)947-5075
Fax: (616)946-2565
Matthew Meadors, Dir.

Oakland Count Small Business Development Center
SOC Bldg.
4555 Corporate Dr., Ste. 201
PO Box 7085
Troy, MI 48098
Phone: (810)641-0088
Fax: (810)267-3809
Daniel V. Belknap, Dir.

Saginaw Valley State University
Small Business Development Center
7400 Bay Rd.
7400 Bay Rd.
University Center, MI 48710-0001
Phone: (517)791-7746
Fax: (517)249-1955
Christine Greve, Dir.

Macomb Community College
SBDC
14500 12 Mile Rd.
Warren, MI 48093
Phone: (810)445-7348
Fax: (810)445-7316
Geary Maiurini, Dir.

Warren - Centerline - Sterling Heights Chamber of Commerce
Small Business Development Center
30500 Van Dyke, Ste. 118
Warren, MI 48093
Phone: (313)751-3939
Fax: (313)751-3995
Janet Masi, Dir.

Minnesota

Northwest Technical College
SBDC
905 Grant Ave., SE
Bemidji, MN 56601
Phone: (218)755-4286
Fax: (218)755-4289
Susan Kozojed, Dir.

Normandale Community College (Bloomington)
Small Business Development Center
9700 France Ave. S
Bloomington, MN 55431
Phone: (612)832-6398
Fax: (612)832-6352
Scott Harding, Dir.

Central Lakes College
Small Business Development Center
501 W. College Dr.
Brainerd, MN 56401
Phone: (218)825-2028
Fax: (218)828-2053
Pamela Thomsen, Dir.

University of Minnesota at Duluth
Small Business Development Center
School of Business and Economics, Rm. 150
10 University Dr.
Duluth, MN 55812-2496
Phone: (218)726-8758
Fax: (218)726-6338
Lee Jensen, Dir.

Itasca Development Corp.
Grand Rapids Small Business Development Center
19 NE 3rd St.
Grand Rapids, MN 55744

Phone: (218)327-2241
Fax: (218)327-2242
Kirk Bustrom, Dir.

Hibbing Community College
Small Business Development Center
1515 E. 25th St.
Hibbing, MN 55746
Phone: (218)262-6703
Fax: (218)262-6717
Jim Antilla, Dir.

Rainy River Community College
Small Business Development Center
1501 Hwy. 71
International Falls, MN 56649
Phone: (218)285-2255
Fax: (218)285-2239
Tom West, Dir.

Region Nine Development Commission
SBDC
410 Jackson St.
PO Box 3367
Mankato, MN 56002-3367
Phone: (507)389-8863
Fax: (507)387-7105
Jill Miller, Dir.

Southwest State University
Small Business Development Center
Science and Technical Resource Center, Ste. 105
1501 State St.
Marshall, MN 56258
Phone: (507)537-7386
Fax: (507)387-7105
Jack Hawk, Dir.

Minnesota Project Innovation
Small Business Development Center
111 3rd Ave. S., Ste. 100
Minneapolis, MN 55401
Phone: (612)347-6751
Fax: (612)338-3483
Pat Dillon, Dir.

University of St. Thomas
SBDC
Mail Stop 25H 225
Ste. MPL 100
Minneapolis, MN 55403
Phone: (612)962-4500
Fax: (612)962-4810
Gregg Schneider, Dir.

Moorhead State University
Small Business Development Center
1104 7th Ave. S.
MSU Box 303
Moorhead, MN 56563
Phone: (218)236-2289
Fax: (218)236-2280
Len Sliwoski, Dir.

Owatonna Incubator, Inc.
SBDC
560 Dunnell Dr., Ste. 203
PO Box 505
Owatonna, MN 55060
Phone: (507)451-0517
Fax: (507)455-2788
Ken Henrickson, Dir.

Pine Technical College
Small Business Development Center
1100 4th St.
Pine City, MN 55063
Phone: (320)629-7340
Fax: (320)629-7603
John Sparling, Dir.

Hennepin Technical College
SBDC
1820 N. Xenium Ln.
Plymouth, MN 55441
Phone: (612)550-7218
Fax: (612)550-7272
Danelle Wolf, Dir.

Pottery Business and Tech. Center
Small Business Development Center
2000 Pottery Pl. Dr., Ste. 339
Red Wing, MN 55066
Phone: (612)388-4079
Fax: (612)385-2251
Marv Bollum, Dir.

Rochester Community and Tech. College
Small Business Development Center
Riverland Hall
851 30th Ave. SE
Rochester, MN 55904
Phone: (507)285-7425
Fax: (507)285-7110
Michelle Pyfferoen, Dir.

Dakota County Technical College
Small Business Development Center
1300 E. 145th St.
Rosemount, MN 55068
Phone: (612)423-8262
Fax: (612)322-5156
Tom Trutna, Dir.

Southeast Minnesota Development Corp.
SBDC
111 W. Jessie St.
PO Box 684
Rushford, MN 55971
Phone: (507)864-7557
Fax: (507)864-2091
Terry Erickson, Dir.

St. Cloud State University
Small Business Development Center
720 4th Ave. S.
St. Cloud, MN 56301-3761
Phone: (320)255-4842
Fax: (320)255-4957
Dawn Jensen-Ragnier, Dir.

Department of Trade and Economic Development
Minnesota SBDC
500 Metro Sq.
121 7th Pl. E.
St. Paul, MN 55101-2146
Phone: (612)297-5770
Fax: (612)296-1290
Mary Kruger, State Dir.

Minnesota Technology, Inc.
Small Business Development Center
Olcott Plaza Bldg., Ste. 140
820 N. 9th St.
Virginia, MN 55792
Phone: (218)741-4241
Fax: (218)741-4249
John Freeland, Dir.

Wadena Chamber of Commerce
SBDC
222 2nd St., SE
Wadena, MN 56482
Phone: (218)631-1502
Fax: (218)631-2396
Paul Kinn, Dir.

Century College
SBDC
3300 Century Ave., N., Ste. 200-D
White Bear Lake, MN 55110-1894
Phone: (612)773-1794
Fax: (612)779-5802
Ernie Brodtmann, Dir.

Mississippi

Northeast Mississippi Community College
SBDC
Holiday Hall, 2nd Fl.

Cunningham Blvd.
Booneville, MS 38829
Phone: (601)720-7448
Fax: (601)720-7464
Kenny Holt, Dir.

Delta State University
Small Business Development Center
PO Box 3235 DSU
Cleveland, MS 38733
Phone: (601)846-4236
Fax: (601)846-4235
David Holman, Dir.

East Central Community College
SBDC
Broad St.
PO Box 129
Decatur, MS 39327
Phone: (601)635-2111
Fax: (601)635-4031
Ronald Westbrook, Dir.

Jones County Junior College
SBDC
900 Court St.
Ellisville, MS 39437
Phone: (601)477-4165
Fax: (601)477-4166
Gary Suddith, Dir.

Mississippi Gulf Coast Community College
SBDC
Jackson County Campus
PO Box 100
Gautier, MS 39553
Phone: (601)497-7723
Fax: (601)497-7788
Janice Mabry, Dir.

Mississippi Delta Community College
Small Business Development Center
PO Box 5607
Greenville, MS 38704-5607
Phone: (601)378-8183
Fax: (601)378-5349
Chuck Herring, Dir.

Mississippi Contract Procurement Center
SBDC
3015 12th St.
PO Box 610
Gulfport, MS 39502-0610
Phone: (601)864-2961
Fax: (601)864-2969
C. W. "Skip" Ryland, Exec. Dir.

Pearl River Community College
Small Business Development Center
5448 U.S. Hwy. 49 S.
Hattiesburg, MS 39401
Phone: (601)544-0030
Fax: (601)544-9149
Heidi McDuffie, Dir.

Mississippi Valley State University
Affiliate SBDC
PO Box 992
Itta Bena, MS 38941
Phone: (601)254-3601
Fax: (601)254-6704
Dr. Jim Breyley, Dir.

Jackson State University
Small Business Development Center
Jackson Enterprise Center, Ste. A-1
931 Hwy. 80 W
Box 43
Jackson, MS 39204
Phone: (601)968-2795
Fax: (601)968-2796
Henry Thomas, Dir.

University of Southern Mississippi
Small Business Development Center
136 Beach Park Pl.
Long Beach, MS 39560
Phone: (601)865-4578
Fax: (601)865-4581
Lucy Betcher, Dir.

Alcorn State University
SBDC
552 West St.
PO Box 90
Lorman, MS 39096-9402
Phone: (601)877-6684
Fax: (601)877-6256
Sharon Witty, Dir.

Meridian Community College
Small Business Development Center
910 Hwy. 19 N
Meridian, MS 39307
Phone: (601)482-7445
Fax: (601)482-5803
Mac Hodges, Dir.

Mississippi State University
Small Business Development Center
1 Research Bldg., Ste 201
PO Drawer 5288
Mississippi State, MS 39762
Phone: (601)325-8684
Fax: (601)325-4016
Sonny Fisher, Dir.

Copiah-Lincoln Community College
Small Business Development Center
11 County Line Circle
Natchez, MS 39120
Phone: (601)445-5254
Fax: (601)446-1221
Bob D. Russ, Dir.

Hinds Community College
Small Business Development Center/International Trade Center
1500 Raymond Lake Rd., 2nd Fl.
Raymond, MS 39154
Phone: (601)857-3536
Fax: (601)857-3474
Marguerite Wall, Dir.

Holmes Community College
SBDC
412 W. Ridgeland Ave.
Ridgeland, MS 39157
Phone: (601)853-0827
Fax: (601)853-0844
John Deddens, Dir.

Northwest Mississippi Community College
SBDC
DeSoto Ctr.
5197 W.E. Ross Pkwy.
Southaven, MS 38671
Phone: (601)280-7648
Fax: (601)280-7648
Jody Dunning, Dir.

Southwest Mississippi Community College
SBDC
College Dr.
Summit, MS 39666
Phone: (601)276-3890
Fax: (601)276-3883
Kathryn Durham, Dir.

Itawamba Community College
Small Business Development Center
653 Eason Blvd.
Tupelo, MS 38801
Phone: (601)680-8515
Fax: (601)680-8547
Rex Hollingsworth, Dir.

University of Mississippi
Mississippi SBDC
N.C.P.A., Rm. 1082
University, MS 38677
Phone: (601)234-2120
Fax: (601)232-4220
Michael Vanderlip, Dir.

University of Mississippi
SBDC
Old Chemistry Bldg., Ste. 216
University, MS 38677
Phone: (601)232-5001
Fax: (601)232-5650
Walter D. Gurley, Jr.

Missouri

Camden County
SBDC Extension Center
113 Kansas
PO Box 1405
Camdenton, MO 65020
Phone: (573)882-0344
Fax: (573)884-4297
Jackie Rasmussen, B&I Spec.

Missouri PAC - Southeastern
Missouri State University
SBDC
222 N. Pacific
Cape Girardeau, MO 63701
Phone: (573)290-5965
Fax: (573)651-5005
George Williams, Dir.

Southeast Missouri State University
Small Business Development Center
University Plaza
MS 5925
Cape Girardeau, MO 63701
Phone: (573)290-5965
Fax: (573)651-5005
E-mail: sbdc-cg@ext.missouri.edu
Frank "Buz" Sutherland, Dir.

Chillicothe City Hall
SBDC
715 Washington St.
Chillicothe, MO 64601-2229
Phone: (660)646-6920
Fax: (660)646-6811
Nanette Anderjaska, Dir.

East Central Missouri - St. Louis County
Extension Center
121 S. Meramac, Ste. 501
Clayton, MO 63105
Phone: (314)889-2911
Fax: (314)854-6147
Carole Leriche-Price, B&I Specialist

Boone County Extension Center
SBDC
1012 N. Hwy. UU
Columbia, MO 65203
Phone: (573)445-9792
Fax: (573)445-9807
Mr. Casey Venters, B&I Specialist

MO PAC-Central Region
University of Missouri-Columbia
SBDC
University Pl., Ste. 1800
1205 University Ave.
Columbia, MO 65211
Phone: (573)882-3597
Fax: (573)884-4297
E-mail: mopcol@ext.missouri.edu
Morris Hudson, Dir.

University of Missouri
Missouri SBDC System
1205 University Ave., Ste. 300
Columbia, MO 65211
Phone: (573)882-0344
Fax: (573)884-4297
E-mail: sbdc-mso@ext.missouri.edu
Max E. Summers, State Dir.

University of Missouri—Columbia
Small Business Development Center
University Pl., Ste. 1800
1205 University Ave.
Columbia, MO 65211
Phone: (573)882-7096
Fax: (573)882-6156
E-mail: sbdc-c@ext.missouri.edu
Frank Siebert, Dir.

Hannibal Satellite Center
Hannibal, MO 63401
Phone: (816)385-6550
Fax: (816)385-6568

Jefferson County
Extension Center
Courthouse, Annex 203
725 Maple St.
PO Box 497
Hillsboro, MO 63050
Phone: (573)789-5391
Fax: (573)789-5059

Cape Girardeau County
SBDC Extension Center
815 Hwy. 25S
PO Box 408
Jackson, MO 63755
Phone: (573)243-3581
Fax: (573)243-1606
Richard Sparks, B&I Specialist

Cole County Extension Center
SBDC
2436 Tanner Bridge Rd.
Jefferson City, MO 65101
Phone: (573)634-2824
Fax: (573)634-5463
Mr. Chris Bouchard, B&I Specialist

Missouri Southern State College
Small Business Development Center
Matthews Hall, Ste. 107
3950 Newman Rd.
Joplin, MO 64801-1595
Phone: (417)625-9313
Fax: (417)625-9782
E-mail: sbdc-j@ext.missouri.edu
Jim Krudwig, Dir.

Rockhurst College
Small Business Development Center
1100 Rockhurst Rd.
VanAckeren Hall, Rm. 205
Kansas City, MO 64110-2508
Phone: (816)501-4572
Fax: (816)501-4646
Rhonda Gerke, Dir.

Truman State University
Small Business Development Center
100 E. Norman
Kirksville, MO 63501-4419
Phone: (816)785-4307
Fax: (816)785-4357
E-mail: sbdc-k@ext.missouri.edu
Glen Giboney, Dir.

Thomas Hill Enterprise Center
SBDC
1409 N. Prospect Dr.
PO Box 246
Macon, MO 63552
Phone: (816)385-6550
Fax: (816)562-3071
Jane Vanderham, Dir.

Northwest Missouri State University
Small Business Development Center
423 N. Market St.
Maryville, MO 64468-1614
Phone: (660)562-1701
Fax: (660)582-3071
Brad Anderson, Dir.

Audrain County Extension Center
SBDC
Courthouse, 4th Fl.
101 Jefferson
Mexico, MO 65265
Phone: (573)581-3231
Fax: (573)581-2766
Virgil Woolridge, B&I Specialist

Randolph County
Extension Center
417 E. Urbandale
Moberly, MO 65270
Phone: (816)263-3534
Fax: (816)263-1874
Ray Marshall, B&I Specialist

Mineral Area College
SBDC
PO Box 1000
Park Hills, MO 63601-1000
Phone: (573)431-4593
Fax: (573)431-2144
E-mail: sbdc-fr@ext.missouri.edu
Eugene Cherry, Dir.

Telecommunications Community
Resource Center
Longhead Learning Center
Small Business Development Center
1121 Victory Ln.
3019 Fair St.
Poplar Bluff, MO 63901
Phone: (573)840-9450
Fax: (573)840-9456
Judy Moss, Dir.

Washington County SBDC
102 N. Missouri
Potosi, MO 63664
Phone: (573)438-2671
Fax: (573)438-2079
LaDonna McCuan, B&I Specialist

Center for Technology Transfer and
Economic Development
Nagogami Ter., Bldg. 1, Rm. 104
Rolla, MO 65401-0249
Phone: (573)341-4559
Fax: (573)346-2694
Fred Goss, Dir.

Phelps County
SBDC Extension Center
Courthouse
200 N. Main
PO Box 725
Rolla, MO 65401
Phone: (573)364-3147
Fax: (573)364-0436
Paul Cretin, B&I Specialist

University of Missouri at Rolla
SBDC
Nagogami Terrace, Bldg. 1, Rm. 104
Rolla, MO 65401-0249
Phone: (573)341-4559
Fax: (573)341-6495
E-mail: sbdc-rt@ext.missouri.edu
Fred Goss, Dir.

Missouri PAC - Eastern Region
SBDC
3830 Washington Ave.
St. Louis, MO 63108
Phone: (314)534-4413
Fax: (314)534-3237
E-mail: mopstl@ext.missouri.edu
Ken Konchel, Dir.

St. Louis County
Extension Center
207 Marillac, UMSL
8001 Natural Bridge Rd.
St. Louis, MO 63121
Phone: (314)553-5944
John Henschke, Specialist

St. Louis University
Small Business State University
SBDC
3750 Lindell Blvd.
St. Louis, MO 63108-3412
Phone: (314)977-7232
Fax: (314)977-7241
E-mail: sbdc-stl@ext.missouri.edu
Virginia Campbell, Dir.

St. Louis / St. Charles County
Economic Council
SBDC Extension Center
260 Brown Rd.
St. Peters, MO 63376
Phone: (314)970-3000
Fax: (314)274-3310
Tim Wathen, B&I Specialist

Pettis County
Extension Center
1012A Thompson Blvd.
Sedalia, MO 65301
Phone: (816)827-0591
Fax: (816)827-4888
Betty Lorton, B&I Specialist

Southwest Missouri State University
Center for Business Research
Small Business Development Center
901 S. National
Box 88
Springfield, MO 65804-0089
Phone: (417)836-5685
Fax: (417)836-7666
Jane Peterson, Dir.

Franklin County
SBDC Extension Center
414 E. Main
PO Box 71
Union, MO 63084
Phone: (573)583-5141
Fax: (573)583-5145
Rebecca How, B&I Specialist

Central Missouri State University
Center for Technology
Grinstead, No. 75
Warrensburg, MO 64093-5037
Phone: (816)543-4402
Fax: (816)747-1653
Cindy Tanck, Coordinator

Central Missouri State University
SBDC
Grinstead, No. 9
Warrensburg, MO 64093-5037
Phone: (816)543-4402
Fax: (816)543-8159
Wes Savage, Coordinator

Howell County
SBDC Extension Center
217 S. Aid Ave.
West Plains, MO 65775
Phone: (417)256-2391
Fax: (417)256-8569
Mick Gilliam, B&I Specialist

Montana

Montana Tradepost Authority
Small Business Development Center
2722 3rd Ave., Ste. W300
Billings, MT 59101
Phone: (406)256-6871
Fax: (406)256-6877
Tom McKerlick, Contact

Bozeman Small Business
Development Center
222 E. Main St., Ste. 102
Bozeman, MT 59715
Phone: (406)587-3113
Fax: (406)587-9565
Michele DuBose, Contact

Butte Small Business Development
Center
305 W. Mercury, Ste. 211
Butte, MT 59701
Phone: (406)782-7333
Fax: (406)782-9675
John Donovan, Contact

High Plains Development Authority
Great Falls SBDC

710 1st. Ave. N.
PO Box 2568
Great Falls, MT 59403
Phone: (406)454-1934
Fax: (406)454-2995
Suzie David

Havre Small Business Development Center
PO Box 170
Havre, MT 59501
Phone: (406)265-9226
Fax: (406)265-5602
Randy Hanson, Contact

Montana Department of Commerce
Montana SBDC
1424 9th Ave.
PO Box 200505
Helena, MT 59620
Phone: (406)444-2463
Fax: (406)444-1872
Ralph Kloser, State Dir.

Kalispell Small Business Development Center
PO Box 8300
Kalispell, MT 59901
Phone: (406)758-5412
Fax: (406)758-6582
Dan Manning, Contact

Missoula Small Business Development Center
127 N. Higgins, 3rd Fl.
Missoula, MT 59802
Phone: (406)728-9234
Fax: (406)721-4584
Brett George, Contact

Sidney Small Business Development Center
123 W. Main
Sidney, MT 59270
Phone: (406)482-5024
Fax: (406)482-5306
Dwayne Heintz, Contact

Nebraska

Chadron State College
SBDC
Administration Bldg.
1000 Main St.
Chadron, NE 69337
Phone: (308)432-6282
Fax: (308)432-6430
Cliff Hanson, Dir.

University of Nebraska at Kearney
SBDC
Welch Hall
19th St. and College Dr.
Kearney, NE 68849-3035
Phone: (308)865-8344
Fax: (308)865-8153
Susan Jensen, Dir.

University of Nebraska at Lincoln
SBDC
1135 M St., No. 200
11th and Cornhusker Hwy.
Lincoln, NE 68521
Phone: (402)472-3358
Fax: (402)472-3363
Cliff Mosteller, Dir.

Mid-Plains Community College
SBDC
416 N. Jeffers, Rm. 26
North Platte, NE 69101
Phone: (308)534-5115
Fax: (308)534-5117
Dean Kurth, Dir.

Nebraska Small Business Development Center
Omaha Business and Technology Center
2505 N. 24 St., Ste. 101
Omaha, NE 68110
Phone: (402)595-3511
Fax: (402)595-3524
Tom McCabe, Dir.

University of Nebraska at Omaha
Nebraska Business Development Center
College of Business Administration, Rm. 407
60th & Dodge Sts.
CBA Rm. 407
Omaha, NE 68182
Phone: (402)554-2521
Fax: (402)554-3747
Robert Bernier, State Dir.

University of Nebraska at Omaha
Peter Kiewit Conference Center
SBDC
1313 Farnam-on-the-Mall, Ste. 132
Omaha, NE 68182-0248
Phone: (402)595-2381
Fax: (402)595-2385
Nate Brei, Dir.

Peru State College
SBDC
T.J. Majors Hall, Rm. 248
Peru, NE 68421
Phone: (402)872-2274
Fax: (402)872-2422
Jerry Brazil, Dir.

Western Nebraska Community College
SBDC
Nebraska Public Power Bldg., Rm. 408
1721 Broadway
Scottsbluff, NE 69361
Phone: (308)635-7513
Fax: (308)635-6596
Ingrid Battershell, Dir.

Wayne State College
SBDC
Gardner Hall
1111 Main St.
Wayne, NE 68787
Phone: (402)375-7575
Fax: (402)375-7574
Loren Kucera, Dir.

Nevada

Carson City Chamber of Commerce
Small Business Development Center
1900 S. Carson St., Ste. 100
Carson City, NV 89701
Phone: (702)882-1565
Fax: (702)882-4179
Larry Osborne, Dir.

Great Basin College
Small Business Development Center
1500 College Pkwy.
Elko, NV 89801
Phone: (702)753-2205
Fax: (702)753-2242
John Pryor, Dir.

Incline Village Chamber of Commerce
SBDC
969 Tahoe Blvd.
Incline Village, NV 89451
Phone: (702)831-4440
Fax: (702)832-1605
Sheri Woods, Exec. Dir.

Las Vegas SBDC
SBDC
3720 Howard Hughes Pkwy., Ste. 130
Las Vegas, NV 89109

Phone: (702)734-7575
Fax: (702)734-7633
Robert Holland, Bus. Dev. Specialist

University of Nevada at Las Vegas
Small Business Development Center
4505 Maryland Pkwy.
Box 456011
Las Vegas, NV 89154-6011
Phone: (702)895-0852
Fax: (702)895-4095
Nancy Buist, Business Development Specialist

North Las Vegas Small Business Development Center
19 W. Brooks Ave., Ste. B
North Las Vegas, NV 89030
Phone: (702)399-6300
Fax: (702)895-4095
Janis Stevenson, Business Development Specialist

University of Nevada at Reno
Small Business Development Center
College of Business Administration
Nazir Ansari Business Bldg., Rm. 411
Reno, NV 89557-0100
Phone: (702)784-1717
Fax: (702)784-4337
E-mail: nsbdc@scs.unr.edu
Sam Males, Dir.

Tri-County Development Authority
Small Business Development Center
50 W. 4th St.
PO Box 820
Winnemucca, NV 89446
Phone: (702)623-5777
Fax: (702)623-5999
Teri Williams, Dir.

New Hampshire

University of New Hampshire
Small Business Development Center
108 McConnell Hall
15 College Rd.
Durham, NH 03824-3593
Phone: (603)862-2200
Fax: (603)862-4876
Mary Collins, State Dir.

Keene State College
Small Business Development Center
Mail Stop 210
Keene, NH 03435-2101
Phone: (603)358-2602
Fax: (603)358-2612
Gary Cloutier, Regional Mgr.

Littleton Small Business Development Center
120 Main St.
Littleton, NH 03561
Phone: (603)444-1053
Fax: (603)444-5463
Liz Ward, Regional Mgr.

Manchester Small Business Development Center
1000 Elm St., 14th Fl.
Manchester, NH 03101
Phone: (603)624-2000
Fax: (603)634-2449
Bob Ebberson, Regional Mgr.

Office of Economic Initiatives
SBDC
1000 Elm St., 14th Fl.
Manchester, NH 03101
Phone: (603)634-2796
E-mail: ahj@hopper.unh.edu
Amy Jennings, Dir.

New Hampshire Small Business Development Center
1 Indian Head Plz., Ste. 510
Nashua, NH 03060
Phone: (603)886-1233
Fax: (603)598-1164
Bob Wilburn, Regional Mgr.

Plymouth State College
Small Business Development Center
Outreach Center, MSC24A
Plymouth, NH 03264-1595
Phone: (603)535-2523
Fax: (603)535-2850
Janice Kitchen, Regional Mgr.

Small Business Development Center, Rochester
18 S. Main St., Ste. 3A
Rochester, NH 03867
Phone: (603)330-1929
Fax: (603)330-1948

New Jersey

Greater Atlantic City Chamber of Commerce
Small Business Development Center
1301 Atlantic Ave.
Atlantic City, NJ 08401
Phone: (609)345-5600
Fax: (609)345-1666
William R. McGinley, Dir.

Rutgers University At Camden
Small Business Development Center
227 Penn St., 3rd Fl., Rm. 334
Camden, NJ 08102
Phone: (609)757-6221
Fax: (609)225-6231
Patricia Peacock, Dir.

Brookdale Community College
Small Business Development Center
Newman Springs Rd.
Lincroft, NJ 07738
Phone: (732)842-1900
Fax: (732)842-0203
Larry Novick, Dir.

Rutgers University
New Jersey SBDC
Graduate School of Management
49 Bleeker St.
Newark, NJ 07102
Phone: (973)353-5950
Fax: (973)353-1110
Brenda B. Hopper, State Dir.

Bergen County Community College
SBDC
400 Paramus Rd., Rm. A333
Paramus, NJ 07652-1595
Phone: (201)447-7841
Fax: (201)447-7495
Melody Irvin, Dir.

Mercer County Community College
Small Business Development Center
West Windsor Campus
1200 Old Trenton Rd.
PO Box B
Trenton, NJ 08690
Phone: (609)586-4800
Fax: (609)890-6338
Herb Spiegel, Dir.

Kean College
Small Business Development Center
East Campus, Rm. 242
Union, NJ 07083
Phone: (908)527-2946
Fax: (908)527-2960
Mira Kostak, Dir.

Warren County Community College
Small Business Development Center
Skylands 475
Rte. 57 W.
Washington, NJ 07882-9605
Phone: (908)689-9620
Fax: (908)689-2247
James Smith, Dir.

New Mexico

New Mexico State University at Alamogordo
Small Business Development Center
2230 Lawrence Blvd.
Alamogordo, NM 88310
Phone: (505)434-5272
Fax: (505)439-3643
Dwight Harp, Dir.

Albuquerque Technical-Vocational Institute
Small Business Development Center
525 Buena Vista SE
Albuquerque, NM 87106
Phone: (505)224-4246
Fax: (505)224-4251
Ray Garcia, Dir.

South Valley SBDC
SBDC
70 4th St. SW, Ste. A
Albuquerque, NM 87102
Phone: (505)248-0132
Fax: (505)248-0127
Steven Becerra, Dir.

New Mexico State University at Carlsbad
Small Business Development Center
301 S. Canal St.
PO Box 1090
Carlsbad, NM 88220
Phone: (505)887-6562
Fax: (505)885-0818
Larry Coalson, Dir.

Clovis Community College
Small Business Development Center
417 Schepps Blvd.
Clovis, NM 88101
Phone: (505)769-4136
Fax: (505)769-4190
Sandra Taylor-Smith

Northern New Mexico Community College
Small Business Development Center
1002 N. Onate St.
Espanola, NM 87532
Phone: (505)747-2236
Fax: (505)757-2234
Ralph Prather, Dir.

San Juan College
Small Business Development Center
4601 College Blvd.
Farmington, NM 87402
Phone: (505)599-0528
Fax: (505)599-0385
Cal Tingey, Dir.

University of New Mexico at Gallup
Small Business Development Center
103 W. Hwy. 66
Gallup, NM 87305
Phone: (505)722-2220
Fax: (505)863-6006
Elsie Sanchez, Dir.

New Mexico State University at Grants
Small Business Development Center
709 E. Roosevelt Ave.
Grants, NM 87020
Phone: (505)287-8221
Fax: (505)287-2125
Clemente Sanchez, Dir.

New Mexico Junior College
Small Business Development Center
5317 Lovington Hwy.
Hobbs, NM 88240
Phone: (505)392-5549
Fax: (505)392-2527
Don Leach, Dir.

Dona Ana Branch Community College
Small Business Development Center
3400 S. Espina St.
Dept. 3DA, Box 30001
Las Cruces, NM 88003-0001
Phone: (505)527-7601
Fax: (505)527-7515
Terry Sullivan, Dir.

Luna Vocational-Technical Institute
Small Business Development Center
Camp Luna Site
Hot Springs Blvd.
PO Box 1510
Las Vegas, NM 87701
Phone: (505)454-2595
Fax: (505)454-2588
Don Bustos, Dir.

University of New Mexico at Los Alamos
Small Business Development Center
901 18th St., No. 18
PO Box 715
Los Alamos, NM 87544
Phone: (505)662-0001
Fax: (505)662-0099
Jay Wechsler, Interim Dir.

University of New Mexico at Valencia
Small Business Development Center
280 La Entrada
Los Lunas, NM 87031
Phone: (505)925-8980
Fax: (505)925-8987
David Ashley, Dir.

Eastern New Mexico University at Roswell
Small Business Development Center
57 University Ave.
PO Box 6000
Roswell, NM 88201-6000
Phone: (505)624-7133
Fax: (505)624-7132
Eugene D. Simmons, Dir.

Santa Fe Community College
New Mexico SBDC
6401 Richards Ave.
Santa Fe, NM 87505
Phone: (505)438-1362
Free: (800)281-SBDC
Fax: (505)471-1469
Roy Miller, State Dir.

Western New Mexico University
Small Business Development Center
PO Box 2672
Silver City, NM 88062
Phone: (505)538-6320
Fax: (505)538-6341
Linda K. Jones, Dir.

Mesa Technical College
Small Business Development Center
911 S. 10th St.
Tucumcari, NM 88401
Phone: (505)461-4413
Fax: (505)461-1901
Carl Reiney, Dir.

New York

State University of New York at Albany
Small Business Development Center
Draper Hall, Rm. 107
135 Western Ave.
Albany, NY 12222
Phone: (518)442-5577
Fax: (518)442-5582
Peter George, III

State University of New York (Suny)
New York SBDC
Suny Plaza, S-523

Albany, NY 12246
Phone: (518)443-5398
Free: (800)732-SBDC
Fax: (518)465-4992
E-mail: kingjl@cc.sunycentral.edu
James L. King, State Dir.

Binghamton University
Small Business Development Center
PO Box 6000
Binghamton, NY 13902-6000
Phone: (607)777-4024
Fax: (607)777-4029
E-mail: sbdcbu@spectra.net
Joanne Bauman, Dir.

State University of New York
Small Business Development Center
74 N. Main St.
Brockport, NY 14420
Phone: (716)637-6660
Fax: (716)637-2102
Wilfred Bordeau, Dir.

Bronx Community College
Small Business Development Center
McCracken Hall, Rm. 14
W. 181st St. & University Ave.
Bronx, NY 10453
Phone: (718)563-3570
Fax: (718)563-3572
Adi Israeli, Dir.

Bronx Outreach Center
Con Edison
SBDC
560 Cortlandt Ave.
Bronx, NY 10451
Phone: (718)563-9204
David Bradley

Downtown Brooklyn Outreach Center
Kingsborough Community College
SBDC
395 Flatbush Ave., Extension Rm. 413
Brooklyn, NY 11201
Phone: (718)260-9783
Fax: (718)260-9797
Stuart Harker, Assoc. Dir.

Kingsborough Community College
Small Business Development Center
2001 Oriental Blvd., Bldg. T4, Rm. 4204
Manhattan Beach
Brooklyn, NY 11235
Phone: (718)368-4619
Fax: (718)368-4629
Edward O'Brien, Dir.

State University of New York at Buffalo
Small Business Development Center
Bacon Hall 117
1300 Elmwood Ave.
Buffalo, NY 14222
Phone: (716)878-4030
Fax: (716)878-4067
Susan McCartney, Dir.

Canton Outreach Center (SUNY)
Jefferson Community College
SBDC
Canton, NY 13617
Phone: (315)386-7312
Fax: (315)386-7945

Cobleskill Outreach Center
SBDC
SUNY Cobleskill
Warner Hall, Rm. 218
Cobleskill, NY 12043
Phone: (518)234-5528
Fax: (518)234-5272
Peter Desmond, Business Advisor

Corning Community College
Small Business Development Center
24 Denison Pkwy. W
Corning, NY 14830
Phone: (607)962-9461
Free: (800)358-7171
Fax: (607)936-6642
Bonnie Gestwicki, Dir.

Mercy College/Westchester Outreach Center
SBDC
555 Broadway
Dobbs Ferry, NY 10522-1189
Phone: (914)674-7485
Fax: (914)693-4996
Tom Milton, Coordinator

State University of New York at Farmingdale
Small Business Development Center
Campus Commons Bldg.
2350 Route 110
Farmingdale, NY 11735
Phone: (516)420-2765
Fax: (516)293-5343
Joseph Schwartz, Dir.

Dutchess Outreach Center
SBDC
Fishkill Extension Center
2600 Rte. 9, Unit 90
Fishkill, NY 12524-2001
Phone: (914)897-2607
Fax: (914)897-4653

Suny Geneseo Outreach Center
SBDC
South Hall, No. 111
1 College Circle
Geneseo, NY 14454
Phone: (716)245-5429
Fax: (716)245-5430
Charles VanArsdale, Dir.

Geneva Outreach Center
SBDC
122 N. Genesee St.
Geneva, NY 14456
Phone: (315)781-1253
Sandy Bordeau, Administrative Dir.

Hempstead Outreach Center
SBDC
269 Fulton Ave.
Hempstead, NY 11550
Phone: (516)564-8672
Fax: (516)481-4938
Lloyd Clarke, Asst. Dir.

York College/City University of New York
Small Business Development Center
Science Bldg., Rm. 107
94-50 159th St.
Jamaica, NY 11451
Phone: (718)262-2880
Fax: (718)262-2881
James A. Heyliger

Jamestown Community College
Small Business Development Center
525 Falconer St.
PO Box 20
Jamestown, NY 14702-0020
Phone: (716)665-5754
Free: (800)522-7232
Fax: (716)665-6733
Irene Dobies, Dir.

Kingston Small Business Development Center
1 Development Ct.
Kingston, NY 12401
Phone: (914)339-0025
Fax: (914)339-1631
Patricia La Susa, Dir.

Baruch College
Mid-Town Outreach Center
SBDC

360 Park Ave. S., Rm. 1101
New York, NY 10010
Phone: (212)802-6620
Fax: (212)802-6613
Cheryl Fenton, Dir.

East Harlem Outreach Center
SBDC
145 E. 116th St., 3rd Fl.
New York, NY 10029
Phone: (212)346-1900
Fax: (212)534-4576
Anthony Sanchez, Coordinator

Harlem Outreach Center
SBDC
163 W. 125th St., Rm. 1307
New York, NY 10027
Phone: (212)346-1900
Fax: (212)534-4576
Anthony Sanchez, Coordinator

Mid-Town Outreach Ctr.
Baruch College
SBDC
360 Park Ave. S. Rm. 1101
New York, NY 10010
Phone: (212)802-6620
Fax: (212)802-6613
Barrie Phillip, Coordinator

Pace University
Small Business Development Center
1 Pace Plz., Rm. W483
New York, NY 10038
Phone: (212)346-1900
Fax: (212)346-1613
Ira Davidson, Dir.

Niagara Falls Satellite Office
SBDC / International Trade Center
Carborundum Center
345 3rd St.
Niagara Falls, NY 14303-1117
Phone: (716)285-4793
Fax: (716)285-4797

SUNY at Oswego
Operation Oswego County
SBDC
44 W. Bridge St.
Oswego, NY 13126
Phone: (315)343-1545
Fax: (315)343-1546

Clinton Community College
SBDC
Lake Shore Rd., Rte. 9 S.
136 Clinton Point Dr.
Plattsburgh, NY 12901
Phone: (518)562-4260
Fax: (518)563-9759
Merry Gwynn, Coordinator

Suffolk County Community College
Riverhead Outreach Center
SBDC
Orient Bldg., Rm. 132
Riverhead, NY 11901
Phone: (516)369-1409
Fax: (516)369-3255
Al Falkowski, Contact

SUNY at Brockport
SBDC
Sibley Bldg.
228 E. Main St.
Rochester, NY 14604
Phone: (716)232-7310
Fax: (716)637-2182

Niagara County Community College at Sanborn
Small Business Development Center
3111 Saunders Settlement Rd.
Sanborn, NY 14132
Phone: (716)693-1910
Fax: (716)731-3595
Richard Gorko, Dir.

Long Island University at Southhampton/Southampton Outreach Center
SBDC
Abney Peak, Montauk Hwy.
Southampton, NY 11968
Phone: (516)287-0059
Fax: (516)287-8287
George Tulmany, Business Advisor

College of Staten Island
SBDC
Bldg. 1A, Rm. 111
2800 Victory Blvd.
Staten Island, NY 10314-9806
Phone: (718)982-2560
Fax: (718)982-2323
Dr. Martin Schwartz, Dir.

SUNY at Stony Brook
SBDC
Harriman Hall, Rm. 103
Stony Brook, NY 11794-3775
Phone: (516)632-9070
Fax: (516)632-7176
Judith McEvoy, Dir.

Rockland Community College
Small Business Development Center
145 College Rd.
Suffern, NY 10901-3620
Phone: (914)356-0370
Fax: (914)356-0381
Thomas J. Morley, Dir.

Onondaga Community College
Small Business Development Center
Excell Bldg., Rm. 108
4969 Onondaga Rd.
Syracuse, NY 13215-1944
Phone: (315)498-6070
Fax: (315)492-3704
Robert Varney, Dir.

Manufacturing Field Office
SBDC
Rensselaer Technology Park
385 Jordan Rd.
Troy, NY 12180-7602
Phone: (518)286-1014
Fax: (518)286-1006
Bill Brigham, Dir.

State University Institute of Technology
Small Business Development Center
PO Box 3050
Utica, NY 13504-3050
Phone: (315)792-7546
Fax: (315)792-7554
David Mallen, Dir.

SUNY Institute of Technology at Utica/Rome
SBDC
PO Box 3050
Utica, NY 13504-3050
Phone: (315)792-7546
Fax: (315)792-7554
David Mallen, Dir.

Jefferson Community College
Small Business Development Center
Coffeen St.
Watertown, NY 13601
Phone: (315)782-9262
Fax: (315)782-0901
John F. Tanner, Dir.

SBDC Outreach Small Business Resource Center
222 Bloomingdale Rd., 3rd Fl.
White Plains, NY 10605-1500
Phone: (914)644-4116
Fax: (914)644-2184
Kathleen Cassels, Coordinator

North Carolina

Asheville SBTDC
Haywood St.
PO Box 2570
Asheville, NC 28805
Phone: (704)251-6025
Fax: (704)251-6025

Appalachian State University
Small Business and Technology Development Center (Northwestern Region)
Walker College of Business
2123 Raley Hall
Boone, NC 28608
Phone: (704)262-2492
Fax: (704)262-2027
Bill Parrish, Regional Dir.

University of North Carolina at Chapel Hill
Central Carolina Regional Small Business Development Center
608 Airport Rd., Ste. B
Chapel Hill, NC 27514
Phone: (919)962-0389
Fax: (919)962-3291
Dan Parks, Dir.

University of North Carolina at Charlotte
Small Business and Technology Development Center (Southern Piedmont Region)
The Ben Craig Center
8701 Mallard Creek Rd.
Charlotte, NC 28262
Phone: (704)548-1090
Fax: (704)548-9050
George McAllister, Dir.

Western Carolina University
Small Business and Technology Development Center (Western Region)
Center for Improving Mountain Living
Bird Bldg.
Cullowhee, NC 28723
Phone: (704)227-7494
Fax: (704)227-7422
Allan Steinburg, Dir.

Elizabeth City State University
Small Business and Technology Development Center (Northeastern Region)
1704 Weeksville Rd.
PO Box 874
Elizabeth City, NC 27909
Phone: (919)335-3247
Fax: (919)335-3648
Wauna Dooms, Dir.

Fayetteville State University
Cape Fear Small Business and Technology Development Center
PO Box 1334
Fayetteville, NC 28302
Phone: (910)486-1727
Fax: (910)486-1949
Dr. Sid Gautam, Regional Dir.

North Carolina A&T State University
Northern Piedmont Small Business and Technology Development Center (Eastern Region)
C. H. Moore Agricultural Research Center
1601 E. Market St.
PO Box D-22
Greensboro, NC 27411
Phone: (910)334-7005
Fax: (910)334-7073
Cynthia Clemons, Dir.

East Carolina University
Small Business and Technology Development Center (Eastern Region)
Willis Bldg.
300 East 1st St.
Greenville, NC 27858-4353
Phone: (919)328-6157
Fax: (919)328-6992
Walter Fitts, Dir.

Catawba Valley Region
SBTDC
514 Hwy. 321 NW, Ste. A
Hickory, NC 28601
Phone: (704)345-1110
Fax: (704)326-9117
Rand Riedrich, Dir.

Pembroke State University
Office of Economic Development and SBTDC
SBDC
Pembroke, NC 28372
Phone: (910)521-6603
Fax: (910)521-6550

North Carolina SBTDC
SBDC
333 Fayette St. Mall, Ste. 1150
Raleigh, NC 27601
Phone: (919)715-7272
Fax: (919)715-7777
Scott R. Daugherty, Executive Dir.

North Carolina State University
Capital Region
SBTDC
MCI Small Business Resource Center
800 S. Salisbury St.
Raleigh, NC 27601
Phone: (919)715-0520
Fax: (919)715-0518
Mike Seibert, Dir.

North Carolina Wesleyan College
SBTDC
3400 N. Wesleyan Blvd.
Rocky Mount, NC 27804
Phone: (919)985-5130
Fax: (919)977-3701

University of North Carolina at Wilmington
Small Business and Technology Development Center (Southeast Region)
601 S. College Rd.
Cameron Hall, Rm. 131
Wilmington, NC 28403
Phone: (910)395-3744
Fax: (910)350-3990
Mike Bradley, Dir.

University of North Carolina at Wilmington
Southeastern Region
SBTDC
601 S. College Rd.
Wilmington, NC 28403
Phone: (910)395-3744
Fax: (910)350-3014
Dr. Warren Guiko, Acting Dir.

Winston-Salem State University
Northwestern Piedmont Region Small Business and Technology Center
PO Box 13025
Winston Salem, NC 27110
Phone: (910)750-2030
Fax: (910)750-2031
Bill Dowe, Dir.

North Dakota

Bismarck Regional Small Business Development Center
700 E. Main Ave., 2nd Fl.
Bismarck, ND 58502
Phone: (701)328-5865

Fax: (701)250-4304
Jan M. Peterson, Regional Dir.

Devils Lake Outreach Center
SBDC
417 5th St.
Devils Lake, ND 58301
Free: (800)445-7232
Gordon Synder, Regional Dir.

Dickinson Regional Small Business Development Center
Small Business Development Center
314 3rd Ave. W
Drawer L
Dickinson, ND 58602
Phone: (701)227-2096
Fax: (701)225-0049
Bryan Vendsel, Regional Dir.

Procurement Assistance Center
SBDC
PO Box 1309
Fargo, ND 58107-1309
Phone: (701)237-9678
Free: (800)698-5726
Fax: (701)237-9734
Eric Nelson

Tri-County Economic Development Corp.
Fargo Regional Small Business Development Center
657 2nd Ave. N, Rm. 279
PO Box 1309
Fargo, ND 58103
Phone: (701)237-0986
Fax: (701)237-9734
Jon Grinager, Regional Mgr.

Grafton Outreach Center
Red River Regional Planning Council
SBDC
SBDC
PO Box 633
Grafton, ND 58237
Free: (800)445-7232
Gordon Snyder, Regional Dir.

Grand Forks Regional Small Business Development Center
202 N. 3rd St., Ste. 200
The Hemmp Center
Grand Forks, ND 58203
Phone: (701)772-8502
Fax: (701)772-9238
Gordon Snyder, Regional Dir.

University of North Dakota
North Dakota SBDC
118 Gamble Hall
University Station, Box 7308
Grand Forks, ND 58202-7308
Phone: (701)777-3700
Fax: (701)777-3225
Walter "Wally" Kearns, State Dir.

Jamestown Outreach Center
North Dakota Small Business Development Center
210 10th St. SE
PO Box 1530
Jamestown, ND 58402
Phone: (701)252-9243
Fax: (701)251-2488
Jon Grinager, Regional Dir.

Jamestown Outreach Ctr.
SBDC
210 10th St.
S.E.P.O Box 1530
Jamestown, ND 58402
Phone: (701)252-9243
Fax: (701)251-2488
Jon Grinager, Regional Dir.

Minot Regional Small Business Development Center
SBDC
900 N. Broadway, Ste. 300
Minot, ND 58703
Phone: (701)852-8861
Fax: (701)858-3831
Brian Argabright, Regional Dir.

Williston Outreach Center
SBDC
PO Box 2047
Williston, ND 58801
Free: (800)445-7232
Bryan Vendsel, Regional Dir.

Ohio

Akron Regional Development Board
Small Business Development Center
1 Cascade Plz., 8th Fl.
Akron, OH 44308-1192
Phone: (330)379-3170
Fax: (330)379-3164
Charles Smith, Dir.

Women's Entrepreneurial Growth Organization
Small Business Development Center
Buckingham Bldg., Rm. 55
PO Box 544
Akron, OH 44309
Phone: (330)972-5179
Fax: (330)972-5513
Dr. Penny Marquette, Exec. Dir.

Women's Network
SBDC
1540 West Market St., Ste. 100
Akron, OH 44313
Phone: (330)864-5636
Fax: (330)884-6526
Marlene Miller, Dir.

Enterprise Development Corp.
SBDC
900 E. State St.
Athens, OH 45701
Phone: (614)592-1188
Fax: (614)593-8283
Karen Patton, Dir.

Ohio University Innovation Center
Small Business Development Center
Enterprise & Technical Bldg., Rm. 155
20 East Circle Dr.
Athens, OH 45701
Phone: (614)593-1797
Fax: (614)593-1795
Debra McBride, Dir.

WSOS Community Action Commission, Inc.
Wood County SBDC
121 E. Wooster St.
PO Box 539
Bowling Green, OH 43402
Phone: (419)352-3817
Fax: (419)353-3291
Pat Fligor, Dir.

Kent State University, Stark Campus
SBDC
6000 Frank Ave., NW
Canton, OH 44720
Phone: (330)499-9600
Fax: (330)494-6121
Annette Chunko, Contact

Women's Business Development Center
SBDC
2400 Cleveland Ave., NW
Canton, OH 44709
Phone: (330)453-3867
Fax: (330)773-2992

Wright State University—Lake Campus
Small Business Development Center
West Central Office

7600 State Rte. 703
Celina, OH 45882
Phone: (419)586-0355
Free: (800)237-1477
Fax: (419)586-0358
Tom Knapke, Dir.

Clermont County Chamber of Commerce
Clermont County Area SBDC
4440 Glen Este-Withamsville Rd.
Cincinnati, OH 45245
Phone: (513)753-7141
Fax: (513)753-7146
Matt VanSant, Dir.

University of Cincinnati
SBDC
1111 Edison Ave.
Cincinnati, OH 45216-2265
Phone: (513)948-2051
Fax: (513)948-2109
Mark Sauter, Dir.

Greater Cleveland Growth Association
Small Business Development Center
200 Tower City Center
50 Public Sq.
Cleveland, OH 44113-2291
Phone: (216)621-1294
Fax: (216)621-4617
JoAnn Uhlik, Dir.

Northern Ohio Manufacturing
SBDC
Prospect Park Bldg.
4600 Prospect Ave.
Cleveland, OH 44103-4314
Phone: (216)432-5300
Fax: (216)361-2900
Gretchen Faro, Dir.

Central Ohio Manufacturing
SBDC
1250 Arthur E. Adams Dr.
Columbus, OH 43221
Phone: (614)688-5136
Fax: (614)688-5001

Department of Development
Ohio SBDC
77 S. High St., 28th Fl.
Columbus, OH 43216-1001
Phone: (614)466-2711
Fax: (614)466-0829
Holly I. Schick, State Dir.

Greater Columbus Area Chamber of Commerce
Central Ohio SBDC
37 N. High St.
Columbus, OH 43215-3065
Phone: (614)225-6910
Fax: (614)469-8250
Linda Steward, Dir.

Dayton Area Chamber of Commerce
Small Business Development Center
Chamber Plz.
5th & Main Sts.
Dayton, OH 45402-2400
Phone: (937)226-8239
Fax: (937)226-8254
Harry Bumgarner, Dir.

Wright State University/Dayton
SBDC
Center for Small Business Assistance
College of Business
Rike Hall, Rm. 120C
Dayton, OH 45435
Phone: (937)873-3503
Dr. Mike Body, Dir.

Northwest Private Industry Council
SBDC
197-2-B1 Park Island Ave.
Defiance, OH 43512
Phone: (419)784-6270
Fax: (419)782-6273
Don Wright, Dir.

Northwest Technical College
Small Business Development Center
1935 E. 2nd St., Ste. D
Defiance, OH 43512
Phone: (419)784-3777
Fax: (419)782-4649
Don Wright, Dir.

Terra Community College
Small Business Development Center
North Central Fremont Office
1220 Cedar St.
Fremont, OH 43420
Phone: (419)334-8400
Fax: (419)334-9414
Joe Wilson, Dir.

Enterprise Center
Small Business Development Center
129 E. Main St.
PO Box 756
Hillsboro, OH 45133
Phone: (937)393-9599
Fax: (937)393-8159
Bill Grunkemeyer, Interim Dir.

Ashtabula County Economic Development Council, Inc.
Small Business Development Center
36 W. Walnut St.
Jefferson, OH 44047
Phone: (216)576-9134
Fax: (216)576-5003
Sarah Bogardus, Dir.

Kent State University Partnership
SBDC
College of Business Administration, Rm. 300A
Summit and Terrace
Kent, OH 44242
Phone: (330)672-2772
Fax: (330)672-2448
Linda Yost, Dir.

EMTEC/Southern Area Manufacturing
SBDC
3155 Research Park, Ste. 206
Kettering, OH 45420
Phone: (513)258-6180
Fax: (513)258-8189
Harry Bumgarner, Dir.

Lake County Economic Development Center
SBDC
Lakeland Community College
7750 Clocktower Dr.
Kirtland, OH 44080
Phone: (216)951-1290
Fax: (216)951-7336
Cathy Haworth, Dir.

Lima Technical College
Small Business Development Center
West Central Office
545 W. Market St., Ste. 305
Lima, OH 45801-4717
Phone: (419)229-5320
Fax: (419)229-5424
Gerald J. Biedenharn, Dir.

Lorain County Chamber of Commerce
SBDC
6100 S. Boadway
Lorain, OH 44053
Phone: (216)233-6500
Dennis Jones, Dir.

Mid-Ohio Small Business
Development Center
246 E. 4th St.
PO Box 1208
Mansfield, OH 44901
Phone: (419)521-2655
Free: (800)366-7232
Fax: (419)522-6811
Barbara Harmony, Dir.

Marietta College
SBDC
213 Fourth St., 2nd Fl.
Marietta, OH 45750
Phone: (614)376-4832
Fax: (614)376-4832
Emerson Shimp, Dir.

Marion Area Chamber of Commerce
SBDC
206 S. Prospect St.
Marion, OH 43302
Phone: (614)387-0188
Fax: (614)387-7722
Lynn Lovell, Dir.

Tuscarawas SBDC
300 University Dr., NE
Kent State University
300 University Dr., NE
New Philadelphia, OH 44663-9447
Phone: (330)339-3391
Fax: (330)339-2637
Tom Farbizo, Dir.

Miami University
Small Business Development Center
Department of Decision Sciences
336 Upham Hall
Oxford, OH 45056
Phone: (513)529-4841
Fax: (513)529-1469
Dr. Michael Broida, Dir.

Upper Valley Joint Vocational School
Small Business Development Center
8811 Career Dr.
N. Country Rd., 25A
Piqua, OH 45356
Phone: (937)778-8419
Free: (800)589-6963
Fax: (937)778-9237
Jon Heffner, Dir.

Ohio Valley Minority Business
Association
SBDC
1208 Waller St.
PO Box 847
Portsmouth, OH 45662
Phone: (614)353-8395
Fax: (614)353-3695
Clemmy Womack, Dir.

Department of Development
CIC of Belmont County
Small Business Development Center
100 E. Main St.
St. Clairsville, OH 43950
Phone: (614)695-9678
Fax: (614)695-1536
Mike Campbell, Dir.

Kent State University/Salem Campus
SBDC
2491 State Rte. 45 S.
Salem, OH 44460
Phone: (330)332-0361
Fax: (330)332-9256
Deanne Taylor, Dir.

Lawrence County Chamber of
Commerce
Small Business Development Center
U.S. Rte. 52 & Solida Rd.
PO Box 488
South Point, OH 45680
Phone: (740)894-3838
Fax: (740)894-3836
Lou-Ann Walden, Dir.

Springfield Small Business
Development Center
300 E. Auburn Ave.
Springfield, OH 45505
Phone: (937)322-7821
Fax: (937)322-7824
Ed Levanthal, Dir.

Greater Steubenville Chamber of
Commerce
Jefferson County Small Business
Development Center
630 Market St.
PO Box 278
Steubenville, OH 43952
Phone: (614)282-6226
Fax: (614)282-6285
Tim McFadden, Dir.

Toledo Small Business Development
Center
300 Madison Ave., Ste. 200
Toledo, OH 43604-1575
Phone: (419)243-8191
Fax: (419)241-8302
Wendy Gramza, Dir.

Youngstown/Warren SBDC
Region Chamber of Commerce
180 E. Market St., Ste. 225
Warren, OH 44482
Phone: (330)393-2565
Jim Rowlands, Mgr.

Youngstown State University
SBDC
241 Federal Plaza W.
Youngstown, OH 44503
Phone: (330)746-3350
Fax: (330)746-3324
Patricia Veisz, Mgr.

Zanesville Area Chamber of
Commerce
Mid-East Small Business
Development Center
217 N. 5th St.
Zanesville, OH 43701
Phone: (614)452-4868
Fax: (614)454-2963
Bonnie J. Winnett, Dir.

Oklahoma

East Central University
Small Business Development Center
1036 E. 10th St.
Ada, OK 74820
Phone: (405)436-3190
Fax: (405)436-3190
Frank Vater

Northwestern Oklahoma State
University
Small Business Development Center
709 Oklahoma Blvd.
Alva, OK 73717
Phone: (405)327-8608
Fax: (405)327-0560
Clance Doelling, Dir.

Southeastern Oklahoma State
University
Oklahoma SBDC
517 University
Station A, Box 2584
Durant, OK 74701
Phone: (405)924-0277
Free: (800)522-6154
Fax: (405)920-7471
Dr. Grady Pennington, State Dir.

Phillips University
Small Business Development Center
100 S. University Ave.
Enid, OK 73701

Phone: (405)242-7989
Fax: (405)237-1607
Bill Gregory, Coordinator

Langston University Center
Small Business Development Center
Minority Assistance Center
Hwy. 33 E.
Langston, OK 73050
Phone: (405)466-3256
Fax: (405)466-2909
Robert Allen, Dir.

Lawton Satellite
Small Business Development Center
American National Bank Bldg.
601 SW D Ave., Ste. 209
Lawton, OK 73501
Phone: (405)248-4946
Fax: (405)355-3560
Jim Elliot, Business Development Specialists

Northeastern Oklahoma A&M
Miami Satellite
SBDC
Dyer Hall, Rm. 307
215 I St.
Miami, OK 74354
Phone: (918)540-0575
Fax: (918)540-0575
Hugh Simon, Business Development Specialist

Rose State College
SBDC
Procurement Speciality Center
6420 Southeast 15th St.
Midwest City, OK 73110
Phone: (405)733-7348
Fax: (405)733-7495
Judy Robbins, Dir.

University of Central Oklahoma
Small Business Development Center
115 Park Ave.
Oklahoma City, OK 73102-9005
Phone: (405)232-1968
Fax: (405)232-1967
E-mail: sbdc@aix1.ucok.edu
Website: http://www.osbdc.org/osbdc.htm
Susan Urbach

Carl Albert College
Small Business Development Center
1507 S. McKenna
Poteau, OK 74953
Phone: (918)647-4019
Fax: (918)647-1218
Dean Qualls, Dir.

Northeastern Oklahoma State University
Small Business Development Center
Oklahoma Small Business Development Center
Tahlequah, OK 74464
Phone: (918)458-0802
Fax: (918)458-2105
Danielle Coursey, Business Development Specialist

Tulsa Satellite
Small Business Development Center
State Office Bldg.
616 S. Boston, Ste. 100
Tulsa, OK 74119
Phone: (918)583-2600
Fax: (918)599-6173
Jeff Horvath, Dir.

Southwestern Oklahoma State University
Small Business Development Center
100 Campus Dr.
Weatherford, OK 73096
Phone: (405)774-1040
Fax: (405)774-7091
Chuck Felz, Dir.

Oregon

Linn-Benton Community College
Small Business Development Center
6500 SW Pacific Blvd.
Albany, OR 97321
Phone: (541)917-4923
Fax: (541)917-4445
Dennis Sargent, Dir.

Southern Oregon State College/Ashland
Small Business Development Center
Regional Services Institute
Ashland, OR 97520
Phone: (541)482-5838
Fax: (541)482-1115
Liz Shelby, Dir.

Central Oregon Community College
Small Business Development Center
2600 NW College Way
Bend, OR 97701
Phone: (541)383-7290
Fax: (541)317-3445
Bob Newhart, Dir.

Southwestern Oregon Community College
Small Business Development Center
2110 Newmark Ave.
Coos Bay, OR 97420
Phone: (541)888-7100
Fax: (541)888-7113
Jon Richards, Dir.

Columbia Gorge Community College
SBDC
400 E. Scenic Dr., Ste. 257
The Dalles, OR 97058
Phone: (541)298-3118
Fax: (541)298-3119
Mr. Bob Cole, Dir.

Lane Community College
Oregon SBDC
44 W. Broadway, Ste. 501
Eugene, OR 97401-3021
Phone: (541)726-2250
Fax: (541)345-6006
Dr. Edward Cutler, State Dir.

Rogue Community College
Small Business Development Center
214 SW 4th St.
Grants Pass, OR 97526
Phone: (541)471-3515
Fax: (541)471-3589
Lee Merritt, Dir.

Mount Hood Community College
Small Business Development Center
323 NE Roberts St.
Gresham, OR 97030
Phone: (503)667-7658
Fax: (503)666-1140
Don King, Dir.

Oregon Institute of Technology
Small Business Development Center
3201 Campus Dr. S. 314
Klamath Falls, OR 97601
Phone: (541)885-1760
Fax: (541)885-1855
Jamie Albert, Dir.

Eastern Oregon State College
Small Business Development Center
Regional Services Institute
1410 L Ave.
La Grande, OR 97850
Phone: (541)962-3391
Free: (800)452-8639
Fax: (541)962-3668
John Prosnik, Dir.

Oregon Coast Community College
Small Business Development Center
4157 NW Hwy. 101, Ste. 123
PO Box 419
Lincoln City, OR 97367
Phone: (541)994-4166
Fax: (541)996-4958
Guy Faust, Contact

Southern Oregon State College/
Medford
Small Business Development Center
Regional Services Institute
332 W. 6th St.
Medford, OR 97501
Phone: (541)772-3478
Fax: (541)734-4813
Liz Shelby, Dir.

Clackamas Community College
Small Business Development Center
7616 SE Harmony Rd.
Milwaukie, OR 97222
Phone: (503)656-4447
Fax: (503)652-0389
Jan Stennick, Dir.

Treasure Valley Community College
Small Business Development Center
650 College Blvd.
Ontario, OR 97914
Phone: (541)889-6493
Fax: (541)881-2743
Kathy Simko, Dir.

Blue Mountain Community College
Small Business Development Center
37 SE Dorion
Pendleton, OR 97801
Phone: (541)276-6233
Fax: (541)276-6819
Gerald Wood, Dir.

Portland Community College
Small Business Development Center
2701 NW Vaughn St., No. 499
Portland, OR 97209
Phone: (503)978-5080
Fax: (503)228-6350
Robert Keyser, Dir.

Portland Community College
Small Business International Trade
Program
121 SW Salmon St., Ste. 210
Portland, OR 97204
Phone: (503)274-7482
Fax: (503)228-6350
Tom Niland, Dir.

Umpqua Community College
Small Business Development Center
744 SE Rose
Roseburg, OR 97470
Phone: (541)672-2535
Fax: (541)672-3679
Terry Swagerty, Dir.

Chemeketa Community College
Small Business Development Center
365 Ferry St. SE
Salem, OR 97301
Phone: (503)399-5088
Fax: (503)581-6017
Tom Nelson, Dir.

Clatsop Community College
Small Business Development Center
1761 N. Holladay
Seaside, OR 97138
Phone: (503)738-3347
Fax: (503)738-7843
Lori Martin, Dir.

Tillamook Bay Community College
Small Business Development Center
401 B Main St.
Tillamook, OR 97141
Phone: (503)842-2551
Fax: (503)842-2555
Kathy Wilkes, Dir.

Pennsylvania

Lehigh University
Small Business Development Center
Rauch Business Ctr., No. 37
621 Taylor St.
Bethlehem, PA 18015
Phone: (610)758-3980
Fax: (610)758-5205
Dr. Larry A. Strain, Dir.

Clarion University of Pennsylvania
Small Business Development Center
Dana Still Bldg., Rm. 102
Clarion, PA 16214
Phone: (814)226-2060
Fax: (814)226-2636
Dr. Woodrow Yeaney, Dir.

Bucks County SBDC Outreach Center
2 E. Court St.
Doylestown, PA 18901
Phone: (215)230-7150
Bruce Love, Dir.

Gannon University
Small Business Development Center
120 W. 9th St.
Erie, PA 16501
Phone: (814)871-7714
Fax: (814)871-7383
Ernie Post, Dir.

Kutztown University
Small Business Development Center
2986 N. 2nd St.
Harrisburg, PA 17110
Phone: (717)720-4230
Fax: (717)720-4262
Katherine Wilson, Dir.

Indiana University of Pennsylvania
SBDC
208 Eberly College of Business
Indiana, PA 15705
Phone: (412)357-7915
Fax: (412)357-5985
Dr. Tony Palamone, Dir.

St. Vincent College
Small Business Development Center
Alfred Hall, 4th Fl.
300 Fraser Purchase Rd.
Latrobe, PA 15650
Phone: (412)537-4572
Fax: (412)537-0919
Jack Fabean, Dir.

Bucknell University
Small Business Development Center
126 Dana Engineering Bldg., 1st Fl.
Lewisburg, PA 17837
Phone: (717)524-1249
Fax: (717)524-1768
Charles Knisely, Dir.

St. Francis College
Small Business Development Center
Business Resource Center
Loretto, PA 15940
Phone: (814)472-3200
Fax: (814)472-3202
Edward Huttenhower, Dir.

LaSalle University
Small Business Development Center
1900 W. Olney Ave.
Box 365
Philadelphia, PA 19141
Phone: (215)951-1416
Fax: (215)951-1597
Andrew Lamas, Dir.

Temple University
Small Business Development Center
1510 Cecil B. Moore Ave.

Philadelphia, PA 19121
Phone: (215)204-7282
Fax: (215)204-4554
Geraldine Perkins, Dir.

University Of Pennsylvania
Pennsylvania SBDC
The Wharton School
423 Vance Hall
3733 Spruce St.
Philadelphia, PA 19104-6374
Phone: (215)898-1219
Fax: (215)573-2135
E-mail:
ghiggins@sec1.wharton.upenn.edu
Gregory L. Higgins, Jr.

Duquesne University
Small Business Development Center
Rockwell Hall, Rm. 10, Concourse
600 Forbes Ave.
Pittsburgh, PA 15282
Phone: (412)396-6233
Fax: (412)396-5884
Dr. Mary T. McKinney, Dir.

University of Pittsburgh
Small Business Development Center
The Joseph M. Katz Graduate School of Business
208 Bellefield Hall
315 S. Bellefield Ave.
Pittsburgh, PA 15213
Phone: (412)648-1544
Fax: (412)648-1636
Ann Dugan, Dir.

University of Scranton
Small Business Development Center
St. Thomas Hall, Rm. 588
Scranton, PA 18510
Phone: (717)941-7588
Fax: (717)941-4053
Elaine M. Tweedy, Dir.

West Chester University
SBDC
319 Anderson Hall
211 Carter Dr.
West Chester, PA 19383
Phone: (610)436-2162
Fax: (610)436-2577

Wilkes University
Small Business Development Center
Hollenback Hall
192 S. Franklin St.
Wilkes Barre, PA 18766-0001
Phone: (717)831-4340
Free: (800)572-4444
Fax: (717)824-2245
Jeffrey Alves, Dir.

Puerto Rico

Small Business Development Center
Edificio Union Plaza, Ste. 701
416 Ponce de Leon Ave.
Hato Rey, PR 00918
Phone: (787)763-6811
Fax: (787)763-4629
Carmen Marti, State Dir.

Rhode Island

Northern Rhode Island Chamber of Commerce
SBDC
6 Blackstone Valley Pl., Ste. 105
Lincoln, RI 02865-1105
Phone: (401)334-1000
Fax: (401)334-1009
Shelia Hoogeboom, Program Mgr.

Newport County Chamber of Commerce
E. Bay Small Business Development Center
45 Valley Rd.
Middletown, RI 02842-6377
Phone: (401)849-6900
Fax: (401)841-0570
Samuel Carr, Program Mgr.

Fishing Community Program Office
SBDC
PO Box 178
Narragansett, RI 02882
Phone: (401)783-2466
Angela Caporelli, Program Mgr.

South County SBDC
QP/D Industrial Park
35 Belver Ave., Rm. 212
North Kingstown, RI 02852-7556
Phone: (401)294-1227
Fax: (401)294-6897
Elizabeth Kroll, Program Mgr.

Bryant College
Small Business Development Center
30 Exchange Terrace, 4th Fl.
Providence, RI 02903-1793
Phone: (401)831-1330
Fax: (401)274-5410
Ann Marie Marshall, Case Mgr.

Enterprise Community SBDC/BIC
550 Broad St.
Providence, RI 02907
Phone: (401)272-1083
Fax: (401)272-1186
Simon Goudiaby, Program Mgr.

Bell Atlantic Telecommunications Center
1150 Douglas Pke.
Smithfield, RI 02917-1284
Phone: (401)232-0220
Fax: (401)232-0242
Kate Dolan, Managing Dir.

Bryant College
Export Assistance Center
SBDC
1150 Douglas Pike
Smithfield, RI 02917
Phone: (401)232-6407
Fax: (401)232-6416
Raymond Fogarty, Dir.

Bryant College
Rhode Island SBDC
1150 Douglas Pike
Smithfield, RI 02917-1284
Phone: (401)232-6111
Fax: (401)232-6933
Douglas H. Jobling, State Dir.

Entrepreneurship Training Program
Bryant College
SBDC
1150 Douglas Pike
Smithfield, RI 02917-1284
Phone: (401)232-6115
Fax: (401)232-6933
Sydney Okashige, Program Mgr.

Bristol County Chamber of Commerce
SBDC
PO Box 250
Warren, RI 02885-0250
Phone: (401)245-0750
Fax: (401)245-0110
Samuel Carr, Program Mgr.

Central Rhode Island Chamber of Commerce
SBDC
3288 Post Rd.
Warwick, RI 02886-7151
Phone: (401)732-1100
Fax: (401)732-1107
Mr. Elizabeth Kroll, Program Mgr.

South Carolina

University of South Carolina at Aiken
Aiken Small Business Development Center
171 University Pkwy.
Box 9
Aiken, SC 29801
Phone: (803)641-3646
Fax: (803)641-3647
Jackie Moore, Area Mgr.

University of South Carolina at Beaufort
Small Business Development Center
800 Carteret St.
Beaufort, SC 29902
Phone: (803)521-4143
Fax: (803)521-4142
Martin Goodman, Area Mgr.

Clemson University
Small Business Development Center
College of Business and Public Affairs
425 Sirrine Hall
Box 341392
Clemson, SC 29634-1392
Phone: (803)656-3227
Fax: (803)656-4869
Becky Hobart, Regional Dir.

University of South Carolina
College of Business Administration
South Carolina SBDC
Hipp Bldg.
1710 College St.
Columbia, SC 29208
Phone: (803)777-4907
Fax: (803)777-4403
John Lenti, State Director

University of South Carolina
Small Business Development Center
College of Business Administration
Columbia, SC 29208
Phone: (803)777-5118
Fax: (803)777-4403
James Brazell, Dir.

Coastal Carolina College
Small Business Development Center
School of Business Administration
PO Box 261954
Conway, SC 29526-6054
Phone: (803)349-2170
Fax: (803)349-2455
Tim Lowery, Area Mgr.

Florence-Darlington Technical College
Small Business Development Center
PO Box 100548
Florence, SC 29501-0548
Phone: (803)661-8256
Fax: (803)661-8041
David Raines, Area Mgr.

Greenville Manufacturing Field Office
SBDC
53 E. Antrim Dr.
Greenville, SC 29607
Phone: (803)271-3005

University Center
Upstate Area Office Small Business Development Center
216 S. Pleasantburg Dr., Rm. 140
Greenville, SC 29607
Phone: (864)250-8894
Fax: (864)250-8897

Upper Savannah Council of Government
Small Business Development Center
Exchange Building
222 Phoenix St., Ste. 200
PO Box 1366
Greenwood, SC 29648
Phone: (803)941-8071
Fax: (803)941-8090
George Long, Area Mgr.

University of South Carolina at Hilton Head
Small Business Development Center
1 College Center Dr.
10 Office Park Rd.
Hilton Head, SC 29928-7535
Phone: (803)785-3995
Fax: (803)785-3995
Pat Cameron, Consultant

Charleston SBDC
5900 Core Dr., Ste. 104
North Charleston, SC 29406
Phone: (803)740-6160
Fax: (803)740-1607
Merry Boone, Area Mgr.

South Carolina State College
Small Business Development Center
School of Business Administration
Algernon Belcher Hall
300 College Ave.
Campus Box 7176
Orangeburg, SC 29117
Phone: (803)536-8445
Fax: (803)536-8066
John Gadson, Regional Dir.

Winthrop University
Winthrop Regional Small Business Development Center
College of Business Administration
118 Thurmond Bldg.
Rock Hill, SC 29733
Phone: (803)323-2283
Fax: (803)323-4281
Nate Barber, Regional Dir.

Spartanburg Chamber of Commerce
Small Business Development Center
105 Pine St.
PO Box 1636
Spartanburg, SC 29304
Phone: (803)594-5080
Fax: (803)594-5055
John Keagle, Area Mgr.

South Dakota

Aberdeen Small Business Development Center (Northeast Region)
620 15th Ave., SE
Aberdeen, SD 57401
Phone: (605)626-2565
Fax: (605)626-2667
Belinda Engelhart, Regional Dir.

Pierre Small Business Development Center
105 S. Euclid, Ste. C
Pierre, SD 57501
Phone: (605)773-5941
Fax: (605)773-5942
Greg Sund, Dir.

Rapid City Small Business Development Center (Western Region)
444 N. Mount Rushmore Rd., Rm. 208
Rapid City, SD 57701
Phone: (605)394-5311
Fax: (605)394-6140
Carl Gustafson, Regional Dir.

Sioux Falls Region
SBDC
405 S. 3rd Ave., Ste. 101
Sioux Falls, SD 57104
Phone: (605)367-5757
Fax: (605)367-5755
Wade Bruin, Regional Dir.

University of South Dakota
South Dakota SBDC
School of Business
414 E. Clark
Vermillion, SD 57069
Phone: (605)677-5498
Fax: (605)677-5272
E-mail: sbdc@sundance.usd.edu
Robert E. Ashley. Jr.

Watertown Small Business Development Center
124 1st. Ave., NW
PO Box 1207
Watertown, SD 57201
Phone: (605)886-7224
Fax: (605)882-5049
Belinda Engelhart, Regional Dir.

Tennessee

Chattanooga State Technical Community College
SBDC
100 Cherokee Blvd., No. 202
Chattanooga, TN 37405-3878
Phone: (423)752-1774
Fax: (423)752-1925
Donna Marsh, Specialist

Southeast Tennessee Development District
Small Business Development Center
25 Cherokee Blvd.
PO Box 4757
Chattanooga, TN 37405-0757
Phone: (423)266-5781
Fax: (423)267-7705
Sherri Bishop, Dir.

Austin Peay State University
Small Business Development Center
College of Business
Clarksville, TN 37044
Phone: (615)648-7764
Fax: (615)648-5985
John Volker, Dir.

Cleveland State Community College
Small Business Development Center
PO Box 3570
PO Box 3570
Cleveland, TN 37320-3570
Phone: (423)478-6247
Fax: (423)478-6251
Don Green, Dir.

Small Business Development Center (Columbia)
Maury County Chamber of Commerce Bldg.
106 W. 6th St.
PO Box 8069
Columbia, TN 38402-8069
Phone: (615)898-2745
Fax: (615)893-7089
Eugene Osekowsky, Small Business Specialist

Tennessee Technological University
SBDC
College of Business Administration
PO Box 5023
Cookeville, TN 38505
Phone: (931)372-3648
Fax: (931)372-6249
Dorothy Vaden, Senior Small Bus. Specialist

Dyersburg State Community College
Small Business Development Center
1510 Lake Rd.
Dyersburg, TN 38024-2450
Phone: (901)286-3201
Fax: (901)286-3271
Bob Wylie

Four Lakes Regional Industrial Development Authority
SBDC
PO Box 63
Hartsville, TN 37074-0063
Phone: (615)374-9521
Fax: (615)374-4608
Dorothy Vaden, Senior Small Bus. Specialist

Jackson State Community College
Small Business Development Center
McWherter Center, Rm. 213
2046 N. Parkway St.
Jackson, TN 38301-3797
Phone: (901)424-5389
Fax: (901)425-2641
David L. Brown

Lambuth University
SBDC
705 Lambuth Blvd.
Jackson, TN 38301
Phone: (901)425-3326
Fax: (901)425-3327
Phillip Ramsey, SB Specialist

East Tennessee State University
College of Business
SBDC
PO Box 70625
Johnson City, TN 37614-0625
Phone: (423)929-5630
Fax: (423)461-7080
Bob Justice, Dir.

Knoxville Area Chamber Partnership
International Trade Center
SBDC
Historic City Hall
601 W. Summit Hill Dr.
Knoxville, TN 37902-2011
Phone: (423)632-2990
Fax: (423)521-6367
Richard Vogler, IT Specialist

Pellissippi State Technical Community College
Small Business Development Center
Historic City Hall
601 W. Summit Hill Dr.
Knoxville, TN 37902-2011
Phone: (423)632-2980
Fax: (423)971-4439
Teri Brahams, Consortium Dir.

University of Memphis
International Trade Center
SBDC
320 S. Dudley St.
Memphis, TN 38152-0001
Phone: (901)678-4174
Fax: (901)678-4072
Philip Johnson, Dir.

University of Memphis
Tennessee SBDC
320 S. Dudley St.
Building No. 1
Memphis, TN 38152
Phone: (901)678-2500
Fax: (901)678-4072
Dr. Kenneth J. Burns, State Dir.

Walters State Community College
Tennessee Small Business Development Center
500 S. Davy Crockett Pkwy.
Morristown, TN 37813
Phone: (423)585-2675
Fax: (423)585-2679
Jack Tucker, Dir.

Middle Tennessee State University
Small Business Development Center
Chamber of Commerce Bldg.
501 Memorial Blvd.
PO Box 487
Murfreesboro, TN 37129-0001
Phone: (615)898-2745

Fax: (615)890-7600
Patrick Geho, Dir.

Tennessee State University
Small Business Development Center
College of Business
330 10th Ave. N.
Nashville, TN 37203-3401
Phone: (615)963-7179
Fax: (615)963-7160
Billy E. Lowe, Dir.

Texas

Abilene Christian University
Small Business Development Center
College of Business Administration
648 E. Hwy. 80
Abilene, TX 79601
Phone: (915)670-0300
Fax: (915)670-0311
Judy Wilhelm, Dir.

Sul Ross State University
Big Bend SBDC Satellite
PO Box C-47, Rm. 319
Alpine, TX 79832
Phone: (915)837-8694
Fax: (915)837-8104
Michael Levine, Dir.

Alvin Community College
Small Business Development Center
3110 Mustang Rd.
Alvin, TX 77511-4898
Phone: (713)388-4686
Fax: (713)388-4903
Gina Mattei, Dir.

West Texas A&M University
Small Business Development Center
T. Boone Pickens School of Business
1800 S. Washington, Ste. 209
Amarillo, TX 79102
Phone: (806)372-5151
Fax: (806)372-5261
Don Taylor, Dir.

Trinity Valley Community College
Small Business Development Center
500 S. Prairieville
Athens, TX 75751
Phone: (903)675-7403
Free: (800)335-7232
Fax: (903)675-5199
Judy Loden, Dir.

Lower Colorado River Authority
Small Business Development Center
3701 Lake Austin Blvd.
PO Box 220
Austin, TX 78703
Phone: (512)473-3510
Fax: (512)473-3285
Larry Lucero, Dir.

Lee College
Small Business Development Center
Rundell Hall
PO Box 818
Baytown, TX 77522-0818
Phone: (281)425-6309
Fax: (713)425-6309
Tommy Hathaway, Dir.

Lamar University
Small Business Development Center
855 Florida Ave.
Beaumont, TX 77705
Phone: (409)880-2367
Fax: (409)880-2201
Gene Arnold, Dir.

Bonham Satellite
Small Business Development Center
SBDC
Sam Rayburn Library, Bldg. 2
1201 E. 9th St.
Bonham, TX 75418
Phone: (903)583-7565
Fax: (903)583-6706
Darroll Martin, Coordinator

Blinn College
Small Business Development Center
902 College Ave.
Brenham, TX 77833
Phone: (409)830-4137
Fax: (409)830-4135
Phillis Nelson, Dir.

Brazos Valley Small Business
Development Center
Small Business Development Center
4001 E. 29th St., Ste. 175
PO Box 3695
Bryan, TX 77805-3695
Phone: (409)260-5222
Fax: (409)260-5229
Sam Harwell, Dir.

Greater Corpus Christi Business
Alliance
Small Business Development Center
1201 N. Shoreline
Corpus Christi, TX 78401
Phone: (512)881-1847
Fax: (512)882-4256
Rudy Ortiz, Dir.

Navarro Small Business Development
Center
120 N. 12th St.
Corsicana, TX 75110
Phone: (903)874-0658
Free: (800)320-7232
Fax: (903)874-4187
Leon Allard, Dir.

Dallas County Community College
North Texas SBDC
1402 Corinth St.
Dallas, TX 75215
Phone: 800-350-7232
Fax: (214)860-5813
Elizabeth (Liz) Klimback, Regional
Dir.

International Assistance Center
SBDC
2050 Stemmons Fwy.
PO Box 420451
Dallas, TX 75258
Phone: (214)747-1300
Free: (800)337-7232
Fax: (214)748-5774
Beth Huddleston, Dir.

Bill J. Priest Institute for Economic
Development
North Texas-Dallas Small Business
Development Center
1402 Corinth St.
Dallas, TX 75215
Phone: (214)860-5842
Free: (800)348-7232
Fax: (214)860-5881
Pamela Speraw, Dir.

Technology Assistance Center
SBDC
1402 Corinth St.
Dallas, TX 75215
Phone: 800-355-7232
Fax: (214)860-5881
Pamela Speraw, Dir.

Texas Center for Government
Contracting and Technology
Assistance
Small Business Development Center
1402 Corinth St.
Dallas, TX 75215
Phone: (214)860-5841
Fax: (214)860-5881
Gerald Chandler, Dir.

Grayson County College
Small Business Development Center
6101 Grayson Dr.
Denison, TX 75020
Phone: (903)463-8787
Free: (800)316-7232
Fax: (903)463-5437
Cynthia Flowers-Whitfield, Dir.

Denton Small Business Development Center
PO Drawer P
Denton, TX 76201
Phone: (254)380-1849
Fax: (254)382-0040
Carolyn Birkhead, Coordinator

Best Southwest
SBDC
214 S, Main, Ste. 102A
Duncanville, TX 75116
Phone: (214)709-5878
Free: (800)317-7232
Fax: (214)709-6089
Herb Kamm, Dir.

Best Southwest Small Business Development Center
214 S. Main, Ste. 102A
Duncanville, TX 75116
Phone: (972)709-5878
Free: (800)317-7232
Fax: (972)709-6089
Neil Small, Dir.

University of Texas—Pan American
Small Business Development Center
1201 W. University Dr., Rm. BA-124
Center for Entrepreneurship & Economic Development
Edinburg, TX 78539-2999
Phone: (956)316-2610
Fax: (956)316-2612
Juan Garcia, Dir.

El Paso Community College
Small Business Development Center
103 Montana Ave., Ste. 202
El Paso, TX 79902-3929
Phone: (915)831-4410
Fax: (915)831-4625
Roque R. Segura, Dir.

Small Business Development Center for Enterprise Excellence
SBDC
7300 Jack Newell Blvd., S.
Fort Worth, TX 76118
Phone: (817)272-5930
Fax: (817)272-5932
Jo An Weddle, Dir.

Tarrant County Junior College
Small Business Development Center
Mary Owen Center, Rm. 163
1500 Houston St.
Ft. Worth, TX 76102
Phone: (817)871-2068
Fax: (817)871-0031
David Edmonds, Dir.

North Central Texas College
Small Business Development Center
1525 W. California
Gainesville, TX 76240
Phone: (254)668-4220
Free: (800)351-7232
Fax: (254)668-6049
Cathy Keeler, Dir.

Galveston College
Small Business Development Center
4015 Avenue Q
Galveston, TX 77550
Phone: (409)740-7380
Fax: (409)740-7381
Georgette Peterson, Dir.

Western Bank and Trust Satellite
SBDC
PO Box 461545
Garland, TX 75046
Phone: (214)860-5850
Fax: (214)860-5857
Al Salgado, Dir.

Grand Prairie Satellite
SBDC
Chamber of Commerce
900 Conover Dr.
Grand Prairie, TX 75053
Phone: (214)860-5850
Fax: (214)860-5857
Al Salgado, Dir.

Houston Community College System
Small Business Development Center
10450 Stancliff, Ste. 100
Houston, TX 77099
Phone: (281)933-7932
Fax: (281)568-3690
Joe Harper, Dir.

Houston International Trade Center
Small Business Development Center
1100 Louisiana, Ste. 500
Houston, TX 77002
Phone: (713)752-8404
Fax: (713)756-1500
Mr. Carlos Lopez, Dir.

North Harris Montgomery Community College District
Small Business Development Center
250 N. Sam Houston Pkwy. E.
Houston, TX 77060
Phone: (281)260-3174
Fax: (713)591-3513
Kay Hamilton, Dir.

University of Houston
Southeastern Texas SBDC
1100 Louisiana, Ste. 500
Houston, TX 77002
Phone: (713)752-8444
Fax: (713)756-1500
J.E. "Ted" Cadou, Reg. Dir.

University of Houston
Texas Information Procurement Service
Small Business Development Center
1100 Louisiana, Ste. 500
Houston, TX 77002
Phone: (713)752-8477
Fax: (713)756-1515
Jacqueline Taylor, Dir.

University of Houston
Texas Manufacturing Assistance Center (Gulf Coast)
1100 Louisiana, Ste. 500
Houston, TX 77002
Phone: (713)752-8440
Fax: (713)756-1500
Roy Serpa, Regional Dir.

Sam Houston State University
Small Business Development Center
843 S. Sam Houston Ave.
PO Box 2058
Huntsville, TX 77341-3738
Phone: (409)294-3737
Fax: (409)294-3612
Bob Barragan, Dir.

Kingsville Chamber of Commerce
Small Business Development Center
635 E. King
Kingsville, TX 78363
Phone: (512)595-5088
Fax: (512)592-0866
Marco Garza, Dir.

Brazosport College
Small Business Development Center
500 College Dr.

Lake Jackson, TX 77566
Phone: (409)266-3380
Fax: (409)265-3482
Patricia Leyendecker, Dir.

Laredo Development Foundation
Small Business Development Center
Division of Business Administration
616 Leal St.
Laredo, TX 78041
Phone: (956)722-0563
Fax: (956)722-6247
Araceli Lozano, Acting Dir.

Kilgore College
SBDC
Triple Creek Shopping Plaza
110 Triple Creek Dr., Ste. 70
Longview, TX 75601
Phone: (903)757-5857
Free: (800)338-7232
Fax: (903)753-7920
Brad Bunt, Dir.

Texas Tech University
Northwestern Texas SBDC
Spectrum Plaza
2579 S. Loop 289, Ste. 114
Lubbock, TX 79423
Phone: (806)745-3973
Fax: (806)745-6207
E-mail: odbea@ttacs.ttu.edu
Craig Bean, Regional Dir.

Angelina Community College
Small Business Development Center
Hwy. 59 S.
PO Box 1768
Lufkin, TX 75902
Phone: (409)639-1887
Fax: (409)639-3863
Brian McClain, Dir.

Midlothian SBDC
330 N. 8th St., Ste. 203
Midlothian, TX 76065-0609
Phone: (214)775-4336
Fax: (214)775-4337

Northeast Texarkana
Small Business Development Center
PO Box 1307
Mt. Pleasant, TX 75455
Phone: (903)572-1911
Free: (800)357-7232
Fax: (903)572-0598
Bob Wall, Dir.

University of Texas—Permian Basin
Small Business Development Center
College of Management
4901 E. University Blvd.
Odessa, TX 79762
Phone: (915)552-2455
Fax: (915)552-2433
Arthur L. Connor, III

Paris Junior College
Small Business Development Center
2400 Clarksville St.
Paris, TX 75460
Phone: (903)784-1802
Fax: (903)784-1801
Pat Bell, Dir.

Courtyard Center for Professional and Economic Development
Collin Small Business Development Center
4800 Preston Park Blvd., Ste. A126
Box 15
Plano, TX 75093
Phone: (972)985-3770
Fax: (972)985-3775
Chris Jones, Dir.

Angelo State University
Small Business Development Center
2610 West Ave. N.
Campus Box 10910
San Angelo, TX 76909
Phone: (915)942-2098
Fax: (915)942-2096
Harlan Bruha, Dir.

University of Texas (Downtown San Antonio)
South Texas Border SBDC
1222 N. Main, Ste. 450
San Antonio, TX 78212
Phone: (210)458-2450
Fax: (210)458-2464
E-mail: rmckinle@utsadt.utsa.edu
Robert McKinley, Regional Dir.

University of Texas at San Antonio
International Trade Center
SBDC
1222 N. Main, Ste. 450
San Antonio, TX 78212
Phone: (210)458-2470
Fax: (210)458-2464
Sara Jackson, Dir.

Houston Community College System
Small Business Development Center
13600 Murphy Rd.
Stafford, TX 77477
Phone: (713)499-4870
Fax: (713)499-8194
Ted Charlesworth, Acting Dir.

Tarleton State University
Small Business Development Center
College of Business Administration
Box T-0650
Stephenville, TX 76402
Phone: (817)968-9330
Fax: (817)968-9329
Jim Choate, Dir.

College of the Mainland
Small Business Development Center
1200 Amburn Rd.
Texas City, TX 77591
Phone: (409)938-1211
Free: (800)246-7232
Fax: (409)938-7578
Elizabeth Boudreau, Dir.

Tyler Junior College
Small Business Development Center
1530 South SW Loop 323, Ste. 100
Tyler, TX 75701
Phone: (903)510-2975
Fax: (903)510-2978
Frank Viso, Dir.

Middle Rio Grande Development Council
Small Business Development Center
209 N. Getty St.
Uvalde, TX 78801
Phone: (830)278-2527
Fax: (830)278-2929
Sheri Rutledge, Dir.

University of Houston—Victoria
Small Business Development Center
700 Main Center, Ste. 102
Victoria, TX 77901
Phone: (512)575-8944
Fax: (512)575-8852
Carole Parks, Dir.

McLennan Community College
Small Business Development Center
401 Franklin
Waco, TX 76708
Phone: (254)714-0077
Free: (800)349-7232
Fax: (254)714-1668
Lu Billings, Dir.

LCRA Coastal Plains
SBDC
PO Box 148
Wharton, TX 77488

Phone: (409)532-1007
Fax: (409)532-0056
Lynn Polson, Dir.

Midwestern State University
Small Business Development Center
3410 Taft Blvd.
Wichita Falls, TX 76308
Phone: (817)397-4373
Fax: (817)397-4374
Tim Thomas, Dir.

Utah

Southern Utah University
Small Business Development Center
351 W. Center
Cedar City, UT 84720
Phone: (435)586-5400
Fax: (435)586-5493
Derek Snow, Dir.

Snow College
Small Business Development Center
345 West 100 North
Ephraim, UT 84627
Phone: (435)283-7472
Fax: (435)283-6913
Russell Johnson, Dir.

Utah State University
Small Business Development Center
East Campus Bldg., Rm. 124
Logan, UT 84322
Phone: (435)797-2277
Fax: (435)797-3317
Franklin C. Prante, Dir.

Weber State University
Small Business Development Center
School of Business and Economics
Ogden, UT 84408-3815
Phone: (435)626-6070
Fax: (435)626-7423
Bruce Davis, Dir.

Utah Valley State College
Utah Small Business Development Center
800 West 200 South
Orem, UT 84058
Phone: (435)222-8230
Fax: (435)225-1229
Chuck Cozzens, Contact

South Eastern Utah AOG
Small Business Development Center
Price Center
PO Box 1106
Price, UT 84501
Phone: (435)637-5444
Fax: (435)637-7336
Dennis Rigby, Dir.

Utah State University Extension Office
SBDC
987 E. Lagoon St.
Roosevelt, UT 84066
Phone: (435)722-2294
Fax: (435)789-3689
Mark Holmes, Dir.

Dixie College
Small Business Development Center
225 South 700 East
St. George, UT 84770-3876
Phone: (435)652-7751
Fax: (435)652-7870
Jill Ellis, Dir.

Salt Lake Community College
SBDC
1623 S. State St.
Salt Lake City, UT 84115
Phone: (801)957-3480
Fax: (801)957-3489
Mike Finnerty, State Dir.

Salt Lake Community College
Sandy SBDC
8811 South 700 East
Sandy, UT 84070
Phone: (435)255-5878
Fax: (435)255-6393
Barry Bartlett, Dir.

Vermont

Brattleboro Development Credit Corp.
SBDC
72 Cotton Mill Hill
PO Box 1177
Brattleboro, VT 05301-1177
Phone: (802)257-7731
Fax: (802)258-3886
William McGrath, Executive V. P.

Greater Burlington Industrial Corp.
Northwestern Vermont Small Business Development Center
PO Box 786
Burlington, VT 05402-0786
Phone: (802)658-9228
Fax: (802)860-1899
Thomas D. Schroeder, Specialist

Addison County Economic Development Corp.
SBDC
RD4, Box 1309A
Middlebury, VT 05753
Phone: (802)388-7953
Fax: (802)388-8066
James Stewart, Exec. Dir.

Central Vermont Economic Development Center
SBDC
PO Box 1439
Montpelier, VT 05601-1439
Phone: (802)223-4654
Fax: (802)223-4655
Donald Rowan, Exec. Dir.

Lamoille Economic Development Corp.
SBDC
Sunset Dr.
PO Box 455
Morrisville, VT 05661-0455
Phone: (802)888-4542
Chris D'Elia, Executive Dir.

Bennington County Industrial Corp.
SBDC
PO Box 357
North Bennington, VT 05257-0357
Phone: (802)442-8975
Fax: (802)442-1101
Chris Hunsinger, Executive Dir.

Lake Champlain Islands Chamber of Commerce
SBDC
PO Box 213
North Hero, VT 05474-0213
Phone: (802)372-5683
Fax: (802)372-6104
Barbara Mooney, Exec. Dir.

Vermont Technical College
Small Business Development Center
PO Box 422
Randolph Center, VT 05060-0422
Phone: (802)728-9101
Free: (800)464-7232
Fax: (802)728-3026
Donald L. Kelpinski, State Dir.

Rutland Economic Development Corp.
Southwestern Vermont Small Business Development Center
256 N. Main St.
Rutland, VT 05701-0039

Phone: (802)773-9147
Fax: (802)773-2772
Wendy Wilton, Regional Dir.

Franklin County Industrial
Development Corp.
SBDC
PO Box 1099
St. Albans, VT 05478-1099
Phone: (802)524-2194
Fax: (802)527-5258
Timothy J. Soule, Executive Dir.

Northeastern Vermont Small Business
Development Center
44 Main St.
PO Box 630
St. Johnsbury, VT 05819-0630
Phone: (802)748-1014
Fax: (802)748-1223
Charles E. E. Carter, Exec. Dir.

Springfield Development Corp.
Southeastern Vermont Small Business
Development Center
PO Box 58
Springfield, VT 05156-0058
Phone: (802)885-2071
Fax: (802)885-3027
Steve Casabona, Specialist

Green Mountain Economic
Development Corporation
SBDC
PO Box 246
White River Jct., VT 05001-0246
Phone: (802)295-3710
Fax: (802)295-3779
Lenae Quillen-Blume, SBDC
Specialist

Virgin Islands

University of the Virgin Islands
(Charlotte Amalie)
Small Business Development Center
8000 Nisky Center, Ste. 202
Charlotte Amalie, VI 00802-5804
Phone: (809)776-3206
Fax: (809)775-3756
Ian Hodge, Assoc. State Dir.

University of the Virgin Islands
Small Business Development Center
Sunshine Mall
No.1 Estate Cane, Ste. 104
Frederiksted, VI 00840
Phone: (809)692-5270
Fax: (809)692-5629
Chester Williams, State Dir.

Virginia

Virginia Highlands SBDC
Rte. 382
PO Box 828
Abingdon, VA 24212
Phone: (540)676-5615
Fax: (540)628-7576
Jim Tilley, Dir.

Arlington Small Business
Development Center
George Mason University, Arlington
Campus
4001 N. Fairfax Dr., Ste. 450
Arlington, VA 22203-1640
Phone: (703)993-8129
Fax: (703)430-7293
Paul Hall, Dir.

Virginia Eastern Shore Corp.
SBDC
36076 Lankford Hwy.
PO Box 395
Belle Haven, VA 23306
Phone: (757)442-7179
Fax: (757)442-7181

Mount Empire Community College
Southwest Small Business
Development Center
Drawer 700, Rte. 23, S.
Big Stone Gap, VA 24219
Phone: (540)523-6529
Fax: (540)523-2400
Tim Blankenbecler, Dir.

Central Virginia Small Business
Development Center
918 Emmet St., N., Ste. 200
Charlottesville, VA 22903-4878
Phone: (804)295-8198
Fax: (804)295-7066
Robert A. Hamilton, Jr.

Hampton Roads Chamber of
Commerce
SBDC
400 Volvo Pkwy.
PO Box 1776
Chesapeake, VA 23320
Phone: (757)664-2590
Fax: (757)548-1835
William J. Holoran, Jr.

George Mason University
Northern Virginia Small Business
Development Center
4031 University Dr., Ste. 200
Fairfax, VA 22030
Phone: (703)277-7700
Fax: (703)993-2126
Michael Kehoe, Exec. Dir.

Longwood College (Farmville)
Small Business Development Center
515 Main St.
Farmville, VA 23909
Phone: (804)395-2086
Fax: (804)395-2359
Gerald L. Hughes, Jr.

Rappahannock Region Small
Business Development Center
1301 College Ave.
Seacobeck Hall, Rm. 102
Fredericksburg, VA 22401
Phone: (540)654-1060
Fax: (540)654-1070
Jeffrey R. Sneddon, Exec. Dir.

Hampton Roads Inc.
Small Business Development Center
525 Butler Farm Rd., Ste. 102
Hampton, VA 23666
Phone: (757)825-2957
Fax: (757)825-2960
James Carroll, Dir.

James Madison University
Small Business Development Center
College of Business
Zane Showker Hall, Rm. 527
PO Box MSC 0206
Harrisonburg, VA 22807
Phone: (540)568-3227
Fax: (540)568-3106
Karen Wigginton, Dir.

Lynchburg Regional Small Business
Development Center
147 Mill Ridge Rd.
Lynchburg, VA 24502-4341
Phone: (804)582-6170
Free: (800)876-7232
Fax: (804)582-6106
Barry Lyons, Dir.

Flory Small Business Development
Center
10311 Sudley Manor Dr.
Manassas, VA 20109-2962
Phone: (703)335-2500
Linda Decker, Dir.

SBDC Satellite Office of Longwood
PO Box 709
115 Broad St.
Martinsville, VA 24114
Phone: (540)632-4462
Fax: (540)632-5059
Ken Copeland, Dir.

Lord Fairfax Community College
SBDC
173 Skirmisher Ln.
PO Box 47
Middletown, VA 22645
Phone: (540)869-6649
Fax: (540)868-7002
Robert Crosen, Dir.

Small Business Development Center of Hampton Roads, Inc. (Norfolk)
420 Bank St.
PO Box 327
Norfolk, VA 23501
Phone: (757)664-2528
Fax: (757)622-5563
Warren Snyder, Dir.

New River Valley
SBDC
600-H Norwood St.
PO Box 3726
Radford, VA 24141
Phone: (540)831-6056
Fax: (540)831-6057
David Shanks, Dir.

Southwest Virginia Community College
Southwest Small Business Development Center
PO Box SVCC, Rte. 19
Richlands, VA 24641
Phone: (540)964-7345
Fax: (540)964-5788
Jim Boyd, Dir.

Department of Business Assistance
Virginia SBDC
707 E. Main St., Ste. 300
Richmond, VA 23219
Phone: (804)371-8253
Fax: (804)225-3384
Bob Wilburn, State Dir.

Greater Richmond Small Business Development Center
1 N. 5th St., Ste. 510
Richmond, VA 23219
Phone: (804)648-7838
Free: (800)646-SBDC
Fax: (804)648-7849
Charlie Meacham, Dir.

Regional Chamber Small Business Development Center
Western Virginia SBDC Consortium
212 S. Jefferson St.
Roanoke, VA 24011
Phone: (540)983-0717
Fax: (540)983-0723
Ian Webb, Dir.

South Boston Satellite Office of Longwood
Small Business Development Center
515 Broad St.
PO Box 1116
South Boston, VA 24592
Phone: (804)575-0044
Fax: (804)572-1762
Vincent Decker, Dir.

Loudoun County Small Business Development Center
Satellite Office of Northern Virginia
207 E. Holly Ave., Ste. 214
Sterling, VA 20164
Phone: (703)430-7222
Fax: (703)430-7258
Ted London, Dir.

Warsaw Small Business Development Center
Satellite Office of Rappahannock
5559 W. Richmond Rd.
PO Box 490
Warsaw, VA 22572
Phone: (804)333-0286
Free: (800)524-8915
Fax: (804)333-0187
John Clickener, Dir.

Wytheville Community College
Wytheville Small Business Development Center
1000 E. Main St.
Wytheville, VA 24382
Phone: (540)223-4798
Free: (800)468-1195
Fax: (540)223-4716
Rob Edwards, Dir.

Washington

Bellevue Small Business Development Center
Bellevue Community College
3000 Landerholm Circle SE
Bellevue, WA 98007-6484
Phone: (425)643-2888
Fax: (425)649-3113
Bill Huenefeld, Business Dev. Specialist

Western Washington University
Small Business Development Center
College of Business and Economics
308 Parks Hall
Bellingham, WA 98225-9073
Phone: (360)650-4831
Fax: (360)650-4844
Tom Dorr, Business Dev. Specialist

Centralia Community College
Small Business Development Center
600 W. Locust St.
Centralia, WA 98531
Phone: (360)736-9391
Fax: (360)730-7504
Joanne Baria, Business Dev. Specialist

Columbia Basin College—TRIDEC
Small Business Development Center
901 N. Colorado
Kennewick, WA 99336
Phone: (509)735-6222
Fax: (509)735-6609
Blake Escudier, Business Dev. Specialist

Edmonds Community College
Small Business Development Center
20000 68th Ave. W.
Lynnwood, WA 98036
Phone: (425)640-1435
Fax: (425)640-1532
Jack Wicks, Business Dev. Specialist

Big Bend Community College
Small Business Development Center
7662 Chanute St.
Moses Lake, WA 98837-3299
Phone: (509)762-6306
Fax: (509)762-6329
Ed Baroch, Business Dev. Specialist

Skagit Valley College
Small Business Development Center
2405 College Way
Mount Vernon, WA 98273
Phone: (360)428-1282
Fax: (360)336-6116
Peter Stroosma, Business Dev. Specialist

Wenatchee Valley College
SBDC
PO Box 741

Okanogan, WA 98840
Phone: (509)826-5107
Fax: (509)826-1812
John Rayburn, Business Dev. Specialist

South Puget Sound Community College
Small Business Development Center
721 Columbia St. SW
Olympia, WA 98501
Phone: (360)753-5616
Fax: (360)586-5493
Douglas Hammel, Business Dev. Specialist

Washington State University (Pullman)
Small Business Development Center
501 Johnson Tower
PO Box 644851
Pullman, WA 99164-4727
Phone: (509)335-1576
Fax: (509)335-0949
Carol Riesenberg, State Dir.

International Trade Institute
North Seattle Community College
Small Business Development Center
2001 6th Ave., Ste. 650
Seattle, WA 98121
Phone: (206)553-0052
Fax: (206)553-7253
Ann Tamura, IT Specialist

South Seattle Community College
Duwamish Industrial Education Center
Small Business Development Center
6770 E. Marginal Way S
Seattle, WA 98108-3405
Phone: (206)768-6855
Fax: (206)764-5838
Henry Burton, Business Dev. Specialist

Washington Small Business Development Center (Seattle)
180 Nickerson, Ste. 207
Seattle, WA 98109
Phone: (206)464-5450
Fax: (206)464-6357
Warner Wong, Business Dev. Specialist

Washington State University (Spokane)
Small Business Development Center
665 North Riverpoint Blvd.
Spokane, WA 99202
Phone: (509)358-7894
Fax: (509)358-7896
Richard Thorpe, Business Dev. Specialist

Washington Small Business Development Center (Tacoma)
950 Pacific Ave., Ste. 300
PO Box 1933
Tacoma, WA 98401-1933
Phone: (253)272-7232
Fax: (253)597-7305
Neil Delisanti, Business Dev. Specialist

Columbia River Economic Development Council
Small Business Development Center
217 SE 136th Ave., Ste. 105
Vancouver, WA 98660
Phone: (360)260-6372
Fax: (360)260-6369
Janet Harte, Business Dev. Specialist

Port of Walla Walla SBDC
500 Tausick Way
Rte. 4, Box 174
Walla Walla, WA 99362
Phone: (509)527-4681
Fax: (509)525-3101
Rich Monacelli, Business Dev. Specialist

Quest Small Business Development Center
37 S. Wenatchee Ave., Ste. C
Industrial Bldg. 2, Ste. D.
Wenatchee, WA 98801-2443
Phone: (509)662-8016
Fax: (509)663-0455
Rich Reim, Business Dev. Specialist

Yakima Valley College
Small Business Development Center
PO Box 1647
Yakima, WA 98907
Phone: (509)454-3608
Fax: (509)454-4155
Audrey Rice, Business Dev. Specialist

West Virginia

College of West Virginia
SBDC
PO Box AG
Beckley, WV 25802
Phone: (304)252-7885
Fax: (304)252-9584
Tom Hardiman, Program Mgr.

West Virginia Department Office
West Virginia SBDC
950 Kanawha Blvd. E., Ste. 200
Charleston, WV 25301
Phone: (304)558-2960
Free: (888)WVA-SBDC
Fax: (304)348-0127
Dr. Hazel Kroesser-Palmer, State-Dir.

Fairmont State College (Elkins Satellite)
SBDC
10 Eleventh St., Ste. 1
Elkins, WV 26241
Phone: (304)637-7205
Fax: (304)637-4902
James Martin, Business Analyst

Fairmont State College
Small Business Development Center
1000 Technology Dr., Ste. 1120
Fairmont, WV 26554
Phone: (304)367-2712
Fax: (304)367-2717
Jack Kirby, Program Mgr.

Marshall University
Small Business Development Center
1050 4th Ave.
Huntington, WV 25755-2126
Phone: (304)696-6246
Fax: (304)696-6277
Edna McClain, Program Mgr.

West Virginia Institute of Technology
Small Business Development Center
Engineering Bldg., Rm. 102
Montgomery, WV 25136
Phone: (304)442-5501
Fax: (304)442-3307
James Epling, Program Mgr.

West Virginia University
Fairmont State College Satellite
Small Business Development Center
PO Box 6025
Morgantown, WV 26506-6025
Phone: (304)293-5839
Fax: (304)293-7061
Sharon Stratton, Business Analyst

West Virginia University (Parkersburg)
Small Business Development Center
Rte. 5, Box 167-A
Parkersburg, WV 26101

Phone: (304)424-8277
Fax: (304)424-8315
Greg Hill, Program Mgr.

Shepherd College
Small Business Development Center
120 N. Princess St.
Shepherdstown, WV 25443
Phone: (304)876-5261
Fax: (304)876-5467
Fred Baer, Program Mgr.

West Virginia Northern Community College
Small Business Development Center
1701 Market St.
College Sq.
Wheeling, WV 26003
Phone: (304)233-5900
Fax: (304)232-0965
Ron Trevellini, Program Mgr.

Wisconsin

University of Wisconsin—Eau Claire
Small Business Development Center
Schneider Hall, Rm. 113
PO Box 4004
Eau Claire, WI 54702-4004
Phone: (715)836-5811
Fax: (715)836-5263
Fred Waedt, Dir.

University of Wisconsin—Green Bay
Small Business Development Center
Wood Hall, Rm. 480
2420 Nicolet Dr.
Green Bay, WI 54311
Phone: (920)465-2089
Fax: (920)465-2552
Jan Thornton, Dir.

University of Wisconsin—Parkside
Small Business Development Center
Tallent Hall, Rm. 284
900 Wood Rd.
Kenosha, WI 53141-2000
Phone: (414)595-2189
Fax: (414)595-2471
Patricia Deutsch, Dir.

University of Wisconsin—La Crosse
Small Business Development Center
North Hall, Rm. 120
1701 Farwell St.
La Crosse, WI 54601
Phone: (608)785-8782
Fax: (608)785-6919
Jan Gallagher, Dir.

University of Wisconsin
Wisconsin SBDC
432 N. Lake St., Rm. 423
Madison, WI 53706
Phone: (608)263-7794
Fax: (608)263-7830
Erica McIntire, State Dir.

University of Wisconsin—Madison
Small Business Development Center
975 University Ave., Rm. 3260
Grainger Hall
Madison, WI 53706
Phone: (608)263-2221
Fax: (608)263-0818
Neil Lerner, Dir.

University of Wisconsin—Milwaukee
Small Business Development Center
161 W. Wisconsin Ave., Ste. 600
Milwaukee, WI 53203
Phone: (414)227-3240
Fax: (414)227-3142
Sara Thompson, Dir.

University of Wisconsin—Oshkosh
Small Business Development Center
800 Algoma Blvd.
Oshkosh, WI 54901
Phone: (920)424-1453
Fax: (920)424-7413
John Mozingo, Dir.

University of Wisconsin—Stevens Point
Small Business Development Center
Old Main Bldg., Rm. 103
Stevens Point, WI 54481
Phone: (715)346-3838
Fax: (715)346-4045
Vicki Lobermeier, Acting Dir.

University of Wisconsin—Superior
Small Business Development Center
1800 Grand Ave.
Superior, WI 54880-2898
Phone: (715)394-8352
Fax: (715)394-8592
Laura Urban, Dir.

University of Wisconsin at Whitewater
Wisconsin Innovation Service Center SBDC
416 McCutchen Hall
Whitewater, WI 53190
Phone: (414)472-1365
Fax: (414)472-1600
E-mail: malewicd@uwwvax.uww.edu
Debra Malewicki, Dir.

Wyoming

Casper Small Business Development Center
Region III
111 W. 2nd St., Ste. 502
Casper, WY 82601
Phone: (307)234-6683
Free: (800)348-5207
Fax: (307)577-7014
Leonard Holler, Dir.

Cheyenne SBDC
Region IV
1400 E. College Dr.
Cheyenne, WY 82007-3298
Phone: (307)632-6141
Free: (800)348-5208
Fax: (307)632-6061
Arlene Soto, Regional Dir.

Northwest Community College
Small Business Development Center
Region II
146 South Bent St.
John Dewitt Student Center
Powell, WY 82435
Phone: (307)754-2139
Free: (800)348-5203
Fax: (307)754-0368
Dwane Heintz, Dir.

Rock Springs Small Business Development Center
Region I
PO Box 1168
Rock Springs, WY 82902
Phone: (307)352-6894
Free: (800)348-5205
Fax: (307)352-6876

SERVICE CORPS OF RETIRED EXECUTIVES (SCORE) OFFICES

This section contains a listing of all SCORE offices organized alphabetically by state/U.S. territory, then by city, then by agency name.

Alabama

SCORE Office (Northeast Alabama)
1330 Quintard Ave.
Anniston, AL 36202
Phone: (256)237-3536

SCORE Office (North Alabama)
901 South 15th St, Rm. 201
Birmingham, AL 35294-2060
Phone: (205)934-6868
Fax: (205)934-0538

SCORE Office (Baldwin County)
29750 Larry Dee Cawyer Dr.
Daphne, AL 36526
Phone: (334)928-5838

SCORE Office (Shoals)
Florence, AL 35630
Phone: (256)760-9067

SCORE Office (Mobile)
600 S Court St.
Mobile, AL 36104
Phone: (334)240-6868
Fax: (334)240-6869

SCORE Office (Alabama Capitol City)
600 S. Court St.
Montgomery, AL 36104
Phone: (334)240-6868
Fax: (334)240-6869

SCORE Office (East Alabama)
601 Ave. A
Opelika, AL 36801
Phone: (334)745-4861
E-mail: score636@hotmail.com
Website: http://www.angelfire.com/sc/score636/

SCORE Office (Tuscaloosa)
2200 University Blvd.
Tuscaloosa, AL 35402
Phone: (205)758-7588

Alaska

SCORE Office (Anchorage)
222 W. 8th Ave.
Anchorage, AK 99513-7559
Phone: (907)271-4022
Fax: (907)271-4545

Arizona

SCORE Office (Lake Havasu)
10 S. Acoma Blvd.
Lake Havasu City, AZ 86403
Phone: (520)453-5951
E-mail: SCORE@ctaz.com
Website: http://www.scorearizona.org/lake_havasu/

SCORE Office (East Valley)
Federal Bldg., Rm. 104
26 N. MacDonald St.
Mesa, AZ 85201
Phone: (602)379-3100
Fax: (602)379-3143
E-mail: 402@aol.com
Website: http://www.scorearizona.org/mesa/

SCORE Office (Phoenix)
2828 N. Central Ave., Ste. 800
Central & One Thomas
Phoenix, AZ 85004
Phone: (602)640-2329
Fax: (602)640-2360
E-mail: e-mail@SCORE-phoenix.org
Website: http://www.score-phoenix.org/

SCORE Office (Prescott Arizona)
1228 Willow Creek Rd., Ste. 2
Prescott, AZ 86301
Phone: (520)778-7438
Fax: (520)778-0812
E-mail: score@northlink.com
Website: http://www.scorearizona.org/prescott/

SCORE Office (Tucson)
110 E. Pennington St.
Tucson, AZ 85702
Phone: (520)670-5008
Fax: (520)670-5011
E-mail: score@azstarnet.com
Website: http://www.scorearizona.org/tucson/

SCORE Office (Yuma)
281 W. 24th St., Ste. 116
Yuma, AZ 85364
Phone: (520)314-0480
E-mail: score@C2i2.com
Website: http://www.scorearizona.org/yuma

Arkansas

SCORE Office (South Central)
201 N. Jackson Ave.
El Dorado, AR 71730-5803
Phone: (870)863-6113
Fax: (870)863-6115

SCORE Office (Ozark)
Fayetteville, AR 72701
Phone: (501)442-7619

SCORE Office (Northwest Arkansas)
Glenn Haven Dr., No. 4
Ft. Smith, AR 72901
Phone: (501)783-3556

SCORE Office (Garland County)
Grand & Ouachita
PO Box 6012
Hot Springs Village, AR 71902
Phone: (501)321-1700

SCORE Office (Little Rock)
2120 Riverfront Dr., Rm. 100
Little Rock, AR 72202-1747
Phone: (501)324-5893
Fax: (501)324-5199

SCORE Office (Southeast Arkansas)
121 W. 6th
Pine Bluff, AR 71601
Phone: (870)535-7189
Fax: (870)535-1643

California

SCORE Office (Golden Empire)
1706 Chester Ave., No. 200
Bakersfield, CA 93301
Phone: (805)322-5881
Fax: (805)322-5663

SCORE Office (Greater Chico Area)
1324 Mangrove St., Ste. 114
Chico, CA 95926
Phone: (916)342-8932
Fax: (916)342-8932

SCORE Office (Concord)
2151-A Salvio St., Ste. B
Concord, CA 94520
Phone: (510)685-1181
Fax: (510)685-5623

SCORE Office (Covina)
935 W. Badillo St.
Covina, CA 91723
Phone: (818)967-4191
Fax: (818)966-9660

SCORE Office (Rancho Cucamonga)
8280 Utica, Ste. 160
Cucamonga, CA 91730
Phone: (909)987-1012
Fax: (909)987-5917

SCORE Office (Culver City)
PO Box 707
Culver City, CA 90232-0707
Phone: (310)287-3850
Fax: (310)287-1350

SCORE Office (Danville)
380 Diablo Rd., Ste. 103
Danville, CA 94526
Phone: (510)837-4400

SCORE Office (Downey)
11131 Brookshire Ave.
Downey, CA 90241
Phone: (310)923-2191
Fax: (310)864-0461

SCORE Office (El Cajon)
109 Rea Ave.
El Cajon, CA 92020
Phone: (619)444-1327
Fax: (619)440-6164

SCORE Office (El Centro)
1100 Main St.
El Centro, CA 92243
Phone: (619)352-3681
Fax: (619)352-3246

SCORE Office (Escondido)
720 N. Broadway
Escondido, CA 92025
Phone: (619)745-2125
Fax: (619)745-1183

SCORE Office (Fairfield)
1111 Webster St.
Fairfield, CA 94533
Phone: (707)425-4625
Fax: (707)425-0826

SCORE Office (Fontana)
17009 Valley Blvd., Ste. B
Fontana, CA 92335
Phone: (909)822-4433
Fax: (909)822-6238

SCORE Office (Foster City)
1125 E. Hillsdale Blvd.
Foster City, CA 94404
Phone: (415)573-7600
Fax: (415)573-5201

SCORE Office (Fremont)
2201 Walnut Ave., Ste. 110
Fremont, CA 94538
Phone: (510)795-2244
Fax: (510)795-2240

SCORE Office (Central California)
2719 N. Air Fresno Dr., Ste. 200
Fresno, CA 93727-1547
Phone: (559)487-5605
Fax: (559)487-5636

SCORE Office (Gardena)
1204 W. Gardena Blvd.
Gardena, CA 90247
Phone: (310)532-9905
Fax: (310)515-4893

SCORE Office (Lompoc)
330 N. Brand Blvd., Ste. 190
Glendale, CA 91203-2304
Phone: (818)552-3206
Fax: (818)552-3323

SCORE Office (Los Angeles)
330 N. Brand Blvd., Ste. 190
Glendale, CA 91203-2304
Phone: (818)552-3206
Fax: (818)552-3323

SCORE Office (Glendora)
131 E. Foothill Blvd.
Glendora, CA 91740
Phone: (818)963-4128
Fax: (818)914-4822

SCORE Office (Grover Beach)
177 S. 8th St.
Grover Beach, CA 93433
Phone: (805)489-9091
Fax: (805)489-9091

SCORE Office (Hawthorne)
12477 Hawthorne Blvd.
Hawthorne, CA 90250
Phone: (310)676-1163
Fax: (310)676-7661

SCORE Office (Hayward)
22300 Foothill Blvd., Ste. 303
Hayward, CA 94541
Phone: (510)537-2424

SCORE Office (Hemet)
1700 E. Florida Ave.
Hemet, CA 92544-4679
Phone: (909)652-4390
Fax: (909)929-8543

SCORE Office (Hesperia)
16367 Main St.
PO Box 403656
Hesperia, CA 92340
Phone: (619)244-2135

SCORE Office (Holloster)
321 San Felipe Rd., No. 11
Hollister, CA 95023

SCORE Office (Hollywood)
7018 Hollywood Blvd.
Hollywood, CA 90028
Phone: (213)469-8311
Fax: (213)469-2805

SCORE Office (Indio)
82503 Hwy. 111
PO Drawer TTT
Indio, CA 92202
Phone: (619)347-0676

SCORE Office (Inglewood)
330 Queen St.
Inglewood, CA 90301
Phone: (818)552-3206

SCORE Office (La Puente)
218 N. Grendanda St. D.
La Puente, CA 91744
Phone: (818)330-3216
Fax: (818)330-9524

SCORE Office (La Verne)
2078 Bonita Ave.
La Verne, CA 91750
Phone: (909)593-5265
Fax: (714)929-8475

SCORE Office (Lake Elsinore)
132 W. Graham Ave.
Lake Elsinore, CA 92530
Phone: (909)674-2577

SCORE Office (Lakeport)
PO Box 295
Lakeport, CA 95453
Phone: (707)263-5092

SCORE Office (Lakewood)
5445 E. Del Amo Blvd., Ste. 2
Lakewood, CA 90714
Phone: (213)920-7737

SCORE Office (Long Beach)
1 World Trade Center
Long Beach, CA 90831

SCORE Office (Los Alamitos)
901 W. Civic Center Dr., Ste. 160
Los Alamitos, CA 90720

SCORE Office (Los Altos)
321 University Ave.
Los Altos, CA 94022
Phone: (415)948-1455

SCORE Office (Manhattan Beach)
PO Box 3007
Manhattan Beach, CA 90266
Phone: (310)545-5313
Fax: (310)545-7203

SCORE Office (Merced)
1632 N. St.
Merced, CA 95340
Phone: (209)725-3800
Fax: (209)383-4959

SCORE Office (Milpitas)
75 S. Milpitas Blvd., Ste. 205
Milpitas, CA 95035
Phone: (408)262-2613
Fax: (408)262-2823

SCORE Office (Yosemite)
1012 11th St., Ste. 300
Modesto, CA 95354
Phone: (209)521-9333

SCORE Office (Montclair)
5220 Benito Ave.
Montclair, CA 91763

SCORE Office (Monterey Bay)
380 Alvarado St.
PO Box 1770
Monterey, CA 93940-1770
Phone: (408)649-1770

SCORE Office (Moreno Valley)
25480 Alessandro
Moreno Valley, CA 92553

SCORE Office (Morgan Hill)
25 W. 1st St.
PO Box 786
Morgan Hill, CA 95038
Phone: (408)779-9444
Fax: (408)778-1786

SCORE Office (Morro Bay)
880 Main St.
Morro Bay, CA 93442
Phone: (805)772-4467

SCORE Office (Mountain View)
580 Castro St.
Mountain View, CA 94041
Phone: (415)968-8378
Fax: (415)968-5668

SCORE Office (Napa)
1556 1st St.
Napa, CA 94559
Phone: (707)226-7455
Fax: (707)226-1171

SCORE Office (North Hollywood)
5019 Lankershim Blvd.
North Hollywood, CA 91601
Phone: (818)552-3206

SCORE Office (Northridge)
8801 Reseda Blvd.
Northridge, CA 91324
Phone: (818)349-5676

SCORE Office (Novato)
807 De Long Ave.
Novato, CA 94945
Phone: (415)897-1164
Fax: (415)898-9097

SCORE Office (East Bay)
519 17th St.
Oakland, CA 94612
Phone: (510)273-6611
Fax: (510)273-6015
E-mail: webmaster@eastbayscore.org
Website: http://www.eastbayscore.org

SCORE Office (Oceanside)
928 N. Coast Hwy.
Oceanside, CA 92054
Phone: (619)722-1534

SCORE Office (Ontario)
121 West B. St.
Ontario, CA 91762
Fax: (714)984-6439

SCORE Office (Oxnard)
PO Box 867
Oxnard, CA 93032
Phone: (805)385-8860
Fax: (805)487-1763

SCORE Office (Pacifica)
450 Dundee Way, Ste. 2
Pacifica, CA 94044
Phone: (415)355-4122

SCORE Office (Palm Desert)
72990 Hwy. 111
Palm Desert, CA 92260
Phone: (619)346-6111
Fax: (619)346-3463

SCORE Office (Palm Springs)
650 E. Tahquitz Canyon Way Ste. D
Palm Springs, CA 92262-6706
Phone: (760)320-6682
Fax: (760)323-9426

SCORE Office (Lakeside)
2150 Low Tree
Palmdale, CA 93551
Phone: (805)948-4518
Fax: (805)949-1212

SCORE Office (Palo Alto)
325 Forest Ave.
Palo Alto, CA 94301
Phone: (415)324-3121
Fax: (415)324-1215

SCORE Office (Pasadena)
117 E. Colorado Blvd., Ste. 100
Pasadena, CA 91105
Phone: (818)795-3355
Fax: (818)795-5663

SCORE Office (Paso Robles)
1225 Park St.
Paso Robles, CA 93446-2234
Phone: (805)238-0506
Fax: (805)238-0527

SCORE Office (Petaluma)
799 Baywood Dr., Ste. 3
Petaluma, CA 94954
Phone: (707)762-2785
Fax: (707)762-4721

SCORE Office (Pico Rivera)
9122 E. Washington Blvd.
Pico Rivera, CA 90660

SCORE Office (Pittsburg)
2700 E. Leland Rd.
Pittsburg, CA 94565
Phone: (510)439-2181
Fax: (510)427-1599

SCORE Office (Pleasanton)
777 Peters Ave.
Pleasanton, CA 94566
Phone: (510)846-9697

SCORE Office (Monterey Park)
485 N. Garey
Pomona, CA 91769

SCORE Office (Pomona)
485 N. Garey Ave.
Pomona, CA 91766
Phone: (909)622-1256

SCORE Office (Antelope Valley)
4511 West Ave. M-4
Quartz Hill, CA 93536
Phone: (805)272-0087
E-mail: avscore@ptw.com
Website: http://www.score.av.org/

SCORE Office (Shasta)
737 Auditorium Dr.
Redding, CA 96099
Phone: (916)225-2770

SCORE Office (Redwood City)
1675 Broadway
Redwood City, CA 94063
Phone: (415)364-1722
Fax: (415)364-1729

SCORE Office (Richmond)
3925 MacDonald Ave.
Richmond, CA 94805

SCORE Office (Ridgecrest)
PO Box 771
Ridgecrest, CA 93555
Phone: (619)375-8331
Fax: (619)375-0365

SCORE Office (Riverside)
3685 Main St., Ste. 350
Riverside, CA 92501
Phone: (909)683-7100

SCORE Office (Sacramento)
9845 Horn Rd., 260-B
Sacramento, CA 95827
Phone: (916)361-2322
Fax: (916)361-2164
E-mail: sacchapter@directcon.net

SCORE Office (Salinas)
PO Box 1170
Salinas, CA 93902
Phone: (408)424-7611
Fax: (408)424-8639

SCORE Office (Inland Empire)
777 E. Rialto Ave.
Purchasing
San Bernardino, CA 92415-0760
Phone: (909)386-8278

SCORE Office (San Carlos)
San Carlos Chamber of Commerce
PO Box 1086
San Carlos, CA 94070
Phone: (415)593-1068
Fax: (415)593-9108

SCORE Office (Encinitas)
550 W. C St., Ste. 550
San Diego, CA 92101-3540
Phone: (619)557-7272
Fax: (619)557-5894

SCORE Office (San Diego)
550 West C. St., Ste. 550
San Diego, CA 92101-3540
Phone: (619)557-7272
Fax: (619)557-5894
Website: http://www.score-sandiego.org

SCORE Office (Menlo Park)
1100 Merrill St.
San Francisco, CA 94105
Phone: (415)325-2818
Fax: (415)325-0920

SCORE Office (San Francisco)
455 Market St., 6th Fl.
San Francisco, CA 94105
Phone: (415)744-6827
Fax: (415)744-6750
E-mail: sfscore@sfscore.
Website: http://www.sfscore.com

SCORE Office (San Gabriel)
401 W. Las Tunas Dr.
San Gabriel, CA 91776
Phone: (818)576-2525
Fax: (818)289-2901

SCORE Office (San Jose)
Deanza College
208 S. 1st. St., Ste. 137
San Jose, CA 95113
Phone: (408)288-8479
Fax: (408)535-5541

SCORE Office (Santa Clara County)
280 S. 1st St., Rm. 137
San Jose, CA 95113
Phone: (408)288-8479
Fax: (408)535-5541
E-mail: svscore@Prodigy.net
Website: http://www.svscore.org

SCORE Office (San Luis Obispo)
3566 S. Hiquera, No. 104
San Luis Obispo, CA 93401
Phone: (805)547-0779

SCORE Office (San Mateo)
1021 S. El Camino, 2nd Fl.
San Mateo, CA 94402
Phone: (415)341-5679

SCORE Office (San Pedro)
390 W. 7th St.
San Pedro, CA 90731
Phone: (310)832-7272

SCORE Office (Orange County)
200 W. Santa Anna Blvd., Ste. 700
Santa Ana, CA 92701
Phone: (714)550-7369
Fax: (714)550-0191
Website: http://www.score114.org

SCORE Office (Santa Barbara)
3227 State St.
Santa Barbara, CA 93130
Phone: (805)563-0084

SCORE Office (Central Coast)
509 W. Morrison Ave.
Santa Maria, CA 93454
Phone: (805)347-7755

SCORE Office (Santa Maria)
614 S. Broadway
Santa Maria, CA 93454-5111
Phone: (805)925-2403
Fax: (805)928-7559

SCORE Office (Santa Monica)
501 Colorado, Ste. 150
Santa Monica, CA 90401
Phone: (310)393-9825
Fax: (310)394-1868

SCORE Office (Santa Rosa)
777 Sonoma Ave., Rm. 115E
Santa Rosa, CA 95404
Phone: (707)571-8342
Fax: (707)541-0331
Website: http://www.pressdemo.com/community/score/score.html

SCORE Office (Scotts Valley)
4 Camp Evers Ln.
Scotts Valley, CA 95066
Phone: (408)438-1010
Fax: (408)438-6544

SCORE Office (Simi Valley)
40 W. Cochran St., Ste. 100
Simi Valley, CA 93065
Phone: (805)526-3900
Fax: (805)526-6234

SCORE Office (Sonoma)
453 1st St. E
Sonoma, CA 95476
Phone: (707)996-1033

SCORE Office (Los Banos)
222 S. Shepard St.
Sonora, CA 95370
Phone: (209)532-4212

SCORE Office (Tuolumne County)
39 North Washington St.

Sonora, CA 95370
Phone: (209)588-0128
E-mail: score@mlode.com

SCORE Office (South San Francisco)
445 Market St., Ste. 6th Fl.
South San Francisco, CA 94105
Phone: (415)744-6827
Fax: (415)744-6812

SCORE Office (Stockton)
401 N. San Joaquin St., Rm. 215
Stockton, CA 95202
Phone: (209)946-6293

SCORE Office (Taft)
314 4th St.
Taft, CA 93268
Phone: (805)765-2165
Fax: (805)765-6639

SCORE Office (Conejo Valley)
625 W. Hillcrest Dr.
Thousand Oaks, CA 91360
Phone: (805)499-1993
Fax: (805)498-7264

SCORE Office (Torrance)
3400 Torrance Blvd., Ste. 100
Torrance, CA 90503
Phone: (310)540-5858
Fax: (310)540-7662

SCORE Office (Truckee)
PO Box 2757
Truckee, CA 96160
Phone: (916)587-2757
Fax: (916)587-2439

SCORE Office (Visalia)
113 S. M St,
Tulare, CA 93274
Phone: (209)627-0766
Fax: (209)627-8149

SCORE Office (Upland)
433 N. 2nd Ave.
Upland, CA 91786
Phone: (909)931-4108

SCORE Office (Vallejo)
2 Florida St.
Vallejo, CA 94590
Phone: (707)644-5551
Fax: (707)644-5590

SCORE Office (Van Nuys)
14540 Victory Blvd.
Van Nuys, CA 91411
Phone: (818)989-0300
Fax: (818)989-3836

SCORE Office (Ventura)
5700 Ralston St., Ste. 310
Ventura, CA 93001
Phone: (805)658-2688
Fax: (805)658-2252
E-mail: scoreven@jps.net
Website: http://www.jps.net/scoreven

SCORE Office (Vista)
201 E. Washington St.
Vista, CA 92084
Phone: (619)726-1122
Fax: (619)226-8654

SCORE Office (Watsonville)
PO Box 1748
Watsonville, CA 95077
Phone: (408)724-3849
Fax: (408)728-5300

SCORE Office (West Covina)
811 S. Sunset Ave.
West Covina, CA 91790
Phone: (818)338-8496
Fax: (818)960-0511

SCORE Office (Westlake)
30893 Thousand Oaks Blvd.
Westlake Village, CA 91362
Phone: (805)496-5630
Fax: (818)991-1754

Colorado

SCORE Office (Colorado Springs)
2 N. Cascade Ave., Ste. 110
Colorado Springs, CO 80903
Phone: (719)636-3074
Website: http://www.cscc.org/score02/index.html

SCORE Office (Denver)
US Custom's House, 4th Fl.
721 19th St.
Denver, CO 80201-0660
Phone: (303)844-3985
Fax: (303)844-6490
E-mail: score62@csn.net
Website: http://www.sni.net/score62

SCORE Office (Tri-River)
1102 Grand Ave.
Glenwood Springs, CO 81601
Phone: (970)945-6589

SCORE Office (Grand Junction)
2591 B & 3/4 Rd.
Grand Junction, CO 81503
Phone: (970)243-5242

SCORE Office (Gunnison)
608 N. 11th
Gunnison, CO 81230
Phone: (303)641-4422

SCORE Office (Montrose)
1214 Peppertree Dr.
Montrose, CO 81401
Phone: (970)249-6080

SCORE Office (Pagosa Springs)
PO Box 4381
Pagosa Springs, CO 81157
Phone: (970)731-4890

SCORE Office (Rifle)
0854 W. Battlement Pky., Apt. C106
Parachute, CO 81635
Phone: (970)285-9390

SCORE Office (Pueblo)
302 N. Santa Fe
Pueblo, CO 81003
Phone: (719)542-1704
Fax: (719)542-1624
E-mail: mackey@iex.net
Website: http://www.pueblo.org/score

SCORE Office (Ridgway)
143 Poplar Pl.
Ridgway, CO 81432

SCORE Office (Silverton)
PO Box 480
Silverton, CO 81433
Phone: (303)387-5430

SCORE Office (Minturn)
PO Box 2066
Vail, CO 81658
Phone: (970)476-1224

Connecticut

SCORE Office (Greater Bridgeport)
230 Park Ave.
Bridgeport, CT 06601-0999
Phone: (203)576-4369
Fax: (203)576-4388

SCORE Office (Bristol)
10 Main St. 1st. Fl.
Bristol, CT 06010
Phone: (203)584-4718
Fax: (203)584-4722

SCORE office (Greater Danbury)
246 Federal Rd.
Unit LL2, Ste. 7
Brookfield, CT 06804
Phone: (203)775-1151

SCORE Office (Greater Danbury)
246 Federal Rd., Unit LL2, Ste. 7
Brookfield, CT 06804
Phone: (203)775-1151

SCORE Office (Eastern Connecticut)
Administration Bldg., Rm. 313
PO 625
61 Main St. (Chapter 579)
Groton, CT 06475
Phone: (203)388-9508

SCORE Office (Greater Hartford County)
330 Main St.
Hartford, CT 06106
Phone: (860)548-1749
Fax: (860)240-4659
Website: http://www.score56.org

SCORE Office (Manchester)
20 Hartford Rd.
Manchester, CT 06040
Phone: (203)646-2223
Fax: (203)646-5871

SCORE Office (New Britain)
185 Main St., Ste. 431
New Britain, CT 06051
Phone: (203)827-4492
Fax: (203)827-4480

SCORE Office (New Haven)
25 Science Pk., Bldg. 25, Rm. 366
New Haven, CT 06511
Phone: (203)865-7645

SCORE Office (Fairfield County)
24 Beldon Ave., 5th Fl.
Norwalk, CT 06850
Phone: (203)847-7348
Fax: (203)849-9308

SCORE Office (Old Saybrook)
146 Main St.
Old Saybrook, CT 06475
Phone: (860)388-9508

SCORE Office (Simsbury)
Box 244
Simsbury, CT 06070
Phone: (203)651-7307
Fax: (203)651-1933

SCORE Office (Torrington)
23 North Rd.
Torrington, CT 06791
Phone: (203)482-6586

Delaware

SCORE Office (Dover)
Treadway Towers
PO Box 576
Dover, DE 19903
Phone: (302)678-0892
Fax: (302)678-0189

SCORE Office (Lewes)
PO Box 1
Lewes, DE 19958
Phone: (302)645-8073
Fax: (302)645-8412

SCORE Office (Milford)
204 NE Front St.
Milford, DE 19963
Phone: (302)422-3301

SCORE Office (Wilmington)
824 Market St., Ste. 610
Wilmington, DE 19801
Phone: (302)573-6652
Fax: (302)573-6092
Website: http://www.scoredelaware.com

District of Columbia

SCORE Office (George Mason University)
409 3rd St. SW, 4th Fl.
Washington, DC 20024
Free: (800)634-0245

SCORE Office (Washington DC)
1110 Vermont Ave. NW, 9th Fl.
Washington, DC 20043
Phone: (202)606-4000
Fax: (202)606-4225
E-mail: dcscore@hotmail.com
Website: http://www.scoredc.org/

Florida

SCORE Office (Desota County Chamber of Commerce)
16 South Velucia Ave.
Arcadia, FL 34266
Phone: (941)494-4033

SCORE Office (Suncoast/Pinellas)
Airport Business Ctr.
4707 - 140th Ave. N, No. 311
Clearwater, FL 33755
Phone: (813)532-6800
Fax: (813)532-6800

SCORE Office (DeLand)
336 N. Woodland Blvd.
DeLand, FL 32720
Phone: (904)734-4331
Fax: (904)734-4333

SCORE Office (South Palm Beach)
1050 S. Federal Hwy., Ste. 132
Delray Beach, FL 33483
Phone: (561)278-7752
Fax: (561)278-0288

SCORE Office (Ft. Lauderdale)
Federal Bldg., Ste. 123
299 E. Broward Blvd.
Ft. Lauderdale, FL 33301
Phone: (954)356-7263
Fax: (954)356-7145

SCORE Office (Southwest Florida)
The Renaissance
8695 College Pky., Ste. 345 & 346
Ft. Myers, FL 33919
Phone: (941)489-2935
Fax: (941)489-1170

SCORE Office (Treasure Coast)
Professional Center, Ste. 2
3220 S. US, No. 1
Ft. Pierce, FL 34982
Phone: (561)489-0548

SCORE Office (Gainesville)
101 SE 2nd Pl., Ste. 104
Gainesville, FL 32601
Phone: (904)375-8278

SCORE Office (Hialeah Dade Chamber)
59 W. 5th St.
Hialeah, FL 33010
Phone: (305)887-1515
Fax: (305)887-2453

SCORE Office (Daytona Beach)
921 Nova Rd., Ste. A
Holly Hills, FL 32117
Phone: (904)255-6889
Fax: (904)255-0229
E-mail: score87@dbeach.com

SCORE Office (South Broward)
3475 Sheridian St., Ste. 203
Hollywood, FL 33021
Phone: (305)966-8415

SCORE Office (Citrus County)
5 Poplar Ct.
Homosassa, FL 34446
Phone: (352)382-1037

SCORE Office (Jacksonville)
7825 Baymeadows Way, Ste. 100-B
Jacksonville, FL 32256
Phone: (904)443-1911
Fax: (904)443-1980
E-mail: scorejax@juno.com
Website: http://www.scorejax.org/

SCORE Office (Jacksonville Satellite)
3 Independent Dr.
Jacksonville, FL 32256
Phone: (904)366-6600
Fax: (904)632-0617

SCORE Office (Central Florida)
5410 S. Florida Ave., No. 3
Lakeland, FL 33801
Phone: (941)687-5783
Fax: (941)687-6225

SCORE Office (Lakeland)
100 Lake Morton Dr.
Lakeland, FL 33801
Phone: (941)686-2168

SCORE Office (St. Petersburg)
800 W. Bay Dr., Ste. 505
Largo, FL 33712
Phone: (813)585-4571

SCORE Office (Leesburg)
9501 US Hwy. 441
Leesburg, FL 34788-8751
Phone: (352)365-3556
Fax: (352)365-3501

SCORE Office (Cocoa)
1600 Farno Rd., Unit 205
Melbourne, FL 32935
Phone: (407)254-2288

SCORE Office (Melbourne)
Melbourne Professional Complex
1600 Sarno, Ste. 205
Melbourne, FL 32935
Phone: (407)254-2288
Fax: (407)245-2288

SCORE Office (Merritt Island)
1600 Sarno Rd., Ste. 205
Melbourne, FL 32935
Phone: (407)254-2288
Fax: (407)254-2288

SCORE Office (Space Coast)
Melbourn Professional Complex
1600 Sarno, Ste. 205
Melbourne, FL 32935
Phone: (407)254-2288
Fax: (407)254-2288

SCORE Office (Dade)
49 NW 5th St.
Miami, FL 33128
Phone: (305)371-6889
Fax: (305)374-1882
E-mail: score@netrox.net
Website: http://www.netrox.net/~score/

SCORE Office (Naples of Collier)
International College
2654 Tamiami Trl. E
Naples, FL 34112
Phone: (941)417-1280
Fax: (941)417-1281
E-mail: score@naples.net
Website: http://www.naples.net/clubs/score/index.htm

SCORE Office (Pasco County)
6014 US Hwy. 19, Ste. 302
New Port Richey, FL 34652
Phone: (813)842-4638

SCORE Office (Southeast Volusia)
115 Canal St.
New Smyrna Beach, FL 32168
Phone: (904)428-2449
Fax: (904)423-3512

SCORE Office (Ocala)
110 E. Silver Springs Blvd.
Ocala, FL 34470
Phone: (352)629-5959

Clay County SCORE Office
Clay County Chamber of Commerce
1734 Kingsdey Ave.
PO Box 1441
Orange Park, FL 32073
Phone: (904)264-2651
Fax: (904)269-0363

SCORE Office (Orlando)
80 N. Hughey Ave.
Rm. 445 Federal Bldg.
Orlando, FL 32801
Phone: (407)648-6476
Fax: (407)648-6425

SCORE Office (Emerald Coast)
19 W. Garden St., No. 325
Pensacola, FL 32501
Phone: (904)444-2060
Fax: (904)444-2070

SCORE Office (Charlotte County)
201 W. Marion Ave., Ste. 211
Punta Gorda, FL 33950
Phone: (941)575-1818
E-mail: score@gls3c.com
Website: http://www.charlotte-florida.com/business/scorepg01.htm

SCORE Office (St. Augustine)
1 Riberia St.
St. Augustine, FL 32084
Phone: (904)829-5681
Fax: (904)829-6477

SCORE Office (Bradenton)
2801 Fruitville, Ste. 280
Sarasota, FL 34237
Phone: (813)955-1029

SCORE Office (Manasota)
2801 Fruitville Rd., Ste. 280
Sarasota, FL 34237
Phone: (941)955-1029
Fax: (941)955-5581
E-mail: score116@gte.net
Website: http://www.score-suncoast.org/

SCORE Office (Tallahassee)
200 W. Park Ave.
Tallahassee, FL 32302
Phone: (850)487-2665

SCORE Office (Hillsborough)
4732 Dale Mabry Hwy. N, Ste. 400
Tampa, FL 33614-6509
Phone: (813)870-0125

SCORE Office (Lake Sumter)
122 E. Main St.
Tavares, FL 32778-3810
Phone: (352)365-3556

SCORE Office (Titusville)
2000 S. Washington Ave.
Titusville, FL 32780
Phone: (407)267-3036
Fax: (407)264-0127

SCORE Office (Venice)
257 N. Tamiami Trl.
Venice, FL 34285
Phone: (941)488-2236
Fax: (941)484-5903

SCORE Office (Palm Beach)
500 Australian Ave. S, Ste. 100
West Palm Beach, FL 33401
Phone: (561)833-1672
Fax: (561)833-1712

SCORE Office (Wildwood)
103 N. Webster St.
Wildwood, FL 34785

Georgia

SCORE Office (Atlanta)
Harris Tower, Suite 1900
233 Peachtree Rd., NE
Atlanta, GA 30309
Phone: (404)347-2442
Fax: (404)347-1227

SCORE Office (Augusta)
3126 Oxford Rd.
Augusta, GA 30909
Phone: (706)869-9100

SCORE Office (Columbus)
School Bldg.
PO Box 40
Columbus, GA 31901
Phone: (706)327-3654

SCORE Office (Dalton-Whitfield)
305 S. Thorton Ave.
Dalton, GA 30720
Phone: (706)279-3383

SCORE Office (Gainesville)
PO Box 374
Gainesville, GA 30503
Phone: (770)532-6206
Fax: (770)535-8419

SCORE Office (Macon)
711 Grand Bldg.
Macon, GA 31201
Phone: (912)751-6160

SCORE Office (Brunswick)
4 Glen Ave.
St. Simons Island, GA 31520
Phone: (912)265-0620
Fax: (912)265-0629

SCORE Office (Savannah)
111 E. Liberty St., Ste. 103
Savannah, GA 31401
Phone: (912)652-4335
Fax: (912)652-4184
E-mail: info@scoresav.org
Website: http://www.coastalempire.com/score/index.htm

Guam

SCORE Office (Guam)
Pacific News Bldg., Rm. 103
238 Archbishop Flores St.
Agana, GU 96910-5100
Phone: (671)472-7308

Hawaii

SCORE Office (Hawaii, Inc.)
1111 Bishop St., Ste. 204
PO Box 50207
Honolulu, HI 96813
Phone: (808)522-8132
Fax: (808)522-8135
E-mail: hnlscore@juno.com

SCORE Office (Kahului)
250 Alamaha, Unit N16A
Kahului, HI 96732
Phone: (808)871-7711

SCORE Office (Maui, Inc.)
590 E. Lipoa Pkwy., Ste. 227
Kihei, HI 96753
Phone: (808)875-2380

Idaho

SCORE Office (Treasure Valley)
1020 Main St., No. 290
Boise, ID 83702
Phone: (208)334-1696
Fax: (208)334-9353

SCORE Office (Eastern Idaho)
2300 N. Yellowstone, Ste. 119
Idaho Falls, ID 83401
Phone: (208)523-1022
Fax: (208)528-7127

Illinois

SCORE Office (Fox Valley)
40 W. Downer Pl.
PO Box 277
Aurora, IL 60506
Phone: (630)897-9214
Fax: (630)897-7002

SCORE Office (Greater Belvidere)
419 S. State St.
Belvidere, IL 61008
Phone: (815)544-4357
Fax: (815)547-7654

SCORE Office (Bensenville)
1050 Busse Hwy. Suite 100
Bensenville, IL 60106
Phone: (708)350-2944
Fax: (708)350-2979

SCORE Office (Central Illinois)
402 N. Hershey Rd.
Bloomington, IL 61704
Phone: (309)644-0549
Fax: (309)663-8270
E-mail: webmaster@central-illinois-score.org
Website: http://www.central-illinois-score.org/

SCORE Office (Southern Illinois)
150 E. Pleasant Hill Rd.
Box 1
Carbondale, IL 62901
Phone: (618)453-6654
Fax: (618)453-5040

SCORE Office (Chicago)
Northwest Atrium Ctr.
500 W. Madison St., No. 1250
Chicago, IL 60661
Phone: (312)353-7724
Fax: (312)886-5688
Website: http://www.mcs.net/~bic/

SCORE Office (Chicago—Oliver Harvey College)
Pullman Bldg.
1000 E. 11th St., 7th Fl.
Chicago, IL 60628
Fax: (312)468-8086

SCORE Office (Danville)
28 W. N. Street
Danville, IL 61832
Phone: (217)442-7232
Fax: (217)442-6228

SCORE Office (Decatur)
Milliken University
1184 W. Main St.
Decatur, IL 62522
Phone: (217)424-6297
Fax: (217)424-3993
E-mail: charding@mail.millikin.edu
Website: http://www.millikin.edu/academics/Tabor/score.html

SCORE Office (Downers Grove)
925 Curtis
Downers Grove, IL 60515
Phone: (708)968-4050
Fax: (708)968-8368

SCORE Office (Elgin)
24 E. Chicago, 3rd Fl.
PO Box 648
Elgin, IL 60120
Phone: (847)741-5660
Fax: (847)741-5677

SCORE Office (Freeport Area)
26 S. Galena Ave.
Freeport, IL 61032

Phone: (815)233-1350
Fax: (815)235-4038

SCORE Office (Galesburg)
292 E. Simmons St.
PO Box 749
Galesburg, IL 61401
Phone: (309)343-1194
Fax: (309)343-1195

SCORE Office (Glen Ellyn)
500 Pennsylvania
Glen Ellyn, IL 60137
Phone: (708)469-0907
Fax: (708)469-0426

SCORE Office (Greater Alton)
Alden Hall
5800 Godfrey Rd.
Godfrey, IL 62035-2466
Phone: (618)467-2280
Fax: (618)466-8289
Website: http://www.altonweb.com/score/

SCORE Office (Grayslake)
19351 W. Washington St.
Grayslake, IL 60030
Phone: (708)223-3633
Fax: (708)223-9371

SCORE Office (Harrisburg)
303 S. Commercial
Harrisburg, IL 62946-1528
Phone: (618)252-8528
Fax: (618)252-0210

SCORE Office (Joliet)
100 N. Chicago
Joliet, IL 60432
Phone: (815)727-5371
Fax: (815)727-5374

SCORE Office (Kankakee)
101 S. Schuyler Ave.
Kankakee, IL 60901
Phone: (815)933-0376
Fax: (815)933-0380

SCORE Office (Macomb)
216 Seal Hall, Rm. 214
Macomb, IL 61455
Phone: (309)298-1128
Fax: (309)298-2520

SCORE Office (Matteson)
210 Lincoln Mall
Matteson, IL 60443
Phone: (708)709-3750
Fax: (708)503-9322

SCORE Office (Mattoon)
1701 Wabash Ave.
Mattoon, IL 61938
Phone: (217)235-5661
Fax: (217)234-6544

SCORE Office (Quad Cities)
622 19th St.
Moline, IL 61265
Phone: (309)797-0082
Fax: (309)757-5435
E-mail: score@qconline.com
Website: http://www.qconline.com/business/score/

SCORE Office (Naperville)
131 W. Jefferson Ave.
Naperville, IL 60540
Phone: (708)355-4141
Fax: (708)355-8355

SCORE Office (Northbrook)
2002 Walters Ave.
Northbrook, IL 60062
Phone: (847)498-5555
Fax: (847)498-5510

SCORE Office (Palos Hills)
10900 S. 88th Ave.
Palos Hills, IL 60465
Phone: (847)974-5468
Fax: (847)974-0078

SCORE Office (Peoria)
124 SW Adams, Ste. 300
Peoria, IL 61602
Phone: (309)676-0755
Fax: (309)676-7534

SCORE Office (Prospect Heights)
1375 Wolf Rd.
Prospect Heights, IL 60070
Phone: (847)537-8660
Fax: (847)537-7138

SCORE Office (Quincy Tri-State)
300 Civic Center Plz., Ste. 245
Quincy, IL 62301
Phone: (217)222-8093
Fax: (217)222-3033

SCORE Office (River Grove)
2000 5th Ave.
River Grove, IL 60171
Phone: (708)456-0300
Fax: (708)583-3121

SCORE Office (Northern Illinois)
515 N. Court St.
Rockford, IL 61103
Phone: (815)962-0122
Fax: (815)962-0122

SCORE Office (St. Charles)
103 N. 1st Ave.
St. Charles, IL 60174-1982
Phone: (847)584-8384
Fax: (847)584-6065

SCORE Office (Springfield)
511 W. Capitol Ave., Ste. 302
Springfield, IL 62704
Phone: (217)492-4416
Fax: (217)492-4867

SCORE Office (Sycamore)
112 Somunak St.
Sycamore, IL 60178
Phone: (815)895-3456
Fax: (815)895-0125

SCORE Office (University)
Hwy. 50 & Stuenkel Rd. Ste. C3305
University Park, IL 60466
Phone: (708)534-5000
Fax: (708)534-8457

Indiana

SCORE Office (Anderson)
205 W. 11th St.
Anderson, IN 46015
Phone: (317)642-0264

SCORE Office (Bloomington)
Star Center
216 W. Allen
Bloomington, IN 47403
Phone: (812)335-7334
E-mail: wtfische@indiana.edu
Website: http://www.brainfreezemedia.com/score527/

SCORE Office (South East Indiana)
500 Franklin St.
Box 29
Columbus, IN 47201
Phone: (812)379-4457

SCORE Office (Corydon)
310 N. Elm St.
Corydon, IN 47112
Phone: (812)738-2137
Fax: (812)738-6438

SCORE Office (Crown Point)
Old Courthouse Sq. Ste. 206
PO Box 43
Crown Point, IN 46307
Phone: (219)663-1800

SCORE Office (Elkhart)
418 S. Main St.
Elkhart, IN 46515
Phone: (219)293-1531
Fax: (219)294-1859

SCORE Office (Evansville)
1100 W. Lloyd Expy., Ste. 105
Evansville, IN 47708
Phone: (812)426-6144

SCORE Office (Fort Wayne)
1300 S. Harrison St.
Ft. Wayne, IN 46802
Phone: (219)422-2601
Fax: (219)422-2601

SCORE Office (Gary)
973 W. 6th Ave., Rm. 326
Gary, IN 46402
Phone: (219)882-3918

SCORE Office (Hammond)
7034 Indianapolis Blvd.
Hammond, IN 46324
Phone: (219)931-1000
Fax: (219)845-9548

SCORE Office (Indianapolis)
429 N. Pennsylvania St., Ste. 100
Indianapolis, IN 46204-1873
Phone: (317)226-7264
Fax: (317)226-7259
E-mail: inscore@indy.net
Website: http://www.score-indianapolis.org/

SCORE Office (Jasper)
PO Box 307
Jasper, IN 47547-0307
Phone: (812)482-6866

SCORE Office (Kokomo/Howard Counties)
106 N. Washington St.
Kokomo, IN 46901
Phone: (765)457-5301
Fax: (765)452-4564

SCORE Office (Logansport)
300 E. Broadway, Ste. 103
Logansport, IN 46947
Phone: (219)753-6388

SCORE Office (Madison)
301 E. Main St.
Madison, IN 47250
Phone: (812)265-3135
Fax: (812)265-2923

SCORE Office (Marengo)
Rt. 1 Box 224D
Marengo, IN 47140
Fax: (812)365-2793

SCORE Office (Marion/Grant Counties)
215 S. Adams
Marion, IN 46952
Phone: (765)664-5107

SCORE Office (Merrillville)
255 W. 80th Pl.
Merrillville, IN 46410
Phone: (219)769-8180
Fax: (219)736-6223

SCORE Office (Michigan City)
200 E. Michigan Blvd.
Michigan City, IN 46360
Phone: (219)874-6221
Fax: (219)873-1204

SCORE Office (South Central Indiana)
4100 Charleston Rd.
New Albany, IN 47150-9538
Phone: (812)945-0066

SCORE Office (Rensselaer)
104 W. Washington
Rensselaer, IN 47978

SCORE Office (Salem)
210 N. Main St.
Salem, IN 47167
Phone: (812)883-4303
Fax: (812)883-1467

SCORE Office (South Bend)
300 N. Michigan St.
South Bend, IN 46601
Phone: (219)282-4350
E-mail: chair@southbend-score.org
Website: http://www.southbend-score.org/

SCORE Office (Valparaiso)
150 Lincolnway
Valparaiso, IN 46383
Phone: (219)462-1105
Fax: (219)469-5710

SCORE Office (Vincennes)
27 N. 3rd
PO Box 553
Vincennes, IN 47591
Phone: (812)882-6440
Fax: (812)882-6441

SCORE Office (Wabash)
PO Box 371
Wabash, IN 46992
Phone: (219)563-1168
Fax: (219)563-6920

Iowa

SCORE Office (Burlington)
Federal Bldg.
300 N. Main St.
Burlington, IA 52601
Phone: (319)752-2967

SCORE Office (Cedar Rapids)
Lattner Bldg., Ste. 200
215-4th Avenue, SE, No. 200
Cedar Rapids, IA 52401-1806
Phone: (319)362-6405
Fax: (319)362-7861

SCORE Office (Illowa)
333 4th Ave. S
Clinton, IA 52732
Phone: (319)242-5702

SCORE Office (Council Bluffs)
7 N. 6th St.
Council Bluffs, IA 51502
Phone: (712)325-1000

SCORE Office (Northeast Iowa)
3404 285th St.
Cresco, IA 52136
Phone: (319)547-3377

SCORE Office (Des Moines)
Federal Bldg., Rm. 749
210 Walnut St.
Des Moines, IA 50309-2186
Phone: (515)284-4760

SCORE Office (Ft. Dodge)
Federal Bldg., Rm. 436
205 S. 8th St.
Ft. Dodge, IA 50501
Phone: (515)955-2622

SCORE Office (Independence)
110 1st. St. east
Independence, IA 50644
Phone: (319)334-7178
Fax: (319)334-7179

SCORE Office (Iowa City)
210 Federal Bldg.
PO Box 1853
Iowa City, IA 52240-1853
Phone: (319)338-1662

SCORE Office (Keokuk)
401 Main St.
Pierce Bldg., No. 1
Keokuk, IA 52632
Phone: (319)524-5055

SCORE Office (Central Iowa)
Fisher Community College
709 S. Center
Marshalltown, IA 50158
Phone: (515)753-6645

SCORE Office (River City)
15 West State St.
Mason City, IA 50401
Phone: (515)423-5724

SCORE Office (South Central)
SBDC, Indian Hills Community College
525 Grandview Ave.
Ottumwa, IA 52501
Phone: (515)683-5127
Fax: (515)683-5263

SCORE Office (Dubuque)
10250 Sundown Rd.
Peosta, IA 52068
Phone: (319)556-5110

SCORE Office (Southwest Iowa)
614 W. Sheridan
Shenandoah, IA 51601
Phone: (712)246-3260

SCORE Office (Sioux City)
Federal Bldg.
320 6th St.
Sioux City, IA 51101
Phone: (712)277-2324
Fax: (712)277-2325

SCORE Office (Iowa Lakes)
122 W. 5th St.
Spencer, IA 51301
Phone: (712)262-3059

SCORE Office (Vista)
119 W. 6th St.
Storm Lake, IA 50588
Phone: (712)732-3780

SCORE Office (Waterloo)
215 E. 4th
Waterloo, IA 50703
Phone: (319)233-8431

Kansas

SCORE Office (Southwest Kansas)
501 W. Spruce
Dodge City, KS 67801
Phone: (316)227-3119

SCORE Office (Emporia)
811 Homewood
Emporia, KS 66801
Phone: (316)342-1600

SCORE Office (Golden Belt)
1307 Williams
Great Bend, KS 67530
Phone: (316)792-2401

SCORE Office (Hays)
PO Box 400
Hays, KS 67601
Phone: (913)625-6595

SCORE Office (Hutchinson)
1 E. 9th St.
Hutchinson, KS 67501
Phone: (316)665-8468
Fax: (316)665-7619

SCORE Office (Southeast Kansas)
404 Westminster Pl.
PO Box 886
Independence, KS 67301
Phone: (316)331-4741

SCORE Office (McPherson)
306 N. Main
PO Box 616
McPherson, KS 67460
Phone: (316)241-3303

SCORE Office (Salina)
120 Ash St.
Salina, KS 67401
Phone: (785)243-4290
Fax: (785)243-1833

SCORE Office (Topeka)
1700 College
Topeka, KS 66621
Phone: (785)231-1010

SCORE Office (Wichita)
100 E. English, Ste. 510
Wichita, KS 67202
Phone: (316)269-6273
Fax: (316)269-6499

SCORE Office (Ark Valley)
205 E. 9th St.
Winfield, KS 67156
Phone: (316)221-1617

Kentucky

SCORE Office (Ashland)
PO Box 830
Ashland, KY 41105
Phone: (606)329-8011
Fax: (606)325-4607

SCORE Office (Bowling Green)
812 State St.
PO Box 51
Bowling Green, KY 42101
Phone: (502)781-3200
Fax: (502)843-0458

SCORE Office (Tri-Lakes)
508 Barbee Way
Danville, KY 40422-1548
Phone: (606)231-9902

SCORE Office (Glasgow)
301 W. Main St.
Glasgow, KY 42141
Phone: (502)651-3161
Fax: (502)651-3122

SCORE Office (Hazard)
B & I Technical Center
100 Airport Gardens Rd.
Hazard, KY 41701
Phone: (606)439-5856
Fax: (606)439-1808

SCORE Office (Lexington)
410 W. Vine St., Ste. 290, Civic C
Lexington, KY 40507
Phone: (606)231-9902
Fax: (606)253-3190
E-mail:
scorelex@uky.campus.mci.net

SCORE Office (Louisville)
188 Federal Office Bldg.
600 Dr. Martin L. King Jr. Pl.
Louisville, KY 40202
Phone: (502)582-5976

SCORE Office (Madisonville)
257 N. Main
Madisonville, KY 42431
Phone: (502)825-1399
Fax: (502)825-1396

SCORE Office (Paducah)
Federal Office Bldg.
501 Broadway, Rm. B-36
Paducah, KY 42001
Phone: (502)442-5685

Louisiana

SCORE Office (Central Louisiana)
802 3rd St.
Alexandria, LA 71309
Phone: (318)442-6671

SCORE Office (Baton Rouge)
564 Laurel St.
PO Box 3217
Baton Rouge, LA 70801
Phone: (504)381-7130
Fax: (504)336-4306

SCORE Office (North Shore)
2 W. Thomas
Hammond, LA 70401
Phone: (504)345-4457
Fax: (504)345-4749

SCORE Office (Lafayette)
804 St. Mary Blvd.
Lafayette, LA 70505-1307
Phone: (318)233-2705
Fax: (318)234-8671
E-mail: score302@aol.com

SCORE Office (Lake Charles)
120 W. Pujo St.
Lake Charles, LA 70601
Phone: (318)433-3632

SCORE Office (New Orleans)
365 Canal St., Ste. 3100
New Orleans, LA 70130
Phone: (504)589-2356
Fax: (504)589-2339

SCORE Office (Shreveport)
400 Edwards St.
Shreveport, LA 71101
Phone: (318)677-2536
Fax: (318)677-2541

Maine

SCORE Office (Augusta)
40 Western Ave.
Augusta, ME 04330
Phone: (207)622-8509

SCORE Office (Bangor)
Peabody Hall, Rm. 229
One College Cir.
Bangor, ME 04401
Phone: (207)941-9707

SCORE Office (Central & Northern Arroostock)
111 High St.
Caribou, ME 04736
Phone: (207)492-8010
Fax: (207)492-8010

SCORE Office (Penquis)
South St.
Dover Foxcroft, ME 04426
Phone: (207)564-7021

SCORE Office (Maine Coastal)
Mill Mall
Box 1105
Ellsworth, ME 04605-1105
Phone: (207)667-5800
E-mail: score@arcadia.net

SCORE Office (Lewiston-Auburn)
BIC of Maine-Bates Mill Complex
35 Canal St.
Lewiston, ME 04240-7764
Phone: (207)782-3708
Fax: (207)783-7745

SCORE Office (Portland)
66 Pearl St., Rm. 210
Portland, ME 04101
Phone: (207)772-1147
Fax: (207)772-5581
E-mail: Score53@score.maine.org
Website: http://www.score.maine.org/chapter53/

SCORE Office (Western Mountains)
255 River St.
PO Box 252
Rumford, ME 04257-0252
Phone: (207)369-9976

SCORE Office (Oxford Hills)
166 Main St.
South Paris, ME 04281
Phone: (207)743-0499

Maryland

SCORE Office (Southern Maryland)
2525 Riva Rd., Ste. 110
Annapolis, MD 21401
Phone: (410)266-9553
Fax: (410)573-0981
E-mail: score390@aol.com
Website: http://members.aol.com/score390/index.htm

SCORE Office (Baltimore)
The City Crescent Bldg., 6th Fl.
10 S. Howard St.
Baltimore, MD 21201
Phone: (410)962-2233
Fax: (410)962-1805

SCORE Office (Bel Air)
108 S. Bond St.
Bel Air, MD 21014
Phone: (410)838-2020
Fax: (410)893-4715

SCORE Office (Bethesda)
7910 Woodmont Ave., Ste. 1204
Bethesda, MD 20814
Phone: (301)652-4900
Fax: (301)657-1973

SCORE Office (Bowie)
6670 Race Track Rd.
Bowie, MD 20715
Phone: (301)262-0920
Fax: (301)262-0921

SCORE Office (Dorchester County)
203 Sunburst Hwy.
Cambridge, MD 21613
Phone: (410)228-3575

SCORE Office (Upper Shore)
210 Marlboro Ave.
Easton, MD 21601
Phone: (410)822-4606
Fax: (410)822-7922

SCORE Office (Frederick County)
43A S. Market St.
Frederick, MD 21701
Phone: (301)662-8723
Fax: (301)846-4427

SCORE Office (Gaithersburg)
9 Park Ave.
Gaithersburg, MD 20877
Phone: (301)840-1400
Fax: (301)963-3918

SCORE Office (Glen Burnie)
103 Crain Hwy. SE
Glen Burnie, MD 21061
Phone: (410)766-8282
Fax: (410)766-9722

SCORE Office (Hagerstown)
111 W. Washington St.
Hagerstown, MD 21740
Phone: (301)739-2015
Fax: (301)739-1278

SCORE Office (Laurel)
7901 Sandy Spring Rd. Ste. 501
Laurel, MD 20707
Phone: (301)725-4000
Fax: (301)725-0776

SCORE Office (Salisbury)
300 E. Main St.

Salisbury, MD 21801
Phone: (410)749-0185
Fax: (410)860-9925

Massachusetts

SCORE Office (NE Massachusetts)
100 Cummings Ctr., Ste. 101 K
Beverly, MA 01923
Phone: (978)922-9441
Website: http://www1.shore.net/~score/

SCORE Office (Boston)
10 Causeway St., Rm. 265
Boston, MA 02222-1093
Phone: (617)565-5591
Fax: (617)565-5598
E-mail: boston-score-20@worldnet.att.net
Website: http://www.scoreboston.org/

SCORE office (Bristol/Plymouth County)
53 N. 6th St., Federal Bldg.
Bristol, MA 02740
Phone: (508)994-5093

SCORE Office (SE Massachusetts)
60 School St.
Brockton, MA 02401
Phone: (508)587-2673
Fax: (508)587-1340
Website: http://www.metrosouthchamber.com/score.html

SCORE Office (North Adams)
820 N. State Rd.
Cheshire, MA 01225
Phone: (413)743-5100

SCORE Office (Clinton Satellite)
1 Green St.
Clinton, MA 01510
Fax: (508)368-7689

SCORE Office (Greenfield)
PO Box 898
Greenfield, MA 01302
Phone: (413)773-5463
Fax: (413)773-7008

SCORE Office (Haverhill)
87 Winter St.
Haverhill, MA 01830
Phone: (508)373-5663
Fax: (508)373-8060

SCORE Office (Hudson Satellite)
PO Box 578
Hudson, MA 01749
Phone: (508)568-0360
Fax: (508)568-0360

SCORE Office (Cape Cod)
Independence Pk., Ste. 5B
270 Communications Way
Hyannis, MA 02601
Phone: (508)775-4884
Fax: (508)790-2540

SCORE Office (Lawrence)
264 Essex St.
Lawrence, MA 01840
Phone: (508)686-0900
Fax: (508)794-9953

SCORE Office (Leominster Satellite)
110 Erdman Way
Leominster, MA 01453
Phone: (508)840-4300
Fax: (508)840-4896

SCORE Office (Bristol/Plymouth Counties)
53 N. 6th St., Federal Bldg.
New Bedford, MA 02740
Phone: (508)994-5093

SCORE Office (Newburyport)
29 State St.
Newburyport, MA 01950
Phone: (617)462-6680

SCORE Office (Pittsfield)
66 West St.
Pittsfield, MA 01201
Phone: (413)499-2485

SCORE Office (Haverhill-Salem)
32 Derby Sq.
Salem, MA 01970
Phone: (508)745-0330
Fax: (508)745-3855

SCORE Office (Springfield)
1350 Main St.
Federal Bldg.
Springfield, MA 01103
Phone: (413)785-0314

SCORE Office (Carver)
12 Taunton Green, Ste. 201
Taunton, MA 02780
Phone: (508)824-4068
Fax: (508)824-4069

SCORE Office (Worcester)
33 Waldo St.
Worcester, MA 01608
Phone: (508)753-2929
Fax: (508)754-8560

Michigan

SCORE Office (Allegan)
PO Box 338
Allegan, MI 49010
Phone: (616)673-2479

SCORE Office (Ann Arbor)
425 S. Main St., Ste. 103
Ann Arbor, MI 48104
Phone: (313)665-4433

SCORE Office (Battle Creek)
34 W. Jackson Ste. 4A
Battle Creek, MI 49017-3505
Phone: (616)962-4076
Fax: (616)962-6309

SCORE Office (Cadillac)
222 Lake St.
Cadillac, MI 49601
Phone: (616)775-9776
Fax: (616)768-4255

SCORE Office (Detroit)
477 Michigan Ave., Rm. 515
Detroit, MI 48226
Phone: (313)226-7947
Fax: (313)226-3448

SCORE Office (Flint)
708 Root Rd., Rm. 308
Flint, MI 48503
Phone: (810)233-6846

SCORE Office (Grand Rapids)
111 Pearl St. NW
Grand Rapids, MI 49503-2831
Phone: (616)771-0305
Fax: (616)771-0328
E-mail: scoreone@iserv.net
Website: http://www.iserv.net/~scoreone/

SCORE Office (Holland)
480 State St.
Holland, MI 49423
Phone: (616)396-9472

SCORE Office (Jackson)
209 East Washington
PO Box 80
Jackson, MI 49204
Phone: (517)782-8221
Fax: (517)782-0061

SCORE Office (Kalamazoo)
345 W. Michigan Ave.
Kalamazoo, MI 49007
Phone: (616)381-5382
Fax: (616)384-0096
E-mail: score@nucleus.net

SCORE Office (Lansing)
117 E. Allegan
PO Box 14030
Lansing, MI 48901
Phone: (517)487-6340
Fax: (517)484-6910

SCORE Office (Livonia)
15401 Farmington Rd.
Livonia, MI 48154
Phone: (313)427-2122
Fax: (313)427-6055

SCORE Office (Madison Heights)
26345 John R
Madison Heights, MI 48071
Phone: (810)542-5010
Fax: (810)542-6821

SCORE Office (Monroe)
111 E. 1st
Monroe, MI 48161
Phone: (313)242-3366
Fax: (313)242-7253

SCORE Office (Mt. Clemens)
58 S/B Gratiot
Mt. Clemens, MI 48043
Phone: (810)463-1528
Fax: (810)463-6541

SCORE Office (Muskegon)
PO Box 1087
230 Terrace Plz.
Muskegon, MI 49443
Phone: (616)722-3751
Fax: (616)728-7251

SCORE Office (Petoskey)
401 E. Mitchell St.
Petoskey, MI 49770
Phone: (616)347-4150

SCORE Office (Pontiac)
Executive Office Bldg.
1200 N. Telegraph Rd.
Pontiac, MI 48341
Phone: (810)975-9555

SCORE Office (Pontiac)
PO Box 430025
Pontiac, MI 48343
Phone: (810)335-9600

SCORE Office (Port Huron)
920 Pinegrove Ave.
Port Huron, MI 48060
Phone: (810)985-7101

SCORE Office (Rochester)
71 Walnut Ste. 110
Rochester, MI 48307
Phone: (810)651-6700
Fax: (810)651-5270

SCORE Office (Saginaw)
901 S. Washington Ave.
Saginaw, MI 48601
Phone: (517)752-7161
Fax: (517)752-9055

SCORE Office (Upper Peninsula)
2581 I-75 Business Spur
Sault Ste. Marie, MI 49783
Phone: (906)632-3301

SCORE Office (Southfield)
21000 W. 10 Mile Rd.
Southfield, MI 48075
Phone: (810)204-3050
Fax: (810)204-3099

SCORE Office (Traverse City)
202 E. Grandview Pkwy.
PO Box 387
Traverse City, MI 49685
Phone: (616)947-5075
Fax: (616)946-2565

SCORE Office (Warren)
30500 Van Dyke, Ste. 118
Warren, MI 48093
Phone: (810)751-3939

Minnesota

SCORE Office (Aitkin)
Aitkin, MN 56431
Phone: (218)741-3906

SCORE Office (Albert Lea)
202 N. Broadway Ave.
Albert Lea, MN 56007
Phone: (507)373-7487

SCORE Office (Austin)
PO Box 864
Austin, MN 55912
Phone: (507)437-4561
Fax: (507)437-4869

SCORE Office (South Metro)
Ames Business Ctr.
2500 W. County Rd., No. 42
Burnsville, MN 55337
Phone: (612)898-5645
Fax: (612)435-6972
E-mail: southmetro@scoreminn.org
Website: http://www.scoreminn.org/southmetro/

SCORE Office (Duluth)
1717 Minnesota Ave.
Duluth, MN 55802
Phone: (218)727-8286
Fax: (218)727-3113
E-mail: duluth@scoreminn.org
Website: http://www.scoreminn.org

SCORE Office (Fairmont)
PO Box 826
Fairmont, MN 56031
Phone: (507)235-5547
Fax: (507)235-8411

SCORE Office (Southwest Minnesota)
112 Riverfront St.
Box 999
Mankato, MN 56001
Phone: (507)345-4519
Fax: (507)345-4451
Website: http://www.scoreminn.org/

SCORE Office (Minneapolis)
North Plaza Bldg., Ste. 51
5217 Wayzata Blvd.
Minneapolis, MN 55416
Phone: (612)591-0539
Fax: (612)544-0436
Website: http://www.scoreminn.org/

SCORE Office (Owatonna)
PO Box 331
Owatonna, MN 55060
Phone: (507)451-7970
Fax: (507)451-7972

SCORE Office (Red Wing)
2000 W. Main St., Ste. 324
Red Wing, MN 55066
Phone: (612)388-4079

SCORE Office (Southeastern Minnesota)
220 S. Broadway, Ste. 100
Rochester, MN 55901
Phone: (507)288-1122
Fax: (507)282-8960
Website: http://www.scoreminn.org/

SCORE Office (Brainerd)
St. Cloud, MN 56301

SCORE Office (Central Area)
1527 Northway Dr.
St. Cloud, MN 56301
Phone: (320)240-1332
Fax: (320)255-9050
Website: http://www.scoreminn.org/

SCORE Office (St. Paul)
350 St. Peter St., No. 295
Lowry Professional Bldg.
St. Paul, MN 55102
Phone: (651)223-5010
Fax: (651)223-5048
Website: http://www.scoreminn.org/

SCORE Office (Winona)
Box 870
Winona, MN 55987
Phone: (507)452-2272
Fax: (507)454-8814

SCORE Office (Worthington)
1121 3rd Ave.
Worthington, MN 56187
Phone: (507)372-2919
Fax: (507)372-2827

Mississippi

SCORE Office (Delta)
915 Washington Ave.
PO Box 933
Greenville, MS 38701
Phone: (601)378-3141

SCORE Office (Gulfcoast)
1 Government Plaza
2909 13th St., Ste. 203
Gulfport, MS 39501
Phone: (228)863-0054

SCORE Office (Jackson)
1st Jackson Center, Ste. 400
101 W. Capitol St.
Jackson, MS 39201
Phone: (601)965-5533

SCORE Office (Meridian)
5220 16th Ave.
Meridian, MS 39305
Phone: (601)482-4412

Missouri

SCORE Office (Lake of the Ozark)
University Extension
113 Kansas St.
PO Box 1405
Camdenton, MO 65020
Phone: (573)346-2644
Fax: (573)346-2694
E-mail: score@cdoc.net
Website: http://sites.cdoc.net/score/

Chamber of Commerce (Cape Girardeau)
PO Box 98
Cape Girardeau, MO 63702-0098
Phone: (314)335-3312

SCORE Office (Mid-Missouri)
1705 Halstead Ct.
Columbia, MO 65203
Phone: (573)874-1132

SCORE Office (Ozark-Gateway)
1486 Glassy Rd.
Cuba, MO 65453-1640
Phone: (573)885-4954

SCORE Office (Kansas City)
323 W. 8th St., Ste. 104
Kansas City, MO 64105
Phone: (816)374-6675
Fax: (816)374-6692
E-mail: SCOREBIC@AOL.COM
Website: http://www.crn.org/score/

SCORE Office (Sedalia)
Lucas Place
323 W. 8th St., Ste.104
Kansas City, MO 64105
Phone: (816)374-6675

SCORE office (Tri-Lakes)
PO Box 1148
Kimberling, MO 65686
Phone: (417)739-3041

SCORE Office (Tri-Lakes)
HCRI Box 85
Lampe, MO 65681
Phone: (417)858-6798

SCORE Office (Mexico)
111 N. Washington St.
Mexico, MO 65265
Phone: (314)581-2765

SCORE Office (Southeast Missouri)
Rte. 1, Box 280
Neelyville, MO 63954
Phone: (573)989-3577

SCORE office (Poplar Bluff Area)
806 Emma St.
Poplar Bluff, MO 63901
Phone: (573)686-8892

SCORE Office (St. Joseph)
3003 Frederick Ave.
St. Joseph, MO 64506
Phone: (816)232-4461

SCORE Office (St. Louis)
815 Olive St., Rm. 242
St. Louis, MO 63101-1569
Phone: (314)539-6970
Fax: (314)539-3785
E-mail: info@stlscore.org
Website: http://www.stlscore.org/

SCORE Office (Lewis & Clark)
425 Spencer Rd.
St. Peters, MO 63376
Phone: (314)928-2900
Fax: (314)928-2900
E-mail: score01@mail.win.org

SCORE Office (Springfield)
620 S. Glenstone, Ste. 110
Springfield, MO 65802-3200
Phone: (417)864-7670
Fax: (417)864-4108

SCORE office (Southeast Kansas)
1206 W. First St.
Webb City, MO 64870
Phone: (417)673-3984

Montana

SCORE Office (Billings)
815 S. 27th St.
Billings, MT 59101
Phone: (406)245-4111

SCORE Office (Bozeman)
1205 E. Main St.
Bozeman, MT 59715
Phone: (406)586-5421

SCORE Office (Butte)
1000 George St.
Butte, MT 59701
Phone: (406)723-3177

SCORE Office (Great Falls)
710 First Ave. N
Great Falls, MT 59401
Phone: (406)761-4434
E-mail: scoregtf@in.tch.com

SCORE Office (Havre, Montana)
518 First St.
Havre, MT 59501
Phone: (406)265-4383

SCORE Office (Helena)
Federal Bldg.
301 S. Park

Helena, MT 59626-0054
Phone: (406)441-1081

SCORE Office (Kalispell)
2 Main St.
Kalispell, MT 59901
Phone: (406)756-5271
Fax: (406)752-6665

SCORE Office (Missoula)
723 Ronan
Missoula, MT 59806
Phone: (406)327-8806
E-mail: score@safeshop.com
Website: http://missoula.bigsky.net/score/

Nebraska

SCORE Office (Columbus)
Columbus, NE 68601
Phone: (402)564-2769

SCORE Office (Fremont)
92 W. 5th St.
Fremont, NE 68025
Phone: (402)721-2641

SCORE Office (Hastings)
Hastings, NE 68901
Phone: (402)463-3447

SCORE Office (Lincoln)
8800 O St.
Lincoln, NE 68520
Phone: (402)437-2409

SCORE Office (Panhandle)
150549 CR 30
Minatare, NE 69356
Phone: (308)632-2133
Website: http://www.tandt.com/SCORE

SCORE Office (Norfolk)
3209 S. 48th Ave.
Norfolk, NE 68106
Phone: (402)564-2769

SCORE Office (North Platte)
3301 W. 2nd St.
North Platte, NE 69101
Phone: (308)532-4466

SCORE Office (Omaha)
11145 Mill Valley Rd.
Omaha, NE 68154
Phone: (402)221-3606
Fax: (402)221-3680
E-mail: infoctr@ne.uswest.net
Website: http://www.tandt.com/score/

Nevada

SCORE Office (Incline Village)
969 Tahoe Blvd.
Incline Village, NV 89451
Phone: (702)831-7327
Fax: (702)832-1605

SCORE Office (Carson City)
301 E. Stewart
PO Box 7527
Las Vegas, NV 89125
Phone: (702)388-6104

SCORE Office (Las Vegas)
300 Las Vegas Blvd. S, Ste. 1100
Las Vegas, NV 89101
Phone: (702)388-6104

SCORE Office (Northern Nevada)
SBDC, College of Business Administration
Univ. of Nevada
Reno, NV 89557-0100
Phone: (702)784-4436
Fax: (702)784-4337

New Hampshire

SCORE Office (North Country)
PO Box 34
Berlin, NH 03570
Phone: (603)752-1090

SCORE Office (Concord)
143 N. Main St., Rm. 202A
PO Box 1258
Concord, NH 03301
Phone: (603)225-1400
Fax: (603)225-1409

SCORE Office (Dover)
299 Central Ave.
Dover, NH 03820
Phone: (603)742-2218
Fax: (603)749-6317

SCORE Office (Monadnock)
34 Mechanic St.
Keene, NH 03431-3421
Phone: (603)352-0320

SCORE Office (Lakes Region)
67 Water St., Ste. 105
Laconia, NH 03246
Phone: (603)524-9168

SCORE Office (Upper Valley)
Citizens Bank Bldg., Rm. 310
20 W. Park St.
Lebanon, NH 03766
Phone: (603)448-3491
Fax: (603)448-1908
E-mail: billt@valley.net
Website: http://www.valley.net/~score/

SCORE Office (Merrimack Valley)
275 Chestnut St., Rm. 618
Manchester, NH 03103
Phone: (603)666-7561
Fax: (603)666-7925

SCORE Office (Mt. Washington Valley)
PO Box 1066
North Conway, NH 03818
Phone: (603)383-0800

SCORE Office (Seacoast)
195 Commerce Way, Unit-A
Portsmouth, NH 03801-3251
Phone: (603)433-0575

New Jersey

SCORE Office (Somerset)
Paritan Valley Community College, Rte. 28
Branchburg, NJ 08807
Phone: (908)218-8874
E-mail: nj-score@grizbiz.com.
Website: http://www.nj-score.org/

SCORE Office (Chester)
5 Old Mill Rd.
Chester, NJ 07930
Phone: (908)879-7080

SCORE Office (Greater Princeton)
4 A George Washington Dr.
Cranbury, NJ 08512
Phone: (609)520-1776

SCORE Office (Freehold)
36 W. Main St.
Freehold, NJ 07728
Phone: (908)462-3030
Fax: (908)462-2123

SCORE Office (North West)
Picantinny Innovation Ctr.
3159 Schrader Rd.
Hamburg, NJ 07419
Phone: (973)209-8525
Fax: (973)209-7252
E-mail: nj-score@grizbiz.com
Website: http://www.nj-score.org/

SCORE Office (Monmouth)
765 Newman Springs Rd.

Lincroft, NJ 07738
Phone: (908)224-2573
E-mail: nj-score@grizbiz.com
Website: http://www.nj-score.org/

SCORE Office (Manalapan)
125 Symmes Dr.
Manalapan, NJ 07726
Phone: (908)431-7220

SCORE Office (Jersey City)
2 Gateway Ctr., 4th Fl.
Newark, NJ 07102
Phone: (973)645-3982
Fax: (973)645-2375

SCORE Office (Newark)
2 Gateway Center, 15th Fl.
Newark, NJ 07102-5553
Phone: (973)645-3982
Fax: (973)645-2375
E-mail: nj-score@grizbiz.com
Website: http://www.nj-score.org

SCORE Office (Bergen County)
327 E. Ridgewood Ave.
Paramus, NJ 07652
Phone: (201)599-6090
E-mail: nj-score@grizbiz.com
Website: http://www.nj-score.org/

SCORE Office (Pennsauken)
4900 Rte. 70
Pennsauken, NJ 08109
Phone: (609)486-3421

SCORE Office (Southern New Jersey)
4900 Rte. 70
Pennsauken, NJ 08109
Phone: (609)486-3421
E-mail: nj-score@grizbiz.com
Website: http://www.nj-score.org/

SCORE Office (Greater Princeton)
216 Rockingham Row
Princeton Forrestal Village
Princeton, NJ 08540
Phone: (609)520-1776
Fax: (609)520-9107
E-mail: nj-score@grizbiz.com
Website: http://www.nj-score.org/

SCORE Office (Shrewsbury)
Hwy. 35
Shrewsbury, NJ 07702
Phone: (908)842-5995
Fax: (908)219-6140

SCORE Office (Ocean County)
33 Washington St.
Toms River, NJ 08754
Phone: (732)505-6033
E-mail: nj-score@grizbiz.com
Website: http://www.nj-score.org/

SCORE Office (Wall)
2700 Allaire Rd.
Wall, NJ 07719
Phone: (908)449-8877

SCORE Office (Wayne)
2055 Hamburg Tpke.
Wayne, NJ 07470
Phone: (201)831-7788
Fax: (201)831-9112

New Mexico

SCORE Office (Albuquerque)
525 Buena Vista, SE
Albuquerque, NM 87106
Phone: (505)272-7999
Fax: (505)272-7963

SCORE Office (Las Cruces)
Loretto Towne Center
505 S. Main St., Ste. 125
Las Cruces, NM 88001
Phone: (505)523-5627
Fax: (505)524-2101
E-mail: score.397@zianet.com

SCORE Office (Roswell)
Federal Bldg., Rm. 237
Roswell, NM 88201
Phone: (505)625-2112
Fax: (505)623-2545

SCORE Office (Santa Fe)
Montoya Federal Bldg.
120 Federal Place, Rm. 307
Santa Fe, NM 87501
Phone: (505)988-6302
Fax: (505)988-6300

New York

SCORE Office (Northeast)
1 Computer Dr. S
Albany, NY 12205
Phone: (518)446-1118
Fax: (518)446-1228

SCORE Office (Auburn)
30 South St.
PO Box 675
Auburn, NY 13021
Phone: (315)252-7291

SCORE Office (South Tier Binghamton)
Metro Center, 2nd Fl.
49 Court St.
PO Box 995
Binghamton, NY 13902
Phone: (607)772-8860

SCORE Office (Queens County City)
12055 Queens Blvd., Rm. 333
Borough Hall, NY 11424
Phone: (718)263-8961

SCORE Office (Buffalo)
Federal Bldg., Rm. 1311
111 W. Huron St.
Buffalo, NY 14202
Phone: (716)551-4301
Website: http://www2.pcom.net/score/buf45.html

SCORE Office (Canandaigua)
Chamber of Commerce Bldg.
113 S. Main St.
Canandaigua, NY 14424
Phone: (716)394-4400
Fax: (716)394-4546

SCORE Office (Chemung)
333 E. Water St., 4th Fl.
Elmira, NY 14901
Phone: (607)734-3358

SCORE Office (Geneva)
Chamber of Commerce Bldg.
PO Box 587
Geneva, NY 14456
Phone: (315)789-1776
Fax: (315)789-3993

SCORE Office (Glens Falls)
84 Broad St.
Glens Falls, NY 12801
Phone: (518)798-8463
Fax: (518)745-1433

SCORE Office (Orange County)
40 Matthews St.
Goshen, NY 10924
Phone: (914)294-8080
Fax: (914)294-6121

SCORE Office (Huntington Area)
151 W. Carver St.
Huntington, NY 11743
Phone: (516)423-6100

SCORE Office (Tompkins County)
904 E. Shore Dr.
Ithaca, NY 14850
Phone: (607)273-7080

ORE Office (Harrisburg)
) Chestnut, Ste. 309
rrisburg, PA 17101
one: (717)782-3874

ORE Office (East Montgomery
unty)
ederwood Shopping Center
53 The Fairways, Ste. 204
kintown, PA 19046
one: (215)885-3027

ORE Office (Kittanning)
Butler Rd.
ttanning, PA 16201
one: (412)543-1305
x: (412)543-6206

CORE Office (Lancaster)
8 W. Chestnut St.
ncaster, PA 17603
hone: (717)397-3092

CORE Office (Westmoreland
ounty)
00 Fraser Purchase Rd.
atrobe, PA 15650-2690
hone: (412)539-7505
ax: (412)539-1850

CORE Office (Lebanon)
52 N. 8th St.
O Box 899
ebanon, PA 17042-0899
hone: (717)273-3727
ax: (717)273-7940

CORE Office (Lewistown)
W. Monument Sq., Ste. 204
ewistown, PA 17044
Phone: (717)248-6713
Fax: (717)248-6714

SCORE Office (Delaware County)
602 E. Baltimore Pike
Media, PA 19063
Phone: (610)565-3677
Fax: (610)565-1606

SCORE Office (Milton Area)
112 S. Front St.
Milton, PA 17847
Phone: (717)742-7341
Fax: (717)792-2008

SCORE Office (Mon-Valley)
435 Donner Ave.
Monessen, PA 15062
Phone: (412)684-4277
Fax: (412)684-7688

SCORE Office (Monroeville)
William Penn Plaza
2790 Mosside Blvd., Ste. 295
Monroeville, PA 15146
Phone: (412)856-0622
Fax: (412)856-1030

SCORE Office (Airport Area)
986 Brodhead Rd.
Moon Township, PA 15108-2398
Phone: (412)264-6270
Fax: (412)264-1575

SCORE Office (Northeast)
8601 E. Roosevelt Blvd.
Philadelphia, PA 19152
Phone: (215)332-3400
Fax: (215)332-6050

SCORE Office (Philadelphia)
1315 Walnut St., Ste. 500
Philadelphia, PA 19107
Phone: (215)790-5050
Fax: (215)790-5057
E-mail: score46@bellatlantic.net
Website: http://www.pgweb.net/score46/

SCORE Office (Pittsburgh)
1000 Liberty Ave., Rm. 1122
Pittsburgh, PA 15222
Phone: (412)395-6560
Fax: (412)395-6562

SCORE Office (Tri-County)
801 N. Charlotte St.
Pottstown, PA 19464
Phone: (610)327-2673

SCORE Office (Reading)
601 Penn St.
Reading, PA 19601
Phone: (610)376-3497

SCORE Office (Scranton)
Oppenheim Bldg.
116 N. Washington Ave., Ste. 650
Scranton, PA 18503
Phone: (717)347-4611
Fax: (717)347-4611

SCORE Office (Central Pennsylvania)
200 Innovation Blvd., Ste. 242-B
State College, PA 16803
Phone: (814)234-9415
Fax: (814)238-9686
Website: http://countrystore.org/business/score.htm

SCORE Office (Monroe-Stroudsburg)
556 Main St.
Stroudsburg, PA 18360
Phone: (717)421-4433

SCORE Office (Uniontown)
Federal Bldg.
Pittsburg St.
PO Box 2065 DTS
Uniontown, PA 15401
Phone: (412)437-4222
E-mail: uniontownscore@lcsys.net

SCORE Office (Warren County)
315 2nd Ave.
Warren, PA 16365
Phone: (814)723-9017

SCORE Office (Waynesboro)
323 E. Main St.
Waynesboro, PA 17268
Phone: (717)762-7123
Fax: (717)962-7124

SCORE Office (Chester County)
Government Service Center, Ste. 281
601 Westtown Rd.
West Chester, PA 19382-4538
Phone: (610)344-6910
Fax: (610)344-6919
E-mail: score@locke.ccil.org

SCORE Office (Wilkes-Barre)
7 N. Wilkes-Barre Blvd.
Wilkes Barre, PA 18702-5241
Phone: (717)826-6502
Fax: (717)826-6287

SCORE Office (North Central Pennsylvania)
240 W. 3rd St., Rm. 227
PO Box 725
Williamsport, PA 17703
Phone: (717)322-3720
Fax: (717)322-1607
E-mail: score234@mail.csrlink.net
Website: http://www.lycoming.org/score/

SCORE Office (York)
Cyber Center
2101 Pennsylvania Ave.
York, PA 17404
Phone: (717)845-8830
Fax: (717)854-9333

SCORE Office (Long Island City)
120-55 Queens Blvd.
Jamaica, NY 11424
Phone: (718)263-8961
Fax: (718)263-9032

SCORE Office (Chatauqua)
101 W. 5th St.
Jamestown, NY 14701
Phone: (716)484-1103

SCORE Office (Westchester)
2 Caradon Ln.
Katonah, NY 10536
Phone: (914)948-3907
Fax: (914)948-4645
E-mail: score@w-w-w.com
Website: http://w-w-w.com/score/

SCORE Office (Queens County)
Queens Borough Hall
120-55 Queens Blvd. Rm. 333
Kew Gardens, NY 11424
Phone: (718)263-8961
Fax: (718)263-9032

SCORE Office (Brookhaven)
3233 Rte. 112
Medford, NY 11763
Phone: (516)451-6563
Fax: (516)451-6925

SCORE Office (Melville)
35 Pinelawn Rd., Rm. 207-W
Melville, NY 11747
Phone: (516)454-0771

SCORE Office (Nassau County)
400 County Seat Dr., No. 140
Mineola, NY 11501
Phone: (516)571-3303
E-mail: Counse1998@aol.com
Website: http://members.aol.com/Counse1998/Default.htm

SCORE Office (Mt. Vernon)
4 N. 7th Ave.
Mt. Vernon, NY 10550
Phone: (914)667-7500

SCORE Office (New York)
26 Federal Plz., Rm. 3100
New York, NY 10278
Phone: (212)264-4507
Fax: (212)264-4963
E-mail: score1000@erols.com
Website: http://users.erols.com/score-nyc/

SCORE Office (Newburgh)
47 Grand St.
Newburgh, NY 12550
Phone: (914)562-5100

SCORE Office (Owego)
188 Front St.
Owego, NY 13827
Phone: (607)687-2020

SCORE Office (Peekskill)
1 S. Division St.
Peekskill, NY 10566
Phone: (914)737-3600
Fax: (914)737-0541

SCORE Office (Penn Yan)
2375 Rte. 14A
Penn Yan, NY 14527
Phone: (315)536-3111

SCORE Office (Dutchess)
110 Main St.
Poughkeepsie, NY 12601
Phone: (914)454-1700

SCORE Office (Rochester)
601 Keating Federal Bldg., Rm. 410
100 State St.
Rochester, NY 14614
Phone: (716)263-6473
Fax: (716)263-3146
Website: http://www.ggw.org/score/

SCORE Office (Saranac Lake)
30 Main St.
Saranac Lake, NY 12983
Phone: (315)448-0415

SCORE Office (Suffolk)
286 Main St.
Setauket, NY 11733
Phone: (516)751-3886

SCORE Office (Staten Island)
130 Bay St.
Staten Island, NY 10301
Phone: (718)727-1221

SCORE Office (Ulster)
Clinton Bldg., Rm. 107
Stone Ridge, NY 12484
Phone: (914)687-5035
Fax: (914)687-5015
Website: http://www.scoreulster.org/

SCORE Office (Syracuse)
401 S. Salina, 5th Fl.
Syracuse, NY 13202
Phone: (315)471-9393

SCORE Office (Utica)
SUNY Institute of Technology, Route 12
Utica, NY 13504-3050
Phone: (315)792-7553

SCORE Office (Watertown)
518 Davidson St.
Watertown, NY 13601
Phone: (315)788-1200
Fax: (315)788-8251

North Carolina

SCORE office (Asheboro)
317 E. Dixie Dr.
Asheboro, NC 27203
Phone: (336)626-2626
Fax: (336)626-7077

SCORE Office (Asheville)
Federal Bldg., Rm. 259
151 Patton
Asheville, NC 28801-5770
Phone: (828)271-4786
Fax: (828)271-4009

SCORE Office (Chapel Hill)
104 S. Estes Dr.
PO Box 2897
Chapel Hill, NC 27514
Phone: (919)967-7075

SCORE Office (Coastal Plains)
PO Box 2897
Chapel Hill, NC 27515
Phone: (919)967-7075
Fax: (919)968-6874

SCORE Office (Charlotte)
200 N. College St., Ste. A-2015
Charlotte, NC 28202
Phone: (704)344-6576
Fax: (704)344-6769
E-mail: CharlotteSCORE47@AOL.com
Website: http://www.charweb.org/business/score/

SCORE Office (Durham)
411 W. Chapel Hill St.
Durham, NC 27707
Phone: (919)541-2171

SCORE Office (Gastonia)
PO Box 2168
Gastonia, NC 28053
Phone: (704)864-2621
Fax: (704)854-8723

SCORE Office (Greensboro)
400 W. Market St., Ste. 103
Greensboro, NC 27401-2241
Phone: (910)333-5399

SCORE Office (Henderson)
PO Box 917
Henderson, NC 27536
Phone: (919)492-2061
Fax: (919)430-0460

SCORE Office (Hendersonville)
Federal Bldg., Rm. 108
W. 4th Ave. & Church St.
Hendersonville, NC 28792
Phone: (828)693-8702
E-mail: score@circle.net
Website: http://www.wncguide.com/score/Welcome.html

SCORE Office (Unifour)
PO Box 1828
Hickory, NC 28603
Phone: (704)328-6111

SCORE Office (High Point)
1101 N. Main St.
High Point, NC 27262
Phone: (336)882-8625
Fax: (336)889-9499

SCORE Office (Outer Banks)
Collington Rd. and Mustain
Kill Devil Hills, NC 27948
Phone: (252)441-8144

SCORE Office (Down East)
312 S. Front St., Ste. 6
New Bern, NC 28560
Phone: (252)633-6688
Fax: (252)633-9608

SCORE Office (Kinston)
PO Box 95
New Bern, NC 28561
Phone: (919)633-6688

SCORE Office (Raleigh)
Century Post Office Bldg., Ste. 306
300 Federal St. Mall
Raleigh, NC 27601
Phone: (919)856-4739
E-mail: jendres@ibm.net
Website: http://www.intrex.net/score96/score96.htm

SCORE Office (Sanford)
1801 Nash St.
Sanford, NC 27330
Phone: (919)774-6442
Fax: (919)776-8739

SCORE Office (Sandhills Area)
1480 Hwy. 15-501
PO Box 458
Southern Pines, NC 28387
Phone: (910)692-3926

SCORE Office (Wilmington)
Corps of Engineers Bldg.
96 Darlington Ave., Ste. 207
Wilmington, NC 28403
Phone: (910)815-4576
Fax: (910)815-4658

North Dakota

SCORE Office (Bismarck-Mandan)
700 E. Main Ave., 2nd Fl.
PO Box 5509
Bismarck, ND 58506-5509
Phone: (701)250-4303

SCORE Office (Fargo)
657 2nd Ave., Rm. 225
Fargo, ND 58108-3083
Phone: (701)239-5677

SCORE Office (Upper Red River)
4275 Technology Dr., Rm. 156
Grand Forks, ND 58202-8372
Phone: (701)777-3051

SCORE Office (Minot)
100 1st St. SW
Minot, ND 58701-3846
Phone: (701)852-6883
Fax: (701)852-6905

Ohio

SCORE Office (Akron)
1 Cascade Plz., 7th Fl.
Akron, OH 44308
Phone: (330)379-3163
Fax: (330)379-3164

SCORE Office (Ashland)
Gill Center
47 W. Main St.
Ashland, OH 44805
Phone: (419)281-4584

SCORE Office (Canton)
116 Cleveland Ave. NW, Ste. 601
Canton, OH 44702-1720
Phone: (330)453-6047

SCORE Office (Chillicothe)
165 S. Paint St.
Chillicothe, OH 45601
Phone: (614)772-4530

SCORE Office (Cincinnati)
Ameritrust Bldg., Rm. 850
525 Vine St.
Cincinnati, OH 45202
Phone: (513)684-2812
Fax: (513)684-3251
Website: http://www.score.chapter34.org/

SCORE Office (Cleveland)
Eaton Center, Ste. 620
1100 Superior Ave.
Cleveland, OH 44114-2507
Phone: (216)522-4194
Fax: (216)522-4844

SCORE Office (Columbus)
2 Nationwide Plz., Ste. 1400
Columbus, OH 43215-2542
Phone: (614)469-2357
Fax: (614)469-2391
E-mail: info@scorecolumbus.org
Website: http://www.scorecolumbus.org/

SCORE Office (Dayton)
Dayton Federal Bldg., Rm. 505
200 W. Second St.
Dayton, OH 45402-1430
Phone: (513)225-2887
Fax: (513)225-7667

SCORE Office (Defiance)
615 W. 3rd St.
PO Box 130
Defiance, OH 43512
Phone: (419)782-7946

SCORE Office (Findlay)
123 E. Main Cross St.
PO Box 923
Findlay, OH 45840
Phone: (419)422-3314

SCORE Office (Lima)
147 N. Main St.
Lima, OH 45801
Phone: (419)222-6045
Fax: (419)229-0266

SCORE Office (Mansfield)
55 N. Mulberry St.
Mansfield, OH 44902
Phone: (419)522-3211

SCORE Office (Marietta)
Thomas Hall
Marietta, OH 45750
Phone: (614)373-0268

SCORE Office (Medina)
County Administrative Bldg.

144 N. Broadway
Medina, OH 44256
Phone: (216)764-8650

SCORE Office (Licking County)
50 W. Locust St.
Newark, OH 43055
Phone: (614)345-7458

SCORE Office (Salem)
2491 State Rte. 45 S
Salem, OH 44460
Phone: (216)332-0361

SCORE Office (Tiffin)
62 S. Washington St.
Tiffin, OH 44883
Phone: (419)447-4141
Fax: (419)447-5141

SCORE Office (Toledo)
608 Madison Ave, Ste. 910
Toledo, OH 43624
Phone: (419)259-7598
Fax: (419)259-6460

SCORE Office (Heart of Ohio)
377 W. Liberty St.
Wooster, OH 44691
Phone: (330)262-5735
Fax: (330)262-5745

SCORE Office (Youngstown)
306 Williamson Hall
Youngstown, OH 44555
Phone: (330)746-2687

Oklahoma

SCORE Office (Anadarko)
PO Box 366
Anadarko, OK 73005
Phone: (405)247-665

SCORE Office (Ardmore)
410 W. Main
Ardmore, OK 73401
Phone: (580)226-2620

SCORE Office (Northeast Oklahoma)
210 S. Main
Grove, OK 74344
Phone: (918)787-2796
Fax: (918)787-2796
E-mail: Score595@greencis.net

SCORE Office (Lawton)
4500 W. Lee Blvd., Bldg. 100, Ste. 107
Lawton, OK 73505
Phone: (580)353-8727
Fax: (580)250-5677

SCORE Office (Oklahoma City)
210 Park Ave., No. 1300
Oklahoma City, OK 73102
Phone: (405)231-5163
Fax: (405)231-4876
E-mail: score212@usa.net

SCORE Office (Stillwater)
439 S. Main
Stillwater, OK 74074
Phone: (405)372-5573
Fax: (405)372-4316

SCORE Office (Tulsa)
616 S. Boston, Ste. 406
Tulsa, OK 74119
Phone: (918)581-7462
Fax: (918)581-6908
Website: http://www.ionet.net/~tulscore/

Oregon

SCORE Office (Bend)
63085 N. Hwy. 97
Bend, OR 97701
Phone: (541)923-2849
Fax: (541)330-6900

SCORE Office (Willamette)
1401 Willamette St.
PO Box 1107
Eugene, OR 97401-4003
Phone: (541)465-6600
Fax: (541)484-4942

SCORE Office (Florence)
3149 Oak St.
Florence, OR 97439
Phone: (503)997-8444
Fax: (503)997-8448

SCORE Office (Southern Oregon)
33 N. Central Ave., Ste. 216
Medford, OR 97501
Phone: (541)776-4220
E-mail: pgr134f@prodigy.com

SCORE Office (Portland)
1515 SW 5th Ave., Ste. 1050
Portland, OR 97201
Phone: (503)326-3441
Fax: (503)326-2808
E-mail: gr134@prodigy.com

SCORE Office (Salem)
416 State St. (corner of Liberty)
Salem, OR 97301
Phone: (503)370-289

Pennsylvania

SCORE Office (Altoc
1212 12th Ave.
Altoona, PA 16601-3
Phone: (814)943-8151

SCORE Office (Lehig
Rauch Bldg. 37
Lehigh University
621 Taylor St.
Bethlehem, PA 18015
Phone: (610)758-4496
Fax: (610)758-5205

SCORE Office (Butler
100 N. Main St.
PO Box 1082
Butler, PA 16003
Phone: (412)283-2222
Fax: (412)283-0224

SCORE Office (Harrisb
4211 Trindle Rd.
Camp Hill, PA 17011
Phone: (717)761-4304
Fax: (717)761-4315

SCORE Office (Cumberl
75 S. 2nd St.
Chambersburg, PA 1720
Phone: (717)264-2935

SCORE Office (Monroe
Stroudsburg)
556 Main St.
East Stroudsburg, PA 183
Phone: (717)421-4433

SCORE Office (Erie)
120 W. 9th St.
Erie, PA 16501
Phone: (814)871-5650
Fax: (814)871-7530

SCORE Office (Bucks Cou
409 Hood Blvd.
Fairless Hills, PA 19030
Phone: (215)943-8850
Fax: (215)943-7404

SCORE Office (Hanover)
146 Broadway
Hanover, PA 17331
Phone: (717)637-6130
Fax: (717)637-9127

Puerto Rico

SCORE Office (Puerto Rico & Virgin Islands)
PO Box 12383-96
San Juan, PR 00914-0383
Phone: (787)726-8040
Fax: (787)726-8135

Rhode Island

SCORE Office (Barrington)
281 County Rd.
Barrington, RI 02806
Phone: (401)247-1920
Fax: (401)247-3763

SCORE Office (Woonsocket)
640 Washington Hwy.
Lincoln, RI 02865
Phone: (401)334-1000
Fax: (401)334-1009

SCORE Office (Wickford)
8045 Post Rd.
North Kingstown, RI 02852
Phone: (401)295-5566
Fax: (401)295-8987

SCORE Office (J.G.E. Knight)
380 Westminster St.
Providence, RI 02903
Phone: (401)528-4571
Fax: (401)528-4539
E-mail: feedback@ch13.score.org.
Website: http://chapters.score.org/ch13

SCORE Office (Warwick)
3288 Post Rd.
Warwick, RI 02886
Phone: (401)732-1100
Fax: (401)732-1101

SCORE Office (Westerly)
74 Post Rd.
Westerly, RI 02891
Phone: (401)596-7761
Free: (800)732-7636
Fax: (401)596-2190

South Carolina

SCORE Office (Aiken)
PO Box 892
Aiken, SC 29802
Phone: (803)641-1111
Free: (800)542-4536
Fax: (803)641-4174

SCORE Office (Anderson)
Anderson Mall
3130 N. Main St.
Anderson, SC 29621
Phone: (864)224-0453

SCORE Office (Coastal)
284 King St.
Charleston, SC 29401
Phone: (803)727-4778
Fax: (803)853-2529

SCORE Office (Midlands)
Strom Thurmond Bldg., Rm. 358
1835 Assembly St., Rm 358
Columbia, SC 29201
Phone: (803)765-5131
Fax: (803)765-5962
Website: http://www.scoremidlands.org/

SCORE Office (Piedmont)
Federal Bldg., Rm. B-02
300 E. Washington St.
Greenville, SC 29601
Phone: (864)271-3638

SCORE Office (Greenwood)
PO Drawer 1467
Greenwood, SC 29648
Phone: (864)223-8357

SCORE Office (Hilton Head Island)
52 Savannah Trail
Hilton Head, SC 29926
Phone: (803)785-7107
Fax: (803)785-7110

SCORE Office (Grand Strand)
937 Broadway
Myrtle Beach, SC 29577
Phone: (803)918-1079
Fax: (803)918-1083
E-mail: score381@aol.com

SCORE Office (Spartanburg)
PO Box 1636
Spartanburg, SC 29304
Phone: (864)594-5000
Fax: (864)594-5055

South Dakota

SCORE Office (West River)
Rushmore Plz. Civic Ctr.
444 Mount Rushmore Rd., No. 209
Rapid City, SD 57701
Phone: (605)394-5311
E-mail: score@gwtc.net

SCORE Office (Sioux Falls)
First Financial Center
110 S. Phillips Ave., Ste. 200
Sioux Falls, SD 57104-6727
Phone: (605)330-4231
Fax: (605)330-4231

Tennessee

SCORE Office (Chattanooga)
Federal Bldg., Rm. 26
900 Georgia Ave.
Chattanooga, TN 37402
Phone: (423)752-5190
Fax: (423)752-5335

SCORE Office (Cleveland)
PO Box 2275
Cleveland, TN 37320
Phone: (423)472-6587
Fax: (423)472-2019

SCORE Office (Upper Cumberland Center)
1225 S. Willow Ave.
Cookeville, TN 38501
Phone: (615)432-4111
Fax: (615)432-6010

SCORE Office (Unicoi County)
PO Box 713
Erwin, TN 37650
Phone: (423)743-3000
Fax: (423)743-0942

SCORE Office (Greeneville)
115 Academy St.
Greeneville, TN 37743
Phone: (423)638-4111
Fax: (423)638-5345

SCORE Office (Jackson)
194 Auditorium St.
Jackson, TN 38301
Phone: (901)423-2200

SCORE Office (Northeast Tennessee)
1st Tennessee Bank Bldg.
2710 S. Roan St., Ste. 584
Johnson City, TN 37601
Phone: (423)929-7686
Fax: (423)461-8052

SCORE Office (Kingsport)
151 E. Main St.
Kingsport, TN 37662
Phone: (423)392-8805

SCORE Office (Greater Knoxville)
Farragot Bldg., Ste. 224

530 S. Gay St.
Knoxville, TN 37902
Phone: (423)545-4203
E-mail: scoreknox@ntown.com
Website: http://www.scoreknox.org/

SCORE Office (Maryville)
201 S. Washington St.
Maryville, TN 37804-5728
Phone: (423)983-2241
Free: (800)525-6834
Fax: (423)984-1386

SCORE Office (Memphis)
Federal Bldg., Ste. 390
167 N. Main St.
Memphis, TN 38103
Phone: (901)544-3588

SCORE Office (Nashville)
50 Vantage Way, Ste. 201
Nashville, TN 37228-1500
Phone: (615)736-7621

Texas

SCORE Office (Abilene)
2106 Federal Post Office and Court Bldg.
Abilene, TX 79601
Phone: (915)677-1857

SCORE Office (Austin)
2501 S. Congress
Austin, TX 78701
Phone: (512)442-7235
Fax: (512)442-7528

SCORE Office (Golden Triangle)
450 Boyd St.
Beaumont, TX 77704
Phone: (409)838-6581
Fax: (409)833-6718

SCORE Office (Brownsville)
3505 Boca Chica Blvd., Ste. 305
Brownsville, TX 78521
Phone: (210)541-4508

SCORE Office (Brazos Valley)
3000 Briarcrest, Ste. 302
Bryan, TX 77802
Phone: (409)776-8876
E-mail:
102633.2612@compuserve.com

SCORE Office (Cleburne)
Watergarden Pl., 9th Fl., Ste. 400
Cleburne, TX 76031
Phone: (817)871-6002

SCORE Office (Corpus Christi)
651 Upper North Broadway, Ste. 654
Corpus Christi, TX 78477
Phone: (512)888-4322
Fax: (512)888-3418

SCORE Office (Dallas)
6260 E. Mockingbird
Dallas, TX 75214-2619
Phone: (214)828-2471
Fax: (214)821-8033

SCORE Office (El Paso)
10 Civic Center Plaza
El Paso, TX 79901
Phone: (915)534-0541
Fax: (915)534-0513

SCORE Office (Bedford)
100 E. 15th St., Ste. 400
Ft. Worth, TX 76102
Phone: (817)871-6002

SCORE Office (Ft. Worth)
100 E. 15th St., No. 24
Ft. Worth, TX 76102
Phone: (817)871-6002
Fax: (817)871-6031
E-mail: fwbac@onramp.net

SCORE Office (Garland)
2734 W. Kingsley Rd.
Garland, TX 75041
Phone: (214)271-9224

SCORE Office (Granbury Chamber of Commerce)
416 S. Morgan
Granbury, TX 76048
Phone: (817)573-1622
Fax: (817)573-0805

SCORE Office (Lower Rio Grande Valley)
222 E. Van Buren, Ste. 500
Harlingen, TX 78550
Phone: (956)427-8533
Fax: (956)427-8537

SCORE Office (Houston)
9301 Southwest Fwy., Ste. 550
Houston, TX 77074
Phone: (713)773-6565
Fax: (713)773-6550

SCORE Office (Irving)
3333 N. MacArthur Blvd., Ste. 100
Irving, TX 75062
Phone: (214)252-8484
Fax: (214)252-6710

SCORE Office (Lubbock)
1205 Texas Ave., Rm. 411D
Lubbock, TX 79401
Phone: (806)472-7462
Fax: (806)472-7487

SCORE Office (Midland)
Post Office Annex
200 E. Wall St., Rm. P121
Midland, TX 79701
Phone: (915)687-2649

SCORE Office (Orange)
1012 Green Ave.
Orange, TX 77630-5620
Phone: (409)883-3536
Free: (800)528-4906
Fax: (409)886-3247

SCORE Office (Plano)
1200 E. 15th St.
PO Drawer 940287
Plano, TX 75094-0287
Phone: (214)424-7547
Fax: (214)422-5182

SCORE Office (Port Arthur)
4749 Twin City Hwy., Ste. 300
Port Arthur, TX 77642
Phone: (409)963-1107
Fax: (409)963-3322

SCORE Office (Richardson)
411 Belle Grove
Richardson, TX 75080
Phone: (214)234-4141
Free: (800)777-8001
Fax: (214)680-9103

SCORE Office (San Antonio)
Federal Bldg., Rm. A527
727 E. Durango
San Antonio, TX 78206
Phone: (210)472-5931
Fax: (210)472-5935

SCORE Office (Texarkana State College)
819 State Line Ave.
Texarkana, TX 75501
Phone: (903)792-7191
Fax: (903)793-4304

SCORE Office (East Texas) RTDC
1530 SSW Loop 323, Ste. 100
Tyler, TX 75701
Phone: (903)510-2975
Fax: (903)510-2978

SCORE Office (Waco)
401 Franklin Ave.
Waco, TX 76701
Phone: (817)754-8898
Fax: (817)756-0776
Website: http://www.brc-waco.com/

SCORE Office (Wichita Falls)
Hamilton Bldg.
900 8th St.
Wichita Falls, TX 76307
Phone: (940)723-2741
Fax: (940)723-8773

Utah

SCORE Office (Northern Utah)
160 N. Main
Logan, UT 84321
Phone: (435)752-2161

SCORE Office (Ogden)
1701 E. Windsor Dr.
Ogden, UT 84604
Phone: (801)226-0881
E-mail: score158@netscape.net

SCORE Office (Central Utah)
1071 E. Windsor Dr.
Provo, UT 84604
Phone: (801)226-0881

SCORE Office (Southern Utah)
225 South 700 East
St. George, UT 84770
Phone: (801)652-7741

SCORE Office (Salt Lake)
169 E. 100 S.
Salt Lake City, UT 84111
Phone: (801)364-1331
Fax: (801)364-1310

Vermont

SCORE Office (Champlain Valley)
Winston Prouty Federal Bldg.
11 Lincoln St., Rm. 106
Essex Junction, VT 05452
Phone: (802)951-6762

SCORE Office (Montpelier)
87 State St., Rm. 205
PO Box 605
Montpelier, VT 05601
Phone: (802)828-4422
Fax: (802)828-4485

SCORE Office (Marble Valley)
256 N. Main St.
Rutland, VT 05701-2413
Phone: (802)773-9147

SCORE Office (Northeast Kingdom)
20 Main St.
PO Box 904
St. Johnsbury, VT 05819
Phone: (802)748-5101

Virgin Islands

SCORE Office (St. Croix)
United Plaza Shopping Center
PO Box 4010, Christiansted
St. Croix, VI 00822
Phone: (809)778-5380

SCORE Office (St. Thomas-St. John)
Federal Bldg., Rm. 21
Veterans Dr.
St. Thomas, VI 00801
Phone: (809)774-8530

Virginia

SCORE Office (Arlington)
2009 N. 14th St., Ste. 111
Arlington, VA 22201
Phone: (703)525-2400

SCORE Office (Blacksburg)
141 Jackson St.
Blacksburg, VA 24060
Phone: (540)552-4061

SCORE Office (Bristol)
20 Volunteer Pkwy.
Bristol, VA 24203
Phone: (540)989-4850

SCORE Office (Central Virginia)
1001 E. Market St., Ste. 101
Charlottesville, VA 22902
Phone: (804)295-6712
Fax: (804)295-7066

SCORE Office (Alleghany Satellite)
241 W. Main St.
Covington, VA 24426
Phone: (540)962-2178
Fax: (540)962-2179

SCORE Office (Central Fairfax)
3975 University Dr., Ste. 350
Fairfax, VA 22030
Phone: (703)591-2450

SCORE Office (Falls Church)
PO Box 491
Falls Church, VA 22040
Phone: (703)532-1050
Fax: (703)237-7904

SCORE Office (Glenns)
Glenns Campus
Box 287
Glenns, VA 23149
Phone: (804)693-9650

SCORE Office (Peninsula)
6 Manhattan Sq.
PO Box 7269
Hampton, VA 23666
Phone: (757)766-2000
Fax: (757)865-0339
E-mail: score100@seva.net

SCORE Office (Tri-Cities)
108 N. Main St.
Hopewell, VA 23860
Phone: (804)458-5536

SCORE Office (Lynchburg)
Federal Bldg.
1100 Main St.
Lynchburg, VA 24504-1714
Phone: (804)846-3235

SCORE Office (Greater Prince William)
8963 Center St
Manassas, VA 20110
Phone: (703)368-4813
Fax: (703)368-4733

SCORE Office (Martinsvile)
115 Broad St.
Martinsville, VA 24112-0709
Phone: (540)632-6401
Fax: (540)632-5059

SCORE Office (Hampton Roads)
Federal Bldg., Rm. 737
200 Grandby St.
Norfolk, VA 23510
Phone: (757)441-3733
Fax: (757)441-3733
E-mail: scorehr60@juno.com

SCORE Office (Norfolk)
Federal Bldg., Rm. 737
200 Granby St.
Norfolk, VA 23510
Phone: (757)441-3733
Fax: (757)441-3733

SCORE Office (Virginia Beach)
Chamber of Commerce
200 Grandby St., Rm 737
Norfolk, VA 23510
Phone: (804)441-3733

SCORE Office (Radford)
1126 Norwood St.
Radford, VA 24141
Phone: (540)639-2202

SCORE Office (Richmond)
Federal Bldg.
400 N. 8th St., Ste. 1150
PO Box 10126
Richmond, VA 23240-0126
Phone: (804)771-2400
Fax: (804)771-8018
E-mail: scorechapter12@yahoo.com
Website: http://www.cvco.org/score/

SCORE Office (Roanoke)
Federal Bldg., Rm. 716
250 Franklin Rd.
Roanoke, VA 24011
Phone: (540)857-2834
Fax: (540)857-2043
E-mail: scorerva@juno.com
Website: http://hometown.aol.com/scorerv/Index.html

SCORE Office (Fairfax)
8391 Old Courthouse Rd., Ste. 300
Vienna, VA 22182
Phone: (703)749-0400

SCORE Office (Greater Vienna)
513 Maple Ave. West
Vienna, VA 22180
Phone: (703)281-1333
Fax: (703)242-1482

SCORE Office (Shenandoah Valley)
301 W. Main St.
Waynesboro, VA 22980
Phone: (540)949-8203
Fax: (540)949-7740
E-mail: score427@intelos.net

SCORE Office (Williamsburg)
201 Penniman Rd.
Williamsburg, VA 23185
Phone: (757)229-6511
E-mail: wacc@williamsburgcc.com

SCORE Office (Northern Virginia)
1360 S. Pleasant Valley Rd.
Winchester, VA 22601
Phone: (540)662-4118

Washington

SCORE Office (Gray's Harbor)
506 Duffy St.
Aberdeen, WA 98520
Phone: (360)532-1924
Fax: (360)533-7945

SCORE Office (Bellingham)
101 E. Holly St.
Bellingham, WA 98225
Phone: (360)676-3307

SCORE Office (Everett)
2702 Hoyt Ave.
Everett, WA 98201-3556
Phone: (206)259-8000

SCORE Office (Gig Harbor)
3125 Judson St.
Gig Harbor, WA 98335
Phone: (206)851-6865

SCORE Office (Kennewick)
PO Box 6986
Kennewick, WA 99336
Phone: (509)736-0510

SCORE Office (Puyallup)
322 2nd St. SW
PO Box 1298
Puyallup, WA 98371
Phone: (206)845-6755
Fax: (206)848-6164

SCORE Office (Seattle)
1200 6th Ave., Ste. 1700
Seattle, WA 98101
Phone: (206)553-7320
Fax: (206)553-7044
E-mail: score55@aol.com
Website: http://www.scn.org/civic/score-online/index55.html

SCORE Office (Spokane)
801 W. Riverside Ave., No. 240
Spokane, WA 99201
Phone: (509)353-2820
Fax: (509)353-2600
E-mail: score@dmi.net
Website: http://www.dmi.net/score/

SCORE Office (Clover Park)
PO Box 1933
Tacoma, WA 98401-1933
Phone: (206)627-2175

SCORE Office (Tacoma)
1101 Pacific Ave.
Tacoma, WA 98402
Phone: (253)274-1288
Fax: (253)274-1289

SCORE Office (Fort Vancouver)
1701 Broadway, S-1
Vancouver, WA 98663
Phone: (360)699-1079

SCORE Office (Walla Walla)
500 Tausick Way
Walla Walla, WA 99362
Phone: (509)527-4681

SCORE Office (Mid-Columbia)
1113 S. 14th Ave.
Yakima, WA 98907
Phone: (509)574-4944
Fax: (509)574-2943
Website: http://www.ellensburg.com/~score/

West Virginia

SCORE Office (Charleston)
1116 Smith St.
Charleston, WV 25301
Phone: (304)347-5463
E-mail: score256@juno.com

SCORE Office (Virginia Street)
1116 Smith St., Ste. 302
Charleston, WV 25301
Phone: (304)347-5463

SCORE Office (Marion County)
PO Box 208
Fairmont, WV 26555-0208
Phone: (304)363-0486

SCORE Office (Upper Monongahela Valley)
1000 Technology Dr., Ste. 1111
Fairmont, WV 26555
Phone: (304)363-0486
E-mail: score537@hotmail.com

SCORE Office (Huntington)
1101 6th Ave., Ste. 220
Huntington, WV 25701-2309
Phone: (304)523-4092

SCORE Office (Wheeling)
1310 Market St.
Wheeling, WV 26003
Phone: (304)233-2575
Fax: (304)233-1320

Wisconsin

SCORE Office (Fox Cities)
227 S. Walnut St.
Appleton, WI 54913
Phone: (920)734-7101
Fax: (920)734-7161

SCORE Office (Beloit)
136 W. Grand Ave., Ste. 100
PO Box 717
Beloit, WI 53511
Phone: (608)365-8835
Fax: (608)365-9170

SCORE Office (Eau Claire)
Federal Bldg., Rm. B11
510 S. Barstow St.
Eau Claire, WI 54701
Phone: (715)834-1573
E-mail: score@ecol.net
Website: http://www.ecol.net/~score/

SCORE Office (Fond du Lac)
207 N. Main St.
Fond du Lac, WI 54935
Phone: (414)921-9500
Fax: (414)921-9559

SCORE Office (Green Bay)
835 Potts Ave.
Green Bay, WI 54304
Phone: (414)496-8930
Fax: (414)496-6009

SCORE Office (Janesville)
20 S. Main St., Ste. 11
PO Box 8008
Janesville, WI 53547
Phone: (608)757-3160
Fax: (608)757-3170

SCORE Office (La Crosse)
712 Main St.
La Crosse, WI 54602-0219
Phone: (608)784-4880

SCORE Office (Madison)
505 S. Rosa Rd.
Madison, WI 53719
Phone: (608)441-2820

SCORE Office (Manitowoc)
1515 Memorial Dr.
PO Box 903
Manitowoc, WI 54221-0903
Phone: (414)684-5575
Fax: (414)684-1915

SCORE Office (Milwaukee)
310 W. Wisconsin Ave., Ste. 425
Milwaukee, WI 53203
Phone: (414)297-3942
Fax: (414)297-1377

SCORE Office (Central Wisconsin)
1224 Lindbergh Ave.
Stevens Point, WI 54481
Phone: (715)344-7729

SCORE Office (Superior)
Superior Business Center Inc.
1423 N. 8th St.
Superior, WI 54880
Phone: (715)394-7388
Fax: (715)393-7414

SCORE Office (Waukesha)
223 Wisconsin Ave.
Waukesha, WI 53186-4926
Phone: (414)542-4249

SCORE Office (Wausau)
300 3rd St., Ste. 200
Wausau, WI 54402-6190
Phone: (715)845-6231

SCORE Office (Wisconsin Rapids)
2240 Kingston Rd.
Wisconsin Rapids, WI 54494
Phone: (715)423-1830

Wyoming

SCORE Office (Casper)
Federal Bldg., No. 2215
100 East B St.
Casper, WY 82602
Phone: (307)261-6529
Fax: (307)261-6530

VENTURE CAPITAL & FINANCING COMPANIES

This section contains a listing of financing and loan companies in the United States and Canada. These listings are arranged alphabetically by country, then by state or province, then by city, then by organization name.

CANADA

Alberta

Launchworks Inc.
1902J 11th St., S.E.
Calgary, AB, Canada T2G 3G2
Phone: (403)269-1119
Fax: (403)269-1141
Website: http://www.launchworks.com
Investment Types: Start-up. Industry Preferences: Diversified. Geographic Preferences: Canada.

Native Venture Capital Company, Inc.
21 Artist View Point, Box 7
Site 25, RR 12
Calgary, AB, Canada T3E 6W3
Phone: (903)208-5380
Milt Pahl, President
Investment Types: Seed, start-up, first stage, second stage, and leveraged buyout. Industry Preferences: Diversified. Geographic Preferences: Western Canada.

Miralta Capital Inc.
4445 Calgary Trail South
888 Terrace Plaza Alberta
Edmonton, AB, Canada T6H 5R7
Phone: (780)438-3535
Fax: (780)438-3129
Michael Welsh
Preferred Investment Size: $1,000,000 minimum. Investment Types: First and second stage, and leveraged buyout. Industry Preferences: Diversified communications, computer related, electronics, consumer products, industrial products and equipment. Geographic Preferences: Canada.

Vencap Equities Alberta Ltd.
10180-101st St., Ste. 1980
Edmonton, AB, Canada T5J 3S4
Phone: (403)420-1171
Fax: (403)429-2541
Preferred Investment Size: $1,000,000 minimum. Investment Types: Start-up, first and second stage, control-block purchases, leveraged buyout, and mezzanine. Industry Preferences: Diversified. Geographic Preferences: Northwest, Rocky Mountain region, and Western Canada.

British Columbia

Discovery Capital
5th Fl., 1199 West Hastings
Vancouver, BC, Canada V6E 3T5
Phone: (604)683-3000
Fax: (604)662-3457
E-mail: info@discoverycapital.com
Website: http://www.discoverycapital.com
Investment Types: Early stage and start-up. Industry Preferences:

Internet related. Geographic Preferences: Canada.

Greenstone Venture Partners
1177 West Hastings St.
Ste. 400
Vancouver, BC, Canada V6E 2K3
Phone: (604)717-1977
Fax: (604)717-1976
Website: http://www.greenstonevc.com
Investment Types: Diversified. Industry Preferences: Diversified. Geographic Preferences: Canada.

Growthworks Capital
2600-1055 West Georgia St.
Box 11170 Royal Centre
Vancouver, BC, Canada V6E 3R5
Phone: (604)895-7259
Fax: (604)669-7605
Website: http://www.wofund.com
Mike Philips
Preferred Investment Size: $330,000 to $3,300,000. Investment Types: Seed, start-up, first and second stage, balanced, joint ventures, mezzanine, private placement, research and development, and management buyout. Industry Preferences: Diversified. Geographic Preferences: British Columbia, Canada.

MDS Discovery Venture Management, Inc.
555 W. Eighth Ave., Ste. 305
Vancouver, BC, Canada V5Z 1C6
Phone: (604)872-8464
Fax: (604)872-2977
E-mail: info@mds-ventures.com
David Scott, President
Investment Types: Seed, research and development, start-up, first and second stages. Industry Preferences: Biotechnology and communications. Geographic Preferences: Western Canada and Northwestern U.S.

Ventures West Management Inc.
1285 W. Pender St., Ste. 280
Vancouver, BC, Canada V6E 4B1
Phone: (604)688-9495
Fax: (604)687-2145
Website: http://www.ventureswest.com
Investment Types: Seed, research and development, start-up, first and second stages. Industry Preferences: Diversified technology. Geographic Preferences: Northeast and Western U.S., Canada.

Nova Scotia

ACF Equity Atlantic Inc.
Purdy's Wharf Tower II
Ste. 2106
Halifax, NS, Canada B3J 3R7
Phone: (902)421-1965
Fax: (902)421-1808
David Wilson
Investment Types: Seed, start-up, first and second stage, balanced, mezzanine, and leveraged buyout. Industry Preferences: Diversified. Geographic Preferences: Canada.

Montgomerie, Huck & Co.
146 Bluenose Dr.
PO Box 538
Lunenburg, NS, Canada B0J 2C0
Phone: (902)634-7125
Fax: (902)634-7130
Christopher Huck
Preferred Investment Size: $300,000 to $500,000. Investment Types: First and second stage, leveraged buyout, mezzanine, and special situation. Industry Preferences: Diversified communications, computer related, and industrial machinery. Geographic Preferences: Canada.

Ontario

IPS Industrial Promotion Services Ltd.
60 Columbia Way, Ste. 720
Markham, ON, Canada L3R 0C9
Phone: (905)475-9400
Fax: (905)475-5003
Azim Lalani
Preferred Investment Size: $500,000 minimum. Investment Types: Control-block purchases, leveraged buyout, second stage, and special situation. Industry Preferences: Diversified. Geographic Preferences: U.S. and Canada.

Betwin Investments Inc.
Box 23110
Sault Ste. Marie, ON, Canada P6A 6W6
Phone: (705)253-0744
Fax: (705)253-0744
D.B. Stinson
Preferred Investment Size: $500,000 to $1,000,000. Investment Types: Second stage. Industry Preferences: Diversified. Geographic Preferences: U.S. and Canada.

Bailey & Company, Inc.
594 Spadina Ave.
Toronto, ON, Canada M5S 2H4
Phone: (416)921-6930
Fax: (416)925-4670
Preferred Investment Size: $500,000 to $1,000,000. Investment Types: Research and development, first stage, and special situations. Industry Preferences: Diversified technology. Geographic Preferences: No preference.

BCE Capital
200 Bay St.
South Tower, Ste. 3120
Toronto, ON, Canada M5J 2J2
Phone: (416)815-0078
Fax: (416)941-1073
Website: http://www.bcecapital.com
Preferred Investment Size: $350,000 to $2,000,000. Investment Types: Seed, start-up, early stage, expansion, and research and development. Industry Preferences: Communications, Internet related, electronics, and computer software and services. Geographic Preferences: Ontario and Western Canada.

Castlehill Ventures
55 University Ave., Ste. 500
Toronto, ON, Canada M5J 2H7
Phone: (416)862-8574
Fax: (416)862-8875
Investment Types: Start-up. Industry Preferences: Telecommunications and computer related. Geographic Preferences: Ontario, Canada.

CCFL Mezzanine Partners of Canada
70 University Ave.
Ste. 1450
Toronto, ON, Canada M5J 2M4
Phone: (416)977-1450
Fax: (416)977-6764
E-mail: info@ccfl.com
Website: http://www.ccfl.com
Paul Benson
Preferred Investment Size: $10,000,000. Investment Types:

Generalist PE. Industry Preferences: Diversified. Geographic Preferences: U.S. and Canada.

Celtic House International
100 Simcoe St., Ste. 100
Toronto, ON, Canada M5H 3G2
Phone: (416)542-2436
Fax: (416)542-2435
Website: http://www.celtic-house.com
Investment Types: Early stage. Industry Preferences: Computer software and services, electronics, Internet related, communications, and computer hardware. Geographic Preferences: U.S. and Canada.

Clairvest Group Inc.
22 St. Clair Ave. East
Ste. 1700
Toronto, ON, Canada M4T 2S3
Phone: (416)925-9270
Fax: (416)925-5753
Jeff Parr
Preferred Investment Size: $5,000,000 minimum. Investment Types: Balanced, control-block purchases, later stage, leveraged buyout, and special situation. Industry Preferences: Diversified. Geographic Preferences: U.S. and Canada.

Crosbie & Co., Inc.
One First Canadian Place
9th Fl.
PO Box 116
Toronto, ON, Canada M5X 1A4
Phone: (416)362-7726
Fax: (416)362-3447
E-mail: info@crosbieco.com
Website: http://www.crosbieco.com
Investment Types: Acquisition, distressed debt, expansion, generalist PE, later stage, leveraged and management buyouts, mezzanine, private placement, recaps, special situations, and turnarounds. Industry Preferences: Diversified. Geographic Preferences: Ontario, Canada.

Drug Royalty Corp.
Eight King St. East
Ste. 202
Toronto, ON, Canada M5C 1B5
Phone: (416)863-1865
Fax: (416)863-5161
Harry K. Loveys
Preferred Investment Size: $4,000,000 to $5,000,000. Investment Types: Research and development and special situation. Industry Preferences: Biotechnology and medical/health related. Geographic Preferences: No preference.

Grieve, Horner, Brown & Asculai
8 King St. E, Ste. 1704
Toronto, ON, Canada M5C 1B5
Phone: (416)362-7668
Fax: (416)362-7660
Preferred Investment Size: $300,000 to $500,000. Investment Types: Start-up, first and second stages. Industry Preferences: Diversified. Geographic Preferences: Entire U.S. and Canada.

Jefferson Partners
77 King St. West
Ste. 4010
PO Box 136
Toronto, ON, Canada M5K 1H1
Phone: (416)367-1533
Fax: (416)367-5827
Website: http://www.jefferson.com
Preferred Investment Size: $3,000,000 to $10,000,000. Investment Types: Seed and expansion. Industry Preferences: Communications and media, software, and Internet related. Geographic Preferences: Northeastern U.S. and Canada.

J.L. Albright Venture Partners
Canada Trust Tower, 161 Bay St.
Ste. 4440
PO Box 215
Toronto, ON, Canada M5J 2S1
Phone: (416)367-2440
Fax: (416)367-4604
Website: http://www.jlaventures.com
Jon Prosser
Investment Types: First and second stage. Industry Preferences: Internet related, communications, and computer related. Geographic Preferences: Canada.

McLean Watson Capital Inc.
One First Canadian Place
Ste. 1410
PO Box 129
Toronto, ON, Canada M5X 1A4
Phone: (416)363-2000
Fax: (416)363-2010
Website: http://www.mcleanwatson.com
Matt H. Lawton
Investment Types: First and second stage. Industry Preferences: Diversified communications, computer related, laser related, and fiber optics. Geographic Preferences: U.S. and Canada.

Middlefield Capital Fund
One First Canadian Place
85th Fl.
PO Box 192
Toronto, ON, Canada M5X 1A6
Phone: (416)362-0714
Fax: (416)362-7925
Website: http://www.middlefield.com
David Roode
Preferred Investment Size: $3,000,000 minimum. Investment Types: Second stage, control-block purchases, industry rollups, leveraged buyout, and mezzanine. Industry Preferences: Diversified. Geographic Preferences: U.S. and Canada.

Mosaic Venture Partners
24 Duncan St.
Ste. 300
Toronto, ON, Canada M5V 3M6
Phone: (416)597-8889
Fax: (416)597-2345
Investment Types: Early stage. Industry Preferences: Internet related. Geographic Preferences: U.S. and Canada.

Onex Corp.
161 Bay St.
PO Box 700
Toronto, ON, Canada M5J 2S1
Phone: (416)362-7711
Fax: (416)362-5765
Anthony Munk
Preferred Investment Size: $10,000,000 minimum. Investment Types:
Control-block purchases, leveraged buyout, and special situations. Industry Preferences: Diversified. Geographic Preferences: U.S. and Canada.

Penfund Partners Inc.
145 King St. West
Ste. 1920
Toronto, ON, Canada M5H 1J8

Phone: (416)865-0300
Fax: (416)364-6912
Website: http://www.penfund.com
David Collins
Preferred Investment Size: $667,000 to $4,670,000. Investment Types: Generalist PE, leveraged and management buyouts, and mezzanine. Industry Preferences: Diversified. Geographic Preferences: Canada.

Primaxis Technology Ventures Inc.
1 Richmond St. West, 8th Fl.
Toronto, ON, Canada M5H 3W4
Phone: (416)313-5210
Fax: (416)313-5218
Website: http://www.primaxis.com
Investment Types: Seed and early stage. Industry Preferences: Telecommunications, electronics, and manufacturing. Geographic Preferences: Canada.

Priveq Capital Funds
240 Duncan Mill Rd., Ste. 602
Toronto, ON, Canada M3B 3P1
Phone: (416)447-3330
Fax: (416)447-3331
E-mail: priveq@sympatico.ca
Preferred Investment Size: $1,000,000 minimum. Investment Types: Industry rollups, leveraged buyout, mezzanine, recaps, second stage, and special situation. Industry Preferences: Diversified. Geographic Preferences: Mid Atlantic, Midwest, Northeast, Northwest, and Southeastern U.S.; and Canada.

Roynat Ventures
40 King St. West, 26th Fl.
Toronto, ON, Canada M5H 1H1
Phone: (416)933-2667
Fax: (416)933-2783
Website: http://www.roynatcapital.com
Bob Roy
Investment Types: Early stage and expansion. Industry Preferences: Diversified. Geographic Preferences: Canada.

Tera Capital Corp.
366 Adelaide St. East, Ste. 337
Toronto, ON, Canada M5A 3X9
Phone: (416)368-1024
Fax: (416)368-1427
Investment Types: Balanced. Industry Preferences: Computer related and biotechnology. Geographic Preferences: U.S. and Canada.

Working Ventures Canadian Fund Inc.
250 Bloor St. East, Ste. 1600
Toronto, ON, Canada M4W 1E6
Phone: (416)934-7718
Fax: (416)929-0901
Website: http://www.workingventures.ca
Preferred Investment Size: $334,000 minimum. Investment Types: No preference. Industry Preferences: Diversified. Geographic Preferences: Ontario and Western Canada.

Quebec

Altamira Capital Corp.
202 University
Niveau de Maisoneuve, Bur. 201
Montreal, QC, Canada H3A 2A5
Phone: (514)499-1656
Fax: (514)499-9570
Preferred Investment Size: $1,000,000 minimum. Investment Types: First stage. Industry Preferences: Diversified. Geographic Preferences: No preference.

Federal Business Development Bank
Venture Capital Division
Five Place Ville Marie, Ste. 600
Montreal, QC, Canada H3B 5E7
Phone: (514)283-1896
Fax: (514)283-5455
Preferred Investment Size: $1,000,000. Investment Types: Seed, start-up, first and second stage, mezzanine, research and development, and leveraged buyout. Industry Preferences: Biotechnology; Internet related; computer software, hardware, and services. Geographic Preferences: Canada.

Hydro-Quebec Capitech Inc.
75 Boul, Rene Levesque Quest
Montreal, QC, Canada H2Z 1A4
Phone: (514)289-4783
Fax: (514)289-5420
Website: http://www.hqcapitech.com
Investment Types: Seed, start-up, early, first and second stage, balanced, expansion, and mezzanine. Industry Preferences: Diversified. Geographic Preferences: U.S. and Canada.

Investissement Desjardins
2 complexe Desjardins
C.P. 760
Montreal, QC, Canada H5B 1B8
Phone: (514)281-7131
Fax: (514)281-7808
Website: http://www.desjardins.com/id
Preferred Investment Size: $5,000,000 minimum. Investment Types: Start-up, first and second stage, control-block purchases, mezzanine, and leveraged buyout. Industry Preferences: Diversified. Geographic Preferences: Quebec, Canada.

Marleau Lemire Inc.
One Place Ville-Marie, Ste. 3601
Montreal, QC, Canada H3B 3P2
Phone: (514)877-3800
Fax: (514)875-6415
Jean Francois Perrault
Preferred Investment Size: $3,000,000 minimum. Investment Types: Second stage, mezzanine, leveraged buyout, and special situation. Industry Preferences: Diversified. Geographic Preferences: Canada.

Speirs Consultants Inc.
365 Stanstead
Montreal, QC, Canada H3R 1X5
Phone: (514)342-3858
Fax: (514)342-1977
Derek Speirs
Preferred Investment Size: $1,000,000 minimum. Investment Types: Start-up, first and second stage, control-block purchases, industry rollups, leveraged buyout, mezzanine, research and development, and special situation. Industry Preferences: Diversified. Geographic Preferences: Canada.

Tecnocap Inc.
4028 Marlowe
Montreal, QC, Canada H4A 3M2
Phone: (514)483-6009
Fax: (514)483-6045
Website: http://www.technocap.com

Preferred Investment Size: $1,000,000 minimum. Investment Types: Early stage and expansion. Industry Preferences: Diversified. Geographic Preferences: Northeast and Southwest U.S., and Central Canada.

Telsoft Ventures
1000, Rue de la Gauchetiere
Quest, 25eme Etage
Montreal, QC, Canada H3B 4W5
Phone: (514)397-8450
Fax: (514)397-8451
Investment Types: First and second stage, and mezzanine. Industry Preferences: Computer related. Geographic Preferences: West Coast, and Western Canada.

Saskatchewan

Saskatchewan Government Growth Fund
1801 Hamilton St., Ste. 1210
Canada Trust Tower
Regina, SK, Canada S4P 4B4
Phone: (306)787-2994
Fax: (306)787-2086
Rob M. Duguid, Vice President, Investing
Investment Types: Start-up, first stage, second stage, and mezzanine. Industry Preferences: Diversified. Geographic Preferences: Western Canada.

UNITED STATES

Alabama

FHL Capital Corp.
600 20th Street North
Suite 350
Birmingham, AL 35203
Phone: (205)328-3098
Fax: (205)323-0001
Kevin Keck, Vice President
Preferred Investment Size: Between $500,000 and $1,000,000. Investment Types: Mezzanine, leveraged buyout, and special situations. Geographic Preferences: Southeast.

Harbert Management Corp.
One Riverchase Pkwy. South
Birmingham, AL 35244
Phone: (205)987-5500
Fax: (205)987-5707
Website: http://www.harbert.net
Charles Miller, Vice President
Preferred Investment Size: $5,000,000 to $25,000,000. Investment Types: Leveraged buyout, special situations and industry roll ups. Industry Preferences: Oil and gas not considered. Geographic Preferences: Entire U.S.

Jefferson Capital Fund
PO Box 13129
Birmingham, AL 35213
Phone: (205)324-7709
Preferred Investment Size: From $1,000,000. Investment Types: Leveraged buyout, special situations and control block purchases. Industry Preferences: Telephone communications; consumer leisure and recreational products; consumer and industrial, medical and catalog specialty distribution; industrial products and equipment; medical/health related; publishing and education related. Geographic Preferences: Northeast, Southeast, and Middle Atlantic.

Private Capital Corp.
100 Brookwood Pl., 4th Fl.
Birmingham, AL 35209
Phone: (205)879-2722
Fax: (205)879-5121
William Acker, Vice President
Preferred Investment Size: $1,000,000 to $5,000,000. Investment Types: Start-up, first stage, second stage, mezzanine, leveraged buyout, and special situations. Industry Preferences: Communications; computer related; industrial, and medical product distribution; electronic components and instrumentation; energy/natural resources; medical/health related; education; and finance and insurance. Geographic Preferences: Southeast.

21st Century Health Ventures
One Health South Pkwy.
Birmingham, AL 35243
Phone: (256)268-6250
Fax: (256)970-8928
W. Barry McRae
Preferred Investment Size: $5,000,000. Investment Types: First stage, second stage, and leveraged buyout. Industry Preferences: Medical/Health related. Geographic Preferences: Entire U.S.

FJC Growth Capital Corp.
200 W. Side Sq., Ste. 340
Huntsville, AL 35801
Phone: (256)922-2918
Fax: (256)922-2909
William B. Noojin, President
Preferred Investment Size: $300,000 and $500,000. Investment Types: Mezzanine and second stage. Industry Preferences: Communications, electronics, hotels, and resort. Geographic Preferences: Southeast.

Hickory Venture Capital Corp.
301 Washington St. NW
Suite 301
Huntsville, AL 35801
Phone: (256)539-1931
Fax: (256)539-5130
E-mail: hvcc@hvcc.com
Website: http://www.hvcc.com
J. Thomas Noojin, President
Preferred Investment Size: $1,000,000 - $7,000,000. Investment Types: First stage, late stage, and leverage buyout. Industry Preferences: Communications, computer and Internet-related, energy, consumer, and biotechnology. Geographic Preferences: Southeast, Midwest, and Texas.

Southeastern Technology Fund
7910 South Memorial Pkwy., Ste. F
Huntsville, AL 35802
Phone: (256)883-8711
Fax: (256)883-8558
Preferred Investment Size: $500,000 to $5,000,000. Investment Types: Early, first and second stage, and expansion. Industry Preferences: Internet related, computer related, and communications. Geographic Preferences: Southeast.

Cordova Ventures
4121 Carmichael Rd., Ste. 301
Montgomery, AL 36106
Phone: (334)271-6011
Fax: (334)260-0120

Website: http://
www.cordovaventures.com
Teo F. Dagi
Investment Types: Start-up, early, second and late stage, and expansion. Industry Preferences: Diversified. Geographic Preferences: Southeast.

Small Business Clinic of Alabama/
AG Bartholomew & Associates
PO Box 231074
Montgomery, AL 36123-1074
Phone: (334)284-3640
Preferred Investment Size: From $2,000,000. Investment Types: Start-up, first stage, second stage, leveraged buyout, and special situations. Industry Preferences: Communications, computer related, consumer, distribution, industrial products and equipment, medical/ health related, education, finance and insurance, real estate, specialty consulting, and transportation. Geographic Preferences: Southeast.

Arizona

Miller Capital Corp.
4909 E. McDowell Rd.
Phoenix, AZ 85008
Phone: (602)225-0504
Fax: (602)225-9024
Website: http://
www.themillergroup.com
Rudy R. Miller, Chairman and President
Preferred Investment Size: $1,000,000 to $20,000,000. Investment Types: First stage, second stage, and recapitalizations. Industry Preferences: Communications, computer-related, electronics, financial and business services, and consumer-related. Geographic Preferences: Entire U.S.

The Columbine Venture Funds
9449 North 90th St., Ste. 200
Scottsdale, AZ 85258
Phone: (602)661-9222
Fax: (602)661-6262
Preferred Investment Size: $300,000 - $800,000. Investment Types: Seed, research and development, start-up, and first stage. Industry Preferences: Diversified technology. Geographic Preferences: Southwest, Rocky Mountains, and West Coast.

Koch Ventures
17767 N. Perimeter Dr., Ste. 101
Scottsdale, AZ 85255
Phone: (480)419-3600
Fax: (480)419-3606
Website: http://
www.kochventures.com
Preferred Investment Size: $2,000,000 to $10,000,000. Investment Types: Early stage and expansion. Industry Preferences: Electronics, Internet and computer related, and communications. Geographic Preferences: U.S.

McKee & Co.
7702 E. Doubletree Ranch Rd.
Suite 230
Scottsdale, AZ 85258
Phone: (480)368-0333
Fax: (480)607-7446
Mark Jazwin, Corporate Finance
Preferred Investment Size: From $1,000,000. Investment Types: Second stage, mezzanine, and leveraged buyout. Industry Preferences: Communications, computer related, consumer, distribution, electronic components and instrumentation, energy/natural resources, biosensors, industrial products and equipment, medical and health related, finance, and transportation. Geographic Preferences: Entire U.S.

Merita Capital Ltd.
7350 E. Stetson Dr., Ste. 108-A
Scottsdale, AZ 85251
Phone: (480)947-8700
Fax: (480)947-8766
Investment Types: First and second stage, mezzanine, and special situation. Industry Preferences: Diversified. Geographic Preferences: Western U.S.

Valley Ventures / Arizona Growth Partners L.P.
6720 N. Scottsdale Rd., Ste. 208
Scottsdale, AZ 85253
Phone: (480)661-6600
Fax: (480)661-6262
Investment Types: Second stage, mezzanine, and leveraged buyout. Industry Preferences: Diversified. Geographic Preferences: Southwest and Rocky Mountains.

Estreetcapital.com
660 South Mill Ave., Ste. 315
Tempe, AZ 85281
Phone: (480)968-8400
Fax: (480)968-8480
Website: http://
www.estreetcapital.com
Industry Preferences: Internet related. Geographic Preferences: Entire U.S.

Coronado Venture Fund
PO Box 65420
Tucson, AZ 85728-5420
Phone: (520)577-3764
Fax: (520)299-8491
Preferred Investment Size: $100,000 $500,000. Investment Types: Seed, start-up, first and second stage. Industry Preferences: Communications, computer related, electronic components and instrumentation, genetic engineering, industrial products and equipment, medical and health related, retail, and robotics. Geographic Preferences: No preference.

Arkansas

Arkansas Capital Corp.
225 South Pulaski St.
Little Rock, AR 72201
Phone: (501)374-9247
Fax: (501)374-9425
Website: http://www.arcapital.com
Private firm investing own capital. Interested in financing expansion.

California

Sundance Venture Partners, L.P.
100 Clocktower Place, Ste. 130
Carmel, CA 93923
Phone: (831)625-6500
Fax: (831)625-6590
Preferred Investment Size: $800,000 minimum. Investment Types: First and second stage, mezzanine, leveraged buyout, and special situations. Industry Preferences: No preference. Geographic Preferences: Southwest and West Coast.

Westar Capital (Costa Mesa)
949 South Coast Dr., Ste. 650

Costa Mesa, CA 92626
Phone: (714)481-5160
Fax: (714)481-5166
E-mail: mailbox@westarcapital.com
Website: http://www.westarcapital.com
Alan Sellers, General Partner
Preferred Investment Size: $5,000,000 to $10,000,000. Investment Types: Leveraged buyouts, special situations, control block purchases, and industry roll ups. Industry Preferences: Diversified. Geographic Preferences: Northwest, Southwest, Rocky Mountains, and West Coast.

Alpine Technology Ventures
20300 Stevens Creek Boulevard, Ste. 495
Cupertino, CA 95014
Phone: (408)725-1810
Fax: (408)725-1207
Website: http://www.alpineventures.com
Investment Types: Seed, start-up, research and development, first and second stage. Industry Preferences: Internet-related, communications, computer-related, distribution, electronic components and instrumentation, industrial products and equipment.

Bay Partners
10600 N. De Anza Blvd.
Cupertino, CA 95014-2031
Phone: (408)725-2444
Fax: (408)446-4502
Website: http://www.baypartners.com
Bob Williams, General Partner
Preferred Investment Size: $5,000,000 to $15,000,000. Investment Types: Seed and start-up. Industry Preferences: Internet, communications, and computer related. Geographic Preferences: National.

Novus Ventures
20111 Stevens Creek Blvd., Ste. 130
Cupertino, CA 95014
Phone: (408)252-3900
Fax: (408)252-1713
Website: http://www.novusventures.com
Dan Tompkins, Managing General Partner
Preferred Investment Size: $500,000 to $1 Million. Investment Types: Start-up, first and early stage, expansion, and buyouts. Industry Preferences: Information technology. Geographic Preferences: Western U.S.

Triune Capital
19925 Stevens Creek Blvd., Ste. 200
Cupertino, CA 95014
Phone: (310)284-6800
Fax: (310)284-3290
Preferred Investment Size: $1,000,000 minimum. Investment Types: First, second, and late stage; mezzanine; control block; and special situations. Industry Preferences: Diversified technology. Geographic Preferences: West Coast.

Acorn Ventures
268 Bush St., Ste. 2829
Daly City, CA 94014
Phone: (650)994-7801
Fax: (650)994-3305
Website: http://www.acornventures.com
Preferred Investment Size: $250,000 minimum. Investment Types: Seed, first and second stage, and leveraged buyout. Industry Preferences: Diversified. Geographic Preferences: No preference.

Digital Media Campus
2221 Park Place
El Segundo, CA 90245
Phone: (310)426-8000
Fax: (310)426-8010
E-mail: info@thecampus.com
Website: http://www.digitalmediacampus.com
Investment Types: Seed and early stage. Industry Preferences: Entertainment and leisure, sports, and media. Geographic Preferences: U.S.

BankAmerica Ventures / BA Venture Partners
950 Tower Ln., Ste. 700
Foster City, CA 94404
Phone: (650)378-6000
Fax: (650)378-6040
Website: http://www.baventurepartners.com
George Rossman
Preferred Investment Size: $1,000,000 to $12,000,000. Investment Types: Start-up, first and second stage. Industry Preferences: Computer and Internet related, communications, medical product distribution, electronic components and instrumentation, genetic engineering, and medical/health related. Geographic Preferences: National.

Starting Point Partners
666 Portofino Lane
Foster City, CA 94404
Phone: (650)722-1035
Website: http://www.startingpointpartners.com
Preferred Investment Size: $100,000 to $1,000,000. Investment Types: Early stage. Industry Preferences: Diversified. Geographic Preferences: U.S.

Opportunity Capital Partners
2201 Walnut Ave., Ste. 210
Fremont, CA 94538
Phone: (510)795-7000
Fax: (510)494-5439
Website: http://www.ocpcapital.com
Peter Thompson, Managing Partner
Preferred Investment Size: $100,000 to $1,500,000. Investment Types: Second stage, late stage, mezzanine, leveraged buyout, and industry roll ups. Industry Preferences: Internet related, consumer related, communications, computer, and medical/health related. Geographic Preferences: Entire U.S.

Imperial Ventures Inc.
9920 S. La Cienega Boulevar, 14th Fl.
Inglewood, CA 90301
Phone: (310)417-5409
Fax: (310)338-6115
Preferred Investment Size: $500,000 to $2,000,000. Investment Types: Second stage and leveraged buyout. Industry Preferences: Diversified. Geographic Preferences: No preference.

Ventana Global (Irvine)
18881 Von Karman Ave., Ste. 1150
Irvine, CA 92612
Phone: (949)476-2204

Fax: (949)752-0223
Website: http://
www.ventanaglobal.com
Scott A. Burri, Managing Director
Preferred Investment Size: $1,000,000 minimum. Investment Types: First and second stage, seed, special situation, and mezzanine. Industry Preferences: Diversified technology. Geographic Preferences: Southwest.

Integrated Consortium Inc.
50 Ridgecrest Rd.
Kentfield, CA 94904
Phone: (415)925-0386
Fax: (415)461-2726
Preferred Investment Size: $1,000,000. Investment Types: First and second stage, control-block purchases, industry rollups, leveraged buyouts, and mezzanine. Industry Preferences: Entertainment and leisure, retail, computer stores, franchises, food/beverage, consumer products and services. Geographic Preferences: West Coast.

Enterprise Partners
979 Ivanhoe Ave., Ste. 550
La Jolla, CA 92037
Phone: (858)454-8833
Fax: (858)454-2489
Website: http://www.epvc.com
Preferred Investment Size: $1,000,000 to $20,000,000. Investment Types: Early stage. Industry Preferences: Diversified. Geographic Preferences: Entire U.S.

Domain Associates
28202 Cabot Rd., Ste. 200
Laguna Niguel, CA 92677
Phone: (949)347-2446
Fax: (949)347-9720
Website: http://www.domainvc.com
Preferred Investment Size: $1,000,000 to $20,000,000. Investment Types: Seed, first stage and second stage, expansion, private placement, research and development, and balanced. Industry Preferences: Electronics, computer, biotechnology, and medical/health related. Geographic Preferences: Entire U.S.

Cascade Communications Ventures
60 E. Sir Francis Drake Blvd., Ste. 300
Larkspur, CA 94939
Phone: (415)925-6500
Fax: (415)925-6501
Dennis Brush
Preferred Investment Size: $1,000,000 to $5,000,000. Investment Types: Leveraged buyout and special situations. Industry Preferences: Communications and franchises. Geographic Preferences: Entire U.S and Canada.

Allegis Capital
One First St., Ste. Two
Los Altos, CA 94022
Phone: (650)917-5900
Fax: (650)917-5901
Website: http://
www.allegiscapital.com
Robert R. Ackerman, Jr.
Investment Types: Seed and early stage. Industry Preferences: Diversified. Geographic Preferences: West Coast and District of Columbia.

Aspen Ventures
1000 Fremont Ave., Ste. 200
Los Altos, CA 94024
Phone: (650)917-5670
Fax: (650)917-5677
Website: http://
www.aspenventures.com
Alexander Cilento, Partner
Preferred Investment Size: $500,000 to $3,500,000. Investment Policies: Equity. Investment Types: Seed, and early stage. Industry Preferences: Communications, computer related, medical/health, biotechnology, and electronics. Geographic Preferences: West Coast.

AVI Capital L.P.
1 First St., Ste. 2
Los Altos, CA 94022
Phone: (650)949-9862
Fax: (650)949-8510
Website: http://www.avicapital.com
Brian J. Grossi, General Partner
Preferred Investment Size: $1,000,000 to $2 million. Investment Policies: Equity Only. Investment Types: Seed, start-up, first and second stage, and special situations. Industry Preferences: Computer hardware, software, and services; Internet related; communications; electronics; energy; and medical/health. Geographic Preferences: West Coast.

Bastion Capital Corp.
1999 Avenue of the Stars, Ste. 2960
Los Angeles, CA 90067
Phone: (310)788-5700
Fax: (310)277-7582
E-mail: ga@bastioncapital.com
Website: http://
www.bastioncapital.com
James Villanueva, Vice President
Preferred Investment Size: $10,000,000 minimum. Investment Types: Leveraged buyout, special situations and control block purchases. Industry Preferences: Diversified. Geographic Preferences: Entire U.S. and Canada.

Davis Group
PO Box 69953
Los Angeles, CA 90069-0953
Phone: (310)659-6327
Fax: (310)659-6337
Roger W. Davis, Chairman
Preferred Investment Size: $100,000 minimum. Investment Types: Early stages, leveraged buyouts, and special situations. Industry Preferences: Diversified. Geographic Preferences: International.

Developers Equity Corp.
1880 Century Park East, Ste. 211
Los Angeles, CA 90067
Phone: (213)277-0300
Investment Types: Seed, start-up, and leverage buyout. Industry Preferences: Industrial products and machinery, transportation, and real estate.

Far East Capital Corp.
350 S. Grand Ave., Ste. 4100
Los Angeles, CA 90071
Phone: (213)687-1361
Fax: (213)617-7939
E-mail:
free@fareastnationalbank.com
Preferred Investment Size: $100,000 to $300,000. Investment Types: First stage, second stage, mezzanine, and special situations. Industry Preferences: Communications, computer and Internet related, electronic components and instrumentation, genetic engineering,

medical/health related. Geographic Preferences: West Coast.

Kline Hawkes & Co.
11726 San Vicente Blvd., Ste. 300
Los Angeles, CA 90049
Phone: (310)442-4700
Fax: (310)442-4707
Website: http://www.klinehawkes.com
Robert M. Freiland, Partner
Preferred Investment Size: $4,000,000 to $10,000,000. Investment Types: Second and later stage, private placement, and expansion. Industry Preferences: Diversified technology. Geographic Preferences: West Coast.

Lawrence Financial Group
701 Teakwood
PO Box 491773
Los Angeles, CA 90049
Phone: (310)471-4060
Fax: (310)472-3155
Larry Hurwitz
Preferred Investment Size: $500,000 to $1,000,000. Investment Types: Second stage. Industry Preferences: Diversified. Geographic Preferences: West Coast.

Riordan Lewis & Haden
300 S. Grand Ave., 29th Fl.
Los Angeles, CA 90071
Phone: (213)229-8500
Fax: (213)229-8597
Jonathan Leach
Preferred Investment Size: $2,000,000 minimum. Investment Types: First and second stage, start-up, leveraged buyouts, and special situations. Industry Preferences: Diversified. Geographic Preferences: West Coast.

Union Venture Corp.
445 S. Figueroa St., 9th Fl.
Los Angeles, CA 90071
Phone: (213)236-4092
Fax: (213)236-6329
Preferred Investment Size: $300,000 to $500,000. Investment Types: Second stage, mezzanine, leveraged buyout, and special situations. Industry Preferences: Communications, computer related. Geographic Preferences: National.

Wedbush Capital Partners
1000 Wilshire Blvd.
Los Angeles, CA 90017
Phone: (213)688-4545
Fax: (213)688-6642
Website: http://www.wedbush.com
Preferred Investment Size: $500,000 minimum. Investment Types: Second stage, mezzanine, and leveraged buyouts. Industry Preferences: Diversified computer technology, consumer related, distribution, and healthcare. Geographic Preferences: West Coast.

Advent International Corp.
2180 Sand Hill Rd., Ste. 420
Menlo Park, CA 94025
Phone: (650)233-7500
Fax: (650)233-7515
Website: http://www.adventinternational.com
Preferred Investment Size: $1,000,000 minimum. Investment Types: Start-up, first and second stage, mezzanine, leveraged buyout, special situations, recaps, and acquisitions. Industry Preferences: Diversified. Geographic Preferences: Entire U.S. and Canada.

Altos Ventures
2882 Sand Hill Rd., Ste. 100
Menlo Park, CA 94025
Phone: (650)234-9771
Fax: (650)233-9821
Website: http://www.altosvc.com
Investment Types: Start-up, seed, first and second stage. Industry Preferences: Internet and computer related, consumer related, medical/health. Geographic Preferences: West Coast.

Applied Technology
1010 El Camino Real, Ste. 300
Menlo Park, CA 94025
Phone: (415)326-8622
Fax: (415)326-8163
Ellie McCormack, Partner
Investment Types: Seed, start-up, first and second stage, research and development. Industry Preferences: Diversified. Geographic Preferences: Entire U.S.

APV Technology Partners
535 Middlefield, Ste. 150
Menlo Park, CA 94025
Phone: (650)327-7871
Fax: (650)327-7631
Website: http://www.apvtp.com
Preferred Investment Size: $2,000,000 to $10,000,000. Investment Types: Early stage. Industry Preferences: Diversified. Geographic Preferences: Entire U.S.

August Capital Management
2480 Sand Hill Rd., Ste. 101
Menlo Park, CA 94025
Phone: (650)234-9900
Fax: (650)234-9910
Website: http://www.augustcap.com
Andrew S. Rappaport, General Partner
Preferred Investment Size: $1,000,000 to $5,000,000. Investment Types: Start-up, first stage and special situations. Industry Preferences: Communications, computer related, distribution, and electronic components and instrumentation. Geographic Preferences: Northwest, Southwest, Rocky Mountains and West Coast.

Baccharis Capital Inc.
2420 Sand Hill Rd., Ste. 100
Menlo Park, CA 94025
Phone: (650)324-6844
Fax: (650)854-3025
Michelle von Roedelbronn
Preferred Investment Size: $1,000,000 minimum. Investment Types: Start-up, first stage and second stage, mezzanine and special situations. Industry Preferences: Diversified. Geographic Preferences: West Coast.

Benchmark Capital
2480 Sand Hill Rd., Ste. 200
Menlo Park, CA 94025
Phone: (650)854-8180
Fax: (650)854-8183
E-mail: info@benchmark.com
Website: http://www.benchmark.com
Investment Types: Seed, research and development, start-up, first and second stage, and special situations. Industry Preferences: Communications, computer related, and electronic components and instrumentation. Geographic

Preferences: Southwest and West Coast.

Bessemer Venture Partners (Menlo Park)
535 Middlefield Rd., Ste. 245
Menlo Park, CA 94025
Phone: (650)853-7000
Fax: (650)853-7001
Website: http://www.bvp.com
Investment Types: Seed, research and development, start-up, first stages, leveraged buyout, special situations, and expansion. Industry Preferences: Communications, computer related, consumer products, distribution, and electronics. Geographic Preferences: Entire U.S.

The Cambria Group
1600 El Camino Real Rd., Ste. 155
Menlo Park, CA 94025
Phone: (650)329-8600
Fax: (650)329-8601
Website: http://www.cambriagroup.com
Paul L. Davies, III, Managing Principal
Preferred Investment Size: $3,000,000. Investment Types: Second stage, mezzanine, leveraged buyout, special situations, and control block purchases. Industry Preferences: Diversified. Geographic Preferences: Entire U.S.

Canaan Partners
2884 Sand Hill Rd., Ste. 115
Menlo Park, CA 94025
Phone: (650)854-8092
Fax: (650)854-8127
Website: http://www.canaan.com
Preferred Investment Size: $5,00,000 to $20,000,000. Investment Types: First and second stage, and expansion. Industry Preferences: Diversified. Geographic Preferences: Entire U.S.

Capstone Ventures
3000 Sand Hill Rd., Bldg. One, Ste. 290
Menlo Park, CA 94025
Phone: (650)854-2523
Fax: (650)854-9010
Website: http://www.capstonevc.com
Eugene J. Fischer
Preferred Investment Size: $500,000 to $3,000,000. Investment Types: First and second stage, early, and expansion. Industry Preferences: Diversified high technology. Geographic Preferences: Diversified.

Comdisco Venture Group (Silicon Valley)
3000 Sand Hill Rd., Bldg. 1, Ste. 155
Menlo Park, CA 94025
Phone: (650)854-9484
Fax: (650)854-4026
Preferred Investment Size: $300,000 to $20,000,000. Investment Types: Seed, start-up, first and second stage. Industry Preferences: Diversified. Geographic Preferences: No preference.

Commtech International
535 Middlefield Rd., Ste. 200
Menlo Park, CA 94025
Phone: (650)328-0190
Fax: (650)328-6442
Preferred Investment Size: $300,000 to $500,000. Investment Types: Seed and start-up. Industry Preferences: Diversified. Geographic Preferences: West Coast.

Compass Technology Partners
1550 El Camino Real, Ste. 275
Menlo Park, CA 94025-4111
Phone: (650)322-7595
Fax: (650)322-0588
Website: http://www.compasstechpartners.com
Leon Dulberger, General Partner
Investment Types: Mezzanine, leveraged buyout, and special situations. Industry Preferences: Diversified high technology. Geographic Preferences: National.

Convergence Partners
3000 Sand Hill Rd., Ste. 235
Menlo Park, CA 94025
Phone: (650)854-3010
Fax: (650)854-3015
Website: http://www.convergencepartners.com
Preferred Investment Size: $2,000,000 to $10,000,000. Investment Types: Seed, start-up, research and development, early and late stage, and mezzanine. Industry Preferences: Communications, computer related, electronic components and instrumentation, and interactive media. Geographic Preferences: West Coast.

The Dakota Group
PO Box 1025
Menlo Park, CA 94025
Phone: (650)853-0600
Fax: (650)851-4899
E-mail: info@dakota.com
Stephen A. Meyer, General Partner
Preferred Investment Size: $300,000 to $500,000. Investment Types: Early and later stages, and special situations. Industry Preferences: Diversified computer and communications technology, education, and publishing. Geographic Preferences: National.

Delphi Ventures
3000 Sand Hill Rd.
Bldg. One, Ste. 135
Menlo Park, CA 94025
Phone: (650)854-9650
Fax: (650)854-2961
Website: http://www.delphiventures.com
Preferred Investment Size: $500,000 minimum. Investment Types: Seed, start-up, first and second stage. Industry Preferences: Medical/health related, Internet related, biotechnology, computer software and services. Geographic Preferences: Entire U.S.

El Dorado Ventures
2884 Sand Hill Rd., Ste. 121
Menlo Park, CA 94025
Phone: (650)854-1200
Fax: (650)854-1202
Website: http://www.eldoradoventures.com
Preferred Investment Size: $500,000 to $5,000,000. Investment Types: Seed, start-up, first and second stage. Industry Preferences: Communications, computer and Internet related, electronics, and industrial products and equipment. Geographic Preferences: West Coast.

Glynn Ventures
3000 Sand Hill Rd., Bldg. 4, Ste. 235
Menlo Park, CA 94025
Phone: (650)854-2215

John W. Glynn, Jr., General Partner
Preferred Investment Size: $300,000 to $500,000. Investment Types: Start-up, first and second stage, leveraged buyout, and mezzanine. Industry Preferences: Diversified computer and communications technology, and medical/health. Geographic Preferences: East and West Coast.

Indosuez Ventures
2180 Sand Hill Rd., Ste. 450
Menlo Park, CA 94025
Phone: (650)854-0587
Fax: (650)323-5561
Website: http://www.indosuezventures.com
Preferred Investment Size: $250,000 to $1,500,000. Investment Types: Start-up, first and second stage, and mezzanine. Industry Preferences: Diversified. Geographic Preferences: West Coast.

Institutional Venture Partners
3000 Sand Hill Rd., Bldg. 2, Ste. 290
Menlo Park, CA 94025
Phone: (650)854-0132
Fax: (650)854-5762
Website: http://www.ivp.com
Preferred Investment Size: $500,000 minimum. Investment Types: Seed, start-up, first and second stage, and special situations. Industry Preferences: Diversified. Geographic Preferences: International.

Interwest Partners (Menlo Park)
3000 Sand Hill Rd., Bldg. 3, Ste. 255
Menlo Park, CA 94025-7112
Phone: (650)854-8585
Fax: (650)854-4706
Website: http://www.interwest.com
Preferred Investment Size: $2,000,000 to $25,000,000. Investment Types: Seed, research and development, start-up, first and second stage, expansion, and special situations. Industry Preferences: Diversified. Geographic Preferences: Entire U.S.

Kleiner Perkins Caufield & Byers (Menlo Park)
2750 Sand Hill Rd.
Menlo Park, CA 94025
Phone: (650)233-2750
Fax: (650)233-0300
Website: http://www.kpcb.com
Preferred Investment Size: $500,000. Investment Types: Seed, start-up, first and second stage. Industry Preferences: Diversified. Geographic Preferences: West Coast.

Magic Venture Capital LLC
1010 El Camino Real, Ste. 300
Menlo Park, CA 94025
Phone: (650)325-4149
Patrick Lynn
Preferred Investment Size: $100,000 to $1,000,000. Investment Types: Seed, start-up, first stage. Industry Preferences: Medical/health related. Geographic Preferences: West Coast.

Matrix Partners
2500 Sand Hill Rd., Ste. 113
Menlo Park, CA 94025
Phone: (650)854-3131
Fax: (650)854-3296
Website: http://www.matrixpartners.com
Andrew W. Verlahen, General Partner
Preferred Investment Size: $500,000 to $1,000,000. Investment Types: Start-up, early, first and second stage, and leveraged buyout. Industry Preferences: Communications, computer related, medical/health, and electronic components and instrumentation. Geographic Preferences: Entire U.S.

Mayfield Fund
2800 Sand Hill Rd.
Menlo Park, CA 94025
Phone: (650)854-5560
Fax: (650)854-5712
Website: http://www.mayfield.com
Preferred Investment Size: $250,000 minimum. Investment Types: Seed, start-up, first and second stage, and recapitalization. Industry Preferences: Diversified. Geographic Preferences: Northwest, Rocky Mountains, and West Coast.

McCown De Leeuw and Co. (Menlo Park)
3000 Sand Hill Rd., Bldg. 3, Ste. 290
Menlo Park, CA 94025-7111
Phone: (650)854-6000
Fax: (650)854-0853
Website: http://www.mdcpartners.com
Christopher Crosby, Principal
Preferred Investment Size: $40,000,000 minimum. Investment Types: Leveraged buyout and special situations. Industry Preferences: Diversified. Geographic Preferences: Entire U.S.

Menlo Ventures
3000 Sand Hill Rd., Bldg. 4, Ste. 100
Menlo Park, CA 94025
Phone: (650)854-8540
Fax: (650)854-7059
Website: http://www.menloventures.com
H. DuBose Montgomery, General Partner and Managing Director
Venture capital supplier. Provides start-up and expansion financing to companies with experienced management teams, distinctive product lines, and large growing markets. Primary interest is in technology-oriented, Internet, and computer related companies. Investments range from $5,000,000 to $30 million; also provides capital for research and development.

Merrill Pickard Anderson & Eyre
2480 Sand Hill Rd., Ste. 200
Menlo Park, CA 94025
Phone: (650)854-8600
Fax: (650)854-0345
Preferred Investment Size: $1,000,000 maximum. Investment Types: Seed, start-up, first and second stage. Industry Preferences: Diversified technology. Geographic Preferences: No preference.

New Enterprise Associates (Menlo Park)
2490 Sand Hill Rd.
Menlo Park, CA 94025
Phone: (650)854-9499
Fax: (650)854-9397
Website: http://www.nea.com
Ronald H. Kase, General Partner
Preferred Investment Size: $100,000 minimum. Investment Types: Seed, early, start-up, first and second stage, and mezzanine. Industry Preferences: Diversified technology. Geographic Preferences: No preference.

Onset Ventures
2400 Sand Hill Rd., Ste. 150

Menlo Park, CA 94025
Phone: (650)529-0700
Fax: (650)529-0777
Website: http://www.onset.com
Preferred Investment Size: $100,000 minimum. Investment Types: Early stage. Industry Preferences: Communications, computer related, medical and health related. Geographic Preferences: West Coast.

Paragon Venture Partners
3000 Sand Hill Rd., Bldg. 1, Ste. 275
Menlo Park, CA 94025
Phone: (650)854-8000
Fax: (650)854-7260
Preferred Investment Size: $500,000 to $1,500,000. Investment Types: Start-up, seed, first and second stage, special situation. Industry Preferences: Diversified. Geographic Preferences: No preference.

Pathfinder Venture Capital Funds (Menlo Park)
3000 Sand Hill Rd., Bldg. 3, Ste. 255
Menlo Park, CA 94025
Phone: (650)854-0650
Fax: (650)854-4706
Jack K. Ahrens, II, Investment Officer
Preferred Investment Size: $2,00,000 minimum. Investment Types: Seed, start-up, first and second stage, mezzanine, leveraged buyout, and special situations. Industry Preferences: Diversified technology. Geographic Preferences: Entire U.S. and Canada.

Rocket Ventures
3000 Sandhill Rd., Bldg. 1, Ste. 170
Menlo Park, CA 94025
Phone: (650)561-9100
Fax: (650)561-9183
Website: http://www.rocketventures.com
Preferred Investment Size: $100,000 to $5,000,000. Investment Types: Seed, start-up, and early stage. Industry Preferences: Communications, software, and Internet related. Geographic Preferences: West Coast.

Sequoia Capital
3000 Sand Hill Rd., Bldg. 4, Ste. 280
Menlo Park, CA 94025
Phone: (650)854-3927
Fax: (650)854-2977
E-mail: sequoia@sequioacap.com
Website: http://www.sequoiacap.com
Investment Types: Early, seed, start-up, first and second stage. Industry Preferences: Diversified technology. Geographic Preferences: Western U.S. and international.

Sierra Ventures
3000 Sand Hill Rd., Bldg. 4, Ste. 210
Menlo Park, CA 94025
Phone: (650)854-1000
Fax: (650)854-5593
Website: http://www.sierraventures.com
Preferred Investment Size: $100,000 minimum. Investment Types: Seed, start-up, first and second stage, recapitalization, and leveraged buyout. Industry Preferences: Diversified. Geographic Preferences: No preference.

Sigma Partners
2884 Sand Hill Rd., Ste. 121
Menlo Park, CA 94025-7022
Phone: (650)853-1700
Fax: (650)853-1717
E-mail: info@sigmapartners.com
Website: http://www.sigmapartners.com
Lawrence G. Finch, Partner
Investment Types: Seed, start-up, first and second stage, special situation, recap, and control block purchases. Industry Preferences: Diversified technology. Geographic Preferences: U.S.

Sprout Group (Menlo Park)
3000 Sand Hill Rd.
Bldg. 3, Ste. 170
Menlo Park, CA 94025
Phone: (650)234-2700
Fax: (650)234-2779
Website: http://www.sproutgroup.com
Investment Types: Seed, start-up, first and second stage, mezzanine, leveraged buyout, and special situations. Industry Preferences: Diversified technology. Geographic Preferences: U.S. and foreign countries.

TA Associates (Menlo Park)
70 Willow Rd., Ste. 100
Menlo Park, CA 94025
Phone: (650)328-1210
Fax: (650)326-4933
Website: http://www.ta.com
Michael C. Child, Managing Director
Preferred Investment Size: $20,000,000 to $60,000,000. Investment Types: Control-block purchases, leveraged buyout, and special situations. Industry Preferences: Diversified. Geographic Preferences: No preference.

Thompson Clive & Partners Ltd.
3000 Sand Hill Rd., Bldg. 1, Ste. 185
Menlo Park, CA 94025-7102
Phone: (650)854-0314
Fax: (650)854-0670
E-mail: mail@tcvc.com
Website: http://www.tcvc.com
Greg Ennis, Principal
Preferred Investment Size: $500,000 to $1,000,000. Investment Types: Early stage, management buyouts, and special situations. Industry Preferences: Diversified computer and communications technology, electronic instrumentation, genetic engineering, and medical/health. Geographic Preferences: Entire U.S.; International.

Trinity Ventures Ltd.
3000 Sand Hill Rd., Bldg. 1, Ste. 240
Menlo Park, CA 94025
Phone: (650)854-9500
Fax: (650)854-9501
Website: http://www.trinityventures.com
Lawrence K. Orr, General Partner
Preferred Investment Size: $5,000,000 to $20,000,000. Investment Types: Early stage. Industry Preferences: Communications, computer and Internet related, consumer products and services, and electronics. Geographic Preferences: Mid-Atlantic and Western U.S.

U.S. Venture Partners
2180 Sand Hill Rd., Ste. 300
Menlo Park, CA 94025
Phone: (650)854-9080
Fax: (650)854-3018
Website: http://www.usvp.com

William K. Bowes, Jr., Founding Partner
Preferred Investment Size: $500,000 minimum. Investment Types: Seed, start-up, first and second stage, and late stage. Industry Preferences: Communications, computer related, consumer products and services, distribution, electronics, and medical/health related. Geographic Preferences: Northwest and West Coast.

USVP-Schlein Marketing Fund
2180 Sand Hill Rd., Ste. 300
Menlo Park, CA 94025
Phone: (415)854-9080
Fax: (415)854-3018
Website: http://www.usvp.com
Venture capital fund. Prefers specialty retailing/consumer products companies.

Venrock Associates
2494 Sand Hill Rd., Ste. 200
Menlo Park, CA 94025
Phone: (650)561-9580
Fax: (650)561-9180
Website: http://www.venrock.com
Ted H. McCourtney, Managing General Partner
Preferred Investment Size: $500,000 minimum. Investment Types: Seed, research and development, start-up, first and second stage. Industry Preferences: Diversified. Geographic Preferences: No preference.

Brad Peery Capital Inc.
145 Chapel Pkwy.
Mill Valley, CA 94941
Phone: (415)389-0625
Fax: (415)389-1336
Brad Peery, Chairman
Preferred Investment Size: $100,000 to $300,000. Investment Types: Second stage financing. Industry Preferences: Communications and media. Geographic Preferences: Entire U.S.

Dot Edu Ventures
650 Castro St., Ste. 270
Mountain View, CA 94041
Phone: (650)575-5638
Fax: (650)325-5247
Website: http://www.doteduventures.com
Investment Types: Early stage and seed. Industry Preferences: Internet related. Geographic Preferences: Entire U.S.

Forrest, Binkley & Brown
840 Newport Ctr. Dr., Ste. 480
Newport Beach, CA 92660
Phone: (949)729-3222
Fax: (949)729-3226
Website: http://www.fbbvc.com
Jeff Brown, Partner
Investment Policies: $1,000,000 to $10,000,000. Investment Types: First stage, second stage, expansion, and balanced. Industry Preferences: Communications, computer and Internet related, consumer, electronic components and instrumentation, genetic engineering, industrial products and equipment, and medical/health related. Geographic Preferences: National.

Marwit Capital LLC
180 Newport Center Dr., Ste. 200
Newport Beach, CA 92660
Phone: (949)640-6234
Fax: (949)720-8077
Website: http://www.marwit.com
Thomas W. Windsor, Vice President
Preferred Investment Size: $250,000 minimum. Investment Types: Acquisition, control-block, leveraged buyout, and mezzanine. Industry Preferences: Software, transportation, distribution, and manufacturing. Geographic Preferences: Entire U.S.

Kaiser Permanente / National Venture Development
1800 Harrison St., 22nd Fl.
Oakland, CA 94612
Phone: (510)267-4010
Fax: (510)267-4036
Website: http://www.kpventures.com
Preferred Investment Size: $500,000 to $2,000,000. Investment Types: Balanced, first and second stage, expansion, joint ventures, and private placement. Industry Preferences: Diversified. Geographic Preferences: Entire U.S. and Canada.

Nu Capital Access Group, Ltd.
7677 Oakport St., Ste. 105
Oakland, CA 94621
Phone: (510)635-7345
Fax: (510)635-7068
Preferred Investment Size: $500,000 to $1,000,000. Investment Types: First and second stages, leveraged buyouts, industry rollups, and special situations. Industry Preferences: Diversified consumer products and services, food and industrial product distribution. Geographic Preferences: Western U.S.

Inman and Bowman
4 Orinda Way, Bldg. D, Ste. 150
Orinda, CA 94563
Phone: (510)253-1611
Fax: (510)253-9037
Preferred Investment Size: $1,000,000 minimum. Investment Types: Start-up, first and second stage, leveraged buyout, and special situations. Industry Preferences: Diversified technology. Geographic Preferences: West Coast.

Accel Partners (San Francisco)
428 University Ave.
Palo Alto, CA 94301
Phone: (650)614-4800
Fax: (650)614-4880
Website: http://www.accel.com
Preferred Investment Size: $1,000,000 minimum. Investment Types: Seed, start-up, and early stage. Industry Preferences: Communications, computer related, medical/health, biotechnology, and electronic components and instrumentation. Geographic Preferences: No preference.

Accenture Technology Ventures
1661 Page Mill Rd.
Palo Alto, CA 94304
Phone: (650)213-2500
Fax: (650)213-2222
Website: http://www.accenturetechventures.com
Investment Types: Start-up, early and later stage, balanced, expansion, and mezzanine. Industry Preferences: Internet and computer related, and communications. Geographic Preferences: Entire U.S.

Advanced Technology Ventures
485 Ramona St., Ste. 200
Palo Alto, CA 94301
Phone: (650)321-8601

Fax: (650)321-0934
Website: http://www.atvcapital.com
Steven Baloff, General Partner
Investment Types: Start-up, first stage, second stage, and balanced. Industry Preferences: Diversified. Geographic Preferences: National.

Anila Fund
400 Channing Ave.
Palo Alto, CA 94301
Phone: (650)833-5790
Fax: (650)833-0590
Website: http://www.anila.com
Investment Types: Early stage. Industry Preferences: Telecommunications and Internet related. Geographic Preferences: Entire U.S.

Asset Management Company Venture Capital
2275 E. Bayshore, Ste. 150
Palo Alto, CA 94303
Phone: (650)494-7400
Fax: (650)856-1826
E-mail: postmaster@assetman.com
Website: http://www.assetman.com
Preferred Investment Size: $750,000 minimum. Investment Types: Seed, start-up, and first stage. Industry Preferences: Diversified technology. Geographic Preferences: Northeast, West Coast.

BancBoston Capital / BancBoston Ventures
435 Tasso St., Ste. 250
Palo Alto, CA 94305
Phone: (650)470-4100
Fax: (650)853-1425
Website: http://www.bancbostoncapital.com
Preferred Investment Size: $1,000,000 to $10,000,000. Investment Types: Seed, early stage, acquisition, expansion, later stage, management buyouts, and recapitalizations. Industry Preferences: Diversified. Geographic Preferences: Entire U.S. and Eastern Canada.

Charter Ventures
525 University Ave., Ste. 1400
Palo Alto, CA 94301
Phone: (650)325-6953
Fax: (650)325-4762
Website: http://www.charterventures.com
Investment Types: Seed, start-up, first and second stage, mezzanine, leveraged buyout, and special situations. Industry Preferences: Diversified. Geographic Preferences: No preference.

Communications Ventures
505 Hamilton Avenue, Ste. 305
Palo Alto, CA 94301
Phone: (650)325-9600
Fax: (650)325-9608
Website: http://www.comven.com
Clifford Higgerson, General Partner
Preferred Investment Size: $500,000 to $25,000,000. Investment Types: Seed, start-up, early, first, and second stage. Industry Preferences: Communications, Internet related, electronics, and computer related. Geographic Preferences: No preference.

HMS Group
2468 Embarcadero Way
Palo Alto, CA 94303-3313
Phone: (650)856-9862
Fax: (650)856-9864
Industry Preferences: Communications, computer related, electronics, and industrial products. Geographic Preferences: No preference.

New Vista Capital
540 Cowper St., Ste. 200
Palo Alto, CA 94301
Phone: (650)329-9333
Fax: (650)328-9434
E-mail: fgreene@nvcap.com
Website: http://www.nvcap.com
Frank Greene
Investment Types: Seed, start-up, first stage, second stage. Industry Preferences: Communications, computer related, electronics, and consumer related. Geographic Preferences: Western U.S., Rocky Mountains.

Norwest Equity Partners (Palo Alto)
245 Lytton Ave., Ste. 250
Palo Alto, CA 94301-1426
Phone: (650)321-8000
Fax: (650)321-8010
Website: http://www.norwestvp.com
Charles B. Lennin, Partner
Preferred Investment Size: $1,000,000 to $25,000,000. Investment Types: Seed, early and later stage, and expansion. Industry Preferences: Diversified. Geographic Preferences: No preference.

Oak Investment Partners
525 University Ave., Ste. 1300
Palo Alto, CA 94301
Phone: (650)614-3700
Fax: (650)328-6345
Website: http://www.oakinv.com
Preferred Investment Size: $250,000 to $5,000,000. Investment Types: Seed, start-up, first stage, leveraged buyout, open market, control-block purchases, and special situations. Industry Preferences: communications, computer related, consumer restaurants and retailing, electronics, genetic engineering, and medical/health related. Geographic Preferences: No preference.

Patricof & Co. Ventures, Inc. (Palo Alto)
2100 Geng Rd., Ste. 150
Palo Alto, CA 94303
Phone: (650)494-9944
Fax: (650)494-6751
Website: http://www.patricof.com
Preferred Investment Size: $5,000,000 minimum. Investment Types: Seed, start-up, first and second stage, mezzanine, and leveraged buyout. Industry Preferences: Diversified. Geographic Preferences: No preference.

RWI Group
835 Page Mill Rd.
Palo Alto, CA 94304
Phone: (650)251-1800
Fax: (650)213-8660
Website: http://www.rwigroup.com
Preferred Investment Size: $500,000 to $4,000,000. Investment Types: Seed, start-up, first and second stage. Industry Preferences: Diversified. Geographic Preferences: West Coast.

Summit Partners (Palo Alto)
499 Hamilton Ave., Ste. 200
Palo Alto, CA 94301
Phone: (650)321-1166
Fax: (650)321-1188

Website: http://www.summitpartners.com
Christopher W. Sheeline
Preferred Investment Size: $1,500,000 minimum. Investment Types: First and second stage, mezzanine, leveraged buyout, special situations, and control block purchases. Industry Preferences: Diversified. Geographic Preferences: Entire U.S. and Canada.

Sutter Hill Ventures
755 Page Mill Rd., Ste. A-200
Palo Alto, CA 94304
Phone: (650)493-5600
Fax: (650)858-1854
E-mail: shv@shv.com
Preferred Investment Size: $100,000 minimum. Investment Types: Seed, start-up, first and second stage. Industry Preferences: Diversified. Geographic Preferences: Entire U.S.

Vanguard Venture Partners
525 University Ave., Ste. 600
Palo Alto, CA 94301
Phone: (650)321-2900
Fax: (650)321-2902
Website: http://www.vanguardventures.com
Donald F. Wood, Partner
Preferred Investment Size: $500,000 to $1,000,000. Investment Types: Early stages. Industry Preferences: Diversified computer and communications technology, genetic engineering, and electronics. Geographic Preferences: National.

Venture Growth Associates
2479 East Bayshore St., Ste. 710
Palo Alto, CA 94303
Phone: (650)855-9100
Fax: (650)855-9104
James R. Berdell, Managing Partner
Preferred Investment Size: $1,000,000 to $5,000,000. Investment Types: First and second stage, leveraged buyout, and mezzanine. Industry Preferences: Diversified technology, finance and consumer related. Geographic Preferences: West Coast.

Worldview Technology Partners
435 Tasso St., Ste. 120
Palo Alto, CA 94301
Phone: (650)322-3800
Fax: (650)322-3880
Website: http://www.worldview.com
Mike Orsak, General Partner
Investment Types: Seed, research and development, start-up, first stage, second stage, mezzanine. Industry Preferences: Diversified technology. Geographic Preferences: National.

Jafco America Ventures, Inc.
505 Hamilton Ste. 310
Palto Alto, CA 94301
Phone: (650)463-8800
Fax: (650)463-8801
Website: http://www.jafco.com
Andrew P. Goldfarb, Senior Managing Director
Preferred Investment Size: $500,000 minimum. Investment Types: First and second stage and mezzanine. Industry Preferences: Diversified technology. Geographic Preferences: No preference.

Draper, Fisher, Jurvetson / Draper Associates
400 Seaport Ct., Ste.250
Redwood City, CA 94063
Phone: (415)599-9000
Fax: (415)599-9726
Website: http://www.dfj.com
J.B. Fox
Preferred Investment Size: $1,000,000 to $5,000,000. Investment Types: Seed, start-up, and first stage. Industry Preferences: Communications, computer and Internet related, electronic components and instrumentation. Geographic Preferences: No preference.

Gabriel Venture Partners
350 Marine Pkwy., Ste. 200
Redwood Shores, CA 94065
Phone: (650)551-5000
Fax: (650)551-5001
Website: http://www.gabrielvp.com
Preferred Investment Size: $500,000 to $7,000,000. Investment Types: Seed, early and first stage. Industry Preferences: Internet and computer related, communications, and electronics. Geographic Preferences: West Coast and Mid Atlantic.

Hallador Venture Partners, L.L.C.
740 University Ave., Ste. 110
Sacramento, CA 95825-6710
Phone: (916)920-0191
Fax: (916)920-5188
E-mail: chris@hallador.com
Chris L. Branscum, Managing Director
Preferred Investment Size: $500,000 to $1,000,000. Investment Types: Early and later stages, and research and development. Industry Preferences: Diversified computer and communications technology, and electronic semiconductors. Geographic Preferences: Western U.S.

Emerald Venture Group
12396 World Trade Dr., Ste. 116
San Diego, CA 92128
Phone: (858)451-1001
Fax: (858)451-1003
Website: http://www.emeraldventure.com
Cherie Simoni
Preferred Investment Size: $100,000 to $50,000,000. Investment Types: Start-up, seed, first and second stage, leveraged buyout, mezzanine, and research and development. Industry Preferences: Diversified. Geographic Preferences: No preference.

Forward Ventures
9255 Towne Centre Dr.
San Diego, CA 92121
Phone: (858)677-6077
Fax: (858)452-8799
E-mail: info@forwardventure.com
Website: http://www.forwardventure.com
Standish M. Fleming, Partner
Preferred Investment Size: $500,000 to $10,000,000. Investment Types: Seed, research and development, start-up, first and second stage, mezzanine, and private placement. Industry Preferences: Biotechnology, and medical/health related. Geographic Preferences: Entire U.S.

Idanta Partners Ltd.
4660 La Jolla Village Dr., Ste. 850
San Diego, CA 92122
Phone: (619)452-9690
Fax: (619)452-2013
Website: http://www.idanta.com

Preferred Investment Size: $500,000 minimum. Investment Types: Seed, start-up, first and second stage. Industry Preferences: Diversified. Geographic Preferences: Entire U.S.

Kingsbury Associates
3655 Nobel Dr., Ste. 490
San Diego, CA 92122
Phone: (858)677-0600
Fax: (858)677-0800
Preferred Investment Size: $500,000 to $1,000,000. Investment Types: Start-up, first and second stage. Industry Preferences: Medical/health, biotechnology, computer and Internet related. Geographic Preferences: West Coast.

Kyocera International Inc.
Corporate Development
8611 Balboa Ave.
San Diego, CA 92123
Phone: (858)576-2600
Fax: (858)492-1456
Preferred Investment Size: $300,000 to $500,000. Investment Types: Second stage. Industry Preferences: Diversified. Geographic Preferences: Northeast, Northwest, West Coast.

Sorrento Associates, Inc.
4370 LaJolla Village Dr., Ste. 1040
San Diego, CA 92122
Phone: (619)452-3100
Fax: (619)452-7607
Website: http://www.sorrentoventures.com
Vincent J. Burgess, Vice President
Preferred Investment Size: $500,000 TO $7,000,000. Investment Policies: Equity only. Investment Types: Start-up, first and second stage, leveraged buyout, special situations, and control block purchases. Industry Preferences: Medicine, health, communications, electronics, special retail. Geographic Preferences: West Coast.

Western States Investment Group
9191 Towne Ctr. Dr., Ste. 310
San Diego, CA 92122
Phone: (619)678-0800
Fax: (619)678-0900
Investment Types: Seed, research and development, start-up, first stage, leveraged buyout. Industry Preferences: Computer related, consumer, electronic components and instrumentation, medical/health related. Geographic Preferences: Western U.S.

Aberdare Ventures
One Embarcadero Center, Ste. 4000
San Francisco, CA 94111
Phone: (415)392-7442
Fax: (415)392-4264
Website: http://www.aberdare.com
Preferred Investment Size: $500,000 to $7,000,000. Investment Types: Start-up, first and second stage. Industry Preferences: Diversified. Geographic Preferences: Entire U.S.

Acacia Venture Partners
101 California St., Ste. 3160
San Francisco, CA 94111
Phone: (415)433-4200
Fax: (415)433-4250
Website: http://www.acaciavp.com
Brian Roberts, Senior Associate
Preferred Investment Size: $2,000,000 to $10,000,000. Investment Types: Seed, start-up, first and second stage, mezzanine and leveraged buyout. Industry Preferences: Computer, and medical/health related. Geographic Preferences: Entire U.S.

Access Venture Partners
319 Laidley St.
San Francisco, CA 94131
Phone: (415)586-0132
Fax: (415)392-6310
Website: http://www.accessventurepartners.com
Robert W. Rees, II, Managing Director
Preferred Investment Size: $250,000 to $5 million. Investment Types: Seed, start-up, and first stage. Industry Preferences: Internet related, biotechnology, communications, and computer software and services.Geographic Preferences: Southwest and Rocky Mountain region.

Alta Partners
One Embarcadero Center, Ste. 4050
San Francisco, CA 94111
Phone: (415)362-4022
Fax: (415)362-6178
E-mail: alta@altapartners.com
Website: http://www.altapartners.com
Jean Deleage, Partner
Preferred Investment Size: $1,000,000 to $10,000,000. Investment Types: Seed, start-up, first and second stage, and mezzanine. Industry Preferences: Communications, computer related, distribution, electronic components and instrumentation, genetic engineering, industrial products and equipment, medical/health related. Real estate, oil and natural gas exploration, and environmental not considered. Geographic Preferences: West Coast.

Bangert Dawes Reade Davis & Thom
220 Montgomery St., Ste. 424
San Francisco, CA 94104
Phone: (415)954-9900
Fax: (415)954-9901
E-mail: bdrdt@pacbell.net
Lambert Thom, Vice President
Preferred Investment Size: $500,000 to $5,000,000. Investment Types: Second stage, mezzanine, leveraged buyout and special situations. Industry Preferences: Diversified. Geographic Preferences: No preference.

Berkeley International Capital Corp.
650 California St., Ste. 2800
San Francisco, CA 94108-2609
Phone: (415)249-0450
Fax: (415)392-3929
Website: http://www.berkeleyvc.com
Arthur I. Trueger, Chairman
Preferred Investment Size: $3,000,000 to $15,000,000. Investment Types: Second stage, mezzanine, leveraged buyout and special situations. Industry Preferences: Communications, computer related, distribution, electronic components and instrumentation, industrial products and equipment, and medical/health related. Geographic Preferences: Entire U.S.

Blueprint Ventures LLC
456 Montgomery St., 22nd Fl.
San Francisco, CA 94104
Phone: (415)901-4000
Fax: (415)901-4035

Website: http://www.blueprintventures.com
Preferred Investment Size: $3,000,000 to $10,000,000. Investment Types: Early stage. Industry Preferences: Communications and Internet related. Geographic Preferences: Entire U.S.

Blumberg Capital Ventures
580 Howard St., Ste. 401
San Francisco, CA 94105
Phone: (415)905-5007
Fax: (415)357-5027
Website: http://www.blumberg-capital.com
Mark Pretorius, Principal
Preferred Investment Size: $500,000 to $5,000,000. Investment Types: Seed, start-up, first and early stage, and expansion. Industry Preferences: Diversified. Geographic Preferences: Entire U.S.

Burr, Egan, Deleage, and Co. (San Francisco)
1 Embarcadero Center, Ste. 4050
San Francisco, CA 94111
Phone: (415)362-4022
Fax: (415)362-6178
Private venture capital supplier. Invests start-up, expansion, and acquisitions capital nationwide. Principal concerns are strength of the management team; large, rapidly expanding markets; and unique products for services. Past investments have been made in the fields of biotechnology and pharmaceuticals, cable TV, chemicals/plastics, communications, software, computer systems and peripherals, distributorships, radio common carriers, electronics and electrical components, environmental control, health services, medical devices and instrumentation, and radio and cellular telecommunications. Primarily interested in medical, electronics, and media industries.

Burrill & Company
120 Montgomery St., Ste. 1370
San Francisco, CA 94104
Phone: (415)743-3160
Fax: (415)743-3161
Website: http://www.burrillandco.com
David Collier, Managing Director
Preferred Investment Size: $500,000 to $5,000,000. Investment Types: Start-up, first and second stage, and mezzanine. Industry Preferences: Diversified. Geographic Preferences: No preference.

CMEA Ventures
235 Montgomery St., Ste. 920
San Francisco, CA 94401
Phone: (415)352-1520
Fax: (415)352-1524
Website: http://www.cmeaventures.com
Thomas R. Baruch, General Partner
Preferred Investment Size: $100,000 to $1,000,000. Investment Types: Seed, start-up, first and second stage. Industry Preferences: Diversified high technology. Geographic Preferences: No preference.

Crocker Capital
1 Post St., Ste. 2500
San Francisco, CA 94101
Phone: (415)956-5250
Fax: (415)959-5710
Investment Types: Second stage, leveraged buyout, and start-up. Industry Preferences: Communications, medical/health related, consumer, retail, food/beverage, education, industrial materials, and manufacturing. Geographic Preferences: West Coast.

Dominion Ventures, Inc.
44 Montgomery St., Ste. 4200
San Francisco, CA 94104
Phone: (415)362-4890
Fax: (415)394-9245
Preferred Investment Size: $1,000,000 to $10,000,000. Investment Types: First and second stage, and mezzanine. Industry Preferences: Diversified. Geographic Preferences: No preference.

Dorset Capital
Pier 1
Bay 2
San Francisco, CA 94111
Phone: (415)398-7101
Fax: (415)398-7141
Website: http://www.dorsetcapital.com
Preferred Investment Size: $1,000,000 to $10,000,000. Investment Types: Second and later stage, expansion, generalist PE, leveraged and management buyouts. Industry Preferences: Consumer retail, food and beverage, and business services. Geographic Preferences: Entire U.S.

Gatx Capital
Four Embarcadero Center, Ste. 2200
San Francisco, CA 94904
Phone: (415)955-3200
Fax: (415)955-3449
Preferred Investment Size: $500,000 to $5,000,000. Investment Types: Early and later stages, and leveraged buyouts. Industry Preferences: Diversified technologies, forestry, and agriculture. Geographic Preferences: National and Canada.

IMinds
135 Main St., Ste. 1350
San Francisco, CA 94105
Phone: (415)547-0000
Fax: (415)227-0300
Website: http://www.iminds.com
Preferred Investment Size: $500,000 to $2,000,000. Investment Types: Seed, start-up, and early stage. Industry Preferences: Internet and computer related. Geographic Preferences: West Coast.

LF International Inc.
360 Post St., Ste. 705
San Francisco, CA 94108
Phone: (415)399-0110
Fax: (415)399-9222
Website: http://www.lfvc.com
Preferred Investment Size: $500,000 to $1,000,000. Investment Types: Control-block purchases, first and second stage, expansion, industry rollups, management buyouts, and special situations. Industry Preferences: Consumer related, retail. Geographic Preferences: Entire U.S.

Newbury Ventures
535 Pacific Ave., 2nd Fl.
San Francisco, CA 94133
Phone: (415)296-7408
Fax: (415)296-7416

Website: http://
www.newburyven.com
Preferred Investment Size: $500,000 to $1,000,000. Investment Types: Early and later stages, and leveraged buyout. Industry Preferences: Diversified high technology. Geographic Preferences: Eastern and Western U.S. and Canada.

Quest Ventures (San Francisco)
333 Bush St., Ste. 1750
San Francisco, CA 94104
Phone: (415)782-1414
Fax: (415)782-1415
E-mail: ruby@crownadvisors.com
Lucien Ruby, General Partner
Preferred Investment Size: $100,000 maximum. Investment Types: Seed and special situations. Industry Preferences: Diversified. Geographic Preferences: No preference.

Robertson-Stephens Co.
555 California St., Ste. 2600
San Francisco, CA 94104
Phone: (415)781-9700
Fax: (415)781-2556
Website: http://
www.omegaadventures.com
Private venture capital firm. Considers investments in any attractive merging-growth area, including product and service companies. Key preferences include health care, communications and technology, biotechnology, software, and information services. Maximum investment is $5 million.

Rosewood Capital, L.P.
One Maritime Plaza, Ste. 1330
San Francisco, CA 94111-3503
Phone: (415)362-5526
Fax: (415)362-1192
Website: http://
www.rosewoodvc.com
Kevin Reilly, Vice President
Preferred Investment Size: $1,000,000 to $3,000,000. Investment Policies: Equity. Investment Types: Later stages, leveraged buyout, and special situations. Industry Preferences: Consumer and Internet related. Geographic Preferences: National.

Ticonderoga Capital Inc.
555 California St., No. 4950
San Francisco, CA 94104
Phone: (415)296-7900
Fax: (415)296-8956
Graham K Crooke, Partner
Preferred Investment Size: $5,000,000 maximum. Investment Types: Second stage, mezzanine, leveraged buyout, and consolidation strategies. Industry Preferences: Diversified. Geographic Preferences: Entire U.S. and Canada.

21st Century Internet Venture Partners
Two South Park
2nd Floor
San Francisco, CA 94107
Phone: (415)512-1221
Fax: (415)512-2650
Website: http://www.21vc.com
Shawn Myers
Preferred Investment Size: $5,000,000 maximum. Investment Types: Seed, research and development, start-up, first and second stage, mezzanine, leveraged buyout, and special situations. Industry Preferences: Diversified. Geographic Preferences: Entire U.S. and Canada.

VK Ventures
600 California St., Ste.1700
San Francisco, CA 94111
Phone: (415)391-5600
Fax: (415)397-2744
David D. Horwich, Senior Vice President
Preferred Investment Size: $100,000 to $250,000. Investment Types: Second stage, mezzanine, and leveraged buyout. Industry Preferences: Diversified. Geographic Preferences: West Coast.

Walden Group of Venture Capital Funds
750 Battery St., Seventh Floor
San Francisco, CA 94111
Phone: (415)391-7225
Fax: (415)391-7262
Arthur Berliner
Preferred Investment Size: $1,000,000 to $7,000,000. Investment Types: Seed, start-up, first and second stage. Industry Preferences: Diversified technology. Geographic Preferences: Entire U.S.

Acer Technology Ventures
2641 Orchard Pkwy.
San Jose, CA 95134
Phone: (408)433-4945
Fax: (408)433-5230
James C. Lu, Managing Director
Preferred Investment Size: $500,000 to $5,000,000. Investment Types: Seed, start-up, first and second stage. Industry Preferences: Diversified. Geographic Preferences: Entire U.S. and Canada.

Authosis
226 Airport Pkwy., Ste. 405
San Jose, CA 95110
Phone: (650)814-3603
Website: http://www.authosis.com
Investment Types: Seed, first and second stage. Industry Preferences: Computer software. Geographic Preferences: Entire U.S.

Western Technology Investment
2010 N. First St., Ste. 310
San Jose, CA 95131
Phone: (408)436-8577
Fax: (408)436-8625
E-mail: mktg@westerntech.com
Investment Types: Seed, research and development, start-up, first stage, second stage, mezzanine, leveraged buyout, and special situations. Industry Preferences: Diversified. Geographic Preferences: National.

Drysdale Enterprises
177 Bovet Rd., Ste. 600
San Mateo, CA 94402
Phone: (650)341-6336
Fax: (650)341-1329
E-mail: drysdale@aol.com
George M. Drysdale, President
Preferred Investment Size: $500,000 to $5,000,000. Investment Types: First and second stage, mezzanine, leveraged buyout, and special situations. Industry Preferences: Diversified. Geographic Preferences: West Coast.

Greylock
2929 Campus Dr., Ste. 400
San Mateo, CA 94401
Phone: (650)493-5525
Fax: (650)493-5575

Website: http://www.greylock.com
Preferred Investment Size: $250,000 minimum. Investment Types: Seed, start-up, early and first stage, and expansion. Industry Preferences: Diversified. Geographic Preferences: Entire U.S.

Technology Funding
2000 Alameda de las Pulgas, Ste. 250
San Mateo, CA 94403
Phone: (415)345-2200
Fax: (415)345-1797
Peter F. Bernardoni, Partner
Small business investment corporation. Provides primarily late first-stage, early second-stage, and mezzanine equity financing. Also offers secured debt with equity participation to venture capital backed companies. Investments range from $250,000 to $500,000.

2M Invest Inc.
1875 S. Grant St.
Suite 750
San Mateo, CA 94402
Phone: (650)655-3765
Fax: (650)372-9107
E-mail: 2minfo@2minvest.com
Website: http://www.2minvest.com
Preferred Investment Size: $500,000 to $5 million. Investment Types: Start-up. Industry Preferences: Communications, computer related, electronic components and instrumentation. Non-information technology companies not considered. Geographic Preferences: West Coast.

Phoenix Growth Capital Corp.
2401 Kerner Blvd.
San Rafael, CA 94901
Phone: (415)485-4569
Fax: (415)485-4663
E-mail: nnelson@phxa.com
Preferred Investment Size: $250,000 to $1,000,000. Investment Types: First and second stage, and mezzanine. Industry Preferences: Communications, computer related, consumer retailing, distribution, electronics, genetic engineering, medical/health related, education, publishing, and transportation. Geographic Preferences: Entire U.S.

NextGen Partners LLC
1705 East Valley Rd.
Santa Barbara, CA 93108
Phone: (805)969-8540
Fax: (805)969-8542
Website: http://www.nextgenpartners.com
Preferred Investment Size: $100,000 to $3,000,000. Investment Types: Seed, start-up, first and second stage, expansion, and research and development. Industry Preferences: Diversified. Geographic Preferences: Entire U.S. and Canada.

Denali Venture Capital
1925 Woodland Ave.
Santa Clara, CA 95050
Phone: (408)690-4838
Fax: (408)247-6979
E-mail: wael@denaliventurecapital.com
Website: http://www.denaliventurecapital.com
Preferred Investment Size: $100,000 to $5,000,000. Investment Types: Early stage. Industry Preferences: Medical/health related. Geographic Preferences: West Coast.

Dotcom Ventures LP
3945 Freedom Circle, Ste. 740
Santa Clara, CA 95045
Phone: (408)919-9855
Fax: (408)919-9857
Website: http://www.dotcomventuresatl.com
Investment Types: Early, first stage, and seed. Industry Preferences: Telecommunications and Internet related. Geographic Preferences: Entire U.S.

Silicon Valley Bank
3003 Tasman
Santa Clara, CA 95054
Phone: (408)654-7400
Fax: (408)727-8728
Investment Types: Start-up, first stage, second stage, mezzanine. Industry Preferences: Diversified. Geographic Preferences: National.

Al Shugart International
920 41st Ave.
Santa Cruz, CA 95062
Phone: (831)479-7852
Fax: (831)479-7852
Website: http://www.alshugart.com
Investment Types: Seed, start-up, and early stage. Industry Preferences: Diversified. Geographic Preferences: U.S.

Leonard Mautner Associates
1434 Sixth St.
Santa Monica, CA 90401
Phone: (213)393-9788
Fax: (310)459-9918
Leonard Mautner
Preferred Investment Size: $100,000 to $300,000. Investment Types: Seed, start-up, first stage, and special situation. Industry Preferences: Diversified. Geographic Preferences: West Coast.

Palomar Ventures
100 Wilshire Blvd., Ste. 450
Santa Monica, CA 90401
Phone: (310)260-6050
Fax: (310)656-4150
Website: http://www.palomarventures.com
Preferred Investment Size: $250,000 to $15,000,000. Investment Types: Seed, start-up, first and early stage, and expansion. Industry Preferences: Communications, Internet related, computer software and services. Geographic Preferences: West Coast and Southwest.

Medicus Venture Partners
12930 Saratoga Ave., Ste. D8
Saratoga, CA 95070
Phone: (408)447-8600
Fax: (408)447-8599
Website: http://www.medicusvc.com
Fred Dotzler, General Partner
Preferred Investment Size: $100,000 to $5,000,000. Investment Types: Early stages. Industry Preferences: Genetic engineering and healthcare industry. Geographic Preferences: Western U.S.

Redleaf Venture Management
14395 Saratoga Ave., Ste. 130
Saratoga, CA 95070
Phone: (408)868-0800
Fax: (408)868-0810
E-mail: nancy@redleaf.com
Website: http://www.redleaf.com
Robert von Goeben, Director

Preferred Investment Size: $1,000,000 to $4,000,000. Investment Policies: Equity. Investment Types: Early and late stage. Industry Preferences: Internet business related. Geographic Preferences: Northwest and Silicon Valley.

Artemis Ventures
207 Second St., Ste. E
3rd Fl.
Sausalito, CA 94965
Phone: (415)289-2500
Fax: (415)289-1789
Website: http://www.artemisventures.com
Investment Types: Seed, first and second stage. Industry Preferences: Internet and computer related, electronics, and various products. Geographic Preferences: Northern U.S. and West Coast.

Deucalion Venture Partners
19501 Brooklime
Sonoma, CA 95476
Phone: (707)938-4974
Fax: (707)938-8921
Preferred Investment Size: $500,000 minimum. Investment Types: Seed, start-up, first and second stage. Industry Preferences: Computer software, biotechnology, education, energy conservation, industrial machinery, transportation, financial services, and publishing. Geographic Preferences: West Coast.

Windward Ventures
PO Box 7688
Thousand Oaks, CA 91359-7688
Phone: (805)497-3332
Fax: (805)497-9331
Investment Types: Seed, start-up, first stage, second stage. Industry Preferences: Communications, computer related, electronic components and instrumentation, genetic engineering, industrial products and equipment, medical and health related. Geographic Preferences: West Coast.

National Investment Management, Inc.
2601 Airport Dr., Ste.210
Torrance, CA 90505
Phone: (310)784-7600
Fax: (310)784-7605
E-mail: robins621@aol.com
Preferred Investment Size: $1,000,000 to $5,000,000. Investment Types: Leveraged buyout. Industry Preferences: Consumer products and retailing, distribution, industrial products and equipment, medical/health related, and publishing. Real estate deals not considered. Geographic Preferences: Entire U.S.

Southern California Ventures
406 Amapola Ave. Ste. 125
Torrance, CA 90501
Phone: (310)787-4381
Fax: (310)787-4382
Preferred Investment Size: $300,000 to $1,000,000. Investment Types: Seed, start-up, and first stage. Industry Preferences: Communications, and medical/health related. Geographic Preferences: West Coast.

Sandton Financial Group
21550 Oxnard St., Ste. 300
Woodland Hills, CA 91367
Phone: (818)702-9283
Preferred Investment Size: $100,000 to $250,000. Investment Types: Early and later stages, and special situations. Industry Preferences: No preference. Geographic Preferences: National and Canada.

Woodside Fund
850 Woodside Dr.
Woodside, CA 94062
Phone: (650)368-5545
Fax: (650)368-2416
Website: http://www.woodsidefund.com
Matthew Bolton, Analyst
Investment Types: Seed, start-up, first stage, second stage, and special situations. Industry Preferences: Diversified technology. Geographic Preferences: Western U.S.

Colorado

Colorado Venture Management
Ste. 300
Boulder, CO 80301
Phone: (303)440-4055
Fax: (303)440-4636
Preferred Investment Size: $250,000 to $1,000,000. Investment Types: Seed, start-up, early, and first and second stage. Industry Preferences: Diversified. Geographic Preferences: Midwest and Rocky Mountain region.

Dean & Associates
4362 Apple Way
Boulder, CO 80301
Fax: (303)473-9900
Investment Types: First stage, second stage, and mezzanine. Industry Preferences: Internet related. Geographic Preferences: Western U.S.

Roser Ventures LLC
1105 Spruce St.
Boulder, CO 80302
Phone: (303)443-6436
Fax: (303)443-1885
Website: http://www.roserventures.com
Steven T. Joanis, Associate
Investment Types: Start-up, first stage, second stage, and special situations. Industry Preferences: Communications, computer related, distribution, electronic components and instrumentation, energy/natural resources, industrial products and equipment, medical and health related. Geographic Preferences: National.

Sequel Venture Partners
4430 Arapahoe Ave., Ste. 220
Boulder, CO 80303
Phone: (303)546-0400
Fax: (303)546-9728
E-mail: tom@sequelvc.com
Website: http://www.sequelvc.com
Kinney Johnson, Partner
Preferred Investment Size: $100,000 to $5,000,000. Investment Types: Seed, start-up, and early stage. Industry Preferences: Diversified technology. Geographic Preferences: Rocky Mountains.

New Venture Resources
445C E. Cheyenne Mtn. Blvd.
Colorado Springs, CO 80906-4570
Phone: (719)598-9272
Fax: (719)598-9272
Jeffrey M. Cooper, Managing Director

Preferred Investment Size: $100,000 to $250,000. Investment Types: Seed and start-up. Industry Preferences: Diversified technology. Geographic Preferences: Southwest, rocky mountains.

The Centennial Funds
1428 15th St.
Denver, CO 80202-1318
Phone: (303)405-7500
Fax: (303)405-7575
Website: http://www.centennial.com
Preferred Investment Size: $250,000 to $5,000,000. Investment Types: Seed, start-up, first and second stage, and national consolidations. Industry Preferences: Diversified. Geographic Preferences: No preference.

Rocky Mountain Capital Partners
1125 17th St., Ste. 2260
Denver, CO 80202
Phone: (303)291-5200
Fax: (303)291-5327
Investment Types: Mezzanine and leveraged buyout. Industry Preferences: Diversified. Communications, computer related, consumer, distribution, electronic components and instrumentation, and industrial products and equipment. Geographic Preferences: Western U.S.

Sandlot Capital LLC
600 South Cherry St., Ste. 525
Denver, CO 80246
Phone: (303)893-3400
Fax: (303)893-3403
Website: http://www.sandlotcapital.com
Preferred Investment Size: $250,000 to $20,000,000. Investment Types: Seed, start-up, early and first stage, and special situation. Industry Preferences: Diversified. Geographic Preferences: U.S.

Wolf Ventures
50 South Steele St., Ste. 777
Denver, CO 80209
Phone: (303)321-4800
Fax: (303)321-4848
E-mail: businessplan@wolfventures.com
Website: http://www.wolfventures.com
David O. Wolf
Preferred Investment Size: $500,000 to $3,000,000. Investment Types: First stage, second stage, and special situations. Industry Preferences: Diversified. Geographic Preferences: Rocky mountains.

The Columbine Venture Funds
5460 S. Quebec St., Ste. 270
Englewood, CO 80111
Phone: (303)694-3222
Fax: (303)694-9007
Preferred Investment Size: $100,000 to $250,000. Investment Types: Seed, research and development, start-up, and first stage. Industry Preferences: Diversified technology. Geographic Preferences: Southwest, Rocky Mountains, and West Coast.

Investment Securities of Colorado, Inc.
4605 Denice Dr.
Englewood, CO 80111
Phone: (303)796-9192
Preferred Investment Size: $100,000 to $300,000. Investment Types: Seed and start-up. Industry Preferences: Electronic components, industrial controls and sensors, healthcare industry. Geographic Preferences: Rocky Mountain area.

Kinship Partners
6300 S. Syracuse Way, Ste. 484
Englewood, CO 80111
Phone: (303)694-0268
Fax: (303)694-1707
E-mail: block@vailsys.com
Preferred Investment Size: $250,000 to $1,000,000. Investment Types: Seed, start-up, and early stage. Industry Preferences: Diversified computer and communication technology, specialty retailing, genetic engineering, and healthcare. Geographic Preferences: Within two hours of office.

Boranco Management, L.L.C.
1528 Hillside Dr.
Fort Collins, CO 80524-1969
Phone: (970)221-2297
Fax: (970)221-4787
Preferred Investment Size: $100,000. Investment Types: Early and late stage. Industry Preferences: Agricultural and animal biotechnology. Geographic Preferences: Within two hours of office.

Aweida Ventures
890 West Cherry St., Ste. 220
Louisville, CO 80027
Phone: (303)664-9520
Fax: (303)664-9530
Website: http://www.aweida.com
Investment Types: Seed and first and second stage. Industry Preferences: Software, Internet related, and medical/health related. Geographic Preferences: West Coast.

Access Venture Partners
8787 Turnpike Dr., Ste. 260
Westminster, CO 80030
Phone: (303)426-8899
Fax: (303)426-8828
E-mail: robert.rees@juno.com
Robert W. Rees, Managing Director
Investment Types: Seed, start-up, first stage, and special situations. Industry Preferences: Diversified. Geographic Preferences: Western and Midwestern U.S.

Connecticut

Medmax Ventures LP
1 Northwestern Dr., Ste. 203
Bloomfield, CT 06002
Phone: (860)286-2960
Fax: (860)286-9960
Noam Karstaedt
Preferred Investment Size: $500,000 minimum. Investment Types: Seed, start-up, first and second stage, and research and development. Industry Preferences: Biotechnology and medical/health related. Geographic Preferences: Northeast.

James B. Kobak & Co.
Four Mansfield Place
Darien, CT 06820
Phone: (203)656-3471
Fax: (203)655-2905
Preferred Investment Size: $100,000 maximum. Investment Types: First stage. Industry Preferences: Publishing. Geographic Preferences: National.

Orien Ventures
1 Post Rd.
Fairfield, CT 06430
Phone: (203)259-9933
Fax: (203)259-5288
Anthony Miadich, Managing General Partner
Preferred Investment Size: $500,000 minimum. Investment Types: Start-up, seed, early and first stage. Industry Preferences: Diversified technology. Geographic Preferences: No preference.

ABP Acquisition Corporation
115 Maple Ave.
Greenwich, CT 06830
Phone: (203)625-8287
Fax: (203)447-6187
Preferred Investment Size: $10,000,000 to $30,000,000. Investment Types: Leveraged buyout and acquisition. Industry Preferences: Diversified. Geographic Preferences: Mid Atlantic, Northeast, Ontario, and Quebec.

Catterton Partners
9 Greenwich Office Park
Greenwich, CT 06830
Phone: (203)629-4901
Fax: (203)629-4903
Website: http://www.cpequity.com
Andrew C. Taub
Preferred Investment Size: $5,000,000 minimum. Investment Types: First stage, second stage, leveraged buyout, and special situations. Industry Preferences: Consumer products and services, Internet related, biotechnology. Geographic Preferences: U.S. and Canada.

Consumer Venture Partners
3 Pickwick Plz.
Greenwich, CT 06830
Phone: (203)629-8800
Fax: (203)629-2019
E-mail: lcummin@consumer-venture.com
Linda Cummin, Business Manager
Preferred Investment Size: $10,000,000 minimum. Investment Types: Start-up, first and second stage, and leveraged buyout. Industry Preferences: Internet related, consumer related. Geographic Preferences: Entire U.S.

Insurance Venture Partners
31 Brookside Dr., Ste. 211
Greenwich, CT 06830
Phone: (203)861-0030
Fax: (203)861-2745
Preferred Investment Size: $500,000 to $50,000,000. Investment Types: First and second stage, and leveraged buyouts. Industry Preferences: Insurance. Geographic Preferences: U.S.

The NTC Group
Three Pickwick Plaza
Ste. 200
Greenwich, CT 06830
Phone: (203)862-2800
Fax: (203)622-6538
Preferred Investment Size: $1,000,000 minimum. Investment Types: Seed, first stage, control-block purchases, and leveraged buyout. Industry Preferences: Electronic components, factory automation, and machinery. Geographic Preferences: Entire U.S.

Regulus International Capital Co., Inc.
140 Greenwich Ave.
Greenwich, CT 06830
Phone: (203)625-9700
Fax: (203)625-9706
E-mail: lee@chaossystems.com
Preferred Investment Size: $100,000 minimum. Investment Types: Start-up, seed, research and development. Industry Preferences: Computer software, industrial materials and machinery, and publishing. Geographic Preferences: National.

Axiom Venture Partners
City Place II
185 Asylum St., 17th Fl.
Hartford, CT 06103
Phone: (860)548-7799
Fax: (860)548-7797
Website: http://www.axiomventures.com
Preferred Investment Size: $2,000,000 to $5,000,000. Investment Types: Seed, early and later stages, and expansion. Industry Preferences: Communications, computer and Internet related, distribution, genetic engineering, medical/health related. Geographic Preferences: National.

Conning Capital Partners
City Place II
185 Asylum St.
Hartford, CT 06103-4105
Phone: (860)520-1289
Fax: (860)520-1299
E-mail: pe@conning.com
Website: http://www.conning.com
John B. Clinton, Executive Vice President
Preferred Investment Size: $5,000,000 to $35,000,000. Investment Types: Second and late stage, and expansion. Industry Preferences: Computer related, consumer related, and medical/health related. Geographic Preferences: National.

First New England Capital L.P.
100 Pearl St.
Hartford, CT 06103
Phone: (860)293-3333
Fax: (860)293-3338
E-mail: info@firstnewenglandcapital.com
Website: http://www.firstnewenglandcapital.com
Preferred Investment Size: $100,000 to $1,000,000. Investment Types: Mezzanine, expansion, and management buyouts. Industry Preferences: Communications, computer related, electronics, consumer related, and medical/health related. Geographic Preferences: Northeastern U.S.

Northeast Ventures
One State St., Ste. 1720
Hartford, CT 06103
Phone: (860)547-1414
Fax: (860)246-8755
Preferred Investment Size: $1,000,000 minimum. Investment Types: Secondary. Industry Preferences: Diversified. Geographic Preferences: National.

Windward Holdings
38 Sylvan Rd.
Madison, CT 06443
Phone: (203)245-6870
Fax: (203)245-6865

Preferred Investment Size: $300,000 minimum. Investment Types: Leveraged buyouts, mezzanine, recaps, and special situations. Industry Preferences: Electronics, food/beverage, and industrial products. Geographic Preferences: Northeastern U.S.

Advanced Materials Partners, Inc.
45 Pine St.
PO Box 1022
New Canaan, CT 06840
Phone: (203)966-6415
Fax: (203)966-8448
E-mail: wkb@amplink.com
Preferred Investment Size: $500,000 to $25,000,000. Investment Types: Seed, start-up, early and late stage, leveraged buyout, research and development, and special situations. Industry Preferences: Diversified. Geographic Preferences: National and Canada.

RFE Investment Partners
36 Grove St.
New Canaan, CT 06840
Phone: (203)966-2800
Fax: (203)966-3109
Website: http://www.rfeip.com
James A. Parsons, General Partner
Preferred Investment Size: $15,000,000 minimum. Investment Policies: Prefer equity investments. Investment Types: Later stage, industry rollups, leveraged buyout, mezzanine, and special situations. Industry Preferences: Diversified. Geographic Preferences: Entire U.S.

Connecticut Innovations, Inc.
999 West St.
Rocky Hill, CT 06067
Phone: (860)563-5851
Fax: (860)563-4877
E-mail: pamela.hartley@ctinnovations.com
Website: http://www.ctinnovations.com
Preferred Investment Size: $50,000 minimum to $1,000,000. Investment Types: Start-up, first and second stage, joint ventures, and mezzanine. Industry Preferences: Diversified technology. Geographic Preferences: Northeast.

Canaan Partners
105 Rowayton Ave.
Rowayton, CT 06853
Phone: (203)855-0400
Fax: (203)854-9117
Website: http://www.canaan.com
Preferred Investment Size: $5,000,000 to $20,000,000. Investment Types: Early, first, and second stage; and expansion. Industry Preferences: Diversified. Geographic Preferences: National.

Landmark Partners, Inc.
10 Mill Pond Ln.
Simsbury, CT 06070
Phone: (860)651-9760
Fax: (860)651-8890
Website: http://www.landmarkpartners.com
James P. McConnell, Partner
Preferred Investment Size: $500,000 to $5,000,000. Investment Types: Seed, start-up, first and second stage, and special situations. Industry Preferences: Diversified technology. Geographic Preferences: U.S. and Canada.

Sweeney & Company
PO Box 567
Southport, CT 06490
Phone: (203)255-0220
Fax: (203)255-0220
E-mail: sweeney@connix.com
Preferred Investment Size: $1,000,000 minimum. Investment Types: Seed, research and development, start-up, first stage, second stage, mezzanine, leveraged buyout, and special situations. Industry Preferences: Diversified. Geographic Preferences: Northeast U.S. and Eastern Canada.

Baxter Associates, Inc.
PO Box 1333
Stamford, CT 06904
Phone: (203)323-3143
Fax: (203)348-0622
Preferred Investment Size: $2,000,000 minimum. Investment Types: Seed, start-up, first stage, research and development, leveraged buyout, and special situations. Industry Preferences: Diversified. Geographic Preferences: National.

Beacon Partners Inc.
6 Landmark Sq., 4th Fl.
Stamford, CT 06901-2792
Phone: (203)359-5776
Fax: (203)359-5876
Preferred Investment Size: $300,000 to $1,000,000. Investment Types: First stage, second stage, mezzanine, and leveraged buyout. Industry Preferences: Diversified. Geographic Preferences: Northeast.

Collinson, Howe, and Lennox, LLC
1055 Washington Blvd., 5th Fl.
Stamford, CT 06901
Phone: (203)324-7700
Fax: (203)324-3636
E-mail: info@chlmedical.com
Website: http://www.chlmedical.com
Investment Types: Seed, research and development, start-up, and first stage. Industry Preferences: Medical/health related, biotechnology, and Internet related. Geographic Preferences: National.

Prime Capital Management Co.
550 West Ave.
Stamford, CT 06902
Phone: (203)964-0642
Fax: (203)964-0862
Preferred Investment Size: $300,000 to $800,000. Investment Types: First and second stage, and recaps. Industry Preferences: Diversified. Geographic Preferences: Northeast.

Saugatuck Capital Co.
1 Canterbury Green
Stamford, CT 06901
Phone: (203)348-6669
Fax: (203)324-6995
Website: http://www.saugatuckcapital.com
Preferred Investment Size: $25,000,000 maximum. Investment Types: Leveraged buyout, acquisition, control-block purchases, expansion, later stage, and recaps. Industry Preferences: Diversified. Geographic Preferences: Entire U.S.

Soundview Financial Group Inc.
22 Gatehouse Rd.
Stamford, CT 06902
Phone: (203)462-7200
Fax: (203)462-7350
Website: http://www.sndv.com

Brian Bristol, Managing Director
Preferred Investment Size: $100,000 to $500,000. Investment Types: Second stage and mezzanine. Industry Preferences: Diversified information technology. Geographic Preferences: United States and Canada.

TSG Ventures, L.L.C.
177 Broad St., 12th Fl.
Stamford, CT 06901
Phone: (203)406-1500
Fax: (203)406-1590
Darryl Thompson
Preferred Investment Size: $30,000,000 minimum. Investment Types: Second stage and leveraged buyout. Industry Preferences: Diversified. Geographic Preferences: Entire U.S. and Canada.

Whitney & Company
177 Broad St.
Stamford, CT 06901
Phone: (203)973-1400
Fax: (203)973-1422
Website: http://www.jhwhitney.com
Preferred Investment Size: $1,000,000. Investment Types: Leveraged buyout and expansion. Industry Preferences: Diversified technology. Geographic Preferences: No preference.

Cullinane & Donnelly Venture Partners L.P.
970 Farmington Ave.
West Hartford, CT 06107
Phone: (860)521-7811
Fax: (860)521-7911
Preferred Investment Size: $300,000 to $1,000,000. Investment Types: Seed, first and second stage, and recaps. Industry Preferences: Diversified. Geographic Preferences: Northeast.

The Crestview Investment and Financial Group
431 Post Rd. E, Ste. 1
Westport, CT 06880-4403
Phone: (203)222-0333
Fax: (203)222-0000
Norman Marland, Pres.
Preferred Investment Size: $500,000 to $3,000,000. Investment Types: Seed, research and development, first stage, second stage, and mezzanine. Industry Preferences: Diversified. Geographic Preferences: U.S. and Canada.

Marketcorp Venture Associates, L.P. (MCV)
274 Riverside Ave.
Westport, CT 06880
Phone: (203)222-3030
Fax: (203)222-3033
E. Bulkeley Griswold, General Partner
Preferred Investment Size: $500,000 to $1,000,000. Investment Types: First and second stage, mezzanine, and leveraged buyout. Industry Preferences: Consumer products and services, and computer services. Geographic Preferences: Entire U.S.

Oak Investment Partners (Westport)
1 Gorham Island
Westport, CT 06880
Phone: (203)226-8346
Fax: (203)227-0372
Website: http://www.oakinv.com
Preferred Investment Size: $250,000 to $5,000,000. Investment Types: Start-up; early, first, second, and late stage; leveraged buyout; open market; control-block purchases; open market; and special situations. Industry Preferences: Diversified technology. Geographic Preferences: National.

Oxford Bioscience Partners
315 Post Rd. W
Westport, CT 06880-5200
Phone: (203)341-3300
Fax: (203)341-3309
Website: http://www.oxbio.com
William Greenman
Preferred Investment Size: $500,000 to $5,000,000. Investment Types: Early and first stage, and research and development. Industry Preferences: Genetic engineering and medical/health related, computer related. Geographic Preferences: Entire U.S. and Canada.

Prince Ventures (Westport)
25 Ford Rd.
Westport, CT 06880
Phone: (203)227-8332
Fax: (203)226-5302
Preferred Investment Size: $500,000 to $1,000,000. Investment Types: Seed, start-up, first and second stage, and leveraged buyout. Industry Preferences: Genetic engineering and medical/health related, computer software and services, industrial, and communications. Geographic Preferences: No preference.

LTI Venture Leasing Corp.
221 Danbury Rd.
Wilton, CT 06897
Phone: (203)563-1100
Fax: (203)563-1111
Website: http://www.ltileasing.com
Richard Livingston, Vice President
Preferred Investment Size: $500,000 to $2,000,000. Investment Types: Early, first, second, and late stage; mezzanine; and special situation. Industry Preferences: Communications, computer related, consumer, electronic components and instrumentation, industrial products and equipment, medical and health related. Geographic Preferences: National.

Delaware

Blue Rock Capital
5803 Kennett Pike, Ste. A
Wilmington, DE 19807
Phone: (302)426-0981
Fax: (302)426-0982
Website: http://www.bluerockcapital.com
Preferred Investment Size: $250,000 to $3,000,000. Investment Types: Seed, start-up, and first stage. Industry Preferences: Communication, Internet related, computer, semiconductors, and consumer related. Geographic Preferences: Northeast, Middle Atlantic.

District of Columbia

Allied Capital Corp.
1919 Pennsylvania Ave. NW
Washington, DC 20006-3434
Phone: (202)331-2444
Fax: (202)659-2053
Website: http://www.alliedcapital.com
Tricia Daniels, Sales & Marketing

Preferred Investment Size: $5,000,000 to $40,000,000. Investment Types: Mezzanine, leveraged buyout, acquisition, management buyouts, and recapitalization. Industry Preferences: Diversified. Geographic Preferences: No preference.

Atlantic Coastal Ventures, L.P.
3101 South St. NW
Washington, DC 20007
Phone: (202)293-1166
Fax: (202)293-1181
Website: http://www.atlanticcv.com
Preferred Investment Size: $300,000 minimum. Investment Types: Leveraged buyout, mezzanine, and special situations. Industry Preferences: Communication and computer related, and electronics. Geographic Preferences: East Coast.

Columbia Capital Group, Inc.
1660 L St. NW, Ste. 308
Washington, DC 20036
Phone: (202)775-8815
Fax: (202)223-0544
Erica Batie, Director of Investments
Preferred Investment Size: $100,000 to $250,000. Investment Types: First and second stage, and mezzanine. Industry Preferences: Communication and computer related, electronics, and biotechnology. Geographic Preferences: Mid Atlantic.

Core Capital Partners
901 15th St., NW
9th Fl.
Washington, DC 20005
Phone: (202)589-0090
Fax: (202)589-0091
Website: http://www.core-capitai.com
Preferred Investment Size: $1,000,000 to $10,000,000. Investment Types: Start-up, first and second stage, expansion, and later stage. Industry Preferences: Diversified. Geographic Preferences: Mid Atlantic, Northeast, and Southeast.

Next Point Partners
701 Pennsylvania Ave. NW, Ste. 900
Washington, DC 20004
Phone: (202)661-8703
Fax: (202)434-7400
E-mail: mf@nextpoint.vc
Website: http://www.nextpointvc.com
Michael Faber, Managing General Partner
Investment Types: First and second stage. Industry Preferences: Communications, computer related, and electronic components. Geographic Preferences: National.

Telecommunications Development Fund
2020 K. St. NW
Ste. 375
Washington, DC 20006
Phone: (202)293-8840
Fax: (202)293-8850
Website: http://www.tdfund.com
Preferred Investment Size: $375,000 to $1,000,000. Investment Types: Seed, early stage, and expansion. Industry Preferences: Internet related, computer hardware/software and services, and communications. Geographic Preferences: Entire U.S.

Wachtel & Co., Inc.
1101 4th St. NW
Washington, DC 20005-5680
Phone: (202)898-1144
Preferred Investment Size: $100,000 to $300,000. Investment Types: Start-up, first and second stage, and recaps. Industry Preferences: Diversified. Geographic Preferences: East Coast.

Winslow Partners LLC
1300 Connecticut Ave. NW
Washington, DC 20036-1703
Phone: (202)530-5000
Fax: (202)530-5010
E-mail: winslow@winslowpartners.com
Robert Chartener, Partner
Investment Types: Later stage, acquisition, control-block purchases, expansion, management and leverage buyouts. Industry Preferences: Diversified. Geographic Preferences: Entire U.S.

Women's Growth Capital Fund
1054 31st St., NW
Ste. 110
Washington, DC 20007
Phone: (202)342-1431
Fax: (202)341-1203
Website: http://www.wgcf.com
Preferred Investment Size: $500,000 to $2,000,000. Investment Types: First, second, and later stage. Industry Preferences: Internet related, communications, and computer software and services. Geographic Preferences: Entire U.S.

Florida

Sigma Capital Corp.
22668 Caravelle Circle
Boca Raton, FL 33433
Phone: (561)368-9783
Preferred Investment Size: $100,000 to $300,000. Investment Types: Second stage. Industry Preferences: Diversified communication and computer, consumer products and services, distribution, electronics, genetic engineering, finance, and real estate. Geographic Preferences: Southeast.

North American Business Development Co., L.L.C.
111 East Las Olas Blvd.
Ft. Lauderdale, FL 33301
Phone: (305)463-0681
Fax: (305)527-0904
Website: http://www.northamericanfund.com
Robert Underwood
PIS $10,000,000 minimum. Investment Types: Leveraged buyout, special situations, control block purchases, industry roll ups, and small business with growth potential. Industry Preferences: No preference. Geographic Preferences: Southeast and Midwest.

Chartwell Capital Management Co. Inc.
1 Independent Dr., Ste. 3120
Jacksonville, FL 32202
Phone: (904)355-3519
Fax: (904)353-5833
E-mail: info@chartwellcap.com
Anthony Marinatos
Preferred Investment Size: $5,000,000 minimum. Investment Types: First stage, second stage and leveraged buyout. Industry Preferences: Diversified. Geographic Preferences: Northwest and Southeast.

CEO Advisors
1061 Maitland Center Commons
Ste. 209
Maitland, FL 32751
Phone: (407)660-9327
Fax: (407)660-2109
Preferred Investment Size: $300,000 to $500,000. Investment Types: Seed, start-up, first stage, and research and development. Industry Preferences: Diversified. Geographic Preferences: Southeast.

Henry & Co.
8201 Peters Rd., Ste. 1000
Plantation, FL 33324
Phone: (954)797-7400
June Knaudt
Preferred Investment Size: $500,000 to $1,000,000. Investment Types: First and second stage. Industry Preferences: Healthcare industry. Geographic Preferences: West Coast.

Avery Business Development Services
2506 St. Michel Ct.
Ponte Vedra, FL 32082
Phone: (904)285-6033
Preferred Investment Size: $2,000,000. Investment Types: Seed, research and development, start-up, first stage, leveraged buyout, and special situations. Industry Preferences: Diversified. Geographic Preferences: National.

New South Ventures
5053 Ocean Blvd.
Sarasota, FL 34242
Phone: (941)358-6000
Fax: (941)358-6078
Website: http://www.newsouthventures.com
Preferred Investment Size: $300,000 to $3,000,000. Investment Types: Seed and early stage. Industry Preferences: Diversified. Geographic Preferences: Southeast.

Venture Capital Management Corp.
PO Box 2626
Satellite Beach, FL 32937
Phone: (407)777-1969
Preferred Investment Size: $100,000 to $300,000. Investment Types: First and second stage, and leveraged buyout. Industry Preferences: Diversified. Geographic Preferences: National.

Florida Capital Venture Ltd.
325 Florida Bank Plaza
100 W. Kennedy Blvd.
Tampa, FL 33602
Phone: (813)229-2294
Fax: (813)229-2028
Warren Miller
Preferred Investment Size: $500,000 minimum. Investment Types: Start-up, first and second stage, leveraged buyout, and special situations. Industry Preferences: Diversified. Geographic Preferences: Southeast.

Quantum Capital Partners
339 South Plant Ave.
Tampa, FL 33606
Phone: (813)250-1999
Fax: (813)250-1998
Website: http://www.quantumcapitalpartners.com
Preferred Investment Size: $1,000,000 to $5,000,000. Investment Types: Expansion, later stage, and mezzanine. Industry Preferences: Diversified technology, medical/health, consumer, retail, financial and business services, and manufacturing. Geographic Preferences: Florida.

South Atlantic Venture Fund
614 W. Bay St.
Tampa, FL 33606-2704
Phone: (813)253-2500
Fax: (813)253-2360
E-mail: venture@southatlantic.com
Website: http://www.southatlantic.com
Donald W. Burton, Chairman and Managing Director
Preferred Investment Size: $1,500,000 minimum. Investment Types: First and second stage, special situations, expansion and control block purchases. Industry Preferences: Diversified. Geographic Preferences: Southeast, Middle Atlantic, and Texas.

LM Capital Corp.
120 S. Olive, Ste. 400
West Palm Beach, FL 33401
Phone: (561)833-9700
Fax: (561)655-6587
Website: http://www.lmcapitalsecurities.com
Preferred Investment Size: $5,000,000 minimum. Investment Types: Leveraged buyout. Industry Preferences: Diversified. Geographic Preferences: No preference.

Georgia

Venture First Associates
4811 Thornwood Dr.
Acworth, GA 30102
Phone: (770)928-3733
Fax: (770)928-6455
J. Douglas Mullins
Preferred Investment Size: $500,000 to $5,000,000. Investment Types: Seed, start-up, first and second stage. Industry Preferences: Diversified technology and electronics. Geographic Preferences: Southeast.

Alliance Technology Ventures
8995 Westside Pkwy., Ste. 200
Alpharetta, GA 30004
Phone: (678)336-2000
Fax: (678)336-2001
E-mail: info@atv.com
Website: http://www.atv.com
Preferred Investment Size: $250,000 to $1,000,000. Investment Types: Seed, start-up, first and second stage. Industry Preferences: Diversified technology. Geographic Preferences: Southeast.

Cordova Ventures
2500 North Winds Pkwy., Ste. 475
Alpharetta, GA 30004
Phone: (678)942-0300
Fax: (678)942-0301
Website: http://www.cordovaventures.com
Teo F. Dagi
Preferred Investment Size: $250,000 to $4,000,000. Investment Policies: Equity and/or debt. Investment Types: Early and late stage, start-up, expansion, and balanced. Industry Preferences: Diversified. Geographic Preferences: Southeast.

Advanced Technology Development Fund
1000 Abernathy, Ste. 1420

Atlanta, GA 30328-5614
Phone: (404)668-2333
Fax: (404)668-2333
Preferred Investment Size: $500,000 to $1,500,000. Investment Types: Seed, start-up, first and second stage, and leveraged buyout. Industry Preferences: Diversified. Geographic Preferences: No preference.

CGW Southeast Partners
12 Piedmont Center, Ste. 210
Atlanta, GA 30305
Phone: (404)816-3255
Fax: (404)816-3258
Website: http://www.cgwlp.com
Garrison M. Kitchen, Managing Partner
Preferred Investment Size: $25,000,000 to $200,000,000. Investment Types: Management buyout. Industry Preferences: Diversified. Geographic Preferences: Entire U.S.

Cyberstarts
1900 Emery St., NW
3rd Fl.
Atlanta, GA 30318
Phone: (404)267-5000
Fax: (404)267-5200
Website: http://www.cyberstarts.com
Investment Types: Seed and start-up. Industry Preferences: Internet and financial services. Geographic Preferences: Entire U.S.

EGL Holdings, Inc.
10 Piedmont Center, Ste. 412
Atlanta, GA 30305
Phone: (404)949-8300
Fax: (404)949-8311
Salvatore A. Massaro, Partner
Preferred Investment Size: $1,000,000 minimum. Investment Types: Mezzanine, leveraged buyout, industry roll ups, recapitalization, and second stage. Industry Preferences: Diversified. Geographic Preferences: Southeast and East Coast, Midwest.

Equity South
1790 The Lenox Bldg.
3399 Peachtree Rd. NE
Atlanta, GA 30326
Phone: (404)237-6222
Fax: (404)261-1578
Douglas L. Diamond, Managing Director
Preferred Investment Size: $2,000,000 to $3,000,000. Investment Types: Mezzanine, leveraged buyout, recapitalization, and control block purchases. Industry Preferences: Diversified. Geographic Preferences: Northeast, Southeast, and Southwest.

Five Paces
3400 Peachtree Rd., Ste. 200
Atlanta, GA 30326
Phone: (404)439-8300
Fax: (404)439-8301
Website: http://www.fivepaces.com
Investment Types: Balanced. Industry Preferences: Diversified. Geographic Preferences: Entire U.S.

Frontline Capital, Inc.
3475 Lenox Rd., Ste. 400
Atlanta, GA 30326
Phone: (404)240-7280
Fax: (404)240-7281
Preferred Investment Size: $1,000,000 minimum. Investment Types: First stage. Industry Preferences: Diversified communication and computer technology, consumer products and services, distribution, electronics, business and financial services, and publishing. Geographic Preferences: Southeast.

Fuqua Ventures LLC
1201 W. Peachtree St. NW, Ste. 5000
Atlanta, GA 30309
Phone: (404)815-4500
Fax: (404)815-4528
Website: http://www.fuquaventures.com
Investment Types: Early stage. Industry Preferences: Internet related, biotechnology, communications, and computer software and services. Geographic Preferences: Entire U.S.

Noro-Moseley Partners
4200 Northside Pkwy., Bldg. 9
Atlanta, GA 30327
Phone: (404)233-1966
Fax: (404)239-9280
Website: http://www.noro-moseley.com
Preferred Investment Size: $1,000,000 to $5,000,000. Investment Types: Start-up, first and second stage, mezzanine, leveraged buyout, special situations, and control block purchases. Industry Preferences: Diversified. Geographic Preferences: Southeast.

Renaissance Capital Corp.
34 Peachtree St. NW, Ste. 2230
Atlanta, GA 30303
Phone: (404)658-9061
Fax: (404)658-9064
Larry Edler
Preferred Investment Size: $300,000 minimum. Investment Types: Second stage, mezzanine, and leveraged buyout. Industry Preferences: Diversified. Geographic Preferences: Southeast.

River Capital, Inc.
Two Midtown Plaza
1360 Peachtree St. NE, Ste. 1430
Atlanta, GA 30309
Phone: (404)873-2166
Fax: (404)873-2158
Jerry D. Wethington
Preferred Investment Size: $3,000,000 minimum. Investment Types: Mezzanine, recapitalization, and leveraged buyout. Industry Preferences: Diversified. Geographic Preferences: Southeast, Southwest, Midwest, and Middle Atlantic.

State Street Bank & Trust Co.
3414 Peachtree Rd. NE, Ste. 1010
Atlanta, GA 30326
Phone: (404)364-9500
Fax: (404)261-4469
Preferred Investment Size: $10,000,000 minimum. Investment Types: Leveraged buyout and special situations. Industry Preferences: Diversified technology. Geographic Preferences: National.

UPS Strategic Enterprise Fund
55 Glenlake Pkwy. NE
Atlanta, GA 30328
Phone: (404)828-8814
Fax: (404)828-8088
E-mail: jcacyce@ups.com
Website: http://www.ups.com/sef/sef_home
Preferred Investment Size: $1,000,000. Investment Types: Early and late stage. Industry Preferences:

Diversified communication and computer technology. Geographic Preferences: United States and Canada.

Wachovia
191 Peachtree St. NE, 26th Fl.
Atlanta, GA 30303
Phone: (404)332-1000
Fax: (404)332-1392
Website: http://www.wachovia.com/wca
Preferred Investment Size: $5,000,000 to $15,000,000. Investment Types: Expansion, later stage, management buyouts, mezzanine, private placement, and recaps. Industry Preferences: Diversified. Geographic Preferences: Southeast.

Brainworks Ventures
4243 Dunwoody Club Dr.
Chamblee, GA 30341
Phone: (770)239-7447
Investment Types: Balanced and early and later stage. Industry Preferences: Telecommunications and computers. Geographic Preferences: Southeast.

First Growth Capital Inc.
Best Western Plaza, Ste. 105
PO Box 815
Forsyth, GA 31029
Phone: (912)781-7131
Fax: (912)781-0066
Preferred Investment Size: $100,000 to $300,000. Investment Types: Second stage and special situation. Industry Preferences: Diversified. Geographic Preferences: No preference.

Financial Capital Resources, Inc.
21 Eastbrook Bend, Ste. 116
Peachtree City, GA 30269
Phone: (404)487-6650
Preferred Investment Size: $5,000,000 minimum. Investment Types: Leveraged buyout. Industry Preferences: Machinery. Geographic Preferences: National.

Hawaii

HMS Hawaii Management Partners
Davies Pacific Center
841 Bishop St., Ste. 860
Honolulu, HI 96813
Phone: (808)545-3755
Fax: (808)531-2611
Preferred Investment Size: $500,000 to $1,500,000. Investment Types: Seed, start-up, first stage, and leveraged buyout. Industry Preferences: Internet related, communications, and consumer related. Geographic Preferences: Entire U.S.

Idaho

Sun Valley Ventures
160 Second St.
Ketchum, ID 83340
Phone: (208)726-5005
Fax: (208)726-5094
Preferred Investment Size: $5,000,000. Investment Types: Second stage, leveraged buyout, control-block purchases, and special situations. Industry Preferences: Diversified. Geographic Preferences: Entire U.S. and Canada.

Illinois

Open Prairie Ventures
115 N. Neil St., Ste. 209
Champaign, IL 61820
Phone: (217)351-7000
Fax: (217)351-7051
E-mail: inquire@openprairie.com
Website: http://www.openprairie.com
Dennis D. Spice, Managing Member
Preferred Investment Size: $250,000 to $2,500,000. Investment Types: Early stage. Industry Preferences: Diversified communication and computer technology, electronics, and genetic engineering. Geographic Preferences: Midwest.

ABN AMRO Private Equity
208 S. La Salle St., 10th Fl.
Chicago, IL 60604
Phone: (312)855-7079
Fax: (312)553-6648
Website: http://www.abnequity.com
David Bogetz, Managing Director
Preferred Investment Size: $10,000,000 maximum. Investment Types: Early stage and expansion. Industry Preferences: Diversified. Geographic Preferences: Entire U.S. and Canada.

Alpha Capital Partners, Ltd.
122 S. Michigan Ave., Ste. 1700
Chicago, IL 60603
Phone: (312)322-9800
Fax: (312)322-9808
E-mail: acp@alphacapital.com
William J. Oberholtzer, Vice President
Preferred Investment Size: $2,000,000 minimum. Investment Types: First and second stage, leveraged buyout, and special situations. Industry Preferences: Diversified. Geographic Preferences: Midwest.

Ameritech Development Corp.
30 S. Wacker Dr., 37th Fl.
Chicago, IL 60606
Phone: (312)750-5083
Fax: (312)609-0244
Craig Lee, Director
Preferred Investment Size: $5,000,000 minimum. Investment Types: Start-up, first and second stage. Industry Preferences: Communications, computer related, and electronics. Geographic Preferences: Entire U.S.

Apex Investment Partners
225 W. Washington, Ste. 1450
Chicago, IL 60606
Phone: (312)857-2800
Fax: (312)857-1800
E-mail: apex@apexvc.com
Website: http://www.apexvc.com
Preferred Investment Size: $500,000 to $15,000,000. Investment Types: Early stage. Industry Preferences: Diversified communication and computer technology, consumer products and services, industrial/energy, and electronics. Geographic Preferences: Entire U.S.

Arch Venture Partners
8725 W. Higgins Rd., Ste. 290
Chicago, IL 60631
Phone: (773)380-6600
Fax: (773)380-6606
Website: http://www.archventure.com
Steven Lazarus, Managing Director
Preferred Investment Size: $100,000 to $1,000,000. Investment Types: Seed, start-up, early stage. Industry Preferences: Diversified communication and computer

technology, electronics, and genetic engineering. Geographic Preferences: National.

The Bank Funds
208 South LaSalle St., Ste. 1680
Chicago, IL 60604
Phone: (312)855-6020
Fax: (312)855-8910
Investment Types: Control-block purchases, later stage, leveraged buyout, second stage, and special situation. Industry Preferences: Diversified. Geographic Preferences: No preference.

Batterson Venture Partners
303 W. Madison St., Ste. 1110
Chicago, IL 60606-3309
Phone: (312)269-0300
Fax: (312)269-0021
Website: http://www.battersonvp.com
Preferred Investment Size: $500,000 to $3,000,000. Investment Types: Seed, start-up, first and second stage. Industry Preferences: Diversified. Geographic Preferences: Entire U.S.

William Blair Capital Partners, L.L.C.
222 W. Adams St., Ste. 1300
Chicago, IL 60606
Phone: (312)364-8250
Fax: (312)236-1042
E-mail: privateequity@wmblair.com
Website: http://www.wmblair.com
Maureen Naddy, Office Manager
Preferred Investment Size: $5,000,000 minimum. Investment Types: First and early stage, acquisition and leveraged buyout. Industry Preferences: Communications, computer related, consumer, electronics, energy/natural resources, genetic engineering, and medical/health related. Geographic Preferences: Mid Atlantic, Midwest, and Northeast.

Bluestar Ventures
208 South LaSalle St., Ste. 1020
Chicago, IL 60604
Phone: (312)384-5000
Fax: (312)384-5005
Website: http://
www.bluestarventures.com
Preferred Investment Size: $1,000,000 to $3,000,000. Investment Types: Early, first, and second stage. Industry Preferences: Diversified. Geographic Preferences: Midwest.

The Capital Strategy Management Co.
233 S. Wacker Dr.
Box 06334
Chicago, IL 60606
Phone: (312)444-1170
Eric Von Bauer
Preferred Investment Size: $200,000 to $50,000,000. Investment Types: Various types. Industry Preferences: Diversified communication and computer technology, medical/health, industrial/energy, consumer products and services, distribution, electronics, and utilities. Geographic Preferences: Midwest, Northwest, Southeast, Mid Atlantic.

DN Partners
77 West Wacker Dr., Ste. 4550
Chicago, IL 60601
Phone: (312)332-7960
Fax: (312)332-7979
Investment Types: Leveraged buyout. Industry Preferences: Communications, computer related, electronics, medical/health, consumer related, industrial products, transportation, financial services, publishing, and agriculture related. Geographic Preferences: U.S.

Dresner Capital Inc.
29 South LaSalle St., Ste. 310
Chicago, IL 60603
Phone: (312)726-3600
Fax: (312)726-7448
John Riddle
Preferred Investment Size: $500,000 to $1,000,000. Investment Types: Leveraged buyout, mezzanine, and second stage. Industry Preferences: Diversified. Geographic Preferences: No preference.

Eblast Ventures LLC
11 South LaSalle St., 5th Fl.
Chicago, IL 60603
Phone: (312)372-2600
Fax: (312)372-5621
Website: http://
www.eblastventures.com
Preferred Investment Size: $100,000 to $500,000. Investment Types: Early, seed, start-up, and turnaround. Industry Preferences: Diversified. Geographic Preferences: Midwest.

Essex Woodlands Health Ventures, L.P.
190 S. LaSalle St., Ste. 2800
Chicago, IL 60603
Phone: (312)444-6040
Fax: (312)444-6034
Website: http://
www.essexwoodlands.com
Marc S. Sandroff, General Partner
Preferred Investment Size: $1,000,000 to $12,000,000. Investment Types: Start-up, early and second stage, private placement, and mezzanine. Industry Preferences: Healthcare, biotechnology, Internet related. Geographic Preferences: No preference.

First Analysis Venture Capital
233 S. Wacker Dr., Ste. 9500
Chicago, IL 60606
Phone: (312)258-1400
Fax: (312)258-0334
Website: http://www.firstanalysis.com
Bret Maxwell, CEO
Preferred Investment Size: $3,000,000 to $15,000,000. Investment Types: Early and later stage, and expansion. Industry Preferences: Diversified. Geographic Preferences: No preference.

Frontenac Co.
135 S. LaSalle St., Ste.3800
Chicago, IL 60603
Phone: (312)368-0044
Fax: (312)368-9520
Website: http://www.frontenac.com
Preferred Investment Size: $500,000 minimum. Investment Types: Start-up, first and second stage, leveraged buyout, special situation, and industry roll ups. Industry Preferences: Diversified. Geographic Preferences: Entire U.S.

GTCR Golder Rauner, LLC
6100 Sears Tower
Chicago, IL 60606
Phone: (312)382-2200
Fax: (312)382-2201
Website: http://www.gtcr.com
Bruce V. Rauner
Preferred Investment Size: $10,000,000 minimum. Investment

Types: Leveraged buyout, acquisition, expansion, management buyouts, and recapitalization. Industry Preferences: Diversified. Geographic Preferences: No preference.

High Street Capital LLC
311 South Wacker Dr., Ste. 4550
Chicago, IL 60606
Phone: (312)697-4990
Fax: (312)697-4994
Website: http://www.highstr.com
Preferred Investment Size: $2,000,000 to $10,000,000. Investment Types: Acquisition, control-block purchases, expansion, generalist PE, leveraged and management buyouts, recaps, and special situations. Industry Preferences: Diversified. Geographic Preferences: Entire U.S.

IEG Venture Management, Inc.
70 West Madison
Chicago, IL 60602
Phone: (312)644-0890
Fax: (312)454-0369
Website: http://www.iegventure.com
Preferred Investment Size: $100,000 to $500,000. Investment Types: Seed, start-up, first and second stage. Industry Preferences: Diversified. Geographic Preferences: Midwest.

JK&B Capital
180 North Stetson, Ste. 4500
Chicago, IL 60601
Phone: (312)946-1200
Fax: (312)946-1103
E-mail: gspencer@jkbcapital.com
Website: http://www.jkbcapital.com
Preferred Investment Size: $5,000,000 to $20,000,000. Investment Types: Early and late stage, and expansion. Industry Preferences: Diversified. Geographic Preferences: National.

Kettle Partners L.P.
350 W. Hubbard, Ste. 350
Chicago, IL 60610
Phone: (312)329-9300
Fax: (312)527-4519
Website: http://www.kettlevc.com
Preferred Investment Size: $1,000,000 to $5,000,000. Investment Types: Early, first and second stage, seed, and start-up. Industry Preferences: Internet related, communications, computer related. Geographic Preferences: Entire U.S.

Lake Shore Capital Partners
20 N. Wacker Dr., Ste. 2807
Chicago, IL 60606
Phone: (312)803-3536
Fax: (312)803-3534
Preferred Investment Size: $1,000,000 to $10,000,000. Investment Types: First and second stage, mezzanine, and leveraged buyout. Industry Preferences: Diversified. Geographic Preferences: National.

LaSalle Capital Group Inc.
70 W. Madison St., Ste. 5710
Chicago, IL 60602
Phone: (312)236-7041
Fax: (312)236-0720
Anthony Pesavento
Preferred Investment Size: $1,000,000 minimum. Investment Types: Leveraged buyout and special situation. Industry Preferences: Entertainment and leisure, consumer products, industrial products, and machinery. Geographic Preferences: No preference.

Linc Capital, Inc.
303 E. Wacker Pkwy., Ste. 1000
Chicago, IL 60601
Phone: (312)946-2670
Fax: (312)938-4290
E-mail: bdemars@linccap.com
Martin E. Zimmerman, Chairman
Preferred Investment Size: $500,000 to $2,000,000. Investment Types: Seed, start-up, early and late stage, mezzanine, research and development, and special situations. Industry Preferences: Diversified communication and computer technology, electronics, and medical/health related. Geographic Preferences: National.

Madison Dearborn Partners, Inc.
3 First National Plz., Ste. 3800
Chicago, IL 60602
Phone: (312)895-1000
Fax: (312)895-1001
E-mail: invest@mdcp.com
Website: http://www.mdcp.com
Preferred Investment Size: $20,000,000 to $400,000,000. Investment Types: Start-up, early stage, leveraged buyout, special situations, and expansion. Industry Preferences: Diversified. Geographic Preferences: Entire U.S. and Canada.

Mesirow Private Equity Investments Inc.
350 N. Clark St.
Chicago, IL 60610
Phone: (312)595-6950
Fax: (312)595-6211
Website: http://
www.meisrowfinancial.com
Preferred Investment Size: $4,000,000 to $10,000,000. Investment Types: Second stage, mezzanine, and leveraged buyout. Industry Preferences: Diversified. Geographic Preferences: Entire U.S.

Mosaix Ventures LLC
1822 North Mohawk
Chicago, IL 60614
Phone: (312)274-0988
Fax: (312)274-0989
Website: http://
www.mosaixventures.com
Preferred Investment Size: $500,000 to $3,000,000. Investment Types: Early and later stage, and expansion. Industry Preferences: Medical/health related. Geographic Preferences: U.S.

Nesbitt Burns
111 West Monroe St.
Chicago, IL 60603
Phone: (312)416-3855
Fax: (312)765-8000
Website: http://www.harrisbank.com
I. David Burn
Investment Types: Control-block purchases, leveraged buyout, and special situation. Industry Preferences: Diversified. Geographic Preferences: U.S. and Canada.

Polestar Capital, Inc.
180 N. Michigan Ave., Ste. 1905
Chicago, IL 60601
Phone: (312)984-9090
Fax: (312)984-9877
E-mail: wl@polestarvc.com
Website: http://www.polestarvc.com
Preferred Investment Size: $250,000 to $1,000,000. Investment Policies:

Primarily equity. Investment Types: Start-up, first and second stage. Industry Preferences: Communications, computer related. Geographic Preferences: Entire U.S.

Prince Ventures (Chicago)
10 S. Wacker Dr., Ste. 2575
Chicago, IL 60606-7407
Phone: (312)454-1408
Fax: (312)454-9125
Preferred Investment Size: $500,000 to $1,000,000. Investment Types: Seed, start-up, first and second stage, leveraged buyout. Industry Preferences: Genetic engineering and medical/health related. Geographic Preferences: No preference.

Prism Capital
444 N. Michigan Ave.
Chicago, IL 60611
Phone: (312)464-7900
Fax: (312)464-7915
Website: http://www.prismfund.com
Investment Types: First and second stage, mezzanine, leveraged buyout, and special situations. Industry Preferences: Diversified technology. Geographic Preferences: National.

Third Coast Capital
900 N. Franklin St., Ste. 700
Chicago, IL 60610
Phone: (312)337-3303
Fax: (312)337-2567
E-mail: manic@earthlink.com
Website: http://www.thirdcoastcapital.com
Preferred Investment Size: $2,000,000 to $5,000,000. Industry Preferences: Telecommunications and fiber optics. Geographic Preferences: National.

Thoma Cressey Equity Partners
4460 Sears Tower, 92nd Fl.
233 S. Wacker Dr.
Chicago, IL 60606
Phone: (312)777-4444
Fax: (312)777-4445
Website: http://www.thomacressey.com
Investment Types: Early and later stage, leveraged buyouts, and recapitalization. Industry Preferences: Diversified. Geographic Preferences: U.S. and Canada.

Tribune Ventures
435 N. Michigan Ave., Ste. 600
Chicago, IL 60611
Phone: (312)527-8797
Fax: (312)222-5993
Website: http://www.tribuneventures.com
Frances McCaughan
Preferred Investment Size: $1,000,000 to $10,000,000. Investment Types: Early stage, expansion, first and second stage, seed, and start-up. Industry Preferences: Diversified. Geographic Preferences: Entire U.S.

Wind Point Partners (Chicago)
676 N. Michigan Ave., Ste. 330
Chicago, IL 60611
Phone: (312)649-4000
Website: http://www.wppartners.com
Preferred Investment Size: $10,000,000 to $60,000,000. Investment Types: Later stage, leveraged buyout, acquisition, expansion, and recapitalization. Industry Preferences: Diversified. Geographic Preferences: Midwest.

Marquette Venture Partners
520 Lake Cook Rd., Ste. 450
Deerfield, IL 60015
Phone: (847)940-1700
Fax: (847)940-1724
Website: http://www.marquetteventures.com
Preferred Investment Size: $1,000,000 to $5,000,000. Investment Types: Start-up, first and second stage. Industry Preferences: Diversified. Geographic Preferences: Mid Atlantic, Midwest, Rocky Mountain, and West Coast.

Duchossois Investments Limited, LLC
845 Larch Ave.
Elmhurst, IL 60126
Phone: (630)530-6105
Fax: (630)993-8644
Website: http://www.duchtec.com
Preferred Investment Size: $500,000 to $5,000,000. Investment Types: Early, first and second stage. Industry Preferences: Diversified. Communications and computer related. Geographic Preferences: National.

Evanston Business Investment Corp.
1840 Oak Ave.
Evanston, IL 60201
Phone: (847)866-1840
Fax: (847)866-1808
E-mail: t-parkinson@nwu.com
Website: http://www.ebic.com
Preferred Investment Size: $250,000 to $500,000. Investment Types: Early stages. Industry Preferences: Diversified communication and computer technology, consumer products and services, medical/health, electronics, and publishing. Geographic Preferences: Chicago metropolitan area.

Inroads Capital Partners L.P.
1603 Orrington Ave., Ste. 2050
Evanston, IL 60201-3841
Phone: (847)864-2000
Fax: (847)864-9692
Preferred Investment Size: $1,000,000 to $5,000,000. Investment Types: Expansion and later stage. Industry Preferences: Diversified. Geographic Preferences: Entire U.S.

The Cerulean Fund/WGC Enterprises
1701 E. Lake Ave., Ste. 170
Glenview, IL 60025
Phone: (847)657-8002
Fax: (847)657-8168
Walter G. Cornett, III, Managing Director
Preferred Investment Size: $5,000,000 minimum. Investment Types: Seed, start-up, leveraged buyout, special situations, control block purchases, and research and development. Industry Preferences: Diversified. Geographic Preferences: Midwest.

Ventana Financial Resources, Inc.
249 Market Sq.
Lake Forest, IL 60045
Phone: (847)234-3434
Preferred Investment Size: $5,000,000 minimum. Investment Types: Seed, start-up, first and second stage, research and development, leveraged buyout, and mezzanine. Industry Preferences: Diversified. Geographic Preferences: Midwest, Southeast, and Southwest.

Beecken, Petty & Co.
901 Warrenville Rd., Ste. 205
Lisle, IL 60532
Phone: (630)435-0300
Fax: (630)435-0370
E-mail: hep@bpcompany.com
Website: http://www.bpcompany.com
Preferred Investment Size: $2,000,000 to $12,000,000. Investment Types: Early, first, second, and late stage; expansion; management buyouts; private placement; recapitalization. Industry Preferences: Communications, computer related, genetic engineering, medical and health related. Geographic Preferences: National.

Allstate Private Equity
3075 Sanders Rd., Ste. G5D
Northbrook, IL 60062-7127
Phone: (847)402-8247
Fax: (847)402-0880
Preferred Investment Size: $5,000,000 minimum. Investment Types: Start-up, first and second stage, mezzanine, leveraged buyout, and special situations. Industry Preferences: Diversified. Geographic Preferences: Entire U.S.

KB Partners
1101 Skokie Blvd., Ste. 260
Northbrook, IL 60062-2856
Phone: (847)714-0444
Fax: (847)714-0445
E-mail: keith@kbpartners.com
Website: http://www.kbpartners.com
Keith Bank, Managing Partner
Preferred Investment Size: $1,000,000 to $5,000,000. Investment Types: Seed, start-up, and early, first and second stage. Industry Preferences: Diversified. Geographic Preferences: National.

Transcap Associates Inc.
900 Skokie Blvd., Ste. 210
Northbrook, IL 60062
Phone: (847)753-9600
Fax: (847)753-9090
Ira J. Ederson
Preferred Investment Size: $500,000 to $5,000,000. Investment Types: Mezzanine, second stage, and special situation. Industry Preferences: Diversified. Geographic Preferences: Entire U.S.

Graystone Venture Partners, L.L.C. / Portage Venture Partners
One Northfield Plaza, Ste. 530
Northfield, IL 60093
Phone: (847)446-9460
Fax: (847)446-9470
Website: http://www.portageventures.com
Mathew B. McCall, Vice President
Preferred Investment Size: $250,000 to $3,000,000. Investment Types: Early stage. Industry Preferences: Diversified communication and computer technology, consumer products and services, genetic engineering, and medical/health. Geographic Preferences: National.

Motorola Inc.
1303 E. Algonquin Rd.
Schaumburg, IL 60196-1065
Phone: (847)576-4929
Fax: (847)538-2250
Website: http://www.mot.com/mne
James Burke, New Business Development Manager
Investment Types: Start-up, first and second stage. Industry Preferences: Diversified technology. Geographic Preferences: National.

Indiana

Irwin Ventures LLC
500 Washington St.
Columbus, IN 47202
Phone: (812)373-1434
Fax: (812)376-1709
Website: http://www.irwinventures.com
Preferred Investment Size: $750,000 to $1,250,000. Investment Types: Early and first stage. Industry Preferences: Internet related and financial services. Geographic Preferences: Northeast and Northwest.

Cambridge Venture Partners
4181 East 96th St., Ste. 200
Indianapolis, IN 46240
Phone: (317)814-6192
Fax: (317)944-9815
Jean Wojtowicz, President
Preferred Investment Size: $100,000 maximum. Investment Types: Second stage, mezzanine, and leveraged buyout. Industry Preferences: No preference. Geographic Preferences: Midwest, within 200 miles of office.

CID Equity Partners
One American Square, Ste. 2850
Box 82074
Indianapolis, IN 46282
Phone: (317)269-2350
Fax: (317)269-2355
Website: http://www.cidequity.com
Chris Gough, Associate
Preferred Investment Size: $1,000,000 minimum. Investment Types: Start-up, early and first stage, industry rollups, leveraged buyout, and special situations. Industry Preferences: Diversified. Geographic Preferences: Midwest and Rocky Mountain region.

Gazelle Techventures
6325 Digital Way, Ste. 460
Indianapolis, IN 46278
Phone: (317)275-6800
Fax: (317)275-1101
Website: http://www.gazellevc.com
Preferred Investment Size: $2,000,000 maximum. Investment Types: Early and later stage. Industry Preferences: Diversified. Geographic Preferences: Indiana.

Monument Advisors Inc.
Bank One Center/Circle
111 Monument Circle, Ste. 600
Indianapolis, IN 46204-5172
Phone: (317)656-5065
Fax: (317)656-5060
Website: http://www.monumentadv.com
Preferred Investment Size: $500,000 to $7,000,000. Investment Types: Balanced, leveraged buyout, management buyouts, and mezzanine. Industry Preferences: Business services, distribution, and manufacturing. Geographic Preferences: Midwest and Southeast.

MWV Capital Partners
201 N. Illinois St., Ste. 300
Indianapolis, IN 46204
Phone: (317)237-2323
Fax: (317)237-2325

Website: http://www.mwvcapital.com
Garth Dickey, Managing Director
Preferred Investment Size: $1,000,000 to $5,000,000. Investment Types: Balanced, second and later stage. Industry Preferences: Diversified. Geographic Preferences: Midwest.

First Source Capital Corp.
100 North Michigan St.
PO Box 1602
South Bend, IN 46601
Phone: (219)235-2180
Fax: (219)235-2227
Eugene L. Cavanaugh, Vice President
Preferred Investment Size: $300,000 to $500,000. Investment Types: Second stage, mezzanine, leveraged buyout, and special situations. Industry Preferences: Diversified. Geographic Preferences: Midwest.

Iowa

Allsop Venture Partners
118 Third Ave. SE, Ste. 837
Cedar Rapids, IA 52401
Phone: (319)368-6675
Fax: (319)363-9515
Preferred Investment Size: $500,000 minimum. Investment Types: First stage, industry rollups, leveraged buyout, mezzanine, second stage, and special situation. Industry Preferences: Diversified. Geographic Preferences: Entire U.S.

InvestAmerica Investment Advisors, Inc.
101 2nd St. SE, Ste. 800
Cedar Rapids, IA 52401
Phone: (319)363-8249
Fax: (319)363-9683
Kevin F. Mullane, Vice President
Preferred Investment Size: $500,000 to $1,000,000. Investment Types: First and second stage, leveraged buyout, and special situations. Industry Preferences: Diversified. Geographic Preferences: Entire U.S.

Pappajohn Capital Resources
2116 Financial Center
Des Moines, IA 50309
Phone: (515)244-5746
Fax: (515)244-2346
Website: http://www.pappajohn.com
Joe Dunham, President
Preferred Investment Size: $500,000 to $1,000,000. Investment Policies: Equity. Investment Types: Seed, start-up, first and second stage, leveraged buyout, and special situations. Industry Preferences: Diversified communication and computer technology, electronics, genetic engineering, and healthcare. Geographic Preferences: National.

Berthel Fisher & Company Planning Inc.
701 Tama St.
PO Box 609
Marion, IA 52302
Phone: (319)497-5700
Fax: (319)497-4244
Investment Types: Later stage. Industry Preferences: Diversified. Geographic Preferences: Midwest.

Kansas

Enterprise Merchant Bank
7400 West 110th St., Ste. 560
Overland Park, KS 66210
Phone: (913)327-8500
Fax: (913)327-8505
Preferred Investment Size: $1,000,000 minimum. Investment Types: Second stage, leveraged buyout, mezzanine, and special situations. Geographic Preferences: Midwest.

Kansas Venture Capital, Inc. (Overland Park)
6700 Antioch Plz., Ste. 460
Overland Park, KS 66204
Phone: (913)262-7117
Fax: (913)262-3509
E-mail: jdalton@kvci.com
John S. Dalton, President
Preferred Investment Size: $1,000,000 minimum. Investment Types: First and second stage, mezzanine, and leveraged buyout. Industry Preferences: Diversified. Geographic Preferences: Midwest.

Child Health Investment Corp.
6803 W. 64th St., Ste. 208
Shawnee Mission, KS 66202
Phone: (913)262-1436
Fax: (913)262-1575
Website: http://www.chca.com
Investment Types: Balanced, early stage, first stage, seed, and start-up. Industry Preferences: Diversified. Geographic Preferences: Entire U.S.

Kansas Technology Enterprise Corp.
214 SW 6th, 1st Fl.
Topeka, KS 66603-3719
Phone: (785)296-5272
Fax: (785)296-1160
E-mail: ktec@ktec.com
Website: http://www.ktec.com
Preferred Investment Size: $300,000. Investment Types: Seed, start-up, research and development. Industry Preferences: Diversified communication and computer technology, electronics, genetic engineering, and healthcare. Geographic Preferences: Within two hours of office.

Kentucky

Kentucky Highlands Investment Corp.
362 Old Whitley Rd.
London, KY 40741
Phone: (606)864-5175
Fax: (606)864-5194
Website: http://www.khic.org
Investment Types: Second stage, special situation, and start-up. Industry Preferences: Manufacturing. Geographic Preferences: Kentucky.

Chrysalis Ventures, L.L.C.
1850 National City Tower
Louisville, KY 40202
Phone: (502)583-7644
Fax: (502)583-7648
E-mail: bobsany@chrysalisventures.com
Website: http://www.chrysalisventures.com
Preferred Investment Size: $3,000,000 to $5,000,000. Investment Types: Start-up, first and second stage. Industry Preferences: Diversified communication and computer technology. Geographic Preferences: Southeast and Midwest.

Humana Venture Capital
500 West Main St.
Louisville, KY 40202
Phone: (502)580-3922
Fax: (502)580-2051

E-mail: gemont@humana.com
George Emont, Director
Preferred Investment Size: $10,000,000 minimum. Investment Types: Seed, start-up, first and second stage, leveraged buyout, mezzanine, and research and development. Industry Preferences: Medical/health related, Internet and computer related, and biotechnology. Geographic Preferences: National.

Summit Capital Group, Inc.
6510 Glenridge Park Pl., Ste. 8
Louisville, KY 40222
Phone: (502)332-2700
Preferred Investment Size: $10,000,000 to $40,000,000. Investment Types: Control-block purchases, expansion, leveraged and management buyouts. Industry Preferences: Diversified. Geographic Preferences: Southeast and Southwest.

Louisiana

Bank One Equity Investors, Inc.
451 Florida St.
Baton Rouge, LA 70801
Phone: (504)332-4421
Fax: (504)332-7377
Michael P. Kriby
Preferred Investment Size: $8,000,000 minimum. Investment Types: First and second stage, mezzanine, leveraged buyout, and special situations. Industry Preferences: Diversified. Geographic Preferences: Southeast and Southwest.

Advantage Capital Partners
LLE Tower
909 Poydras St., Ste. 2230
New Orleans, LA 70112
Phone: (504)522-4850
Fax: (504)522-4950
Website: http://www.advantagecap.com
Steven T. Stull, President
Preferred Investment Size: $1,000,000 to $10,000,000. Investment Types: Seed, start-up, early and second stage, and mezzanine. Industry Preferences: Diversified. Geographic Preferences: North and Southeast, and Midwest.

Maine

CEI Ventures / Coastal Ventures LP
2 Portland Fish Pier, Ste. 201
Portland, ME 04101
Phone: (207)772-5356
Fax: (207)772-5503
Website: http://www.ceiventures.com
Investment Types: No preference. Industry Preferences: Diversified. Geographic Preferences: Entire U.S.

Commwealth Bioventures, Inc.
4 Milk St.
Portland, ME 04101
Phone: (207)780-0904
Fax: (207)780-0913
E-mail: cbi4milk@aol.com
Investment Types: Seed. Industry Preferences: Biotechnology based start-ups. Geographic Preferences: No preference.

Maryland

Annapolis Ventures LLC
151 West St., Ste. 302
Annapolis, MD 21401
Phone: (443)482-9555
Fax: (443)482-9565
Website: http://www.annapolisventures.com
Preferred Investment Size: $2,000,000 to $5,000,000. Investment Types: Later stage. Industry Preferences: Diversified. Geographic Preferences: Midwest, Northeast, and Southeast.

Delmag Ventures
220 Wardour Dr.
Annapolis, MD 21401
Phone: (410)267-8196
Fax: (410)267-8017
Website: http://www.delmagventures.com
Preferred Investment Size: $250,000 to $1,000,000. Investment Types: Early stage and seed. Industry Preferences: Diversified. Geographic Preferences: Mid Atlantic.

Abell Venture Fund
111 S. Calvert St., Ste. 2300
Baltimore, MD 21202
Phone: (410)547-1300
Fax: (410)539-6579
Website: http://www.abell.org
Investment Types: Early stage, expansion, first and second stage, and private placement. Industry Preferences: Internet related, electronics, communications, and medical/health related. Geographic Preferences: Maryland.

ABS Ventures (Baltimore)
1 South St., Ste. 2150
Baltimore, MD 21202
Phone: (410)895-3895
Fax: (410)895-3899
Website: http://www.absventures.com
Preferred Investment Size: $500,000 maximum. Investment Types: Start-up, first and second stage, and mezzanine. Industry Preferences: Communications, computer related, genetic engineering, and medical/health related. Geographic Preferences: Entire U.S.

Anthem Capital, L.P.
16 S. Calvert St., Ste. 800
Baltimore, MD 21202-1305
Phone: (410)625-1510
Fax: (410)625-1735
Website: http://www.anthemcapital.com
Preferred Investment Size: $500,000 to $1,000,000. Investment Types: Early and later stage, mezzanine, and special situations. Industry Preferences: Diversified. Geographic Preferences: Middle Atlantic.

Catalyst Ventures
1119 St. Paul St.
Baltimore, MD 21202
Phone: (410)244-0123
Fax: (410)752-7721
Preferred Investment Size: $500,000 maximum. Investment Policies: Equity. Investment Types: Research and development, and early stage. Industry Preferences: Data communications, biotechnology, and medical related. Geographic Preferences: Middle Atlantic.

Maryland Venture Capital Trust
217 E. Redwood St., Ste. 2200
Baltimore, MD 21202
Phone: (410)767-6361
Fax: (410)333-6931
E-mail: rblank@mdbusiness.state.md.us

Preferred Investment Size: $1,000,000 to $5,000,000. Investment Types: Seed, start-up, first and second stage. Industry Preferences: Diversified. Geographic Preferences: Maryland.

New Enterprise Associates (Baltimore)
1119 St. Paul St.
Baltimore, MD 21202
Phone: (410)244-0115
Fax: (410)752-7721
Website: http://www.nea.com
Frank A. Bonsal, Jr., Founding Partner
Preferred Investment Size: $100,000 minimum. Investment Types: Seed, start-up, first and second stage, and mezzanine. Industry Preferences: Diversified. Geographic Preferences: Entire U.S.

T. Rowe Price Threshold Partnerships
100 E. Pratt St., 8th Fl.
Baltimore, MD 21202
Phone: (410)345-2000
Fax: (410)345-2800
Terral Jordan
Preferred Investment Size: $3,000,000 to $5,000,000. Investment Types: Mezzanine and special situations. Industry Preferences: Diversified. Geographic Preferences: Entire U.S.

Spring Capital Partners
16 W. Madison St.
Baltimore, MD 21201
Phone: (410)685-8000
Fax: (410)727-1436
E-mail: mailbox@springcap.com
Robert M. Stewart
Preferred Investment Size: $2,000,000 minimum. Investment Types: Second stage, acquisition, industry rollups, mezzanine, and leveraged buyout. Industry Preferences: Diversified. Geographic Preferences: Mid-Atlantic.

Arete Corporation
3 Bethesda Metro Ctr., Ste. 770
Bethesda, MD 20814
Phone: (301)657-6268
Fax: (301)657-6254
Website: http://www.arete-microgen.com
Jill Wilmoth
Investment Types: Seed, start-up, first stage, and research and development. Industry Preferences: Alternative energy. Geographic Preferences: Entire U.S. and Canada.

Embryon Capital
7903 Sleaford Place
Bethesda, MD 20814
Phone: (301)656-6837
Fax: (301)656-8056
Preferred Investment Size: $300,000 to $1,000,000. Investment Types: Diversified. Industry Preferences: Diversified. Geographic Preferences: Entire U.S.

Potomac Ventures
7920 Norfolk Ave., Ste. 1100
Bethesda, MD 20814
Phone: (301)215-9240
Website: http://www.potomacventures.com
Preferred Investment Size: $400,000 to $1,000,000. Investment Types: Early stage. Industry Preferences: Internet related. Geographic Preferences: Mid Atlantic.

Toucan Capital Corp.
3 Bethesda Metro Center, Ste. 700
Bethesda, MD 20814
Phone: (301)961-1970
Fax: (301)961-1969
Website: http://www.toucancapital.com
Preferred Investment Size: $1,000,000 to $1,000,000. Investment Types: Early stage, seed, and start-up. Industry Preferences: Diversified. Geographic Preferences: Entire U.S.

Kinetic Ventures LLC
2 Wisconsin Cir., Ste. 620
Chevy Chase, MD 20815
Phone: (301)652-8066
Fax: (301)652-8310
Website: http://www.kineticventures.com
Investment Types: Start-up, first stage, second stage, and leveraged buyout. Industry Preferences: Diversified technology. Geographic Preferences: National.

Boulder Ventures Ltd.
4750 Owings Mills Blvd.
Owings Mills, MD 21117
Phone: (410)998-3114
Fax: (410)356-5492
Website: http://www.boulderventures.com
Preferred Investment Size: $2,000,000 to $5,000,000. Investment Types: Early stage, expansion, first stage, and start-up. Industry Preferences: Diversified. Geographic Preferences: Entire U.S.

Grotech Capital Group
9690 Deereco Rd., Ste. 800
Timonium, MD 21093
Phone: (410)560-2000
Fax: (410)560-1910
Website: http://www.grotech.com
Frank A. Adams, President and CEO
Preferred Investment Size: $1,000,000 to $5,000,000. Investment Types: First and second stage, start-up, mezzanine, leveraged buyouts, and special situations. Industry Preferences: Diversified. Geographic Preferences: Southeast and Middle Atlantic.

Massachusetts

Adams, Harkness & Hill, Inc.
60 State St.
Boston, MA 02109
Phone: (617)371-3900
Tim McMahan, Managing Director
Preferred Investment Size: $1,000,000 minimum. Investment Types: Second stage, balanced, mezzanine, and special situation. Industry Preferences: Computer, consumer, electronics, business services, industrial products and equipment, and medical. Geographic Preferences: Northeast.

Advent International
75 State St., 29th Fl.
Boston, MA 02109
Phone: (617)951-9400
Fax: (617)951-0566
Website: http://www.adventinernational.com
Will Schmidt, Managing Director
Preferred Investment Size: $1,000,000 minimum. Investment Types: Seed, first and second stage, mezzanine, leveraged buyout, special situations, research and development, and acquisitions. Industry

Preferences: Diversified. Geographic Preferences: Entire U.S. and Canada.

American Research and Development
30 Federal St.
Boston, MA 02110-2508
Phone: (617)423-7500
Fax: (617)423-9655
Maureen A. White, Administrative Manager
Preferred Investment Size: $100,000 minimum. Investment Types: Seed, start-up, first and second stage. Industry Preferences: Diversified technology. Geographic Preferences: Northeast.

Ascent Venture Partners
255 State St., 5th Fl.
Boston, MA 02109
Phone: (617)270-9400
Fax: (617)270-9401
E-mail: info@ascentvp.com
Website: http://www.ascentvp.com
Leigh E. Michl, Managing Director
Investment Types: First stage and acquisition. Industry Preferences: Diversified. Geographic Preferences: Northeast.

Atlas Venture
222 Berkeley St.
Boston, MA 02116
Phone: (617)488-2200
Fax: (617)859-9292
Website: http://www.atlasventure.com
Preferred Investment Size: $500,000 to $20,000,000. Investment Types: Seed, start-up, research and development, first and second stage, mezzanine, and balanced. Industry Preferences: Communications, computer, genetic engineering, electronics, medical and health related. Geographic Preferences: Entire U.S. and Canada.

Axxon Capital
28 State St., 37th Fl.
Boston, MA 02109
Phone: (617)722-0980
Fax: (617)557-6014
Website: http://www.axxoncapital.com
Preferred Investment Size: $300,000 to $2,500,000. Investment Types: Balanced. Industry Preferences: Communications and media. Geographic Preferences: Northeast.

BancBoston Capital/BancBoston Ventures
175 Federal St., 10th Fl.
Boston, MA 02110
Phone: (617)434-2509
Fax: (617)434-6175
Website: http://www.bancbostoncapital.com
Frederick M. Fritz, President
Preferred Investment Size: $1,000,000 to $100,000,000. Investment Types: Seed, early stage, acquisition, recaps, later stage, management buyouts, expansion, and mezzanine. Industry Preferences: Diversified. Geographic Preferences: Entire U.S. and Eastern Canada.

Boston Capital Ventures
Old City Hall
45 School St.
Boston, MA 02108
Phone: (617)227-6550
Fax: (617)227-3847
E-mail: info@bcv.com
Website: http://www.bcv.com
Alexander Wilmerding
Preferred Investment Size: $250,000 to $8,000,000. Investment Types: Start-up, first and second stage, recaps, and leveraged buyouts. Industry Preferences: Diversified. Geographic Preferences: Entire U.S.

Boston Financial & Equity Corp.
20 Overland St.
PO Box 15071
Boston, MA 02215
Phone: (617)267-2900
Fax: (617)437-7601
E-mail: debbie@bfec.com
Deborah J. Monosson, Senior Vice President
Preferred Investment Size: $500,000 to $1,000,000. Investment Types: Seed, start-up, first and second stage, leveraged buyout, mezzanine, and research and development. Industry Preferences: Diversified. Geographic Preferences: National.

Boston Millennia Partners
30 Rowes Wharf
Boston, MA 02110
Phone: (617)428-5150
Fax: (617)428-5160
Website: http://www.millenniapartners.com
Dana Callow, Managing General Partner
Preferred Investment Size: $5,000,000 to $25,000,000. Investment Policies: Equity. Investment Types: First and second stage, start-up, leveraged buyout, and mezzanine. Industry Preferences: Communication, computer related, consumer services, electronics, genetic engineering, medical, and education. Geographic Preferences: National.

Bristol Investment Trust
842A Beacon St.
Boston, MA 02215-3199
Phone: (617)566-5212
Fax: (617)267-0932
E-mail: bernardberkman@prodigy.net
Preferred Investment Size: $100,000 minimum. Investment Policies: Equity. Investment Types: First and second stage, and mezzanine. Industry Preferences: Restaurants, retailing, consumer distribution, medical/health, and real estate. Geographic Preferences: Northeast.

Brook Venture Management LLC
50 Federal St., 5th Fl.
Boston, MA 02110
Phone: (617)451-8989
Fax: (617)451-2369
Website: http://www.brookventure.com
Preferred Investment Size: $500,000 to $2,500,000. Investment Types: Early and first stage. Industry Preferences: Diversified. Geographic Preferences: Northeast.

Burr, Egan, Deleage, and Co. (Boston)
200 Clarendon St., Ste. 3800
Boston, MA 02116
Phone: (617)262-7770
Fax: (617)262-9779
Preferred Investment Size: $2,000,000. Investment Types: No preference. Industry Preferences: Communications, computer, and medical/health related. Geographic Preferences: Entire U.S.

Cambridge/Samsung Partners
One Exeter Plaza
Ninth Fl.
Boston, MA 02116
Phone: (617)262-4440
Fax: (617)262-5562
Aashish Kalra, Associate
Preferred Investment Size: $100,000 minimum. Investment Policies: Equity. Investment Types: Early stage. Industry Preferences: Diversified. Geographic Preferences: National.

Chestnut Street Partners, Inc.
75 State St., Ste. 2500
Boston, MA 02109
Phone: (617)345-7220
Fax: (617)345-7201
E-mail: chestnut@chestnutp.com
Drew Zalkind, Senior Vice President
Preferred Investment Size: $100,000 to $1,000,000. Investment Types: Seed, research and development, start-up, and first stage. Industry Preferences: Diversified. Geographic Preferences: No preference.

Claflin Capital Management, Inc.
10 Liberty Sq., Ste. 300
Boston, MA 02109
Phone: (617)426-6505
Fax: (617)482-0016
Website: http://www.claflincapital.com
William Wilcoxson, General Partner
Preferred Investment Size: $100,000 minimum. Investment Types: Seed, start-up, and first stage. Industry Preferences: Diversified. Geographic Preferences: Northeast.

Copley Venture Partners
99 Summer St., Ste. 1720
Boston, MA 02110
Phone: (617)737-1253
Fax: (617)439-0699
Preferred Investment Size: $1,000,000 minimum. Investment Types: First and second stage, and start-up. Industry Preferences: Diversified. Geographic Preferences: No preference.

Corning Capital / Corning Technology Ventures
121 High Street, Ste. 400
Boston, MA 02110
Phone: (617)338-2656
Fax: (617)261-3864
Website: http://www.corningventures.com
Preferred Investment Size: $100,000 to $500,000. Investment Policies: Equity. Investment Types: Early stage. Industry Preferences: Diversified technology. Geographic Preferences: Northeast.

Downer & Co.
211 Congress St.
Boston, MA 02110
Phone: (617)482-6200
Fax: (617)482-6201
E-mail: cdowner@downer.com
Website: http://www.downer.com
Charles W. Downer
Preferred Investment Size: $300,000 to $500,000. Investment Types: Start-up, first and second stage, and mezzanine. Industry Preferences: Diversified. Geographic Preferences: Northeastern U.S. and Canada.

Fidelity Ventures
82 Devonshire St.
Boston, MA 02109
Phone: (617)563-6370
Fax: (617)476-9023
Website: http://www.fidelityventures.com
Neal Yanofsky, Vice President
Preferred Investment Size: $1,000,000 to $10,000,000. Investment Types: Start-up, first and second stage, leveraged buyout, and special situations. Industry Preferences: Diversified. Geographic Preferences: Northeast.

Greylock Management Corp. (Boston)
1 Federal St.
Boston, MA 02110-2065
Phone: (617)423-5525
Fax: (617)482-0059
Chris Surowiec
Preferred Investment Size: $250,000 minimum. Investment Types: Seed, start-up, first and early stage, and expansion. Industry Preferences: Diversified. Geographic Preferences: No preference.

Gryphon Ventures
222 Berkeley St., Ste.1600
Boston, MA 02116
Phone: (617)267-9191
Fax: (617)267-4293
E-mail: all@gryphoninc.com
Andrew J. Atkinson, Vice President
Preferred Investment Size: $1,000,000 minimum. Investment Types: Start-up, first stage, second stage. Industry Preferences: Energy/natural resources, genetic engineering, and industrial products and equipment. Geographic Preferences: National.

Halpern, Denny & Co.
500 Boylston St.
Boston, MA 02116
Phone: (617)536-6602
Fax: (617)536-8535
David P. Malm, Partner
Preferred Investment Size: $5,000,000 to $40,000,000. Investment Types: First stage, second stage, control-black purchases, and leveraged buyouts. Industry Preferences: Consumer related, Internet and computer related, communications, industrial/energy, and medical/health. Geographic Preferences: National.

Harbourvest Partners, LLC
1 Financial Center, 44th Fl.
Boston, MA 02111
Phone: (617)348-3707
Fax: (617)350-0305
Website: http://www.hvpllc.com
Kevin Delbridge, Managing Partner
Preferred Investment Size: $5,000,000 minimum. Investment Types: All types. Industry Preferences: Diversified. Geographic Preferences: No preference.

Highland Capital Partners
2 International Pl.
Boston, MA 02110
Phone: (617)981-1500
Fax: (617)531-1550
E-mail: info@hcp.com
Website: http://www.hcp.com
Keith Benjamin, General Partner
Preferred Investment Size: $500,000 to $5,000,000. Investment Types: Seed, start-up, and early, first and second stage. Industry Preferences: Communications, computer and Internet related, genetic engineering,

and medical/health related. Geographic Preferences: Entire U.S. and Canada.

Lee Munder Venture Partners
John Hancock Tower T-53
200 Clarendon St.
Boston, MA 02103
Phone: (617)380-5600
Fax: (617)380-5601
Website: http://www.leemunder.com
Investment Types: Early, first, second, and later stage; expansion; mezzanine; seed; start-up; and special situation. Industry Preferences: Diversified. Geographic Preferences: East Coast, Mid Atlantic, Northeast, and Southeast.

M/C Venture Partners
75 State St., Ste. 2500
Boston, MA 02109
Phone: (617)345-7200
Fax: (617)345-7201
Website: http://www.mcventurepartners.com
Matthew J. Rubins
Preferred Investment Size: $5,000,000 to $20,000,000. Investment Types: Early stage. Industry Preferences: Communications, computer software and services, Internet related. Geographic Preferences: Entire U.S. and Canada.

Massachusetts Capital Resources Co.
420 Boylston St.
Boston, MA 02116
Phone: (617)536-3900
Fax: (617)536-7930
William J. Torpey, Jr., President
Preferred Investment Size: $500,000 to $1,000,000. Investment Policies: Equity. Investment Types: Second stage, leveraged buyout, and mezzanine. Industry Preferences: No preference. Geographic Preferences: Northeast.

Massachusetts Technology Development Corp. (MTDC)
148 State St.
Boston, MA 02109
Phone: (617)723-4920
Fax: (617)723-5983
E-mail: jhodgman@mtdc.com
Website: http://www.mtdc.com
John F. Hodgman, President
Preferred Investment Size: $200,000 to $1,000,000. Investment Types: Early, seed, and start-up. Industry Preferences: Diversified. Geographic Preferences: Massachusetts.

New England Partners
One Boston Place, Ste. 2100
Boston, MA 02108
Phone: (617)624-8400
Fax: (617)624-8999
Website: http://www.nepartners.com
Christopher P. Young
Preferred Investment Size: $1,000,000 to $5,000,000. Investment Types: Balanced, early, and first and second stage. Industry Preferences: Diversified. Geographic Preferences: Entire U.S.

North Hill Ventures
Ten Post Office Square
11th Fl.
Boston, MA 02109
Phone: (617)788-2112
Fax: (617)788-2152
Website: http://www.northhillventures.com
Preferred Investment Size: $1,500,000 to $7,000,000. Investment Types: Balanced, expansion, and later and second stage. Industry Preferences: Communications, computer software, Internet related, consumer and retail related, business services, and financial services. Geographic Preferences: Entire U.S.

OneLiberty Ventures
150 Cambridge Park Dr.
Boston, MA 02140
Phone: (617)492-7280
Fax: (617)492-7290
Website: http://www.oneliberty.com
Stephen J. McCullen, General Partner
Preferred Investment Size: $1,000,000 to $8,000,000. Investment Policies: Equity. Investment Types: Early and late stage. Industry Preferences: Diversified technology. Geographic Preferences: Northeast.

Schroder Ventures
Life Sciences
60 State St., Ste. 3650
Boston, MA 02109
Phone: (617)367-8100
Fax: (617)367-1590
Website: http://www.shroderventures.com
Preferred Investment Size: $250,000 minimum. Investment Types: Balanced, first stage, leveraged buyout, mezzanine, second stage, special situation, and start-up. Industry Preferences: Diversified. Geographic Preferences: Entire U.S. and Canada.

Shawmut Capital Partners
75 Federal St., 18th Fl.
Boston, MA 02110
Phone: (617)368-4900
Fax: (617)368-4910
Website: http://www.shawmutcapital.com
Daniel Doyle, Managing Director
Preferred Investment Size: $5,000,000 minimum. Investment Types: Start-up, first stage, second stage, mezzanine, leveraged buyout, and special situations. Industry Preferences: Financial services and applications. Geographic Preferences: Entire U.S. and Canada.

Solstice Capital LLC
15 Broad St., 3rd Fl.
Boston, MA 02109
Phone: (617)523-7733
Fax: (617)523-5827
E-mail: solticecapital@solcap.com
Henry Newman, Partner
Preferred Investment Size: $250,000 to $1,000,000. Investment Types: Early and seed. Industry Preferences: Diversified. Geographic Preferences: Northeast, Rocky Mountain, Southwest, West Coast.

Spectrum Equity Investors
One International Pl., 29th Fl.
Boston, MA 02110
Phone: (617)464-4600
Fax: (617)464-4601
Website: http://www.spectrumequity.com
William Collatos, Managing General Partner
Preferred Investment Size: $5,000,000 minimum. Investment Types: Balanced. Industry Preferences: Communications and computer related. Geographic Preferences: U.S. and Canada.

Spray Venture Partners
One Walnut St.
Boston, MA 02108
Phone: (617)305-4140
Fax: (617)305-4144
Website: http://www.sprayventure.com
Preferred Investment Size: $50,000 to $4,000,000. Investment Policies: Equity. Investment Types: Seed, start-up, first and second stage, and research and development. Industry Preferences: Medical and health related, and genetic engineering. Geographic Preferences: National.

The Still River Fund
100 Federal St., 29th Fl.
Boston, MA 02110
Phone: (617)348-2327
Fax: (617)348-2371
Website: http://www.stillriverfund.com
Preferred Investment Size: $300,000 to $4,000,000. Investment Types: Early stage, expansion, first and second stage, seed, and start-up. Industry Preferences: Diversified. Geographic Preferences: Entire U.S.

Summit Partners
600 Atlantic Ave., Ste. 2800
Boston, MA 02210-2227
Phone: (617)824-1000
Fax: (617)824-1159
Website: http://www.summitpartners.com
Christopher W. Sheeline
Preferred Investment Size: $1,500,000 minimum. Investment Types: First and second stage, mezzanine, leveraged buyout, special situations, and control block purchases. Industry Preferences: Diversified. Geographic Preferences: Entire U.S. and Canada.

TA Associates, Inc. (Boston)
High Street Tower
125 High St., Ste. 2500
Boston, MA 02110
Phone: (617)574-6700
Fax: (617)574-6728
Website: http://www.ta.com
Brian Conway, Managing Director
Preferred Investment Size: $60,000,000 maximum. Investment Types: Leveraged buyout, special situations, control block purchases. Industry Preferences: Diversified. Geographic Preferences: No preference.

TVM Techno Venture Management
101 Arch St., Ste. 1950
Boston, MA 02110
Phone: (617)345-9320
Fax: (617)345-9377
E-mail: info@tvmvc.com
Website: http://www.tvmvc.com
Helmut Schuehsler, Partner
Investment Types: Seed, start-up, first and early stage. Industry Preferences: Diversified. Geographic Preferences: Entire U.S.

UNC Ventures
64 Burough St.
Boston, MA 02130-4017
Phone: (617)482-7070
Fax: (617)522-2176
Preferred Investment Size: $500,000 to $1,000,000. Investment Types: Leveraged buyout, mezzanine, and second stage. Industry Preferences: Radio and television broadcasting, environmental related, and financial services. Geographic Preferences: Entire U.S.

Venture Investment Management Company (VIMAC)
177 Milk St.
Boston, MA 02190-3410
Phone: (617)292-3300
Fax: (617)292-7979
E-mail: bzeisig@vimac.com
Website: http://www.vimac.com
Preferred Investment Size: $1,000,000 to $7,000,000. Investment Types: Seed, start-up, first and second stage. Industry Preferences: Diversified technology. Geographic Preferences: Northeast U.S. and Eastern Canada.

MDT Advisers, Inc.
125 Cambridge Park Dr.
Cambridge, MA 02140-2314
Phone: (617)234-2200
Fax: (617)234-2210
Website: http://www.mdtai.com
Michael E.A. O'Malley
Preferred Investment Size: $500,000 to $5,000,000. Investment Types: Early stage and expansion. Industry Preferences: Diversified. Geographic Preferences: Northeast.

TTC Ventures
One Main St., 6th Fl.
Cambridge, MA 02142
Phone: (617)528-3137
Fax: (617)577-1715
E-mail: info@ttcventures.com
Investment Types: Seed, start-up, first stage, second stage, and mezzanine. Industry Preferences: Computer related. Geographic Preferences: National.

Zero Stage Capital Co. Inc.
101 Main St., 17th Fl.
Cambridge, MA 02142
Phone: (617)876-5355
Fax: (617)876-1248
Website: http://www.zerostage.com
Paul Kelley, President
Preferred Investment Size: $10,000 to $15,000,000. Investment Types: Early and later stage. Industry Preferences: Diversified technology. Geographic Preferences: Entire U.S.

Atlantic Capital
164 Cushing Hwy.
Cohasset, MA 02025
Phone: (617)383-9449
Fax: (617)383-6040
E-mail: info@atlanticcap.com
Website: http://www.atlanticcap.com
Preferred Investment Size: $300,000 to $500,000. Investment Types: Start-up and first stage. Industry Preferences: Diversified. Geographic Preferences: National.

Seacoast Capital Partners
55 Ferncroft Rd.
Danvers, MA 01923
Phone: (978)750-1300
Fax: (978)750-1301
E-mail: gdeli@seacoastcapital.com
Website: http://www.seacoastcapital.com
Gregory A. Hulecki
Preferred Investment Size: $3,000,000 minimum. Investment Policies: Loans and equity investments. Investment Types: Second stage, industry rollups, leveraged buyout, mezzanine, and special situations. Industry Preferences: Diversified. Geographic Preferences: National.

Sage Management Group
44 South Street
PO Box 2026
East Dennis, MA 02641
Phone: (508)385-7172
Fax: (508)385-7272
E-mail: sagemgt@capecod.net
Charles Bauer
Preferred Investment Size: $500,000 to $1,000,000. Investment Policies: Equity. Investment Types: First and second stage, leveraged buyout, mezzanine, and special situations. Industry Preferences: Diversified technology. Geographic Preferences: National.

Applied Technology
1 Cranberry Hill
Lexington, MA 02421-7397
Phone: (617)862-8622
Fax: (617)862-8367
Ellie McCormack, Analyst
Preferred Investment Size: $100,000 to $2,000,000. Investment Types: Seed, start-up, first and second stage, leveraged buyout, and research and development. Industry Preferences: Diversified. Geographic Preferences: Entire U.S.

Royalty Capital Management
5 Downing Rd.
Lexington, MA 02421-6918
Phone: (781)861-8490
Preferred Investment Size: $100,000 to $300,000. Investment Types: Start-up, first stage, second stage, leveraged buyout, and special situations. Industry Preferences: Diversified. Geographic Preferences: Northeast.

Argo Global Capital
210 Broadway, Ste. 101
Lynnfield, MA 01940
Phone: (781)592-5250
Fax: (781)592-5230
Website: http://www.gsmcapital.com
Investment Types: Balanced and expansion. Industry Preferences: Communications, computer, and Internet related. Geographic Preferences: No preference.

Industry Ventures
6 Bayne Lane
Newburyport, MA 01950
Phone: (978)499-7606
Fax: (978)499-0686
Website: http://
www.industryventures.com
Preferred Investment Size: $250,000 to $2,000,000. Investment Types: Early, first, and second stage; seed, start-up. Industry Preferences: Wireless communications, computer software, Internet related, retail, and media. Geographic Preferences: Mid Atlantic, Northeast, West Coast.

Softbank Capital Partners
10 Langley Rd., Ste. 202
Newton Center, MA 02459
Phone: (617)928-9300
Fax: (617)928-9305
E-mail: clax@bvc.com
Gary Rieschel
Investment Types: Seed, start-up, first stage, second stage, mezzanine, leveraged buyout, and special situations. Industry Preferences: Communications and Internet. Geographic Preferences: Entire U.S. and Canada.

Advanced Technology Ventures (Boston)
281 Winter St., Ste. 350
Waltham, MA 02451
Phone: (781)290-0707
Fax: (781)684-0045
E-mail: info@atvcapital.com
Website: http://www.atvcapital.com
Preferred Investment Size: $15,000,000 to $35,000,000. Investment Types: Start-up, first stage, second stage, and balanced. Industry Preferences: Diversified. Geographic Preferences: No preference.

Castile Ventures
890 Winter St., Ste. 140
Waltham, MA 02451
Phone: (781)890-0060
Fax: (781)890-0065
Website: http://
www.castileventures.com
Preferred Investment Size: $100,000 to $15,000,000. Investment Types: Early, first, and second stage; seed; and start-up. Industry Preferences: Communications and media, and Internet related. Geographic Preferences: Mid Atlantic, Northeast, and Southeast.

Charles River Ventures
1000 Winter St., Ste. 3300
Waltham, MA 02451
Phone: (781)487-7060
Fax: (781)487-7065
Website: http://www.crv.com
Richard M. Burnes, Jr., General Partner
Preferred Investment Size: $1,000,000 to $20,000,000. Investment Types: Seed, start-up, first and second stage. Industry Preferences: Diversified. Geographic Preferences: No preference.

Comdisco Venture Group (Waltham)
Totton Pond Office Center
400-1 Totten Pond Rd.
Waltham, MA 02451
Phone: (617)672-0250
Fax: (617)398-8099
Preferred Investment Size: $300,000 to $20,000,000. Investment Types: Seed, start-up, first and second stage. Industry Preferences: Diversified. Geographic Preferences: National.

Marconi Ventures
890 Winter St., Ste. 310
Waltham, MA 02451
Phone: (781)839-7177
Fax: (781)522-7477
Website: http://www.marconi.com
Preferred Investment Size: $1,000,000 to $10,000,000. Investment Types: Balanced; first, second, and later stage; and start-up. Industry Preferences: Diversified. Geographic Preferences: U.S. and Canada.

Matrix Partners
Bay Colony Corporate Center
1000 Winter St., Ste.4500
Waltham, MA 02451
Phone: (781)890-2244
Fax: (781)890-2288
Website: http://
www.matrixpartners.com
Andrew Marcuvitz, General Partner
Preferred Investment Size: $500,000 to $1,000,000. Investment Types: Start-up, first and second stage, and leveraged buyout. Industry Preferences: Diversified. Geographic Preferences: Entire U.S.

North Bridge Venture Partners
950 Winter St. Ste. 4600
Waltham, MA 02451
Phone: (781)290-0004
Fax: (781)290-0999
E-mail: eta@nbvp.com
Preferred Investment Size: $2,000,000 to $3,000,000. Investment Types: Seed, research and development, start-up, first and second stage. Industry Preferences: Communications, computer related, medical/health, and electronics. Geographic Preferences: Entire U.S. and Canada.

Polaris Venture Partners
Bay Colony Corporate Ctr.
1000 Winter St., Ste. 3500
Waltham, MA 02451
Phone: (781)290-0770
Fax: (781)290-0880
E-mail: partners@polarisventures.com
Website: http://www.polarisventures.com
Michael Hirschland
Preferred Investment Size: $250,000 to $15,000,000. Investment Types: Seed, start-up, first and second stages. Industry Preferences: Information technology, medical and health related. Geographic Preferences: National.

Seaflower Ventures
Bay Colony Corporate Ctr.
1000 Winter St. Ste. 1000
Waltham, MA 02451
Phone: (781)466-9552
Fax: (781)466-9553
E-mail: moot@seaflower.com
Website: http://www.seaflower.com
Alexander Moot, Partner
Investment Types: Seed, research and development, start-up, first and second stage, recaps, and strategic alliances. Industry Preferences: Diversified technology. Geographic Preferences: Eastern U.S. and Midwest.

Ampersand Ventures
55 William St., Ste. 240
Wellesley, MA 02481
Phone: (617)239-0700
Fax: (617)239-0824
E-mail: info@ampersandventures.com
Website: http://www.ampersandventures.com
Paul C. Zigman, Partner
Preferred Investment Size: $5,000,000 to $15,000,000. Investment Types: All types. Industry Preferences: Diversified. Geographic Preferences: No preference.

Battery Ventures (Boston)
20 William St., Ste. 200
Wellesley, MA 02481
Phone: (781)577-1000
Fax: (781)577-1001
Website: http://www.battery.com
David A. Hartwig
Preferred Investment Size: $3,000,000 to $35,000,000. Investment Types: Seed, start-up, first and second stage, mezzanine, and leveraged buyout. Industry Preferences: Communications, computer, computer and communications distribution. Geographic Preferences: No preference.

Commonwealth Capital Ventures, L.P.
20 William St., Ste.225
Wellesley, MA 02481
Phone: (781)237-7373
Fax: (781)235-8627
Website: http://www.ccvlp.com
Preferred Investment Size: $500,000 to $5,000,000. Investment Policies: Equity. Investment Types: Seed, start-up, first stage, leveraged buyout, mezzanine, and special situation. Industry Preferences: Diversified communication and computer technology, consumer products and services, retailing, distribution, electronics, medical and health related. Geographic Preferences: Northeast.

Fowler, Anthony & Company
20 Walnut St.
Wellesley, MA 02481
Phone: (781)237-4201
Fax: (781)237-7718
Preferred Investment Size: $4,000,000 to $5,000,000. Investment Types: All types. Industry Preferences: Diversified. Geographic Preferences: Entire U.S. and Canada.

Gemini Investors
20 William St.
Wellesley, MA 02481
Phone: (781)237-7001
Fax: (781)237-7233
C. Redington Barrett, III, Managing Director
Investment Types: Second stage, mezzanine, leveraged buyout, and special situations. Industry Preferences: Diversified. Geographic Preferences: National.

Grove Street Advisors Inc.
20 William St., Ste. 230
Wellesley, MA 02481
Phone: (781)263-6100
Fax: (781)263-6101
Website: http://www.grovestreetadvisors.com
Preferred Investment Size: $1,000,000 to $7,500,000. Investment Types: First stage, mezzanine, second stage, special situation, and start-up. Industry Preferences: Diversified. Geographic Preferences: U.S.

Mees Pierson Investeringsmaat B.V.
20 William St., Ste. 210
Wellesley, MA 02482
Phone: (781)239-7600
Fax: (781)239-0377
Dennis P. Cameron
Investment Types: First and second stage, and start-up. Industry Preferences: Diversified technology. Geographic Preferences: Entire U.S. and Canada.

Norwest Equity Partners
40 William St., Ste. 305
Wellesley, MA 02481-3902
Phone: (781)237-5870
Fax: (781)237-6270
Website: http://www.norwestvp.com
Charles B. Lennin
Preferred Investment Size: $1,000,000 to $25,000,000. Investment Types: Seed, early and later stage, and expansion. Industry Preferences: Diversified. Geographic Preferences: National.

Bessemer Venture Partners (Wellesley Hills)
83 Walnut St.

Wellesley Hills, MA 02481
Phone: (781)237-6050
Fax: (781)235-7576
E-mail: travis@bvpny.com
Website: http://www.bvp.com
Preferred Investment Size: $100,000 to $15,000,000. Investment Types: Seed, start-up, early stage, first and second stage, and expansion. Industry Preferences: Communications, computer related, consumer products, distribution, and electronics. Geographic Preferences: National.

Venture Capital Fund of New England
20 Walnut St., Ste. 120
Wellesley Hills, MA 02481-2175
Phone: (781)239-8262
Fax: (781)239-8263
E-mail: kjdvcfne3@aol.com
Kevin J. Dougherty, General Partner
Preferred Investment Size: $750,000 to $3,000,000. Investment Types: Start-up, first and second stage. Industry Preferences: Diversified. Geographic Preferences: Northeast.

Prism Venture Partners
100 Lowder Brook Dr., Ste. 2500
Westwood, MA 02090
Phone: (781)302-4000
Fax: (781)302-4040
E-mail: dwbaum@prismventure.com
Preferred Investment Size: $2,000,000 to $10,000,000. Investment Types: Start-up, first stage, second stage, and mezzanine. Industry Preferences: Communications, computer and Internet related, electronic components and instrumentation, medical and health. Geographic Preferences: U.S. and Canada.

Palmer Partners LP
200 Unicorn Park Dr.
Woburn, MA 01801
Phone: (781)933-5445
Fax: (781)933-0698
John Shane
Preferred Investment Size: $250,000 to $1,000,000. Investment Types: Start-up, first and second stage, and special situations. Industry Preferences: Communications, computer, energy/natural resources, industrial, education, finance, and publishing. Geographic Preferences: Northeast, Southeast, Southwest, Midwest, and Middle Atlantic; Central and Eastern Canada.

Michigan

Arbor Partners, L.L.C.
130 South First St.
Ann Arbor, MI 48104
Phone: (734)668-9000
Fax: (734)669-4195
Website: http://
www.arborpartners.com
Preferred Investment Size: $250,000 minimum. Investment Policies: Equity. Investment Types: Early and expansion. Industry Preferences: Diversified technology. Geographic Preferences: Midwest.

EDF Ventures
425 N. Main St.
Ann Arbor, MI 48104
Phone: (734)663-3213
Fax: (734)663-7358
E-mail: edf@edfvc.com
Website: http://www.edfvc.com
Mary Campbell, Partner
Preferred Investment Size: $500,000 to $10,000,000. Investment Types: Seed, start-up, first stage, second stage, expansion, and research and development. Industry Preferences: Diversified technology. Geographic Preferences: Midwest.

White Pines Management, L.L.C.
2401 Plymouth Rd., Ste. B
Ann Arbor, MI 48105
Phone: (734)747-9401
Fax: (734)747-9704
E-mail: ibund@whitepines.com
Website: http://www.whitepines.com
Preferred Investment Size: $1,000,000 to $4,000,000. Investment Types: Second stage, mezzanine, leveraged buyout, and special situations. Industry Preferences: Diversified. Geographic Preferences: Southeast and Midwest.

Wellmax, Inc.
3541 Bendway Blvd., Ste. 100
Bloomfield Hills, MI 48301
Phone: (248)646-3554
Fax: (248)646-6220
Preferred Investment Size: $100,000 to $1,000,000. Investment Policies: Equity. Investment Types: Start-up, early and late stage, leveraged buyout, and special situations. Industry Preferences: Diversified. Geographic Preferences: Midwest, Southeast.

Venture Funding, Ltd.
Fisher Bldg.
3011 West Grand Blvd., Ste. 321
Detroit, MI 48202
Phone: (313)871-3606
Fax: (313)873-4935
Monis Schuster, Vice President
Preferred Investment Size: $1,000,000 minimum. Investment Policies: Equity. Investment Types: Start-up, seed, leveraged buyout, research and development, and special situations. Industry Preferences: Diversified. Geographic Preferences: National.

Investcare Partners L.P. / GMA Capital LLC
32330 W. Twelve Mile Rd.
Farmington Hills, MI 48334
Phone: (248)489-9000
Fax: (248)489-8819
E-mail: gma@gmacapital.com
Website: http://www.gmacapital.com
Malcolm Moss, Managing Director
Investment Types: Second stage and leveraged buyout. Industry Preferences: Medical and health related. Geographic Preferences: National.

Liberty Bidco Investment Corp.
30833 Northwestern Highway, Ste. 211
Farmington Hills, MI 48334
Phone: (248)626-6070
Fax: (248)626-6072
James Zabriskie, Vice President
Preferred Investment Size: $500,000 minimum. Investment Types: Second stage, leveraged buyout, mezzanine, and special situations. Industry Preferences: Diversified. Geographic Preferences: Midwestern U.S. and Ontario, Canada.

Seaflower Ventures
5170 Nicholson Rd.
PO Box 474

Fowlerville, MI 48836
Phone: (517)223-3335
Fax: (517)223-3337
E-mail: gibbons@seaflower.com
Website: http://www.seaflower.com
M. Christine Gibbons, Partner
Investment Types: Seed, research and development, start-up, recaps, strategic alliances, first and second stage. Industry Preferences: Genetic engineering, industrial products and equipment, medical and health related. Geographic Preferences: Midwest, Northeast, and Mid Atlantic.

Ralph Wilson Equity Fund LLC
15400 E. Jefferson Ave.
Gross Pointe Park, MI 48230
Phone: (313)821-9122
Fax: (313)821-9101
Website: http://www.RalphWilsonEquityFund.com
J. Skip Simms, President
Preferred Investment Size: $200,000 to $1,000,000. Investment Types: Balanced, early stage, expansion, and first and second stage. Industry Preferences: Diversified. Geographic Preferences: Entire U.S.

Minnesota

Development Corp. of Austin
1900 Eighth Ave., NW
Austin, MN 55912
Phone: (507)433-0346
Fax: (507)433-0361
E-mail: dca@smig.net
Website: http://www.spamtownusa.com
Preferred Investment Size: $100,000. Investment Types: Start-up, seed, and first stage. Industry Preferences: Diversified. Geographic Preferences: No preference.

Northeast Ventures Corp.
802 Alworth Bldg.
Duluth, MN 55802
Phone: (218)722-9915
Fax: (218)722-9871
Greg Sandbulte, President
Preferred Investment Size: $100,000 to $500,000. Investment Policies: Equity. Investment Types: Start-up, early and late stage, mezzanine, leveraged buyout, and research and development. Industry Preferences: No preference. Geographic Preferences: Midwest.

Medical Innovation Partners, Inc.
6450 City West Pkwy.
Eden Prairie, MN 55344-3245
Phone: (612)828-9616
Fax: (612)828-9596
Mark B. Knudson, Ph.D., Managing Partner
Preferred Investment Size: $100,000 to $5,000,000. Investment Types: Seed, start-up, and first stage. Industry Preferences: Medical technology and healthcare, and communications. Geographic Preferences: Northwest and Midwest.

St. Paul Venture Capital, Inc.
10400 Vicking Dr., Ste. 550
Eden Prairie, MN 55344
Phone: (612)995-7474
Fax: (612)995-7475
Website: http://www.stpaulvc.com
Preferred Investment Size: $500,000 minimum. Investment Types: Early stage. Industry Preferences: Diversified. Geographic Preferences: California, Massachusetts, and Minnesota.

Cherry Tree Investments, Inc.
7601 France Ave. S, Ste. 150
Edina, MN 55435
Phone: (612)893-9012
Fax: (612)893-9036
Website: http://www.cherrytree.com
Sandy Trump
Preferred Investment Size: $100,000 minimum. Investment Types: Balanced and early second stage. Industry Preferences: Diversified. Geographic Preferences: Midwest.

Shared Ventures, Inc.
6550 York Ave. S
Edina, MN 55435
Phone: (612)925-3411
Howard Weiner
Preferred Investment Size: $100,000 to $300,000. Investment Types: First and second stage, start-up, leveraged buyout, control-block purchases, and special situations. Industry Preferences: Consumer, electronics, distribution, energy/natural resources, industrial products and equipment, medical and health related. Geographic Preferences: Midwest.

Sherpa Partners LLC
5050 Lincoln Dr., Ste. 490
Edina, MN 55436
Phone: (952)942-1070
Fax: (952)942-1071
Website: http://www.sherpapartners.com
Preferred Investment Size: $250,000 to $5,000,000. Investment Types: Early stage. Industry Preferences: Telecommunications, computer software, and Internet related. Geographic Preferences: Midwest.

Affinity Capital Management
901 Marquette Ave., Ste. 1810
Minneapolis, MN 55402
Phone: (612)252-9900
Fax: (612)252-9911
Website: http://www.affinitycapital.com
Edson W. Spencer
Preferred Investment Size: $250,000 to $1,100,000. Investment Types: Seed, start-up, first and second stage. Industry Preferences: Medical/Health related, Internet and computer related. Geographic Preferences: Midwest.

Artesian Capital
1700 Foshay Tower
821 Marquette Ave.
Minneapolis, MN 55402
Phone: (612)334-5600
Fax: (612)334-5601
E-mail: artesian@artesian.com
Frank B. Bennett, President
Preferred Investment Size: $300,000 to $500,000. Investment Types: Seed, research and development, leveraged buyout, and start-up. Industry Preferences: Diversified. Geographic Preferences: Midwest.

Coral Ventures
60 S. 6th St., Ste. 3510
Minneapolis, MN 55402
Phone: (612)335-8666
Fax: (612)335-8668
Website: http://www.coralventures.com
Preferred Investment Size: $1,000,000 to $11,000,000. Investment Types: Seed, start-up, first and second stage. Industry

Preferences: Diversified technology. Geographic Preferences: No preference.

Crescendo Venture Management, L.L.C.
800 LaSalle Ave., Ste. 2250
Minneapolis, MN 55402
Phone: (612)607-2800
Fax: (612)607-2801
Website: http://www.crescendoventures.com
Jeffrey R. Tollefson, Partner
Preferred Investment Size: $1,000,000 to $5,000,000. Investment Types: Start-up, seed, early and late stage. Industry Preferences: Diversified information technology. Geographic Preferences: U.S. and Canada.

Gideon Hixon Venture
1900 Foshay Tower
821 Marquette Ave.
Minneapolis, MN 55402
Phone: (612)904-2314
Fax: (612)204-0913
E-mail: bkwhitney@gideonhixon.com
Preferred Investment Size: $300,000 to $500,000. Investment Policies: Equity. Investment Types: Start-up, seed, early and late stage. Industry Preferences: Diversified communication and computer technology, medical/health, and electronics. Geographic Preferences: West Coast.

Norwest Equity Partners
3600 IDS Center
80 S. 8th St.
Minneapolis, MN 55402
Phone: (612)215-1600
Fax: (612)215-1601
Website: http://www.norwestvp.com
Charles B. Lennin, Partner
Preferred Investment Size: $1,000,000 to $25,000,000. Investment Policies: Equity. Investment Types: Seed, expansion, early and later stage. Industry Preferences: Diversified. Geographic Preferences: National.

Oak Investment Partners (Minneapolis)
4550 Norwest Center
90 S. 7th St.
Minneapolis, MN 55402
Phone: (612)339-9322
Fax: (612)337-8017
Website: http://www.oakinv.com
Preferred Investment Size: $250,000 to $5,000,000. Investment Types: Start-up, first stage, second and late stage, leveraged buyout, control-block purchases, open market, and special situations. Industry Preferences: Diversified. Geographic Preferences: Entire U.S.

Pathfinder Venture Capital Funds (Minneapolis)
7300 Metro Blvd., Ste. 585
Minneapolis, MN 55439
Phone: (612)835-1121
Fax: (612)835-8389
E-mail: jahrens620@aol.com
Jack K. Ahrens, II, Investment Officer
Preferred Investment Size: $2,000,000 minimum. Investment Types: Seed, start-up, first and second stage, mezzanine, leveraged buyouts, and special situations. Industry Preferences: Diversified. Geographic Preferences: Entire U.S. and Canada.

U.S. Bancorp Piper Jaffray Ventures, Inc.
800 Nicollet Mall, Ste. 800
Minneapolis, MN 55402
Phone: (612)303-5686
Fax: (612)303-1350
Website: http://www.paperjaffreyventures.com
Preferred Investment Size: $250,000 minimum. Investment Types: Early and late stage, and mezzanine. Industry Preferences: Diversified. Geographic Preferences: Entire U.S.

The Food Fund, Ltd. Partnership
5720 Smatana Dr., Ste. 300
Minnetonka, MN 55343
Phone: (612)939-3950
Fax: (612)939-8106
John Trucano, Managing General Partner
Preferred Investment Size: $800,000 minimum. Investment Types: Start-up, first and second stage, leveraged buyout, and special situations. Industry Preferences: Consumer related, industrial and energy, and electronics. Geographic Preferences: Entire U.S.

Mayo Medical Ventures
200 First St. SW
Rochester, MN 55905
Phone: (507)266-4586
Fax: (507)284-5410
Website: http://www.mayo.edu
Preferred Investment Size: $1,000,000 minimum. Investment Types: Early stage. Industry Preferences: Diversified. Geographic Preferences: Entire U.S.

Missouri

Bankers Capital Corp.
3100 Gillham Rd.
Kansas City, MO 64109
Phone: (816)531-1600
Fax: (816)531-1334
Lee Glasnapp, Vice President
Preferred Investment Size: $100,000 minimum. Investment Types: Leveraged buyout. Industry Preferences: Consumer product and electronics distribution, and industrial equipment and machinery. Geographic Preferences: Midwest.

Capital for Business, Inc. (Kansas City)
1000 Walnut St., 18th Fl.
Kansas City, MO 64106
Phone: (816)234-2357
Fax: (816)234-2952
Website: http://www.capitalforbusiness.com
Hollis A. Huels
Preferred Investment Size: $500,000 to $5,000,000. Investment Types: Expansion, leveraged and management buyouts, and later stage. Industry Preferences: Diversified. Geographic Preferences: Midwest.

De Vries & Co. Inc.
800 West 47th St.
Kansas City, MO 64112
Phone: (816)756-0055
Fax: (816)756-0061
Preferred Investment Size: $500,000 minimum. Investment Types: Acquisition, expansion, later stage, leveraged and management buyout, mezzanine, private placement, recaps, and second stage. Industry

Preferences: Diversified. Geographic Preferences: No preference.

InvestAmerica Venture Group Inc. (Kansas City)
Commerce Tower
911 Main St., Ste. 2424
Kansas City, MO 64105
Phone: (816)842-0114
Fax: (816)471-7339
Kevin F. Mullane, Vice President
Preferred Investment Size: $500,000 to $1,000,000. Investment Types: First and second stage, leveraged buyout, and special situations. Industry Preferences: Diversified. Geographic Preferences: Entire U.S.

Kansas City Equity Partners
233 W. 47th St.
Kansas City, MO 64112
Phone: (816)960-1771
Fax: (816)960-1777
Website: http://www.kcep.com
Preferred Investment Size: $2,000,000 to $8,000,000. Investment Types: Start-up, early stage, expansion, and joint ventures. Industry Preferences: Diversified. Geographic Preferences: Midwest.

Bome Investors, Inc.
8000 Maryland Ave., Ste. 1190
St. Louis, MO 63105
Phone: (314)721-5707
Fax: (314)721-5135
Website: http://www.gatewayventures.com
Gregory R. Johnson
Preferred Investment Size: $500,000 to $1,000,000. Investment Types: Start-up, early and late stage. Industry Preferences: Diversified. Geographic Preferences: Midwest.

Capital for Business, Inc. (St. Louis)
11 S. Meramac St., Ste. 1430
St. Louis, MO 63105
Phone: (314)746-7427
Fax: (314)746-8739
Website: http://www.capitalforbusiness.com
Hollis A. Huels
Preferred Investment Size: $500,000 to $5,000,000. Investment Types: Expansion, leveraged and management buyouts, and later stage. Industry Preferences: Diversified. Geographic Preferences: Midwest.

Crown Capital Corp.
540 Maryville Centre Dr., Ste. 120
Saint Louis, MO 63141
Phone: (314)576-1201
Fax: (314)576-1525
Website: http://www.crown-cap.com
Investment Types: Control-block purchases, first stage, leveraged buyout, mezzanine, second stage, and special situation. Industry Preferences: Diversified. Geographic Preferences: Entire U.S. and Canada.

Gateway Associates L.P.
8000 Maryland Ave., Ste. 1190
St. Louis, MO 63105
Phone: (314)721-5707
Fax: (314)721-5135
John S. McCarthy, Managing General Partner
Preferred Investment Size: $1,000,000 minimum. Investment Types: Start-up, second stage, mezzanine, leveraged buyout, special situations, control block purchases. Industry Preferences: Communications, computer related, electronics, and hospital and other institutional management. Geographic Preferences: Entire U.S.

Harbison Corp.
8112 Maryland Ave., Ste. 250
Saint Louis, MO 63105
Phone: (314)727-8200
Fax: (314)727-0249
Keith Harbison
Preferred Investment Size: $500,000 minimum. Investment Types: Control-block purchases, leveraged buyout, and special situation. Industry Preferences: Diversified. Geographic Preferences: Mid Atlantic and Southeast; Ontario and Quebec, Canada.

Nebraska

Heartland Capital Fund, Ltd.
PO Box 642117
Omaha, NE 68154
Phone: (402)778-5124
Fax: (402)445-2370
Website: http://www.heartlandcapitalfund.com
John G. Gustafson, Vice President
Preferred Investment Size: $500,000 to $3,000,000. Investment Policies: Equity. Investment Types: First and second stage, and expansion. Industry Preferences: Diversified technology. Geographic Preferences: Southwest and Midwest.

Odin Capital Group
1625 Farnam St., Ste. 700
Omaha, NE 68102
Phone: (402)346-6200
Fax: (402)342-9311
Website: http://www.odincapital.com
Preferred Investment Size: $1,000,000 to $5,000,000. Investment Types: Early, first, and second stage, and expansion. Industry Preferences: Internet related and financial services. Geographic Preferences: U.S.

Nevada

Edge Capital Investment Co. LLC
1350 E. Flamingo Rd., Ste. 3000
Las Vegas, NV 89119
Phone: (702)438-3343
E-mail: info@edgecapital.net
Website: http://www.edgecapital.net
Preferred Investment Size: $500,000 to $15,000,000. Investment Types: Seed, start-up, first stage, second stage, mezzanine, leveraged buyout, and special situations. Industry Preferences: Diversified technology. Geographic Preferences: U.S. and Canada.

The Benefit Capital Companies Inc.
PO Box 542
Logandale, NV 89021
Phone: (702)398-3222
Fax: (702)398-3700
Robert Smiley
Preferred Investment Size: $2,500,000 minimum. Investment Types: Leveraged buyout and mezzanine. Industry Preferences: Diversified. Geographic Preferences: Entire U.S.

Millennium Three Venture Group LLC
6880 South McCarran Blvd., Ste. A-11
Reno, NV 89509
Phone: (775)954-2020

Fax: (775)954-2023
Website: http://www.m3vg.com
Preferred Investment Size: $500,000 to $2,000,000. Investment Types: Early stage, expansion, first stage, mezzanine, second stage, and seed. Industry Preferences: Diversified. Geographic Preferences: West Coast.

New Jersey

Alan I. Goldman & Associates
497 Ridgewood Ave.
Glen Ridge, NJ 07028
Phone: (973)857-5680
Fax: (973)509-8856
Alan Goldman
Preferred Investment Size: $500,000 minimum. Investment Types: Control-block purchases, leveraged buyout, mezzanine, second stage, and special situation. Industry Preferences: Diversified. Geographic Preferences: Entire U.S. and Canada.

CS Capital Partners LLC
328 Second St., Ste. 200
Lakewood, NJ 08701
Phone: (732)901-1111
Fax: (212)202-5071
Website: http://www.cs-capital.com
Preferred Investment Size: $500,000 to $3,000,000. Investment Types: Distressed debt, early stage, expansion, first and second stage, and turnaround. Industry Preferences: Internet and computer related, communications, and medical/health related. Geographic Preferences: Entire U.S. and Ontario and Quebec, Canada.

Edison Venture Fund
1009 Lenox Dr., Ste. 4
Lawrenceville, NJ 08648
Phone: (609)896-1900
Fax: (609)896-0066
E-mail: info@edisonventure.com
Website: http://www.edisonventure.com
John H. Martinson, Managing Partner
Preferred Investment Size: $1,000,000 to $6,000,000. Investment Types: Early and later stage, expansion, and management buyouts. Industry Preferences: Diversified. Geographic Preferences: Northeast and Middle Atlantic.

Tappan Zee Capital Corp. (New Jersey)
201 Lower Notch Rd.
PO Box 416
Little Falls, NJ 07424
Phone: (973)256-8280
Fax: (973)256-2841
Jeffrey Birnberg, President
Preferred Investment Size: $100,000 to $250,000. Investment Types: Leveraged buyout. Industry Preferences: Diversified. Geographic Preferences: No preference.

The CIT Group/Venture Capital, Inc.
650 CIT Dr.
Livingston, NJ 07039
Phone: (973)740-5429
Fax: (973)740-5555
Website: http://www.cit.com
Preferred Investment Size: $3,000,000 minimum. Investment Types: First and second stage, mezzanine, and leveraged buyout. Industry Preferences: Diversified. Geographic Preferences: Entire U.S.

Capital Express, L.L.C.
1100 Valleybrook Ave.
Lyndhurst, NJ 07071
Phone: (201)438-8228
Fax: (201)438-5131
E-mail: niles@capitalexpress.com
Website: http://www.capitalexpress.com
Niles Cohen
Preferred Investment Size: $300,000 to $500,000. Investment Policies: Equity. Investment Types: Start-up, first and second stage, and recaps. Industry Preferences: Internet and consumer related, and publishing. Geographic Preferences: East Coast.

Westford Technology Ventures, L.P.
17 Academy St.
Newark, NJ 07102
Phone: (973)624-2131
Fax: (973)624-2008
Preferred Investment Size: $300,000 to $500,000. Investment Types: start-up, first and second stage. Industry Preferences: Diversified communication and computer technology, electronics, industrial products and equipment. Geographic Preferences: No preference.

Accel Partners
1 Palmer Sq.
Princeton, NJ 08542
Phone: (609)683-4500
Fax: (609)683-4880
Website: http://www.accel.com
Preferred Investment Size: $1,000,000 minimum. Investment Types: Seed, start-up and early stage. Industry Preferences: Diversified. Geographic Preferences: National.

Cardinal Partners
221 Nassau St.
Princeton, NJ 08542
Phone: (609)924-6452
Fax: (609)683-0174
Website: http://www.cardinalhealthpartners.com
Lisa Skeete Tatum, Associate
Preferred Investment Size: $1,000,000 to $8,000,000. Investment Types: Seed, start-up, first and second stage. Industry Preferences: Diversified. Geographic Preferences: U.S. and Canada.

Domain Associates L.L.C.
One Palmer Sq., Ste. 515
Princeton, NJ 08542
Phone: (609)683-5656
Fax: (609)683-9789
Website: http://www.domainvc.com
Preferred Investment Size: $1,000,000 to $20,000,000. Investment Types: Seed, start-up, first and second stage, balanced, expansion, mezzanine, private placement, research and development, and late stage. Industry Preferences: Electronic components and instrumentation, genetic engineering, industrial products and equipment, medical and health related. Geographic Preferences: National.

Johnston Associates, Inc.
181 Cherry Valley Rd.
Princeton, NJ 08540
Phone: (609)924-3131
Fax: (609)683-7524
E-mail: jaincorp@aol.com
Preferred Investment Size: $500,000 to $5,000,000. Investment Types: Start-up and early stage. Industry Preferences: Science and healthcare industry. Geographic Preferences: Northeast.

Kemper Ventures
Princeton Forrestal Village
155 Village Blvd.
Princeton, NJ 08540
Phone: (609)936-3035
Fax: (609)936-3051
Richard Secchia, Partner
Investment Types: Seed, research and development, start-up, first and second stage. Industry Preferences: Computer related, medical and health related, financial services. Geographic Preferences: National.

Penny Lane Parnters
One Palmer Sq., Ste. 309
Princeton, NJ 08542
Phone: (609)497-4646
Fax: (609)497-0611
Preferred Investment Size: $1,000,000. Investment Types: Recaps, second stage, and leveraged buyouts. Industry Preferences: Computer related, genetic engineering, medical/health related, and electronics. Geographic Preferences: Eastern U.S.

Early Stage Enterprises L.P.
995 Route 518
Skillman, NJ 08558
Phone: (609)921-8896
Fax: (609)921-8703
Website: http://www.esevc.com
Ronald R. Hahn, Managing Director
Preferred Investment Size: $250,000 to $1,000,000. Investment Types: Seed, start-up, and early stage. Industry Preferences: Diversified. Geographic Preferences: Mid Atlantic.

MBW Management Inc.
1 Springfield Ave.
Summit, NJ 07901
Phone: (908)273-4060
Fax: (908)273-4430
Preferred Investment Size: $1,000,000 minimum. Investment Types: First stage, leveraged buyout, second stage, special situation, and start-up. Industry Preferences: Diversified. Geographic Preferences: No preference.

BCI Advisors, Inc.
Glenpointe Center W.
Teaneck, NJ 07666
Phone: (201)836-3900
Fax: (201)836-6368
E-mail: info@bciadvisors.com
Website: http://www.bcipartners.com
Thomas J. Cusick, General Partner
Preferred Investment Size: $5,000,000 to $25,000,000. Investment Types: Expansion. Industry Preferences: Diversified. Geographic Preferences: Entire U.S.

Demuth, Folger & Wetherill / DFW Capital Partners
Glenpointe Center E., 5th Fl.
300 Frank W. Burr Blvd.
Teaneck, NJ 07666
Phone: (201)836-2233
Fax: (201)836-5666
Website: http://www.dfwcapital.com
Donald F. DeMuth, General Partner
Preferred Investment Size: $500,000 minimum. Investment Policies: Equity. Investment Types: Acquisition, control-block purchases, later stage, leveraged buyout, management buyout, recaps, and speical situations. Industry Preferences: Healthcare, computer, communication, diversified. Geographic Preferences: National.

First Princeton Capital Corp.
189 Berdan Ave., No. 131
Wayne, NJ 07470-3233
Phone: (973)278-3233
Fax: (973)278-4290
Website: http://www.lytellcatt.net
Michael Lytell
Preferred Investment Size: $200,000 minimum. Investment Types: First and second stage, mezzanine, recaps, control-block purchases, and leveraged buyout. Industry Preferences: Diversified. Geographic Preferences: Northeast and East Coast.

Edelson Technology Partners
300 Tice Blvd.
Woodcliff Lake, NJ 07675
Phone: (201)930-9898
Fax: (201)930-8899
Website: http://www.edelsontech.com
Harry Edelson, Managing Partner
Preferred Investment Size: $500,000 to $1,000,000. Investment Types: Seed, start-up, first and second stage, leveraged buyout, and mezzanine. Industry Preferences: Diversified. Geographic Preferences: No preference.

New Mexico

Bruce F. Glaspell & Associates
10400 Academy Rd. NE, Ste. 313
Albuquerque, NM 87111
Phone: (505)292-4505
Fax: (505)292-4258
Bruce Glaspell
Preferred Investment Size: $100,000 to $5,000,000. Investment Types: Seed, start-up, first stage, second stage, late stage, private placement, and expansion. Industry Preferences: Diversified. Geographic Preferences: Entire U.S. and Canada.

High Desert Ventures, Inc.
6101 Imparata St. NE, Ste. 1721
Albuquerque, NM 87111
Phone: (505)797-3330
Fax: (505)338-5147
E-mail: zilenziger@aol.com
Preferred Investment Size: $500,000 to $2,500,000. Investment Types: start-up and early stage. Industry Preferences: Diversified. Geographic Preferences: Northeast and Southwest.

New Business Capital Fund, Ltd.
5805 Torreon NE
Albuquerque, NM 87109
Phone: (505)822-8445
Preferred Investment Size: $100,000. Investment Policies: Equity. Investment Types: Seed, start-up, and first stage. Industry Preferences: Diversified. Geographic Preferences: No preference.

SBC Ventures
10400 Academy Rd. NE, Ste. 313
Albuquerque, NM 87111
Phone: (505)292-4505
Fax: (505)292-4528
Viviana Cloninger, General Partner
Preferred Investment Size: $300,000 to $3,000,000. Investment Types: Seed, research and development, start-up, and first stage. Industry Preferences: Diversified. Geographic Preferences: Entire U.S. and Canada.

Technology Ventures Corp.
1155 University Blvd. SE

Albuquerque, NM 87106
Phone: (505)246-2882
Fax: (505)246-2891
Beverly Bendicksen
Investment Types: Seed, start-up, first and second stage. Industry Preferences: Diversified. Geographic Preferences: Southwest.

New York

New York State Science & Technology Foundation
Small Business Technology Investment Fund
99 Washington Ave., Ste. 1731
Albany, NY 12210
Phone: (518)473-9741
Fax: (518)473-6876
E-mail: jvanwie@empire.state.ny.us
Preferred Investment Size: $100,000 to $300,000. Investment Types: Seed, start-up, first and second stage. Industry Preferences: Diversified technology. Geographic Preferences: Northeast.

Rand Capital Corp.
2200 Rand Bldg.
Buffalo, NY 14203
Phone: (716)853-0802
Fax: (716)854-8480
Website: http://www.randcapital.com
Allen F. Grum, President and CEO
Preferred Investment Size: $25,000 to $500,000. Investment Types: Second stage. Industry Preferences: Diversified. Geographic Preferences: Northeast and Ontario, Canada.

Seed Capital Partners
620 Main St.
Buffalo, NY 14202
Phone: (716)845-7520
Fax: (716)845-7539
Website: http://www.seedcp.com
Investment Types: Early stage. Industry Preferences: Diversified technology, communications, and other products. Geographic Preferences: Northeast.

Coleman Venture Group
5909 Northern Blvd.
PO Box 224
East Norwich, NY 11732
Phone: (516)626-3642
Fax: (516)626-9722
Preferred Investment Size: $100,000 to $1,000,000. Investment Types: First stage, recaps, seed, start-up, and special situation. Industry Preferences: Electronics and consumer products. Geographic Preferences: Northeast and West Coast, and Canada.

Vega Capital Corp.
45 Knollwood Rd.
Elmsford, NY 10523
Phone: (914)345-9500
Fax: (914)345-9505
Ronald Linden
Preferred Investment Size: $300,000 minimum. Investment Types: Second stage, mezzanine, leveraged buyout, and special situations. Industry Preferences: Diversified. Geographic Preferences: Northeast, Southeast, and Middle Atlantic.

Herbert Young Securities, Inc.
98 Cuttermill Rd.
Great Neck, NY 11021
Phone: (516)487-8300
Fax: (516)487-8319
Herbert D. Levine, President
Preferred Investment Size: $1,000,000 minimum. Investment Types: First and second stage, leveraged buyout, mezzanine, and special situation. Industry Preferences: Diversified communications and computer technology, consumer products and services, electronics, genetic engineering, healthcare, and real estate. Geographic Preferences: National.

Sterling/Carl Marks Capital, Inc.
175 Great Neck Rd., Ste. 408
Great Neck, NY 11021
Phone: (516)482-7374
Fax: (516)487-0781
E-mail: stercrlmar@aol.com
Website: http://
www.serlingcarlmarks.com
Preferred Investment Size: $1,000,000 to $2,000,000. Investment Types: Second stage, expansion, management buyouts, and mezzanine. Industry Preferences: Consumer related; distribution of electronics equipment, food and industrial products; and industrial equipment and machinery. Geographic Preferences: Northeast.

Impex Venture Management Co.
PO Box 1570
Green Island, NY 12183
Phone: (518)271-8008
Fax: (518)271-9101
Jay Banker
Preferred Investment Size: $1,000,000 minimum. Investment Types: First stage, leveraged buyout, second stage, special situation, and start-up. Industry Preferences: Diversified. Geographic Preferences: Mid Atlantic and Northeast, and Quebec, Canada.

Corporate Venture Partners L.P.
200 Sunset Park
Ithaca, NY 14850
Phone: (607)257-6323
Fax: (607)257-6128
Preferred Investment Size: $500,000 to $1,000,000. Investment Types: First stage. Industry Preferences: Diversified. Geographic Preferences: Northeast.

Arthur P. Gould & Co.
One Wilshire Dr.
Lake Success, NY 11020
Phone: (516)773-3000
Fax: (516)773-3289
Andrew Gould, Vice President
Preferred Investment Size: $5,000,000 minimum. Investment Types: Seed, research and development, start-up, first stage, second stage, mezzanine, and leveraged buyout. Industry Preferences: Diversified. Geographic Preferences: National.

Dauphin Capital Partners
108 Forest Ave.
Locust Valley, NY 11560
Phone: (516)759-3339
Fax: (516)759-3322
Website: http://
www.dauphincapital.com
Preferred Investment Size: $1,000,000 to $3,000,000. Investment Types: Balanced; and early, first, second, and later stage. Industry Preferences: Diversified technology, education, and business services. Geographic Preferences: Entire U.S.

services, and chemicals and materials. Geographic Preferences: Entire U.S.

InterEquity Capital Partners, L.P.
220 5th Ave.
New York, NY 10001
Phone: (212)779-2022
Fax: (212)779-2103
Website: http://www.interequity-capital.com
Preferred Investment Size: $1,000,000 to $3,000,000. Investment Types: First and second stage, mezzanine, leveraged buyout, and special situations. Industry Preferences: Diversified. Geographic Preferences: Entire U.S.

The Jordan Edmiston Group Inc.
150 East 52nd St., 18th Fl.
New York, NY 10022
Phone: (212)754-0710
Fax: (212)754-0337
Scott Peters
Preferred Investment Size: $1,000,000. Investment Types: Leveraged buyout, mezzanine, second stage, and special situation. Industry Preferences: Publishing. Geographic Preferences: No preference.

Josephberg, Grosz and Co., Inc.
633 3rd Ave., 13th Fl.
New York, NY 10017
Phone: (212)974-9926
Fax: (212)397-5832
Richard Josephberg
Preferred Investment Size: $1,000,000 to $30,000,000. Investment Types: Many types including seed, research and development, start-up, first and second stage, mezzanine, and leveraged buyout. Industry Preferences: Diversified. Geographic Preferences: Entire U.S.

J.P. Morgan Capital Corp.
60 Wall St.
New York, NY 10260-0060
Phone: (212)648-9000
Fax: (212)648-5002
Website: http://www.jpmorgan.com
Lincoln E. Frank, Chief Operating Officer
Preferred Investment Size: $10,000,000 to $20,000,000. Investment Types: Second stage and special situations. Industry Preferences: Diversified. Geographic Preferences: Entire U.S. and Canada.

The Lambda Funds
380 Lexington Ave., 54th Fl.
New York, NY 10168
Phone: (212)682-3454
Fax: (212)682-9231
Preferred Investment Size: $200,000 to $500,000. Investment Types: Early stage, expansion, first and second stage, and management buyout. Industry Preferences: Diversified. Geographic Preferences: Mid Atlantic, Northeast, and West Coast.

Lepercq Capital Management Inc.
1675 Broadway
New York, NY 10019
Phone: (212)698-0795
Fax: (212)262-0155
Michael J. Connelly
Preferred Investment Size: $1,000,000 to $10,000,000. Investment Types: Control-block purchases, leveraged buyout, and second stage. Industry Preferences: Diversified. Geographic Preferences: No preference.

Loeb Partners Corp.
61 Broadway, Ste. 2400
New York, NY 10006
Phone: (212)483-7000
Fax: (212)574-2001
Preferred Investment Size: $100,000. Investment Types: Early stage, acquisition, expansion, leveraged and management buyout. Industry Preferences: Diversified. Geographic Preferences: National.

Madison Investment Partners
660 Madison Ave.
New York, NY 10021
Phone: (212)223-2600
Fax: (212)223-8208
Preferred Investment Size: $5,000,000. Investment Types: Second stage, leveraged buyout, and industry roll ups. Industry Preferences: Diversified. Geographic Preferences: National.

MC Capital Inc.
520 Madison Ave., 16th Fl.
New York, NY 10022
Phone: (212)644-0841
Fax: (212)644-2926
Shunichi Maeda
Preferred Investment Size: $1,000,000 to $30,000,000. Investment Types: Acquisition, expansion, first stage, fund of funds, generalist PE, joint ventures, later stage, leveraged buyout, private placement, second stage, special situation, and turnaround. Industry Preferences: Communications, computers, electronics, biotechnology, and medical/health related. Geographic Preferences: Entire U.S. and Canada.

McCown, De Leeuw and Co. (New York)
65 E. 55th St., 36th Fl.
New York, NY 10022
Phone: (212)355-5500
Fax: (212)355-6283
Website: http://www.mdcpartners.com
Christopher Crosby, Principal
Preferred Investment Size: $40,000,000 minimum. Investment Types: Leveraged buyout and special situations. Industry Preferences: Diversified. Geographic Preferences: Entire U.S.

Morgan Stanley Venture Partners
1221 Avenue of the Americas, 33rd Fl.
New York, NY 10020
Phone: (212)762-7900
Fax: (212)762-8424
E-mail: msventures@ms.com
Website: http://www.msvp.com
Preferred Investment Size: $2,000,000. Investment Types: Second stage, mezzanine, leveraged buyout, and industry roll ups. Industry Preferences: Diversified technology. Geographic Preferences: Entire U.S. and Canada.

Nazem and Co.
645 Madison Ave., 12th Fl.
New York, NY 10022
Phone: (212)371-7900
Fax: (212)371-2150
E-mail: nazem@msn.com
Fred F. Nazem, Managing General Partner
Preferred Investment Size: $1,000,000 minimum. Investment

550 Digital Media Ventures
555 Madison Ave., 10th Fl.
New York, NY 10022
Website: http://www.550dmv.com
Investment Types: Early stage. Industry Preferences: Entertainment and leisure, and media. Geographic Preferences: Entire U.S.

Aberlyn Capital Management Co., Inc.
500 Fifth Ave.
New York, NY 10110
Phone: (212)391-7750
Fax: (212)391-7762
Lawrence Hoffman, Chairman and CEO
Preferred Investment Size: $25,000,000 minimum. Investment Types: Start-up, first and second stage, leveraged buyout, and special situation. Industry Preferences: Diversified computer technology, food and beverage products, genetic engineering, and healthcare. Geographic Preferences: National.

Adler & Company
342 Madison Ave., Ste. 807
New York, NY 10173
Phone: (212)599-2535
Fax: (212)599-2526
Jay Nickse, Treasurer & Chief Financial Officer
Investment Types: Start-up, first and second stage, leveraged buyout, and control-block purchases. Industry Preferences: Diversified. Geographic Preferences: National.

Alimansky Capital Group, Inc.
605 Madison Ave., Ste. 300
New York, NY 10022-1901
Phone: (212)832-7300
Fax: (212)832-7338
Howard Duby, Managing Director
Preferred Investment Size: $2,000,000. Investment Types: First stage, second stage, mezzanine, leveraged buyout, and special situations. Industry Preferences: Diversified. Geographic Preferences: Entire U.S. and Canada.

Allegra Partners
515 Madison Ave., 29th Fl.
New York, NY 10022
Phone: (212)826-9080
Fax: (212)759-2561
Preferred Investment Size: $1,000,000 minimum. Investment Types: First stage, leveraged buyout, recaps, second stage, and special situation. Industry Preferences: Communications, computer related, and consumer related. Geographic Preferences: Mid Atlantic, and Eastern and Western U.S.

The Argentum Group
The Chyrsler Bldg.
405 Lexington Ave.
New York, NY 10174
Phone: (212)949-6262
Fax: (212)949-8294
Website: http://www.argentumgroup.com
Walter H. Barandiaran, Managing Dir.
Preferred Investment Size: $10,000,000 minimum. Investment Types: Second stage, mezzanine, leveraged buyout, and special situations. Industry Preferences: Diversified. Geographic Preferences: Entire U.S.

Axavision Inc.
14 Wall St., 26th Fl.
New York, NY 10005
Phone: (212)619-4000
Fax: (212)619-7202
Preferred Investment Size: $100,000 to $300,000. Investment Types: Seed and start-up. Industry Preferences: Computer services and software, Internet related, and financial services. Geographic Preferences: No preference.

Bedford Capital Corp.
18 East 48th St., Ste. 1800
New York, NY 10017
Phone: (212)688-5700
Fax: (212)754-4699
E-mail: info@bedfordnyc.com
Website: http://www.bedfordnyc.com
Nathan Bernstein
Preferred Investment Size: $100,000 to $300,000. Investment Types: First and second stage, industry rollups, recaps, and leveraged buyout. Industry Preferences: Diversified. Geographic Preferences: Midwest.

Bloom & Co.
950 Third Ave.
New York, NY 10022
Phone: (212)838-1858
Fax: (212)838-1843
Jack S. Bloom, President
Preferred Investment Size: $3,000,000 minimum. Investment Types: Start-up, first and second stage, control-block purchases, leveraged buyout, mezzanine, and special situation. Industry Preferences: No preference. Geographic Preferences: No preference.

Bristol Capital Management
300 Park Ave., 17th Fl.
New York, NY 10022
Phone: (212)572-6306
Fax: (212)705-4292
Investment Types: Leveraged buyout, mezzanine, second stage, and special situation. Industry Preferences: Communications, computer related, electronics, medical/health related, entertainment and leisure, retail, food/beverage, consumer services, machinery, and publishing. Geographic Preferences: Entire U.S.

Citicorp Venture Capital Ltd. (New York City)
399 Park Ave., 14th Fl.
Zone 4
New York, NY 10043
Phone: (212)559-1127
Fax: (212)888-2940
Preferred Investment Size: $5,000,000. Investment Types: Leveraged buyout, second stage, and special situations. Industry Preferences: Diversified. Geographic Preferences: No preference.

CM Equity Partners
135 E. 57th St.
New York, NY 10022
Phone: (212)909-8428
Fax: (212)980-2630
Preferred Investment Size: $2,000,000 minimum. Investment Types: First and second stage, start-up, mezzanine, leveraged buyout, special situations, and industry rollups. Industry Preferences: Diversified. Geographic Preferences: No preference.

Cohen & Co., L.L.C.
800 Third Ave.
New York, NY 10022
Phone: (212)317-2250
Fax: (212)317-2255
E-mail: nlcohen@aol.com
Neil L. Cohen, President
Preferred Investment Size: $10,000,000 minimum. Investment Types: Start-up, seed, early and late stage, mezzanine, leveraged buyout, control-block purchases, and special situations. Industry Preferences: Communications, consumer, distribution, electronics, energy, and healthcare. Geographic Preferences: National.

Cornerstone Equity Investors, L.L.C.
717 5th Ave., Ste. 1100
New York, NY 10022
Phone: (212)753-0901
Fax: (212)826-6798
Website: http://www.cornerstone-equity.com
Mark Rossi, Senior Managing Director
Preferred Investment Size: $50,000,000 maximum. Investment Types: Leveraged buyout, and special situations. Industry Preferences: Diversified. Geographic Preferences: No preference.

CW Group, Inc.
1041 3rd Ave., 2nd fl.
New York, NY 10021
Phone: (212)308-5266
Fax: (212)644-0354
Website: http://www.cwventures.com
Christopher Fenimore
Preferred Investment Size: $100,000 to $5,000,000. Investment Types: Seed, research and development, start-up, first and second stage, leveraged buyout, special situations, and control block purchases. Industry Preferences: Specialize in the medical/health business and biotechnology. Geographic Preferences: Entire U.S.

DH Blair Investment Banking Corp.
44 Wall St., 2nd Fl.
New York, NY 10005
Phone: (212)495-5000
Fax: (212)269-1438
J. Morton Davis, Chairman
Preferred Investment Size: $100,000. Investment Types: Research and development, start-up, first stage, and leveraged buyout. Industry Preferences: Diversified. Geographic Preferences: No preference.

Dresdner Kleinwort Capital
75 Wall St.
New York, NY 10005
Phone: (212)429-3131
Fax: (212)429-3139
Website: http://www.dresdnerkb.com
Richard Wolf, Partner
Preferred Investment Size: $5,000,000 minimum. Investment Types: Early and second stage, expansion, mezzanine, and leveraged buyout. Industry Preferences: Diversified. Geographic Preferences: National.

East River Ventures, L.P.
645 Madison Ave., 22nd Fl.
New York, NY 10022
Phone: (212)644-2322
Fax: (212)644-5498
Montague H. Hackett
Preferred Investment Size: $500,000 to $5,000,000. Investment Types: Early and late stage, and mezzanine. Industry Preferences: Diversified communication and computer technology, consumer services, and medical. Geographic Preferences: National.

Easton Hunt Capital Partners
641 Lexington Ave., 21st Fl.
New York, NY 10017
Phone: (212)702-0950
Fax: (212)702-0952
Website: http://www.eastoncapital.com
Investment Types: First stage, mezzanine, and special situations. Industry Preferences: Diversified. Geographic Preferences: Entire U.S.

Elk Associates Funding Corp.
747 3rd Ave., Ste. 4C
New York, NY 10017
Phone: (212)355-2449
Fax: (212)759-3338
Gary C. Granoff, Pres.
Preferred Investment Size: $100,000 to $300,000. Investment Types: Second stage and leveraged buyout. Industry Preferences: Radio and TV, consumer franchise businesses, hotel and resort areas, and transportation. Geographic Preferences: Southeast and Midwest.

EOS Partners, L.P.
320 Park Ave., 22nd Fl.
New York, NY 10022
Phone: (212)832-5800
Fax: (212)832-5815
E-mail: mfirst@eospartners.com
Website: http://www.eospartners.com
Mark L. First, Managing Director
Preferred Investment Size: $3,000,000. Investment Policies: Equity and equity-oriented debt. Investment Types: Industry rollups, leveraged buyout, mezzanine, second stage, and special situation. Industry Preferences: Diversified. Geographic Preferences: Entire United States and Canada.

Euclid Partners
45 Rockefeller Plaza, Ste. 3240
New York, NY 10111
Phone: (212)218-6880
Fax: (212)218-6877
E-mail: graham@euclidpartners.com
Website: http://www.euclidpartners.com
Preferred Investment Size: $500,000 to $5,000,000. Investment Types: start-up, first and second stage. Industry Preferences: Internet related, computer software and services, genetic engineering, and medical/health related. Geographic Preferences: No preference.

Evergreen Capital Partners, Inc.
150 East 58th St.
New York, NY 10155
Phone: (212)813-0758
Fax: (212)813-0754
E-mail: rysmith@evergreencapital.com
Preferred Investment Size: $1,000,000 to $300,000,000. Investment Types: No preference. Industry Preferences: Diversified. Geographic Preferences: National.

Exeter Capital L.P.
10 E. 53rd St.
New York, NY 10022
Phone: (212)872-1172
Fax: (212)872-1198
E-mail: exeter@usa.net
Karen J. Watai, Partner
Preferred Investment Size: $1,000,000 minimum. Investment Policies: Loans and equity investments. Investment Types: Leveraged buyout, mezzanine, second stage, and special situation. Industry Preferences: Diversified. Geographic Preferences: National.

Financial Technology Research Corp.
518 Broadway
Penthouse
New York, NY 10012
Phone: (212)625-9100
Fax: (212)431-0300
E-mail: fintek@financier.com
Neal Bruckman, President
Preferred Investment Size: $300,000 to $500,000. Investment Types: Seed, research and development, start-up, first stage, second stage, and special situations. Industry Preferences: Diversified. Geographic Preferences: Entire U.S. and Canada.

4C Ventures
237 Park Ave., Ste. 801
New York, NY 10017
Phone: (212)692-3680
Fax: (212)692-3685
Website: http://www.4cventures.com
Ted Hobart, Partner
Preferred Investment Size: $500,000 to $1,000,000. Investment Types: Seed, research and development, start-up, first and second stage. Industry Preferences: Communications, computer related, and consumer. Geographic Preferences: Entire U.S. and Canada.

Fusient Ventures
99 Park Ave., 20th Fl.
New York, NY 10016
Phone: (212)972-8999
Fax: (212)972-9876
E-mail: info@fusient.com
Website: http://www.fusient.com
Preferred Investment Size: $500,000 to $3,000,000. Investment Types: Early and first stage, and seed. Industry Preferences: Internet, entertainment and leisure, and media. Geographic Preferences: U.S.

Generation Capital Partners
551 Fifth Ave., Ste. 3100
New York, NY 10176
Phone: (212)450-8507
Fax: (212)450-8550
Website: http://www.genpartners.com
Preferred Investment Size: $5,000,000. Investment Types: Start-up, early and late stage, and leveraged buyout. Industry Preferences: Diversified communications and computer technology, consumer products and services, and industrial products and equipment. Geographic Preferences: United States and Canada.

Golub Associates, Inc.
555 Madison Ave.
New York, NY 10022
Phone: (212)750-6060
Fax: (212)750-5505
Evelyn Mordechai, Vice President
Preferred Investment Size: $1,000,000 to $10,000,000. Investment Types: Second stage, mezzanine, leveraged buyout, recaps, and special situations. Industry Preferences: Diversified. Geographic Preferences: Eastern U.S.

Hambro America Biosciences Inc.
650 Madison Ave., 21st Floor
New York, NY 10022
Phone: (212)223-7400
Fax: (212)223-0305
Preferred Investment Size: $2,500,000 to $5,000,000. Investment Types: First and second stage, and special situations. Industry Preferences: Genetic engineering, chemicals and materials, and medical/health related. Geographic Preferences: Entire U.S.

Hanover Capital Corp.
505 Park Ave., 15th Fl.
New York, NY 10022
Phone: (212)755-1222
Fax: (212)935-1787
Michael Wainstein
Preferred Investment Size: $300,000 minimum. Investment Types: Leveraged buyout, mezzanine, and second stage. Industry Preferences: Diversified. Geographic Preferences: Entire U.S.

Harvest Partners, Inc.
280 Park Ave, 33rd Fl.
New York, NY 10017
Phone: (212)559-6300
Fax: (212)812-0100
Website: http://www.harvpart.com
Harvey Mallement
Preferred Investment Size: $15,000,000 to $100,000,000. Investment Types: Acquisition, leveraged buyout, management buyouts, private placements, special situations, and turnaround. Industry Preferences: Consumer products and services, communications, distribution, fiberoptics, and medical/health related. Geographic Preferences: No preference.

Holding Capital Group, Inc.
10 E. 53rd St., 30th Fl.
New York, NY 10022
Phone: (212)486-6670
Fax: (212)486-0843
James W. Donaghy, President
Preferred Investment Size: $5,000,000. Investment Types: Leveraged buyout. Industry Preferences: No preference. Geographic Preferences: Entire U.S.

Hudson Venture Partners
660 Madison Ave., 14th Fl.
New York, NY 10021-8405
Phone: (212)644-9797
Fax: (212)644-7430
Website: http://www.hudsonptr.com
Marilyn Adler
Preferred Investment Size: $500,000 to $2,800,000. Investment Types: Seed, start-up, first and early stages, and expansion. Industry Preferences: Diversified. Geographic Preferences: Entire U.S.

IBJS Capital Corp.
1 State St., 9th Fl.
New York, NY 10004
Phone: (212)858-2018
Fax: (212)858-2768
George Zombeck, Chief Operating Officer
Preferred Investment Size: $2,000,000. Investment Types: Mezzanine, leveraged buyout, and special situations. Industry Preferences: Consumer products and

Types: Seed, start-up, first and second stage, mezzanine, leveraged buyout, and special situations. Industry Preferences: Diversified. Geographic Preferences: No preference.

Needham Capital Management, L.L.C.
445 Park Ave.
New York, NY 10022
Phone: (212)371-8300
Fax: (212)705-0299
Website: http://www.needhamco.com
Joseph Abramoff
Preferred Investment Size: $1,000,000 to $10,000,000. Investment Policies: Equity. Investment Types: Expansion, later stage, leveraged buyout, management buyout, and mezzanine. Industry Preferences: Diversified technology. Geographic Preferences: National.

Norwood Venture Corp.
1430 Broadway, Ste. 1607
New York, NY 10018
Phone: (212)869-5075
Fax: (212)869-5331
E-mail: nvc@mail.idt.net
Website: http://www.norven.com
Mark Littell
Preferred Investment Size: $500,000 to $1,000,000. Investment Types: Mezzanine, leveraged buyout, and special situations. Industry Preferences: Diversified. Geographic Preferences: National.

Noveltek Venture Corp.
521 Fifth Ave., Ste. 1700
New York, NY 10175
Phone: (212)286-1963
Preferred Investment Size: $1,000,000 minimum. Investment Types: Control-block purchases, first stage, mezzanine, second stage, special situation, and start-up. Industry Preferences: Diversified. Geographic Preferences: Entire U.S. and Canada.

Paribas Principal, Inc.
787 7th Ave.
New York, NY 10019
Phone: (212)841-2005
Fax: (212)841-3558
Gary Binning
Preferred Investment Size: $50,000,000. Investment Types: Leveraged buyout, special situations, and control block purchases. Industry Preferences: Diversified. Geographic Preferences: Entire U.S.

Patricof & Co. Ventures, Inc. (New York)
445 Park Ave.
New York, NY 10022
Phone: (212)753-6300
Fax: (212)319-6155
Website: http://www.patricof.com
Preferred Investment Size: $500,000 minimum. Investment Types: Seed, start-up, first and second stage, mezzanine, and leveraged buyout. Industry Preferences: Diversified. Geographic Preferences: No preference.

The Platinum Group, Inc.
350 Fifth Ave, Ste. 7113
New York, NY 10118
Phone: (212)736-4300
Fax: (212)736-6086
Website: http://www.platinumgroup.com
Michael Grant, Analyst
Investment Types: Start-up, first stage, second stage, and leveraged buyout. Industry Preferences: Diversified. Geographic Preferences: National.

Pomona Capital
780 Third Ave., 28th Fl.
New York, NY 10017
Phone: (212)593-3639
Fax: (212)593-3987
Website: http://www.pomonacapital.com
Karen Macleod
Preferred Investment Size: $1,000,000 minimum. Investment Types: Various investment types. Industry Preferences: Diversified. Geographic Preferences: Entire U.S.

Prospect Street Ventures
10 East 40th St., 44th Fl.
New York, NY 10016
Phone: (212)448-0702
Fax: (212)448-9652
E-mail: wkohler@prospectstreet.com
Website: http://www.prospectstreet.com
Edward Ryeom, Vice President
Preferred Investment Size: $1,000,000 minimum. Investment Types: First and second stage, start-up, control-block purchases, recaps, and special situations. Industry Preferences: Internet related, computer software and services, computer hardware, and communications. Geographic Preferences: East and West Coast, and Eastern Canada.

Regent Capital Management
505 Park Ave., Ste. 1700
New York, NY 10022
Phone: (212)735-9900
Fax: (212)735-9908
E-mail: ninamcle@aol.com
Richard Hochman, Managing Director
Preferred Investment Size: $3,500,000 minimum. Investment Types: Second stage, mezzanine, and leveraged buyout. Industry Preferences: Communications, consumer products and services. Geographic Preferences: National.

Rothschild Ventures, Inc.
1251 Avenue of the Americas, 51st Fl.
New York, NY 10020
Phone: (212)403-3500
Fax: (212)403-3652
Website: http://www.nmrothschild.com
Preferred Investment Size: $500,000 to $5,000,000. Investment Types: Seed, research and development, start-up, first and second stage, mezzanine, and leveraged buyout. Industry Preferences: Diversified. Geographic Preferences: Entire U.S. and Canada.

Sandler Capital Management
767 Fifth Ave., 45th Fl.
New York, NY 10153
Phone: (212)754-8100
Fax: (212)826-0280
Preferred Investment Size: $20,000,000 minimum. Investment Policies: Equity. Investment Types: Seed, start-up, first and second stage, control-block purchases, leveraged buyout, mezzanine, research and development, and special situation.

Industry Preferences: Diversified communication and computer technology, consumer products and services, education, and publishing. Geographic Preferences: United States and Canada.

Siguler Guff & Company
630 Fifth Ave., 16th Fl.
New York, NY 10111
Phone: (212)332-5100
Fax: (212)332-5120
Maria Boyazny, Associate
Investment Types: Start-up, first stage, second stage, control-block purchases, mezzanine, leveraged buyout, and special situations. Industry Preferences: Diversified. Geographic Preferences: National.

Spencer Trask Ventures Inc.
535 Madison Ave.
New York, NY 10022
Phone: (212)355-5565
Fax: (212)751-3362
Website: http://www.spencertrask.com
A. Emerson Martin, II, Senior Managing Director
Preferred Investment Size: $3,000,000 minimum. Investment Types: Start-up, first stage, second stage, and special situations. Industry Preferences: Diversified. Geographic Preferences: National.

Sprout Group (New York City)
277 Park Ave.
New York, NY 10172
Phone: (212)892-3600
Fax: (212)892-3444
E-mail: info@sproutgroup.com
Website: http://www.sproutgroup.com
Patrick J. Boroian, General Partner
Preferred Investment Size: $5,000,000 to $50,000,000. Investment Types: Seed, start-up, first and second stage, mezzanine, leveraged buyout, and special situations. Industry Preferences: Diversified technology. Geographic Preferences: Entire U.S.

US Trust Private Equity
114 W.47th St.
New York, NY 10036
Phone: (212)852-3949
Fax: (212)852-3759
Website: http://www.ustrust.com/privateequity
Jim Ruler
Preferred Investment Size: $5,000,000 minimum. Investment Types: Early, first stage, and second stage. Industry Preferences: Diversified. Geographic Preferences: National.

Vencon Management Inc.
301 West 53rd St., Ste. 10F
New York, NY 10019
Phone: (212)581-8787
Fax: (212)397-4126
Website: http://www.venconinc.com
Ingrid Yang
Preferred Investment Size: $500,000 to $10,000,000. Investment Types: First and second stage, leveraged buyout, seed, special situation, and start-up. Industry Preferences: Diversified. Geographic Preferences: Entire U.S. and Canada.

Venrock Associates
30 Rockefeller Plaza, Ste. 5508
New York, NY 10112
Phone: (212)649-5600
Fax: (212)649-5788
Website: http://www.venrock.com
Preferred Investment Size: $500,000 minimum. Investment Types: Seed, research and development, start-up, first and second stages. Industry Preferences: Diversified. Geographic Preferences: National.

Venture Capital Fund of America, Inc.
509 Madison Ave., Ste. 812
New York, NY 10022
Phone: (212)838-5577
Fax: (212)838-7614
E-mail: mail@vcfa.com
Website: http://www.vcfa.com
Dayton T. Carr, General Partner
Preferred Investment Size: $500,000 to $100,000,000. Investment Types: Secondary partnership interests. Industry Preferences: Does not consider tax shelters, real estate, or direct investments in companies. Geographic Preferences: Entire U.S.

Venture Opportunities Corp.
150 E. 58th St.
New York, NY 10155
Phone: (212)832-3737
Fax: (212)980-6603
E-mail: jerryvoc@aol.com
Jerry March
Preferred Investment Size: $2,000,000 minimum. Investment Types: Start-up, first and second stage, mezzanine, leveraged buyout, and special situations. Industry Preferences: Diversified. Geographic Preferences: Entire U.S.

Warburg Pincus Ventures, Inc.
466 Lexington Ave., 11th Fl.
New York, NY 10017
Phone: (212)878-9309
Fax: (212)878-9200
Website: http://www.warburgpincus.com
Preferred Investment Size: $1,000,000 to $500,000,000. Investment Types: Many types including seed, start-up, first and second stage, mezzanine, leveraged buyouts, private placements, recaps, and special situations. Industry Preferences: Diversified. Geographic Preferences: U.S. and Canada.

Wasserstein, Perella & Co. Inc.
31 W. 52nd St., 27th Fl.
New York, NY 10019
Phone: (212)702-5691
Fax: (212)969-7879
Perry W. Steiner
Investment Types: Leveraged buyout. Industry Preferences: Diversified. Geographic Preferences: National.

Welsh, Carson, Anderson, & Stowe
320 Park Ave., Ste. 2500
New York, NY 10022-6815
Phone: (212)893-9500
Fax: (212)893-9575
Patrick J. Welsh, General Partner
Preferred Investment Size: $25,000,000 minimum. Investment Types: Leveraged buyout and special situations. Industry Preferences: Computer related and medical/health related. Geographic Preferences: Entire U.S.

Whitney and Co. (New York)
630 Fifth Ave. Ste. 3225
New York, NY 10111
Phone: (212)332-2400

Fax: (212)332-2422
Website: http://www.jhwitney.com
Preferred Investment Size: $1,000,000. Investment Types: Leveraged buyout and expansion. Industry Preferences: Diversified technology. Geographic Preferences: No preference.

Winthrop Ventures
74 Trinity Place, Ste. 600
New York, NY 10006
Phone: (212)422-0100
Cyrus Brown
Preferred Investment Size: $1,000,000 minimum. Investment Types: Start-up, early and late stage, and leveraged buyout. Industry Preferences: Diversified. Geographic Preferences: National.

The Pittsford Group
8 Lodge Pole Rd.
Pittsford, NY 14534
Phone: (716)223-3523
Preferred Investment Size: $100,000 to $300,000. Investment Types: start-up, first and second stage, and control-block purchases. Industry Preferences: Diversified technology. Geographic Preferences: Eastern U.S. and Canada.

Genesee Funding
70 Linden Oaks, 3rd Fl.
Rochester, NY 14625
Phone: (716)383-5550
Fax: (716)383-5305
Preferred Investment Size: $200,000. Investment Types: Second stage, mezzanine, and leveraged buyout. Industry Preferences: Diversified. Geographic Preferences: Northeast.

Gabelli Multimedia Partners
One Corporate Center
Rye, NY 10580
Phone: (914)921-5395
Fax: (914)921-5031
E-mail: fsommer@gabelli.com
Preferred Investment Size: $250,000 to $500,000. Investment Policies: Equity. Investment Types: Seed, start-up, first and second stage. Industry Preferences: Diversified communications. Geographic Preferences: Northeast.

Stamford Financial
108 Main St.
Stamford, NY 12167
Phone: (607)652-3311
Fax: (607)652-6301
Website: http://www.stamfordfinancial.com
Alexander C. Brosda
Preferred Investment Size: $1,000,000 to $2,500,000. Investment Types: Expansion and mezzanine. Industry Preferences: Diversified. Geographic Preferences: Entire U.S.

Northwood Ventures LLC
485 Underhill Blvd., Ste. 205
Syosset, NY 11791
Phone: (516)364-5544
Fax: (516)364-0879
E-mail: northwood@northwood.com
Website: http://www.northwoodventures.com
Paul Homer, Associate
Preferred Investment Size: $1,000,000 to $10,000,000. Investment Types: First and second stage, acquisition, expansion, leveraged buyout, private placement, special situations, and industry roll ups. Industry Preferences: Diversified. Geographic Preferences: Entire U.S. and Canada.

Exponential Business Development Co.
216 Walton St.
Syracuse, NY 13202-1227
Phone: (315)474-4500
Fax: (315)474-4682
E-mail: dirksonn@aol.com
Website: http://www.exponential-ny.com
Dirk E. Sonneborn, Partner
Preferred Investment Size: $100,000 to $600,000. Investment Types: Early and first stage. Industry Preferences: No preference. Geographic Preferences: New York.

Onondaga Venture Capital Fund Inc.
714 State Tower Bldg.
Syracuse, NY 13202
Phone: (315)478-0157
Fax: (315)478-0158
Irving Schwartz
Preferred Investment Size: $100,000 to $250,000. Investment Types: Expansion, later stage, and mezzanine. Industry Preferences: Diversified. Geographic Preferences: Mid Atlantic and Northeast.

Bessemer Venture Partners (Westbury)
1400 Old Country Rd., Ste. 109
Westbury, NY 11590
Phone: (516)997-2300
Fax: (516)997-2371
E-mail: bob@bvpny.com
Website: http://www.bvp.com
Investment Types: Seed, research and development, start-up, first stages, leveraged buyout, special situations, and expansion. Industry Preferences: Communications, computer related, consumer products, distribution, and electronics. Geographic Preferences: Entire U.S.

Ovation Capital Partners
120 Bloomingdale Rd., 4th Fl.
White Plains, NY 10605
Phone: (914)258-0011
Fax: (914)684-0848
Website: http://www.ovationcapital.com
Preferred Investment Size: $500,000 to $4,000,000. Investment Types: Early stage. Industry Preferences: Internet related. Geographic Preferences: Northeast.

North Carolina

Carolinas Capital Investment Corp.
1408 Biltmore Dr.
Charlotte, NC 28207
Phone: (704)375-3888
Fax: (704)375-6226
E-mail: ed@carolinacapital.com
Edward Goode
Preferred Investment Size: $200,000 to $1,000,000. Investment Types: Seed, research and development, leveraged buyout, start-up, first and second stages. Industry Preferences: Communications, electronic components and instrumentation. Geographic Preferences: No preference.

First Union Capital Partners
1st Union Center, 12th Fl.
301 S. College St.
Charlotte, NC 28288-0732
Phone: (704)383-0000

Fax: (704)374-6711
Website: http://www.fucp.com
L. Watts Hamrick, III, Partner
Preferred Investment Size: $5,000,000 minimum. Investment Types: Seed, start-up, first and second stage, mezzanine, expansion, leveraged buyout, special situations, and control block purchases. Industry Preferences: Diversified. Geographic Preferences: No preference.

Frontier Capital LLC
525 North Tryon St., Ste. 1700
Charlotte, NC 28202
Phone: (704)414-2880
Fax: (704)414-2881
Website: http://www.frontierfunds.com
Preferred Investment Size: $500,000 to $3,000,000. Investment Types: Early stage and expansion. Industry Preferences: Telecommunications, computer related, electronics, and energy. Geographic Preferences: Mid Atlantic and Southeast.

Kitty Hawk Capital
2700 Coltsgate Rd., Ste. 202
Charlotte, NC 28211
Phone: (704)362-3909
Fax: (704)362-2774
Website: http://www.kittyhawkcapital.com
Stephen W. Buchanan, General Partner
Preferred Investment Size: $1,000,000 to $7,000,000. Investment Types: Expansion, first and early stage. Industry Preferences: Diversified. Geographic Preferences: Southeast.

Piedmont Venture Partners
One Morrocroft Centre
6805 Morisson Blvd., Ste. 380
Charlotte, NC 28211
Phone: (704)731-5200
Fax: (704)365-9733
Website: http://www.piedmontvp.com
Preferred Investment Size: $250,000 to $5,000,000. Investment Types: Early stage. Industry Preferences: Diversified. Geographic Preferences: Southeast.

Ruddick Investment Co.
1800 Two First Union Center
Charlotte, NC 28282
Phone: (704)372-5404
Fax: (704)372-6409
Richard N. Brigden, Vice President
Preferred Investment Size: $500,000 to $1,000,000. Investment Types: First and second stage, and mezzanine. Industry Preferences: Diversified. Geographic Preferences: Southeast.

The Shelton Companies Inc.
3600 One First Union Center
301 S. College St.
Charlotte, NC 28202
Phone: (704)348-2200
Fax: (704)348-2260
Preferred Investment Size: $1,000,000 to $10,000,000. Investment Types: Control-block purchases, leveraged buyouts, recaps, and second stage. Industry Preferences: Diversified. Geographic Preferences: Mid Atlantic, Midwest, Southeast, and Southwest.

Wakefield Group
1110 E. Morehead St.
PO Box 36329
Charlotte, NC 28236
Phone: (704)372-0355
Fax: (704)372-8216
Website: http://www.wakefieldgroup.com
Anna Nelson, Partner
Preferred Investment Size: $1,000,000 to $5,000,000. Investment Types: Early stage. Industry Preferences: Diversified. Geographic Preferences: Southeast.

Aurora Funds, Inc.
2525 Meridian Pkwy., Ste. 220
Durham, NC 27713
Phone: (919)484-0400
Fax: (919)484-0444
Website: http://www.aurorafunds.com
Preferred Investment Size: $250,000 to $1,500,000. Investment Types: start-up, seed, early and first stage. Industry Preferences: Diversified. Geographic Preferences: Eastern United States.

Intersouth Partners
3211 Shannon Rd., Ste. 610
Durham, NC 27707
Phone: (919)493-6640
Fax: (919)493-6649
E-mail: info@intersouth.com
Website: http://www.intersouth.com
Jonathan Perl
Preferred Investment Size: $2,000,000 to $10,000,000. Investment Types: Seed, start-up, first and early stages. Industry Preferences: Diversified. Geographic Preferences: Southeast and Southwest.

Geneva Merchant Banking Partners
PO Box 21962
Greensboro, NC 27420
Phone: (336)275-7002
Fax: (336)275-9155
Website: http://www.genevamerchantbank.com
Preferred Investment Size: $1,000,000 to $7,000,000. Investment Types: Balanced, distressed debt, expansion, leveraged and management buyout, mezzanine, second stage, and special situation. Industry Preferences: Diversified. Geographic Preferences: Mid Atlantic, Midwest, and Southeast.

The North Carolina Enterprise Fund, L.P.
3600 Glenwood Ave., Ste. 107
Raleigh, NC 27612
Phone: (919)781-2691
Fax: (919)783-9195
Website: http://www.ncef.com
Charles T. Closson, President and CEO
Preferred Investment Size: $2,000,000 minimum. Investment Policies: Equity. Investment Types: Start-up, first stage, and mezzanine. Industry Preferences: Diversified. Geographic Preferences: North Carolina and Southeast.

Ohio

Senmend Medical Ventures
4445 Lake Forest Dr., Ste. 600
Cincinnati, OH 45242
Phone: (513)563-3264
Fax: (513)563-3261
Preferred Investment Size: $500,000 to $1,000,000. Investment Types: Second stage and mezzanine. Industry Preferences: Genetic engineering,

medical and health related. Geographic Preferences: National.

The Walnut Group
312 Walnut St., Ste. 1151
Cincinnati, OH 45202
Phone: (513)651-3300
Fax: (513)929-4441
Website: http://www.thewalnutgroup.com
Preferred Investment Size: $500,000 to $5,000,000. Investment Types: Balanced. Geographic Preferences: Northeast.

Brantley Venture Partners
20600 Chagrin Blvd., Ste. 1150
Cleveland, OH 44122
Phone: (216)283-4800
Fax: (216)283-5324
Kevin J. Cook, Associate
Preferred Investment Size: $1,000,000 to $5,000,000. Investment Types: Industry rollups, seed, start-up, and first stage. Industry Preferences: Diversified. Geographic Preferences: Entire U.S.

Clarion Capital Corp.
1801 E. 9th St., Ste. 1120
Cleveland, OH 44114
Phone: (216)687-1096
Fax: (216)694-3545
Preferred Investment Size: $250,000 to $500,000. Investment Types: Early, first and second stage. Industry Preferences: Diversified. Geographic Preferences: East Coast, Midwest, and West Coast.

Crystal Internet Venture Fund, L.P.
1120 Chester Ave., Ste. 418
Cleveland, OH 44114
Phone: (216)263-5515
Fax: (216)263-5518
E-mail: jf@crystalventure.com
Website: http://www.crystalventure.com
Daniel Kellog, Partner
Preferred Investment Size: $1,000,000 to $6,000,000. Investment Policies: Equity. Investment Types: Balanced and early stage. Industry Preferences: Diversified communications and computer technology. Geographic Preferences: National.

Key Equity Capital Corp.
127 Public Sq., 28th Fl.
Cleveland, OH 44114
Phone: (216)689-3000
Fax: (216)689-3204
Website: http://www.keybank.com
Cindy J. Babitt
Preferred Investment Size: $1,000,000 minimum. Investment Policies: Willing to make equity investments. Investment Types: Expansion, industry rollups, leveraged buyout, second stage, and special situation. Industry Preferences: Diversified. Geographic Preferences: National.

Morgenthaler Ventures
Terminal Tower
50 Public Square, Ste. 2700
Cleveland, OH 44113
Phone: (216)416-7500
Fax: (216)416-7501
Website: http://www.morgenthaler.com
Robert C. Belles, Jr., General Partner
Preferred Investment Size: $500,000 minimum. Investment Types: Start-up, first and second stage, acquisition, leveraged and management buyout, special situations, and expansion. Industry Preferences: Diversified. Geographic Preferences: Entire U.S. and Ontario, Canada.

National City Equity Partners Inc.
1965 E. 6th St.
Cleveland, OH 44114
Phone: (216)575-2491
Fax: (216)575-9965
E-mail: nccap@aol.com
Website: http://www.nccapital.com
Carl E. Baldassarre, Managing Director
Preferred Investment Size: $1,000,000 to $20,000,000. Investment Types: Second stage, mezzanine, leveraged buyout, special situations, recaps, management buyouts, and expansion. Industry Preferences: Diversified. Geographic Preferences: Entire U.S.

Primus Venture Partners, Inc.
5900 LanderBrook Dr., Ste. 2000
Cleveland, OH 44124-4020
Phone: (440)684-7300
Fax: (440)684-7342
E-mail: info@primusventure.com
Website: http://www.primusventure.com
Jeffrey J. Milius, Investment Manager
Preferred Investment Size: $5,000,000 minimum. Investment Types: Early stage, start-up, expansion and balanced. Industry Preferences: Diversified. Geographic Preferences: Entire U.S.

Banc One Capital Partners (Columbus)
150 East Gay St., 24th Fl.
Columbus, OH 43215
Phone: (614)217-1100
Fax: (614)217-1217
Suzanne B. Kriscunas, Managing Director
Preferred Investment Size: $1,000,000 minimum. Investment Types: Later stage, leveraged buyout, mezzanine, industry rollups, and special situations. Industry Preferences: Diversified. Geographic Preferences: Entire U.S.

Battelle Venture Partners
505 King Ave.
Columbus, OH 43201
Phone: (614)424-7005
Fax: (614)424-4874
Preferred Investment Size: $500,000 to $1,000,000. Investment Types: start-up, first and second stage. Industry Preferences: Energy/natural resources, industrial products and equipment. Geographic Preferences: National.

Ohio Partners
62 E. Board St., 3rd Fl.
Columbus, OH 43215
Phone: (614)621-1210
Fax: (614)621-1240
E-mail: mcox@ohiopartners.com
Investment Types: Start-up, first and second stage. Industry Preferences: Computer related. Geographic Preferences: Western U.S. and Midwest.

Capital Technology Group, L.L.C.
400 Metro Place North, Ste. 300
Dublin, OH 43017
Phone: (614)792-6066
Fax: (614)792-6036
E-mail: info@capitaltech.com

Website: http://www.capitaltech.com
Preferred Investment Size: $250,000 to $1,000,000. Investment Types: Seed, early and start-up. Industry Preferences: Diversified electronics, alternative energy, and Internet related. Geographic Preferences: National.

Northwest Ohio Venture Fund
4159 Holland-Sylvania R., Ste. 202
Toledo, OH 43623
Phone: (419)824-8144
Fax: (419)882-2035
E-mail: bwalsh@novf.com
Barry P. Walsh, Managing Partner
Preferred Investment Size: $250,000 minimum. Investment Types: Seed, early and late stage, leveraged buyout, mezzanine, research and development. Industry Preferences: Diversified. Geographic Preferences: Midwest.

Oklahoma

Moore & Associates
1000 W. Wilshire Blvd., Ste. 370
Oklahoma City, OK 73116
Phone: (405)842-3660
Fax: (405)842-3763
Preferred Investment Size: $500,000 minimum. Investment Types: Start-up, first and second stage, mezzanine, and leveraged buyout. Industry Preferences: Diversified technology. Geographic Preferences: National.

Chisholm Private Capital Partners
100 West 5th St., Ste. 805
Tulsa, OK 74103
Phone: (918)584-0440
Fax: (918)584-0441
Website: http://www.chisholmvc.com
James Bode, General Partner
Preferred Investment Size: $1,000,000 to $4,000,000. Investment Types: start-up, early and late stage. Industry Preferences: Diversified communications and computer, consumer products and retailing, electronics, alternative energy, and medical. Geographic Preferences: Entire U.S.

Davis, Tuttle Venture Partners (Tulsa)
320 S. Boston, Ste. 1000
Tulsa, OK 74103-3703
Phone: (918)584-7272
Fax: (918)582-3404
Website: http://www.davistuttle.com
Preferred Investment Size: $5,000,000 minimum. Investment Types: First and second stage, mezzanine, and leveraged buyout. Industry Preferences: Diversified. Geographic Preferences: Southwest.

RBC Ventures
2627 E. 21st St.
Tulsa, OK 74114
Phone: (918)744-5607
Fax: (918)743-8630
K.Y. Vargas, Vice President
Preferred Investment Size: $2,000,000 minimum. Investment Policies: Equity. Investment Types: Control-block purchases, leveraged buyout, mezzanine, second stage, and special situations. Industry Preferences: Diversified transportation. Geographic Preferences: Southwest.

Oregon

Utah Ventures II LP
10700 SW Beaverton-Hillsdale Hwy., Ste. 548
Beaverton, OR 97005
Phone: (503)574-4125
E-mail: adishlip@uven.com
Website: http://www.uven.com
Preferred Investment Size: $1,000,000 to $7,000,000. Investment Types: Early stages. Industry Preferences: Diversified technology. Geographic Preferences: Northwest and Rocky Mountains.

Orien Ventures
14523 SW Westlake Dr.
Lake Oswego, OR 97035
Phone: (503)699-1680
Fax: (503)699-1681
Anthony Miadich, Managing General Partner
Preferred Investment Size: $500,000 minimum. Investment Types: Start-up, seed, early and first stage. Industry Preferences: Diversified technology. Geographic Preferences: No preference.

OVP Venture Partners (Lake Oswego)
340 Oswego Pointe Dr., Ste. 200
Lake Oswego, OR 97034
Phone: (503)697-8766
Fax: (503)697-8863
E-mail: info@ovp.com
Website: http://www.ovp.com
Preferred Investment Size: $1,000,000 to $10,000,000. Investment Types: Seed, start-up, and early stage. Industry Preferences: Communications, computer and Internet related, electronics, genetic engineering, and medical health related. Geographic Preferences: Western U.S. and Western Canada.

Oregon Resource and Technology Development Fund
4370 NE Halsey St., Ste. 233
Portland, OR 97213-1566
Phone: (503)282-4462
Fax: (503)282-2976
Preferred Investment Size: $100,000 to $300,000. Investment Types: Seed, start-up, research and development. Industry Preferences: Biotechnology, electronics, computer software and services, and medical/health related. Geographic Preferences: West Coast.

Shaw Venture Partners
400 SW 6th Ave., Ste. 1100
Portland, OR 97204-1636
Phone: (503)228-4884
Fax: (503)227-2471
Website: http://
www.shawventures.com
Preferred Investment Size: $250,000 to $3,000,000. Investment Types: Seed, start-up, first and second stage, leveraged buyout, and special situations. Industry Preferences: Diversified. Geographic Preferences: Northwest.

Pennsylvania

Mid-Atlantic Venture Funds
125 Goodman Dr.
Bethlehem, PA 18015
Phone: (610)865-6550
Fax: (610)865-6427
Website: http://www.mavf.com
Thomas A. Smith
Preferred Investment Size: $500,000 to $8,000,000. Investment Types: Seed, research and development, first and second stage, leveraged buyout. Industry Preferences: Diversified.

Geographic Preferences: Middle Atlantic and Northeast.

Newspring Ventures
100 W. Elm St., Ste. 101
Conshohocken, PA 19428
Phone: (610)567-2380
Fax: (610)567-2388
Website: http://www.newsprintventures.com
Preferred Investment Size: $1,000,000 minimum. Investment Types: Early stage and expansion. Industry Preferences: Communications, computer related, medical products, industrial products, and business services. Geographic Preferences: Mid Atlantic.

Patricof & Co. Ventures, Inc.
455 S. Gulph Rd., Ste. 410
King of Prussia, PA 19406
Phone: (610)265-0286
Fax: (610)265-4959
Website: http://www.patricof.com
Preferred Investment Size: $500,000 minimum. Investment Types: Seed, start-up, first and second stage, mezzanine, and leveraged buyout. Industry Preferences: Diversified. Geographic Preferences: No preference.

Loyalhanna Venture Fund
527 Cedar Way, Ste. 104
Oakmont, PA 15139
Phone: (412)820-7035
Fax: (412)820-7036
James H. Knowles, Jr.
Preferred Investment Size: $300,000 to $1,000,000. Investment Types: First and second stage, and leveraged buyout. Industry Preferences: No preference. Geographic Preferences: Entire U.S.

Innovest Group Inc.
2000 Market St., Ste. 1400
Philadelphia, PA 19103
Phone: (215)564-3960
Fax: (215)569-3272
Richard Woosnam
Preferred Investment Size: $500,000 to $1,000,000. Investment Types: First stage, leveraged buyout, recaps, second stage, special situation, and start-up. Industry Preferences: Diversified. Geographic Preferences: Mid Atlantic, Midwest, Northeast, and Southeast.

Keystone Venture Capital Management Co.
1601 Market St., Ste. 2500
Philadelphia, PA 19103
Phone: (215)241-1200
Fax: (215)241-1211
Website: http://www.keystonevc.com
Peter Ligeti
Preferred Investment Size: $2,000,000 to $5,000,000. Investment Types: First and second stage, balanced, and expansion. Industry Preferences: Diversified. Geographic Preferences: Middle Atlantic.

Liberty Venture Partners
2005 Market St., Ste. 200
Philadelphia, PA 19103
Phone: (215)282-4484
Fax: (215)282-4485
E-mail: info@libertyvp.com
Website: http://www.libertyvp.com
Thomas Morse
Preferred Investment Size: $3,000,000 to $7,000,000. Investment Types: Early stage and expansion. Industry Preferences: Diversified technology. Geographic Preferences: National.

Penn Janney Fund, Inc.
1801 Market St., 11th Fl.
Philadelphia, PA 19103
Phone: (215)665-4447
Fax: (215)557-0820
William Rulon-Miller
Preferred Investment Size: $1,000,000 minimum. Investment Types: Second stage, mezzanine, leveraged buyout, and special situations. Industry Preferences: Diversified. Geographic Preferences: Northeast, West Coast, and Middle Atlantic.

Philadelphia Ventures, Inc.
The Bellevue
200 S. Broad St.
Philadelphia, PA 19102
Phone: (215)732-4445
Fax: (215)732-4644
Walter M. Aikman, Managing Director
Preferred Investment Size: $500,000 maximum. Investment Types: Start-up, first and second stage, mezzanine, and leveraged buyout. Industry Preferences: Diversified technology. Geographic Preferences: Entire U.S.

Birchmere Ventures Inc.
2000 Technology Dr.
Pittsburgh, PA 15219-3109
Phone: (412)803-8000
Fax: (412)687-8139
Website: http://www.birchmerevc.com
Investment Types: Early stage, expansion, first and later stage, and start-up. Industry Preferences: Diversified. Geographic Preferences: Mid Atlantic.

CEO Venture Fund
2000 Technology Dr., Ste. 160
Pittsburgh, PA 15219-3109
Phone: (412)687-3451
Fax: (412)687-8139
E-mail: ceofund@aol.com
Website: http://www.ceoventurefund.com
Ned Renzi, General Partner
Preferred Investment Size: $1,000,000 to $2,000,000. Investment Types: start-up, first stage, second stage, leveraged buyout, and special situations. Industry Preferences: Diversified technology. Geographic Preferences: Middle Atlantic states.

Innovation Works Inc.
2000 Technology Dr., Ste. 250
Pittsburgh, PA 15219
Phone: (412)681-1520
Fax: (412)681-2625
Website: http://www.innovationworks.org
Preferred Investment Size: $100,000 to $500,000. Investment Types: Early and first stage, seed, and start-up. Industry Preferences: Diversified technology. Geographic Preferences: Pennsylvania.

Keystone Minority Capital Fund L.P.
1801 Centre Ave., Ste. 201
Williams Sq.
Pittsburgh, PA 15219
Phone: (412)338-2230
Fax: (412)338-2224
Earl Hord, General Partner
Preferred Investment Size: $500,000 minimum. Investment Types: Start-

up, first stage, second stage, mezzanine, and leveraged buyout. Industry Preferences: Diversified. Geographic Preferences: Middle Atlantic states.

Mellon Ventures, Inc.
One Mellon Bank Ctr., Rm. 3500
Pittsburgh, PA 15258
Phone: (412)236-3594
Fax: (412)236-3593
Website: http://www.mellonventures.com
Preferred Investment Size: $2,000,000 to $25,000,000. Investment Types: Mezzanine, leveraged buyout, and special situations. Industry Preferences: Diversified. Geographic Preferences: National.

Pennsylvania Growth Fund
5850 Ellsworth Ave., Ste. 303
Pittsburgh, PA 15232
Phone: (412)661-1000
Fax: (412)361-0676
Barry Lhormer, Partner
Preferred Investment Size: $500,000 minimum. Investment Types: Leveraged buyout, mezzanine, second stage, and special situation. Industry Preferences: Diversified. Geographic Preferences: Middle Atlantic, Midwest, Northeast, and Southeast.

Point Venture Partners
The Century Bldg.
130 Seventh St., 7th Fl.
Pittsburgh, PA 15222
Phone: (412)261-1966
Fax: (412)261-1718
Kent Engelmeier, General Partner
Preferred Investment Size: $2,000,000. Investment Types: Start-up, first stage, second stage, mezzanine, recaps, and leveraged buyout. Industry Preferences: Diversified. Geographic Preferences: Eastern and Midwestern U.S.

Cross Atlantic Capital Partners
5 Radnor Corporate Center, Ste. 555
Radnor, PA 19087
Phone: (610)995-2650
Fax: (610)971-2062
Website: http://www.xacp.com
Preferred Investment Size: $1,000,000 to $10,000,000. Investment Types: Balanced, early stage, expansion, seed, and start-up. Industry Preferences: Diversified. Geographic Preferences: Entire U.S.

Meridian Venture Partners (Radnor)
The Radnor Court Bldg., Ste. 140
259 Radnor-Chester Rd.
Radnor, PA 19087
Phone: (610)254-2999
Fax: (610)254-2996
E-mail: mvpart@ix.netcom.com
Kenneth E. Jones
Preferred Investment Size: $1,000,000 to $2,000,000. Investment Types: Second stage, leveraged buyout, and special situations. Industry Preferences: Diversified. Geographic Preferences: Entire U.S.

TDH
919 Conestoga Rd., Bldg. 1, Ste. 301
Rosemont, PA 19010
Phone: (610)526-9970
Fax: (610)526-9971
J.B. Doherty, Managing General Partner
Preferred Investment Size: $1,500,000 minimum. Investment Types: Start-up, first and second stage, mezzanine, recaps, and leveraged buyout. Industry Preferences: Diversified. Geographic Preferences: Eastern U.S. and Midwest.

Adams Capital Management
500 Blackburn Ave.
Sewickley, PA 15143
Phone: (412)749-9454
Fax: (412)749-9459
Website: http://www.acm.com
Joel Adams, General Partner
Investment Types: Early and first stages. Industry Preferences: Diversified technology. Geographic Preferences: National.

S.R. One, Ltd.
Four Tower Bridge
200 Barr Harbor Dr., Ste. 250
W. Conshohocken, PA 19428
Phone: (610)567-1000
Fax: (610)567-1039
Barbara Dalton, Vice President
Preferred Investment Size: $500,000 to $5,000,000. Investment Types: Start-up, first and second stage, and late stage. Industry Preferences: Healthcare and genetic engineering, and computer software and services. Geographic Preferences: No preference.

Greater Philadelphia Venture Capital Corp.
351 East Conestoga Rd.
Wayne, PA 19087
Phone: (610)688-6829
Fax: (610)254-8958
Fred Choate, Manager
Preferred Investment Size: $100,000 to $300,000. Investment Types: First and second stage, leveraged buyout, mezzanine, and special situations. Industry Preferences: Diversified. Geographic Preferences: Middle Atlantic.

PA Early Stage
435 Devon Park Dr., Bldg. 500, Ste. 510
Wayne, PA 19087
Phone: (610)293-4075
Fax: (610)254-4240
Website: http://www.paearlystage.com
Preferred Investment Size: $100,000 to $10,000,000. Investment Types: Early, first, and second stage; seed; and start-up. Industry Preferences: Diversified. Geographic Preferences: Mid Atlantic.

The Sandhurst Venture Fund, L.P.
351 E. Constoga Rd.
Wayne, PA 19087
Phone: (610)254-8900
Fax: (610)254-8958
Preferred Investment Size: $500,000 to $1,000,000. Investment Types: Second stage, recaps, and leveraged buyout. Industry Preferences: Computer stores, disposable medical/health related, and industrial products. Geographic Preferences: East Coast and Middle Atlantic.

TL Ventures
700 Bldg.
435 Devon Park Dr.
Wayne, PA 19087-1990
Phone: (610)975-3765
Fax: (610)254-4210
Website: http://www.tlventures.com

Pam Strisofsky,
pstrisofsky@tlventures.com
Preferred Investment Size: $2,000,000 minimum. Investment Types: Seed and early stage. Industry Preferences: Diversified technology. Geographic Preferences: National.

Rockhill Ventures, Inc.
100 Front St., Ste. 1350
West Conshohocken, PA 19428
Phone: (610)940-0300
Fax: (610)940-0301
E-mail: chuck@rockhillventures.com
Preferred Investment Size: $1,000,000 to $2,000,000. Investment Types: Seed, research and development, start-up, first and second stage, leveraged buyout, and recaps. Industry Preferences: Genetic engineering and medical/health related. Geographic Preferences: Eastern U.S.

Puerto Rico

Advent-Morro Equity Partners
Banco Popular Bldg.
206 Tetuan St., Ste. 903
San Juan, PR 00902
Phone: (787)725-5285
Fax: (787)721-1735
Cyril L. Meduna, General Partner
Preferred Investment Size: $500,000 to $3,000,000. Investment Types: No preference. Industry Preferences: Diversified. Geographic Preferences: Puerto Rico.

North America Investment Corp.
Mercantil Plaza, Ste. 813
PO Box 191831
San Juan, PR 00919
Phone: (787)754-6178
Fax: (787)754-6181
Marcelino D. Pastrana-Torres, President
Preferred Investment Size: $25,000 to $250,000. Investment Types: Early stage and expansion. Industry Preferences: Consumer products and retailing, consumer distribution, industrial equipment, therapeutic equipment, real estate, and business services. Geographic Preferences: Puerto Rico.

Rhode Island

Manchester Humphreys, Inc.
40 Westminster St., Ste. 900
Providence, RI 02903
Phone: (401)454-0400
Fax: (401)454-0403
Preferred Investment Size: $500,000 minimum. Investment Types: Leveraged and management buyouts. Industry Preferences: Diversified. Geographic Preferences: National.

Navis Partners
50 Kennedy Plaza, 12th Fl.
Providence, RI 02903
Phone: (401)278-6770
Fax: (401)278-6387
Website: http://www.navispartners.com
Rory B. Smith, General Partner
Preferred Investment Size: $20,000,000 to $75,000,000. Investment Policies: Equity. Investment Types: Acquisition, early and later stage, leveraged and management buyouts, recaps, and expansion. Industry Preferences: Diversified. Geographic Preferences: U.S. and Canada.

South Carolina

Capital Insights, L.L.C.
PO Box 27162
Greenville, SC 29616-2162
Phone: (864)242-6832
Fax: (864)242-6755
E-mail: jwarner@capitalinsights.com
Website: http://www.capitalinsights.com
Preferred Investment Size: $500,000 to $5,000,000. Investment Policies: Equity. Investment Types: Early and late stage. Industry Preferences: Communications and consumer-related services. Geographic Preferences: Southeast.

Transamerica Mezzanine Financing
7 N. Laurens St., Ste. 603
Greenville, SC 29601
Phone: (864)232-6198
Fax: (864)241-4444
J. Phillip Falls, Investment Officer
Investment Types: Seed, start-up, first stage, second stage, and mezzanine. Industry Preferences: Diversified technology. Geographic Preferences: Southeast.

Tennessee

Valley Capital Corp.
Krystal Bldg.
100 W. Martin Luther King Blvd., Ste. 212
Chattanooga, TN 37402
Phone: (423)265-1557
Fax: (423)265-1588
Faye Robinson
Preferred Investment Size: $200,000 minimum. Investment Types: Second stage, mezzanine, and leveraged buyout. Industry Preferences: Diversified. Geographic Preferences: Southeast.

Coleman Swenson Booth Inc.
237 2nd Ave. S
Franklin, TN 37064-2649
Phone: (615)791-9462
Fax: (615)791-9636
Website: http://www.colemanswenson.com
Larry H. Coleman, Ph.D., Managing Partner
Preferred Investment Size: $1,000,000 to $7,000,000. Investment Types: Seed, start-up, first and second stage, and mezzanine. Industry Preferences: Diversified. Geographic Preferences: No preference.

Capital Services & Resources, Inc.
5159 Wheelis Dr., Ste. 106
Memphis, TN 38117
Phone: (901)761-2156
Fax: (907)767-0060
Charles Y. Bancroft, Treasurer
Preferred Investment Size: $300,000 minimum. Investment Policies: Equity. Investment Types: Second stage, leveraged buyout, and special situations. Industry Preferences: Diversified. Geographic Preferences: United States and Canada.

Paradigm Capital Partners LLC
6410 Poplar Ave., Ste. 395
Memphis, TN 38119
Phone: (901)682-6060
Fax: (901)328-3061
Preferred Investment Size: $500,000 to $6,000,000. Investment Types: First and second stage, and seed.

Industry Preferences: Diversified. Geographic Preferences: Southeast.

SSM Ventures
845 Crossover Ln., Ste. 140
Memphis, TN 38117
Phone: (901)767-1131
Fax: (901)767-1135
Website: http://www.ssmventures.com
R. Wilson Orr, III
Preferred Investment Size: $2,000,000 to $10,000,000. Investment Types: start-up, leveraged buyout, and expansion. Industry Preferences: Diversified. Geographic Preferences: Southeast and Southwest U.S.

Capital Across America L.P.
501 Union St., Ste. 201
Nashville, TN 37219
Phone: (615)254-1414
Fax: (615)254-1856
Website: http://www.capitalacrossamerica.com
Investment Types: Balanced. Industry Preferences: Diversified; women/minority-owned businesses. Geographic Preferences: Entire U.S.

Equitas L.P.
2000 Glen Echo Rd., Ste. 101
PO Box 158838
Nashville, TN 37215-8838
Phone: (615)383-8673
Fax: (615)383-8693
Preferred Investment Size: $500.000. Investment Types: Second stage, leveraged buyout, mezzanine, recaps, and special situation. Industry Preferences: Diversified. Geographic Preferences: Southeast and Midwest.

Massey Burch Capital Corp.
One Burton Hills Blvd., Ste. 350
Nashville, TN 37215
Phone: (615)665-3221
Fax: (615)665-3240
E-mail: tcalton@masseyburch.com
Website: http://www.masseyburch.com
Lucious E. Burch, IV, Partner
Preferred Investment Size: $1,000,000 to $5,000,000. Investment Types: Seed, start-up, early and first stage. Industry Preferences: Communication and computer related. Geographic Preferences: Southeast.

Nelson Capital Corp.
3401 West End Ave., Ste. 300
Nashville, TN 37203
Phone: (615)292-8787
Fax: (615)385-3150
Preferred Investment Size: $500,000 minimum. Investment Types: First and second stage, leveraged buyout, and mezzanine. Industry Preferences: Diversified. Geographic Preferences: Southeast.

Texas

Phillips-Smith Specialty Retail Group
5080 Spectrum Dr., Ste. 805 W
Addison, TX 75001
Phone: (972)387-0725
Fax: (972)458-2560
E-mail: pssrg@aol.com
Website: http://www.phillips-smith.com
G. Michael Machens, General Partner
Preferred Investment Size: $1,000,000 minimum. Investment Types: Seed, start-up, first and second stage, mezzanine, and leveraged buyout. Industry Preferences: Retail and Internet related. Geographic Preferences: Entire U.S.

Austin Ventures, L.P.
701 Brazos St., Ste. 1400
Austin, TX 78701
Phone: (512)485-1900
Fax: (512)476-3952
E-mail: info@ausven.com
Website: http://www.austinventures.com
Joseph C. Aragona, General Partner
Preferred Investment Size: $1,000,000 to $15,000,000. Investment Types: Seed, start-up, first and second stage, leveraged buyout, and special situations. Industry Preferences: Diversified. Geographic Preferences: Southwest and Texas.

The Capital Network
3925 West Braker Lane, Ste. 406
Austin, TX 78759-5321
Phone: (512)305-0826
Fax: (512)305-0836
Preferred Investment Size: $100,000 to $500,000. Investment Types: Seed, early and late stage, leveraged buyout, mezzanine, research and development, and special situations. Industry Preferences: Diversified. Geographic Preferences: United States and Canada.

Techxas Ventures LLC
5000 Plaza on the Lake
Austin, TX 78746
Phone: (512)343-0118
Fax: (512)343-1879
E-mail: bruce@techxas.com
Website: http://www.techxas.com
Bruce Ezell, General Partner
Preferred Investment Size: $500,000 to $5,000,000. Investment Types: Seed, start-up, first stage, second stage, balanced, joint ventures, and special situations. Industry Preferences: Diversified technology. Geographic Preferences: Texas.

Alliance Financial of Houston
218 Heather Ln.
Conroe, TX 77385-9013
Phone: (936)447-3300
Fax: (936)447-4222
Preferred Investment Size: $300,000 to $500,000. Investment Types: Second stage, mezzanine, leveraged buyout, and special situations. Industry Preferences: Sales, distribution, and manufacturing. Geographic Preferences: Gulf states.

Amerimark Capital Corp.
1111 W. Mockingbird, Ste. 1111
Dallas, TX 75247
Phone: (214)638-7878
Fax: (214)638-7612
E-mail: amerimark@amcapital.com
Website: http://www.amcapital.com
Preferred Investment Size: $500,000 minimum. Investment Types: Second stage, mezzanine, and leveraged buyout. Industry Preferences: Diversified. Geographic Preferences: National.

AMT Venture Partners / AMT Capital Ltd.
5220 Spring Valley Rd., Ste. 600
Dallas, TX 75240
Phone: (214)905-9757
Fax: (214)905-9761
Website: http://www.amtcapital.com

Preferred Investment Size: $100,000 to $500,000. Investment Types: First and second stages, and expanion. Industry Preferences: Industrial products and equipment, electronic components and instruments. Geographic Preferences: National.

Arkoma Venture Partners
5950 Berkshire Lane, Ste. 1400
Dallas, TX 75225
Phone: (214)739-3515
Fax: (214)739-3572
E-mail: joelf@arkomavp.com
Joel Fontenot, Executive Vice President
Preferred Investment Size: $250,000 to $2,500,000. Investment Policies: Equity. Investment Types: Seed, start-up, early and second stage, and expansion. Industry Preferences: Communications, computer, and electronics. Geographic Preferences: Southwest.

Capital Southwest Corp.
12900 Preston Rd., Ste. 700
Dallas, TX 75230
Phone: (972)233-8242
Fax: (972)233-7362
Website: http://www.capitalsouthwest.com
Howard Thomas, Investment Associate
Preferred Investment Size: $1,000,000 to $6,000,000. Investment Types: First and second stage, leveraged buyout, acquisition, expansion, management buyout, and late stage. Industry Preferences: Diversified. Geographic Preferences: Entire U.S.

Dali, Hook Partners
One Lincoln Center, Ste. 1550
5400 LBJ Freeway
Dallas, TX 75240
Phone: (972)991-5457
Fax: (972)991-5458
E-mail: dhook@hookpartners.com
Website: http://www.hookpartners.com
David J. Hook
Preferred Investment Size: $100,000 to $5,000,000. Investment Types: Balanced, first, and second stage. Industry Preferences: Diversified. Geographic Preferences: Southwest and West Coast.

HO2 Partners
Two Galleria Tower
13455 Noel Rd., Ste. 1670
Dallas, TX 75240
Phone: (972)702-1144
Fax: (972)702-8234
Website: http://www.ho2.com
Preferred Investment Size: $750,000 to $3,000,000. Investment Types: First and second stage, and seed. Industry Preferences: Diversified technology. Geographic Preferences: Texas.

Interwest Partners (Dallas)
2 Galleria Tower
13455 Noel Rd., Ste. 1670
Dallas, TX 75240
Phone: (972)392-7279
Fax: (972)490-6348
Website: http://www.interwest.com
Preferred Investment Size: $2,000,000 to $25,000,000. Investment Types: Seed, research and development, start-up, first and second stage, expansion, and special situations. Industry Preferences: Diversified. Geographic Preferences: Entire U.S.

Kahala Investments, Inc.
8214 Westchester Dr., Ste. 715
Dallas, TX 75225
Phone: (214)987-0077
Fax: (214)987-2332
Lee R. Slaughter, Jr., President
Preferred Investment Size: $10,000,000 minimum. Investment Types: Mezzanine, leveraged buyout, special situations, control block purchases, and industry roll ups. Industry Preferences: Diversified. Geographic Preferences: Southeast and Southwest.

MESBIC Ventures Holding Co.
2435 North Central Expressway, Ste. 200
Dallas, TX 75080
Phone: (972)991-1597
Fax: (972)991-4770
Website: http://www.mvhc.com
Jeff Schaefer
Preferred Investment Size: $1,000,000 minimum. Investment Policies: Loans and/or equity. Investment Types: Leveraged buyout, mezzanine, and second stage. Industry Preferences: Diversified. Geographic Preferences: Southeast and Southwest.

North Texas MESBIC, Inc.
9500 Forest Lane, Ste. 430
Dallas, TX 75243
Phone: (214)221-3565
Fax: (214)221-3566
Preferred Investment Size: $300,000 minimum. Investment Types: Second stage, mezzanine, and leveraged buyout. Industry Preferences: Consumer food and beverage products, restaurants, retailing, consumer and food distribution. Geographic Preferences: Southwest.

Richard Jaffe & Company, Inc,
7318 Royal Cir.
Dallas, TX 75230
Phone: (214)265-9397
Fax: (214)739-1845
E-mail: rjaffe@pssi.net
Richard R. Jaffe, President
Preferred Investment Size: $100,000 to $300,000. Investment Types: start-up, first stage, leveraged buyouts, and special situations. Industry Preferences: Diversified. Geographic Preferences: Southwest.

Sevin Rosen Management Co.
13455 Noel Rd., Ste. 1670
Dallas, TX 75240
Phone: (972)702-1100
Fax: (972)702-1103
E-mail: info@srfunds.com
Website: http://www.srfunds.com
John V. Jaggers, Partner
Preferred Investment Size: $500,000 minimum. Investment Types: Start-up, early and first stage. Industry Preferences: Diversified technology. Geographic Preferences: Entire U.S.

Stratford Capital Partners, L.P.
300 Crescent Ct., Ste. 500
Dallas, TX 75201
Phone: (214)740-7377
Fax: (214)720-7393
E-mail: stratcap@hmtf.com
Michael D. Brown, Managing Partner
Preferred Investment Size: $1,000,000 minimum. Investment

Policies: Equity, sub debt with equity. Investment Types: Expansion, later stage, acquisition, leveraged and management buyout, mezzanine, and recaps. Industry Preferences: Diversified. Geographic Preferences: National.

Sunwestern Investment Group
12221 Merit Dr., Ste. 935
Dallas, TX 75251
Phone: (972)239-5650
Fax: (972)701-0024
Preferred Investment Size: $500,000 to $1,000,000. Investment Types: Second stage, leveraged buyout, and special situations. Industry Preferences: Diversified. Geographic Preferences: Southwest and West Coast.

Wingate Partners
750 N. St. Paul St., Ste. 1200
Dallas, TX 75201
Phone: (214)720-1313
Fax: (214)871-8799
Preferred Investment Size: $20,000,000 minimum. Investment Types: Leveraged buyout and control block purchases. Industry Preferences: Diversified. Geographic Preferences: Entire U.S. and Canada.

Buena Venture Associates
201 Main St., 32nd Fl.
Fort Worth, TX 76102
Phone: (817)339-7400
Fax: (817)390-8408
Website: http://www.buenaventure.com
Preferred Investment Size: $1,000,000 to $50,000,000. Investment Types: Early, first and second stage; seed; and start-up. Industry Preferences: Diversified technology, and health services. Geographic Preferences: Entire U.S.

The Catalyst Group
3 Riverway, Ste. 770
Houston, TX 77056
Phone: (713)623-8133
Fax: (713)623-0473
E-mail: herman@thecatalystgroup.net
Website: http://www.thecatalystgroup.net
Rick Herman, Partner
Preferred Investment Size: $1,000,000 minimum. Investment Types: Second stage, mezzanine, leveraged buyout, and control block purchases. Industry Preferences: Diversified. Geographic Preferences: No preference.

Cureton & Co., Inc.
1100 Louisiana, Ste. 3250
Houston, TX 77002
Phone: (713)658-9806
Fax: (713)658-0476
Stewart Cureton, Jr., President
Preferred Investment Size: $10,000,000 minimum. Investment Types: First and second stage, leveraged buyout, and special situations. Industry Preferences: Diversified. Geographic Preferences: Southwest.

Davis, Tuttle Venture Partners (Dallas)
8 Greenway Plaza, Ste. 1020
Houston, TX 77046
Phone: (713)993-0440
Fax: (713)621-2297
Website: http://www.davistuttle.com
Phillip Tuttle, Partner
Preferred Investment Size: $5,000,000 minimum. Investment Types: First and second stage, mezzanine, and leveraged buyout. Industry Preferences: Diversified. Geographic Preferences: Southwest.

Houston Partners
401 Louisiana, 8th Fl.
Houston, TX 77002
Phone: (713)222-8600
Fax: (713)222-8932
Preferred Investment Size: $500,000 to $1,000,000. Investment Types: Start-up, first and second stage, and expansion. Industry Preferences: Diversified industry preference. Geographic Preferences: Entire U.S.

Southwest Venture Group
10878 Westheimer, Ste. 178
Houston, TX 77042
Phone: (713)827-8947
Fax: (713)461-1470
David M. Klausmeyer, Partner
Preferred Investment Size: $50,000,000 minimum. Investment Types: Diversified. Industry Preferences: Diversified. Geographic Preferences: U.S. and Canada.

Triad Ventures
AM Fund
4600 Post Oak Place, Ste. 100
Houston, TX 77027
Phone: (713)627-9111
Fax: (713)627-9119
David Mueller
Preferred Investment Size: $800,000 maximum. Investment Types: First and second stage, and mezzanine. Industry Preferences: Medical, consumer, computer-related. Geographic Preferences: Southwest and Texas.

Ventex Management, Inc.
3417 Milam St.
Houston, TX 77002-9531
Phone: (713)659-7870
Fax: (713)659-7855
Preferred Investment Size: $1,000,000 to $5,000,000. Investment Types: Second stage, mezzanine, leveraged buyout, and special situations. Industry Preferences: Diversified. Geographic Preferences: Southwest.

MBA Venture Group
1004 Olde Town Rd., Ste. 102
Irving, TX 75061
Phone: (972)986-6703
John Mason
Preferred Investment Size: $1,000,000 minimum. Investment Types: First stage, leveraged buyout, mezzanine, research and development, second stage, seed, start-up. Industry Preferences: Diversified. Geographic Preferences: Entire U.S.

First Capital Group Management Co.
750 East Mulberry St., Ste. 305
PO Box 15616
San Antonio, TX 78212
Phone: (210)736-4233
Fax: (210)736-5449
Jeffrey P. Blanchard, Managing Partner
Preferred Investment Size: $1,000,000 minimum. Investment Types: First and second stage, mezzanine, leveraged buyout, and

special situations. Industry Preferences: Diversified. Geographic Preferences: Southwest.

The Southwest Venture Partnerships
16414 San Pedro, Ste. 345
San Antonio, TX 78232
Phone: (210)402-1200
Fax: (210)402-1221
E-mail: swvp@aol.com
Preferred Investment Size: $500,000 to $5,000,000. Investment Types: start-up, first and second stage, and leveraged buyout. Industry Preferences: Diversified. Geographic Preferences: Southwest.

Medtech International Inc.
1742 Carriageway
Sugarland, TX 77478
Phone: (713)980-8474
Fax: (713)980-6343
Dave Banker
Preferred Investment Size: $100,000 to $500,000. Investment Types: First stage, leveraged buyout, mezzanine, research and development, second stage, seed, special situation, and start-up. Industry Preferences: Diversified. Geographic Preferences: No preference.

Utah

First Security Business Investment Corp.
15 East 100 South, Ste. 100
Salt Lake City, UT 84111
Phone: (801)246-5737
Fax: (801)246-5740
Preferred Investment Size: $300,000 to $800,000. Investment Policies: Loans and/or equity. Investment Types: Leveraged buyout, mezzanine, and second stage. Industry Preferences: Diversified. Geographic Preferences: West Coast, Rocky Mountains.

Utah Ventures II, L.P.
423 Wakara Way, Ste. 206
Salt Lake City, UT 84108
Phone: (801)583-5922
Fax: (801)583-4105
Website: http://www.uven.com
James C. Dreyfous, Managing General Partner
Preferred Investment Size: $1,000,000 to $7,000,000. Investment Types: Early stage. Industry Preferences: Diversified technology. Geographic Preferences: Northwest and Rocky Mountain region.

Wasatch Venture Corp.
1 S. Main St., Ste. 1400
Salt Lake City, UT 84133
Phone: (801)524-8939
Fax: (801)524-8941
E-mail: mail@wasatchvc.com
Todd Stevens, Manager
Preferred Investment Size: $500,000 to $2,000,000. Investment Policies: Equity and debt. Investment Types: Early stage. Industry Preferences: High technology. Geographic Preferences: Western U.S.

Vermont

North Atlantic Capital Corp.
76 Saint Paul St., Ste. 600
Burlington, VT 05401
Phone: (802)658-7820
Fax: (802)658-5757
Website: http://www.northatlanticcapital.com
Preferred Investment Size: $1,500,000 minimum. Investment Types: First and second stage, mezzanine, and leveraged buyout. Industry Preferences: Diversified technology. Geographic Preferences: Northeast.

Green Mountain Advisors Inc.
PO Box 1230
Quechee, VT 05059
Phone: (802)296-7800
Fax: (802)296-6012
Website: http://www.gmtcap.com
Michael Sweatman, President
Preferred Investment Size: $100,000 to $500,000. Investment Types: Second stage, expansion, and mezzanine. Industry Preferences: Technology, communications. Geographic Preferences: Entire U.S.

Virginia

Oxford Financial Services Corp.
Alexandria, VA 22314
Phone: (703)519-4900
Fax: (703)519-4910
E-mail: oxford133@aol.com
J. Alden Philbrick
Preferred Investment Size: $1,000,000. Investment Types: Seed, research and development, start-up, first stage, second stage, and mezzanine. Industry Preferences: Diversified technology. Geographic Preferences: National.

Continental SBIC
4141 N. Henderson Rd.
Arlington, VA 22203
Phone: (703)527-5200
Fax: (703)527-3700
Michael W. Jones, Senior Vice President
Preferred Investment Size: $300,000 to $5,000,000. Investment Types: No preference. Industry Preferences: Diversified. Geographic Preferences: Northeast, Southeast, Middle Atlantic, and Central Canada.

Novak Biddle Venture Partners
1750 Tysons Blvd., Ste. 1190
McLean, VA 22102
Phone: (703)847-3770
Fax: (703)847-3771
E-mail: roger@novakbiddle.com
Website: http://www.novakbiddle.com
Roger Novak, General Partner
Preferred Investment Size: $1,000,000 to $5,000,000. Investment Types: Seed and early stage. Industry Preferences: Communications and computer related. Geographic Preferences: Eastern U.S.

Spacevest
11911 Freedom Dr., Ste. 500
Reston, VA 20190
Phone: (703)904-9800
Fax: (703)904-0571
E-mail: spacevest@spacevest.com
Website: http://www.spacevest.com
Roger P. Widing, Managing Director
Preferred Investment Size: $250,000 to $10,000,000. Investment Policies: Equity. Investment Types: Early and late stage, expansion, and mezzanine. Industry Preferences: Diversified. Geographic Preferences: U.S. and Canada.

Virginia Capital
1801 Libbie Ave., Ste. 201
Richmond, VA 23226
Phone: (804)648-4802
Fax: (804)648-4809
E-mail: webmaster@vacapital.com
Website: http://www.vacapital.com
Thomas E. Deardorff, Vice President
Investment Types: Acquisition, balanced, expansion, and leveraged and management buyouts. Industry Preferences: Communications, consumer, medical and health related. Geographic Preferences: Mid Atlantic.

Calvert Social Venture Partners
402 Maple Ave. W
Vienna, VA 22180
Phone: (703)255-4930
Fax: (703)255-4931
E-mail: calven2000@aol.com
John May, Managing General Partner
Preferred Investment Size: $100,000 to $700,000. Investment Types: First stages. Industry Preferences: Diversified. Geographic Preferences: Middle Atlantic states.

Fairfax Partners
8000 Towers Crescent Dr., Ste. 940
Vienna, VA 22182
Phone: (703)847-9486
Fax: (703)847-0911
E-mail: bgouldey@fairfaxpartners.com
Bruce K. Gouldey, Managing Director
Investment Types: Start-up, first stage, second stage, and leveraged buyout. Industry Preferences: Computer related, Medical and health related. Geographic Preferences: Middle Atlantic States.

Global Internet Ventures
8150 Leesburg Pike, Ste. 1210
Vienna, VA 22182
Phone: (703)442-3300
Fax: (703)442-3388
Website: http://www.givinc.com
Preferred Investment Size: $500,000 to $3,000,000. Investment Types: Early stage. Industry Preferences: Communications, computer, and Internet related. Geographic Preferences: Entire U.S.

Walnut Capital Corp. (Vienna)
8000 Towers Crescent Dr., Ste. 1070
Vienna, VA 22182
Phone: (703)448-3771
Fax: (703)448-7751
Preferred Investment Size: $300,000 to $500,000. Investment Types: start-up, first and second stage, mezzanine, and leveraged buyout. Industry Preferences: Diversified. Geographic Preferences: No preference.

Washington

Encompass Ventures
777 108th Ave. NE, Ste. 2300
Bellevue, WA 98004
Phone: (425)486-3900
Fax: (425)486-3901
E-mail: info@evpartners.com
Website: http://www.encompassventures.com
Preferred Investment Size: $300,000 to $3,000,000. Investment Types: Research and development, start-up, first and second stages. Industry Preferences: Computer related, medical and health related. Geographic Preferences: Western U.S. and Canada.

Fluke Venture Partners
11400 SE Sixth St., Ste. 230
Bellevue, WA 98004
Phone: (425)453-4590
Fax: (425)453-4675
E-mail: gabelein@flukeventures.com
Website: http://www.flukeventures.com
Dennis Weston, Managing Director
Preferred Investment Size: $250,000 to $2,500,000. Investment Types: start-up, seed, first stage, second stage, expansion, and mezzanine. Industry Preferences: Diversified. Geographic Preferences: Northwest.

Pacific Northwest Partners SBIC, L.P.
15352 SE 53rd St.
Bellevue, WA 98006
Phone: (425)455-9967
Fax: (425)455-9404
Preferred Investment Size: $500,000 minimum. Investment Policies: Private equity investments. Investment Types: Seed, start-up, and early and first stage. Industry Preferences: Diversified. Geographic Preferences: Entire U.S.

Materia Venture Associates, L.P.
3435 Carillon Pointe
Kirkland, WA 98033-7354
Phone: (425)822-4100
Fax: (425)827-4086
Preferred Investment Size: $500,000 to $1,000,000. Investment Types: start-up, first and second stage, and mezzanine. Industry Preferences: Advanced industrial products and equipment. Geographic Preferences: Entire U.S.

OVP Venture Partners (Kirkland)
2420 Carillon Pt.
Kirkland, WA 98033
Phone: (425)889-9192
Fax: (425)889-0152
E-mail: info@ovp.com
Website: http://www.ovp.com
Preferred Investment Size: $1,000,000 to $10,000,000. Investment Types: Seed, start-up, early stage. Industry Preferences: Diversified technology. Geographic Preferences: Western U.S. and Canada.

Digital Partners
999 3rd Ave., Ste. 1610
Seattle, WA 98104
Phone: (206)405-3607
Fax: (206)405-3617
Website: http://www.digitalpartners.com
Preferred Investment Size: $250,000 to $3,000,000. Investment Types: Early, first and second stage, and seed. Industry Preferences: Diversified technology. Geographic Preferences: Northwest and Western Canada.

Frazier & Company
601 Union St., Ste. 3300
Seattle, WA 98101
Phone: (206)621-7200
Fax: (206)621-1848
E-mail: jon@frazierco.com
Jon Gilbert, General Partner
Preferred Investment Size: $2,000,000 to $3,000,000. Investment Types: No preference. Industry Preferences: Diversified. Geographic Preferences: National.

Kirlan Venture Capital, Inc.
221 First Ave. W, Ste. 108
Seattle, WA 98119-4223
Phone: (206)281-8610
Fax: (206)285-3451
E-mail: bill@kirlanventure.com
Website: http://www.kirlanventure.com
Preferred Investment Size: $300,000 to $500,000. Investment Types: First stage, second stage, and mezzanine. Industry Preferences: Diversified technology. Geographic Preferences: Western U.S. and Canada.

Phoenix Partners
1000 2nd Ave., Ste. 3600
Seattle, WA 98104
Phone: (206)624-8968
Fax: (206)624-1907
E-mail: djohnsto@interserv.com
William B. Horne, Chief Financial Officer
Preferred Investment Size: $2,000,000 to $3,000,000. Investment Types: Seed, research and development, start-up, first and second stage, and mezzanine. Industry Preferences: Diversified. Geographic Preferences: No preference.

Voyager Capital
800 5th St., Ste. 4100
Seattle, WA 98103
Phone: (206)470-1180
Fax: (206)470-1185
E-mail: info@voyagercap.com
Website: http://www.voyagercap.com
Erik Benson, Senior Associate
Preferred Investment Size: $5,000,000 to $10,000,000. Investment Policies: Equity. Investment Types: Start-up, early and late stage. Industry Preferences: Diversified communications and computer related. Geographic Preferences: West Coast and Western Canada.

Northwest Venture Associates
221 N. Wall St., Ste. 628
Spokane, WA 99201
Phone: (509)747-0728
Fax: (509)747-0758
Website: http://www.nwva.com
Christopher Brookfield
Preferred Investment Size: $1,000,000 to $2,000,000. Investment Types: Seed, research and development, start-up, first stage, second stage, and mezzanine. Industry Preferences: Diversified. Geographic Preferences: Northwest and Rocky Mountains.

Wisconsin

Venture Investors Management, L.L.C.
University Research Park
505 S. Rosa Rd.
Madison, WI 53719
Phone: (608)441-2700
Fax: (608)441-2727
E-mail: roger@ventureinvestors.com
Website: http://www.ventureinvesters.com

Appendix C - Glossary of Small Business Terms

Glossary of Small Business Terms

Absolute liability
Liability that is incurred due to product defects or negligent actions. Manufacturers or retail establishments are held responsible, even though the defect or action may not have been intentional or negligent.

ACE
See Active Corps of Executives

Accident and health benefits
Benefits offered to employees and their families in order to offset the costs associated with accidental death, accidental injury, or sickness.

Account statement
A record of transactions, including payments, new debt, and deposits, incurred during a defined period of time.

Accounting system
System capturing the costs of all employees and/or machinery included in business expenses.

Accounts payable
See Trade credit

Accounts receivable
Unpaid accounts which arise from unsettled claims and transactions from the sale of a company's products or services to its customers.

Active Corps of Executives (ACE)
(See also Service Corps of Retired Executives)
A group of volunteers for a management assistance program of the U.S. Small Business Administration; volunteers provide one-on-one counseling and teach workshops and seminars for small firms.

ADA
See Americans with Disabilities Act

Adaptation
The process whereby an invention is modified to meet the needs of users.

Adaptive engineering
The process whereby an invention is modified to meet the manufacturing and commercial requirements of a targeted market.

Adverse selection
The tendency for higher-risk individuals to purchase health care and more comprehensive plans, resulting in increased costs.

Advertising
A marketing tool used to capture public attention and influence purchasing decisions for a product or service. Utilizes various forms of media to generate consumer response, such as flyers, magazines, newspapers, radio, and television.

Age discrimination
The denial of the rights and privileges of employment based solely on the age of an individual.

Agency costs
Costs incurred to insure that the lender or investor maintains control over assets while allowing the borrower or entrepreneur to use them. Monitoring and information costs are the two major types of agency costs.

Agribusiness
The production and sale of commodities and products from the commercial farming industry.

America Online
(See also Prodigy)
An online service which is accessible by computer modem. The service features Internet access, bulletin boards, online periodicals, electronic mail, and other services for subscribers.

Americans with Disabilities Act (ADA)
Law designed to ensure equal access and opportunity to handicapped persons.

Annual report
(See also Securities and Exchange Commission)
Yearly financial report prepared by a business that adheres to the requirements set forth by the Securities and Exchange Commission (SEC).

Antitrust immunity
(See also Collective ratemaking)
Exemption from prosecution under antitrust laws. In the

transportation industry, firms with antitrust immunity are permitted—under certain conditions—to set schedules and sometimes prices for the public benefit.

Applied research
Scientific study targeted for use in a product or process.

Asians
A minority category used by the U.S. Bureau of the Census to represent a diverse group that includes Aleuts, Eskimos, American Indians, Asian Indians, Chinese, Japanese, Koreans, Vietnamese, Filipinos, Hawaiians, and other Pacific Islanders.

Assets
Anything of value owned by a company.

Audit
The verification of accounting records and business procedures conducted by an outside accounting service.

Average cost
Total production costs divided by the quantity produced.

Balance Sheet
A financial statement listing the total assets and liabilities of a company at a given time.

Bankruptcy
(See also Chapter 7 of the 1978 Bankruptcy Act; Chapter 11 of the 1978 Bankruptcy Act)
The condition in which a business cannot meet its debt obligations and petitions a federal district court either for reorganization of its debts (Chapter 11) or for liquidation of its assets (Chapter 7).

Basic research
Theoretical scientific exploration not targeted to application.

Basket clause
A provision specifying the amount of public pension funds that may be placed in investments not included on a state's legal list (see separate citation).

BBS
See Bulletin Board Service

BDC
See Business development corporation

Benefit
Various services, such as health care, flextime, day care, insurance, and vacation, offered to employees as part of a hiring package. Typically subsidized in whole or in part by the business.

BIDCO
See Business and industrial development company

Billing cycle
A system designed to evenly distribute customer billing throughout the month, preventing clerical backlogs.

Birth
See Business birth

Blue chip security
A low-risk, low-yield security representing an interest in a very stable company.

Blue sky laws
A general term that denotes various states' laws regulating securities.

Bond
(See also General obligation bond; Taxable bonds; Treasury bonds)
A written instrument executed by a bidder or contractor (the principal) and a second party (the surety or sureties) to assure fulfillment of the principal's obligations to a third party (the obligee or government) identified in the bond. If the principal's obligations are not met, the bond assures payment to the extent stipulated of any loss sustained by the obligee.

Bonding requirements
Terms contained in a bond (see separate citation).

Bonus
An amount of money paid to an employee as a reward for achieving certain business goals or objectives.

Brainstorming
A group session where employees contribute their ideas for solving a problem or meeting a company objective without fear of retribution or ridicule.

Brand name
The part of a brand, trademark, or service mark that can be spoken. It can be a word, letter, or group of words or letters.

Continuation coverage
Health coverage offered for a specified period of time to employees who leave their jobs and to their widows, divorced spouses, or dependents.

Contractions
See Business contractions

Convertible preferred stock
A class of stock that pays a reasonable dividend and is convertible into common stock (see separate citation). Generally the convertible feature may only be exercised after being held for a stated period of time. This arrangement is usually considered second-round financing when a company needs equity to maintain its cash flow.

Convertible securities
A feature of certain bonds, debentures, or preferred stocks that allows them to be exchanged by the owner for another class of securities at a future date and in accordance with any other terms of the issue.

Copayment
See Coinsurance

Copyright
A legal form of protection available to creators and authors to safeguard their works from unlawful use or claim of ownership by others. Copyrights may be acquired for works of art, sculpture, music, and published or unpublished manuscripts. All copyrights should be registered at the Copyright Office of the Library of Congress.

Corporate financial ratios
(See also Industry financial ratios)
The relationship between key figures found in a company's financial statement expressed as a numeric value. Used to evaluate risk and company performance. Also known as Financial averages, Operating ratios, and Business ratios.

Corporation
A legal entity, chartered by a state or the federal government, recognized as a separate entity having its own rights, privileges, and liabilities distinct from those of its members.

Cost containment
Actions taken by employers and insurers to curtail rising health care costs; for example, increasing employee cost sharing (see separate citation), requiring second opinions, or preadmission screening.

Cost sharing
The requirement that health care consumers contribute to their own medical care costs through deductibles and coinsurance (see separate citations). Cost sharing does not include the amounts paid in premiums. It is used to control utilization of services; for example, requiring a fixed amount to be paid with each health care service.

Cottage industry
(See also Home-based business)
Businesses based in the home in which the family members are the labor force and family-owned equipment is used to process the goods.

Credit Rating
A letter or number calculated by an organization (such as Dun & Bradstreet) to represent the ability and disposition of a business to meet its financial obligations.

Customer service
Various techniques used to ensure the satisfaction of a customer.

Cyclical peak
The upper turning point in a business cycle.

Cyclical trough
The lower turning point in a business cycle.

DBA
See Business name

Death
See Business death

Debenture
A certificate given as acknowledgment of a debt (see separate citation) secured by the general credit of the issuing corporation. A bond, usually without security, issued by a corporation and sometimes convertible to common stock.

Debt
(See also Long-term debt; Mid-term debt; Securitized debt; Short-term debt)
Something owed by one person to another. Financing in which a company receives capital that must be repaid; no ownership is transferred.

Bridge financing
A short-term loan made in expectation of intermediate-term or long-term financing. Can be used when a company plans to go public in the near future.

Broker
One who matches resources available for innovation with those who need them.

Budget
An estimate of the spending necessary to complete a project or offer a service in comparison to cash-on-hand and expected earnings for the coming year, with an emphasis on cost control.

Bulletin Board Service (BBS)
An online service enabling users to communicate with each other about specific topics.

Business and industrial development company (BIDCO)
A private, for-profit financing corporation chartered by the state to provide both equity and long-term debt capital to small business owners (see separate citations for equity and debt capital).

Business birth
The formation of a new establishment or enterprise. The appearance of a new establishment or enterprise in the Small Business Data Base (see separate citation).

Business conditions
Outside factors that can affect the financial performance of a business.

Business contractions
The number of establishments that have decreased in employment during a specified time.

Business cycle
A period of economic recession and recovery. These cycles vary in duration.

Business death
The voluntary or involuntary closure of a firm or establishment. The disappearance of an establishment or enterprise from the Small Business Data Base (see separate citation).

Business development corporation (BDC)
A business financing agency, usually composed of the financial institutions in an area or state, organized to assist in financing businesses unable to obtain assistance through normal channels; the risk is spread among various members of the business development corporation, and interest rates may vary somewhat from those charged by member institutions. A venture capital firm in which shares of ownership are publicly held and to which the Investment Act of 1940 applies.

Business dissolution
For enumeration purposes, the absence of a business that was present in the prior time period from any current record.

Business entry
See Business birth

Business ethics
Moral values and principles espoused by members of the business community as a guide to fair and honest business practices.

Business exit
See Business death

Business expansions
The number of establishments that added employees during a specified time.

Business failure
Closure of a business causing a loss to at least one creditor.

Business format franchising
(See also Franchising)
The purchase of the name, trademark, and an ongoing business plan of the parent corporation or franchisor by the franchisee.

Business license
A legal authorization issued by municipal and state governments and required for business operations.

Business name
(See also Business license; Trademark)
Enterprises must register their business names with local governments usually on a "doing business as" (DBA) form. (This name is sometimes referred to as a "fictional name.") The procedure is part of the business licensing process and prevents any other business from using that same name for a similar business in the same locality.

Business norms
See Financial ratios

Business permit
See Business license

Business plan
A document that spells out a company's expected course of action for a specified period, usually including a detailed listing and analysis of risks and uncertainties. For the small business, it should examine the proposed products, the market, the industry, the management policies, the marketing policies, production needs, and financial needs. Frequently, it is used as a prospectus for potential investors and lenders.

Business proposal
See Business plan

Business service firm
An establishment primarily engaged in rendering services to other business organizations on a fee or contract basis.

Business start
For enumeration purposes, a business with a name or similar designation that did not exist in a prior time period.

Cafeteria plan
See Flexible benefit plan

Capacity
Level of a firm's, industry's, or nation's output corresponding to full practical utilization of available resources.

Capital
Assets less liabilities, representing the ownership interest in a business. A stock of accumulated goods, especially at a specified time and in contrast to income received during a specified time period. Accumulated goods devoted to production. Accumulated possessions calculated to bring income.

Capital expenditure
Expenses incurred by a business for improvements that will depreciate over time.

Capital gain
The monetary difference between the purchase price and the selling price of capital. Capital gains are taxed at a rate of 28% by the federal government.

Capital intensity
(See also Debt capital; Equity midrisk venture capital; Informal capital; Internal capital; Owner's capital; Secondhand capital; Seed capital; Venture capital)
The relative importance of capital in the production process, usually expressed as the ratio of capital to labor but also sometimes as the ratio of capital to output.

Capital resource
The equipment, facilities and labor used to create products and services.

Caribbean Basin Initiative
An interdisciplinary program to support commerce among the businesses in the nations of the Caribbean Basin and the United States. Agencies involved include: the Agency for International Development, the U.S. Small Business Administration, the International Trade Administration of the U.S. Department of Commerce, and various private sector groups.

Catastrophic care
Medical and other services for acute and long-term illnesses that cost more than insurance coverage limits or that cost the amount most families may be expected to pay with their own resources.

CDC
See Certified development corporation

CD-ROM
Compact disc with read-only memory used to store large amounts of digitized data.

Certified development corporation (CDC)
A local area or statewide corporation or authority (for profit or nonprofit) that packages U.S. Small Business Administration (SBA), bank, state, and/or private money into financial assistance for existing business capital improvements. The SBA holds the second lien on its maximum share of 40 percent involvement. Each state has at least one certified development corporation. This program is called the SBA 504 Program.

Certified lenders
Banks that participate in the SBA guaranteed loan program (see separate citation). Such banks must have a good track record with the U.S. Small Business Administration (SBA) and must agree to certain conditions set forth by the agency. In return, the SBA agrees to process any guaranteed loan application within three business days.

Champion
An advocate for the development of an innovation.

Channel of distribution
The means used to transport merchandise from the manufacturer to the consumer.

Chapter 7 of the 1978 Bankruptcy Act
Provides for a court-appointed trustee who is responsible for liquidating a company's assets in order to settle outstanding debts.

Chapter 11 of the 1978 Bankruptcy Act
Allows the business owners to retain control of the company while working with their creditors to reorganize their finances and establish better business practices to prevent liquidation of assets.

Closely held corporation
A corporation in which the shares are held by a few persons, usually officers, employees, or others close to the management; these shares are rarely offered to the public.

Code of Federal Regulations
Codification of general and permanent rules of the federal government published in the Federal Register.

Code sharing
See Computer code sharing

Coinsurance
(See also Cost sharing)
Upon meeting the deductible payment, health insurance participants may be required to make additional health care cost-sharing payments. Coinsurance is a payment of a fixed percentage of the cost of each service; copayment is usually a fixed amount to be paid with each service.

Collateral
Securities, evidence of deposit, or other property pledged by a borrower to secure repayment of a loan.

Collective ratemaking
(See also Antitrust immunity)
The establishment of uniform charges for services by a group of businesses in the same industry.

Commercial insurance plan
See Underwriting

Commercial loans
Short-term renewable loans used to finance specific capital needs of a business.

Commercialization
The final stage of the innovation process, including production and distribution.

Common stock
The most frequently used instrument for purchasing ownership in private or public companies. Common stock generally carries the right to vote on certain corporate actions and may pay dividends, although it rarely does in venture investments. In liquidation, common stockholders are the last to share in the proceeds from the sale of a corporation's assets; bondholders and preferred shareholders have priority. Common stock is often used in first-round start-up financing.

Community development corporation
A corporation established to develop economic programs for a community and, in most cases, to provide financial support for such development.

Competitor
A business whose product or service is marketed for the same purpose/use and to the same consumer group as the product or service of another.

Computer code sharing
An arrangement whereby flights of a regional airline are identified by the two-letter code of a major carrier in the computer reservation system to help direct passengers to new regional carriers.

Consignment
A merchandising agreement, usually referring to second-hand shops, where the dealer pays the owner of an item a percentage of the profit when the item is sold.

Consortium
A coalition of organizations such as banks and corporations for ventures requiring large capital resources.

Consultant
An individual that is paid by a business to provide advice and expertise in a particular area.

Consumer price index
A measure of the fluctuation in prices between two points in time.

Consumer research
Research conducted by a business to obtain information about existing or potential consumer markets.

Debt capital
Business financing that normally requires periodic interest payments and repayment of the principal within a specified time.

Debt financing
See Debt capital

Debt securities
Loans such as bonds and notes that provide a specified rate of return for a specified period of time.

Deductible
A set amount that an individual must pay before any benefits are received.

Demand shock absorbers
A term used to describe the role that some small firms play by expanding their output levels to accommodate a transient surge in demand.

Demographics
Statistics on various markets, including age, income, and education, used to target specific products or services to appropriate consumer groups.

Demonstration
Showing that a product or process has been modified sufficiently to meet the needs of users.

Deregulation
The lifting of government restrictions; for example, the lifting of government restrictions on the entry of new businesses, the expansion of services, and the setting of prices in particular industries.

Desktop Publishing
Using personal computers and specialized software to produce camera-ready copy for publications.

Disaster loans
Various types of physical and economic assistance available to individuals and businesses through the U.S. Small Business Administration (SBA). This is the only SBA loan program available for residential purposes.

Discrimination
The denial of the rights and privileges of employment based on factors such as age, race, religion, or gender.

Diseconomies of scale
The condition in which the costs of production increase faster than the volume of production.

Dissolution
See Business dissolution

Distribution
Delivering a product or process to the user.

Distributor
One who delivers merchandise to the user.

Diversified company
A company whose products and services are used by several different markets.

Doing business as (DBA)
See Business name

Dow Jones
An information services company that publishes the Wall Street Journal and other sources of financial information.

Dow Jones Industrial Average
An indicator of stock market performance.

Earned income
A tax term that refers to wages and salaries earned by the recipient, as opposed to monies earned through interest and dividends.

Economic efficiency
The use of productive resources to the fullest practical extent in the provision of the set of goods and services that is most preferred by purchasers in the economy.

Economic indicators
Statistics used to express the state of the economy. These include the length of the average work week, the rate of unemployment, and stock prices.

Economically disadvantaged
See Socially and economically disadvantaged

Economies of scale
See Scale economies

EEOC
See Equal Employment Opportunity Commission

8(a) Program
A program authorized by the Small Business Act that directs federal contracts to small businesses owned and operated by socially and economically disadvantaged individuals.

Electronic mail (e-mail)
The electronic transmission of mail via phone lines.

E-mail
See Electronic mail

Employee leasing
A contract by which employers arrange to have their workers hired by a leasing company and then leased back to them for a management fee. The leasing company typically assumes the administrative burden of payroll and provides a benefit package to the workers.

Employee tenure
The length of time an employee works for a particular employer.

Employer identification number
The business equivalent of a social security number. Assigned by the U.S. Internal Revenue Service.

Enterprise
An aggregation of all establishments owned by a parent company. An enterprise may consist of a single, independent establishment or include subsidiaries and other branches under the same ownership and control.

Enterprise zone
A designated area, usually found in inner cities and other areas with significant unemployment, where businesses receive tax credits and other incentives to entice them to establish operations there.

Entrepreneur
A person who takes the risk of organizing and operating a new business venture.

Entry
See Business entry

Equal Employment Opportunity Commission (EEOC)
A federal agency that ensures nondiscrimination in the hiring and firing practices of a business.

Equal opportunity employer
An employer who adheres to the standards set by the Equal Employment Opportunity Commission (see separate citation).

Equity
(See also Common Stock; Equity midrisk venture capital)
The ownership interest. Financing in which partial or total ownership of a company is surrendered in exchange for capital. An investor's financial return comes from dividend payments and from growth in the net worth of the business.

Equity capital
See Equity; Equity midrisk venture capital

Equity financing
See Equity; Equity midrisk venture capital

Equity midrisk venture capital
An unsecured investment in a company. Usually a purchase of ownership interest in a company that occurs in the later stages of a company's development.

Equity partnership
A limited partnership arrangement for providing start-up and seed capital to businesses.

Equity securities
See Equity

Equity-type
Debt financing subordinated to conventional debt.

Establishment
A single-location business unit that may be independent (a single-establishment enterprise) or owned by a parent enterprise.

Establishment and Enterprise Microdata File
See U.S. Establishment and Enterprise Microdata File

Establishment birth
See Business birth

Establishment Longitudinal Microdata File
See U.S. Establishment Longitudinal Microdata File

Ethics
See Business ethics

Evaluation
Determining the potential success of translating an invention into a product or process.

Exit
See Business exit

Experience rating
See Underwriting

Export
A product sold outside of the country.

Export license
A general or specific license granted by the U.S. Department of Commerce required of anyone wishing to export goods. Some restricted articles need approval from the U.S. Departments of State, Defense, or Energy.

Failure
See Business failure

Fair share agreement
(See also Franchising)
An agreement reached between a franchisor and a minority business organization to extend business ownership to minorities by either reducing the amount of capital required or by setting aside certain marketing areas for minority business owners.

Feasibility study
A study to determine the likelihood that a proposed product or development will fulfill the objectives of a particular investor.

Federal Trade Commission (FTC)
Federal agency that promotes free enterprise and competition within the U.S.

Federal Trade Mark Act of 1946
See Lanham Act

Fictional name
See Business name

Fiduciary
An individual or group that hold assets in trust for a beneficiary.

Financial analysis
The techniques used to determine money needs in a business. Techniques include ratio analysis, calculation of return on investment, guides for measuring profitability, and break-even analysis to determine ultimate success.

Financial intermediary
A financial institution that acts as the intermediary between borrowers and lenders. Banks, savings and loan associations, finance companies, and venture capital companies are major financial intermediaries in the United States.

Financial ratios
See Corporate financial ratios; Industry financial ratios

Financial statement
A written record of business finances, including balance sheets and profit and loss statements.

Financing
See First-stage financing; Second-stage financing; Third-stage financing

First-stage financing
(See also Second-stage financing; Third-stage financing)
Financing provided to companies that have expended their initial capital, and require funds to start full-scale manufacturing and sales. Also known as First-round financing.

Fiscal year
Any twelve-month period used by businesses for accounting purposes.

504 Program
See Certified development corporation

Flexible benefit plan
A plan that offers a choice among cash and/or qualified benefits such as group term life insurance, accident and health insurance, group legal services, dependent care assistance, and vacations.

FOB
See Free on board

Format franchising
See Business format franchising; Franchising

401(k) plan
A financial plan where employees contribute a percentage of their earnings to a fund that is invested in stocks, bonds, or money markets for the purpose of saving money for retirement.

Four Ps
Marketing terms referring to Product, Price, Place, and Promotion.

Franchising
A form of licensing by which the owner—the franchisor—distributes or markets a product, method, or service through affiliated dealers called franchisees. The product, method, or service being marketed is identified by a brand name, and the franchisor maintains control over the

marketing methods employed. The franchisee is often given exclusive access to a defined geographic area.

Free on board (FOB)
A pricing term indicating that the quoted price includes the cost of loading goods into transport vessels at a specified place.

Frictional unemployment
See Unemployment

FTC
See Federal Trade Commission

Fulfillment
The systems necessary for accurate delivery of an ordered item, including subscriptions and direct marketing.

Full-time workers
Generally, those who work a regular schedule of more than 35 hours per week.

Garment registration number
A number that must appear on every garment sold in the U.S. to indicate the manufacturer of the garment, which may or may not be the same as the label under which the garment is sold. The U.S. Federal Trade Commission assigns and regulates garment registration numbers.

Gatekeeper
A key contact point for entry into a network.

GDP
See Gross domestic product

General obligation bond
A municipal bond secured by the taxing power of the municipality. The Tax Reform Act of 1986 limits the purposes for which such bonds may be issued and establishes volume limits on the extent of their issuance.

GNP
See Gross national product

Good Housekeeping Seal
Seal appearing on products that signifies the fulfillment of the standards set by the Good Housekeeping Institute to protect consumer interests.

Goods sector
All businesses producing tangible goods, including agriculture, mining, construction, and manufacturing businesses.

GPO
See Gross product originating

Gross domestic product (GDP)
The part of the nation's gross national product (see separate citation) generated by private business using resources from within the country.

Gross national product (GNP)
The most comprehensive single measure of aggregate economic output. Represents the market value of the total output of goods and services produced by a nation's economy.

Gross product originating (GPO)
A measure of business output estimated from the income or production side using employee compensation, profit income, net interest, capital consumption, and indirect business taxes.

HAL
See Handicapped assistance loan program

Handicapped assistance loan program (HAL)
Low-interest direct loan program through the U.S. Small Business Administration (SBA) for handicapped persons. The SBA requires that these persons demonstrate that their disability is such that it is impossible for them to secure employment, thus making it necessary to go into their own business to make a living.

Health maintenance organization (HMO)
Organization of physicians and other health care professionals that provides health services to subscribers and their dependents on a prepaid basis.

Health provider
An individual or institution that gives medical care. Under Medicare, an institutional provider is a hospital, skilled nursing facility, home health agency, or provider of certain physical therapy services.

Hispanic
A person of Cuban, Mexican, Puerto Rican, Latin American (Central or South American), European Spanish, or other Spanish-speaking origin or ancestry.

HMO
See Health maintenance organization

Home-based business
(See also Cottage industry)

A business with an operating address that is also a residential address (usually the residential address of the proprietor).

Hub-and-spoke system
A system in which flights of an airline from many different cities (the spokes) converge at a single airport (the hub). After allowing passengers sufficient time to make connections, planes then depart for different cities.

Human Resources Management
A business program designed to oversee recruiting, pay, benefits, and other issues related to the company's work force, including planning to determine the optimal use of labor to increase production, thereby increasing profit.

Idea
An original concept for a new product or process.

Import
Products produced outside the country in which they are consumed.

Income
Money or its equivalent, earned or accrued, resulting from the sale of goods and services.

Income statement
A financial statement that lists the profits and losses of a company at a given time.

Incorporation
The filing of a certificate of incorporation with a state's secretary of state, thereby limiting the business owner's liability.

Incubator
A facility designed to encourage entrepreneurship and minimize obstacles to new business formation and growth, particularly for high-technology firms, by housing a number of fledgling enterprises that share an array of services, such as meeting areas, secretarial services, accounting, research library, on-site financial and management counseling, and word processing facilities.

Independent contractor
An individual considered self-employed (see separate citation) and responsible for paying Social Security taxes and income taxes on earnings.

Indirect health coverage
Health insurance obtained through another individual's health care plan; for example, a spouse's employer-sponsored plan.

Industrial development authority
The financial arm of a state or other political subdivision established for the purpose of financing economic development in an area, usually through loans to nonprofit organizations, which in turn provide facilities for manufacturing and other industrial operations.

Industry financial ratios
(See also Corporate financial ratios)
Corporate financial ratios averaged for a specified industry. These are used for comparison purposes and reveal industry trends and identify differences between the performance of a specific company and the performance of its industry. Also known as Industrial averages, Industry ratios, Financial averages, and Business or Industrial norms.

Inflation
Increases in volume of currency and credit, generally resulting in a sharp and continuing rise in price levels.

Informal capital
Financing from informal, unorganized sources; includes informal debt capital such as trade credit or loans from friends and relatives and equity capital from informal investors.

Initial public offering (IPO)
A corporation's first offering of stock to the public.

Innovation
The introduction of a new idea into the marketplace in the form of a new product or service or an improvement in organization or process.

Intellectual property
Any idea or work that can be considered proprietary in nature and is thus protected from infringement by others.

Internal capital
Debt or equity financing obtained from the owner or through retained business earnings.

Internet
A government-designed computer network that contains large amounts of information and is accessible through various vendors for a fee.

Intrapreneurship
The state of employing entrepreneurial principles to nonentrepreneurial situations.

Invention
The tangible form of a technological idea, which could include a laboratory prototype, drawings, formulas, etc.

IPO
See Initial public offering

Job description
The duties and responsibilities required in a particular position.

Job tenure
A period of time during which an individual is continuously employed in the same job.

Joint marketing agreements
Agreements between regional and major airlines, often involving the coordination of flight schedules, fares, and baggage transfer. These agreements help regional carriers operate at lower cost.

Joint venture
Venture in which two or more people combine efforts in a particular business enterprise, usually a single transaction or a limited activity, and agree to share the profits and losses jointly or in proportion to their contributions.

Keogh plan
Designed for self-employed persons and unincorporated businesses as a tax-deferred pension account.

Labor force
Civilians considered eligible for employment who are also willing and able to work.

Labor force participation rate
The civilian labor force as a percentage of the civilian population.

Labor intensity
(See also Capital intensity)
The relative importance of labor in the production process, usually measured as the capital-labor ratio; i.e., the ratio of units of capital (typically, dollars of tangible assets) to the number of employees. The higher the capital-labor ratio exhibited by a firm or industry, the lower the capital intensity of that firm or industry is said to be.

Labor surplus area
An area in which there exists a high unemployment rate. In procurement (see separate citation), extra points are given to firms in counties that are designated a labor surplus area; this information is requested on procurement bid sheets.

Labor union
An organization of similarly-skilled workers who collectively bargain with management over the conditions of employment.

Laboratory prototype
See Prototype

LAN
See Local Area Network

Lanham Act
Refers to the Federal Trade Mark Act of 1946. Protects registered trademarks, trade names, and other service marks used in commerce.

Large business-dominated industry
Industry in which a minimum of 60 percent of employment or sales is in firms with more than 500 workers.

LBO
See Leveraged buy-out

Leader pricing
A reduction in the price of a good or service in order to generate more sales of that good or service.

Legal list
A list of securities selected by a state in which certain institutions and fiduciaries (such as pension funds, insurance companies, and banks) may invest. Securities not on the list are not eligible for investment. Legal lists typically restrict investments to high quality securities meeting certain specifications. Generally, investment is limited to U.S. securities and investment-grade blue chip securities (see separate citation).

Leveraged buy-out (LBO)
The purchase of a business or a division of a corporation through a highly leveraged financing package.

Liability
An obligation or duty to perform a service or an act. Also defined as money owed.

License
(See also Business license)
A legal agreement granting to another the right to use a technological innovation.

Export
A product sold outside of the country.

Export license
A general or specific license granted by the U.S. Department of Commerce required of anyone wishing to export goods. Some restricted articles need approval from the U.S. Departments of State, Defense, or Energy.

Failure
See Business failure

Fair share agreement
(See also Franchising)
An agreement reached between a franchisor and a minority business organization to extend business ownership to minorities by either reducing the amount of capital required or by setting aside certain marketing areas for minority business owners.

Feasibility study
A study to determine the likelihood that a proposed product or development will fulfill the objectives of a particular investor.

Federal Trade Commission (FTC)
Federal agency that promotes free enterprise and competition within the U.S.

Federal Trade Mark Act of 1946
See Lanham Act

Fictional name
See Business name

Fiduciary
An individual or group that hold assets in trust for a beneficiary.

Financial analysis
The techniques used to determine money needs in a business. Techniques include ratio analysis, calculation of return on investment, guides for measuring profitability, and break-even analysis to determine ultimate success.

Financial intermediary
A financial institution that acts as the intermediary between borrowers and lenders. Banks, savings and loan associations, finance companies, and venture capital companies are major financial intermediaries in the United States.

Financial ratios
See Corporate financial ratios; Industry financial ratios

Financial statement
A written record of business finances, including balance sheets and profit and loss statements.

Financing
See First-stage financing; Second-stage financing; Third-stage financing

First-stage financing
(See also Second-stage financing; Third-stage financing)
Financing provided to companies that have expended their initial capital, and require funds to start full-scale manufacturing and sales. Also known as First-round financing.

Fiscal year
Any twelve-month period used by businesses for accounting purposes.

504 Program
See Certified development corporation

Flexible benefit plan
A plan that offers a choice among cash and/or qualified benefits such as group term life insurance, accident and health insurance, group legal services, dependent care assistance, and vacations.

FOB
See Free on board

Format franchising
See Business format franchising; Franchising

401(k) plan
A financial plan where employees contribute a percentage of their earnings to a fund that is invested in stocks, bonds, or money markets for the purpose of saving money for retirement.

Four Ps
Marketing terms referring to Product, Price, Place, and Promotion.

Franchising
A form of licensing by which the owner—the franchisor—distributes or markets a product, method, or service through affiliated dealers called franchisees. The product, method, or service being marketed is identified by a brand name, and the franchisor maintains control over the

marketing methods employed. The franchisee is often given exclusive access to a defined geographic area.

Free on board (FOB)
A pricing term indicating that the quoted price includes the cost of loading goods into transport vessels at a specified place.

Frictional unemployment
See Unemployment

FTC
See Federal Trade Commission

Fulfillment
The systems necessary for accurate delivery of an ordered item, including subscriptions and direct marketing.

Full-time workers
Generally, those who work a regular schedule of more than 35 hours per week.

Garment registration number
A number that must appear on every garment sold in the U.S. to indicate the manufacturer of the garment, which may or may not be the same as the label under which the garment is sold. The U.S. Federal Trade Commission assigns and regulates garment registration numbers.

Gatekeeper
A key contact point for entry into a network.

GDP
See Gross domestic product

General obligation bond
A municipal bond secured by the taxing power of the municipality. The Tax Reform Act of 1986 limits the purposes for which such bonds may be issued and establishes volume limits on the extent of their issuance.

GNP
See Gross national product

Good Housekeeping Seal
Seal appearing on products that signifies the fulfillment of the standards set by the Good Housekeeping Institute to protect consumer interests.

Goods sector
All businesses producing tangible goods, including agriculture, mining, construction, and manufacturing businesses.

GPO
See Gross product originating

Gross domestic product (GDP)
The part of the nation's gross national product (see separate citation) generated by private business using resources from within the country.

Gross national product (GNP)
The most comprehensive single measure of aggregate economic output. Represents the market value of the total output of goods and services produced by a nation's economy.

Gross product originating (GPO)
A measure of business output estimated from the income or production side using employee compensation, profit income, net interest, capital consumption, and indirect business taxes.

HAL
See Handicapped assistance loan program

Handicapped assistance loan program (HAL)
Low-interest direct loan program through the U.S. Small Business Administration (SBA) for handicapped persons. The SBA requires that these persons demonstrate that their disability is such that it is impossible for them to secure employment, thus making it necessary to go into their own business to make a living.

Health maintenance organization (HMO)
Organization of physicians and other health care professionals that provides health services to subscribers and their dependents on a prepaid basis.

Health provider
An individual or institution that gives medical care. Under Medicare, an institutional provider is a hospital, skilled nursing facility, home health agency, or provider of certain physical therapy services.

Hispanic
A person of Cuban, Mexican, Puerto Rican, Latin American (Central or South American), European Spanish, or other Spanish-speaking origin or ancestry.

HMO
See Health maintenance organization

Home-based business
(See also Cottage industry)

Limited partnerships
See Venture capital limited partnerships

Liquidity
The ability to convert a security into cash promptly.

Loans
See Commercial loans; Disaster loans; SBA direct loans; SBA guaranteed loans; SBA special lending institution categories

Local Area Network (LAN)
Computer networks contained within a single building or small area; used to facilitate the sharing of information.

Local development corporation
An organization, usually made up of local citizens of a community, designed to improve the economy of the area by inducing business and industry to locate and expand there. A local development corporation establishes a capability to finance local growth.

Long-haul rates
Rates charged by a transporter in which the distance traveled is more than 800 miles.

Long-term debt
An obligation that matures in a period that exceeds five years.

Low-grade bond
A corporate bond that is rated below investment grade by the major rating agencies (Standard and Poor's, Moody's).

Macro-efficiency
(See also Economic efficiency)
Efficiency as it pertains to the operation of markets and market systems.

Managed care
A cost-effective health care program initiated by employers whereby low-cost health care is made available to the employees in return for exclusive patronage to program doctors.

Management Assistance Programs
See SBA Management Assistance Programs

Management and technical assistance
A term used by many programs to mean business (as opposed to technological) assistance.

Mandated benefits
Specific treatments, providers, or individuals required by law to be included in commercial health plans.

Market evaluation
The use of market information to determine the sales potential of a specific product or process.

Market failure
The situation in which the workings of a competitive market do not produce the best results from the point of view of the entire society.

Market information
Data of any type that can be used for market evaluation, which could include demographic data, technology forecasting, regulatory changes, etc.

Market research
A systematic collection, analysis, and reporting of data about the market and its preferences, opinions, trends, and plans; used for corporate decision-making.

Market share
In a particular market, the percentage of sales of a specific product.

Marketing
Promotion of goods or services through various media.

Master Establishment List (MEL)
A list of firms in the United States developed by the U.S. Small Business Administration; firms can be selected by industry, region, state, standard metropolitan statistical area (see separate citation), county, and zip code.

Maturity
(See also Term)
The date upon which the principal or stated value of a bond or other indebtedness becomes due and payable.

Medicaid (Title XIX)
A federally aided, state-operated and administered program that provides medical benefits for certain low-income persons in need of health and medical care who are eligible for one of the government's welfare cash payment programs, including the aged, the blind, the disabled, and members of families with dependent children where one parent is absent, incapacitated, or unemployed.

Medicare (Title XVIII)
A nationwide health insurance program for disabled and aged persons. Health insurance is available to insured persons without regard to income. Monies from payroll taxes cover hospital insurance and monies from general revenues and beneficiary premiums pay for supplementary medical insurance.

MEL
See Master Establishment List

MESBIC
See Minority enterprise small business investment corporation

MET
See Multiple employer trust

Metropolitan statistical area (MSA)
A means used by the government to define large population centers that may transverse different governmental jurisdictions. For example, the Washington, D.C. MSA includes the District of Columbia and contiguous parts of Maryland and Virginia because all of these geopolitical areas comprise one population and economic operating unit.

Mezzanine financing
See Third-stage financing

Micro-efficiency
(See also Economic efficiency)
Efficiency as it pertains to the operation of individual firms.

Microdata
Information on the characteristics of an individual business firm.

Mid-term debt
An obligation that matures within one to five years.

Midrisk venture capital
See Equity midrisk venture capital

Minimum premium plan
A combination approach to funding an insurance plan aimed primarily at premium tax savings. The employer self-funds a fixed percentage of estimated monthly claims and the insurance company insures the excess.

Minimum wage
The lowest hourly wage allowed by the federal government.

Minority Business Development Agency
Contracts with private firms throughout the nation to sponsor Minority Business Development Centers which provide minority firms with advice and technical assistance on a fee basis.

Minority Enterprise Small Business Investment Corporation (MESBIC)
A federally funded private venture capital firm licensed by the U.S. Small Business Administration to provide capital to minority-owned businesses (see separate citation).

Minority-owned business
Businesses owned by those who are socially or economically disadvantaged (see separate citation).

Mom and Pop business
A small store or enterprise having limited capital, principally employing family members.

Moonlighter
A wage-and-salary worker with a side business.

MSA
See Metropolitan statistical area

Multi-employer plan
A health plan to which more than one employer is required to contribute and that may be maintained through a collective bargaining agreement and required to meet standards prescribed by the U.S. Department of Labor.

Multi-level marketing
A system of selling in which you sign up other people to assist you and they, in turn, recruit others to help them. Some entrepreneurs have built successful companies on this concept because the main focus of their activities is their product and product sales.

Multimedia
The use of several types of media to promote a product or service. Also, refers to the use of several different types of media (sight, sound, pictures, text) in a CD-ROM (see separate citation) product.

Multiple employer trust (MET)
A self-funded benefit plan generally geared toward small employers sharing a common interest.

NAFTA
See North American Free Trade Agreement

NASDAQ
See National Association of Securities Dealers Automated Quotations

National Association of Securities Dealers Automated Quotations
Provides price quotes on over-the-counter securities as well as securities listed on the New York Stock Exchange.

National income
Aggregate earnings of labor and property arising from the production of goods and services in a nation's economy.

Net assets
See Net worth

Net income
The amount remaining from earnings and profits after all expenses and costs have been met or deducted. Also known as Net earnings.

Net profit
Money earned after production and overhead expenses (see separate citations) have been deducted.

Net worth
(See also Capital)
The difference between a company's total assets and its total liabilities.

Network
A chain of interconnected individuals or organizations sharing information and/or services.

New York Stock Exchange (NYSE)
The oldest stock exchange in the U.S. Allows for trading in stocks, bonds, warrants, options, and rights that meet listing requirements.

Niche
A career or business for which a person is well-suited. Also, a product which fulfills one need of a particular market segment, often with little or no competition.

Nodes
One workstation in a network, either local area or wide area (see separate citations).

Nonbank bank
A bank that either accepts deposits or makes loans, but not both. Used to create many new branch banks.

Noncompetitive awards
A method of contracting whereby the federal government negotiates with only one contractor to supply a product or service.

Nonmember bank
A state-regulated bank that does not belong to the federal bank system.

Nonprofit
An organization that has no shareholders, does not distribute profits, and is without federal and state tax liabilities.

Norms
See Financial ratios

North American Free Trade Agreement (NAFTA)
Passed in 1993, NAFTA eliminates trade barriers among businesses in the U.S., Canada, and Mexico.

NYSE
See New York Stock Exchange

Occupational Safety & Health Administration (OSHA)
Federal agency that regulates health and safety standards within the workplace.

Optimal firm size
The business size at which the production cost per unit of output (average cost) is, in the long run, at its minimum.

Organizational chart
A hierarchical chart tracking the chain of command within an organization.

OSHA
See Occupational Safety & Health Administration

Overhead
Expenses, such as employee benefits and building utilities, incurred by a business that are unrelated to the actual product or service sold.

Owner's capital
Debt or equity funds provided by the owner(s) of a business; sources of owner's capital are personal savings, sales of assets, or loans from financial institutions.

P & L
See Profit and loss statement

Part-time workers
Normally, those who work less than 35 hours per week. The Tax Reform Act indicated that part-time workers who work less than 17.5 hours per week may be excluded from health plans for purposes of complying with federal nondiscrimination rules.

Part-year workers
Those who work less than 50 weeks per year.

Partnership
Two or more parties who enter into a legal relationship to conduct business for profit. Defined by the U.S. Internal Revenue Code as joint ventures, syndicates, groups, pools, and other associations of two or more persons organized for profit that are not specifically classified in the IRS code as corporations or proprietorships.

Patent
A grant made by the government assuring an inventor the sole right to make, use, and sell an invention for a period of 17 years.

PC
See Professional corporation

Peak
See Cyclical peak

Pension
A series of payments made monthly, semiannually, annually, or at other specified intervals during the lifetime of the pensioner for distribution upon retirement. The term is sometimes used to denote the portion of the retirement allowance financed by the employer's contributions.

Pension fund
A fund established to provide for the payment of pension benefits; the collective contributions made by all of the parties to the pension plan.

Performance appraisal
An established set of objective criteria, based on job description and requirements, that is used to evaluate the performance of an employee in a specific job.

Permit
See Business license

Plan
See Business plan

Pooling
An arrangement for employers to achieve efficiencies and lower health costs by joining together to purchase group health insurance or self-insurance.

PPO
See Preferred provider organization

Preferred lenders program
See SBA special lending institution categories

Preferred provider organization (PPO)
A contractual arrangement with a health care services organization that agrees to discount its health care rates in return for faster payment and/or a patient base.

Premiums
The amount of money paid to an insurer for health insurance under a policy. The premium is generally paid periodically (e.g., monthly), and often is split between the employer and the employee. Unlike deductibles and coinsurance or copayments, premiums are paid for coverage whether or not benefits are actually used.

Prime-age workers
Employees 25 to 54 years of age.

Prime contract
A contract awarded directly by the U.S. Federal Government.

Private company
See Closely held corporation

Private placement
A method of raising capital by offering for sale an investment or business to a small group of investors (generally avoiding registration with the Securities and Exchange Commission or state securities registration agencies). Also known as Private financing or Private offering.

Pro forma
The use of hypothetical figures in financial statements to represent future expenditures, debts, and other potential financial expenses.

Proactive
Taking the initiative to solve problems and anticipate future events before they happen, instead of reacting to an already existing problem or waiting for a difficult situation to occur.

Procurement
(See also 8(a) Program; Small business set asides)
A contract from an agency of the federal government for goods or services from a small business.

Prodigy
(See also America Online)
An online service which is accessible by computer modem. The service features Internet access, bulletin boards, online periodicals, electronic mail, and other services for subscribers.

Product development
The stage of the innovation process where research is translated into a product or process through evaluation, adaptation, and demonstration.

Product franchising
An arrangement for a franchisee to use the name and to produce the product line of the franchisor or parent corporation.

Production
The manufacture of a product.

Production prototype
See Prototype

Productivity
A measurement of the number of goods produced during a specific amount of time.

Professional corporation (PC)
Organized by members of a profession such as medicine, dentistry, or law for the purpose of conducting their professional activities as a corporation. Liability of a member or shareholder is limited in the same manner as in a business corporation.

Profit and loss statement (P & L)
The summary of the incomes (total revenues) and costs of a company's operation during a specific period of time. Also known as Income and expense statement.

Proposal
See Business plan

Proprietorship
The most common legal form of business ownership; about 85 percent of all small businesses are proprietorships. The liability of the owner is unlimited in this form of ownership.

Prospective payment system
A cost-containment measure included in the Social Security Amendments of 1983 whereby Medicare payments to hospitals are based on established prices, rather than on cost reimbursement.

Prototype
A model that demonstrates the validity of the concept of an invention (laboratory prototype); a model that meets the needs of the manufacturing process and the user (production prototype).

Prudent investor rule or standard
A legal doctrine that requires fiduciaries to make investments using the prudence, diligence, and intelligence that would be used by a prudent person in making similar investments. Because fiduciaries make investments on behalf of third-party beneficiaries, the standard results in very conservative investments. Until recently, most state regulations required the fiduciary to apply this standard to each investment. Newer, more progressive regulations permit fiduciaries to apply this standard to the portfolio taken as a whole, thereby allowing a fiduciary to balance a portfolio with higher-yield, higher-risk investments. In states with more progressive regulations, practically every type of security is eligible for inclusion in the portfolio of investments made by a fiduciary, provided that the portfolio investments, in their totality, are those of a prudent person.

Public equity markets
Organized markets for trading in equity shares such as common stocks, preferred stocks, and warrants. Includes markets for both regularly traded and nonregularly traded securities.

Public offering
General solicitation for participation in an investment opportunity. Interstate public offerings are supervised by the U.S. Securities and Exchange Commission (see separate citation).

Quality control
The process by which a product is checked and tested to ensure consistent standards of high quality.

Rate of return
(See also Yield)
The yield obtained on a security or other investment based on its purchase price or its current market price. The total rate of return is current income plus or minus capital appreciation or depreciation.

Real property
Includes the land and all that is contained on it.

Realignment
See Resource realignment

Recession
Contraction of economic activity occurring between the peak and trough (see separate citations) of a business cycle.

Regulated market
A market in which the government controls the forces of supply and demand, such as who may enter and what price may be charged.

Regulation D
A vehicle by which small businesses make small offerings and private placements of securities with limited disclosure requirements. It was designed to ease the burdens imposed on small businesses utilizing this method of capital formation.

Regulatory Flexibility Act
An act requiring federal agencies to evaluate the impact of their regulations on small businesses before the regulations are issued and to consider less burdensome alternatives.

Research
The initial stage of the innovation process, which includes idea generation and invention.

Research and development financing
A tax-advantaged partnership set up to finance product development for start-ups as well as more mature companies.

Resource mobility
The ease with which labor and capital move from firm to firm or from industry to industry.

Resource realignment
The adjustment of productive resources to interindustry changes in demand.

Resources
The sources of support or help in the innovation process, including sources of financing, technical evaluation, market evaluation, management and business assistance, etc.

Retained business earnings
Business profits that are retained by the business rather than being distributed to the shareholders as dividends.

Revolving credit
An agreement with a lending institution for an amount of money, which cannot exceed a set maximum, over a specified period of time. Each time the borrower repays a portion of the loan, the amount of the repayment may be borrowed yet again.

Risk capital
See Venture capital

Risk management
The act of identifying potential sources of financial loss and taking action to minimize their negative impact.

Routing
The sequence of steps necessary to complete a product during production.

S corporations
See Sub chapter S corporations

SBA
See Small Business Administration

SBA direct loans
Loans made directly by the U.S. Small Business Administration (SBA); monies come from funds appropriated specifically for this purpose. In general, SBA direct loans carry interest rates slightly lower than those in the private financial markets and are available only to applicants unable to secure private financing or an SBA guaranteed loan.

SBA 504 Program
See Certified development corporation

SBA guaranteed loans
Loans made by lending institutions in which the U.S. Small Business Administration (SBA) will pay a prior agreed-upon percentage of the outstanding principal in the event the borrower of the loan defaults. The terms of the loan and the interest rate are negotiated between the

borrower and the lending institution, within set parameters.

SBA loans
See Disaster loans; SBA direct loans; SBA guaranteed loans; SBA special lending institution categories

SBA Management Assistance Programs
(See also Active Corps of Executives; Service Corps of Retired Executives; Small business institutes program) Classes, workshops, counseling, and publications offered by the U.S. Small Business Administration.

SBA special lending institution categories.
U.S. Small Business Administration (SBA) loan program in which the SBA promises certified banks a 72-hour turnaround period in giving its approval for a loan, and in which preferred lenders in a pilot program are allowed to write SBA loans without seeking prior SBA approval.

SBDB
See Small Business Data Base

SBDC
See Small business development centers

SBI
See Small business institutes program

SBIC
See Small business investment corporation

SBIR Program
See Small Business Innovation Development Act of 1982

Scale economies
The decline of the production cost per unit of output (average cost) as the volume of output increases.

Scale efficiency
The reduction in unit cost available to a firm when producing at a higher output volume.

SCORE
See Service Corps of Retired Executives

SEC
See Securities and Exchange Commission

SECA
See Self-Employment Contributions Act

Second-stage financing
(See also First-stage financing; Third-stage financing) Working capital for the initial expansion of a company that is producing, shipping, and has growing accounts receivable and inventories. Also known as Second-round financing.

Secondary market
A market established for the purchase and sale of outstanding securities following their initial distribution.

Secondary worker
Any worker in a family other than the person who is the primary source of income for the family.

Secondhand capital
Previously used and subsequently resold capital equipment (e.g., buildings and machinery).

Securities and Exchange Commission (SEC)
Federal agency charged with regulating the trade of securities to prevent unethical practices in the investor market.

Securitized debt
A marketing technique that converts long-term loans to marketable securities.

Seed capital
Venture financing provided in the early stages of the innovation process, usually during product development.

Self-employed person
One who works for a profit or fees in his or her own business, profession, or trade, or who operates a farm.

Self-Employment Contributions Act (SECA)
Federal law that governs the self-employment tax (see separate citation).

Self-employment income
Income covered by Social Security if a business earns a net income of at least $400.00 during the year. Taxes are paid on earnings that exceed $400.00.

Self-employment retirement plan
See Keogh plan

Self-employment tax
Required tax imposed on self-employed individuals for the provision of Social Security and Medicare. The tax must be paid quarterly with estimated income tax statements.

Self-funding
A health benefit plan in which a firm uses its own funds to pay claims, rather than transferring the financial risks of

paying claims to an outside insurer in exchange for premium payments.

Service Corps of Retired Executives (SCORE)
(See also Active Corps of Executives)
Volunteers for the SBA Management Assistance Program who provide one-on-one counseling and teach workshops and seminars for small firms.

Service firm
See Business service firm

Service sector
Broadly defined, all U.S. industries that produce intangibles, including the five major industry divisions of transportation, communications, and utilities; wholesale trade; retail trade; finance, insurance, and real estate; and services.

Set asides
See Small business set asides

Short-haul service
A type of transportation service in which the transporter supplies service between cities where the maximum distance is no more than 200 miles.

Short-term debt
An obligation that matures in one year.

SIC codes
See Standard Industrial Classification codes

Single-establishment enterprise
See Establishment

Small business
An enterprise that is independently owned and operated, is not dominant in its field, and employs fewer than 500 people. For SBA purposes, the U.S. Small Business Administration (SBA) considers various other factors (such as gross annual sales) in determining size of a business.

Small Business Administration (SBA)
An independent federal agency that provides assistance with loans, management, and advocating interests before other federal agencies.

Small Business Data Base
(See also U.S. Establishment and Enterprise Microdata File; U.S. Establishment Longitudinal Microdata File)
A collection of microdata (see separate citation) files on individual firms developed and maintained by the U.S. Small Business Administration.

Small business development centers (SBDC)
Centers that provide support services to small businesses, such as individual counseling, SBA advice, seminars and conferences, and other learning center activities. Most services are free of charge, or available at minimal cost.

Small business development corporation
See Certified development corporation

Small business-dominated industry
Industry in which a minimum of 60 percent of employment or sales is in firms with fewer than 500 employees.

Small Business Innovation Development Act of 1982
Federal statute requiring federal agencies with large extramural research and development budgets to allocate a certain percentage of these funds to small research and development firms. The program, called the Small Business Innovation Research (SBIR) Program, is designed to stimulate technological innovation and make greater use of small businesses in meeting national innovation needs.

Small business institutes (SBI) program
Cooperative arrangements made by U.S. Small Business Administration district offices and local colleges and universities to provide small business firms with graduate students to counsel them without charge.

Small business investment corporation (SBIC)
A privately owned company licensed and funded through the U.S. Small Business Administration and private sector sources to provide equity or debt capital to small businesses.

Small business set asides
Procurement (see separate citation) opportunities required by law to be on all contracts under $10,000 or a certain percentage of an agency's total procurement expenditure.

Smaller firms
For U.S. Department of Commerce purposes, those firms not included in the Fortune 1000.

SMSA
See Metropolitan statistical area

Socially and economically disadvantaged
Individuals who have been subjected to racial or ethnic prejudice or cultural bias without regard to their qualities as individuals, and whose abilities to compete are impaired because of diminished opportunities to obtain capital and credit.

Sole proprietorship
An unincorporated, one-owner business, farm, or professional practice.

Special lending institution categories
See SBA special lending institution categories

Standard Industrial Classification (SIC) codes
Four-digit codes established by the U.S. Federal Government to categorize businesses by type of economic activity; the first two digits correspond to major groups such as construction and manufacturing, while the last two digits correspond to subgroups such as home construction or highway construction.

Standard metropolitan statistical area (SMSA)
See Metropolitan statistical area

Start-up
A new business, at the earliest stages of development and financing.

Start-up costs
Costs incurred before a business can commence operations.

Start-up financing
Financing provided to companies that have either completed product development and initial marketing or have been in business for less than one year but have not yet sold their product commercially.

Stock
(See also Common stock; Convertible preferred stock)
A certificate of equity ownership in a business.

Stop-loss coverage
Insurance for a self-insured plan that reimburses the company for any losses it might incur in its health claims beyond a specified amount.

Strategic planning
Projected growth and development of a business to establish a guiding direction for the future. Also used to determine which market segments to explore for optimal sales of products or services.

Structural unemployment
See Unemployment

Sub chapter S corporations
Corporations that are considered noncorporate for tax purposes but legally remain corporations.

Subcontract
A contract between a prime contractor and a subcontractor, or between subcontractors, to furnish supplies or services for performance of a prime contract (see separate citation) or a subcontract.

Surety bonds
Bonds providing reimbursement to an individual, company, or the government if a firm fails to complete a contract. The U.S. Small Business Administration guarantees surety bonds in a program much like the SBA guaranteed loan program (see separate citation).

Swing loan
See Bridge financing

Target market
The clients or customers sought for a business' product or service.

Targeted Jobs Tax Credit
Federal legislation enacted in 1978 that provides a tax credit to an employer who hires structurally unemployed individuals.

Tax number
(See also Employer identification number)
A number assigned to a business by a state revenue department that enables the business to buy goods without paying sales tax.

Taxable bonds
An interest-bearing certificate of public or private indebtedness. Bonds are issued by public agencies to finance economic development.

Technical assistance
See Management and technical assistance

Technical evaluation
Assessment of technological feasibility.

Technology
The method in which a firm combines and utilizes labor and capital resources to produce goods or services; the

application of science for commercial or industrial purposes.

Technology transfer
The movement of information about a technology or intellectual property from one party to another for use.

Tenure
See Employee tenure

Term
(See also Maturity)
The length of time for which a loan is made.

Terms of a note
The conditions or limits of a note; includes the interest rate per annum, the due date, and transferability and convertibility features, if any.

Third-party administrator
An outside company responsible for handling claims and performing administrative tasks associated with health insurance plan maintenance.

Third-stage financing
(See also First-stage financing; Second-stage financing)
Financing provided for the major expansion of a company whose sales volume is increasing and that is breaking even or profitable. These funds are used for further plant expansion, marketing, working capital, or development of an improved product. Also known as Third-round or Mezzanine financing.

Time deposit
A bank deposit that cannot be withdrawn before a specified future time.

Time management
Skills and scheduling techniques used to maximize productivity.

Trade credit
Credit extended by suppliers of raw materials or finished products. In an accounting statement, trade credit is referred to as "accounts payable."

Trade name
The name under which a company conducts business, or by which its business, goods, or services are identified. It may or may not be registered as a trademark.

Trade periodical
A publication with a specific focus on one or more aspects of business and industry.

Trade secret
Competitive advantage gained by a business through the use of a unique manufacturing process or formula.

Trade show
An exhibition of goods or services used in a particular industry. Typically held in exhibition centers where exhibitors rent space to display their merchandise.

Trademark
A graphic symbol, device, or slogan that identifies a business. A business has property rights to its trademark from the inception of its use, but it is still prudent to register all trademarks with the Trademark Office of the U.S. Department of Commerce.

Translation
See Product development

Treasury bills
Investment tender issued by the Federal Reserve Bank in amounts of $10,000 that mature in 91 to 182 days.

Treasury bonds
Long-term notes with maturity dates of not less than seven and not more than twenty-five years.

Treasury notes
Short-term notes maturing in less than seven years.

Trend
A statistical measurement used to track changes that occur over time.

Trough
See Cyclical trough

UCC
See Uniform Commercial Code

UL
See Underwriters Laboratories

Underwriters Laboratories (UL)
One of several private firms that tests products and processes to determine their safety. Although various firms can provide this kind of testing service, many local and insurance codes specify UL certification.

Underwriting
A process by which an insurer determines whether or not and on what basis it will accept an application for insurance. In an experience-rated plan, premiums are based on a firm's or group's past claims; factors other than prior claims are used for community-rated or manually rated plans.

Unfair competition
Refers to business practices, usually unethical, such as using unlicensed products, pirating merchandise, or misleading the public through false advertising, which give the offending business an unequitable advantage over others.

Unfunded accrued liability
The excess of total liabilities, both present and prospective, over present and prospective assets.

Unemployment
The joblessness of individuals who are willing to work, who are legally and physically able to work, and who are seeking work. Unemployment may represent the temporary joblessness of a worker between jobs (frictional unemployment) or the joblessness of a worker whose skills are not suitable for jobs available in the labor market (structural unemployment).

Uniform Commercial Code (UCC)
A code of laws governing commercial transactions across the U.S., except Louisiana. Their purpose is to bring uniformity to financial transactions.

Uniform product code (UPC symbol)
A computer-readable label comprised of ten digits and stripes that encodes what a product is and how much it costs. The first five digits are assigned by the Uniform Product Code Council, and the last five digits by the individual manufacturer.

Unit cost
See Average cost

UPC symbol
See Uniform product code

U.S. Establishment and Enterprise Microdata (USEEM) File
A cross-sectional database containing information on employment, sales, and location for individual enterprises and establishments with employees that have a Dun & Bradstreet credit rating.

U.S. Establishment Longitudinal Microdata (USELM) File
A database containing longitudinally linked sample microdata on establishments drawn from the U.S. Establishment and Enterprise Microdata file (see separate citation).

U.S. Small Business Administration 504 Program
See Certified development corporation

USEEM
See U.S. Establishment and Enterprise Microdata File

USELM
See U.S. Establishment Longitudinal Microdata File

VCN
See Venture capital network

Venture capital
(See also Equity; Equity midrisk venture capital)
Money used to support new or unusual business ventures that exhibit above-average growth rates, significant potential for market expansion, and are in need of additional financing to sustain growth or further research and development; equity or equity-type financing traditionally provided at the commercialization stage, increasingly available prior to commercialization.

Venture capital company
A company organized to provide seed capital to a business in its formation stage, or in its first or second stage of expansion. Funding is obtained through public or private pension funds, commercial banks and bank holding companies, small business investment corporations licensed by the U.S. Small Business Administration, private venture capital firms, insurance companies, investment management companies, bank trust departments, industrial companies seeking to diversify their investment, and investment bankers acting as intermediaries for other investors or directly investing on their own behalf.

Venture capital limited partnerships
Designed for business development, these partnerships are an institutional mechanism for providing capital for young, technology-oriented businesses. The investors' money is pooled and invested in money market assets until venture investments have been selected. The general partners are experienced investment managers who select and invest the equity and debt securities of firms with high

growth potential and the ability to go public in the near future.

Venture capital network (VCN)
A computer database that matches investors with entrepreneurs.

WAN
See Wide Area Network

Wide Area Network (WAN)
Computer networks linking systems throughout a state or around the world in order to facilitate the sharing of information.

Withholding
Federal, state, social security, and unemployment taxes withheld by the employer from employees' wages; employers are liable for these taxes and the corporate umbrella and bankruptcy will not exonerate an employer from paying back payroll withholding. Employers should escrow these funds in a separate account and disperse them quarterly to withholding authorities.

Workers' compensation
A state-mandated form of insurance covering workers injured in job-related accidents. In some states, the state is the insurer; in other states, insurance must be acquired from commercial insurance firms. Insurance rates are based on a number of factors, including salaries, firm history, and risk of occupation.

Working capital
Refers to a firm's short-term investment of current assets, including cash, short-term securities, accounts receivable, and inventories.

Yield
(See also Rate of return)
The rate of income returned on an investment, expressed as a percentage. Income yield is obtained by dividing the current dollar income by the current market price of the security. Net yield or yield to maturity is the current income yield minus any premium above par or plus any discount from par in purchase price, with the adjustment spread over the period from the date of purchase to the date of maturity.

Appendix D - Cumulative Index

Index

Listings in this index are arranged alphabetically by business plan type (in bold), then alphabetically by business plan name. Users are provided with the volume number in which the plan appears.